JESUS
the
CHRIST

JESUS *the* CHRIST

JAMES E. TALMAGE

Covenant Communications, Inc.

Cover image: *Christ Healing the Man with the Withered Hand*, by Robert T. Barrett. © Intellectual Reserve, Inc. Courtesy of the Museum of Church History and Art.

Cover design copyrighted © 2006 by Covenant Communications, Inc.

Published by Covenant Communications, Inc.
American Fork, Utah

Printed in the United States of America
First Printing: October 2006

20 19 18   16 15 14 13 12 11 10

ISBN 978-1-59811-195-8

TABLE of CONTENTS

the Pharisees, Sadducees, and Herodians.—Peter's great confession, "Thou art the Christ."

Barren Fig Tree.—A woman healed on the Sabbath.—Many or few to be saved?—Jesus warned of Herod's design.

nent.—The Voice of the Lord Jesus Christ heard.—His visitations to the Nephites.—The Nephite Twelve.—Baptism among Nephites.—The Mosaic law fulfilled.—Address to Nephites compared with Sermon on the Mount.—Sacrament of bread and wine instituted among Nephites.—Name of Christ's Church. — The Three Nephites.—Growth of the Church.—Final apostasy of Nephite nation.

CHAPTER 1

INTRODUCTION

It is a matter of history that, at or near the beginning of what has since come to be known as the Christian era, the Man Jesus, surnamed the Christ, was born in Bethlehem of Judea.[a] The principal data as to His birth, life, and death are so well attested as to be reasonably indisputable; they are facts of record, and are accepted as essentially authentic by the civilized world at large. True, there are diversities of deduction based on alleged discrepancies in the records of the past as to circumstantial details; but such differences are of strictly minor importance, for none of them nor all taken together cast a shadow of rational doubt upon the historicity of the earthly existence of the Man known in literature as Jesus of Nazareth.

As to who and what He was there are dissensions of grave moment dividing the opinions of men; and this divergence of conception and belief is most pronounced upon those matters to which the greatest importance attaches. The solemn testimonies of millions dead and of millions living unite in proclaiming Him as divine, the Son of the Living God, the Redeemer and Savior of the human race, the Eternal Judge of the souls of men, the Chosen and Anointed of the Father—in short, the Christ. Others there are who deny His Godhood while extolling the transcendent qualities of His unparalleled and unapproachable Manhood.

To the student of history this Man among men stands first, foremost, and alone, as a directing personality in the world's progression.

---

[a] As to the year of Christ's birth, see chapter 8.

Mankind has never produced a leader to rank with Him. Regarded solely as a historic personage He is unique. Judged by the standard of human estimation, Jesus of Nazareth is supreme among men by reason of the excellence of His personal character, the simplicity, beauty, and genuine worth of His precepts, and the influence of His example and doctrines in the advancement of the race. To these distinguishing characteristics of surpassing greatness the devout Christian soul adds an attribute that far exceeds the sum of all the others—the divinity of Christ's origin and the eternal reality of His status as Lord and God.

Christian and unbeliever alike acknowledge His supremacy as a Man, and respect the epoch-making significance of His birth. Christ was born in the meridian of time;[b] and His life on earth marked at once the culmination of the past and the inauguration of an era distinctive in human hope, endeavor, and achievement. His advent determined a new order in the reckoning of the years; and by common consent the centuries antedating His birth have been counted backward from the pivotal event and are designated accordingly. The rise and fall of dynasties, the birth and dissolution of nations, all the cycles of history as to war and peace, as to prosperity and adversity, as to health and pestilence, seasons of plenty and of famine, the awful happenings of earthquake and storm, the triumphs of invention and discovery, the epochs of man's development in godliness and the long periods of his dwindling in unbelief—all the occurrences that make history—are chronicled throughout Christendom by reference to the year before or after the birth of Jesus Christ.

His earthly life covered a period of thirty-three years; and of these but three were spent by Him as an acknowledged Teacher openly engaged in the activities of public ministry. He was brought to a violent death before He had attained what we now regard as the age of manhood's prime. As an individual He was personally known to but few; and His fame as a world character became general only after His death.

Brief account of some of His words and works has been preserved to us; and this record, fragmentary and incomplete though it be, is

[b] See chapter 6.

rightly esteemed as the world's greatest treasure. The earliest and most extended history of His mortal existence is embodied within the compilation of scriptures known as the New Testament; indeed but little is said of Him by secular historians of His time. Few and short as are the allusions to Him made by nonscriptural writers in the period immediately following that of His ministry, enough is found to corroborate the sacred record as to the actuality and period of Christ's earthly existence.

No adequate biography of Jesus as Boy and Man has been or can be written, for the sufficing reason that a fullness of data is lacking. Nevertheless, man never lived of whom more has been said and sung, none to whom is devoted a greater proportion of the world's literature. He is extolled by Christian, Mohammedan and Jew, by skeptic and infidel, by the world's greatest poets, philosophers, statesmen, scientists, and historians. Even the profane sinner in the foul sacrilege of his oath acclaims the divine supremacy of Him whose name he desecrates.

The purpose of the present treatise is that of considering the life and mission of Jesus *as* the Christ. In this undertaking we are to be guided by the light of both ancient and modern scriptures; and, thus led, we shall discover, even in the early stages of our course, that the word of God as revealed in latter days is effective in illuming and making plain the Holy Writ of ancient times, and this, in many matters of the profoundest import.ᶜ

Instead of beginning our study with the earthly birth of the Holy Babe of Bethlehem, we shall consider the part taken by the Firstborn Son of God in the primeval councils of heaven, at the time when He was chosen and ordained to be the Savior of the unborn race of mortals, the Redeemer of a world then in its formative stages of development. We are to study Him as the Creator of the world, as the Word of Power, through whom the purposes of the Eternal Father were realized in the preparation of the earth for the abode of His myriad spirit children during the appointed period of their mortal probation. Jesus Christ was and is Jehovah, the God of Adam and of

ᶜ The Holy Bible, the Book of Mormon, the Doctrine and Covenants, and the Pearl of Great Price constitute the standard works of The Church of Jesus Christ of Latter-day Saints. These will be cited alike as Scriptures in the following pages, for such they are.

Noah, the God of Abraham, Isaac, and Jacob, the God of Israel, the God at whose instance the prophets of the ages have spoken, the God of all nations, and He who shall yet reign on earth as King of kings and Lord of lords.

His wondrous yet natural birth, His immaculate life in the flesh, and His voluntary death as a consecrated sacrifice for the sins of mankind, shall claim our reverent attention; as shall also His redeeming service in the world of disembodied spirits; His literal Resurrection from bodily death to immortality; His several appearings to men and His continued ministry as the Resurrected Lord on both continents; the reestablishment of His Church through His personal presence and that of the Eternal Father in the latter days; and His coming to His temple in the current dispensation. All these developments in the ministration of the Christ are already of the past. Our proposed course of investigation will lead yet onward, into the future concerning which the word of divine revelation is of record. We shall consider the conditions incident to the Lord's return in power and glory to inaugurate the dominion of the Kingdom of Heaven on earth, and to usher in the predicted Millennium of peace and righteousness. And yet beyond we shall follow Him, through the post-Millennial conflict between the powers of heaven and the forces of hell, to the completion of His victory over Satan, sin, and death, when He shall present the glorified earth and its sanctified hosts, spotless and celestialized, unto the Father.

The Church of Jesus Christ of Latter-day Saints affirms her possession of divine authority for the use of the sacred name, Jesus Christ, as the essential part of her distinctive designation. In view of this exalted claim, it is pertinent to inquire as to what special or particular message the Church has to give to the world concerning the Redeemer and Savior of the race, and as to what she has to say in justification of her solemn affirmation, or in vindication of her exclusive name and title. As we proceed with our study, we shall find that among the specific teachings of the Church respecting the Christ are these:

(1) The unity and continuity of His mission in all ages—this of necessity involving the verity of His preexistence and foreordination. (2) The fact of His antemortal Godship. (3) The actuality of His

birth in the flesh as the natural issue of divine and mortal parentage. (4) The reality of His death and physical Resurrection, as a result of which the power of death shall be eventually overcome. (5) The literalness of the Atonement wrought by Him, including the absolute requirement of individual compliance with the laws and ordinances of His gospel as the means by which salvation may be attained. (6) The restoration of His Priesthood and the reestablishment of His Church in the current age, which is verily the Dispensation of the Fullness of Times. (7) The certainty of His return to earth in the near future, with power and great glory, to reign in Person and bodily presence as Lord and King.

CHAPTER 2

PREEXISTENCE AND FOREORDINATION
OF THE CHRIST

We affirm, on the authority of Holy Scripture, that the Being who is known among men as Jesus of Nazareth, and by all who acknowledge His Godhood as Jesus the Christ, existed with the Father prior to birth in the flesh; and that in the preexistent state He was chosen and ordained to be the one and only Savior and Redeemer of the human race. Foreordination implies and comprises preexistence as an essential condition; therefore scriptures bearing upon the one are germane to the other; and consequently in this presentation no segregation of evidence as applying specifically to the preexistence of Christ or to His foreordination will be attempted.

John the Revelator beheld in vision some of the scenes that had been enacted in the spirit world before the beginning of human history. He witnessed strife and contention between loyalty and rebellion, with the hosts defending the former led by Michael the archangel, and the rebellious forces captained by Satan, who is also called the devil, the serpent, and the dragon. We read: "And there was war in heaven: Michael and his angels fought against the dragon; and the dragon fought and his angels."[a]

In this struggle between unembodied hosts the forces were unequally divided; Satan drew to his standard only a third part of the children of God, who are symbolized as the "stars of heaven";[b] the majority either fought with Michael, or at least refrained from active opposition, thus accomplishing the purpose of their "first estate";

[a] Rev. 12:7; see also verses 8 and 9.
[b] Rev. 12:4; see also D&C 29:36–38; and 76:25–27.

while the angels who arrayed themselves on the side of Satan "kept not their first estate,"[c] and therefore rendered themselves ineligible for the glorious possibilities of an advanced condition or "second estate."[d] The victory was with Michael and his angels; and Satan or Lucifer, theretofore a "son of the morning," was cast out of heaven, yea "he was cast out into the earth, and his angels were cast out with him."[e] The prophet Isaiah, to whom these momentous occurrences had been revealed about eight centuries prior to the time of John's writings, laments with inspired pathos the fall of so great a one; and specifies selfish ambition as the occasion: "How art thou fallen from heaven, O Lucifer, son of the morning! how art thou cut down to the ground, which didst weaken the nations! For thou hast said in thine heart, I will ascend into heaven, I will exalt my throne above the stars of God: I will sit also upon the mount of the congregation, in the sides of the north: I will ascend above the heights of the clouds; I will be like the most High. Yet thou shalt be brought down to hell, to the sides of the pit."[f]

Justification for citing these scriptures in connection with our present consideration will be found in the cause of the great contention—the conditions that led to this war in heaven. It is plain from the words of Isaiah that Lucifer, already of exalted rank, sought to aggrandize himself without regard to the rights and agency of others. The matter is set forth, in words that none may misapprehend, in a revelation given to Moses and repeated through the first prophet of the present dispensation: "And I, the Lord God, spake unto Moses, saying: That Satan, whom thou hast commanded in the name of mine Only Begotten, is the same which was from the beginning, and he came before me, saying—Behold, here am I, send me, I will be thy son, and I will redeem all mankind, that one soul shall not be lost, and surely I will do it; wherefore give me thine honor. But, behold, my Beloved Son, which was my Beloved and Chosen from the beginning, said unto me—Father, thy will be done, and the glory be thine forever. Wherefore, because that Satan rebelled against me, and

[c] Jude 6.
[d] Abr. 3:26.
[e] Rev. 12:9.
[f] Isa. 14: 12–15; compare D&C 29:36–38; and 76:23–27.

sought to destroy the agency of man, which I, the Lord God, had given him, and also, that I should give unto him mine own power; by the power of mine Only Begotten, I caused that he should be cast down; and he became Satan, yea, even the devil, the father of all lies, to deceive and to blind men, and to lead them captive at his will, even as many as would not hearken unto my voice."[g]

Thus it is shown that prior to the placing of man upon the earth, how long before we do not know, Christ and Satan, together with the hosts of the spirit children of God, existed as intelligent individuals,[h] possessing power and opportunity to choose the course they would pursue and the leaders whom they would follow and obey.[i] In that great concourse of spirit intelligences, the Father's plan, whereby His children would be advanced to their second estate, was submitted and doubtless discussed. The opportunity so placed within the reach of the spirits who were to be privileged to take bodies upon the earth was so transcendently glorious that those heavenly multitudes burst forth into song and shouted for joy.[j]

Satan's plan of compulsion, whereby all would be safely conducted through the career of mortality, bereft of freedom to act and agency to choose, so circumscribed that they would be compelled to do right—that one soul would not be lost—was rejected; and the humble offer of Jesus the Firstborn—to assume mortality and live among men as their Exemplar and Teacher, observing the sanctity of man's agency but teaching men to use aright that divine heritage—was accepted. The decision brought war, which resulted in the vanquishment of Satan and his angels, who were cast out and deprived of the boundless privileges incident to the mortal or second estate.

In that august council of the angels and the Gods, the Being who later was born in flesh as Mary's Son, Jesus, took prominent part, and there was He ordained of the Father to be the Savior of mankind. As to time, the term being used in the sense of all duration past, this is

[g] P. of G. P., Moses 4: 1–4; see also Abr. 3:27, 28.
[h] For a further treatment of the preexistence of spirits see the author's *Articles of Faith*, 10: 189–94.
[i] Note 1, end of chapter.
[j] Job 38:7.

our earliest record of the Firstborn among the sons of God; to us who read, it marks the beginning of the written history of Jesus the Christ.[k]

Old Testament scriptures, while abounding in promises relating to the actuality of Christ's advent in the flesh, are less specific in information concerning His antemortal existence. By the children of Israel, while living under the law and still unprepared to receive the gospel, the Messiah was looked for as one to be born in the lineage of Abraham and David, empowered to deliver them from personal and national burdens, and to vanquish their enemies. The actuality of the Messiah's status as the chosen Son of God, who was with the Father from the beginning, a Being of preexistent power and glory, was but dimly perceived, if conceived at all, by the people in general; and although to prophets specially commissioned in the authorities and privileges of the Holy Priesthood, revelation of the great truth was given,[l] they transmitted it to the people rather in the language of imagery and parable than in words of direct plainness. Nevertheless the testimony of the evangelists and the apostles, the attestation of the Christ Himself while in the flesh, and the revelations given in the present dispensation leave us without dearth of scriptural proof.

In the opening lines of the Gospel book written by John the apostle, we read: "In the beginning was the Word, and the Word was with God, and the Word was God. The same was in the beginning with God. All things were made by him; and without him was not anything made that was made. . . . And the Word was made flesh, and dwelt among us, (and we beheld his glory, the glory as of the only begotten of the Father,) full of grace and truth."[m]

The passage is simple, precise and unambiguous. We may reasonably give to the phrase "In the beginning" the same meaning as attaches thereto in the first line of Genesis; and such signification must indicate a time antecedent to the earliest stages of human existence upon the earth. That the Word is Jesus Christ, who was with the Father in that beginning and who was Himself invested with the powers and rank of Godship, and that He came into the world and dwelt among men,

---

[k] Note 2, end of chapter.

[l] Ps. 25:14; Amos 3:7.

[m] John 1:1–3, 14; see also 1 John 1:1; 5:7; Rev. 19:13; compare D&C 93:1–17, 21.

are definitely affirmed. These statements are corroborated through a revelation given to Moses, in which he was permitted to see many of the creations of God, and to hear the voice of the Father with respect to the things that had been made: "And by the word of my power, have I created them, which is mine Only Begotten Son, who is full of grace and truth."[n]

John the apostle repeatedly affirms the preexistence of the Christ and the fact of His authority and power in the antemortal state.[o] To the same effect is the testimony of Paul[p] and of Peter. Instructing the saints concerning the basis of their faith, the last-named apostle impressed upon them that their redemption was not to be secured through corruptible things nor by the outward observance of traditional requirements, "But with the precious blood of Christ, as of a lamb without blemish and without spot: who verily was foreordained before the foundation of the world, but was manifest in these last times for you."[q]

Even more impressive and yet more truly conclusive are the personal testimonies of the Savior as to His own preexistent life and the mission among men to which He had been appointed. No one who accepts Jesus as the Messiah can consistently reject these evidences of His eternal nature. When, on a certain occasion, the Jews in the synagogue disputed among themselves and murmured because of their failure to understand aright His doctrine concerning Himself, especially as touching His relationship with the Father, Jesus said unto them: "For I came down from heaven, not to do mine own will, but the will of him that sent me." And then, continuing the lesson based upon the contrast between the manna with which their fathers had been fed in the wilderness and the bread of life which He had to offer, He added: "I am the living bread which came down from heaven," and again declared "the living Father hath sent me." Not a few of the disciples failed to comprehend His teachings; and their complaints

[n] Moses 1:32, 33; see also 2:5.
[o] 1 John 1:1–3; 2:13, 14; 4:9; Rev. 3:14.
[p] 2 Tim. 1:9, 10; Rom. 16:25; Eph. 1:4; 3:9, 11; Titus 1:2. See especially Rom. 3:25; and note the marginal rendering—"foreordained"—making the passage read: "Whom God hath foreordained to be a propitiation."
[q] 1 Pet. 1:19, 20.

drew from Him these words: "Doth this offend you? What and if ye shall see the Son of man ascend up where he was before?"[r]

To certain wicked Jews, wrapped in the mantle of racial pride, boastful of their descent through the lineage of Abraham, and seeking to excuse their sins through an unwarranted use of the great patriarch's name, our Lord thus proclaimed His own preeminence: "Verily, verily, I say unto you, Before Abraham was, I am."[s] The fuller significance of this remark will be treated later; suffice it in the present connection to consider this scripture as a plain avowal of our Lord's seniority and supremacy over Abraham. But as Abraham's birth had preceded that of Christ by more than nineteen centuries, such seniority must have reference to a state of existence antedating that of mortality.

When the hour of His betrayal was near, in the last interview with the apostles prior to His agonizing experience in Gethsemane, Jesus comforted them saying: "For the Father himself loveth you, because ye have loved me, and have believed that I came out from God. I came forth from the Father, and am come into the world: again, I leave the world, and go to the Father."[t] Furthermore, in the course of upwelling prayer for those who had been true to their testimony of His Messiahship, He addressed the Father with this solemn invocation: "And this is life eternal, that they might know thee the only true God, and Jesus Christ, whom thou hast sent. I have glorified thee on the earth: I have finished the work which thou gavest me to do. And now, O Father glorify thou me with thine own self with the glory which I had with thee before the world was."[u]

Book of Mormon scriptures are likewise explicit in proof of the preexistence of the Christ and of His foreappointed mission. One only of the many evidences therein found will be cited here. An ancient prophet, designated in the record as the brother of Jared,[v] once pleaded with the Lord in special supplication: "And the Lord said unto him, Believest thou the words which I shall speak? And he

---

[r] John 6:38, 51, 57, 61, 62.
[s] John 8:58; see also 17:5, 24; and compare Ex. 3:14.
[t] John 16:27–28; see also 13:3.
[u] John 17:3–5; see also verses 24, 25.
[v] Note 3, end of chapter.

answered, Yea, Lord, I know that thou speakest the truth, for thou art a God of truth, and canst not lie. And when he had said these words, behold, the Lord shewed himself unto him, and said, Because thou knowest these things, ye are redeemed from the fall; therefore ye are brought back into my presence; therefore I shew myself unto you. Behold, I am he who was prepared from the foundation of the world to redeem my people. Behold, I am Jesus Christ. I am the Father and the Son. In me shall all mankind have light, and that eternally, even they who shall believe on my name; and they shall become my sons and my daughters. And never have I shewed myself unto man whom I have created, for never has man believed in me as thou hast. Seest thou that ye are created after mine own image? Yea, even all men were created in the beginning, after mine own image. Behold, this body, which ye now behold, is the body of my spirit; and man have I created after the body of my spirit; and even as I appear unto thee to be in the spirit, will I appear unto my people in the flesh."ᵂ The main facts attested by this scripture as having a direct bearing upon our present subject are those of the Christ manifesting Himself while yet in His antemortal state, and of His declaration that He had been chosen from the foundation of the world as the Redeemer.

Revelation given through the prophets of God in the present dispensation is replete with evidence of Christ's appointment and ordination in the primeval world; and the whole tenor of the scriptures contained in the Doctrine and Covenants may be called in witness. The following instances are particularly in point. In a communication to Joseph Smith the prophet, in May, 1833, the Lord declared Himself as the One who had previously come into the world from the Father, and of whom John had borne testimony as the Word; and the solemn truth is reiterated that He, Jesus Christ, "was in the beginning, before the world was," and further, that He was the Redeemer who "came into the world, because the world was made by him, and in him was the life of men and the light of men." Again, He is referred to as "the Only Begotten of the Father, full of grace and truth, even the Spirit of truth, which came and dwelt in the flesh." In the course

---

ᵂ Ether 3:11–16. See also 1 Ne. 17:30; 19:7; 2 Ne. 9:5; 11:7; 25:12; 26:12; Mosiah 3:5; 4:2; 7:27; 13:34; 15:1; Alma 11:40; Hel. 14:12; 3 Ne. 9:15.

of the same revelation the Lord said: "And now, verily I say unto you, I was in the beginning with the Father and am the firstborn."ˣ On an earlier occasion, as the modern prophet testifies, he and an associate in the priesthood were enlightened by the Spirit so that they were able to see and understand the things of God—"Even those things which were from the beginning before the world was, which were ordained of the Father, through his Only Begotten Son, who was in the bosom of the Father, even from the beginning; Of whom we bear record, and the record which we bear is the fulness of the gospel of Jesus Christ, who is the Son, whom we saw and with whom we conversed in the heavenly vision."ʸ

The testimony of scriptures written on both hemispheres, that of records both ancient and modern, the inspired utterances of prophets and apostles, and the words of the Lord Himself, are of one voice in proclaiming the preexistence of the Christ and His ordination as the chosen Savior and Redeemer of mankind—in the beginning, yea, even before the foundation of the world.

NOTES TO CHAPTER 2

1. Graded Intelligences in the Antemortal State.—That the spirits of men existed as individual intelligences, of varying degrees of ability and power, prior to the inauguration of the mortal state upon this earth and even prior to the creation of the world as a suitable abode for human beings, is shown in great plainness through a divine revelation to Abraham: "Now the Lord had shown unto me, Abraham, the intelligences that were organized before the world was; and among all these there were many of the noble and great ones; and God saw these souls that they were good, and he stood in the midst of them, and he said: These I will make my rulers; for he stood among those that were spirits, and he saw that they were good; and he said unto me: Abraham, thou art one of them; thou wast chosen before thou wast born" (Abr. 3:22–23).

That both Christ and Satan were among those exalted intelligences, and that Christ was chosen while Satan was rejected as the future Savior of mankind, are shown by the portions of the revelation immediately following that above quoted: "And there stood one among them that was like unto God, and he said unto those who were with him: We will go down, for there is space there, and we will take of these materials, and we will make an earth whereon these may dwell; and we will

ˣ D&C 93:1–17, 21.
ʸ D&C 76:13, 14.

prove them herewith, to see if they will do all things whatsoever the Lord their God shall command them; and they who keep their first estate shall be added upon, and they who keep not their first estate shall not have glory in the same kingdom with those who keep their first estate; and they who keep their second estate shall have glory added upon their heads forever and ever. And the Lord said: Whom shall I send? And one answered like unto the Son of Man: Here am I, send me. And another answered and said: Here am I, send me. And the Lord said: I will send the first. And the second was angry, and kept not his first estate; and, at that day, many followed after him" (Abr. 3:24–28).

2. The Primeval Council in the Heavens.—"It is definitely stated in the Book of Genesis that God said, 'Let us make man in our image, after our likeness'; and again, after Adam had taken of the forbidden fruit the Lord said, 'Behold, the man has become as one of us'; and the inference is direct that in all that related to the work of the creation of the world there was a consultation; and though God spake as it is recorded in the Bible, yet it is evident He counseled with others. The scriptures tell us there are 'Gods many and Lords many. But to us there is but one God, the Father' (I Cor. 8:5). And for this reason, though there were others engaged in the creation of the worlds, it is given to us in the Bible in the shape that it is; for the fulness of these truths is only revealed to highly favored persons for certain reasons known to God; as we are told in the scriptures: 'The secret of the Lord is with them that fear him; and he will show them his covenant.'—Psalm 25:14.

"It is consistent to believe that at this Council in the heavens the plan that should be adopted in relation to the sons of God who were then spirits, and had not yet obtained tabernacles, was duly considered. For, in view of the creation of the world and the placing of men upon it, whereby it would be possible for them to obtain tabernacles, and in those tabernacles obey laws of life, and with them again be exalted among the Gods, we are told that at that time, 'the morning stars sang together, and all the sons of God shouted for joy.' The question then arose, how, and upon what principle, should the salvation, exaltation and eternal glory of God's sons be brought about? It is evident that at that Council certain plans had been proposed and discussed, and that after a full discussion of those principles, and the declaration of the Father's will pertaining to His design, Lucifer came before the Father with a plan of his own, saying, 'Behold [here am] I; send me, I will be thy son, and I will redeem all mankind, that one soul shall not be lost, and surely I will do it; wherefore, give me thine honor.' But Jesus, on hearing this statement made by Lucifer, said, 'Father, thy will be done, and the glory be thine forever.' From these remarks made by the well beloved Son, we should naturally infer that in the discussion of this subject the Father had made known His will and developed His plan and design pertaining to these matters, and all that His well beloved Son wanted to do was to carry out the will of His Father, as it would appear had been before expressed. He also wished the glory to be given to His Father, who, as God the Father, and the originator and designer of the plan, had a right to all the honor and glory. But Lucifer wanted to introduce a plan contrary to the will of his Father, and then wanted His honor, and said: 'I will save every soul of man, wherefore give me thine honor.' He wanted to go contrary to the will of his Father, and presumptuously sought to deprive man of his free agency, thus making him a serf, and placing him in a position in which it was impossible for him to obtain that exaltation which God designed should be man's, through obedience to the law which He had suggested; and again, Lucifer wanted the honor and power of his Father, to enable him to carry out principles which were contrary to the Father's wish."—John Taylor, *Mediation and Atonement*, pp. 93–94.

3. The Jaredites.—"Of the two nations whose histories constitute the Book of Mormon, the first in order of time consisted of the people of Jared, who followed their leader from the Tower of Babel at the time of the confusion of tongues. Their history was written on twenty-four plates of gold by Ether, the last of their prophets, who, foreseeing the destruction of his people because of their wickedness, hid away the historical plates. They were afterward found, 123 B.C. , by an expedition sent out by King Limhi, a Nephite ruler. The record engraved on these plates was subsequently abridged by Moroni, and the condensed account was attached by him to the Book of Mormon record; it appears in the modern translation under the name of the Book of Ether.

"The first and chief prophet of the Jaredites is not mentioned by name in the record as we have it; he is known only as the brother of Jared. Of the people, we learn that, amid the confusion of Babel, Jared and his brother importuned the Lord that He would spare them and their associates from the impending disruption. Their prayer was heard, and the Lord led them with a considerable company, who, like themselves, were free from the taint of idolatry, away from their homes, promising to conduct them to a land choice above all other lands. Their course of travel is not given with exactness; we learn only that they reached the ocean, and there constructed eight vessels, called barges, in which they set out upon the waters. These vessels were small and dark within; but the Lord made luminous certain stones, which gave light to the imprisoned voyagers. After a passage of three hundred and forty-four days, the colony landed on the western shore of North America, probably at a place south of the Gulf of California, and north of the Isthmus of Panama.

"Here they became a flourishing nation; but, giving way in time to internal dissensions, they divided into factions, which warred with one another until the people were totally destroyed. This destruction, which occurred near the hill Ramah, afterward known among the Nephites as Cumorah, probably took place at about the time of Lehi's landing in South America—590 B.C."—James E. Talmage, *Articles of Faith*, pp. 260–62.

CHAPTER 3

THE NEED OF A REDEEMER

We have heretofore shown that the entire human race existed as spirit beings in the primeval world, and that for the purpose of making possible to them the experiences of mortality this earth was created. They were endowed with the powers of agency or choice while yet but spirits; and the divine plan provided that they be free-born in the flesh, heirs to the inalienable birthright of liberty to choose and to act for themselves in mortality. It is undeniably essential to the eternal progression of God's children that they be subjected to the influences of both good and evil, that they be tried and tested and proved withal, "to see if they will do all things whatsoever the Lord their God shall command them."[a] Free agency is an indispensable element of such a test.

The Eternal Father well understood the diverse natures and varied capacities of His spirit offspring; and His infinite foreknowledge made plain to Him, even in the beginning, that in the school of life some of His children would succeed and others would fail; some would be faithful, others false; some would choose the good, others the evil; some would seek the way of life while others would elect to follow the road to destruction. He further foresaw that death would enter the world, and that the possession of bodies by His children would be of but brief individual duration. He saw that His commandments would be disobeyed and His law violated; and that men, shut out from His presence and left to themselves, would sink rather than rise, would

---

[a] Abr. 3:25. For a fuller treatment of man's free agency, see the author's *Articles of Faith*, 3: 52–63, and the numerous references there given.

retrogress rather than advance, and would be lost to the heavens. It was necessary that a means of redemption be provided, whereby erring man might make amends, and by compliance with established law achieve salvation and eventual exaltation in the eternal worlds. The power of death was to be overcome, so that, though men would of necessity die, they would live anew, their spirits clothed with immortalized bodies over which death could not again prevail.

Let not ignorance and thoughtlessness lead us into the error of assuming that the Father's foreknowledge as to what *would be*, under given conditions, determined that such *must be*. It was not His design that the souls of mankind be lost; on the contrary it was and is His work and glory, "to bring to pass the immortality and eternal life of man."[b] Nevertheless He saw the evil into which His children would assuredly fall, and with infinite love and mercy did He ordain means of averting the dire effect, provided the transgressor would elect to avail himself thereof.[c] The offer of the firstborn Son to establish through His own ministry among men the gospel of salvation, and to sacrifice Himself, through labor, humiliation and suffering even unto death, was accepted and made the foreordained plan of man's redemption from death, of his eventual salvation from the effects of sin, and of his possible exaltation through righteous achievement.

In accordance with the plan adopted in the council of the Gods, man was created as an embodied spirit; his tabernacle of flesh was composed of the elements of earth.[d] He was given commandment and law, and was free to obey or disobey—with the just and inevitable condition that he should enjoy or suffer the natural results of his choice.[e] Adam, the first man[f] placed upon the earth in pursuance of the established plan, and Eve who was given unto him as companion and associate, indispensable to him in the appointed mission of peopling the earth, disobeyed the express commandment of God and so brought about the "fall of man," whereby the mortal state, of which

[b] Moses 1:39; compare 6:59. Note 1, end of chapter.
[c] Note 2, end of chapter.
[d] Gen. 1:26, 27; 2:7; compare Moses 2:26–27; 3:7; Abr. 4:26–28; 5:7.
[e] Gen. 1:28–31; 2:16–17; compare Moses 2:28–31; 3:16, 17; Abr. 4:28–31; 5:12, 13.
[f] Gen. 2:8; compare statement in verse 5—that prior to that time there was "not a man to till the ground"; see also Moses 3:7; Abr. 1:3; and 1 Ne. 5:11.

death is an essential element was inaugurated.[g] It is not proposed to consider here at length the doctrine of the fall; for the present argument it is sufficient to establish the fact of the momentous occurrence and its portentous consequences.[h] The woman was deceived, and in direct violation of counsel and commandment partook of the food that had been forbidden, as a result of which act her body became degenerate and subject to death. Adam realized the disparity that had been brought between him and his companion, and with some measure of understanding followed her course, thus becoming her partner in bodily degeneracy. Note in this matter the words of Paul the apostle: "Adam was not deceived, but the woman being deceived was in the transgression."[i]

The man and the woman had now become mortal; through indulgence in food unsuited to their nature and condition and against which they had been specifically warned, and as the inevitable result of their disobeying the divine law and commandment, they became liable to the physical ailments and bodily frailties to which mankind has since been the natural heir.[j] Those bodies, which before the Fall had been perfect in form and function, were now subject for eventual dissolution or death. The arch-tempter through whose sophistries, half-truths and infamous falsehoods, Eve had been beguiled, was none other than Satan, or Lucifer, that rebellious and fallen "son of the morning," whose proposal involving the destruction of man's liberty had been rejected in the council of the heavens, and who had been "cast out into the earth," he and all his angels as unembodied spirits, never to be tabernacled in bodies of their own.[k] As an act of diabolic reprisal following his rejection in the council, his defeat by Michael and the heavenly hosts, and his ignominious expulsion from heaven, Satan planned to destroy the bodies in which the faithful spirits—those who had kept their first estate—would be born; and his beguilement of Eve was but an early stage of that infernal scheme.

[g] Gen. chap. 3; compare Moses, chap. 4.
[h] See *Articles of Faith,* pp. 63–70.
[i] 1 Tim. 2:14; see also 2 Cor. 11:3.
[j] Note 3, end of chapter.
[k] See page 9.

Death has come to be the universal heritage; it may claim its victim in infancy or youth, in the period of life's prime, or its summons may be deferred until the snows of age have gathered upon the hoary head; it may befall as the result of accident or disease, by violence, or as we say, through natural causes; but come it must, as Satan well knows; and in this knowledge is his present though but temporary triumph. But the purposes of God, as they ever have been and ever shall be, are infinitely superior to the deepest designs of men or devils; and the Satanic machinations to make death inevitable, perpetual and supreme were provided against even before the first man had been created in the flesh. The Atonement to be wrought by Jesus the Christ was ordained to overcome death and to provide a means of ransom from the power of Satan.

As the penalty incident to the Fall came upon the race through an individual act, it would be manifestly unjust, and therefore impossible as part of the divine purpose, to make all men suffer the results thereof without provision for deliverance.[l] Moreover, since by the transgression of one man sin came into the world and death was entailed upon all, it is consistent with reason that the atonement thus made necessary should be wrought by one.[m] "Wherefore, as by one man sin entered into the world, and death by sin; and so death passed upon all men, for that all have sinned: . . . Therefore as by the offence of one judgment came upon all men to condemnation; even so by the righteousness of one the free gift came upon all men unto justification of life."[n] So taught the apostle Paul; and, further, "For since by man came death, by man came also the resurrection of the dead. For as in Adam all die, even so in Christ shall all be made alive."[o]

The atonement was plainly to be a vicarious sacrifice, voluntary and love-inspired on the Savior's part, universal in its application to mankind so far as men shall accept the means of deliverance thus placed within their reach. For such a mission only one who was without sin could be eligible. Even the altar victims of ancient Israel

[l] Note 4, end of chapter.
[m] Note 5, end of chapter.
[n] Rom. 5:12, 18.
[o] 1 Cor. 15:21, 22.

offered as a provisional propitiation for the offenses of the people under the Mosaic law had to be clean and devoid of spot or blemish; otherwise they were unacceptable and the attempt to offer them was sacrilege.[p] Jesus Christ was the only Being suited to the requirements of the great sacrifice:

1—As the one and only sinless Man;

2—As the Only Begotten of the Father and therefore the only Being born to earth possessing in their fulness the attributes of both Godhood and manhood;

3—As the One who had been chosen in the heavens and foreordained to this service.

What other man has been without sin, and therefore wholly exempt from the dominion of Satan, and to whom death, the wage of sin, is not naturally due? Had Jesus Christ met death as other men have done—the result of the power that Satan has gained over them through their sins—His death would have been but an individual experience, expiatory in no degree of any faults or offenses but His own. Christ's absolute sinlessness made Him eligible, His humility and willingness rendered Him acceptable to the Father, as the atoning sacrifice whereby propitiation could be made for the sins of all men.

What other man has lived with power to withstand death, over whom death could not prevail except through his own submission? Yet Jesus Christ could not be slain until His "hour had come," and that, the hour in which He voluntarily surrendered His life, and permitted His own decease through an act of will. Born of a mortal mother He inherited the capacity to die; begotten by an immortal Sire He possessed as a heritage the power to withstand death indefinitely. He literally gave up His life; to this effect is His own affirmation: "Therefore doth my Father love me, because I lay down my life, that I might take it again. No man taketh it from me, but I lay it down of myself. I have power to lay it down, and I have power to take it again."[q] And further: "For as the Father hath life in himself; so hath he given to the Son to have life in himself."[r] Only such a One could conquer death;

p Lev. 22:20; Deut. 15:21; 17:1; Mal. 1:8, 14; compare Heb. 9:14; 1 Pet. 1:19.
q John 10: 17–18.
r John 5:26.

in none but Jesus the Christ was realized this requisite condition of a Redeemer of the world.

What other man has come to earth with such appointment, clothed with the authority of such foreordination? The atoning mission of Jesus Christ was no self-assumption. True, He had offered Himself when the call was made in the heavens; true, He has been accepted, and in due time came to earth to carry into effect the terms of that acceptance; but He was chosen by One greater than Himself. The burden of His confession of authority was ever to the effect that He operated under the direction of the Father, as witness these words: "I came down from heaven, not to do mine own will, but the will of him that sent me."ˢ "My meat is to do the will of him that sent me, and to finish his work."ᵗ "I can of mine own self do nothing: as I hear, I judge: and my judgment is just; because I seek not mine own will but the will of the Father which hath sent me."ᵘ

Through the Atonement accomplished by Jesus Christ—a redeeming service, vicariously rendered in behalf of mankind, all of whom have become estranged from God by the effects of sin both inherited and individually incurred—the way is opened for a reconciliation whereby man may come again into communion with God, and be made fit to dwell anew and forever in the presence of his Eternal Father. This basal thought is admirably implied in our English word, "atonement," which, as its syllables attest, is *at-one-ment*, "denoting reconciliation, or the bringing into agreement of those who have been estranged."ᵛ The effect of the Atonement may be conveniently considered as twofold:

1—The universal redemption of the human race from death invoked by the Fall of our first parents; and,

2—Salvation, whereby means of relief from the results of individual sin are provided.

The victory over death was made manifest in the Resurrection of the crucified Christ; He was the first to pass from death to immortality

---

ˢ John 6:38.
ᵗ John 4:34.
ᵘ John 5:30; see also verse 19; also Matt. 26:42; compare D&C 19:2; 20:24.
ᵛ New Standard Dictionary under "propitiation."

and so is justly known as "the first fruits of them that slept."[w] That the resurrection of the dead so inaugurated is to be extended to every one who has or shall have lived is proved by an abundance of scriptural evidence. Following our Lord's Resurrection, others who had slept in the tomb arose and were seen of many, not as spirit apparitions but as resurrected beings possessing immortalized bodies: "And the graves were opened; and many bodies of the saints which slept arose, and came out of the graves after his resurrection, and went into the holy city, and appeared unto many."[x]

Those who thus early came forth are spoken of as "the saints"; and other scriptures confirm the fact that only the righteous shall be brought forth in the earlier stages of the resurrection yet to be consummated; but that all the dead shall in turn resume bodies of flesh and bones is placed beyond doubt by the revealed word. The Savior's direct affirmation ought to be conclusive: "Verily, verily, I say unto you, The hour is coming, and now is, when the dead shall hear the voice of the Son of God: and they that hear shall live. . . . Marvel not at this: for the hour is coming, in the which all that are in the graves shall hear his voice, and shall come forth; they that have done good, unto the resurrection of life; and they that have done evil, unto the resurrection of damnation."[y] The doctrine of a universal resurrection was taught by the apostles of old,[z] as also by the Nephite prophets;[aa] and the same is confirmed by revelation incident to the present dispensation.[bb] Even the heathen who have not known God shall be brought forth from their graves; and, inasmuch as they have lived and died in ignorance of the saving law, a means of making the plan of salvation known unto them is provided. "And then shall the heathen nations be redeemed, and they that knew no law shall have part in the first resurrection."[cc]

[w] 1 Cor. 15:20; see also Acts 26:23; Col. 1:18; Rev. 1:5.
[x] Matt. 27:52–53.
[y] John 5:25, 28, 29. A modern scripture attesting the same truth reads: "They who have done good in the resurrection of the just; and they who have done evil in the resurrection of the unjust."—D&C 76:17.
[z] Acts 24:15; Rev. 20:12, 13.
[aa] For instances see 2 Ne. 9:6, 12, 13, 21, 22; Hel. 14: 15–17; Mosiah 15:20–24; Alma 40:2–16; Morm. 9: 13, 14.
[bb] For instances see D&C 18: 11, 12; 45:44, 45; 88:95–98.
[cc] D&C 45:54.

Jacob, a Nephite prophet, taught the universality of the resurrection, and set forth the absolute need of a Redeemer, without whom the purposes of God in the creation of man would be rendered futile. His words constitute a concise and forceful summary of revealed truth directly bearing upon our present subject:

"For as death hath passed upon all men, to fulfil the merciful plan of the great Creator, there must needs be a power of resurrection, and the resurrection must needs come unto man by reason of the fall; and the Fall came by reason of transgression; and because man became fallen, they were cut off from the presence of the Lord; wherefore it must needs be an infinite atonement; save it should be an infinite atonement, this corruption could not put on incorruption. Wherefore, the first judgment which came upon man, must needs have remained to an endless duration. And if so, this flesh must have laid down to rot and to crumble to its mother earth, to rise no more. O the wisdom of God! his mercy and grace! For behold, if the flesh should rise no more, our spirits must become subject to that angel who fell from before the presence of the eternal God, and became the devil, to rise no more. And our spirits must have become like unto him, and we become devils, angels to a devil, to be shut out from the presence of our God, and to remain with the father of lies, in misery, like unto himself; yea, to that being who beguiled our first parents; who transformeth himself nigh unto an angel of light, and stirreth up the children of men unto secret combinations of murder, and all manner of secret works of darkness. O how great the goodness of our God, who prepareth a way for our escape from the grasp of this awful monster; yea, that monster, death and hell, which I call the death of the body, and also the death of the spirit. And because of the way of deliverance of our God, the Holy One of Israel, this death, of which I have spoken, which is the temporal, shall deliver up its dead; which death is the grave. And this death of which I have spoken, which is the spiritual death, shall deliver up its dead; which spiritual death is hell; wherefore, death and hell must deliver up their dead, and hell must deliver up its captive spirits, and the grave must deliver up its captive bodies, and the bodies and the spirits of men will be restored one to the other; and it is by the power of the resurrection of the Holy One of Israel. O how great the plan of our God!

For on the other hand, the paradise of God must deliver up the spirits of the righteous, and the grave deliver up the body of the righteous; and the spirit and the body is restored to itself again, and all men become incorruptible, and immortal, and they are living souls, having a perfect knowledge like unto us in the flesh; save it be that our knowledge shall be perfect."dd

The application of the Atonement to individual transgression, whereby the sinner may obtain absolution through compliance with the laws and ordinances embodied in the gospel of Jesus Christ, is conclusively attested by scripture. Since forgiveness of sins can be secured in none other way, there being either in heaven or earth no name save that of Jesus Christ whereby salvation shall come unto the children of men,ee every soul stands in need of the Savior's mediation, since all are sinners. "For all have sinned and come short of the glory of God," said Paul of oldff and John the apostle added his testimony in these words: "If we say that we have no sin we deceive ourselves, and the truth is not in us."gg

Who shall question the justice of God, which denies salvation to all who will not comply with the prescribed conditions on which alone it is declared obtainable? Christ is "the author of eternal salvation unto all them that obey him,"hh and God "will render to every man according to his deeds: to them who by patient continuance in well doing seek for glory and honor and immortality, eternal life: but unto them that are contentious, and do not obey the truth, but obey unrighteousness, indignation and wrath, tribulation and anguish, upon every soul of man that doeth evil."ii

Such then is the need of a Redeemer, for without Him mankind would forever remain in a fallen state, and as to hope of eternal progression would be inevitably lost.jj The mortal probation is

---

dd 2 Ne. 9:6–13; read the entire chapter.
ee Moses 6:52; compare 2 Ne. 25:20; Mosiah 3:17; 5:8; D&C 76:1.
ff Rom. 3:23; see also verse 9; Gal. 3:22.
gg 1 John 1:8.
hh Heb. 5:9.
ii Rom. 2:6–9.
jj No special treatment relating to the Fall, the Atonement, or the Resurrection has been either attempted or intended in this chapter. For such the student is referred to doctrinal works dealing with these subjects. See the author's *Articles of Faith*, lectures 3, 4, and 21.

provided as an opportunity for advancement; but so great are the difficulties and the dangers, so strong is the influence of evil in the world, and so weak is man in resistance thereto, that without the aid of a power above that of humanity no soul would find its way back to God from whom it came. The need of a Redeemer lies in the inability of man to raise himself from the temporal to the spiritual plane, from the lower kingdom to the higher. In this conception we are not without analogies in the natural world. We recognize a fundamental distinction between inanimate and living matter, between the inorganic and the organic, between the lifeless mineral on the one hand and the living plant or animal on the other. Within the limitations of its order the dead mineral grows by accretion of substance, and may attain a relatively perfect condition of structure and form as is seen in the crystal. But mineral matter, though acted upon favorably by the forces of nature—light, heat, electric energy and others—can never become a living organism; nor can the dead elements, through any process of chemical combination dissociated from life, enter into the tissues of the plant as essential parts thereof. But the plant, which is of a higher order, sends its rootlets into the earth, spreads its leaves in the atmosphere, and through these organs absorbs the solutions of the soil, inspires the gases of the air, and from such lifeless materials weaves the tissue of its wondrous structure. No mineral particle, no dead chemical substance has ever been made a constituent of organic tissue except through the agency of life. We may, perhaps with profit, carry the analogy a step farther. The plant is unable to advance its own tissue to the animal plane. Though it be the recognized order of nature that the "animal kingdom" is dependent upon the "vegetable kingdom" for its sustenance, the substance of the plant may become part of the animal organism only as the latter reaches down from its higher plane and by its own vital action incorporates the vegetable compounds with itself. In turn, animal matter can never become, even transitorily, part of a human body, except as the living man assimilates it, and by the vital processes of his own existence lifts, for the time being, the substance of the animal that supplied him food to the higher plane of his own existence. The comparison herein employed is admittedly defective if carried beyond reasonable limits of application; for the raising of mineral matter to the plane of the plant, vegetable tissue to the level of the animal, and the elevation of either to the human plane, is but a temporary change; with the dissolution of the higher tissues the material thereof falls again to the level of the inanimate and the dead. But, as a means of illustration the analogy may not be wholly without value.

So, for the advancement of man from his present fallen and relatively degenerate state to the higher condition of spiritual life, a power above his own must cooperate. Through the operation of the laws obtaining in the higher kingdom man may be reached and lifted; himself he cannot save by his own unaided effort.[kk] A Redeemer and Savior of mankind is beyond all question essential to the realization of the plan of the Eternal Father, "to bring to pass the immortality and eternal life of man";[ll] and that Redeemer and Savior is Jesus the Christ, beside whom there is and can be none other.

NOTES TO CHAPTER 3

1. God's Foreknowledge Not a Determining Cause.—"Respecting the foreknowledge of God, let it not be said that divine omniscience is of itself a determining cause whereby events are inevitably brought to pass. A mortal father, who knows the weaknesses and frailties of his son, may by reason of that knowledge sorrowfully predict the calamities and sufferings awaiting his wayward boy. He may foresee in that son's future a forfeiture of blessings that could have been won, loss of position, self-respect, reputation and honor; even the dark shadows of a felon's cell and the night of a drunkard's grave may appear in the saddening visions of that fond father's soul; yet, convinced by experience of the impossibility of bringing about that son's reform, he foresees the dread developments of the future, and he finds but sorrow and anguish in his knowledge. Can it be said that the father's foreknowledge is a cause of the son's sinful life? The son, perchance, has reached his maturity; he is the master of his own destiny; a free agent unto himself. The father is powerless to control by force or to direct by arbitrary command; and, while he would gladly make any effort or sacrifice to save his son from the fate impending, he fears for what seems to be an awful certainty. But surely that thoughtful, prayerful, loving parent does not, because of his knowledge, contribute to the son's waywardness. To reason otherwise would be to say that a neglectful father, who takes not the trouble to study the nature and character of his son, who shuts his eyes to sinful

[kk] A comparison related to that given in the text is treated at length by Henry Drummond in his essay "Biogenesis," which the reader may study with profit.
[ll] Moses 1:39.

tendencies, and rests in careless indifference as to the probable future, will by his very heartlessness be benefiting his child, because his lack of forethought cannot operate as a contributory cause to dereliction.

"Our Heavenly Father has a full knowledge of the nature and disposition of each of His children, a knowledge gained by long observation and experience in the past eternity of our primeval childhood; a knowledge compared with which that gained by earthly parents through mortal experience with their children is infinitesimally small. By reason of that surpassing knowledge, God reads the future of child and children, of men individually and of men collectively as communities and nations; He knows what each will do under given conditions, and sees the end from the beginning. His foreknowledge is based on intelligence and reason. He foresees the future as a state which naturally and surely will be; not as one which must be because He has arbitrarily willed that it shall be."—James E. Talmage, *The Great Apostasy*, pp. 19, 20.

2. Man Free to Choose for Himself.—"The father of souls has endowed His children with the divine birthright of free agency; He does not and will not control them by arbitrary force; He impels no man toward sin; He compels none to righteousness. Unto man has been given freedom to act for himself; and, associated with this independence, is the fact of strict responsibility and the assurance of individual accountability. In the judgment with which we shall be judged, all the conditions and circumstances of our lives shall be considered. The inborn tendencies due to heredity, the effect of environment whether conducive to good or evil, the wholesome teachings of youth, or the absence of good instruction—these and all other contributory elements must be taken into account in the rendering of a just verdict as to the soul's guilt or innocence. Nevertheless, the divine wisdom makes plain what will be the result with given conditions operating on known natures and dispositions of men, while every individual is free to choose good or evil within the limits of the many conditions existing and operative."—*The Great Apostasy*, p. 21; see also *Articles of Faith*, 3: pp. 52–53.

3. The Fall a Process of Physical Degeneracy.—A modern revelation given to the Church in 1833 (D&C 89), prescribes rules for right living, particularly as regards the uses of stimulants, narcotics, and foods unsuited to the body. Concerning the physical causes by which the Fall was brought about, and the close relation between those causes and current violations of the Word of Wisdom embodied in the revelation referred to above, the following is in point. "This, [the Word of Wisdom] like other revelations that have come in the present dispensation, is not wholly new. It is as old as the human race. The principle of the Word of Wisdom was revealed unto Adam. All the essentials of the Word of Wisdom were made known unto him in his immortal state, before he had taken into his body those things that made of it a thing of earth. He was warned against that very practice. He was not told to treat his body as something to be tortured. He was not told to look upon it as the fakir of India has come to look upon his body, or professes to look upon it, as a thing to be utterly condemned; but he was told that he must not take into that body certain things which were there at hand. He was warned that, if he did, his body would lose the power which it then held of living for ever, and that he would become subject to death. It was pointed out to him, as it has been pointed out to you, that there are many good fruits to be plucked, to be eaten, to be enjoyed. We believe in enjoying good food. We think that these good things are given us of God. We believe in getting all the enjoyment out of eating that we can; and, therefore, we should avoid gluttony, and we should avoid extremes in all our habits of eating; and as was told unto Adam, so is it told unto us: Touch not these things, for in the day that thou doest it thy life shall be shortened and thou shalt die.

"Here let me say that therein consisted the fall—the eating of things unfit, the taking into the body of the things that made of that body a thing of earth: and I take this occasion to raise my voice against the false interpretation of scripture, which has been adopted by certain people, and is current in their minds, and is referred to in a hushed and half-secret way, that the Fall of man consisted in some offense against the laws of chastity and virtue. Such a doctrine is an abomination. What right have we to turn the scriptures from their proper sense and meaning? What right have we to declare that God meant not what He said? The fall was a natural process, resulting through the incorporation into the bodies of our first parents of the things that came from food unfit, through the violation of the command of God regarding what they should eat. Don't go around whispering that the Fall consisted in the mother of the race losing her chastity and her virtue. It is not true; the human race is not born of fornication. These bodies that are given unto us are given in the way that God has provided. Let it not be said that the patriarch of the race, who stood with the gods before he came here upon the earth, and his equally royal consort, were guilty of any such foul offense. The adoption of that belief has led many to excuse departures from the path of chastity and the path of virtue, by saying that it is the sin of the race, that it is as old as Adam. It was not introduced by Adam. It was not committed by Eve. It was the introduction of the devil and came in order that he might sow the seeds of early death in the bodies of men and women, that the race should degenerate as it has degenerated whenever the laws of virtue and of chastity have been transgressed.

"Our first parents were pure and noble, and when we pass behind the veil we shall perhaps learn something of their high estate, more than we know now. But be it known that they were pure; they were noble. It is true that they disobeyed the law of God, in eating things they were told not to eat; but who amongst you can rise up and condemn?"—From an address by the author at the Eighty-fourth Semiannual Conference of the Church, Oct. 6, 1913; *Conference Report*, pp. 118–19.

4. Christ Wrought Redemption from the Fall.—"The Savior thus becomes master of the situation—the debt is paid, the redemption made, the covenant fulfilled, justice satisfied, the will of God done, and all power is now given into the hands of the Son of God—the power of the resurrection, the power of the redemption, the power of salvation, the power to enact laws for the carrying out and accomplishment of this design. Hence life and immortality are brought to light, the gospel is introduced, and He becomes the author of eternal life and exaltation. He is the Redeemer, the Resurrector, the Savior of man and the world; and He has appointed the law of the gospel as the medium which must be complied with in this world or the next, as He complied with His Father's law; hence 'he that believeth shall be saved, and he that believeth not shall be damned.' The plan, the arrangement, the agreement, the covenant was made, entered into and accepted before the foundation of the world; it was prefigured by sacrifices, and was carried out and consummated on the cross. Hence being the mediator between God and man, He becomes by right the dictator and director on earth and in heaven for the living and for the dead, for the past, the present and the future, pertaining to man as associated with this earth or the heavens, in time or eternity, the Captain of our salvation, the Apostle and High Priest of our profession, the Lord and Giver of life."—John Taylor, *Mediation and Atonement*, p. 171.

5. Redemption from the Effect of the Fall.—"'Mormonism' accepts the doctrine of the fall, and the account of the transgression in Eden, as set forth in Genesis; but it affirms that none but Adam is or shall be answerable for Adam's disobedience; that mankind in general are absolutely absolved from responsibility for that 'original sin,' and that each shall account for his own transgressions alone; that the Fall was fore-known of God, that it was turned to good effect by which the necessary condition of mortality should be inaugurated; and that a Redeemer was provided before the world was; that general salvation, in the sense of redemption from the effects of the fall, comes to all without their seeking it; but that individual salvation or rescue from the effects of personal sins is to be acquired by each for himself by faith and good works through the redemption wrought by Jesus Christ."—James E. Talmage, *Story and Philosophy of 'Mormonism,'* p. 111.

CHAPTER 4

THE ANTEMORTAL GODSHIP OF CHRIST

It now becomes our purpose to inquire as to the position and status of Jesus the Christ in the antemortal world, from the period of the solemn council in heaven, in which He was chosen to be the future Savior and Redeemer of mankind, to the time at which He was born in the flesh.

We claim scriptural authority for the assertion that Jesus Christ was and is God the Creator, the God who revealed Himself to Adam, Enoch, and all the antediluvial patriarchs and prophets down to Noah; the God of Abraham, Isaac and Jacob; the God of Israel as a united people, and the God of Ephraim and Judah after the disruption of the Hebrew nation; the God who made Himself known to the prophets from Moses to Malachi; the God of the Old Testament record; and the God of the Nephites. We affirm that Jesus Christ was and is Jehovah, the Eternal One.

The scriptures specify three personages in the Godhead; (1) God the Eternal Father, (2) His Son Jesus Christ, and (3) the Holy Ghost. These constitute the Holy Trinity, comprising three physically separate and distinct individuals, who together constitute the presiding council of the heavens.ᵃ At least two of these appear as directing participants in the work of creation; this fact is instanced by the plurality expressed in Genesis: "And God said, Let us make man in our image, after our likeness"; and later, in the course of consultation concerning Adam's act of transgression, "the Lord God said, Behold,

---

ᵃ See "God and the Godhead," in the author's *Articles of Faith*, lecture 2.

the man is become as one of us."[b] From the words of Moses, as revealed anew in the present dispensation, we learn more fully of the Gods who were actively engaged in the creation of this earth: "And I, God, said unto mine Only Begotten, which was with me from the beginning: Let us make man in our image, after our likeness." Then, further, with regard to the condition of Adam after the fall: "I, the Lord God, said unto mine Only Begotten: Behold, the man is become as one of us."[c] In the account of the creation recorded by Abraham, "the Gods" are repeatedly mentioned.[d]

As heretofore shown in another connection, the Father operated in the work of creation through the Son, who thus became the executive through whom the will, commandment, or word of the Father was put into effect. It is with incisive appropriateness therefore, that the Son, Jesus Christ, is designated by the apostle John as the Word; or as declared by the Father "the word of my power."[e] The part taken by Jesus Christ in the creation, a part so prominent as to justify our calling Him the Creator, is set forth in many scriptures. The author of the Epistle to the Hebrews refers in this wise distinctively to the Father and the Son as separate though associated Beings: "God, who at sundry times and in divers manners spake in time past unto the fathers by the prophets, hath in these last days spoken unto us by his Son, whom he hath appointed heir of all things, by whom also he made the worlds."[f] Paul is even more explicit in his letter to the Colossians, wherein, speaking of Jesus the Son, he says: "For by him were all things created, that are in heaven, and that are in earth, visible and invisible, whether they be thrones, or dominions, or principalities, or powers: all things were created by him, and for him: and he is before all things, and by him all things consist."[g] And here let be repeated the testimony of John, that by the Word, who was with God, and who was God even in the beginning, all things were made; "and without him was not anything made that was made."[h]

[b] Gen. 1:26 and 3:22.
[c] Moses 2:26 and 4:28.
[d] Abr. 4 and 5.
[e] See John 1:1 and Moses 1:32.
[f] Heb. 1:1, 2; see also 1 Cor. 8:6.
[g] Col. 1:16, 17.
[h] John 1:1–3.

That the Christ who was to come was in reality God the Creator was revealed in plainness to the prophets on the western hemisphere. Samuel, the converted Lamanite, in preaching to the unbelieving Nephites justified his testimony as follows: "And also that ye might know of the coming of Jesus Christ, the Son of God, the Father of heaven and of earth, the Creator of all things, from the beginning; and that ye might know of the signs of his coming, to the intent that ye might believe on his name."[i]

To these citations of ancient scripture may most properly be added the personal testimony of the Lord Jesus after He had become a resurrected Being. In His visitation to the Nephites He thus proclaimed Himself: "Behold, I am Jesus Christ the Son of God. I created the heavens and the earth, and all things that in them are. I was with the Father from the beginning. I am in the Father, and the Father in me; and in me hath the Father glorified his name."[j] To the Nephites, who failed to comprehend the relation between the gospel declared unto them by the Resurrected Lord, and the Mosaic law which they held traditionally to be in force, and who marveled at His saying that old things had passed away, He explained in this wise: "Behold I say unto you, that the law is fulfilled that was given unto Moses. Behold, I am he that gave the law, and I am he who covenanted with my people Israel: therefore, the law in me is fulfilled, for I have come to fulfil the law; therefore it hath an end."[k]

Through revelation in the present or last dispensation the voice of Jesus Christ, the Creator of heaven and earth, has been heard anew: "Hearken, O ye people of my church to whom the kingdom has been given—hearken ye and give ear to him who laid the foundation of the earth, who made the heavens and all the hosts thereof, and by whom all things were made which live, and move, and have a being."[l] And again, "Behold, I am Jesus Christ the Son of the living God, who created the heavens and the earth; a light which cannot be hid in darkness."[m]

---

[i] Hel. 14: 12; see also Mosiah 3:8; 4:2; Alma 11:39.
[j] 3 Ne. 9:15.
[k] 3 Ne.15:4, 5.
[l] D&C 45:1.
[m] D&C 14:9; see also 29:1, 31; 76:24.

The divinity of Jesus Christ is indicated by the specific names and titles authoritatively applied to Him. According to man's judgment there may be but little importance attached to names; but in the nomenclature of the Gods every name is a title of power or station. God is righteously zealous of the sanctity of His own name[n] and of names given by His appointment. In the case of children of promise names have been prescribed before birth; this is true of our Lord Jesus and of the Baptist, John, who was sent to prepare the way for the Christ. Names of persons have been changed by divine direction, when not sufficiently definite as titles denoting the particular service to which the bearers were called, or the special blessings conferred upon them.[o]

Jesus is the individual name of the Savior, and as thus spelled is of Greek derivation; its Hebrew equivalent was *Yehoshua* or *Yeshua*, or, as we render it in English, *Joshua*. In the original the name was well understood as meaning "Help of Jehovah," or "Savior." Though as common an appellation as John or Henry or Charles today, the name was nevertheless divinely prescribed, as already stated. Thus, unto Joseph, the espoused husband of the Virgin, the angel said, "And thou shalt call his name JESUS: for he shall save his people from their sins."[p]

Christ is a sacred title, and not an ordinary appellation or common name; it is of Greek derivation, and in meaning is identical with its Hebrew equivalent *Messiah* or *Messias*, signifying the *Anointed One*.[q] Other titles, each possessing a definitive meaning, such as *Emmanuel, Savior, Redeemer, Only Begotten Son, Lord, Son of God, Son of Man*, and many more, are of scriptural occurrence; the fact of main present importance to us is that these several titles are expressive of our Lord's divine origin and Godship. As seen, the essential names or titles of Jesus the Christ were made known before His birth, and were revealed to prophets who preceded Him in the mortal state.[r]

[n] Ex. 20:7; Lev. 19:12; Deut. 5:11.

[o] Note 1, end of chapter.

[p] Matt. 1:21; see also verses 23, 25; Luke 1:31.

[q] John 1:41; 4:25.

[r] Luke 1:31; 2:21; Matt. 1:21, 25; see also verse 23 and compare Isa. 7:14; Luke 2:11. See further Moses 6:51, 57; 7:20; 8:24;   1 Ne. 10:4; 2 Ne. 10:3; Mosiah 3:8.

Jehovah is the Anglicized rendering of the Hebrew, *Yahveh* or *Jahveh*, signifying the *Self-existent One*, or *The Eternal*. This name is generally rendered in our English version of the Old Testament as LORD, printed in capitals.ˢ The Hebrew, *Ehyeh*, signifying *I Am*, is related in meaning and through derivation with the term *Yahveh* or *Jehovah,* and herein lies the significance of this name by which the Lord revealed Himself to Moses when the latter received the commission to go into Egypt and deliver the children of Israel from bondage: "Moses said unto God, Behold, when I come unto the children of Israel, and shall say unto them, The God of your fathers hath sent me unto you; and they shall say to me, What is his name? what shall I say unto them? And God said unto Moses, I AM THAT I AM: and he said, Thus shalt thou say unto the children of Israel, I AM hath sent me unto you."ᵗ In the succeeding verse the Lord declares Himself to be "the God of Abraham, the God of Isaac, and the God of Jacob." While Moses was in Egypt, the Lord further revealed Himself, saying "I am the LORD: and I appeared unto Abraham, unto Isaac, and unto Jacob, by thy name of God Almighty, but by my name JEHOVAH was I not known to them."ᵘ The central fact connoted by this name, *I Am*, or *Jehovah*, the two having essentially the same meaning, is that of existence or duration that shall have no end, and which, judged by all human standards of reckoning, could have had no beginning; the name is related to such other titles as *Alpha and Omega*, the first and the last, the beginning and the end.ᵛ

Jesus, when once assailed with question and criticism from certain Jews who regarded their Abrahamic lineage as an assurance of divine preferment, met their abusive words with the declaration: "Verily, verily, I say unto you, Before Abraham was, I am."ʷ The true significance of this saying would be more plainly expressed were the sentence

---

ˢ The name appears thus in Gen. 2:5; see also Ex. 6:2–4; and read for comparison Gen. 17:1; 35:11.

ᵗ Ex. 3:13, 14; compare with respect to the fact of eternal duration expressed in this name, Isa. 44:6; John 8:58; Col. 1: 17; Heb. 13:8; Rev. 1:4; see also Moses 1:3 and the references there given.

ᵘ Ex. 6:2, 3. Note 2, end of chapter.

ᵛ Rev. 1:11, 17; 2:8; 22:13; compare Isa. 41:4; 44:6; 48:12.

ʷ John 8:58.

punctuated and pointed as follows: "Verily, verily, I say unto you, Before Abraham, was I AM"; which means the same as had He said—Before Abraham, was I, Jehovah. The captious Jews were so offended at hearing Him use a name which, through an erroneous rendering of an earlier scripture,[x] they held was not to be uttered on pain of death, that they immediately took up stones with the intent of killing Him. The Jews regarded *Jehovah* as an ineffable name, not to be spoken; they substituted for it the sacred, though to them the not-forbidden name, *Adonai*, signifying *the Lord.* The original of the terms *Lord* and *God* as they appear in the Old Testament, was either *Yahveh* or *Adonai*; and the divine Being designated by these sacred names was, as shown by the scriptures cited, Jesus the Christ. John, evangelist and apostle, positively identifies Jesus Christ with Adonai, or the Lord who spoke through the voice of Isaiah,[y] and with Jehovah who spoke through Zechariah.[z]

The name *Elohim* is of frequent occurrence in the Hebrew texts of the Old Testament, though it is not found in our English versions. In form the word is a Hebrew plural noun;[aa] but it connotes the plurality of excellence or intensity, rather than distinctively of number. It is expressive of supreme or absolute exaltation and power. *Elohim*, as understood and used in the restored Church of Jesus Christ, is the name-title of God the Eternal Father, whose firstborn Son in the spirit is *Jehovah*—the Only Begotten in the flesh, Jesus Christ.

Jesus of Nazareth, who in solemn testimony to the Jews declared Himself the *I Am* or *Jehovah*, who was God before Abraham lived on earth, was the same Being who is repeatedly proclaimed as the God who made covenant with Abraham, Isaac, and Jacob; the God who led Israel from the bondage of Egypt to the freedom of the promised land, the one and only God known by direct and personal revelation to the Hebrew prophets in general.

The identity of Jesus Christ with the Jehovah of the Israelites was well understood by the Nephite prophets, and the truth of their

[x] Lev. 24: 16. Note 3, end of chapter.

[y] Isa. 6:8–11; and compare John 12:40, 41.

[z] Zech. 12:10; compare John 19:37.

[aa] The singular "Eloah," appears only in poetic usage.

teachings was confirmed by the risen Lord who manifested Himself unto them shortly after His ascension from the midst of the apostles at Jerusalem. This is the record: "And it came to pass that the Lord spake unto them saying, Arise and come forth unto me, that ye may thrust your hands into my side, and also that ye may feel the prints of the nails in my hands and in my feet, that ye may know that I am the God of Israel, and the God of the whole earth, and have been slain for the sins of the world."[bb]

It would appear unnecessary to cite at greater length in substantiating our affirmation that Jesus Christ was God even before He assumed a body of flesh. During that antemortal period there was essential difference between the Father and the Son, in that the former had already passed through the experiences of mortal life, including death and resurrection, and was therefore a Being possessed of a perfect, immortalized body of flesh and bones, while the Son was yet unembodied. Through His death and subsequent Resurrection Jesus the Christ is today a Being like unto the Father in all essential characteristics.

A general consideration of scriptural evidence leads to the conclusion that God the Eternal Father has manifested Himself to earthly prophets or revelators on very few occasions, and then principally to attest the divine authority of His Son, Jesus Christ. As before shown, the Son was the active executive in the work of creation; throughout the creative scenes the Father appears mostly in a directing or consulting capacity. Unto Adam, Enoch, Noah, Abraham and Moses the Father revealed Himself, attesting the Godship of the Christ, and the fact that the Son was the chosen Savior of mankind.[cc] On the occasion of the baptism of Jesus, the Father's voice was heard, saying, "This is my beloved Son, in whom I am well pleased";[dd] and at the transfiguration a similar testimony was given by the Father.[ee] On an occasion yet later, while Jesus prayed in anguish of soul, submitting

---

[bb] 3 Ne. 11:13, 14; also 1 Ne. 17:40 and observe from verse 30 that the Redeemer is here spoken of as the God who delivered Israel. See further Mosiah 7:19. Chapter 39 herein.

[cc] Moses 1:6, 31–33; 2:1; 4:2, 3; 6:57; compare 7:35, 39, 47, 53–59; 8:16, 19, 23, 24; Abr. 3:22–28. See chapter 5 herein.

[dd] Matt. 3:17; also Mark 1:11; Luke 3:22.

[ee] Matt. 17:5; Luke 9:35.

Himself that the Father's purposes be fulfilled and the Father's name glorified, "Then came there a voice from heaven, saying, I have both glorified it, and will glorify it again."ᶠᶠ The resurrected and glorified Christ was announced by the Father to the Nephites on the western hemisphere, in these words: "Behold my beloved Son, in whom I am well pleased, in whom I have glorified my name: hear ye him."ᵍᵍ From the time of the occurrence last noted, the voice of the Father was not heard again among men, so far as the scriptures aver, until the spring of 1820, when both the Father and the Son ministered unto the prophet Joseph Smith, the Father saying, "This is my beloved Son, hear him!"ʰʰ These are the instances of record in which the Eternal Father has been manifest in personal utterance or other revelation to man apart from the Son. God the Creator, the Jehovah of Israel, the Savior and Redeemer of all nations, kindreds and tongues, are the same, and He is Jesus the Christ.

NOTES TO CHAPTER 4

1. Names Given of God.—The significance of names when given of God finds illustration in many scriptural instances. The following are examples: "Jesus," meaning *Savior* (Matt. 1:21; Luke 1:31); "John," signifying *Jehovah's gift*, specifically applied to the Baptist, who was sent to earth to prepare the way for Jehovah's coming in the flesh (Luke 1:13); "Ishmael," signifying *God shall hear him* (Gen. 16:11); "Isaac," meaning laughter (Gen. 17:19, compare 18:10–15). As instances of names changed by divine authority to express added blessings, or special callings, consider the following: "Abram," which connoted *nobility* or *exaltation* and as usually rendered, *father of elevation*, was changed to "Abraham," *father of a multitude* which expressed the reason for the change as given at the time thereof, "for a father of many nations have I made thee" (Gen. 17:5). "Sarai," the name of Abraham's wife, and of uncertain distinctive meaning, was substituted by "Sarah" which signified *the princess* (Gen. 17:15). "Jacob," a name given to the son of Isaac with reference to a circumstance attending his birth, and signifying *a supplanter*, was superseded by "Israel" meaning *a soldier of God, a prince of God*, as expressed in the words effecting the change, "Thy name shall be called no more Jacob, but Israel, for as a prince hast thou power with God and with men, and hast prevailed." (Gen. 32:28; compare 35:9–10.) "Simon," meaning *a hearer*, the name of the man

ᶠᶠ John 12:28.
ᵍᵍ 3 Ne. 11:7.
ʰʰ Joseph Smith—*History* 2:17.

who became the chief apostle of Jesus Christ, was changed by the Lord to "Cephas" (Aramaic) or "Peter" (Greek) meaning *a rock* John (1:42; Matt. 16:18; Luke 6:14). On James and John the sons of Zebedee, the Lord conferred the name or title "Boanerges" meaning *sons of thunder* (Mark 3:17).

The following is an instructive excerpt: "*Name* in the scriptures not only = that by which a person is designated, but frequently = all that is known to belong to the person having this designation, and the person himself. Thus 'the name of God' or 'of Jehovah,' etc., indicates His authority (Deut. 18:20; Matt. 21:9, etc.), His dignity and glory (Isa. 48:9, etc.), His protection and favor (Prov. 18:10, etc.), His character (Ex. 34:5, 14, compare 6–7, etc.), His divine attributes in general (Matt. 6:9, etc.), etc. The Lord is said to set or put His name where the revelation or manifestation of His perfections is made (Deut. 12:5, 14:24, etc.). To believe in or on the name of Christ is to receive and treat Him in accordance with the revelation which the scriptures make of Him (John 1:12; 2:23), etc."—Smith's *Comprehensive Dictionary of the Bible*, "Name."

2. Jesus Christ, the God of Israel.—"That Jesus Christ was the same Being who called Abraham from his native country, who led Israel out of the land of Egypt with mighty miracles and wonders, who made known to them His law amid the thunderings of Sinai, who delivered them from their enemies, who chastened them for their disobedience, who inspired their prophets, and whose glory filled Solomon's temple, is evident from all the inspired writings, and in none more so than in the Bible.

"His lamentation over Jerusalem evidences that, in His humanity, He had not forgotten His former exalted position: 'O Jerusalem, Jerusalem, thou that killest the prophets, and stonest them which are sent unto thee, how often would I have gathered thy children together, . . . and ye would not!' (Matt. 23:37). It was this Creator of the world, this mighty Ruler, this Controller of the destinies of the human family, who, in His last moments, cried out in the agony of His soul, 'My God, my God, why hast thou forsaken me?'" (Mark 15:34.)—Franklin D. Richards and James A. Little, *Compendium of the Doctrines of the Gospel.*

3. "Jehovah" a Name Not Uttered by the Jews.—Long prior to the time of Christ, certain schools among the Jews, ever intent on the observance of the letter of the law, though not without disregard of its spirit, had taught that the mere utterance of the name of God was blasphemous, and that the sin of so doing constituted a capital offense. This extreme conception arose from the accepted though uninspired interpretation of Lev. 24:16, "And he that blasphemeth the name of the Lord, he shall surely be put to death, and all the congregation shall certainly stone him: as well the stranger, as he that is born in the land, when he blasphemeth the name of the Lord, shall be put to death." We take the following from Smith's *Comprehensive Dictionary of the Bible*, article "Jehovah": "The true pronunciation of this name, [Yehovah] by which God was known to the Hebrews, has been entirely lost, the

Jews themselves scrupulously avoiding every mention of it, and substituting in its stead one or other of the words with whose proper vowel-points it may happen to be written [*Adonai*, Lord, or *Elohim*, God]. . . . According to Jewish tradition it was pronounced but once a year by the high priest on the day of atonement when he entered the Holy of Holies; but on this point there is some doubt."

CHAPTER 5

EARTHLY ADVENT OF THE CHRIST PREDICTED

The coming of Christ to earth to tabernacle in the flesh was no unexpected or unheralded event. For centuries prior to the great occurrence the Jews had professed to be looking for the advent of their King; and, in the appointed ceremonials of worship as in private devotions, the coming of the promised Messiah was prominent as a matter of the supplication of Israel to Jehovah. True, there was much diversity in lay opinion and in rabbinical exposition as to the time and manner of His appearing; but the certainty thereof was fundamentally established in the beliefs and hopes of the Hebrew nation.

The records known to us as the books of the Old Testament, together with other inspired writings once regarded as authentic but excluded from later compilations as not strictly canonical, were current among the Hebrews at and long before the time of Christ's birth. These scriptures had their beginning in the proclamation of the law through Moses,[a] who wrote the same, and delivered the writing into the official custody of the priests with an express command that it be read in the assemblies of the people at stated times. To these earlier writings were added the utterances of divinely commissioned prophets, the records of appointed historians, and the songs of inspired poets, as the centuries passed; so that at the time of our Lord's ministry the Jews possessed a great accumulation of writings accepted and revered by them as authoritative.[b] These records are rich in prediction and promise respecting the earthly advent of the Messiah, as are other scriptures to which the Israel of old had not access.

[a] Deut. 31:9, 24–26; compare 17:18–20.
[b] *Articles of Faith*, chapter 13.

Adam, the patriarch of the race, rejoiced in the assurance of the Savior's appointed ministry, through the acceptance of which, he, the transgressor, might gain redemption. Brief mention of the plan of salvation, the author of which is Jesus Christ, appears in the promise given of God following the fall—that though the devil, represented by the serpent in Eden, should have power to bruise the heel of Adam's posterity, through the seed of the woman should come the power to bruise the adversary's head.[c] It is significant that this assurance of eventual victory over sin and its inevitable effect, death, both of which were introduced to earth through Satan the arch-enemy of mankind, was to be realized through the offspring of woman; the promise was not made specifically to the man, nor to the pair. The only instance of offspring from woman dissociated from mortal fatherhood is the birth of Jesus the Christ, who was the earthly Son of a mortal mother, begotten by an immortal Father. He is the Only Begotten of the Eternal Father in the flesh, and was born of woman.

Through scriptures other than those embodied in the Old Testament we learn with greater fulness of the revelations of God to Adam respecting the coming of the Redeemer. As a natural and inevitable result of his disobedience, Adam had forfeited the high privilege he once enjoyed—that of holding direct and personal association with his God; nevertheless in his fallen state he was visited by an angel of the Lord, who revealed unto him the plan of redemption: "And after many days an angel of the Lord appeared unto Adam, saying: Why dost thou offer sacrifices unto the Lord? And Adam said unto him: I know not, save the Lord commanded me. And then the angel spake, saying: This thing is a similitude of the sacrifice of the Only Begotten of the Father, which is full of grace and truth. Wherefore, thou shalt do all that thou doest in the name of the Son, and thou shalt repent and call upon God in the name of the Son for evermore. And in that day the Holy Ghost fell upon Adam, which beareth record of the Father and the Son, saying: I am the Only Begotten of the Father from the beginning, henceforth and for ever, that as thou hast fallen thou mayest be redeemed, and all mankind, even as many as will."[d]

[c] Gen. 3:15; compare Heb. 2:14; Rev. 12:9; 20:3.

[d] Moses 5:6–9. Note 1, end of chapter.

The Lord's revelation to Adam making known the ordained plan whereby the Son of God was to take upon Himself flesh in the meridian of time, and become the Redeemer of the world, was attested by Enoch, son of Jared and father of Methuselah. From the words of Enoch we learn that to him as to his great progenitor, Adam, the very name by which the Savior would be known among men was revealed—"which is Jesus Christ, the only name which shall be given under heaven, whereby salvation shall come unto the children of men."[e] The recorded covenant of God with Abraham, and the reiteration and confirmation thereof with Isaac and in turn with Jacob—that through their posterity should all nations of the earth be blessed—presaged the birth of the Redeemer through that chosen lineage.[f] Its fulfillment is the blessed heritage of the ages.

In pronouncing his patriarchal blessing upon the head of Judah, Jacob prophesied: "The sceptre shall not depart from Judah, nor a lawgiver from between his feet, until Shiloh come; and unto him shall the gathering of the people be."[g] That by Shiloh is meant the Christ is evidenced by the fulfillment of the conditions set forth in the prediction, in the state of the Jewish nation at the time of our Lord's birth.[h]

Moses proclaimed the coming of a great Prophet in Israel, whose ministry was to be of such importance that all men who would not accept Him would be under condemnation; and that this prediction had sole reference to Jesus Christ is conclusively shown by later scriptures. Thus spake the Lord unto Moses: "I will raise them up a Prophet from among their brethren, like unto thee, and will put my words in his mouth; and he shall speak unto them all that I shall command him. And it shall come to pass, that whosoever will not hearken unto my words which he shall speak in my name, I will require it of him."[i] The system of sacrifice expressly enjoined in the

---

[e] Moses 6:52; study also vss. 50–56. See also Gen. 5:18, 21–24; Jude 14. Note 4, end of chapter.

[f] Gen. 12:3; 18:18; 22:18; 26:4; 28:14; compare Acts 3:25; Gal. 3:8.

[g] Gen. 49:10.

[h] Note 2, end of chapter.

[i] Deut. 18:15–19; compare John 1:45; Acts 3:22; 7:37; see also a specific confirmation by our Lord after His Resurrection, 3 Ne. 20:23.

Mosaic code was essentially a prototype of the sacrificial death to be accomplished by the Savior on Calvary. The blood of countless altar victims, slain by Israel's priests in the course of prescribed ritual, ran throughout the centuries from Moses to Christ as a prophetic flood in similitude of the blood of the Son of God appointed to be shed as an expiatory sacrifice for the redemption of the race. But, as already shown, the institution of bloody sacrifice as a type of the future death of Jesus Christ dates from the beginning of human history; since the offering of animal sacrifices through the shedding of blood was required of Adam, to whom the significance of the ordinance, as "a similitude of the sacrifice of the Only Begotten of the Father," was expressly defined.[j]

The paschal lamb, slain for every Israelitish household at the annually recurring feast of the Passover, was a particular type of the Lamb of God who in due time would be slain for the sins of the world. The crucifixion of Christ was effected at the Passover season; and the consummation of the supreme Sacrifice, of which the paschal lambs had been but lesser prototypes, led Paul the apostle to affirm in later times: "For even Christ our passover is sacrificed for us."[k]

Job in the day of dire affliction rejoiced in his testimony of the coming Messiah, and declared with prophetic conviction: "I know that my redeemer liveth, and that he shall stand at the latter day upon the earth."[l] The songs of David the psalmist abound in oft-recurring allusion to the earthly life of Christ, many circumstances of which are described in detail, and, as to these, corroboration of the utterances is found in New Testament scriptures.[m]

---

[j] Note 1, end of chapter.

[k] 1 Cor. 5:7. For references to Christ as the Lamb of God, see John 1:29, 36; 1 Pet. 1:19; Rev. 5, 6, 7, 12, 13, 14, 15, 17, 19, 21, 22; also 1 Ne. 10:10; 11, 12, 13, 14; 2 Ne. 31:4, 5, 6; 33:14; Alma 7:14; Morm. 9:2, 3; D&C 58:11; 132:19.

[l] Job 19:25; see also verses 26–27.

[m] Instances: Ps. 2:7; compare Acts 13:33; Heb. 1:5; 5:5. Ps. 16:10; compare Acts 13:34–37; Ps. 22:18; compare Matt. 27:35; Mark 15:24; Luke 23:34; John 19:24. Ps. 41:9; compare John 13:18; Ps. 69:9, 21; compare Matt. 27:34, 48; Mark 15:23; John 19:29; and John 2:17; Ps. 110:1, 4; compare Matt. 22:44; Mark 12:35–37; Luke 20:41–44; Heb. 5:6; Ps. 118:22, 23; compare Matt. 21:42; Mark 12:10; Luke 20:17; Acts 4:11; Eph. 2:20; 1 Pet. 2:4, 7. The following are known specifically as Messianic Psalms: 2, 21, 22, 45, 67, 69, 89, 96, 110, 132; in them the psalmist extols in poetic measure the excellencies of the Messiah and the certainty of His coming.

Isaiah, whose prophetic office was honored by the personal testimony of Christ and the apostles, manifested in numerous passages the burden of his conviction relating to the great event of the Savior's advent and ministry on earth. With the forcefulness of direct revelation he told of the Virgin's divine maternity, whereof Immanuel should be born, and his prediction was reiterated by the angel of the Lord, over seven centuries later.[n] Looking down through the ages the prophet saw the accomplishment of the divine purposes as if already achieved, and sang in triumph: "For unto us a child is born, unto us a son is given: and the government shall be upon his shoulder: and his name shall be called Wonderful, Counselor, The mighty God, The everlasting Father, The Prince of Peace. Of the increase of his government and peace there shall be no end, upon the throne of David, and upon his kingdom, to order it, and to establish it with judgment and with justice from henceforth even forever."[o]

Immediately prior to its fulfillment, the blessed promise was repeated by Gabriel, sent from the presence of God to the Chosen Virgin of Nazareth.[p] As made known to the prophet and by him proclaimed, the coming Lord was the living Branch that should spring from the undying root typified in the family of Jesse;[q] the foundation Stone insuring the stability of Zion;[r] the Shepherd of the house of Israel;[s] the Light of the world,[t] to Gentile as well as Jew; the Leader and Commander of His people.[u] The same inspired voice predicted the forerunner who should cry in the wilderness: "Prepare ye the way of the Lord, make straight in the desert a highway for our God."[v]

[n] Isa. 7:14; compare Matt. 1:21–23.

[o] Isa.9:6, 7.

[p] Luke 1:26–33.

[q] Isa. 11:1, 10; compare Rom. 15:12; Rev. 5:5; 22:16; see also Jer. 23:5, 6.

[r] Isa. 28:16; compare Ps. 118:22; Matt. 21:42; Acts 4:11; Rom. 9:33; 10:11; Eph. 2:20; 1 Pet. 2:6–8.

[s] Isa. 40:9–11; compare John 10:11, 14; Heb. 13:20; 1 Pet. 2:25; 5:4; see also Ezek. 34:23.

[t] Isa. 42: 1; see also 9:2; 49:6; 60:3; compare Matt. 4:14–16; Luke 2:32; Acts 13:47; 26:18; Eph. 5:8, 14.

[u] Isa. 55:4; compare John 18:37.

[v] Isa. 40:3; compare Matt. 3:3; Mark 1:3; Luke 3:4; John 1:23.

Isaiah was permitted to read the scroll of futurity as to many distinguishing conditions to attend the Messiah's lowly life and atoning death. In Him the prophet saw One who would be despised and rejected of men, a Man of sorrows, acquainted with grief, One to be wounded and bruised for the transgressions of the race, on whom would be laid the iniquity of us all—a patient and willing Sacrifice, silent under affliction, as a lamb brought to the slaughter. The Lord's dying with sinners, and His burial in the tomb of the wealthy were likewise declared with prophetic certainty.[w]

Unto Jeremiah came the word of the Lord in terms of plainness, declaring the sure advent of the King by whom the safety of both Judah and Israel should be assured;[x] the Prince of the House of David, through whom the divine promise to the son of Jesse should be realized.[y] Under the same spirit prophesied Ezekiel,[z] Hosea[aa] and Micah[bb] Zechariah broke off in the midst of fateful prediction to voice the glad song of thanksgiving and praise as he beheld in vision the simple pageantry of the King's triumphal entry into the city of David.[cc] Then the prophet bewailed the grief of the conscience-smitten nation, by whom, as was foreseen, the Savior of humankind would be pierced, even unto death;[dd] and showed that, when subdued by contrition His own people would ask, "What are these wounds in thy hands?", the Lord would answer: "Those with which I was wounded in the house of my friends."[ee] The very price to be paid for the betrayal of the Christ to His death was foretold as in parable.[ff]

The fact, that these predictions of the Old Testament prophets had reference to Jesus Christ and to Him only, is put beyond question

[w] Isa. 53; study the entire chapter; compare Acts 8:32–35.

[x] Jer. 23:5, 6; see also 33:14–16.

[y] Jer. 30:9.

[z] Ezek. 34:23; 37:24, 25.

[aa] Hos. 11:11; compare Matt. 2:15.

[bb] Mic. 5:2; compare Matt. 2:6; John 7:42.

[cc] Zech. 9:9; compare Matt. 21:4–9.

[dd] Zech. 12:10; compare John 19:37.

[ee] Zech. 13:6.

[ff] Zech. 11:12, 13; compare Matt. 26:15; 27:3–10.

by the attestation of the resurrected Lord. To the assembled apostles He said: "These are the words which I spake unto you, while I was yet with you, that all things must be fulfilled, which were written in the law of Moses, and in the prophets, and in the psalms, concerning me. Then opened he their understanding, that they might understand the scriptures, and said unto them, Thus it is written, and thus it behoved Christ to suffer, and to rise from the dead the third day."[gg]

John the Baptist, whose ministry immediately preceded that of the Christ, proclaimed the coming of One mightier than himself, One who should baptize with the Holy Ghost, and specifically identified Jesus of Nazareth as that One, the Son of God, the Lamb who should assume the burden of the world's sins.[hh]

The predictions thus far cited as relating to the life, ministry, and death of the Lord Jesus, are the utterances of prophets who, excepting Adam and Enoch, lived and died on the eastern hemisphere. All save John the Baptist are of Old Testament record, and he, a contemporary of the Christ in mortality, figures in the early chapters of the Gospels. It is important to know that the scriptures of the western hemisphere are likewise explicit in the declaration of the great truth that the Son of God would be born in the flesh. The Book of Mormon contains a history of a colony of Israelites, of the tribe of Joseph, who left Jerusalem 600 B.C., during the reign of Zedekiah, king of Judah, on the eve of the subjugation of Judea by Nebuchadnezzar and the inauguration of the Babylonian captivity. This colony was led by divine guidance to the American continent, whereon they developed into a numerous and mighty people; though, divided by dissension, they formed two opposing nations known respectively as Nephites and Lamanites. The former cultivated the arts of industry and refinement, and preserved a record embodying both history and scripture, while the latter became degenerate and debased. The Nephites suffered extinction about A.D. 400, but the Lamanites lived on in their degraded course, and are today extant upon the land as the American Indians.[ii]

[gg] Luke 24:44, 46; see also verses 25–27.
[hh] Matt. 3:11; Mark 1:8; Luke 3:16; John 1:15, 26, 27, 29–36; see also Acts 1:5, 8; 11:16; 19:4.
[ii] Note 3, end of chapter.

The Nephite annals from the beginning thereof down to the time of our Lord's birth abound in prediction and promise of the Christ; and this chronicle is followed by a record of the actual visitation of the resurrected Savior to the Nephites, and the establishment of His Church among them. Unto Lehi, the leader of the colony, the Lord revealed the time, place, and manner of Christ's then future advent, together with many important facts of His ministry, and the preparatory work of John the forerunner. This revelation was given while the company was journeying in the wilderness of Arabia, prior to their crossing the great waters. The prophecy is thus written by Nephi, a son of Lehi and his successor in the prophetic calling: "Yea, even six hundred years from the time that my father left Jerusalem, a prophet would the Lord God raise up among the Jews; even a Messiah; or, in other words, a Savior of the world. And he also spake concerning the prophets, how great a number had testified of these things concerning this Messiah, of whom he had spoken, or this Redeemer of the world. Wherefore all mankind were in a lost and in a fallen state, and ever would be, save they should rely on this Redeemer. And he spake also concerning a prophet who should come before the Messiah, to prepare the way of the Lord; yea, even he should go forth and cry in the wilderness, Prepare ye the way of the Lord, and make his paths straight; for there standeth one among you whom ye know not; and he is mightier than I, whose shoe's latchet I am not worthy to unloose. And much spake my father concerning this thing. And my father said he should baptize in Bethabara, beyond Jordan; and he also said he should baptize with water; even that he should baptize the Messiah with water. And after he had baptized the Messiah with water, he should behold and bear record, that he had baptized the Lamb of God, who should take away the sins of the world. And it came to pass after my father had spoken these words, he spake unto my brethren concerning the gospel which should be preached among the Jews; and also concerning the dwindling of the Jews in unbelief. And after they had slain the Messiah, who should come, and after he had been slain, he should rise from the dead, and should make himself manifest, by the Holy Ghost, unto the Gentiles."[jj]

---

jj 1 Ne. 10:4–11.

At a later time Nephi writes, not as his father's scribe, but as a prophet and revelator voicing the word of God as made known to himself. He was permitted to behold in vision and to declare to his people the circumstances of the Messiah's birth, His baptism by John and the ministration of the Holy Ghost with its accompanying sign of the dove; he beheld our Lord moving as a Teacher of righteousness among the people, healing the afflicted and rebuking spirits of evil; he saw and bore record of the dread scenes of Calvary; he beheld and predicted the calling of the chosen Twelve, the apostles of the Lamb, for so these were designated by Him who vouchsafed the vision. Moreover he told of the iniquity of the Jews, who were seen in contention with the apostles; and thus concludes the portentous prophecy: "And the angel of the Lord spake unto me again, saying, Thus shall be the destruction of all nations, kindreds, tongues, and people, that shall fight against the twelve apostles of the Lamb."[kk] Soon after the defection whereby the distinction between Nephites and Lamanites was established, Jacob, a brother of Nephi, continued in prophecy of the assured coming of the Messiah, specifically declaring that He would minister at Jerusalem and affirming the necessity of His atoning death as the ordained means of human redemption.[ll] The prophet Abinadi, in his fearless denunciation of sin to the wicked king Noah, preached the Christ who was to come;[mm] and righteous Benjamin, who was at once prophet and king, proclaimed the same great truth to his people about 125 B.C. So taught Alma[nn] in his inspired admonition to his wayward son, Corianton; and so also Amulek[oo] in his contention with Zeezrom. So proclaimed the Lamanite prophet, Samuel, only five years prior to the actual occurrence; furthermore he specified the signs by which the birth of Jesus in Judea would be made known to the people of the western world. Said he: "Behold, I give unto you a sign; for five years more cometh, and behold, then cometh the Son of God to redeem all those

[kk] 1 Ne. chapters 11 and 12; see also 19:10.

[ll] 2 Ne. 9:5, 6; 10:3. See also Nephi's prophecy 25:12–14; and 26.

[mm] Mosiah 13:33–35; 15:1–13.

[nn] Alma 39:15; 40:1–3.

[oo] Alma 11:31–44.

who shall believe on his name. And behold, this will I give unto you for a sign at the time of his coming; for behold, there shall be great lights in heaven, insomuch that in the night before he cometh there shall be no darkness, insomuch that it shall appear unto man as if it was day, therefore there shall be one day and a night, and a day, as if it were One day, and there were no night; and this shall be unto you for a sign; for ye shall know of the rising of the sun, and also of its setting; therefore they shall know of a surety that there shall be two days and a night; nevertheless the night shall not be darkened; and it shall be the night before he is born. And behold there shall a new star arise, such an one as ye never have beheld; and this also shall be a sign unto you. And behold this is not all, there shall be many signs and wonders in heaven."[pp]

Thus the scriptures of both hemispheres and in all ages of ante-meridian time bore solemn testimony to the certainty of Messiah's advent; thus the holy prophets of old voiced the word of revelation predicting the coming of the world's King and Lord, through whom alone is salvation provided, and redemption from death made sure. It is a characteristic of prophets sent of God that they possess and proclaim a personal assurance of the Christ, "for the testimony of Jesus is the spirit of prophecy."[qq] Not a word of inspired prophecy relating to the great event has been found void. The literal fulfilment of the predictions is ample attestation of their origin in divine revelation, and proof conclusive of the divinity of Him whose coming was so abundantly foretold.

NOTES TO CHAPTER 5

1. The Antiquity of Sacrifice as a Prototype of Christ's Atoning Death.—While the Biblical record expressly attests the offering of sacrifices long prior to Israel's exodus from Egypt—e.g. by Abel and by Cain (Gen. 4:3, 4); by Noah after the deluge (Gen. 8:20); by Abraham (Gen. 22:2, 13); by Jacob (Gen. 31:54; 46:1)—it is silent concerning the divine origin of sacrifice as a propitiatory requirement prefiguring the atoning death of Jesus Christ. The difficulty of determining time and circumstance, under which the offering of symbolical sacrifices originated

pp Hel. 14:1–6; compare 3 Ne. 1:4–21.
qq Rev. 19:10.

amongst mankind, is recognized by all investigators save those who admit the validity of modern revelation. The necessity of assuming early instruction from God to man on the subject has been asserted by many Bible scholars. Thus, the writer of the article "Sacrifice" in the Cassell *Bible Dictionary* says: "The idea of sacrifice is prominent throughout the scriptures, and one of the most ancient and widely recognized in the rites of religion throughout the world. There is also a remarkable similarity in the developments and applications of the idea. On these and other accounts it has been judiciously inferred that sacrifice formed an element in the primeval worship of man; and that its universality is not merely an indirect argument for the unity of the human race, but an illustration and confirmation of the first inspired pages of the world's history. The notion of sacrifice can hardly be viewed as a product of unassisted human nature, and must therefore be traced to a higher source and viewed as a divine revelation to primitive man."

Smith's *Dictionary of the Bible* presents the following: "In tracing the history of sacrifice from its first beginning to its perfect development in the Mosaic ritual, we are at once met by the long-disputed question as to the origin of sacrifice, whether it arose from a natural instinct of man, sanctioned and guided by God, or was the subject of some distinct primeval revelation. There can be no doubt that sacrifice was sanctioned by God's Law, with a special, typical reference to the Atonement of Christ; its universal prevalence, independent of, and often opposed to, man's natural reasonings on his relation to God, shows it to have been primeval, and deeply rooted in the instincts of humanity. Whether it was first enjoined by an external command, or was based on that sense of sin and lost communion with God, which is stamped by His hand on the heart of man—is an historical question, perhaps insoluble."

The difficulty vanishes, and the "historical question" as to the origin of sacrifice is definitely solved by the revelations of God in the current dispensation, whereby parts of the record of Moses—not contained in the Bible—have been restored to human knowledge. The scripture quoted in the text (p. 44) makes clear the fact that the offering of sacrifices was required of Adam after his transgression, and that the significance of the divinely established requirement was explained in fullness to the patriarch of the race. The shedding of the blood of animals in sacrifice to God, as a prototype "of the sacrifice of the Only Begotten of the Father," dates from the time immediately following the fall. Its origin is based on a specific revelation to Adam. See Moses 5:5–8.

2. Jacob's Prophecy Concerning "Shiloh."—The prediction of the patriarch Jacob—that the sceptre should not depart from Judah before the coming of Shiloh—has given rise to much disputation among Bible students. Some insist that "Shiloh" is the name of a place and not that of a person. That there was a place known by that name is beyond question (see Josh. 18:1; 19:51; 21:2; 22:9; 1 Sam. 1:3; Jer. 7:12); but the name occurring in Gen. 49:10 is plainly that of a person. It should be known that the use of the word in the King James or authorized version of the Bible is held to be correct by many eminent authorities. Thus, in Dummelow's *Commentary on the Holy Bible*, we read: "This verse has always been regarded by both Jews and Christians as a remarkable prophecy of the coming of the Messiah. . . . On the rendering given above, the whole verse foretells that Judah would retain authority until the advent of the rightful ruler, the Messiah, to whom all peoples would gather. And, broadly speaking, it may be said that the last traces of Jewish legislative power (as vested in the Sanhedrin) did not disappear until the coming of Christ and the destruction of Jerusalem, from which time His kingdom was set up among men."

Adam Clarke, in his exhaustive Bible Commentary, briefly analyzes the objections urged against the admissibility of this passage as applying to the Messiah's advent, and dismisses them all as unfounded. His conclusion as to the meaning of the passage is thus worded: "Judah shall continue a distinct tribe until the Messiah shall come; and it did so; and after His coming it was confounded with the others, so that all distinction has been ever since lost."

Prof. Douglas, as cited in Smith's *Dictionary*, "claims that something of Judah's sceptre still remained, a total eclipse being no proof that the day is at an end—that the proper fulfillment of the prophecy did not begin till David's time, and is consummated in Christ according to Luke 1:32, 33."

The accepted meaning of the word by derivation is "Peaceable," and this is applicable to the attributes of the Christ, who in Isa. 9:6, is designated the prince of peace.

Eusebius, who lived between A.D. 260 and 339, and is known in ecclesiastical history as Bishop of Caesarea, wrote: "At the time that Herod was king, who was the first foreigner that reigned over the Jewish people, the prophecy recorded by Moses received it fulfillment, viz. 'That a prince should not fail of Judah, nor a ruler from his loins, until He should come for whom it is reserved, the expectation of nations.'" (The quoted passage is founded on the Septuagint rendering of Genesis 49:10.)

Some critics have held that in Jacob's use of the word "Shiloh" he did not intend it as a name or proper noun at all. The writer of the article "Shiloh" in Cassell's *Bible Dictionary* says: "The preponderance of evidence is in favor of the Messianic interpretation, but opinions are very divided respecting the retention of the word 'Shiloh' as a proper name. . . . Notwithstanding all the objections that are urged against it being so regarded, we are of the opinion that it is rightly considered to be a proper name, and that the English version represents the true sense of the passage. We recommend those who wish to enter more fully into a question which cannot well be discussed without Hebrew criticism, to the excellent notes upon Gen. 49:10 in the 'Commentary on the Pentateuch' by Keil and Delitzsch. Here the text is thus rendered: "The sceptre shall not depart from Judah, nor the ruler's staff from between his feet, till Shiloh come, and the willing obedience of the nations be to him."

"Notwithstanding the slight put upon the Messianic interpretation by some writers, even those from whom we should scarcely expect it, we see this explanation confirmed and not weakened in the events of history. The text is not taken to mean that Judah should at no time be without a royal ruler of his own, but that the regal power should not finally cease from Judah until Shiloh had come. The objections founded on the Babylonian captivity, and similar intermissions, are of no force, because it is the complete and final termination which is pointed out, and that only happened after the time of Christ." See further *The Book of Prophecy*, by G. Smith, L.L.D., p. 320. See also *Compendium of the Doctrines of the Gospel*, by Franklin D. Richards and James A. Little, article "Christ's First Coming."

3. Nephites and Lamanites.—The progenitors of the Nephite nation were led from Jerusalem, 600 B.C., by Lehi, a Jewish prophet of the tribe of Manasseh. His immediate family, at the time of their departure from Jerusalem, comprised his wife Sariah, and their sons, Laman, Lemuel, Sam, and Nephi; at a later stage of the history, daughters are mentioned, but whether any of these were born before the family exodus we are not told. Beside his own family, the colony of Lehi included Zoram, and Ishmael, the latter an Israelite of the tribe of Ephraim. Ishmael, with his family, joined Lehi in the wilderness; and his descendants were numbered with the nation of whom we are speaking. The company journeyed somewhat east of south, keeping near the borders of the Red Sea; then, changing their course to the eastward, crossed the peninsula of Arabia; and there, on the shores of the Arabian Sea, built and provisioned a vessel in which they committed themselves to divine care upon the waters. Their voyage carried them eastward across the Indian Ocean, then over the south Pacific Ocean to the western coast of South America, whereon they landed (590 B.C.). . . . The people established themselves on what to them was the land of promise; many children were born, and in the course of a few generations a numerous posterity held possession of the land. After the death of Lehi, a division occurred, some of the people accepting as their leader, Nephi, who had been duly appointed to the prophetic office; while the rest proclaimed Laman, the eldest of Lehi's sons, as their chief. Henceforth the divided people were known as Nephites and Lamanites respectively. At times they observed toward each other fairly friendly relations; but generally they were opposed, the Lamanites manifesting implacable hatred and hostility toward their Nephite kindred. The Nephites advanced in the arts of civilization, built large cities and established prosperous commonwealths; yet they often fell into transgression; and the Lord chastened them by allowing their foes to become victorious. They spread northward, occupying the northern part of South America; then, crossing the Isthmus, they extended their domain over the southern, central and eastern portions of what is now the United States of America. The Lamanites, while increasing in numbers, fell under the curse of darkness; they became dark in skin and benighted in spirit, forgot the God of their fathers, lived a wild nomadic life, and degenerated into the fallen state in which the American Indians—their lineal descendants—were found by those who rediscovered the western continent in later times. See Talmage, *Articles of Faith*, pp. 258–60.

4. The First Gospel Dispensation.—The gospel of Jesus Christ was revealed to Adam. Faith in God the Eternal Father, and in His Son the Savior of Adam and all his posterity, repentance of sin, water baptism by immersion, and the reception of the Holy Ghost as a divine bestowal were proclaimed in the beginning of human history as the essentials to salvation. The following scriptures attest this fact. "And thus the Gospel began to be preached, from the beginning, being declared by holy angels sent forth from the presence of God, and by his own voice, and by the gift of the Holy Ghost" (Moses 5:58). The prophet Enoch thus testified: "But God hath made known unto our fathers that all men must repent. And he called upon our father Adam by his own voice, saying: I am God; I made the world, and men before they were in the flesh. And he also said unto him: If thou wilt turn unto me, and hearken unto my voice, and believe, and repent of all thy transgressions, and be baptized, even in water, in the name of mine Only Begotten Son, who is full of grace and truth, which is Jesus Christ, the only name which shall be given under heaven, whereby salvation shall come unto the children of men, ye shall receive the gift of the Holy Ghost, asking all things in his name, and whatsoever ye shall ask, it shall be given you" (Moses 6:50–52; read also 53–61). "And now, behold, I say unto you: This is the plan of salvation unto all men, through the blood of mine Only Begotten, who shall come in the meridian of time" (62). "And it came to pass, when the Lord had spoken with Adam, our father, that Adam cried unto the Lord, and he was caught away by the Spirit of the Lord, and was carried down into the water, and was laid under the water, and was brought forth out of the water. And thus he was baptized, and the Spirit of God descended upon him, and thus he was born of the Spirit, and became quickened in the inner man. And he heard a voice out of heaven, saying: Thou art baptized with fire, and with the Holy Ghost. This is the record of the Father, and the Son, from henceforth and for ever" (64–66). Compare D&C 29:42.

CHAPTER 6
THE MERIDIAN OF TIME

Unto Moses, with whom the Lord spake "face to face, as a man speaketh unto his friend,"[a] the course of the human race, both as then past and future, was made known; and the coming of the Redeemer was recognized by him as the event of greatest import in all the happenings to which the earth and its inhabitants would be witness. The curse of God had aforetime fallen upon the wicked, and upon the earth because of them, "For they would not hearken unto his voice, nor believe on his Only Begotten Son, even him whom he declared should come in the meridian of time, who was prepared from before the foundation of the world."[b] In this scripture appears the earliest mention of the expressive and profoundly significant designation of the period in which the Christ should appear—the meridian of time. If the expression be regarded as figurative, be it remembered the figure is the Lord's.

The term "meridian," as commonly used, conveys the thought of a principal division of time or space;[c] thus we speak of the hours before the daily noon as ante-meridian (a.m.) and those after noon as post-meridian (p.m.). So the years and the centuries of human history are divided by the great event of the birth of Jesus Christ. The years preceding that epoch-making occurrence are now designated as time

[a] Ex.33:11; see also Num. 12:8; Deut. 34:10; compare Moses 1:2, 11, 31.

[b] Moses 5:57; for later mention of the "meridian of time," see 6:56–62; and 7:46; and compare D&C 20:26; 39:3.

[c] "Meridian: . . . figuratively, the highest point or culminating point of anything; the zenith; as the meridian of life."—*New Standard Dictionary.*

Before Christ (B.C.); while subsequent years are each specified as a certain *Year of our Lord*, or, as in the Latin tongue, *Anno Domini* (A.D.). Thus the world's chronology has been adjusted and systematized with reference to the time of the Savior's birth; and this method of reckoning is in use among all Christian nations. It is instructive to note that a similar system was adopted by the isolated branch of the house of Israel that had been brought from the land of Palestine to the western continent; for from the appearance of the promised sign among the people betokening the birth of Him who had been so abundantly predicted by their prophets, the Nephite reckoning of the years, starting with the departure of Lehi and his colony from Jerusalem, was superseded by the annals of the new era.[d]

The occasion of the Savior's advent was preappointed; and the time thereof was specifically revealed through authorized prophets on each of the hemispheres. The long history of the Israelitish nation had unfolded a succession of events that found a relative culmination in the earthly mission of the Messiah. That we may the better comprehend the true significance of the Lord's life and ministry while in the flesh, some consideration should be given to the political, social, and religious condition of the people amongst whom He appeared and with whom He lived and died. Such consideration involves at least a brief review of the antecedent history of the Hebrew nation. The posterity of Abraham through Isaac and Jacob had early come to be known by the title in which they took undying pride and found inspiring promise, Israelites, or the children of Israel.[e] Collectively they were so designated throughout the dark days of their bondage in Egypt;[f] so during the four decades of the exodus and the return to the land of promise,[g] and on through the period of their prosperity as a mighty people under the administration of the judges, and as a united monarchy during the successive reigns of Saul, David, and Solomon.[h]

---

[d] 3 Ne. 2:8; compare 4 Ne. 1:1, 21; Morm. 8:6; Moro. 10:1.

[e] Gen. 32:28; 35:10.

[f] Ex. 1:1, 7; 9:6, 7; 12:3, etc.

[g] Ex. 12:35, 40; 13:19; 15:1; Num. 20:1, 19, 24, etc.

[h] See mention throughout the books of Judges, 1 and 2 Samuel, 1 and 2 Kings, and references therein.

Immediately following the death of Solomon, about 975 B.C. according to the most generally accepted chronology, the nation was disrupted by revolt. The tribe of Judah, part of the tribe of Benjamin, and small remnants of a few other tribes remained true to the royal succession, and accepted Rehoboam, son of Solomon, as their king; while the rest, usually spoken of as the Ten Tribes, broke their allegiance to the house of David, and made Jeroboam, an Ephraimite, their king. The Ten Tribes retained the title Kingdom of Israel though also known as Ephraim.[i] Rehoboam and his adherents were distinctively called the Kingdom of Judah. For about two hundred and fifty years the two kingdoms maintained their separate autonomy; then, about 722 or 721 B.C., the independent status of the Kingdom of Israel was destroyed, and the captive people were transported to Assyria by Shalmanezer and others. Subsequently they disappeared so completely as to be called the Lost Tribes. The Kingdom of Judah was recognized as a nation for about one hundred and thirty years longer; then, about 588 B.C., it was brought into subjection by Nebuchadnezzar, through whom the Babylonian captivity was inaugurated. For three score years and ten Judah was kept in exile and virtual bondage, in consequence of their transgression as had been predicted through Jeremiah.[j] Then the Lord softened the hearts of their captors, and their restoration was begun under the decree of Cyrus the Persian, who had subdued the Babylonian kingdom. The Hebrew people were permitted to return to Judea, and to enter upon the work of rebuilding the temple at Jerusalem.[k]

A great company of the exiled Hebrews availed themselves of this opportunity to return to the lands of their fathers, though many elected to remain in the country of their captivity, preferring Babylon to Israel. The "whole congregation" of the Jews who returned from the Babylonian exile were but "forty and two thousand three hundred and three score, beside their servants and their maids, of whom there were seven thousand three hundred thirty and seven." The relatively small size of the migrating nation is further shown by the register of

[i] Isa. 11:13; 17:3; Ezek. 37:16–22; Hos. 4:17.

[j] Jer. 25:11, 12; see also 29:10.

[k] Ezra 1:1–4; the author, *House of the Lord*, pp. 39-44; also *Articles of Faith*, chapter 17.

their beasts of burden.[l] While those who did return strove valiantly to reestablish themselves as the house of David, and to regain some measure of their former prestige and glory, the Jews were never again a truly independent people. In turn they were preyed upon by Greece, Egypt, and Syria; but about 164–163 B.C., the people threw off, in part at least, the alien yoke, as a result of the patriotic revolt led by the Maccabees, the most prominent of whom was Judas Maccabeus. The temple service, which had been practically abolished through the proscription of victorious foes, was reestablished.[m] In the year 163 B.C., the sacred structure was rededicated, and the joyful occasion was thereafter celebrated in annual festival as the Feast of Dedication.[n] During the reign of the Maccabees, however, the temple fell into an almost ruinous condition, more as a result of the inability of the reduced and impoverished people to maintain it than through any further decline of religious zeal. In the hope of insuring a greater measure of national protection, the Jews entered into an unequal alliance with the Romans and eventually became tributary to them, in which condition the Jewish nation continued throughout the period of our Lord's ministry. In the meridian of time Rome was virtually mistress of the world. When Christ was born, Augustus Caesar[o] was emperor of Rome, and the Idumean, Herod,[p] surnamed the Great, was the vassal king of Judea.

Some semblance of national autonomy was maintained by the Jews under Roman dominion, and their religious ceremonials were not seriously interfered with. The established orders in the priesthood were recognized, and the official acts of the national council, or Sanhedrin,[q] were held to be binding by Roman law; though the judicial powers of this body did not extend to the infliction of capital punishment without the sanction of the imperial executive. It was the established policy of Rome to allow to her tributary and vassal

[l] Ezra 2:64–67.

[m] *House of the Lord*, pp. 42–44.

[n] Josephus, Ant. xii:6, 7; 2 Maccabees 2:19; 10:1–8; also John 10:22.

[o] Luke 2:1.

[p] Matt. 2:1.

[q] Note 1, end of chapter.

peoples freedom in worship so long as the mythological deities, dear to the Romans, were not maligned nor their altars desecrated.[r]

Needless to say, the Jews took not kindly to alien domination, though for many generations they had been trained in that experience, their reduced status having ranged from nominal vassalage to servile bondage. They were already largely a dispersed people. All the Jews in Palestine at the time of Christ's birth constituted but a small remnant of the great Davidic nation. The Ten Tribes, distinctively the aforetime kingdom of Israel, had then long been lost to history, and the people of Judah had been widely scattered among the nations.

In their relations with other peoples the Jews generally endeavored to maintain a haughty exclusiveness, which brought upon them Gentile ridicule. Under Mosaic law Israel had been required to keep apart from other nations; they attached supreme importance to their Abrahamic lineage as children of the covenant, "an holy people unto the Lord," whom He had chosen "to be a special people unto himself, above all people that are upon the face of the earth."[s] Judah had experienced the woeful effects of dalliance with pagan nations, and, at the time we are now considering, a Jew who permitted himself unnecessary association with a Gentile became an unclean being requiring ceremonial cleansing to free him from defilement. Only in strict isolation did the leaders find hope of insuring the perpetuity of the nation.

It is no exaggeration to say that the Jews hated all other peoples and were reciprocally despised and contemned by all others. They manifested special dislike for the Samaritans, perhaps because this people persisted in their efforts to establish some claim of racial relationship. These Samaritans were a mixed people, and were looked upon by the Jews as a mongrel lot, unworthy of decent respect. When the Ten Tribes were led into captivity by the king of Assyria, foreigners were sent to populate Samaria.[t] These intermarried with such Israelites as had escaped the captivity; and some modification of the religion of Israel, embodying at least the profession of Jehovah

[r] Note 6, end of chapter.

[s] Deut. 7:6; see also 10:15; Ex. 19:5, 6; Ps. 135:4; Isa. 41:8; 45:4; compare 1 Pet. 2:9.

[t] 2 Kgs. 17:24.

worship, survived in Samaria. The Samaritan rituals were regarded by the Jews as unorthodox, and the people as reprobate. At the time of Christ the enmity between Jew and Samaritan was so intense that travelers between Judea and Galilee would make long detours rather than pass through the province of Samaria which lay between. The Jews would have no dealings with the Samaritans.[u]

The proud feeling of self-sufficiency, the obsession for exclusiveness and separation—so distinctively a Jewish trait at that time—was inculcated at the maternal knee and emphasized in synagog and school. The Talmud,[v] which in codified form postdates the time of Christ's ministry, enjoined all Jews against reading the books of alien nations, declaring that none who so offended could consistently hope for Jehovah's favor.[w] Josephus gives his endorsement to similar injunction, and records that wisdom among the Jews meant only familiarity with the law and ability to discourse thereon.[x] A thorough acquaintanceship with the law was demanded as strongly as other studies were discountenanced. Thus the lines between learned and unlearned came to be rigidly drawn; and, as an inevitable consequence those who were accounted learned, or so considered themselves, looked down upon their unscholarly fellows as a class distinct and inferior.[y]

Long before the birth of Christ, the Jews had ceased to be a united people even in matters of the law, though the law was their chief reliance as a means of maintaining national solidarity. As early as four score years after the return from the Babylonian exile, and we know not with accuracy how much earlier, there had come to be recognized, as men having authority, certain scholars afterward known as scribes, and honored rabbis[z] or teachers. In the days of Ezra and Nehemiah these specialists in the law constituted a titled class, to whom deference and honor were paid. Ezra is designated "the priest, the scribe, even a scribe of the words of the commandments of the

---

[u] John 4:9; Luke 9:51–53.

[v] Note 2, end of chapter.

[w] Bab. Talmud, Sanhedrin, 90.

[x] Josephus, Ant. xx, 11:2.

[y] Note the emphasis given to this distinction in John 7:45–49; see also 9:34.

[z] Note 3, end of chapter.

Lord, and of his statutes to Israel."[aa] The scribes of those days did valuable service under Ezra, and later under Nehemiah, in compiling the sacred writings then extant; and in Jewish usage those appointed as guardians and expounders of the law came to be known as members of the Great Synagog, or Great Assembly, concerning which we have little information through canonical channels. According to Talmudic record, the organization consisted of one hundred and twenty eminent scholars. The scope of their labors, according to the admonition traditionally perpetuated by themselves, is thus expressed: *Be careful in judgment; set up many scholars, and make a hedge about the law.* They followed this behest by much study and careful consideration of all traditional details in administration; by multiplying scribes and rabbis unto themselves; and, as some of them interpreted the requirement of setting up many scholars, by writing many books and tractates; moreover, they made a fence or hedge about the law by adding numerous rules, which prescribed with great exactness the officially established proprieties for every occasion.

Scribes and rabbis were exalted to the highest rank in the estimation of the people, higher than that of the Levitical or priestly orders; and rabbinical sayings were given precedence over the utterances of the prophets, since the latter were regarded as but messengers or spokesmen, whereas the living scholars were of themselves sources of wisdom and authority. Such secular powers as Roman suzerainty permitted the Jews to retain were vested in the hierarchy, whose members were able thus to gather unto themselves practically all official and professional honors. As a natural result of this condition, there was practically no distinction between Jewish civil and ecclesiastical law, either as to the code or its administration. Rabbinism comprised as an essential element the doctrine of the equal authority of oral rabbinical tradition with the written word of the law. The aggrandizement implied in the application of the title "Rabbi" and the self-pride manifest in welcoming such adulation were especially forbidden by the Lord, who proclaimed Himself the one Master; and, as touching the interpretation of the title held by some as "father," Jesus proclaimed

---

[aa] Ezra 7:11; see also verses 6, 10, 12.

but one Father and He in heaven: "But be not ye called Rabbi: for one is your Master, even Christ; and all ye are brethren. And call no man your father upon the earth: for one is your Father, which is in heaven. Neither be ye called masters: for one is Master, even Christ."[bb]

The scribes, whether so named or designated by the more distinguishing appellation, rabbis, were repeatedly denounced by Jesus, because of the dead literalism of their teachings, and the absence of the spirit of righteousness and virile morality therefrom; and in such denunciations the Pharisees are often coupled with the scribes. The judgment of the Christ upon them is sufficiently expressed by His withering imprecation: "Woe unto you, scribes and Pharisees, hypocrites!"[cc]

The origin of the Pharisees is not fixed by undisputed authority as to either time or circumstance; though it is probably that the sect or party had a beginning in connection with the return of the Jews from the Babylonian captivity. New ideas and added conceptions of the meaning of the law were promulgated by Jews who had imbibed of the spirit of Babylon; and the resulting innovations were accepted by some and rejected by others. The name "Pharisee" does not occur in the Old Testament, nor in the Apocrypha, though it is probable that the Assideans mentioned in the books of the Maccabees[dd] were the original Pharisees. By derivation the name expresses the thought of separatism; the Pharisee, in the estimation of his class, was distinctively set apart from the common people, to whom he considered himself as truly superior as the Jews regarded themselves in contrast with other nations. Pharisees and scribes were one in all essentials of profession, and rabbinism was specifically their doctrine.

In the New Testament the Pharisees are often mentioned as in opposition to the Sadducees; and such were the relations of the two parties that it becomes a simpler matter to contrast one with the other

---

[bb] Matt. 23:8–10; see also John 1:38; 3:2.

[cc] Matt. 23:13, 14, 15, 23, etc., read the entire chapter; compare Mark 12:38–40; Luke 20:46; see also as instances of special denunciation of the Pharisees Luke 11:37–44. Note also that the lawyers, who were professionally associated with the scribes, are included in the sweeping criticism: verses 45–54.

[dd] 1 Maccabees 2:42; 7:13–17; 2 Maccabees 14:6.

than to consider each separately. The Sadducees came into existence as a reactionary organization during the second century B.C., in connection with an insurgent movement against the Maccabean party. Their platform was that of opposition to the ever increasing mass of traditional lore, with which the law was not merely being fenced or hedged about for safety, but under which it was being buried. The Sadducees stood for the sanctity of the law as written and preserved, while they rejected the whole mass of rabbinical precept both as orally transmitted and as collated and codified in the records of the scribes. The Pharisees formed the more popular party; the Sadducees figured as the aristocratic minority. At the time of Christ's birth the Pharisees existed as an organized body numbering over six thousand men, with Jewish women very generally on their side in sympathy and effort;[ee] while the Sadducees were so small a faction and of such limited power that, when they were placed in official positions, they generally followed the policy of the Pharisees as a matter of incumbent expediency. The Pharisees were the Puritans of the time, unflinching in their demand for compliance with the traditional rules as well as the original law of Moses. In this connection note Paul's confession of faith and practice when arraigned before Agrippa—"That after the most straitest sect of our religion I lived a Pharisee."[ff] The Sadducees prided themselves on strict compliance with the law, as they construed it, irrespective of all scribes or rabbis. The Sadducees stood for the temple and its prescribed ordinances, the Pharisees for the synagog and its rabbinical teachings. It is difficult to decide which were the more technical if we judge each party by the standard of its own profession. By way of illustration: the Sadducees held to the literal and full exaction of the Mosaic penalty—an eye for an eye and a tooth for a tooth[gg]—while the Pharisees contended on the authority of rabbinical dictum, that the wording was figurative, and that therefore the penalty could be met by a fine in money or goods.

Pharisees and Sadducees differed on many important if not fundamental matters of belief and practice, including the preexistence

[ee] Josephus, *Antiquities* xvii, 2:4.

[ff] Acts 26:5; see also 23:6; Philip. 3:5.

[gg] Ex. 21:23–35; Lev. 24:20; Deut. 19:21; contrast Matt. 5:38–44.

of spirits, the reality of a future state involving reward and punishment, the necessity for individual self-denial, the immortality of the soul, and the resurrection from the dead; in each of which the Pharisees stood for the affirmative while the Sadducees denied.[hh] Josephus avers—the doctrine of the Sadducees is that the soul and body perish together; the law is all that they are concerned to observe.[ii] They were "a skeptical school of aristocratic traditionalists; adhering only to the Mosaic law."[jj]

Among the many other sects and parties established on the ground of religious or political differences, or both, are the Essenes, the Nazarites, the Herodians and the Galileans. The Essenes were characterized by professions of ultrapiety; they considered even the strictness of Pharisaic profession as weak and insufficient; they guarded membership in their order by severe exactions extending through a first and a second novitiate; they were forbidden even to touch food prepared by strangers; they practiced strict temperance and rigid self-denial, indulged in hard labor—preferably that of agriculture, and were forbidden to trade as merchants, to take part in war, or to own or employ slaves.[kk] Nazarites are not named in the New Testament, though of specific record in the earlier scriptures;[ll] and from sources other than scriptural we learn of their existence at and after the time of Christ. The Nazarite was one of either sex who was bound to abstinence and sacrifice by a voluntary vow for special service to God; the period of the vow might be limited or for life. While the Essenes cultivated an ascetic brotherhood, the Nazarites were devoted to solitary discipline.

The Herodians constituted a politico-religious party who favored the plans of the Herods under the professed belief that through that dynasty alone could the status of the Jewish people be maintained and a reestablishment of the nation be secured. We find mention of the Herodians laying aside their partisan antipathies and acting in

---

[hh] Note 4, end of chapter.

[ii] Josephus, *Antiquities* xviii, 1:4.

[jj] *New Standard Dictionary*, under "Sadducees."

[kk] Josephus, *Antiquities* xviii, 1:5.

[ll] Num. 6:2–21; Judges 13:5, 7; 16:17; Amos 2:11, 12.

concert with the Pharisees in the effort to convict the Lord Jesus and bring Him to death.[mm] The Galileans or people of Galilee were distinguished from their fellow Israelites of Judea by greater simplicity and less ostentatious devotion in matters pertaining to the law. They were opposed to innovations, yet were generally more liberal or less bigoted than some of the professedly devout Judeans. They were prominent as able defenders in the wars of the people, and won for themselves a reputation for bravery and patriotism. They are mentioned in connection with certain tragical occurrences during our Lord's lifetime.[nn]

The authority of the priesthood was outwardly acknowledged by the Jews at the time of Christ; and the appointed order of service for priest and Levite was duly observed. During the reign of David, the descendants of Aaron, who were the hereditary priests in Israel, had been divided into twenty-four courses,[oo] and to each course the labors of the sanctuary were allotted in turn. Representatives of but four of these courses returned from the captivity, but from these the orders were reconstructed on the original plan. In the days of Herod the Great the temple ceremonies were conducted with great display and outward elaborateness, as an essential matter of consistency with the splendor of the structure, which surpassed in magnificence all earlier sanctuaries.[pp] Priests and Levites, therefore, were in demand for continuous service, though the individuals were changed at short intervals according to the established system. In the regard of the people the priests were inferior to the rabbis, and the scholarly attainments of a scribe transcended in honor that pertaining to ordination in the priesthood. The religion of the time was a matter of ceremony and formality, of ritual and performance; it had lost the very spirit of worship, and the true conception of the relationship between Israel and Israel's God was but a dream of the past.

Such in brief were the principal features of the world's condition, and particularly as concerns the Jewish people, when Jesus the Christ was born in the meridian of time.

[mm] Matt. 22:15, 16; Mark 12:13.
[nn] Josephus, *Antiquities* xviii, 1:4.
[oo] 1 Chron. 24:1–18.
[pp] Note 5, end of chapter.

NOTES TO CHAPTER 6

1. The Sanhedrin.—This, the chief court or high council of the Jews, derives its name from Greek *sunedrion*, signifying "a council." In English it is sometimes though inaccurately written "Sanhedrim." The Talmud traces the origin of this body to the calling of the seventy elders whom Moses associated with himself, making seventy-one in all, to administer as judges in Israel (Num. 11:16, 17). The Sanhedrin in the time of Christ, as also long before, comprised seventy-one members, including the high priest who presided in the assembly. It appears to have been known in its earlier period as the Senate, and was occasionally so designated even after Christ's death, (Josephus, *Antiquities* xii, 3:3; compare Acts 5:21); the name "Sanhedrin" came into general use during the reign of Herod the Great; but the term is not of Biblical usage; its equivalent in the New Testament is "council" (Matt. 5:22; 10:17; 26:59) though it must be remembered that the same term is applied to courts of lesser jurisdiction than that of the Sanhedrin, and to local tribunals. (Matt. 5:22; 10:17; 26:59; Mark 13:9; see also Acts 25:12.)

The following, from the *Standard Bible Dictionary*, is instructive: "Those qualified to be members were in general of the priestly house and especially of the Sadducean nobility. But from the days of Queen Alexandra (69–68 B.C.) onward, there were with these chief priests also many Pharisees in it under the name of scribes and elders. These three classes are found combined in Matt. 27:41; Mark 11:27; 14:43, 53; 15:1. How such members were appointed is not entirely clear. The aristocratic character of the body and the history of its origin forbid the belief that it was by election. Its nucleus probably consisted of the members of certain ancient families, to which, however, from time to time others were added by the secular rulers. The presiding officer was the high priest, who at first exercised in it more than the authority of a member, claiming a voice equal to that of the rest of the body. But after the reduction of the high priesthood from a hereditary office to one bestowed by the political ruler according to his pleasure, and the frequent changes in the office introduced by the new system, the high priest naturally lost his prestige. Instead of holding in his hands the 'government of the nation,' he came to be but one of many to share this power; those who had served as high priests being still in esteem among their nation, and having lost their office not for any reason that could be considered valid by the religious sense of the community, exerted a large influence over the decisions of the assembly. In the New Testament they are regarded as the rulers (Matt. 26:59; 27:41; Acts 4:5, 8; Luke 23:13, 35; John 7:26), and Josephus' testimony supports this view. The functions of the Sanhedrin were religious and moral, and also political. In the latter capacity they further exercised administrative as well as judicial functions. As a religious tribunal, the Sanhedrin wielded a potent influence over the whole of the Jewish world (Acts 9:2); but as a court of justice, after the division of the country upon the death of Herod, its jurisdiction was limited to Judea. Here, however, its power was absolute even to the passing of sentence of death (Josephus, *Antiquities* xiv, 9:3, 4; Matt. 26:3; Acts 4:5;

6:12; 22:30), although it had no authority to carry the sentence into execution except as approved and ordered by the representative of the Roman government. The law by which the Sanhedrin governed was naturally the Jewish, and in the execution of it this tribunal had a police of its own, and made arrests at its discretion (Matt. 26:47). . . . While the general authority of the Sanhedrin extended over the whole of Judea, the towns in the country had local councils of their own (Matt. 5:22; 10:17; Mark 13:9; Josephus, B.J. ii, 14:1), for the administration of local affairs. These were constituted of elders (Luke 7:3), at least seven in number, (Josephus, Ant. iv, 8:14; B. J. ii, 20:5), and in some of the largest towns as many as twenty-three. What the relation of these to the central council in Jerusalem was does not appear clearly. . . . Some sort of mutual recognition existed among them; for whenever the judges of the local court could not agree it seems that they were in the habit of referring their cases to the Sanhedrin in Jerusalem. (Josephus, Ant. iv, 8:14; Mishna, Sanh. 11:2)."

2. Talmud.—"The body of Jewish civil and religious law (and discussion directly or remotely relating thereto) not comprised in the Pentateuch, commonly including the *Mishna* and the *Gemara*, but sometimes limited to the latter; written in Aramaic. It exists in two great collections, the *Palestinian Talmud*, or *Talmud of the Land of Israel*, or *Talmud of the West*, or more popularly, *Jerusalem Talmud*, embodying the discussions on the Mishna, of the Palestinian doctors from the 2d to the middle of the 5th century; and the Babylonian, embodying those of the Jewish doctors in Babylonia, from about 190 to the 7th century."—*New Standard Dict.* The Mishna comprises the earlier portions of the Talmud; the Gemara is made up of later writings and is largely an exposition of the Mishna. An edition of the Babylonian Talmud alone (issued at Vienna in 1682) comprised twenty-four tomes. (Geikie.)

3. Rabbis.—The title Rabbi is equivalent to our distinctive appellations Doctor, Master, or Teacher. By derivation it means Master or my Master, thus connoting dignity and rank associated with politeness of address. A definite explanation of the term is given by John (1:38), and the same meaning attaches by implication to its use as recorded by Matthew (23:8). It was applied as a title of respect to Jesus on several occasions (Matt. 23:7, 8; 26:25, 49; Mark 9:5; 11:21; 14:45; John 1:38, 49; 3:2, 26; 4:31; 6:25; 9:2; 11:8). The title was of comparatively recent usage in the time of Christ, as it appears to have first come into general use during the reign of Herod the Great, though the earlier teachers, of the class without the name of Rabbis, were generally revered, and the title was carried back to them by later usage. Rab was an inferior title and Rabban a superior one to Rabbi. Rabboni was expressive of most profound respect, love and honor (see John 20:16). At the time of our Lord's ministry the Rabbis were held in high esteem, and rejoiced in the afflations of precedence and honor among men. They were almost exclusively of the powerful Pharisaic party.

The following is from Geikie's *Life and Words of Christ*, vol. 1, chap. 6: "If the most important figures in the society of Christ's day were the Pharisees, it was

because they were the Rabbis or teachers of the Law. As such they received superstitious honor, which was, indeed, the great motive, with many, to court the title or
join the party. The Rabbis were classed with Moses, the patriarchs, and the
prophets, and claimed equal reverence. Jacob and Joseph were both said to have
been Rabbis. The Targum of Jonathan substitutes Rabbis, or Scribes, for the word
'prophets' where it occurs. Josephus speaks of the prophets of Saul's day as Rabbis.
In the Jerusalem Targum all the patriarchs are learned Rabbis. . . . They were to be
dearer to Israel than father or mother—because parents avail only in this world [as
was then taught] but the Rabbi forever. They were set above kings, for is it not
written 'Through me kings reign'? Their entrance into a house brought a blessing;
to live or to eat with them was the highest good fortune . . . . The Rabbis went even
further than this in exalting their order. The Mishna declares that it is a greater
crime to speak anything to their discredit, than to speak against the words of the
Law. . . . Yet in form, the Law received boundless honor. Every saying of the Rabbis
had to be based on some words of it, which were, however, explained in their own
way. The spirit of the times, the wild fanaticism of the people, and their own bias,
tended alike to make them set value only on ceremonies and worthless externalisms,
to the utter neglect of the spirit of the sacred writings. Still it was held that the Law
needed no confirmation, while the words of the Rabbis did. So far as the Roman
authority under which they lived left them free, the Jews willingly put all power in
the hands of the Rabbis. They or their nominees filled every office, from the highest
in the priesthood to the lowest in the community. They were the casuists, the
teachers, the priests, the judges, the magistrates, and the physicians of the nation. . . .
The central and dominant characteristic of the teaching of the Rabbis was the
certain advent of a great national Deliverer—the Messiah or Anointed of God or in
the Greek translation of the title, the Christ. In no other nation than the Jews has
such a conception ever taken such root or shown such vitality. . . . It was agreed
among the Rabbis that His birthplace must be Bethlehem, and that He must rise
from the tribe of Judah."

Individual rabbis gathered disciples about them, and, inevitably, rivalry became
manifest. Rabbinical schools and academies were established, each depending for its
popularity on the greatness of some rabbi. The most famous of these institutions in
the time of Herod I were the school of Hillel and that of his rival Shammai. Later,
tradition invested these with the title "the fathers of old." It appears from the trifling
matters over which the followers of these two disagreed, that only by opposition could
either maintain a distinguishing status. Hillel is reputed as the grandfather of
Gamaliel, the rabbi and doctor of the law at whose feet Saul of Tarsus, afterward
Paul the apostle, received his early instruction (Acts 22:3). So far as we have historic
record of the views, principles or beliefs advocated by the rival schools of Hillel and
Shammai, it appears that the former stood for a greater degree of liberality and
tolerance, while the later emphasized a strict and possibly narrow interpretation of
the law and its associated traditions. The dependence of the rabbinical schools on
the authority of tradition is illustrated by an incident of record to the effect that

even the prestige of the great Hillel did not insure him against uproar when once he spoke without citing precedent; only when he added that so had his masters Abtalion and Shemajah spoken did the tumult subside.

4. Sadducean Denial of the Resurrection.—As set forth in the text, the Sadducees formed an association numerically small as compared with the more popular and influential Pharisees. In the Gospels the Pharisees are of frequent mention, and very commonly in connection with the scribes, while the Sadducees are less frequently named. In the Acts of the Apostles, the Sadducees appear frequently as opponents of the Church. This condition was doubtless due to the prominence given the resurrection from the dead among the themes of the apostolic preaching, the Twelve continually bearing testimony to the actual Resurrection of Christ. Sadducean doctrine denied the actuality and possibility of a bodily resurrection, the contention resting mainly on the ground that Moses, who was regarded as the supreme mortal lawgiver in Israel, and the chief mouthpiece of Jehovah, had written nothing concerning life after death. The following is taken from Smith's *Dictionary of the Bible*, article "Sadducees," as touching this matter: "The denial of man's resurrection after death followed in the conception of the Sadducees as a logical conclusion from their denial that Moses had revealed to the Israelites the Oral Law. For on a point so momentous as a second life beyond the grave, no religious party among the Jews would have deemed themselves bound to accept any doctrine as an article of faith, unless it had been proclaimed by Moses, their great legislator; and it is certain that in the written Law of the Pentateuch there is a total absence of any assertion by Moses of the resurrection of the dead. This fact is presented to Christians in a striking manner by the well-known words of the pentateuch which are quoted by Christ in argument with the Sadducees on this subject (Ex. 3:6, 16; Mark 12:26, 27; Matt. 22:31, 32; Luke 20:37). It cannot be doubted that in such a case Christ would quote to His powerful adversaries the most cogent text in the Law; and yet the text actually quoted does not do more than suggest an inference on this great doctrine. It is true that passages in other parts of the Old Testament express a belief in the resurrection (Isa. 26:19; Dan. 12:2; Job 19:26; and in some of the Psalms); and it may at first sight be a subject of surprise that the Sadducees were not convinced by the authority of those passages. But although the Sadducees regarded the books which contained these passages as sacred, it is more than doubtful whether any of the Jews regarded them as sacred in precisely the same sense as the written Law. To the Jews Moses was and is a colossal form, preeminent in authority above all subsequent prophets."

5. The Temple of Herod.—"Herod's purpose in the great undertaking (that of restoring the temple, and of enlarging it on a plan of unprecedented magnificence) was that of aggrandizing himself and the nation, rather than the rendering of homage to Jehovah. His proposition to rebuild or restore the temple on a scale of increased magnificence was regarded with suspicion and received with disfavor by the Jews, who feared that were the ancient edifice demolished, the arbitrary monarch might abandon his plan and the people would be left without a temple. To allay these fears the king proceeded to reconstruct and restore the old edifice, part by part, directing the work so that at no time was the temple service seriously interrupted. So little of the ancient structure was allowed to stand, however, that the temple of Herod must be regarded as a new creation. The work was begun about sixteen years before the birth of Christ; and while the Holy House itself was practically completed within a year and a half, this part of the labor having been performed by a body of one thousand priests specially trained for the purpose, the temple area was a scene of uninterrupted building operations down to the year A.D. 63. We read that in the time of Christ's ministry the temple had been forty-six years in building; and at that time it was unfinished.

"The Biblical record gives us little information regarding this the last and the greatest of ancient temples; for what we know concerning it we are indebted mainly to Josephus, with some corroborative testimony found in the Talmud. In all essentials the Holy House, or Temple proper, was similar to the two earlier houses of sanctuary, though externally far more elaborate and imposing than either; but in the matter of surrounding courts and associated buildings, the Temple of Herod preeminently excelled. . . . Yet its beauty and grandeur lay in architectural excellence rather than in the sanctity of its worship or in the manifestation of the Divine Presence within its walls. Its ritual and service were largely man-prescribed; for while the letter of the Mosaic Law was professedly observed, the law had been supplemented and in many features supplanted by rule and priestly prescription. The Jews professed to consider it holy, and by them it was proclaimed as the House of the Lord. Devoid though it was of the divine accompaniments of earlier shrines accepted of God, and defiled as it was by priestly arrogance and usurpation, as also by the selfish interest of traffic and trade, it was nevertheless recognized even by our Lord the Christ as His Father's House. (Matt. 21:12; compare Mark 11:15; Luke 19:45.) . . . For thirty or more years after the death of Christ, the Jews continued the work of adding to and embellishing the temple buildings. The elaborate design conceived and projected by Herod had been practically completed; the temple was well-nigh finished, and, as soon afterward appeared, was ready for destruction. Its fate had been definitely foretold by the Savior Himself."—From the author's *House of the Lord*, pp. 54–61.

6. State of the World at the Time of the Savior's Birth.—At the beginning of the Christian era, the Jews, in common with most other nations, were subjects of the Roman empire. They were allowed a considerable degree of liberty in maintaining their religious observances and national customs generally, but their status was far from that of a free and independent people. The period was one of comparative peace—a time marked by fewer wars and less dissension than the empire had known for many years. These conditions were favorable for the mission of the Christ, and for the founding of His Church on earth. The religious systems extant at the time of Christ's earthly ministry may be classified in a general way as Jewish and Pagan, with a minor system—the Samaritan—which was essentially a mixture of the other two. The children of Israel alone proclaimed the existence of the true and living God; they alone looked forward to the advent of the Messiah, whom mistakenly they awaited as a prospective conqueror coming to crush the enemies of their nation. All other nations, tongues, and peoples, bowed to pagan deities, and their worship comprised naught but the sensual rites of heathen idolatry. Paganism was a religion of form and ceremony, based on polytheism—a belief in the existence of a multitude of gods, which deities were subject to all the vices and passions of humanity, while distinguished by immunity from death. Morality and virtue were unknown as elements of heathen service; and the dominant idea in pagan worship was that of propitiating the gods, in the hope of averting their anger and purchasing their favor.—See the author's *The Great Apostasy*, 1:2–4, and notes following the chapter cited.

CHAPTER 7

GABRIEL'S ANNUNCIATION OF JOHN AND OF JESUS

JOHN THE FORERUNNER

Associated with the prophecies of the birth of Christ are predictions concerning one who should precede Him, going before to prepare the way. It is not surprising that the annunciation of the immediate advent of the forerunner was speedily followed by that of the Messiah; nor that the proclamations were made by the same heavenly ambassador—Gabriel, sent from the presence of God.[a]

About fifteen months prior to the Savior's birth, Zacharias, a priest of the Aaronic order, was officiating in the functions of his office in the temple at Jerusalem. His wife, Elisabeth, was also of a priestly family, being numbered among the descendants of Aaron. The couple had never been blessed with children; and at the time of which we speak they were both well stricken in years and had sorrowfully given up hope of posterity. Zacharias belonged to the course of priests named after Abijah, and known in later time as the course of Abia. This was the eighth in the order of the twenty-four courses established by David the king, each course being appointed to serve in turn a week at the sanctuary.[b] It will be remembered that on the return of the people from Babylon only four of the courses were represented; but of these four each averaged over fourteen hundred men.[c]

During his week of service each priest was required to maintain scrupulously a state of ceremonial cleanliness of person; he had to

[a] Luke 1:19, 26; see also Dan. 8:16; 9:21–23.

[b] Luke 1:5; compare 1 Chr. 24:10.

[c] Ezra 2:36–39.

abstain from wine, and from food except that specifically prescribed; he had to bathe frequently; he lived within the temple precincts and thus was cut off from family association; he was not allowed to come near the dead, nor to mourn in the formal manner if death should rob him of even his nearest and dearest of kin. We learn that the daily selection of the priest who should enter the Holy Place, and there burn incense on the golden altar, was determined by lot;[d] and furthermore we gather, from nonscriptural history, that because of the great number of priests the honor of so officiating seldom fell twice to the same person.

On this day the lot had fallen to Zacharias. It was a very solemn occasion in the life of the humble Judean priest—this one day in his life on which the special and particularly sacred service was required of him. Within the Holy Place he was separated by the veil of the temple only from the Oracle or Holy of Holies—the inner sanctuary into which none but the high priest might enter, and he only on the Day of Atonement, after long ceremonial preparation.[e] The place and the time were conducive to the highest and most reverential feelings. As Zacharias ministered within the Holy Place, the people without bowed themselves in prayer, watching for the clouds of incense smoke to appear above the great partition which formed the barrier between the place of general assembly and the Holy Place, and awaiting the reappearance of the priest and his pronouncement of the benediction.

Before the astonished gaze of Zacharias, at this supreme moment of his priestly service, there appeared, standing on the right of the golden altar of incense, an angel of the Lord. Many generations had passed in Jewry since any visible presence other than mortal had been manifest within the temple, either in the Holy Place or the Holy of Holies; the people regarded personal visitations of heavenly beings as occurrences of the past; they had come almost to believe that there were no longer prophets in Israel. Nevertheless, there was always a feeling of anxiety, akin to that of troubled expectancy, whenever a priest approached the inner sanctuary, which was regarded as the particular

[d] Luke 1:8, 9; read the entire chapter.

[e] Lev. chap. 16; Heb. 9:1–7; see also *House of the Lord*, p. 59, and compare pp. 24 and 39. Note 6, end of chapter.

abode of Jehovah should He ever again condescend to visit His people. In view of these conditions we read without surprise that this angelic presence troubled Zacharias and caused fear to fall upon him. The words of the heavenly visitant, however, were comforting though of startling import, embodying as they did the unqualified assurance that the man's prayers had been heard, and that his wife should bear him a son, who must be named John.[f] The promise went even further, specifying that the child to be born of Elisabeth would be a blessing to the people; many would rejoice at his birth; he would be great in the sight of the Lord, and must be guarded against wine and strong drink;[g] he would be filled with the Holy Ghost, would be the means of turning many souls to God, and would go before to make ready a people prepared to receive the Messiah.

Doubtless Zacharias recognized in the predicted future of the yet unborn child, the great forerunner, of whom the prophets had told and the psalmist had sung; but that such a one should be offspring of himself and his aged wife seemed impossible despite the angel's promise. The man doubted, and asked whereby he should know that what his visitant had spoken was true: "And the angel answering said unto him, I am Gabriel, that stand in the presence of God; and am sent to speak unto thee, and to shew thee these glad tidings. And, behold, thou shalt be dumb, and not able to speak, until the day that these things shall be performed, because thou believest not my words, which shall be fulfilled in their season."[h] When the highly blessed though sorely smitten priest at length came from within and appeared before the expectant congregation, already made anxious by his delayed return, he could but mutely dismiss the assembly and by signs indicate that he had seen a vision. The penalty for doubt was already operative: Zacharias was dumb.

In due time the child was born, there in the hill country of Judea [i] where Zacharias and Elisabeth had their home; and, on the eighth

---

[f] For other instances of children promised in spite of barrenness due to age or other causes, see Isaac (Gen. 17:16, 17; 21:1–3); Samson (Judg. 13); Samuel (1 Sam. 1); son of the Shunammite (2 Kgs. 4:14–17).

[g] Note 1, end of chapter.

[h] Luke 1:19–20.

[i] Luke 1:57; compare verse 39.

day following the birth the family assembled in accordance with custom and Mosaic requirement, to name the babe in connection with the rite of circumcision.[j] All suggestions that he be called after his father were overruled by Zacharias, who wrote with decisive finality: "His name is John." Thereupon the dumb[k] priest's tongue was loosed, and being filled with the Holy Ghost he burst forth in prophecy, praise and song; his inspired utterances have been set to music and are sung in worship by many Christian congregations as the Benedictus:

"Blessed be the Lord God of Israel; for he hath visited and redeemed his people, and hath raised up an horn of salvation for us in the house of his servant David; as he spake by the mouth of his holy prophets, which have been since the world began: that we should be saved from our enemies, and from the hand of all that hate us; to perform the mercy promised to our fathers, and to remember his holy covenant; the oath which he sware to our father Abraham, that he would grant unto us, that we being delivered out of the hand of our enemies might serve him without fear, in holiness and righteousness before him, all the days of our life. And thou, child, shalt be called the prophet of the Highest: for thou shalt go before the face of the Lord to prepare his ways; to give knowledge of salvation unto his people by the remission of their sins, through the tender mercy of our God; whereby the dayspring from on high hath visited us, to give light to them that sit in darkness and in the shadow of death, to guide our feet into the way of peace."[l]

The last words Zacharias had uttered prior to the infliction of dumbness were words of doubt and unbelief, words in which he had called for a sign as proof of authority of one who came from the presence of the Almighty; the words with which he broke his long silence were words of praise unto God in whom he had all assurance, words that were as a sign to all who heard, and the fame whereof spread throughout the region.

The unusual circumstances attending the birth of John, notably the months of dumbness passed by the father and his sudden recovery

[j] Note 2, end of chapter.

[k] Note 3, end of chapter.

[l] Luke 1:68–79.

of speech on the bestowal of the foreappointed name, caused many to marvel and some to fear, as they asked: "What manner of child shall this be!" When, a man grown, John raised his voice in the wilderness, again in fulfillment of prophecy, the people questioned as to whether he was not the Messiah.[m] Of his life between infancy and the beginning of his public ministry, a period of approximately thirty years, we have of record but a single sentence: "And the child grew, and waxed strong in spirit, and was in the deserts till the day of his shewing unto Israel."[n]

THE ANNUNCIATION TO THE VIRGIN

Six months after the visitation of Gabriel to Zacharias, and three months prior to the birth of John, the same heavenly messenger was sent to a young woman named Mary, who lived at Nazareth, a town in Galilee. She was of the lineage of David; and though unmarried was betrothed or espoused to a man named Joseph, who also was of royal descent through the Davidic line. The angel's salutation, while full of honor and blessing, caused Mary to wonder and to feel troubled. "Hail, thou that art highly favoured, the Lord is with thee: blessed art thou among women";[o] thus did Gabriel greet the virgin.

In common with other daughters of Israel, specifically those of the tribe of Judah and of known descent from David, Mary had doubtless contemplated, with holy joy and ecstasy, the coming of the Messiah through the royal line; she knew that some Jewish maiden was yet to become the mother of the Christ. Was it possible that the angel's words to her had reference to this supreme expectation and hope of the nation? She had little time to turn these things in her mind, for the angel continued: "Fear not, Mary: for thou hast found favour with God. And, behold, thou shalt conceive in thy womb, and bring forth a son, and shalt call his name JESUS. He shall be great, and shall be called the Son of the Highest: and the Lord God shall give unto him the throne of his father David: and he shall reign over the house of Jacob for ever; and of his kingdom there shall be no end."[p]

---

[m] Luke 1:65, 66; see also 3:15.

[n] Luke 1:80.

[o] Luke 1:28.

[p] Luke 1:30–33.

Even yet she comprehended but in part the import of this momentous visitation. Not in the spirit of doubt such as had prompted Zacharias to ask for a sign, but through an earnest desire for information and explanation, Mary, conscious of her unmarried status and sure of her virgin condition, asked: "How shall this be, seeing I know not a man?" The answer to her natural and simple inquiry was the announcement of a miracle such as the world had never known—not a miracle in the sense of a happening contrary to nature's law, nevertheless a miracle through the operation of higher law, such as the human mind ordinarily fails to comprehend or regard as possible. Mary was informed that she would conceive and in time bring forth a Son, of whom no mortal man would be the father:— "And the angel answered and said unto her, The Holy Ghost shall come upon thee, and the power of the Highest shall overshadow thee: therefore also that holy thing which shall be born of thee shall be called the Son of God."[q]

Then the angel told her of the blessed condition of her cousin Elisabeth, who had been barren; and by way of sufficient and final explanation added: "For with God nothing shall be impossible." With gentle submissiveness and humble acceptance, the pure young virgin replied: "Behold the handmaid of the Lord; be it unto me according to thy word."

His message delivered, Gabriel departed, leaving the chosen Virgin of Nazareth to ponder over her wondrous experience. Mary's promised Son was to be "The Only Begotten" of the Father in the flesh; so it had been both positively and abundantly predicted. True, the event was unprecedented; true also it has never been paralleled; but that the virgin birth would be unique was as truly essential to the fulfillment of prophecy as that it should occur at all. That Child to be born of Mary was begotten of Elohim, the Eternal Father, not in violation of natural law but in accordance with a higher manifestation thereof; and, the offspring from that association of supreme sanctity, celestial Sireship, and pure though mortal maternity, was of right to be called the "Son of the Highest." In His nature would be combined

---

[q] Luke 1:35; see also preceding verses, 31–33.

the powers of Godhood with the capacity and possibilities of mortality; and this through the ordinary operation of the fundamental law of heredity, declared of God, demonstrated by science, and admitted by philosophy, that living beings shall propagate—after their kind. The Child Jesus was to inherit the physical, mental, and spiritual traits, tendencies, and powers that characterized His parents— one immortal and glorified—God, the other human—woman.

Jesus Christ was to be born of mortal woman, but was not directly the offspring of mortal man, except so far as His mother was the daughter of both man and woman. In our Lord alone has been fulfilled the word of God spoken in relation to the Fall of Adam, that the seed of the woman should have power to overcome Satan by bruising the serpent's head.[r]

In respect to place, condition, and general environment, Gabriel's annunciation to Zacharias offers strong contrast to the delivery of his message to Mary. The prospective forerunner of the Lord was announced to his father within the magnificent temple, and in a place the most exclusively sacred save one other in the Holy House, under the light shed from the golden candlestick, and further illumined by the glow of living coals on the altar of gold; the Messiah was announced to His mother in a small town far from the capital and the temple, most probably within the walls of a simple Galilean cottage.

MARY'S VISIT TO HER COUSIN ELISABETH

It was natural that Mary, left now to herself with a secret in her soul, holier, greater, and more thrilling than any ever borne before or since, should seek companionship, and that of someone of her own sex, in whom she could confide, from whom she might hope to derive comfort and support, and to whom it would be not wrong to tell what at that time was probably known to no mortal save herself. Her heavenly visitant had indeed suggested all this in his mention of Elisabeth, Mary's cousin, herself a subject of unusual blessing, and a woman through whom another miracle of God had been wrought. Mary set out with haste from Nazareth for the hill country of Judea,

[r] Gen. 3:15.

on a journey of about a hundred miles if the traditional account be true that the little town of Juttah was the home of Zacharias. There was mutual joy in the meeting between Mary the youthful virgin, and Elisabeth, already well advanced in life. From what of Gabriel's words her husband had communicated, Elisabeth must have known that the approaching birth of her son would soon be followed by that of the Messiah, and that therefore the day for which Israel had waited and prayed through the long dark centuries was about to dawn. When Mary's salutation fell upon her ears, the Holy Ghost bore witness that the chosen mother of the Lord stood before her in the person of her cousin; and as she experienced the physical thrill incident to the quickening spirit of her own blessed conception, she returned the greeting of her visitor with reverence: "Blessed art thou among women, and blessed is the fruit of thy womb. And whence is this to me, that the mother of my Lord should come to me?"ˢ Mary responded with that glorious hymn of praise, since adopted in the musical ritual of churches as the Magnificat:

"My soul doth magnify the Lord, and my spirit hath rejoiced in God my Saviour. For he hath regarded the low estate of his handmaiden: for, behold, from henceforth all generations shall call me blessed. For he that is mighty hath done to me great things; and holy is his name. And his mercy is on them that fear him from generation to generation. He hath shewed strength with his arm; he hath scattered the proud in the imagination of their hearts. He hath put down the mighty from their seats, and exalted them of low degree. He hath filled the hungry with good things; and the rich he hath sent empty away. He hath holpen his servant Israel, in remembrance of his mercy; as he spake to our fathers, to Abraham, and to his seed for ever."ᵗ

MARY AND JOSEPH

The visit lasted about three months, after which time Mary returned to Nazareth. The real embarrassment of her position she had now to meet. At the home of her cousin she had been understood; her condition had served to confirm the testimony of Zacharias and

---

ˢLuke 1:42; read verses 39–56.

ᵗ Luke 1:46–55.

Elisabeth; but how would her word be received at her own home? And especially, how would she be regarded by her espoused husband?[u] Betrothal, or espousal, in that time was in some respects as binding as the marriage vow, and could only be set aside by a ceremonial separation akin to divorce; yet an espousal was but an engagement to marry, not a marriage. When Joseph greeted his promised bride after her three months' absence, he was greatly distressed over the indications of her prospective maternity. Now the Jewish law provided for the annulment of a betrothal in either of two ways—by public trial and judgment, or by private agreement attested by a written document signed in the presence of witnesses. Joseph was a just man, a strict observer of the law, yet no harsh extremist; moreover he loved Mary and would save her all unnecessary humiliation, whatever might be his own sorrow and suffering. For Mary's sake he dreaded the thought of publicity; and therefore determined to have the espousal annulled with such privacy as the law allowed. He was troubled and thought much of his duty in the matter, when, "behold, the angel of the Lord appeared unto him in a dream, saying, Joseph, thou son of David, fear not to take unto thee Mary thy wife: for that which is conceived in her is of the Holy Ghost. And she shall bring forth a son, and thou shalt call his name JESUS: for he shall save his people from their sins."[v]

Great was Joseph's relief of mind; and great his joy in the realization that the long predicted coming of the Messiah was at hand; the words of the prophets would be fulfilled; a virgin, and she the one in the world most dear to him, had conceived, and in due time would bring forth that blessed Son, Emmanuel, which name by interpretation means "God with us."[w] The angel's salutation was significant; "Joseph, thou son of David," was the form of address; and the use of that royal title must have meant to Joseph that, though he was of kingly lineage, marriage with Mary would cast no shadow upon his family status. Joseph waited not; to insure Mary all possible protection and establish his full legal right as her lawful guardian he hastened the solemnization of the marriage, and "did as the angel of the Lord had bidden him,

[u] Note 4, end of chapter.

[v] Matt. 1:20, 21; read 18–25.

[w] Matt. 1:22–23; compare Isa. 7:14; see also 9:6.

and took unto him his wife: and knew her not till she had brought forth her firstborn son and he called his name JESUS."[x]

The national hope of a Messiah based on promise and prophecy had become confused in the Jewish mind, through the influence of rabbinism with its many vagaries, and its "private interpretation"[y] made to appear authoritative by the artificially sustained prestige of the expositors; yet certain conditions had been emphasized as essential, even by the rabbis, and by these essentials would be judged the claim of any Jew who might declare himself to be the long expected One. It was beyond question that the Messiah was to be born within the tribe of Judah and through the line of descent from David, and, being of David He must of necessity be of the lineage of Abraham, through whose posterity, according to the covenant, all nations of the earth were to be blessed.[z]

Two genealogical records purporting to give the lineage of Jesus are found in the New Testament, one in the first chapter of Matthew, the other in the third chapter of Luke. These records present several apparent discrepancies, but such have been satisfactorily reconciled by the research of specialists in Jewish genealogy. No detailed analysis of the matter will be attempted here; but it should be borne in mind that the consensus of judgment on the part of investigators is that Matthew's account is that of the royal lineage, establishing the order of sequence among the legal successors to the throne of David, while the account given by Luke is a personal pedigree, demonstrating descent from David without adherence to the line of legal succession to the throne through primogeniture or nearness of kin.[aa] Luke's record is regarded by many, however, as the pedigree of Mary, while Matthew's is accepted as that of Joseph. The all-important fact to be remembered is that the Child promised by Gabriel to Mary, the virginal bride of Joseph, would be born in the royal line. A personal genealogy of Joseph was essentially that of Mary also, for they were cousins. Joseph is named

---

[x] Matt. 1:24, 25.

[y] 2 Pet. 1:20.

[z] Gen. 12:3; 18:18; 22:18; 26:4; compare Acts 3:25; Gal. 3:8.

[aa] Note 5, end of chapter.

as son of Jacob by Matthew, and as son of Heli by Luke; but Jacob and Heli were brothers, and it appears that one of the two was the father of Joseph and the other the father of Mary and therefore father-in-law to Joseph. That Mary was of Davidic descent is plainly set forth in many scriptures; for since Jesus was to be born of Mary, yet was not begotten by Joseph, who was the reputed, and according to the law of the Jews, the legal, father, the blood of David's posterity was given to the body of Jesus through Mary alone. Our Lord, though repeatedly addressed as Son of David, never repudiated the title but accepted it as rightly applied to Himself.[bb] Apostolic testimony stands in positive assertion of the royal heirship of Christ through earthly lineage, as witness the affirmation of Paul, the scholarly Pharisee: "Concerning his Son Jesus Christ our Lord, which was made of the seed of David according to the flesh"; and again: "Remember that Jesus Christ of the seed of David was raised from the dead."[cc]

In all the persecutions waged by His implacable haters, in all the false accusations brought against Him, in the specific charges of sacrilege and blasphemy based on His acknowledgment of the Messiahship as His own, no mention is found of even an insinuation that He could not be the Christ through any ineligibility based on lineage. Genealogy was assiduously cared for by the Jews before, during, and after the time of Christ; indeed their national history was largely genealogical record; and any possibility of denying the Christ because of unattested descent would have been used to the fullest extent by insistent Pharisee, learned scribe, haughty rabbi, and aristocratic Sadducee.

At the time of the Savior's birth, Israel was ruled by alien monarchs. The rights of the royal Davidic family were unrecognized; and the ruler of the Jews was an appointee of Rome. Had Judah been a free and independent nation, ruled by her rightful sovereign, Joseph the carpenter would have been her crowned king; and his lawful successor to the throne would have been Jesus of Nazareth, the King of the Jews.

[bb] For instances see Matt. 9:27; 15:22; 21:9; 20:30, 31, with which compare Luke 18:38, 39.

[cc] Rom. 1:3; 2 Tim. 2:8; see also Acts 2:30; 13:23; compare Ps. 132:11; see also Luke 1:32.

Gabriel's annunciation to Mary was that of the Son of David, on whose coming the hope of Israel rested as on a sure foundation. The One, thus announced, was Emmanuel, even God who was to dwell in flesh with His people,[dd] the Redeemer of the world, Jesus the Christ.

NOTES TO CHAPTER 7

1. John the Baptist Regarded as a Nazarite.—The instruction of the angel Gabriel to Zacharias, that the promised son, John, was to "drink neither wine nor strong drink," and the adult life of John as a dweller in the desert, together with his habit of wearing rough garb, have led commentators and Biblical specialists to assume that he was a "Nazarite for life." It is to be remembered, however, that nowhere in scripture extant is John the Baptist definitely called a Nazarite. A Nazarite, the name signifying *consecrated* or *separated,* was one, who by personal vow or by that made for him by his parents, was set apart to some special labor or course of life involving self-denial. (See page 67.) Smith's *Comp. Dict. of the Bible* says: "There is no notice in the Pentateuch of Nazarites for life; but the regulations for the vow of a Nazarite of days are given (Num. 6:1–2). The Nazarite, during the term of his consecration, was bound to abstain from wine, grapes, and every production of the vine, and from every kind of intoxicating drink. He was forbidden to cut the hair of his head, or to approach any dead body, even that of his nearest relation." The sole instance of a Nazarite for life named in the scriptures is that of Samson, whose mother was required to put herself under Nazarite observances prior to his birth, and the child was to be a Nazarite to God from his birth (Judg. 13:3–7, 14). In the strictness of his life, John the Baptist is to be credited with all the personal discipline required of Nazarites whether he was under voluntary or parental vows or was not so bound.

2. Circumcision, while not exclusively a Hebrew or an Israelitish practice, was made a definite requirement through the revelations of God to Abraham, as the sign of the covenant between Jehovah and the patriarch. (Gen. 17:9–14.) This covenant was made to include the establishment of Abraham's posterity as a great nation, and provided that through his descendants should all nations of the earth be blessed (Gen. 22:18)—a promise which has been proved to mean that through that lineage should the Messiah be born. Circumcision was a binding condition; and its practice therefore became a national characteristic. Every male was to be circumcised eight days after birth (Gen. 17:12; Lev. 12:3). This requirement as to age came to be so rigidly enforced, that even if the eighth day fell on a Sabbath the rite had to be performed on that day (John 7:22, 23). All male slaves had to be circumcised

---

dd Matt. 1:23.

(Gen. 17:12, 13) and even strangers who sojourned with the Hebrews and desired to partake of the Passover with them had to submit to the requirement (Ex. 12:48). From the *Standard Bible Dictionary* we take the following: "The ceremony indicated the casting off of uncleanness as a preparation for entrance into the privileges of membership in Israel. In the New Testament, with its transfer of emphasis from the external and formal to the inner and spiritual side of things, it was first declared unnecessary for Gentile converts to the gospel to be circumcised (Acts 15:28), and afterward the rite was set aside even by Jewish Christians." It became customary to name a child at the time it was circumcised, as is instanced in the case of John, son of Zacharias (Luke 1:59).

3. Zacharias's Affliction.—The sign for which Zacharias asked was thus given by the angel: "Behold, thou shalt be dumb, and not able to speak, until the day that these things shall be performed, because thou believest not my words, which shall be fulfilled in their season." (Luke 1:20.) From the account of the circumcision and naming of the boy, John, it is held by some that the afflicted father was also deaf, as the company "made signs" to him as to how he would have his son named (verse 62).

4. Jewish Betrothal.—The vow of espousal, or betrothal, has always been regarded as sacred and binding in Jewish law. In a manner it was as binding as a marriage ceremony, though it carried none of the particular rights of marriage. The following succinct statements are taken from Geikie's *Life and Words of Christ*, vol. 1, p. 99: "Among the Jews of Mary's day it was even more of an actual engagement [than it later came to be]. The betrothal was formally made with rejoicings in the house of the bride under a tent or slight canopy raised for the purpose. It was called the 'making sacred' as the bride thenceforth was sacred to her husband in the strictest sense. To make it legal, the bridegroom gave his betrothed a piece of money, or the worth of it, before witnesses, with the words, 'Lo, thou art betrothed unto me,' or by a formal writing in which similar words and the maiden's name were given, and this in the same way was handed to her before witnesses."

5. Genealogies of Joseph and Mary.—"It is now almost certain that the genealogies in both Gospels are genealogies of Joseph, which if we may rely on early traditions of their consanguinity involve genealogies of Mary also. The Davidic descent of Mary is implied in Acts 2:30; 13:23; Rom. 1:3; Luke 1:32, etc. St. Matthew gives the legal descent of Joseph through the elder and regal line, as heir to the throne of David; St. Luke gives the natural descent. Thus, the real father of Salathiel was heir of the house of Nathan, but the childless Jeconiah (Jer. 22:30) was the last lineal representative of the elder kingly line. The omission of some obscure names and the symmetrical arrangement into tesseradecads were common Jewish customs. It is not too much to say that after the labors of Mill (*On the Mythical Interpretation of the Gospels*, pp. 147–217) and Lord A. C. Hervey (*On the Genealogies of our Lord*, 1853) scarcely a single difficulty remains in reconciling the apparent divergencies.

And thus in this as in so many other instances, the very discrepancies which appear to be most irreconcilable, and most fatal to the historic accuracy of the four evangelists, turn out, on closer and more patient investigation, to be fresh proofs that they are not only entirely independent, but also entirely trustworthy."—Farrar, *Life of Christ*, p. 27, note.

The writer of the article "Genealogy of Jesus Christ" in Smith's *Bible Dict.* says: "The New Testament gives us the genealogy of but one person, our Savior (Matt. 1; Luke 3). . . . The following propositions will explain the true construction of these genealogies (so Lord A. C. Hervey): 1. They are both the genealogies of Joseph, i.e. of Jesus Christ, as the reputed and legal son of Joseph and Mary. 2. The genealogy of Matthew is, as Grotius asserted, Joseph's genealogy as legal successor to the throne of David. That of Luke is Joseph's private genealogy, exhibiting his real birth, as David's son, and thus showing why he was heir to Solomon's crown. The simple principle that one evangelist exhibits that genealogy which contained the successive heirs to David's and Solomon's throne, while the other exhibits the paternal stem of him who was the heir, explains all the anomalies of the two pedigrees, their agreements as well as their discrepancies, and the circumstance of their being two at all. 3. Mary, the mother of Jesus, was probably the daughter of Jacob, and first cousin to Joseph her husband."

A valuable contribution to the literature of this subject appears in the *Journal of the Transactions of the Victoria Institute, or Philosophical Society of Great Britain*, 1912, vol. 44, pp. 9–36, as an article, "The Genealogies of our Lord," by Mrs. A. S. Lewis, and discussion thereof by many scholars of acknowledged ability. The author, Mrs. Lewis, is an authority on Syriac manuscripts, and is one of the two women who, in 1892, discovered in the library of St. Catherine's monastery on Mount Sinai, the Syriac palimpsest MS. of the four Gospels. The gifted author holds that Matthew's account attests the royal pedigree of Joseph, and that Luke's genealogical table proves the equally royal descent of Mary. Mrs. Lewis says: "The Sinai Palimpsest also tells us that Joseph and Mary went to Bethlehem, to be enrolled there, because they were both of the house and lineage of David."

Canon Girdlestone, in discussing the article, says in pertinent emphasis of Mary's status as a princess of royal blood through descent from David: "When the angel was foretelling to Mary the birth of the Holy Child, he said, 'The Lord God shall give Him the throne of His father David.' Now if Joseph, her betrothed, had alone been descended from David, Mary would have answered, 'I am not yet married to Joseph,' whereas she did answer simply, 'I am an unmarried woman,' which plainly implies—if I were married, since I am descended from David, I could infuse my royal blood into a son, but how can I have a royal son while I am a virgin?'"

After brief mention of the Jewish law relating to adoption, wherein it is provided (according to Hammurabi's Code, section 188), that if a man teach his adopted son a handicraft, the son is thereby confirmed in all the rights of heirship, Canon Girdlestone adds: "If the crown of David had been assigned to his successor in the days of Herod it would have been placed on the head of Joseph. And who would have been the legal successor to Joseph? Jesus of Nazareth would have been then the King of the Jews, and the title on the cross spoke the truth. God had raised Him up to the house of David."

6. The Inner Sanctuary of the Temple.—The Holy of Holies in the Temple of Herod retained the form and dimensions of the Oracle in the Temple of Solomon; it was therefore a cube, twenty cubits in each principal measurement. Between this and the Holy Place hung a double veil, of finest material, elaborately embroidered. The outer of the two veils was open at the north end, the inner at the south; so that the high priest who entered at the appointed time once a year could pass between the veils without exposing the Holy of Holies. The sacred chamber was empty save for a large stone upon which the high priest sprinkled the sacrificial blood on the Day of Atonement; this stone occupied the place of the Ark and its Mercy Seat. Outside the veil, in the Holy Place, stood the altar of incense, the seven-branched candlestick, and the table of shewbread.—*The House of the Lord*, p. 59.

CHAPTER 8

THE BABE OF BETHLEHEM

THE BIRTH OF JESUS

Equally definite with the prophecies declaring that the Messiah would be born in the lineage of David are the predictions that fix the place of His birth at Bethlehem, a small town in Judea. There seems to have been no difference of opinion among priests, scribes, or rabbis on the matter, either before or since the great event. Bethlehem, though small and of little importance in trade or commerce, was doubly endeared to the Jewish heart as the birthplace of David and as that of the prospective Messiah. Mary and Joseph lived in Nazareth of Galilee, far removed from Bethlehem of Judea; and, at the time of which we speak, the maternity of the Virgin was fast approaching.

At that time a decree went out from Rome ordering a taxing of the people in all kingdoms and provinces tributary to the empire; the call was of general scope, it provided "that all the world should be taxed."[a] The taxing herein referred to may properly be understood as an enrolment[b] or a registration, whereby a census of Roman subjects would be secured, upon which as a basis the taxation of the different peoples would be determined. This particular census was the second of three such general registrations recorded by historians as occurring at intervals of about twenty years. Had the census been taken by the usual Roman method, each person would have been enrolled at the town of his residence; but the Jewish custom, for which the Roman law had respect, necessitated registration at the cities or towns claimed by the

---

[a] Luke 2:1; see also verses 2–4. Note 1, end of chapter.

[b] Note marginal reading, Oxford and Bagster Bibles.

respective families as their ancestral homes. As to whether the requirement was strictly mandatory that every family should thus register at the city of its ancestors, we need not be specially concerned; certain it is that Joseph and Mary went to Bethlehem, the city of David, to be inscribed under the imperial decree.[c]

The little town was crowded at the time, most likely by the multitude that had come in obedience to the same summons; and, in consequence, Joseph and Mary failed to find the most desirable accommodations and had to be content with the conditions of an improvised camp, as travelers unnumbered had done before, and as uncounted others have done since, in that region and elsewhere. We cannot reasonably regard this circumstance as evidence of extreme destitution; doubtless it entailed inconvenience, but it gives us no assurance of great distress or suffering.[d] It was while she was in this situation that Mary the Virgin gave birth to her firstborn, the Son of the Highest, the Only Begotten of the Eternal Father, Jesus the Christ.

But few details of attendant circumstances are furnished us. We are not told how soon the birth occurred after the arrival of Mary and her husband at Bethlehem. It may have been the purpose of the evangelist who made the record to touch upon matters of purely human interest as lightly as was consistent with the narration of fact, in order that the central truth might neither be hidden nor overshadowed by unimportant incident. We read in Holy Writ this only of the actual birth: "And so it was, that, while they were there, the days were accomplished that she should be delivered. And she brought forth her firstborn son, and wrapped him in swaddling clothes, and laid him in a manger; because there was no room for them in the inn."[e]

In vivid contrast with the simplicity and brevity of the scriptural account and of its paucity of incidental details, is the mass of circumstance supplied by the imagination of men, much of which is wholly unsupported by authoritative record and in many respects is plainly inconsistent and untrue. It is the part of prudence and wisdom to

[c] Note 1, end of chapter.

[d] Note 2, end of chapter.

[e] Luke 2:6, 7.

segregate and keep distinctly separate the authenticated statements of fact, in so momentous a matter, from the fanciful commentaries of historians, theologians, and writers of fiction, as also from the emotional rhapsodies of poets and artistic extravaganzas wrought by chisel or brush.

From the period of its beginning, Bethlehem had been the home of people engaged mostly in pastoral and agricultural pursuits. It is quite in line with what is known of the town and its environs to find at the season of Messiah's birth, which was in the springtime of the year, that flocks were in the field both night and day under the watchful care of their keepers. Unto certain of these humble shepherds came the first proclamation that the Savior had been born. Thus runs the simple record: "And there were in the same country shepherds abiding in the field, keeping watch over their flock by night. And, lo, the angel of the Lord came upon them, and the glory of the Lord shone round about them: and they were sore afraid. And the angel said unto them, Fear not: for, behold, I bring you good tidings of great joy, which shall be to all people. For unto you is born this day in the city of David a Saviour, which is Christ the Lord. And this shall be a sign unto you: Ye shall find a babe wrapped in swaddling clothes, lying in a manger. And suddenly there was with the angel a multitude of the heavenly host praising God, and saying, Glory to God in the highest, and on earth peace, good will toward men."[f]

Tidings of such import had never before been delivered by angel or received by man—good tidings of great joy, given to but few and those among the humblest of earth, but destined to spread to all people. There is sublime grandeur in the scene, as there is divine authorship in the message, and the climax is such as the mind of man could never have conceived—the sudden appearance of a multitude of the heavenly host, singing audibly to human ears the briefest, most consistent and most truly complete of all the songs of peace ever attuned by mortal or spirit choir. What a consummation to be wished—Peace on earth! But how can such come except through the

[f] Luke 2:8–14.

maintenance of good will toward men? And through what means could glory to God in the highest be more effectively rendered?

The trustful and unsophisticated keepers of sheep had not asked for sign or confirmation; their faith was in unison with the heavenly communication; nevertheless the angel had given them what he called a sign, to guide them in their search. They waited not, but went in haste, for in their hearts they believed, yea, more than believed, they knew, and this was the tenor of their resolve: "Let us now go even unto Bethlehem, and see this thing which is come to pass, which the Lord hath made known unto us."[g] They found the Babe in the manger, with the mother and Joseph near by; and, having seen, they went out and testified to the truth concerning the Child. They returned to their flocks, glorifying and praising God for all they had heard and seen.

There is meaning as deep as the pathos that all must feel in the seemingly parenthetical remark by Luke. "But Mary kept all these things, and pondered them in her heart."[h] It is apparent that the great truth as to the personality and mission of her divine Son had not yet unfolded itself in its fulness to her mind. The whole course of events, from the salutation of Gabriel to the reverent testimony of the shepherds concerning the announcing angel and the heavenly hosts, was largely a mystery to that stainless mother and wife.

REQUIREMENTS OF THE LAW STRICTLY OBSERVED

The Child was born a Jew; the mother was a Jewess, and the reputed and legal father, Joseph, was a Jew. The true paternity of the Child was known to but few, perhaps at that time to none save Mary, Joseph, and possibly Elisabeth and Zacharias; as He grew He was regarded by the people as Joseph's son.[i] The requirements of the law were carried out with exactitude in all matters pertaining to the Child. When eight days old He was circumcised, as was required of every male born in Israel;[j] and at the same time He received as an earthly bestowal the name that had been prescribed at the annunciation.

[g] Luke 2:15.

[h] Luke 2:19.

[i] Luke 4:22; Matt. 13:55; Mark 6:3.

[j] Gen. 17:12, 13; Lev. 12:3; compare John 7:22.

He was called JESUS, which, being interpreted is Savior; the name was rightfully His for He came to save the people from their sins.[k]

Part of the law given through Moses to the Israelites in the wilderness and continued in force down through the centuries, related to the procedure prescribed for women after childbirth.[l] In compliance therewith, Mary remained in retirement forty days following the birth of her Son; then she and her husband brought the Boy for presentation before the Lord as prescribed for the male firstborn of every family. It is manifestly impossible that all such presentations could have taken place in the temple, for many Jews lived at great distances from Jerusalem; it was the rule, however, that parents should present their children in the temple when possible. Jesus was born within five or six miles from Jerusalem; He was accordingly taken to the temple for the ceremonial of redemption from the requirement applying to the firstborn of all Israelites except Levites. It will be remembered that the children of Israel had been delivered from the bondage of Egypt with the accompaniment of signs and wonders. Because of Pharaoh's repeated refusals to let the people go, plagues had been brought upon the Egyptians, one of which was the death of the firstborn throughout the land, excepting only the people of Israel. In remembrance of this manifestation of power, the Israelites were required to dedicate their firstborn sons to the service of the sanctuary.[m] Subsequently the Lord directed that all males belonging to the tribe of Levi should be devoted to this special labor instead of the firstborn in every tribe; nevertheless the eldest son was still claimed as particularly the Lord's own, and had to be formally exempted from the earlier requirement of service by the paying of a ransom.[n]

In connection with the ceremony of purification, every mother was required to furnish a yearling lamb for a burnt offering, and a young pigeon or dove for a sin offering; but in the case of any woman who was unable to provide a lamb, a pair of doves or pigeons might be offered. We learn of the humble circumstances of Joseph and Mary

[k] Luke 2:21; compare 1:31; Matt. 1:21, 25.

[l] Lev. 12.

[m] Ex. 12:29; 13:2, 12; 22:29, 30.

[n] Num. 8:15–18; 18:15, 16.

from the fact that they brought the less costly offering, two doves or pigeons, instead of one bird and a lamb.

Among the righteous and devout Israelites were some who, in spite of traditionalism, rabbinism, and priestly corruption, still lived in righteous expectation of inspired confidence, awaiting patiently the consolation of Israel.° One of these was Simeon, then living in Jerusalem. Through the power of the Holy Ghost he had gained the promise that he should not see death until he had looked upon the Lord's Christ in the flesh. Prompted by the Spirit he repaired to the temple on the day of the presentation of Jesus, and recognized in the Babe the promised Messiah. In the moment of realization that the hope of his life had found glorious consummation, Simeon raised the Child reverently in his arms, and, with the simple but undying eloquence that comes of God uttered this splendid supplication, in which thanksgiving, resignation and praise are so richly blended:

"Lord, now lettest thou thy servant depart in peace, according to thy word: for mine eyes have seen thy salvation, which thou hast prepared before the face of all people; a light to lighten the Gentiles, and the glory of thy people Israel."ᴾ

Then under the spirit of prophecy, Simeon told of the greatness of the Child's mission, and of the anguish that the mother would be called to endure because of Him, which would be even like unto that of a sword piercing her soul. The Spirit's witness to the divinity of Jesus was not to be confined to a man. There was at that time in the temple a godly woman of great age, Anna, a prophetess who devoted herself exclusively to temple service; and she, being inspired of God, recognized her Redeemer, and testified of Him to all about her. Both Joseph and Mary marveled at the things that were spoken of the Child; seemingly they were not yet able to comprehend the majesty of Him who had come to them through so miraculous a conception and so marvelous a birth.

°Luke 2:25; see also verse 38; Mark 15:43; compare Ps. 40: 1.

ᴾ Luke 2:29–32. These verses are known in Christian hymnology as the Nunc Dimittis; the name has reference to the first two words of the Latin version.

WISE MEN SEARCH FOR THE KING

Some time after the presentation of Jesus in the temple, though how long we are not told, possibly but a few days, possibly weeks or even months, Herod, king of Judea, was greatly troubled, as were the people of Jerusalem in general, over the report that a Child of Prophecy—one destined to become King of the Jews—had been born. Herod was professedly an adherent of the religion of Judah, though by birth an Idumean, by descent an Edomite or one of the posterity of Esau, all of whom the Jews hated; and of all Edomites not one was more bitterly detested than was Herod the king. He was tyrannical and merciless, sparing neither foe nor friend who came under suspicion of being a possible hindrance to his ambitious designs. He had his wife and several of his sons, as well as others of his blood kindred, cruelly murdered; and he put to death nearly all of the great national council, the Sanhedrin. His reign was one of revolting cruelty and unbridled oppression. Only when in danger of inciting a national revolt or in fear of incurring the displeasure of his imperial master, the Roman emperor, did he stay his hand in any undertaking.[q]

Rumors of the birth of Jesus reached Herod's ears in this way. There came to Jerusalem certain men from afar, wise men they were called, and they asked, "Where is he that is born King of the Jews? for we have seen his star in the east, and are come to worship him."[r] Herod summoned "all the chief priests and scribes of the people," and demanded of them where, according to the prophets, Christ should be born. They answered him: "In Bethlehem of Judea: for thus it is written by the prophet, And thou Bethlehem, in the land of Juda, art not the least among the princes of Juda: for out of thee shall come a Governor, that shall rule my people Israel."[s]

Herod sent secretly for the wise men, and inquired of them as to the source of their information, and particularly as to the time at which the star, to which they attached such significance, had appeared. Then he directed them to Bethlehem, saying: "Go and

[q] Note 3, end of chapter.

[r] Matt. 2:2; read 1–10.

[s] Matt. 2:5, 6; compare Micah 5:2; John 7:42.

search diligently for the young child; and when ye have found him, bring me word again, that I may come and worship him also." As the men set out from Jerusalem on the last stage of their journey of inquiry and search, they rejoiced exceedingly, for the new star they had seen in the east was again visible. They found the house wherein Mary was living with her husband and the Babe, and as they recognized the royal Child they "fell down, and worshipped him: and when they had opened their treasures, they presented unto him gifts; gold, and frankincense, and myrrh."[t] Having thus gloriously accomplished the purpose of their pilgrimage, these devout and learned travelers prepared to return home, and would have stopped at Jerusalem to report to the king as he had requested, but "being warned of God in a dream that they should not return to Herod, they departed into their own country another way."[u]

Much has been written, beyond all possible warrant of scriptural authority, concerning the visit of the magi, or wise men, who thus sought and found the infant Christ. As a matter of fact, we are left without information as to their country, nation, or tribal relationship; we are not even told how many they were, though unauthenticated tradition has designated them as "the three wise men," and has even given them names; whereas they are left unnamed in the scriptures, the only true record of them extant, and may have numbered but two or many. Attempts have been made to identify the star whose appearance in their eastern sky had assured the magi that the King was born; but astronomy furnished no satisfactory confirmation. The recorded appearance of the star has been associated by both ancient and modern interpreters with the prophecy of Balaam, who, though not an Israelite had blessed Israel, and under divine inspiration had predicted: "there shall come a Star out of Jacob, and a Sceptre shall rise out of Israel."[v] Moreover, as already shown, the appearance of a new star was a predicted sign recognized and acknowledged among the people of the western world as witness of Messiah's birth.[w]

[t] Note 4, end of chapter.

[u] Note 5, end of chapter.

[v] Num. 24:17.

[w] Hel. 14:5; 3 Ne. 1:21.

THE FLIGHT INTO EGYPT

Herod's perfidy in directing the magi to return and report to him where the royal Infant was to be found, falsely professing that he wished to worship Him also, while in his heart he purposed taking the Child's life, was thwarted by the divine warning given to the wise men as already noted. Following their departure, the angel of the Lord appeared to Joseph, saying: "Arise, and take the young child and his mother, and flee into Egypt, and be thou there until I bring thee word: for Herod will seek the young child to destroy him."[x] In obedience to this command, Joseph took Mary and her Child, and set out by night on the journey to Egypt; and there the family remained until divinely directed to return. When it was apparent to the king that the wise men had ignored his instructions, he was exceedingly angry; and, estimating the earliest time at which the birth could have occurred according to the magis' statement of the star's appearing, he ruthlessly ordered the slaughter of "all the children that were in Bethlehem, and in all the coasts thereof, from two years old and under."[y] In this massacre of the innocents, the evangelist found a fulfillment of Jeremiah's fateful voicing of the word of the Lord, spoken six centuries earlier and expressed in the forceful past tense as though then already accomplished: "In Rama was there a voice heard, lamentation, and weeping, and great mourning, Rachel weeping for her children, and would not be comforted, because they are not."[z]

BIRTH OF JESUS MADE KNOWN TO THE NEPHITES

As heretofore shown, the prophets of the western hemisphere had foretold in great plainness the earthly advent of the Lord, and had specifically set forth the time, place, and circumstances of His birth.[aa] As the time drew near the people were divided by conflicting opinions concerning the reliability of these prophecies; and intolerant unbelievers cruelly persecuted those, who, like Zacharias, Simeon, Anna, and other righteous ones in Palestine, had maintained in faith

[x] Matt. 2:13.

[y] Matt. 2:16.

[z] Matt. 2:17, 18; compare Jer. 31:15.

[aa] Pages 48–49.

and trust their unwavering expectation of the coming of the Lord. Samuel, a righteous Lamanite, who, because of his faithfulness and sacrificing devotion, had been blessed with the spirit and power of prophecy, fearlessly proclaimed the birth of Christ as near: "And behold, he said unto them, Behold I give unto you a sign; for five years more cometh, and behold, then cometh the Son of God to redeem all those who shall believe on his name."[bb] The prophet told of many signs and wonders, which were to mark the great event. As the five years ran their course, the believers grew more steadfast, the unbelievers more violent, until the last day of the specified period dawned; and this was the "day set apart by the unbelievers, that all those who believed in those traditions should be put to death, except the sign should come to pass which had been given by Samuel the prophet."[cc]

Nephi, a prophet of the time, cried unto the Lord in anguish of soul because of the persecution of which his people were the victims; "and behold, the voice of the Lord came unto him, saying, Lift up your head and be of good cheer; for behold, the time is at hand, and on this night shall the sign be given, and on the morrow come I into the world, to show unto the world that I will fulfil all that which I have caused to be spoken by the mouth of my holy prophets. Behold, I come unto my own, to fulfil all things which I have made known unto the children of men, from the foundation of the world, and to do the will, both of the Father, and of the Son—of the Father because of me, and of the Son because of my flesh. And behold, the time is at hand, and this night shall the sign be given."[dd]

The words of the prophet were fulfilled that night; for though the sun set in its usual course there was no darkness; and on the morrow the sun rose on a land already illumined; a day and a night and another day had been as one day; and this was but one of the signs. A new star appeared in the firmament of the west, even as was seen by the magi in the east; and there were many other marvelous manifestations as the prophets had predicted. All these things occurred on what is

[bb] Hel. 14:2; read 1–9.

[cc] 3 Ne. 1:9; read verses 4–21.

[dd] 3 Ne. 1:12–21.

now known as the American continent, six hundred years after Lehi and his little company had left Jerusalem to come hither.

THE TIME OF THE BIRTH OF JESUS

The time of the Messiah's birth is a subject upon which specialists in theology and history, and those who are designated in literature "the learned," fail to agree. Numerous lines of investigation have been followed, only to reach divergent conclusions, both as to the year and as to the month and day within the year at which the "Christian era" in reality began. The establishment of the birth of Christ as an event marking a time from which chronological data should be calculated, was first effected about A.D. 532 by Dionysius Exiguus; and as a basis for the reckoning of time this method has come to be known as the Dionysian system, and takes for its fundamental datum A.U.C. 753, that is to say 753 years after the founding of Rome, as the year of our Lord's birth. So far as there exists any consensus of opinion among later scholars who have investigated the subject, it is to the effect that the Dionysian calculation is wrong, in that it places the birth of Christ between three and four years too late; and that therefore our Lord was born in the third or fourth year before the beginning of what is designated by the scholars of Oxford and Cambridge, "the Common Account called Anno Domini."[ee]

Without attempting to analyze the mass of calculation data relating to this subject, we accept the Dionysian basis as correct with respect to the year, which is to say that we believe Christ to have been born in the year known to us as 1 B.C., and, as shall be shown, in an early month of that year. In support of this belief we cite the inspired record known as the "Revelation on Church Government, given through Joseph the Prophet, in April, 1830," which opens with these words: "The rise of the Church of Christ in these last days, being one thousand eight hundred and thirty years since the coming of our Lord and Saviour Jesus Christ in the flesh."[ff]

Another evidence of the correctness of our commonly accepted chronology is furnished by the Book of Mormon record. Therein we

---

[ee] Marginal reading, Oxford and Bagster Bibles, Matt. 2:1.

[ff] D&C 20:1; compare 21:3; note 6, end of chapter.

read that "in the commencement of the first year of the reign of Zedekiah, king of Judah," the word of the Lord came to Lehi at Jerusalem, directing him to take his family and depart into the wilderness.[gg] In the early stages of their journey toward the sea, Lehi prophesied, as had been shown him of the Lord, concerning the impending destruction of Jerusalem and the captivity of the Jews. Furthermore, he predicted the eventual return of the people of Judah from their exile in Babylon, and the birth of the Messiah, which latter event he definitely declared would take place six hundred years from the time he and his people had left Jerusalem.[hh] This specification of time was repeated by later prophecy;[ii] and the signs of the actual fulfillment are recorded as having been realized "six hundred years from the time that Lehi left Jerusalem.[jj] These scriptures fix the time of the beginning of Zedekiah's reign as six hundred years before the birth of Christ. According to the commonly accepted reckoning, Zedekiah was made king in the year 597 B.C.[kk] This shows a discrepancy of about three years between the commonly accepted date of Zedekiah's inauguration as king and that given in the Book of Mormon statement; and, as already seen, there is a difference of between three and four years between the Dionysian reckoning and the nearest approach to an agreement among scholars concerning the beginning of the current era. Book of Mormon chronology therefore sustains the correctness of the common or Dionysian system.

As to the season of the year in which Christ was born, there is among the learned as great a diversity of opinion as that relating to the year itself. It is claimed by many Biblical scholars that December 25th, the day celebrated in Christendom as Christmas, cannot be the correct date. We believe April 6th to be the birthday of Jesus Christ as indicated in a revelation of the present dispensation already cited[ll] in

---

[gg] 1 Ne. 1:4; 2:2–4.

[hh] 1 Ne. 10:4.

[ii] 1 Ne 19:8; 2 Ne. 25:19.

[jj] 3 Ne. 1:1.

[kk] Standard Bible Dictionary, ed. Jacobus, Nourse, and Zenos, Funk & Wagnalls Co., New York and London, 1909, p. 915, article "Zedekiah."

[ll] D&C 20:1; compare 21:3.

which that day is made without qualification the completion of the one thousand eight hundred and thirtieth year since the coming of the Lord in the flesh. This acceptance is admittedly based on faith in modern revelation, and in no wise is set forth as the result of chronological research or analysis. We believe that Jesus Christ was born in Bethlehem of Judea, April 6, B.C. 1.

NOTES TO CHAPTER 8

1. The "Taxing."—Regarding the presence of Joseph and Mary in Bethlehem, far from their Galilean home, and the imperial decree by compliance with which they were led there, the following notes are worthy of consideration. Farrar (*Life of Christ*, p. 24, note), says: "It appears to be uncertain whether the journey of Mary with her husband was obligatory or voluntary. . . . Women were liable to a capitation tax, if this enrolment also involved taxation. But, apart from any legal necessity, it may easily be imagined that at such a moment Mary would desire not to be left alone. The cruel suspicion of which she had been the subject, and which had almost led to the breaking off of her betrothal (Matt. 1:19) would make her cling all the more to the protection of her husband." The following excerpt is from Geikie's *Life and Words of Christ*, vol. 1, chap. 9; p. 108: "The Jewish nation had paid tribute to Rome, through their rulers, since the days of Pompey; and the methodical Augustus, who now reigned, and had to restore order and soundness to the finances of the empire, after the confusion and exhaustion of the civil wars, took good care that this obligation should neither be forgotten nor evaded. He was accustomed to require a census to be taken periodically in every province of his vast dominions, that he might know the number of soldiers he could levy in each, and the amount of taxes due to the treasury. . . . In an empire embracing the then known world, such a census could hardly have been made simultaneously, or in any short or fixed time; more probably it was the work of years, in successive provinces or kingdoms. Sooner or later, however, even the dominions of vassal kings like Herod had to furnish the statistics demanded by their master. He had received his kingdom on the footing of a subject, and grew more entirely dependent on Augustus as years passed, asking his sanction at every turn for steps he proposed to take. He would, thus, be only too ready to meet his wish, by obtaining the statistics he sought, as may be judged from the fact that in one of the last years of his life, just before Christ's birth, he made the whole Jewish nation take a solemn oath of allegiance to the emperor as well as to himself.

"It is quite probable that the mode of taking the required statistics was left very much to Herod, at once to show respect to him before his people, and from the known opposition of the Jews to anything like a general numeration, even apart from the taxation to which it was designed to lead. At the time to which the narrative refers, a simple registration seems to have been made, on the old Hebrew plan of enrolling by families in their ancestral districts, of course for future use; and thus it passed over quietly. . . . The proclamation having been made through the land, Joseph had no choice but to go to Bethlehem, the city of David, the place in which his family descent, from the house and lineage of David, required him to be inscribed."

2. Jesus Born Amidst Poor Surroundings.—Undoubtedly the accommodations for physical comfort amidst which Jesus was born were few and poor. But the environment, considered in the light of the customs of the country and time, was far from the state of abject deprivation which modern and western ways would make it appear. "Camping out" was no unusual exigency among travelers in Palestine at the time of our Lord's birth; nor is it considered such today. It is, however, beyond question that Jesus was born into a comparatively poor family, amidst humble surroundings associated with the inconveniences incident to travel. Cunningham Geikie, *Life and Words of Christ*, chap. 9, pp. 112, 113, says: "It was to Bethlehem that Joseph and Mary were coming, the town of Ruth and Boaz, and the early home of their own great forefather David. As they approached it from Jerusalem they would pass, at the last mile, a spot sacred to Jewish memory, where the light of Jacob's life went out, when his first love, Rachel, died, and was buried, as her tomb still shows, 'in the way to Ephrath, which is Bethlehem.'. . . Traveling in the East has always been very different from Western ideas. As in all thinly-settled countries, private hospitality, in early times, supplied the want of inns, but it was the peculiarity of the East that this friendly custom continued through a long series of ages. On the great roads through barren or uninhabited parts, the need of shelter led, very early, to the erection of rude and simple buildings, of varying size, known as khans, which offered the wayfarer the protection of walls and a roof, and water, but little more. The smaller structures consisted of sometimes only a single empty room, on the floor of which the traveler might spread his carpet for sleep; the larger ones, always built in a hollow square, enclosing a court for the beasts, with water in it for them and their masters. From immemorial antiquity it has been a favorite mode of benevolence to raise such places of shelter, as we see so far back as the times of David, when Chimham built a great khan near Bethlehem, on the caravan road to Egypt."

Canon Farrar (*Life of Christ*, chap. 1) accepts the traditional belief that the shelter within which Jesus was born was that of one of the numerous limestone caves which abound in the region, and which are still used by travelers as resting places. He says: "In Palestine it not infrequently happens that the entire khan, or at any rate the portion of it in which the animals are housed, is one of those innumerable caves which abound in the limestone rocks of its central hills. Such seems to have been in the case at the little town of Bethlehem-Ephratah, in the land of Judah. Justin Martyr, the Apologist, who, from his birth at Shechem, was familiar with Palestine, and who lived less than a century after the time of our Lord, places the scene of the nativity in a cave. This is, indeed, the ancient and constant tradition both of the Eastern and the Western Churches, and it is one of the few to which, though unrecorded in the Gospel history, we may attach a reasonable probability."

3. Herod the Great.—The history of Herod I, otherwise known as Herod the Great, must be sought in special works, in which the subject is treated at length. Some of the principal facts should be considered in our present study, and for the assistance of the student a few extracts from works regarded as reliable are presented herewith.

Condensed from part of article in the *Standard Bible Dictionary*, edited by Jacobus, Nourse, and Zenos; published by Funk and Wagnalls Co., 1909:—Herod I, the son of Antipater, was early given office by his father, who had been made procurator of Judea. The first office which Herod held was that of governor of Galilee. He was then a young man of about twenty-five, energetic and athletic. Immediately he set about the eradication of the robber bands that infested his district, and soon was able to execute the robber chief Hezekiah and several of his followers. For this he was summoned to Jerusalem by the Sanhedrin, tried and condemned, but with the connivance of Hyrcanus II [the high priest and ethnarch] he escaped by night.—He went to Rome where he was appointed King of Judea by Antony and Octavius.—For the next two years he was engaged in fighting the forces of Antigonus, whom he finally defeated, and in 37 B.C. gained possession of Jerusalem.—As king Herod confronted serious difficulties. The Jews objected to him because of his birth and reputation. The Asmonean family regarded him as a usurper, notwithstanding the fact that he had married Mariamne. The Pharisees were shocked at his Hellenistic sympathies, as well as at his severe methods of government. On the other hand the Romans held him responsible for the order of his kingdom, and the protection of the eastern frontier of the Republic. Herod met these various difficulties with characteristic energy and even cruelty, and generally with cold sagacity. Although he taxed the people severely, in times of famine he remitted their dues and even sold his plate to get means to buy them food. While he never became actually friendly with the Pharisees, they profited by his hostility to the party of the Asmoneans, which led at the beginning of his reign to the execution of a number of Sadducees who were members of the Sanhedrin.

From Smith's *Comprehensive Dictionary of the Bible*:—The latter part "of the reign of Herod was undisturbed by external troubles, but his domestic life was embittered by an almost uninterrupted series of injuries and cruel acts of vengeance. The terrible acts of bloodshed which Herod perpetrated in his own family were accompanied by others among his subjects equally terrible, from the number who fell victims to them. According to the well-known story, he ordered the nobles whom he had called to him in his last moments to be executed immediately after his decease, that so at least his death might be attended by universal mourning. It was at the time of his fatal illness that he must have caused the slaughter of the infants at Bethlehem" (Matt. 2:16–18).

The mortal end of the tyrant and multi-murderer is thus treated by Farrar in his *Life of Christ*, pp. 54, 55:—"It must have been very shortly after the murder of the innocents that Herod died. Only five days before his death he had made a frantic attempt at suicide, and had ordered the execution of his eldest son Antipater.

His deathbed, which once more reminds us of Henry VIII, was accompanied by circumstances of peculiar horror; and it has been asserted that he died of a loathsome disease, which is hardly mentioned in history, except in the case of men who have been rendered infamous by an atrocity of persecuting zeal. On his bed of intolerable anguish, in that splendid and luxurious palace which he had built for himself, under the palms of Jericho, swollen with disease and scorched by thirst, ulcerated externally and glowing inwardly with a, soft slow fire,' surrounded by plotting sons and plundering slaves, detesting all and detested by all, longing for death as a release from his tortures yet dreading it as the beginning of worse terrors, stung by remorse yet still unslaked with murder, a horror to all around him yet in his guilty conscience a worse terror to himself, devoured by the premature corruption of an anticipated grave, eaten of worms as though visibly smitten by the finger of God's wrath after seventy years of successful villainy, the wretched old man, whom men had called the Great, lay in savage frenzy awaiting his last hour. As he knew that none would shed one tear for him, he determined that they should shed many for themselves, and issued an order that, under pain of death, the principal families of the kingdom and the chiefs of the tribes should come to Jericho. They came, and then, shutting them in the hippodrome, he secretly commanded his sister Salome that at the moment of his death they should all be massacred. And so, choking as it were with blood, devising massacres in its very delirium, the soul of Herod passed forth into the night."

For mention of the Temple of Herod see Note 5, following Chapter 6.

4. Gifts from the Wise Men to the Child Jesus.—The scriptural account of the visit of the wise men to Jesus and His mother states that they "fell down and worshipped him," and furthermore that "when they had opened their treasures, they presented unto him gifts: gold, and frankincense, and myrrh." The offering of gifts to a superior in rank, either as to worldly status or recognized spiritual endowment, was a custom of early days and still prevails in many oriental lands. It is worthy of note that we have no record of these men from the east offering gifts to Herod in his palace; they did, however, impart of their treasure to the lowly Infant, in whom they recognized the King they had come to seek. The tendency to ascribe occult significance to even trifling details mentioned in scripture, and particularly as regards the life of Christ, has led to many fanciful suggestions concerning the gold and frankincense and myrrh specified in this incident. Some have supposed a half-hidden symbolism therein—gold a tribute to His royal estate, frankincense an offering in recognition of His priesthood, and myrrh for His burial. The sacred record offers no basis for such conjecture. Myrrh and frankincense are aromatic resins derived from plants indigenous to eastern lands, and they have been used from very early times in medicine and in the preparation of perfumes and incense mixtures. They were presumably among the natural productions of the lands from which the magi came, though probably even there they were costly and highly esteemed. Such, together with gold, which is of value among all nations, were most appropriate as gifts for a king. Any mystical significance one may choose to attach to the presents must be remembered as his own supposition or fancy, and not as based on scriptural warrant.

5. Testimonies from Shepherds and Magi.—The following instructive note on the testimonies relating to Messiah's birth, is taken from the *Young Men's Mutual Improvement Association Manual* for 1897–8: "It will be observed that the testimonies concerning the birth of the Messiah are from two extremes, the lowly shepherds in the Judean field, and the learned magi from the far east. We cannot think this is the result of mere chance, but that in it may be discerned the purpose and wisdom of God. All Israel was looking forward to the coming of the Messiah, and in the birth of Jesus at Bethlehem, the hope of Israel—though unknown to Israel—is fulfilled. Messiah, of whom the prophet spake, is born. But there must be those who can testify of that truth, and hence to the shepherds who watched their flocks by night an angel was sent to say: 'Fear not, behold I bring you good tidings of great joy, which shall be to all people; for unto you is born this day, in the city of David, a Saviour, which is Christ, the Lord.' And for a sign of the truth of the message, they were to find the child wrapped in swaddling clothes, lying in a manger in Bethlehem. And they went with haste and found Mary and Joseph, and the babe lying in a manger; and when they had seen it, they made known abroad the saying which was told them concerning this child. God had raised up to Himself witnesses among the people to testify that Messiah was born, that the hope of Israel was fulfilled. But there were classes of people among the Jews whom these lowly shepherd witnesses could not reach, and had they been able to reach them, the story of the angel's visit, and the concourse of angels singing the magnificent song of "Peace on earth, good will to men" would doubtless have been accounted an idle tale of superstitious folk, deceived by their own overwrought imaginations or idle dreams. Hence God raised up another class of witnesses—the 'wise men from the east'— witnesses that could enter the royal palace of proud King Herod and boldly ask: 'Where is he that is born king of the Jews? for we have seen his star in the east, and are come to worship him'; a testimony that startled Herod and troubled all Jerusalem. So that indeed God raised up witnesses for Himself to meet all classes and conditions of men—the testimony of angels for the poor and the lowly; the testimony of wise men for the haughty king and proud priests of Judea. So that of the things concerning the birth of Messiah, no less than of the things of His death and Resurrection from the dead, His disciples could say, 'these things were not done in a corner.'"

6. The Year of Christ's Birth.—In treating this topic Dr. Charles F. Deems (*The Light of the Nations*, p. 28), after giving careful consideration of the estimates, calculations, and assumptions of men who have employed many means in their investigation and reach only discordant results says: "It is annoying to see learned men use the same apparatus of calculation and reach the most diverse results. It is bewildering to attempt a reconciliation of these varying calculations." In an appended note the same author states: "For example: the birth of our Lord is placed in 1 B.C. by Pearson and Hug; 2 B.C. by Scalinger; 3 B.C. by Baronius and Paulus; 4 B.C. by Bengel, Wieseler, and Greswell; 5 B.C. by Usher and Petavius; 6 B.C. by Strong, Luvin, and Clark; 7 B.C. by Ideler and Sanclemente."

CHAPTER 9

THE BOY OF NAZARETH

Joseph, Mary, and her Son remained in Egypt until after the death of Herod the Great, which event was made known by another angelic visitation. Their stay in the foreign land was probably brief, for Herod did not long survive the babes he had slain in Bethlehem. In the return of the family from Egypt the evangelist finds a fulfillment of Hosea's prophetic vision of what should be: "Out of Egypt have I called my son."[a]

It appears to have been Joseph's intention to make a home for the family in Judea, possibly at Bethlehem—the city of his ancestors and a place now even more endeared to him as the birthplace of Mary's Child—but, learning on the way that Herod's son Archelaus ruled in the place of his wicked father, Joseph modified his purpose; and, "being warned of God in a dream, he turned aside into the parts of Galilee: and he came and dwelt in a city called Nazareth: that it might be fulfilled which was spoken by the prophets, He shall be called a Nazarene."[b]

While Archelaus, who appears to have been a natural heir to his infamous father's wickedness and cruelty, ruled in Judea,[c] for a short time as king, then with the less exalted title of ethnarch, which had been decreed to him by the emperor, his brother Antipas governed as tetrarch in Galilee. Herod Antipas was well nigh as vicious and reprobate as others of his unprincipled family, but he was less aggressive in vindictiveness, and in that period of his reign was comparatively tolerant.[d]

[a] Matt. 2:15; compare Hos. 11:1.

[b] Matt. 2:19–23. Note 5, end of chapter.

[c] Note 1, end of chapter.

[d] Note 2, end of chapter.

Concerning the home life of Joseph and his family in Nazareth, the scriptural record makes but brief mention. The silence with which the early period of the life of Jesus is treated by the inspired historians is impressive; while the fanciful accounts written in later years by unauthorized hands are full of fictitious detail, much of which is positively revolting in its puerile inconsistency. None but Joseph, Mary, and the other members of the immediate family or close associates of the household could have furnished the facts of daily life in the humble home at Nazareth; and from these qualified informants Matthew and Luke probably derived the knowledge of which they wrote. The record made by those who knew is marked by impressive brevity. In this absence of detail we may see evidence of the genuineness of the scriptural account. Inventive writers would have supplied, as, later, such did supply, what we seek in vain within the chapters of the Gospels. With hallowed silence do the inspired scribes honor the boyhood of their Lord; he who seeks to invent circumstances and to invest the life of Christ with fictitious additions, dishonors Him. Read thoughtfully the attested truth concerning the Childhood of the Christ: "And the child grew, and waxed strong in spirit, filled with wisdom: and the grace of God was upon him."[e]

In such simplicity is the normal, natural development of the Boy Jesus made clear. He came among men to experience all the natural conditions of mortality; He was born as truly a dependent, helpless babe as is any other child; His infancy was in all common features as the infancy of others; His boyhood was actual boyhood, His development was as necessary and as real as that of all children. Over His mind had fallen the veil of forgetfulness common to all who are born to earth, by which the remembrance of primeval existence is shut off. The Child grew, and with growth there came to Him expansion of mind, development of faculties, and progression in power and understanding. His advancement was from one grace to another, not from gracelessness to grace; from good to greater good, not from evil to good, from favor with God to greater favor, not from estrangement because of sin to reconciliation through repentance and propitiation.[f]

---

[e] Luke 2:40.
[f] Note 3, end of chapter.

Our knowledge of Jewish life in that age justifies the inference that the Boy was well taught in the law and the scriptures, for such was the rule. He garnered knowledge by study, and gained wisdom by prayer, thought, and effort. Beyond question He was trained to labor, for idleness was abhorred then as it is now; and every Jewish boy, whether carpenter's son, peasant's child, or rabbi's heir, was required to learn and follow a practical and productive vocation. Jesus was all that a boy should be, for His development was unretarded by the dragging weight of sin; He loved and obeyed the truth and therefore was free.[g]

Joseph and Mary, devout and faithful in all observances of the law, went up to Jerusalem every year at the feast of the Passover. This religious festival, it should be remembered, was one of the most solemn and sacred among the many ceremonial commemorations of the Jews; it had been established at the time of the peoples' exodus from Egypt, in remembrance of the outstretched arm of power by which God had delivered Israel after the angel of destruction had slain the firstborn in every Egyptian home and had mercifully passed over the houses of the children of Jacob.[h] It was of such importance that its annual recurrence was made the beginning of the new year. The law required all males to present themselves before the Lord at the feast. The rule was that women should likewise attend if not lawfully detained; and Mary appears to have followed both the spirit of the law and the letter of the rule, for she habitually accompanied her husband to the annual gathering at Jerusalem.

When Jesus had attained the age of twelve years He was taken by His mother and Joseph to the feast as the law required; whether the Boy had ever before been present on such an occasion we are not told. At twelve years of age a Jewish boy was recognized as a member of his home community; he was required then to enter with definite purpose upon his chosen vocation; he attained an advanced status as an individual in that thereafter he could not be arbitrarily disposed of as a bondservant by his parents; he was appointed to higher studies in school and home; and, when accepted by the priests, he became a

[g] Compare His teachings after He had reached manhood, e.g., John 8:32.

[h] Deut. 16:1–6; compare Ex. 12:2.

"son of the law." It was the common and very natural desire of parents to have their sons attend the feast of the Passover and be present at the temple ceremonies as recognized members of the congregation when of the prescribed age. Thus came the Boy Jesus to the temple.

The feast proper lasted seven days, and in the time of Christ was annually attended by great concourses of Jews; Josephus speaks of such a Passover gathering as "an innumerable multitude."[i] The people came from distant provinces in large companies and caravans, as a matter of convenience and as a means of common protection against the marauding bands which are known to have infested the country. As members of such a company Joseph and his family traveled.

When, following the conclusion of the Passover, the Galilean company had gone a day's journey toward home, Joseph and Mary discovered to their surprise and deep concern that Jesus was not with their company. After a fruitless search among their friends and acquaintances, they turned back toward Jerusalem seeking the Boy. Their inquiries brought little comfort or assistance until three days had passed; then "they found him in the temple, sitting in the midst of the doctors, both hearing them and asking them questions."[j] It was no unusual thing for a twelve year old boy to be questioned by priests, scribes, or rabbis, nor to be permitted to ask questions of these professional expounders of the law, for such procedure was part of the educational training of Jewish youths; nor was there anything surprising in such a meeting of students and teachers within the temple courts, for the rabbis of that time were accustomed to give instruction there; and people, young and old, gathered about them, sitting at their feet to learn; but there was much that was extraordinary in this interview as the demeanor of the learned doctors showed, for never before had such a student been found, inasmuch as "all that heard him were astonished at his understanding and answers." The incident furnishes evidence of a well spent boyhood and proof of unusual attainments.[k]

---

[i] Josephus: *Wars of the Jews,* ii, 1:3.

[j] Luke 2:46; read 41–52.

[k] Compare Matt. 7:28, 29; 13:54; Mark 6:2; Luke 4:22.

The amazement of Mary and her husband on finding the Boy in such distinguished company, and so plainly the object of deference and respect, and the joy of seeing again the beloved One who to them had been lost, did not entirely banish the memory of the anguish His absence had caused them. In words of gentle yet unmistakable reproof the mother said: "Son, why hast thou thus dealt with us? behold, thy father and I have sought thee sorrowing." The Boy's reply astonished them, in that it revealed, to an extent they had not before realized, His rapidly maturing powers of judgment and understanding. Said He: "How is it that ye sought me? wist ye not that I must be about my Father's business?"

Let us not say that there was unkind rebuke or unfilial reproof in the answer of this most dutiful of sons to His mother. His reply was to Mary a reminder of what she seems to have forgotten for the moment—the facts in the matter of her Son's paternity. She had used the words "thy father and I"; and her Son's response had brought anew to her mind the truth that Joseph was not the Boy's father. She appears to have been astonished that One so young should so thoroughly understand His position with respect to herself. He had made plain to her the inadvertent inaccuracy of her words; His Father had not been seeking Him; for was He not even at that moment in His Father's house, and particularly engaged in His Father's business, the very work to which His Father had appointed Him?

He had in no wise intimated a doubt as to Mary's maternal relationship to Himself; though He had indisputably shown that He recognized as His Father, not Joseph of Nazareth, but the God of Heaven. Both Mary and Joseph failed to comprehend the full import of His words. Though He understood the superior claim of duty based On His divine Sonship, and had shown to Mary that her authority as earthly mother was subordinate to that of His Immortal and divine Father, nevertheless He obeyed her. Interested as were the doctors in this remarkable Boy, much as He had given them to ponder over through His searching questions and wise answers, they could not detain Him, for the very law they professed to uphold enjoined strict obedience to parental authority. "And he went down with them, and came to Nazareth, and was subject unto them: but his mother kept all these sayings in her heart."

What marvelous and sacred secrets were treasured in that mother's heart; and what new surprises and grave problems were added day after day in the manifestations of unfolding wisdom displayed by her more than mortal Son! Though she could never have wholly forgotten, at times she seemingly lost sight of her Son's exalted personality. That such conditions should exist was perhaps divinely appointed. There could scarcely have been a full measure of truly human experience in the relationship between Jesus and His mother, or between Him and Joseph, had the fact of His divinity been always dominant or even prominently apparent. Mary appears never to have fully understood her Son; at every new evidence of His uniqueness she marveled and pondered anew. He was hers, and yet in a very real sense not wholly hers. There was about their relation to each other a mystery, awful yet sublime, a holy secret which that chosen and blessed mother hesitated even to tell over to herself. Fear must have contended with joy within her soul because of Him. The memory of Gabriel's glorious promises, the testimony of the rejoicing shepherds, and the adoration of the magi must have struggled with that of Simeon's portentous prophecy, directed to herself in person: "Yea, a sword shall pierce through thy own soul also."[l]

As to the events of the eighteen years following the return of Jesus from Jerusalem to Nazareth, the scriptures are silent save for one rich sentence of greatest import: "And Jesus increased in wisdom and stature, and in favor with God and man."[m] Plainly this Son of the Highest was not endowed with a fulness of knowledge, nor with the complete investiture of wisdom, from the cradle.[n] Slowly the assurance of His appointed mission as the Messiah, of whose coming He read in the law, the prophets, and the psalms, developed within His soul; and in devoted preparation for the ministry that should find culmination on the cross He passed the years of youth and early manhood. From the chronicles of later years we learn that He was reputed without question to be the son of Joseph and Mary, and was regarded as the brother of other and younger children of the family. He was spoken

[l] Luke 2:35.

[m] Luke 2:52.

[n] Note 3, end of chapter.

of both as a carpenter and a carpenter's son; and, until the beginning of His public ministry He appears to have been of little prominence even in the small home community.[o]

He lived the simple life, at peace with His fellows, in communion with His Father, thus increasing in favor with God and men. As shown by His public utterances after He had become a man, these years of seclusion were spent in active effort, both physical and mental. Jesus was a close observer of nature and men. He was able to draw illustrations with which to point His teachings from the varied occupations, trades and professions; the ways of the lawyer and the physician, the manners of the scribe, the Pharisee and the rabbi, the habits of the poor, the customs of the rich, the life of the shepherd, the farmer, the vinedresser and the fisherman—were all known to Him. He considered the lilies of the field, and the grass in meadow and upland, the birds which sowed not nor gathered into barns but lived on the bounty of their Maker, the foxes in their holes, the petted house dog and the vagrant cur, the hen sheltering her brood beneath protecting wings—all these had contributed to the wisdom in which He grew, as had also the moods of the weather, the recurrence of the seasons, and all the phenomena of natural change and order.

Nazareth was the abode of Jesus until He was about thirty years of age; and, in accordance with the custom of designating individuals by the names of their home towns as additions to their personal names,[p] our Lord came to be generally known as Jesus of Nazareth.[q] He is also referred to as a Nazarene, or a native of Nazareth, and this fact is cited by Matthew as a fulfillment of earlier prediction, though our current compilation of scriptures constituting the Old Testament contains no record of such prophecy. It is practically certain that this prediction was contained in someone of the many scriptures extant in earlier days but since lost.[r] That Nazareth was an obscure village, of little

[o] Matt. 13:55, 56; Mark 6:3; Luke 4:22; compare Matt. 12:46, 47; Gal. 1:19.

[p] For illustrative examples see Joseph of Arimathea (Mark 15:43); Mary Magdalene, so known from her native town of Magdala (Matt. 27:56); Judas Iscariot, possibly named after his home in Kerioth (Matt. 10:4).

[q] Matt. 21:11; John 18:5; 19:19; Acts 2:22; 3:6; see also Luke 4:16.

[r] Note 4, end of chapter.

honor or renown, is evidenced by the almost contemptuous question of Nathanael, who, on being informed that the Messiah had been found in Jesus of Nazareth, asked: "Can there any good thing come out of Nazareth?"[s] The incredulous query had passed into a proverb current even today as expressive of any unpopular or unpromising source of good. Nathanael lived in Cana, but a few miles from Nazareth, and his surprise at the tidings brought by Philip concerning the Messiah incidentally affords evidence of seclusion in which Jesus had lived.

So passed the boyhood, youth, and early manhood of the Savior of mankind.

NOTES TO CHAPTER 9

1. Archelaus Reigned in Herod's Stead.—"At his death Herod [the Great] left a will according to which his kingdom was to be divided among his three sons. Archelaus was to have Judea, Idumea, and Samaria, with the title of king (Matt. 2:22). Herod Antipas was to receive Galilee and Perea, with the title of tetrarch; Philip was to come into possession of the trans-Jordan territory with the title of tetrarch (Luke 3:1). This will was ratified by Augustus with the exception of the title given to Archelaus. Archelaus, after the ratification of Herod's will by Augustus, succeeded to the rule of Judea, Samaria, and Idumea, having the title of ethnarch, with the understanding that, if he ruled well, he was to become king. He was, however, highly unpopular with the people, and his reign was marked by disturbances and acts of oppression. The situation became finally so intolerable that the Jews appealed to Augustus, and Archelaus was removed and sent into exile. This accounts for the statement in Matt. 2:22, and possibly also suggested the point of the parable (Luke 19:12, etc.)."—*Standard Bible Dictionary*, Funk and Wagnalls Co., article "Herod." Early in his reign he wreaked summary vengeance on the people who ventured to protest against a continuation of his father's violence, by slaughtering three thousand or more; and the awful deed of carnage was perpetrated in part within the precincts of the temple. (Josephus, *Antiquities* xvii, 9:1–3.)

2. Herod Antipas.—Son of Herod I (the Great) by a Samaritan woman, and full brother to Archelaus. By the will of his father he became tetrarch of Galilee and Perea (Matt. 14:1; Luke 3:19; 9:7; Acts 13:1; compare Luke 3:1). He repudiated his wife, a daughter of Aretas, king of Arabia Petrea, and entered into an unlawful union with Herodias, the wife of his half-brother Herod Philip I (not the tetrarch

[s] John 1:45, 46.

Philip). John the Baptist was imprisoned and finally put to death, through the anger of Herodias over his denunciation of her union with Herod Antipas. Herodias urged Antipas to go to Rome and petition Caesar for the title of king (compare Mark 6:14, etc.). Antipas is the Herod most frequently mentioned in the New Testament (Mark 6:17; 8:15; Luke 3:1; 9:7; 13:31; Acts 4:27; 13:1). He was the Herod to whom Pilate sent Jesus for examination, taking advantage of Christ being known as a Galilean, and of the coincident fact of Herod's presence in Jerusalem at the time in attendance at the Passover (Luke 23:6, etc.). For further details see Smith's, Cassell's, or the *Standard Bible Dictionary*.

3. Testimony of John the Apostle Concerning Christ's Development in Knowledge and Grace.—In a modern revelation, Jesus the Christ has confirmed the record of John the apostle, which record appears but in part in our compilation of ancient scriptures. John thus attests the actuality of natural development in the growth of Jesus from childhood to maturity: "And I, John, saw that he received not of the fulness at the first, but received grace for grace; And he received not of the fulness at first, but continued from grace to grace, until he received a fulness; And thus he was called the Son of God, because he received not of the fulness at the first" (D&C 93:12–14). Notwithstanding this graded course of growth and development after His birth in the flesh, Jesus Christ had been associated with the Father from the beginning, as is set forth in the revelation cited. We read therein: "And he [John] bore record, saying, I saw his glory that he was in the beginning before the world was; therefore in the beginning the Word was, for he was the Word, even the messenger of salvation, the light and the Redeemer of the world; the Spirit of truth, who came into the world, because the world was made by him, and in him was the life of men and the light of men. The worlds were made by him: men were made by him: all things were made by him, and through him, and of him. And I, John, bear record that I beheld his glory, as the glory of the Only Begotten of the Father, full of grace and truth, even the Spirit of truth, which came and dwelt in the flesh, and dwelt among us" (verses 7–11).

4. Missing Scripture.—Matthew's commentary on the abode of Joseph, Mary and Jesus at Nazareth, "and he came and dwelt in a city called Nazareth: that it might be fulfilled which was spoken by the prophets, he shall be called a Nazarene" (2:23), with the fact that no such saying of the prophets is found in any of the books contained in the Bible, suggests the certainty of lost scripture. Those who oppose the doctrine of continual revelation between God and His Church, on the ground that the Bible is complete as a collection of sacred scriptures, and that alleged revelation not found therein must therefore be spurious, may profitably take note of the many books not included in the Bible, yet mentioned therein, generally in such a way as to leave no doubt that they were once regarded as authentic. Among these extra-Biblical scriptures, the following may be named; some of them are in existence today, and are classed with the Apocrypha; but the greater number are unknown.

We read of the Book of the Covenant (Ex. 24:7); Book of the Wars of the Lord (Num. 21:14); Book of Jasher (Josh. 10:13); Book of the Statutes (1 Sam. 10:25); Book of Enoch (Jude 14); Book of the Acts of Solomon (1 Kgs. 11:41); Book of Nathan the Prophet, and that of Gad the Seer (1 Chr. 29:29); Book of Ahijah the Shilonite, and visions of Iddo the Seer (2 Chr. 9:29); Book of Shemaiah (2 Chr. 12:15); Story of the Prophet Iddo (2 Chr. 13:22); Book of Jehu (2 Chr. 20:34); the Acts of Uzziah, by Isaiah, the son of Amoz (2 Chr. 26:22); Sayings of the Seers (2 Chr. 33:19); a missing epistle of Paul to the Corinthians (1 Cor. 5:9); a missing epistle to the Ephesians (Eph. 3:3); missing epistle to the Colossians, written from Laodicea (Col. 4:16); a missing epistle of Jude (Jude 3).

5. Nazareth.—A town or "city" in Galilee, of which Biblical mention is found in the New Testament only. Josephus says nothing concerning the place. The name of the existing village, or the Nazareth of today, is *En-Nazirah*. This occupies an upland site on the southerly ridge of Lebanon, and "commands a splendid view of the Plain of Esdraelon and Mount Carmel, and is very picturesque in general" (Zenos). The author of the article "Nazareth" in Smith's *Bible Dict.* identifies the modern En-Nazirah, with the Nazareth of old on the following grounds: "It is on the lower declivities of a hill or mountain (Luke 4:29); it is within the limits of the province of Galilee (Mark 1:9); it is near Cana (John 2:1, 2, 11); a precipice exists in the neighborhood (Luke 4:29); and a series of testimonials reaching back to Eusebius represent the place as having occupied the same position." The same writer adds: "Its population is 3000 or 4000; a few are Mohammedans, the rest Latin and Greek Christians. Most of the houses are well built of stone, and appear neat and comfortable. The streets or lanes are narrow and crooked, and after rain are so full of mud and mire as to be almost impassable." At the time of Christ's life the town was not only regarded as unimportant by the Judeans who professed but little respect for Galilee or the Galileans, but as without honor by the Galileans themselves, as appears from the fact that the seemingly contemptuous question, "Can there any good thing come out of Nazareth?" was uttered by Nathanael (John 1:46), who was a Galilean and a native of Cana, a neighboring town to Nazareth (John 21:2). Nazareth owes its celebrity to its association with events in the life of Jesus Christ (Matt. 2:23; 13:54; Mark 1:9; 6:1; Luke 1:26; 2:4; 4:23, 34; John 1:45, 46; 19:19; Acts 2:22).

CHAPTER 10

IN THE WILDERNESS OF JUDEA

THE VOICE IN THE WILDERNESS

At a time definitely stated as the fifteenth year of the reign of Tiberius Caesar, emperor of Rome, the people of Judea were greatly aroused over the strange preaching of a man theretofore unknown. He was of priestly descent, but untrained in the schools; and, without authorization of the rabbis or license from the chief priests, he proclaimed himself as one sent of God with a message to Israel. He appeared not in the synagogs nor within the temple courts, where scribes and doctors taught, but cried aloud in the wilderness. The people of Jerusalem and of adjacent rural parts went out in great multitudes to hear him. He disdained the soft garments and flowing robes of comfort, and preached in his rough desert garb, consisting of a garment of camel's hair held in place by a leathern girdle. The coarseness of his attire was regarded as significant. Elijah the Tishbite, that fearless prophet whose home had been the desert, was known in his day as "an hairy man, and girt with a girdle of leather about his loins";[a] and rough garments had come to be thought of as a distinguishing characteristic of prophets.[b] Nor did this strange preacher eat the food of luxury and ease, but fed on what the desert supplied, locusts and wild honey.[c]

The man was John, son of Zacharias, soon to be known as the Baptist. He had spent many years in the desert, apart from the abodes of men, years of preparation for his particular mission. He had been a

[a] 2 Kgs. 1:8.

[b] Note 1, end of chapter.

[c] Matt. 3:1–5; compare Lev. 11:22; see also Mark 1:1–8. Note 2, end of chapter.

student under the tutelage of divine teachers; and there in the wilderness of Judea the word of the Lord reached him;[d] as in similar environment it had reached Moses[e] and Elijah[f] of old. Then was heard "The voice of one crying in the wilderness, Prepare ye the way of the Lord, make his paths straight."[g] It was the voice of the herald, the messenger who, as the prophets had said, should go before the Lord to prepare His way.[h] The burden of his message was "Repent ye, for the kingdom of heaven is at hand." And to such as had faith in his words and professed repentance, confessing their sins, he administered baptism by immersion in water—proclaiming the while, "I indeed baptize you with water unto repentance: but he that cometh after me is mightier than I, whose shoes I am not worthy to bear: he shall baptize you with the Holy Ghost, and with fire."[i]

Neither the man nor his message could be ignored; his preaching was specific in promise to the repentant soul, and scathingly denunciatory to the hypocrite and the hardened sinner. Where Pharisees and Sadducees came to his baptism, prating of the law, the spirit of which they ceased not to transgress, and of the prophets, whom they dishonored, he denounced them as a generation of vipers, and demanded of them: "Who hath warned you to flee from the wrath to come?" He brushed aside their oft-repeated boasts that they were the children of Abraham, saying, "Bring forth therefore fruits meet for repentance: and think not to say within yourselves, We have Abraham to our father: for I say unto you, that God is able of these stones to raise up children unto Abraham."[j] The ignoring of their claims to preferment as the children of Abraham was a strong rebuke, and a cause of sore affront alike to aristocratic Sadducee and rule-bound Pharisee. Judaism held that the posterity of Abraham had an assured place in the kingdom of the expected Messiah, and that no proselyte from

[d] Luke 3:2.

[e] Ex. 3:1, 2.

[f] 1 Kgs. 17:2–7.

[g] Mark 1:3.

[h] Mark 1:2; compare Isa. 40:3; Mal. 3:1; Matt. 11:10; Luke 7:27.

[i] Matt. 3:11.

[j] Matt. 3:7–10; see also Luke 3:3–9.

among the Gentiles could possibly attain the rank and distinction of which the "children" were sure. John's forceful assertion that God could raise up, from the stones on the river bank, children to Abraham, meant to those who heard that even the lowest of the human family might be preferred before themselves unless they repented and reformed.[k] Their time of wordy profession had passed; fruits were demanded, not barren though leafy profusion; the ax was ready, aye, at the very root of the tree; and every tree that produced not good fruit was to be hewn down and cast into the fire.

The people were astonished; and many, seeing themselves in their actual condition of dereliction and sin, as John, with burning words laid bare their faults, cried out: "What shall we do then?"[l] His reply was directed against ceremonialism, which had caused spirituality to wither almost to death in the hearts of the people. Unselfish charity was demanded—"He that hath two coats, let him impart to him that hath none; and he that hath meat, let him do likewise." The publicans or tax-farmers and collectors, under whose unjust and unlawful exactions the people had suffered so long, came asking: "Master, what shall we do? And he said unto them, Exact no more than that which is appointed you." To the soldiers who asked what to do he replied: "Do violence to no man, neither accuse any falsely; and be content with your wages."[m]

The spirit of his demands was that of a practical religion, the only religion of any possible worth—the religion of right living. With all his vigor, in spite of his brusqueness, notwithstanding his forceful assaults on the degenerate customs of the times, this John was no agitator against established institutions, no inciter of riot, no advocate of revolt, no promoter of rebellion. He did not assail the tax system but the extortions of the corrupt and avaricious publicans; he did not denounce the army, but the iniquities of the soldiers, many of whom had taken advantage of their position to bear false witness for the sake of gain and to enrich themselves by forcible seizure. He preached, what in the now current dispensation we call the first fundamental principles of the gospel—"the beginning of the gospel of Jesus Christ,

[k] Compare a later instance, in which Christ similarly taught (John 8:33–59).

[l] Luke 3:10; compare Acts 2:37.

[m] Luke 3:10–15.

the Son of God,"[n] comprising faith, which is vitalized belief, in God; genuine repentance, which comprises contrition for past offenses and a resolute determination to turn from sin; baptism by immersion in water at his hands as the hands of one having authority; and the higher baptism by fire or the bestowal of the Holy Ghost by an authority greater than that possessed by himself. His preaching was positive, and in many respects opposed to the conventions of the times; he made no appeal to the people through the medium of miraculous manifestations;[o] and though many of his hearers attached themselves to him as disciples,[p] he established no formal organization, nor did he attempt to form a cult. His demand for repentance was an individual call, as unto each acceptable applicant the rite of baptism was individually administered.

To the Jews, who were living in a state of expectancy, waiting for the long-predicted Messiah, the words of this strange prophet in the wilderness were fraught with deep portent. Could it be that he was the Christ? He spoke of One yet to come, mightier than himself, whose shoe-latchet he was not worthy to loosen,[q] One who would separate the people as the thresher, fan in hand, blew the chaff from the wheat; and, he added, that mightier One "will gather the wheat into his garner; but the chaff he will burn with fire unquenchable."[r]

In such wise did the predicted herald of the Lord deliver his message. Himself he would not exalt; his office, however, was sacred to him, and with its functions he brooked no interference from priest, Levite, or rabbi. He was no respecter of persons; sin he denounced, sinners he excoriated, whether in priestly vestments, peasant garb, or royal robes. All the claims the Baptist had made for himself and his mission were later confirmed and vindicated by the specific testimony of Christ.[s] John was the harbinger not alone of the kingdom but of the King; and to him the King in person came.

---

[n] Mark 1:1.

[o] John 10:41.

[p] John 1:35, 37; Matt. 11:2; Luke 7:18.

[q] Note 3, end of chapter.

[r] Luke 3:17; see also Matt. 3:12; compare Mal. 3:2.

[s] Matt. 11:11–14; 17:12; Luke 7:24–30.

THE BAPTISM OF JESUS—
TO FULFILL ALL RIGHTEOUSNESS

When Jesus "began to be about thirty years of age"[t] He journeyed from His home in Galilee, to Jordan unto John, to be baptized of him. But John forbad him, saying, I have need to be baptized of thee, and comest thou to me? And Jesus answering said unto him, Suffer it to be so now; for thus it becometh us to fulfil all righteousness. Then he suffered him."[u]

John and Jesus were second cousins; as to whether there had existed any close companionship between the two as boys or men we are not told. It is certain, however, that when Jesus presented Himself for baptism, John recognized in Him a sinless Man who stood in no need of repentance; and, as the Baptist had been commissioned to baptize for the remission of sins, he saw no necessity of administering the ordinance to Jesus. He who had received the confessions of multitudes now reverently confessed to One whom he knew was more righteous than himself. In the light of later events it appears that at this time John did not know that Jesus was the Christ, the Mightier One for whom he waited and whose forerunner he knew himself to be. When John expressed his conviction that Jesus needed no baptismal cleansing, our Lord, conscious of His own sinlessness, did not deny the Baptist's imputation, but nevertheless pressed His application for baptism with the significant explanation: "Thus it becometh us to fulfil all righteousness." If John was able to comprehend the deeper meaning of this utterance, he must have found therein the truth that water baptism is not alone the means provided for gaining remission of sins, but is also an indispensable ordinance established in righteousness and required of all mankind as an essential condition for membership in the kingdom of God.[v]

Jesus Christ thus humbly complied with the will of the Father, and was baptized of John by immersion in water. That His baptism was accepted as a pleasing and necessary act of submission was

[t] Luke 3:23.

[u] Matt. 3:13–15.

[v] For treatment of Baptism as a universal requirement, see the author's *Articles of Faith*, pp. 128–34. Note 6, end of chapter.

attested by what immediately ensued: "And Jesus, when he was baptized, went up straightway out of the water: and, lo, the heavens were opened unto him, and he saw the Spirit of God descending like a dove, and lighting upon him: and lo a voice from heaven, saying, This is my beloved Son, in whom I am well pleased."ᵂ Then John knew his Redeemer.

The four Gospel-writers record the descent of the Holy Ghost upon the baptized Jesus as accompanied by a visible manifestation "like a dove"; and this sign had been indicated to John as the fore-appointed means by which the Messiah should be made known to him; and to that sign, before specified, was now added the supreme testimony of the Father as to the literal Sonship of Jesus. Matthew records the Father's acknowledgment as given in the third person, "This is my beloved Son"; while both Mark and Luke give the more direct address, "Thou art my beloved Son." The variation, slight and essentially unimportant as it is though bearing on so momentous a subject, affords evidence of independent authorship and discredits any insinuation of collusion among the writers.

The incidents attending the emergence of Jesus from the baptismal grave demonstrate the distinct individuality of the three Personages of the Godhead. On that solemn occasion Jesus the Son was present in the flesh; the presence of the Holy Ghost was manifest through the accompanying sign of the dove, and the voice of the Eternal Father was heard from heaven. Had we no other evidence of the separate personality of each member of the Holy Trinity, this instance should be conclusive; but other scriptures confirm the great truth.ˣ

THE TEMPTATIONS OF CHRIST

Soon after His baptism, immediately thereafter as Mark asserts, Jesus was constrained by the promptings of the Spirit to withdraw from men and the distractions of community life, by retiring into the wilderness where He would be free to commune with His God. So

---

ʷ Matt. 3:16, 17; compare Mark 1:9–11; Luke 3:21, 22.

ˣ Shortly before His death, the Savior promised the apostles that the Father would send unto them the Comforter, which is the Holy Ghost (John 14:26; 15:26). See the author's *Articles of Faith*, pp. 39–42.

strong was the influence of the impelling force that He was led thereby, or, as stated by the evangelist, driven, into solitary seclusion, in which He remained during forty days, "with the wild beasts" of the desert. This remarkable episode in our Lord's life is described, though not with equal fulness, in three of the Gospels;[y] John is silent thereon.

The circumstances attending this time of exile and test must have been related by Jesus Himself, for of other human witnesses there were none. The recorded narratives deal principally with events marking the close of the forty-day period, but considered in their entirety they place beyond doubt the fact that the season was one of fasting and prayer. Christ's realization that He was the chosen and foreordained Messiah came to Him gradually. As shown by His words to His mother on the occasion of the memorable interview with the doctors in the temple courts, He knew, when but a Boy of twelve years, that in a particular and personal sense He was the Son of God; yet it is evident that a comprehension of the full purport of His earthly mission developed within Him only as He progressed step by step in wisdom. His acknowledgment by the Father, and the continued companionship of the Holy Ghost, opened His soul to the glorious fact of His divinity. He had much to think about, much that demanded prayer and the communion with God that prayer alone could insure. Throughout the period of retirement, he ate not, but chose to fast, that His mortal body might the more completely be subjected to His divine spirit.

Then, when He was hungry and physically weak, the tempter came with the insidious suggestion that He use His extraordinary powers to provide food. Satan had chosen the most propitious time for his evil purpose. What will mortals not do, to what lengths have men not gone, to assuage the pangs of hunger? Esau bartered his birthright for a meal. Men have fought like brutes for food. Women have slain and eaten their own babes rather than endure the gnawing pangs of starvation. All this Satan knew when he came to the Christ in the hour of extreme physical need, and said unto Him: "If thou be the Son of God, command that these stones be made bread." During

---

[y] Matt. 4:1–11; Mark 1:12, 13; Luke 4:1–13.

the long weeks of seclusion, our Lord had been sustained by the exaltation of spirit that would naturally attend such all-absorbing concentration of mind as His protracted meditation and communion with the heavens undoubtedly produced; in such profound devotion of spirit, bodily appetites were subdued and superseded; but the reaction of the flesh was inevitable.

Hungry as Jesus was, there was a temptation in Satan's words even greater than that embodied in the suggestion that He provide food for His famishing body—the temptation to put to proof the possible doubt implied in the tempter's "If." The Eternal Father had proclaimed Jesus as His Son; the devil tried to make the Son doubt that divine relationship. Why not prove the Father's interest in His Son at this moment of dire necessity? Was it proper that the Son of God should go hungry? Had the Father so soon forgotten as to leave His Beloved Son thus to suffer? Was it not reasonable that Jesus, faint from long abstinence, should provide for Himself, and particularly so since He could provide, and that by a word of command, *if* the voice heard at His baptism was that of the Eternal Father. *If* thou be in reality the Son of God, demonstrate thy power, and at the same time satisfy thy hunger—such was the purport of the diabolical suggestion. To have yielded would have been to manifest positive doubt of the Father's acknowledgment.

Moreover, the superior power that Jesus possessed had not been given to Him for personal gratification, but for service to others. He was to experience all the trials of mortality; another man, as hungry as He, could not provide for himself by a miracle; and though by miracle such a one might be fed, the miraculous supply would have to be given, not provided by himself. It was a necessary result of our Lord's dual nature, comprising the attributes of both God and man, that He should endure and suffer as a mortal while possessing at all times the ability to invoke the power of His own Godhood by which all bodily needs could be supplied or overcome. His reply to the tempter was sublime and positively final: "It is written, Man shall not live by bread alone, but by every word that proceedeth out of the mouth of God."[z]

---

[z] Matt. 4:4; compare Deut. 8:3.

The word that had proceeded from the mouth of God, upon which Satan would have cast mistrust, was that Jesus was the Beloved Son with whom the Father was well pleased. The devil was foiled; Christ was triumphant.

Realizing that he had utterly failed in his attempt to induce Jesus to use His inherent power for personal service, and to trust in Himself rather than rely upon the Father's providence, Satan went to the other extreme and tempted Jesus to wantonly throw Himself upon the Father's protection.[aa] Jesus was standing upon one of the high parts of the temple, a pinnacle or battlement, overlooking the spacious courts, when the devil said unto Him: "If thou be the Son of God, cast thyself down: for it is written, He shall give his angels charge concerning thee: and in their hands they shall bear thee up, lest at any time thou dash thy foot against a stone." Again appears the implication of doubt.[bb] *If* Jesus was in fact the Son of God, could He not trust His Father to save Him, and particularly so as it was written[cc] that angels would guard Him and bear Him up? Christ's reply to the tempter in the wilderness had embodied a scriptural citation, and this He had introduced with the impressive formula common to expounders of sacred writ—"It is written." In the second attempt, the devil tried to support his suggestion by scripture, and employed a similar expression—"for it is written." Our Lord met and answered the devil's quotation with another, saying: "It is written again, Thou shalt not tempt the Lord thy God."[dd]

Beside the provocation to sin by wantonly placing Himself in danger, so that the Father's love might be manifested in a miraculous rescue, or by refusing so to challenge the Father's interposition demonstrate that He doubted His status as the Beloved Son, there lurked an appeal to the human side of Christ's nature, in thought of the fame which an astounding exploit, such as that of leaping from the dizzy height of the temple turrets and alighting unhurt, would surely bring. We cannot resist the thought, though we be not justified

---

aa Note 4, end of chapter.
bb Note 5, end of chapter.
cc Matt. 4:6; Ps. 91:11, 12.
dd Matt. 4:5–7; compare Deut. 6: 16.

in saying that any such had even momentary place in the Savior's mind, that to act upon Satan's suggestion, provided of course the outcome proved to be such as he had indicated, would have been to insure public recognition of Jesus as a Being superior to mortals. It would have been a sign and a wonder indeed, the fame of which would have spread as fire in the dry grass; and all Jewry would have been aflame with excitement and interest in the Christ.

The glaring sophistry of Satan's citation of scripture was unworthy a categorical reply; his doctrine deserved neither logic nor argument; his misapplication of the written word was nullified by scripture that was germane; the lines of the psalmist were met by the binding fiat of the prophet of the exodus, in which he had commanded Israel that they should not provoke nor tempt the Lord to work miracles among them. Satan tempted Jesus to tempt the Father. It is as truly a blasphemous interference with the prerogatives of Deity to set limitations or make fixations of time or place at which the divine power shall be made manifest as it is to attempt to usurp that power. God alone must decide when and how His wonders shall be wrought. Once more the purposes of Satan were thwarted and Christ again was victor.

In the third temptation the devil refrained from further appeal to Jesus to put either His own power or that of the Father to the test. Twice completely foiled, the tempter abandoned that plan of assault; and, discarding all disguise of purpose, submitted a definite proposition. From the top of a high mountain Jesus looked over the land with its wealth of city and field, of vineyard and orchard, of flocks and of herds; and in vision He saw the kingdoms of the world and contemplated the wealth, the splendor, the earthly glory of them all. Then saith Satan unto Him. "All these things will I give thee, if thou wilt fall down and worship me." So wrote Matthew; the more extended version by Luke follows: "And the devil said unto him, All this power will I give thee, and the glory of them: for that is delivered unto me; and to whomsoever I will I give it. If thou therefore wilt worship me, all shall be thine." We need not concern ourselves with conjecture as to whether Satan could have made good his promise in the event of Christ's doing him homage; certain it is Christ could have reached out, and have gathered to Himself the wealth and glory of the world had He willed so to do, and thereby have failed in His Messianic mission. This fact Satan knew full well. Many men have sold themselves to the devil for a kingdom and for less, aye, even for a few paltry pence.

The effrontery of his offer was of itself diabolical. Christ, the Creator of heaven and earth, tabernacled as He then was in mortal flesh, may not have remembered His preexistent state, nor the part He had taken in the great council of the Gods;[ee] while Satan, an unembodied spirit—he the disinherited, the rebellious and rejected son—seeking to tempt the Being through whom the world was created by promising Him part of what was wholly His, still may have had, as indeed he may yet have, a remembrance of those primeval scenes. In that distant past, antedating the creation of the earth, Satan, then Lucifer, a son of the morning, had been rejected; and the Firstborn Son had been chosen. Now that the Chosen One was subject to the trials incident to mortality, Satan thought to thwart the divine purpose by making the Son of God subject to himself. He who had been vanquished by Michael and his hosts and cast down as a defeated rebel, asked the embodied Jehovah to worship him. "Then saith Jesus unto him, Get thee hence, Satan: for it is written, Thou shalt worship the Lord thy God, and him only shalt thou serve. Then the devil leaveth him, and behold, angels came and ministered unto him."[ff]

It is not to be supposed that Christ's victorious emergence from the dark clouds of the three specified temptations exempted Him from further assaults by Satan, or insured Him against later trials of faith, trust, and endurance. Luke closes his account of the temptations following the forty-day fast as follows: "And when the devil had ended all the temptation, he departed from him for a season."[gg] This victory over the devil and his wiles, this triumph over the cravings of the flesh, the harassing doubts of the mind, the suggested reaching out for fame and material wealth, were great but not final successes in the struggle between Jesus, the embodied God, and Satan, the fallen angel of light. That Christ was subject to temptation during the

[ee] Pages 7–10.

[ff] Matt.4:10, 11; compare Ex. 20:3; Deut. 6:13; 10:20; Josh. 24:14; 1 Sam. 7:3.

[gg] Luke 4:13.

period of His association with the apostles He expressly affirmed.[hh] That His temptations extended even to the agony in Gethsemane will appear as we proceed with this study. It is not given to the rest of us, nor was it given to Jesus, to meet the foe, to fight and overcome in a single encounter, once for all time. The strife between the immortal spirit and the flesh, between the offspring of God on the one hand, the world and the devil on the other, is persistent through life.

Few events in the evangelical history of Jesus of Nazareth have given rise to more discussion, fanciful theory, and barren speculation, than have the temptations. All such surmises we may with propriety ignore. To any believer in the holy scriptures, the account of the temptations therein given is sufficiently explicit to put beyond doubt or question the essential facts; to the unbeliever neither the Christ nor His triumph appeals. What shall it profit us to speculate as to whether Satan appeared to Jesus in visible form, or was present only as an unseen spirit; whether he spoke in audible voice, or aroused in the mind of his intended victim the thoughts later expressed by the written lines; whether the three temptations occurred in immediate sequence or were experienced at longer intervals? With safety we may reject all theories of myth or parable in the scriptural account, and accept the record as it stands; and with equal assurance may we affirm that the temptations were real, and that the trials to which our Lord was put constituted an actual and crucial test. To believe otherwise, one must regard the scriptures as but fiction.

A question deserving some attention in this connection is that of the peccability or impeccability of Christ—the question as to whether He was capable of sinning. Had there been no possibility of His yielding to the lures of Satan, there would have been no real test in the temptations, no genuine victory in the result. Our Lord was sinless yet peccable; He had the capacity, the ability to sin had He willed so to do. Had He been bereft of the faculty to sin, He would have been shorn of His free agency; and it was to safeguard and insure the agency of man that He had offered Himself, before the world was, as a redeeming sacrifice. To say that He could not sin because He was

[hh] Luke 22:28.

the embodiment of righteousness is no denial of His agency of choice between evil and good. A thoroughly truthful man cannot culpably lie; nevertheless his insurance against falsehood is not that of external compulsion, but of internal restraint due to his cultivated companionship of the spirit of truth. A really honest man will neither take nor covet his neighbor's goods, indeed it may be said that he cannot steal; yet he is capable of stealing should he so elect. His honesty is an armor against temptation; but the coat of mail, the helmet, the breastplate, and the greaves, are but an outward covering; the man within may be vulnerable if he can be reached.

But why proceed with labored reasoning, which can lead to but one conclusion, when our Lord's own words and other scriptures confirm the fact? Shortly before His betrayal, when admonishing the Twelve to humility, He said: "Ye are they which have continued with me in my temptations."[ii] While here we find no exclusive reference to the temptations immediately following His baptism, the exposition is plain that He had endured temptations, and by implication, these had continued throughout the period of His ministry. The writer of the epistle to the Hebrews expressly taught that Christ was peccable, in that He was tempted "in all points" as are the rest of mankind. Consider the unambiguous declaration: "Seeing then that we have a great high priest, that is passed into the heavens, Jesus the Son of God, let us hold fast our profession. For we have not an high priest which cannot be touched with the feeling of our infirmities; but was in all points tempted like as we are, yet without sin."[jj] And further: "Though he were a Son, yet learned he obedience by the things he suffered."[kk]

NOTES TO CHAPTER 10

1. Raiment of Camel's Hair.—Through the prophet Zechariah (13:4) a time was foretold in which professing prophets would no longer "wear a rough garment to deceive." Of the raiment of camel's hair worn by John the Baptist, the Oxford and other marginal readings render the expression "a garment of hair" as more literal than the Bible text. Deems (*Light of the Nations*, p. 74, note) says: "The garment of

[ii] Luke 22:28
[jj] Heb. 4:14,15.
[kk] Heb. 5:8.

camel's hair was not the camel's skin with the hair on, which would be too heavy to wear, but raiment woven of camel's hair, such as Josephus speaks of (B. J. i, 24:3)."

2. Locusts and Wild Honey.—Insects of the locust or grasshopper kind were specifically declared clean and suitable for food in the law given to Israel in the wilderness. "Yet these may ye eat of every flying creeping thing that goeth upon all four, which have legs above their feet, to leap withal upon the earth; even these of them ye may eat; the locust after his kind, and the bald locust after his kind, and the beetle after his kind, and the grasshopper after his kind." (Lev. 11:21, 22.) At the present time locusts are used as food by many oriental peoples, though usually by the poorer classes only. Of the passage referring to locusts as part of the Baptist's food while he lived as a recluse in the desert, Farrar (*Life of Christ*, p. 97, note,) says: "The fancy that it means the pods of the so-called locust tree (carob) is a mistake. Locusts are sold as articles of food in regular shops for the purpose at Medina; they are plunged into salt boiling water, dried in the sun, and eaten with butter, but only by the poorest beggars." Geikie (*Life and Words of Christ*, vol. i, pp. 354, 355) gives place to the following as applied to the Baptist's life: "His only food was the locusts which leaped or flew on the bare hills, and the honey of wild bees which he found, here and there, in the clifts of the rocks, and his only drink a draught of water from some rocky hollow. Locusts are still the food of the poor in many parts of the East. 'All the Bedouins of Arabia, and the inhabitants of towns in Nedj and Hedjaz, are accustomed to eat them,' says Burckhardt. 'I have seen at Medina and Tayf, locust shops, where they are sold by measure. In Egypt and Nubia they are eaten only by the poorest beggars. The Arabs, in preparing them for eating, throw them alive into boiling water, with which a good deal of salt has been mixed, taking them out after a few minutes, and drying them in the sun. The head, feet, and wings, are then torn off, the bodies cleansed from the salt, and perfectly dried. They are sometimes eaten boiled in butter, or spread on unleavened bread mixed with butter.' In Palestine, they are eaten only by the Arabs on the extreme frontiers; elsewhere they are looked on with disgust and loathing, and only the very poorest use them. Tristram, however, speaks of them as 'very palatable.' 'I found them very good,' says he, 'when eaten after the Arab fashion, stewed with butter. They tasted somewhat like shrimps, but with less flavour.' In the wilderness of Judea, various kinds abound at all seasons, and spring up with a drumming sound, at every step, suddenly spreading their bright hind wings, of scarlet, crimson, blue, yellow, white, green, or brown, according to the species. They were 'clean,' under the Mosaic Law, and hence could be eaten by John without offence."

Concerning the mention of wild honey as food used by John, the author last quoted says in a continuation of the same paragraph: "The wild bees in Palestine are far more numerous than those kept in hives, and the greater part of the honey sold in the southern districts is obtained from wild swarms. Few countries, indeed, are better adapted for bees. The dry climate, and the stunted but varied flora, consisting largely of aromatic thymes, mints, and other similar plants, with crocuses in the spring, are very favourable to them, while the dry recesses of the limestone rocks everywhere afford them shelter and protection for their combs. In the wilderness of

Judea, bees are far more numerous than in any other part of Palestine, and it is, to this day, part of the homely diet of the Bedouins, who squeeze it from the combs and store it in skins."

3. John's Inferiority to the Mightier One He Proclaimed.—"One mightier than I cometh, the latchet of whose shoes I am not worthy to unloose" (Luke 3:16), or "whose shoes I am not worthy to bear" (Matt. 3:11); this was the way by which the Baptist declared his inferiority to the Mightier One, who was to succeed and supersede him; and a more effective illustration would be difficult to frame. To loosen the shoe latchet or sandal thong, or to carry the shoes of another, "was a menial office betokening great inferiority on the part of the person performing it." (Smith's *Dict. of the Bible*.) A passage in the Talmud (*Tract. Kidduschin* xxii: 2) requires a disciple to do for his teacher whatever a servant might be required to do for his master, except the loosing of his sandal thong. Some teachers urged that a disciple should carry his humility even to the extreme of carrying his master's shoes. The humility of the Baptist, in view of the widespread interest his call aroused, is impressive.

4. The Order in which the Temptations Were Presented.—But two of the Gospel-writers specify the temptations to which Christ was subjected immediately after His baptism; Mark merely mentions the fact that Jesus was tempted. Matthew and Luke place first the temptation that Jesus provide for Himself by miraculously creating bread; the sequence of the later trials is not the same in the two records. The order followed in the text is that of Matthew.

5. The Devil's "If."—Note the later taunting use of that diabolical *if* as the Christ hung upon the cross. The rulers of the Jews, mocking the crucified Jesus in His agony said, "Let him save himself *if* he be the Christ." And the soldier, reading the inscription at the head of the cross derided the dying God, saying: "*If* thou be the king of the Jews, save thyself." And yet again, the unrepentant malefactor by His side cried out, "*If* thou be Christ, save thyself and us." (Luke 23:35–39.) How literally did those railers and mockers quote the very words of their father the devil (see John 8:44).

6. Baptism Required of All.—Baptism is required of all persons who live to the age of accountability in the flesh. None are exempt. Jesus Christ, who lived as a Man without sin in the midst of a sinful world, was baptized "to fulfil all righteousness." Six centuries before this event, Nephi, prophesying to the people on the western continent, foretold the baptism of the Savior, and thus drew therefrom the necessity of baptism as a universal requirement: "And now, if the Lamb of God, he being holy, should have need to be baptized by water, to fulfil all righteousness, O then, how much more need have we, being unholy, to be baptized, yea, even by water. . . . Know ye not that he was holy? But notwithstanding he being holy, he sheweth unto the children of men, that according to the flesh, he humbleth himself before the Father, and witnesseth unto the Father that he would be obedient unto him in keeping his commandments" (2 Ne. 31:5, 7).

CHAPTER 11

FROM JUDEA TO GALILEE

THE BAPTIST'S TESTIMONY OF JESUS

During the period of our Lord's retirement in the wilderness the Baptist continued his ministry, crying repentance to all who would pause to hear, and administering baptism to such as came duly prepared and asking with right intent. The people generally were greatly concerned over the identity of John; and as the real import of the voice[a] dawned upon them, their concern deepened into fear. The ever recurring question was, Who is this new prophet? Then the Jews, by which expression we may understand the rulers of the people, sent a delegation of priests and Levites of the Pharisaic party to personally question him. He answered without evasion, "I am not the Christ," and with equal decisiveness denied that he was Elias, or more accurately, Elijah, the prophet who, the rabbis said through a misinterpretation of Malachi's prediction, was to return to earth as the immediate precursor of the Messiah.[b] Furthermore, he declared that he was not "that prophet," by which was meant the Prophet whose coming Moses had foretold,[c] and who was not universally identified in the Jewish mind with the expected Messiah. "Then said they unto him, Who art thou? that we may give an answer to them that sent us. What sayest thou of thyself? He said, I am the voice of one crying in the wilderness, Make straight the way of the Lord, as said the prophet Esaias."[d] The Pharisaic envoys

[a] Luke 3:4.

[b] John 1:21; compare Mal. 4:5. Note 1, end of chapter.

[c] Deut. 18:15, 18.

[d] John 1:22, 23; compare Isa. 40:3.

then demanded of him his authority for baptizing; in reply he affirmed that the validity of his baptisms would be attested by One who even then was amongst them, though they knew Him not, and averred: "He it is, who coming after me is preferred before me, whose shoe's latchet I am not worthy to unloose."[e]

John's testimony, that Jesus was the Redeemer of the world, was declared as boldly as had been his message of the imminent coming of the Lord. "Behold the Lamb of God, which taketh away the sin of the world," he proclaimed; and, that none might fail to comprehend his identification of the Christ, he added: "This is he of whom I said, After me cometh a man which is preferred before me: for he was before me. And I knew him not: but that he should be made manifest to Israel, therefore am I come baptizing with water."[f] That the attestation of the ministering presence of the Holy Ghost through the material appearance "like a dove" was convincing to John is shown by his further testimony: "And John bare record, saying, I saw the Spirit descending from heaven like a dove, and it abode upon him. And I knew him not: but he that sent me to baptize with water, the same said unto me, Upon whom thou shalt see the Spirit descending, and remaining on him, the same is he which baptizeth with the Holy Ghost. And I saw, and bare record that this is the Son of God."[g] On the day following that of the utterance last quoted, John repeated his testimony to two of his disciples, or followers, as Jesus passed, saying again: "Behold the Lamb of God."[h]

THE FIRST DISCIPLES OF JESUS [i]

Two of the Baptist's followers, specifically called disciples, were with him when for the second time he expressly designated Jesus as the Lamb of God. These were Andrew and John; the latter came to be known in after years as the author of the fourth Gospel. The first is mentioned by name, while the narrator suppresses his own name as

[e] John 1:25–27.

[f] John 1:29–31.

[g] John 1:32, 34; also verses 35, 36. Note 2, end of chapter.

[h] Note 3, end of chapter.

[i] John 1:35–51.

that of the second disciple. Andrew and John were so impressed by the Baptist's testimony that they immediately followed Jesus; and He, turning toward them asked: "What seek ye?" Possibly somewhat embarrassed by the question, or with a real desire to learn where He might be found later, they replied by another inquiry: "Rabbi, where dwellest thou?" Their use of the title Rabbi was a mark of honor and respect, to which Jesus did not demur. His courteous reply to their question assured them that their presence was no unwelcome intrusion. "Come and see," said He.[j] The two young men accompanied Him, and remained with Him to learn more. Andrew, filled with wonder and joy over the interview so graciously accorded, and thrilled with the spirit of testimony that had been enkindled within his soul, hastened to seek his brother Simon, to whom he said: "We have found the Messias." He brought Simon to see and hear for himself; and Jesus, looking upon Andrew's brother, called him by name and added an appellation of distinction by which he was destined to be known throughout all later history: "Thou art Simon the son of Jona; thou shalt be called Cephas." The new name thus bestowed is the Aramaic or Syro-Chaldaic equivalent of the Greek "Petros," and of the present English "Peter," meaning "a stone."[k]

On the following day Jesus set out for Galilee, possibly accompanied by some or all of his newly-made disciples; and on the way He found a man named Philip, in whom He recognized another choice son of Israel. Unto Philip He said: "Follow me." It was customary with rabbis and other teachers of that time to strive for popularity that many might be drawn to them to sit at their feet and be known as their disciples. Jesus, however, selected His own immediate associates; and, as He found them and discerned in them the spirits who, in their preexistent state had been chosen for the earthly mission of the apostleship, He summoned them. They were the servants; He was the Master.[l]

Philip soon found his friend Nathanael, to whom he testified that He of whom Moses and the prophets had written had at last been

---

[j] Note 4, end of chapter.

[k] The name thus given was afterward confirmed, with accompaniments of promise; Matt. 16:18.

[l] To the apostles the Lord said on a subsequent occasion: "Ye have not chosen me, but I have chosen you" (John 15:16; see also 6:70).

found; and that He was none other than Jesus of Nazareth. Nathanael, as his later history demonstrates, was a righteous man, earnest in his hope and expectation of the Messiah, yet seemingly imbued with the belief common throughout Jewry—that the Christ was to come in royal state as seemed befitting the Son of David. The mention of such a One coming from Nazareth, the reputed son of a humble carpenter, provoked wonder if not incredulity in the guileless mind of Nathanael, and he exclaimed: "Can there any good thing come out of Nazareth?" Philip's answer was a repetition of Christ's words to Andrew and John—"Come and see." Nathanael left his seat under the fig tree,[m] where Philip had found him, and went to see for himself. As he approached, Jesus said, "Behold an Israelite indeed, in whom is no guile." Nathanael saw that Jesus could read his mind, and asked in surprise: "Whence knowest thou me?" In reply Jesus showed even greater powers of penetration and perception under conditions that made ordinary observation unlikely if not impossible: "Before that Philip called thee, when thou wast under the fig tree, I saw thee." Nathanael replied with conviction: "Rabbi, thou art the Son of God; thou art the King of Israel." Earnest as the man's testimony was, it rested mainly on his recognition of what he took to be a supernatural power in Jesus; our Lord assured him that he should see yet greater things: "And he saith unto him, Verily, verily, I say unto you, Hereafter ye shall see heaven open, and the angels of God ascending and descending upon the Son of man."

"THE SON OF MAN"

In the promise and prediction made by Christ to Nathanael, we find the significant title—The Son of Man—appearing for the first time, chronologically speaking, in the New Testament. It recurs, however, about forty times, excluding repetitions in parallel accounts in the several Gospels. In each of these passages it is used by the Savior distinctively to designate Himself. In three other instances the title appears In the New Testament, outside the Gospels; and in each case it is applied to the Christ with specific reference to His exalted attributes as Lord and God.[n]

---

[m] A favorite situation for rest, meditation, and study; 1 Kings. 4:25; Micah 4:4.

[n] Acts 7:56; Rev. 1:13; 14:14.

In the Old Testament, the phrase "son of man" occurs in ordinary usage, denoting any human son;[o] and it appears over ninety times as an appellation by which Jehovah addressed Ezekiel, though it is never applied by the prophet to himself.[p] The context of the passages in which Ezekiel is addressed as "son of man" indicates the divine intention of emphasizing the human status of the prophet as contrasted with the divinity of Jehovah.

The title is used in connection with the record of Daniel's vision,[q] in which was revealed the consummation, yet future, when Adam— the Ancient of Days—shall sit to judge his posterity;[r] on which great occasion, the Son of Man is to appear and receive a dominion that shall be everlasting, transcendently superior to that of the Ancient of Days, and embracing every people and nation, all of whom shall serve the Lord, Jesus Christ, the Son of Man.[s]

In applying the designation to Himself, the Lord invariably uses the definite article. "The Son of Man" was and is, specifically and exclusively, Jesus Christ. While as a matter of solemn certainty He was the only male human being from Adam down who was not the son of a mortal man, He used the title in a way to conclusively demonstrate that it was peculiarly and solely His own. It is plainly evident that the expression is fraught with a meaning beyond that conveyed by the words in common usage. The distinguishing appellation has been construed by many to indicate our Lord's humble station as a mortal, and to connote that He stood as the type of humanity, holding a particular and unique relationship to the entire human family. There is, however, a more profound significance attaching to the Lord's use of the title "The Son of Man"; and this lies in the fact that He knew His Father to be the one and only supremely exalted Man,[t] whose Son Jesus was both in spirit and in body—the Firstborn among all the

---

[o] Job 25:6; Ps. 144:3; 146:3; see also 8:4 and compare Heb. 2:6–9.

[p] Ezek. 2:1, 3, 6, 8; 3:1, 3, 4; 4:1; etc.

[q] Dan. 7:13.

[r] D&C 27:11; 78:15, 16; 107:54–57; 116.

[s] D&C 49:6; 58:65; 65:5; 122:8. Observe that in modern revelation the title is used only as applying to the Christ in His resurrected and glorified state.

[t] Note 5, end of chapter.

spirit children of the Father, the Only Begotten in the flesh—and therefore, in a sense applicable to Himself alone, He was and is the Son of the "Man of Holiness," Elohim,[u] the Eternal Father. In His distinctive titles of Sonship, Jesus expressed His spiritual and bodily descent from, and His filial submission to, that exalted Father.

As revealed to Enoch the Seer, "Man of Holiness" is one of the names by which God the Eternal Father is known; "and the name of his Only Begotten is the Son of Man, even Jesus Christ." We learn further that the Father of Jesus Christ thus proclaimed Himself to Enoch: "Behold, I am God; Man of Holiness is my name; Man of Counsel is my name; and Endless and Eternal is my name, also."[v] "The Son of Man" is in great measure synonymous with "The Son of God," as a title denoting divinity, glory, and exaltation; for the "Man of Holiness," whose Son Jesus Christ reverently acknowledges Himself to be, is God the Eternal Father.

THE MIRACLE AT CANA IN GALILEE

Soon after the arrival of Jesus in Galilee we find Him and His little company of disciples at a marriage party in Cana, a neighboring town to Nazareth. The mother of Jesus was at the feast, and for some reason not explained in John's narrative,[w] she manifested concern and personal responsibility in the matter of providing for the guests. Evidently her position was different from that of one present by ordinary invitation. Whether this circumstance indicates the marriage to have been that of one of her own immediate family, or some more distant relative, we are not informed.

It was customary to provide at wedding feasts a sufficiency of wine, the pure though weak product of the local vineyards, which was the ordinary table beverage of the time. On this occasion the supply of wine was exhausted, and Mary told Jesus of the deficiency. Said

---

[u] Page 28.

[v] Moses 6:57; 7:35; see also 7:24, 47, 54, 59, 65. Observe that Satan addressed Moses as "son of man" in a blasphemous attempt to coerce Moses into worshiping him by emphasizing the mortal weakness and inferiority of the man in contrast with his own false pretension of godship. (Moses 1:12.)

[w] John 2:1–11.

He: "Woman, what have I to do with thee? mine hour is not yet come." The noun of address, "Woman," as applied by a son to his mother may sound to our ears somewhat harsh, if not disrespectful; but its use was really an expression of opposite import.[x] To every son the mother ought to be preeminently the woman of women; she is the one woman in the world to whom the son owes his earthly existence; and though the title "Mother" belongs to every woman who has earned the honors of maternity, yet to no child is there more than one woman whom by natural right he can address by that title of respectful acknowledgment. When, in the last dread scenes of His mortal experience, Christ hung in dying agony upon the cross, He looked down upon the weeping Mary, His mother, and commended her to the care of the beloved apostle John, with the words: "Woman, behold thy son!"[y] Can it be thought that in this supreme moment, our Lord's concern for the mother from whom He was about to be separated by death was associated with any emotion other than that of honor, tenderness and love?[z]

Nevertheless, His words to Mary at the marriage feast may have conveyed a gentle reminder of her position as the mother of a Being superior to herself; even as on that earlier occasion when she had found her Boy, Jesus, in the temple, He had brought home to her the fact that her jurisdiction over Him was not supreme. The manner in which she told Him of the insufficiency of wine probably suggested an intimation that He use His more than human power, and by such means supply the need. It was not her function to direct or even to suggest the exercise of the power inherent in Him as the Son of God; such had not been inherited from her. "What have I to do with thee?" He asked; and added: "Mine hour is not yet come." Here we find no disclaimer of the ability to do what she apparently wanted Him to do, but the plain implication that He would act only when the time was right for the purpose, and that He, not she, must decide when that

[x] "The address 'Woman' was so respectful that it might be, and was, addressed to the queen-liest."—(Farrar, *The Life of Christ*, p. 134.)

[y] John 19:26.

[z] On a few occasions Jesus used the address "Woman" in a general way: Matt. 15:28; Luke 13:12; John 4:21; 8:10; etc.

time had come. She understood His meaning, in part at least, and contented herself by instructing the servants to do whatsoever He directed. Here again is evidence of her position of responsibility and domestic authority at the social gathering.

The time for His intervention soon arrived. There stood within the place six water pots;[aa] these He directed the servants to fill with water. Then, without audible command or formula of invocation, as best we know, He caused to be effected a transmutation within the pots, and when the servants drew therefrom, it was wine, not water that issued. At a Jewish social gathering, such as was this wedding festival, someone, usually a relative of the host or hostess, or some other one worthy of the honor, was made governor of the feast, or, as we say in this day, chairman, or master of ceremonies. To this functionary the new wine was first served; and he, calling the bridegroom, who was the real host, asked him why he had reserved his choice wine till the last, when the usual custom was to serve the best at the beginning, and the more ordinary later. The immediate result of this, the first recorded of our Lord's miracles, is thus tersely stated by the inspired evangelist: "This beginning of miracles did Jesus in Cana of Galilee, and manifested forth his glory; and his disciples believed on him."[bb]

The circumstances incident to the miraculous act are instructive to contemplate. The presence of Jesus at the marriage, and His contribution to the successful conduct of the feast, set the seal of His approval upon the matrimonial relationship and upon the propriety of social entertainment. He was neither a recluse nor an ascetic; He moved among men, eating and drinking, as a natural, normal Being.[cc] On the occasion of the feast He recognized and heeded the demands of the liberal hospitality of the times, and provided accordingly. He, who but a few days before had revolted at the tempter's suggestion that He provide bread for His impoverished body, now used His power to supply a luxury for others. One effect

---

[aa] Note 6, end of chapter.

[bb] John 2:11.

[cc] The absence of all false austerity and outward show of abnormal abstinence in His life furnished an imagined excuse for unfounded charges of excess, through which He was said to be a glutton and a winebibber. (Matt. 11:19; Luke 7:34.)

of the miracle was to confirm the trust of those whose belief in Him as the Messiah was yet young and untried. "His disciples believed on him"; surely they had believed in some measure before, otherwise they would not have followed Him; but their belief was now strengthened and made to approach, if indeed it did not attain, the condition of abiding faith in their Lord. The comparative privacy attending the manifestation is impressive; the moral and spiritual effect was for the few, the inauguration of the Lord's ministry was not to be marked by public display.

MIRACLES IN GENERAL

The act of transmutation whereby water became wine was plainly a miracle, a phenomenon not susceptible of explanation, far less of demonstration, by what we consider the ordinary operation of natural law. This was the beginning of His miracles, or as expressed in the revised version of the New Testament, "his signs." In many scriptures miracles are called signs, as also wonders, powers, works, wonderful works, mighty works,[dd] etc. The spiritual effect of miracles would be unattained were the witnesses not caused to inwardly wonder, marvel, ponder and inquire; mere surprise or amazement may be produced by deception and artful trickery. Any miraculous manifestation of divine power would be futile as a means of spiritual effect were it unimpressive. Moreover, every miracle is a sign of God's power; and signs in this sense have been demanded of prophets who professed to speak by divine authority, though such signs have not been given in all cases. The Baptist was credited with no miracle, though he was pronounced by the Christ as more than a prophet;[ee] and the chronicles of some earlier prophets[ff] are devoid of all mention of miracles. On the other hand, Moses, when commissioned to deliver Israel from Egypt, was made to understand that the Egyptians would look for the testimony of miracles, and he was abundantly empowered therefor.[gg]

---

dd Matt. 7:22; 11:20; 12:38; 16:1; 24:24; Mark 6:14; Luke 10:13; John 2:18; 7:21; 10:25; 14:11; Acts 6:8; 8:6; 14:3; 19:11; Rom. 15:19; Rev. 13:13; etc.

ee John 10:41; Matt. 11:9.

ff For example Zechariah and Malachi.

gg Ex. 3:20; 4:1–9. Note 8, end of chapter.

Miracles cannot be in contravention of natural law, but are wrought through the operation of laws not universally or commonly recognized. Gravitation is everywhere operative, but the local and special application of other agencies may appear to nullify it—as by muscular effort or mechanical impulse a stone is lifted from the ground, poised aloft, or sent hurtling through space. At every stage of the process, however, gravity is in full play, though its effect is modified by that of other and locally superior energy. The human sense of the miraculous wanes as comprehension of the operative process increases. Achievements made possible by modern invention of telegraph and telephone with or without wires, the transmutation of mechanical power into electricity with its manifold present applications and yet future possibilities, the development of the gasoline motor, the present accomplishments in aerial navigation—these are no longer miracles in man's estimation, because they are all in some degree understood, are controlled by human agency, and, moreover, are continuous in their operation and not phenomenal. We arbitrarily classify as miracles only such phenomena as are unusual, special, transitory, and wrought by an agency beyond the power of man's control.

In a broader sense, all nature is miracle. Man has learned that by planting the seed of the grape in suitable soil, and by due cultivation, he may conduce to the growth of what shall be a mature and fruitful vine; but is there no miracle, even in the sense of inscrutable processes, in that development? Is there less of real miracle in the so-called natural course of plant development—the growth of root, stem, leaves, and fruit, with the final elaboration of the rich nectar of the vine— than there was in what appears supernatural in the transmutation of water into wine at Cana?

In the contemplation of the miracles wrought by Christ, we must of necessity recognize the operation of a power transcending our present human understanding. In this field, science has not yet advanced far enough to analyze and explain. To deny the actuality of miracles on the ground that, because we cannot comprehend the means, the reported results are fictitious, is to arrogate to the human mind the attribute of omniscience, by implying that what man cannot comprehend cannot be, and that therefore he is able to comprehend all that is. The miracles of record in the Gospels are as fully supported by evidence as are many of the historical events which call forth neither protest nor demand for further proof. To the believer in the divinity of Christ, the miracles are sufficiently attested; to the unbeliever they appear but as myths and fables.[hh]

To comprehend the works of Christ, one must know Him as the Son of God; to the man who has not yet learned to know, to the honest soul who would inquire after the Lord, the invitation is ready; let him "Come and see."

NOTES TO CHAPTER 11

1. Misunderstanding of Malachi's Prediction.—In the closing chapter of the compilation of scriptures known to us as the Old Testament, the prophet Malachi thus describes a condition incident to the last days, immediately preceding the Second Coming of Christ: "For, behold, the day cometh, that shall burn as an oven; and all the proud, yea, and all that do wickedly, shall be stubble: and the day that cometh shall burn them up, saith the Lord of hosts, that it shall leave them neither root nor branch. But unto you that fear my name shall the Sun of righteousness arise with healing in his wings." The fateful prophecy concludes with the following blessed and far-reaching promise: "Behold, I will send you Elijah the prophet before the coming of the great and dreadful day of the Lord: and he shall turn the heart of the fathers to the children, and the heart of the children to their fathers, lest I come and smite the earth with a curse." (Mal. 4:1, 2, 5, 6.) It has been held by theologians and Bible commentators that this prediction had reference to the birth and ministry of John the Baptist (compare Matt. 11:14; 17:11; Mark 9:11; Luke 1:17), upon whom rested the spirit and power of Elias (Luke 1:17). However, we have no record of Elijah having ministered unto the Baptist, and furthermore, the latter's ministry, glorious though it was, justifies no conclusion that in him did the prophecy find its full realization. In addition, it should be remembered, that the Lord's declaration through Malachi, relative to the day of burning in which the wicked would be destroyed as stubble, yet awaits fulfillment. It is evident, therefore, that the commonly accepted interpretation is at fault, and that we must look to a later date than the time of John for the fulfillment of Malachi's prediction. The later occasion has come; it belongs to the present dispensation, and marks the inauguration of a work specially reserved for the Church in these latter days. In the course of a glorious manifestation to Joseph Smith and Oliver Cowdery, in the temple at Kirtland, Ohio, April 3, 1836, there appeared unto them Elijah, the prophet of old, who had been taken from earth while still in the body. He declared unto them: "Behold, the time has fully come, which was spoken of by the mouth of Malachi, testifying that he (Elijah) should be

[hh] Note 7, end of chapter.

sent before the great and dreadful day of the Lord come, to turn the hearts of the fathers to the children, and the children to the fathers, lest the whole earth be smitten with a curse. Therefore the keys of this dispensation are committed into your hands, and by this ye may know that the great and dreadful day of the Lord is near, even at the doors." (D&C 110:13–16.) See also *The House of the Lord,* pp. 82–83.

2. The Sign of the Dove.—"John the Baptist . . . had the privilege of beholding the Holy Ghost descend in the form of a dove, or rather in the *sign* of the dove, in witness of that administration. The sign of the dove was instituted before the creation of the world, a witness for the Holy Ghost, and the devil cannot come in the sign of a dove. The Holy Ghost is a personage, and is in the form of a personage. It does not confine itself to the *form* of the dove, but in *sign* of the dove. The Holy Ghost cannot be transformed into a dove; but the sign of a dove was given to John to signify the truth of the deed, as the dove is an emblem or token of truth and innocence."— From Sermon by Joseph Smith, *History of the Church,* vol. 5, pp. 260–61.

3. The Testimony of John the Baptist.—Observe that the Baptist's testimony to the divinity of Christ's mission is recorded as having been given after the period of our Lord's forty-day fast and temptations, and therefore approximately six weeks subsequent to the baptism of Jesus. To the deputation of priests and Levites of the Pharisaic party, who visited him by direction of the rulers, probably by appointment from the Sanhedrin, John, after disavowing that he was the Christ or any one of the prophets specified in the inquiry, said: "There standeth one among you whom ye know not; he it is who coming after me is preferred before me." On the next day, and again on the day following that, he bore public testimony to Jesus as the Lamb of God; and on the third day after the visit of the priests and Levites to John, Jesus started on the journey to Galilee (John 1:19–43).

John's use of the designation "Lamb of God" implied his conception of the Messiah as One appointed for sacrifice, and his use of the term is the earliest mention found in the Bible. For later Biblical applications, direct or implied, see Acts 8:32; 1 Pet. 1:19; Rev. 5:6, 8, 12, 13; 6:1, 16; 7:9, 10, 17; etc.

4. "Come and See."—The spirit of our Lord's invitation to the young truth seekers, Andrew and John, is manifest in a similar privilege extended to all. The man who would know Christ must come to Him, to see and hear, to feel and know. Missionaries may carry the good tidings, the message of the gospel, but the response must be an individual one. Are you in doubt as to what that message means today? Then come and see for yourself. Would you know where Christ is to be found? Come and see.

5. The Eternal Father a Resurrected, Exalted Being.—"As the Father hath power in himself, so hath the Son power in himself, to lay down his life and take it again, so he has a body of his own. The Son doeth what he hath seen the Father do: then the Father hath some day laid down his life and taken it again; so he has a body of his own; each one will be in his own body."—Joseph Smith; see *History of the Church*, vol. 5, p. 426.

"God himself was once as we are now, and is an exalted Man, and sits enthroned in yonder heavens! That is the great secret. If the veil was rent today, and the Great God who holds this world in its orbit, and who upholds all worlds and all things by his power, was to make himself visible,—I say, if you were to see him today, you would see him like a man in form—like yourselves in all the person, image, and very form as a man; for Adam was created in the very fashion, image, and likeness of God, and received instruction from, and walked, talked and conversed with him, as one man talks and communes with another."—Joseph Smith; see *Compendium*, p. 190.

6. Waterpots for Ceremonial Cleansing.—In the house at Cana there stood in a place specially reserved, six waterpots of stone "after the manner of the purifying of the Jews." Vessels of water were provided, as a matter of prescribed order in Jewish homes, to facilitate the ceremonial washings enjoined by the law. From these pots or jars the water was drawn off as required; they were reservoirs holding the supply, not vessels used in the actual ablution.

7. "The Attitude of Science Towards Miracles" is the subject of a valuable article by Prof. H. L. Orchard, published in *Journal of the Transactions of the Victoria Institute, or Philosophical Society of Great Britain*, 1910, vol. 42, pp. 81–122. This article was the Gunning Prize Essay for 1909. After a lengthy analytical treatment of his subject, the author presents the following summation, which was concurred in by those who took part in the ensuing discussions: "We here complete our scientific investigation of Bible Miracles. It has embraced (1) the *nature* of the phenomenon; (2) the *conditions* under which it is alleged to have occurred; (3) the character of the *testimony* to its occurrence. To the inquiry—Were the Bible miracles probable? science answers in the affirmative. To the further inquiry—Did they actually occur? the answer of science is again, and very emphatically, in the affirmative. If we liken them to gold, she has made her assay and says the gold is pure. Or the Bible miracles may be compared to a string of pearls. If science seeks to know whether the pearls are genuine, she may apply chemical and other tests to the examination of their *character*; she may search into the *conditions and circumstances* in which the alleged pearls were found. Were they first found in an oyster, or in some manufacturing laboratory? And she may investigate the *testimony* of experts. Should the result of any one of these examinations affirm the genuineness of the pearls, science will be slow to believe that they are 'paste'; if all the results declare their genuineness, science will not hesitate to say that they are true pearls. This, as we have seen, is the case of the Bible miracles. Science, therefore, affirms *their actual occurrence*."

8. The Testimony of Miracles.—"The Savior's promise in a former day (Mark 16:17–18), as in the present dispensation (D&C 84:65–73), is definite, to the effect that specified gifts of the Spirit are to follow the believer as signs of divine favor. The possession and exercise of such gifts may be taken therefore as essential features of the Church of Christ. Nevertheless we are not justified in regarding the evidence of miracles as infallible testimony of authority from heaven; on the other hand, the scriptures furnish abundant proof that spiritual powers of the baser sort have wrought miracles, and will continue so to do, to the deceiving of many who lack discernment. If miracles be accepted as infallible evidence of godly power, the magicians of Egypt, through the wonders which they accomplished in opposition to the ordained plan for Israel's deliverance, have as good a claim to our respect as has Moses (Ex. 7:11). John the Revelator saw in vision a wicked power working miracles, and thereby deceiving many; doing great wonders, even bringing fire from heaven (Rev. 13:11–18). Again he saw three unclean spirits, whom he knew to be 'the spirits of devils working miracles' (Rev. 16:13–14). Consider, in connection with this, the prediction made by the Savior:—'There shall arise false Christs, and false prophets, and shall show great signs and wonders, insomuch that, if it were possible, they shall deceive the very elect' (Matt. 24:24). The invalidity of miracles as a proof of righteousness is indicated in an utterance of Jesus Christ regarding the events of the great judgment:—'Many will say to me in that day, Lord, Lord, have we not prophesied in thy name? and in thy name have cast out devils? and in thy name done many wonderful works? And then will I profess unto them, I never knew you; depart from me, ye that work iniquity' (Matt. 7:22–23). The Jews, to whom these teachings were addressed, knew that wonders could be wrought by evil powers; for they charged Christ with working miracles by the authority of Beelzebub the prince of devils" (Matt. 12:22–30; Mark 3:22; Luke 11:15).— From *The Articles of Faith*, pp. 230–31.

CHAPTER 12

EARLY INCIDENTS IN OUR LORD'S PUBLIC MINISTRY

FIRST CLEARING OF THE TEMPLE

Soon after the marriage festivities in Cana, Jesus, accompanied by His disciples, as also by His mother and other members of the family, went to Capernaum, a town pleasantly situated near the northerly end of the Sea of Galilee or Lake of Gennesaret[a] and the scene of many of our Lord's miraculous works; indeed it came to be known as His own city.[b] Because of the unbelief of its people it became a subject of lamentation to Jesus when in sorrow He prefigured the judgment that would befall the place.[c] The exact site of the city is at present unknown. On this occasion Jesus tarried but a few days at Capernaum; for the time of the annual Passover was near, and in compliance with Jewish law and custom He went up to Jerusalem.

The synoptic Gospels,[d] which are primarily devoted to the labors of Christ in Galilee, contain no mention of His attendance at the paschal festival between His twelfth year and the time of His death; to John alone are we indebted for the record of this visit at the beginning of Christ's public ministry. It is not improbable that Jesus had been present at other Passovers during the eighteen years over which the evangelists pass in complete and reverent silence; but at any or all such earlier visits, He, not being thirty years old, could not have assumed the right or privilege of a teacher without contravening

[a] Note 1, end of chapter.

[b] John 2:12; compare Matt. 4:13; 9:1.

[c] Matt. 11:23; Luke 10:15.

[d] Note 2, end of chapter.

established customs.[e] It is worth our attention to note that on this, the first recorded appearance of Jesus in the temple subsequent to His visit as a Boy, He should resume His "Father's business" where He had before been engaged. It was in His Father's service that He had been found in discussion with the doctors of the law,[f] and in His Father's cause He was impelled to action on this later occasion.

The multitudinous and mixed attendance at the Passover celebration has already received passing mention;[g] some of the unseemly customs that prevailed are to be held in mind. The law of Moses had been supplemented by a cumulative array of rules, and the rigidly enforced requirements as to sacrifices and tribute had given rise to a system of sale and barter within the sacred precincts of the House of the Lord. In the outer courts were stalls of oxen, pens of sheep, cages of doves and pigeons; and the ceremonial fitness of these sacrificial victims was cried aloud by the sellers, and charged for in full measure. It was the custom also to pay the yearly poll tribute of the sanctuary at this season—the ransom offering required of every male in Israel, and amounting to half a shekel[h] for each, irrespective of his relative poverty or wealth. This was to be paid "after the shekel of the sanctuary," which limitation, as rabbis had ruled, meant payment in temple coin. Ordinary money, varieties of which bore effigies and inscriptions of heathen import, was not acceptable, and as a result, money changers plied a thriving trade on the temple grounds.

Righteously indignant at what He beheld, zealous for the sanctity of His Father's House, Jesus essayed to clear the place;[i] and, pausing not for argument in words, He promptly applied physical force almost approaching violence—the one form of figurative language that those corrupt barterers for pelf could best understand. Hastily improvising a whip of small cords, He laid about Him on every side, liberating and driving out sheep, oxen, and human traffickers, upsetting the tables of the exchangers and pouring out their heterogeneous

[e] Note 3, end of chapter.

[f] Luke 2:46–49.

[g] Note 4, end of chapter.

[h] Ex. 30:11–16. Note 11, end of chapter.

[i] John 2:14–17.

accumulations of coin. With tender regard for the imprisoned and helpless birds He refrained from assaulting their cages; but to their owners He said: "Take these things hence"; and to all the greedy traders He thundered forth a command that made them quail: "Make not my Father's house an house of merchandise." His disciples saw in the incident a realization of the psalmist's line: "The zeal of thine house hath eaten me up."[j]

The Jews, by which term we mean the priestly officials and rulers of the people, dared not protest this vigorous action on the ground of unrighteousness; they, learned in the law, stood self-convicted of corruption, avarice, and of personal responsibility for the temple's defilement. That the sacred premises were in sore need of a cleansing they all knew; the one point upon which they dared to question the Cleanser was as to why He should thus take to Himself the doing of what was their duty. They practically submitted to His sweeping intervention, as that of one whose possible investiture of authority they might be yet compelled to acknowledge. Their tentative submission was based on fear, and that in turn upon their sin-convicted consciences. Christ prevailed over those haggling Jews by virtue of the eternal principle that right is mightier than wrong, and of the psychological fact that consciousness of guilt robs the culprit of valor when the imminence of just retribution is apparent to his soul.[k] Yet, fearful lest He should prove to be a prophet with power, such as no living priest or rabbi even professed to be, they timidly asked for credentials of His authority—"What sign shewest thou unto us, seeing that thou doest these things?" Curtly, and with scant respect for this demand, so common to wicked and adulterous men,[l] Jesus replied: "Destroy this temple and in three days I will raise it up."[m]

Blinded by their own craft, unwilling to acknowledge the Lord's authority, yet fearful of the possibility that they were opposing one who had the right to act, the perturbed officials found in the words of Jesus reference to the imposing temple of masonry within whose walls

---

[j] Compare Ps. 69:9.

[k] Note 5, end of chapter.

[l] Matt. 12:38, 39; compare 16:1; Mark 8:11; John 6:30; 1 Cor. 1:22.

[m] John 2:19; read verses 18–22.

they stood. They took courage; this strange Galilean, who openly flouted their authority, spoke irreverently of their temple, the visible expression of the profession they so proudly flaunted in words—that they were children of the covenant, worshipers of the true and living God, and hence superior to all heathen and pagan peoples. With seeming indignation they rejoined: "Forty and six years was this temple in building, and wilt thou rear it up in three days?"[n] Though frustrated in their desire to arouse popular indignation against Jesus at this time, the Jews refused to forget or forgive His words. When afterward He stood an undefended prisoner, undergoing an illegal pretense of trial before a sin-impeached court, the blackest perjury uttered against Him was that of the false witnesses who testified: "We heard him say, I will destroy this temple that is made with hands, and within three days I will build another made without hands."[o] And while He hung in mortal suffering, the scoffers who passed by the cross wagged their heads and taunted the dying Christ with "Ah, thou that destroyest the temple, and buildest it in three days, save thyself, and come down from the cross."[p] Yet His words to the Jews who had demanded the credentials of a sign had no reference to the colossal Temple of Herod, but to the sanctuary of His own body, in which, more literally than in the man-built Holy of Holies, dwelt the ever living Spirit of the Eternal God. "The Father is in me" was His doctrine.[q]

"He spake of the temple of His body," the real tabernacle of the Most High.[r] This reference to the destruction of the temple of His body, and the renewal thereof after three days, is His first recorded prediction relating to His appointed death and Resurrection. Even the disciples did not comprehend the profound meaning of His words until after His Resurrection from the dead; then they remembered and understood. The priestly Jews were not as dense as they appeared to be, for we find them coming to Pilate while the body of the crucified Christ lay in the tomb, saying: "Sir, we remember that that

[n] Note 6, end of chapter.

[o] Mark 14:58.

[p] Mark 15:29, 30.

[q] John 10:38; 17:21.

[r] John 2:19–22; compare 1 Cor. 3:16, 17; 6:19; 2 Cor. 6:16; see further Col. 2:9; Heb. 8:2.

deceiver said, while he was yet alive, After three days I will rise again."[s] Though we have many records of Christ having said that He would die and on the third day would rise again, the plainest of such declarations were made to the apostles rather than openly to the public. The Jews who waited upon Pilate almost certainly had in mind the utterance of Jesus when they had stood, nonplussed before Him, at the clearing of the temple courts.[t]

Such an accomplishment as that of defying priestly usage and clearing the temple purlieus by force could not fail to impress, with varied effect, the people in attendance at the feast; and they, returning to their homes in distant and widely separated provinces, would spread the fame of the courageous Galilean Prophet. Many in Jerusalem believed on Him at the time, mainly because they were attracted by the miracles He wrought; but He refused to "commit himself unto them," realizing the insecure foundation of their professions. Popular adulation was foreign to His purpose; He wanted no motley following, but would gather around Him such as received the testimony of His Messiahship from the Father. "He knew all men, and needed not that any should testify of man: for he knew what was in man."[u]

The incident of Christ's forcible clearing of the temple is a contradiction of the traditional conception of Him as of One so gentle and unassertive in demeanor as to appear unmanly. Gentle He was, and patient under affliction, merciful and long-suffering in dealing with contrite sinners, yet stern and inflexible in the presence of hypocrisy, and unsparing in His denunciation of persistent evildoers. His mood was adapted to the conditions to which He addressed Himself; tender words of encouragement or burning expletives of righteous indignation issued with equal fluency from His lips. His nature was no poetic conception of cherubic sweetness ever present, but that of a Man, with the emotions and passions essential to manhood and manliness. He, who often wept with compassion, at other times evinced in word and action the righteous anger of a God. But of all His passions,

[s] Matt. 27:63.

[t] As Canon Farrar has tersely written, "Unless the 'we remember' was a distinct falsehood, they could have been referring to no other occasion than this." (*Life of Christ*, p. 155.)

[u] John 2:23–25.

however gently they rippled or strongly surged, He was ever master. Contrast the gentle Jesus moved to hospitable service by the needs of a festal party in Cana, with the indignant Christ plying His whip, and amidst commotion and turmoil of His own making, driving cattle and men before Him as an unclean herd.

JESUS AND NICODEMUS [v]

That the wonderful deeds wrought by Christ at and about the time of this memorable Passover had led some of the learned, in addition to many of the common people, to believe in Him, is evidenced by the fact that Nicodemus, who was a Pharisee in profession and who occupied a high place as one of the rulers of the Jews, came to Him on an errand of inquiry. There is significance in the circumstance that this visit was made at night. Apparently the man was impelled by a genuine desire to learn more of the Galilean, whose works could not be ignored; though pride of office and fear of possible suspicion that he had become attached to the new Prophet led him to veil his undertaking with privacy.[w] Addressing Jesus by the title he himself bore, and which he regarded as one of honor and respect, he said: "Rabbi, we know that thou art a teacher come from God: for no man can do these miracles that thou doest, except God be with him."[x] Whether his use of the plural pronoun "we" indicates that he was sent by the Sanhedrin, or by the society of Pharisees—the members of which were accustomed to so speak, as representatives of the order—or was employed in the rhetorical sense as indicating himself alone, is of little importance. He acknowledged Jesus as a "teacher come from God," and gave reasons for so regarding Him. Whatever of feeble faith might have been stirring in the heart of the man, such was founded on the evidence of miracles, supported mainly by the psychological effect of signs and wonders. We must accord him credit for sincerity and honesty of purpose.

Without waiting for specific questions, "Jesus answered and said unto him, Verily, verily, I say unto thee, Except a man be born again,

[v] John 3:1–21.

[w] Note 7, end of chapter.

[x] John 3:2; read verses 1–21.

he cannot see the kingdom of God." Nicodemus appears to have been puzzled; he asked how such a rejuvenation was possible. "How can a man be born when he is old? can he enter the second time into his mother's womb, and be born?" We do Nicodemus no injustice in assuming that he as a rabbi, a man learned in the scriptures, ought to have known that there was other meaning in the words of Jesus than that of a mortal, literal birth. Moreover, were it possible that a man could be born a second time literally and in the flesh, how could such a birth profit him in spiritual growth? It would be but a reentrance on the stage of physical existence, not an advancement. The man knew that the figure of a new birth was common in the teachings of his day. Every proselyte to Judaism was spoken of at the time of his conversion as one new-born.

The surprise manifested by Nicodemus was probably due, in part at least, to the universality of the requirement as announced by Christ. Were the children of Abraham included? The traditionalism of centuries was opposed to any such view. Pagans had to be born again through a formal acceptance of Judaism, if they would become even small sharers of the blessings that belonged as a heritage to the house of Israel; but Jesus seemed to treat all alike, Jews and Gentiles, heathen idolaters and the people who, with their lips at least, called Jehovah God.

Jesus repeated the declaration, and with precision, emphasizing by the impressive "Verily, verily," the greatest lesson that had ever saluted the ears of this ruler in Israel: "Verily, verily, I say unto thee, Except a man be born of water and of the Spirit, he cannot enter into the kingdom of God." That the new birth thus declared to be absolutely essential as a condition of entrance into the kingdom of God, applicable to every man, without limitation or qualification, was a spiritual regeneration, was next explained to the wondering rabbi: "That which is born of the flesh is flesh; and that which is born of the Spirit is spirit. Marvel not that I said unto thee, Ye must be born again." Still the learned Jew pondered yet failed to comprehend. Possibly the sound of the night breeze was heard at that moment; if so, Jesus was but utilizing the incident as a skillful teacher would do to impress a lesson when He continued: "The wind bloweth where it listeth, and thou hearest the sound thereof, but canst not tell whence it cometh, and whither it goeth: so is every one that is born of the Spirit." Plainly stated, Nicodemus was given to understand that his worldly learning and official status availed him nothing in any effort to understand the things of God; through the physical sense of hearing he knew that the wind blew; by sight he could be informed of its passage; yet what did he know of the ultimate cause of even this simple phenomenon? If Nicodemus would really be instructed in spiritual matters, he had to divest himself of the bias due to his professed knowledge of lesser things.

Rabbi and eminent Sanhedrist though he was, there at the humble lodging of the Teacher from Galilee, he was in the presence of a Master. In the bewilderment of ignorance he asked, "How can these things be?" The reply must have been humbling if not humiliating to the man: "Art thou a master of Israel, and knowest not these things?" Plainly a knowledge of some of the fundamental principles of the gospel had been before accessible; Nicodemus was held in reproach for his lack of knowledge, particularly as he was a teacher of the people. Then our Lord graciously expounded at greater length, testifying that He spoke from sure knowledge, based upon what He had seen, while Nicodemus and his fellows were unwilling to accept the witness of His words. Furthermore, Jesus averred His mission to be that of the Messiah, and specifically foretold His death and the manner thereof—that He, the Son of Man, must be lifted up, even as Moses had lifted the serpent in the wilderness as a prototype, whereby Israel might escape the fatal plague.[y]

The purpose of the foreappointed death of the Son of Man was: "That whosoever believeth in him should not perish, but have eternal life"; for to this end, and out of His boundless love to man had the Father devoted His Only Begotten Son. And further, while it was true that in His mortal advent the Son had not come to sit as a judge, but to teach, persuade and save, nevertheless condemnation would surely follow rejection of that Savior, for light had come, and wicked men avoided the light, hating it in their preference for the darkness in which they hoped to hide their evil deeds. Here again,

[y] Num. 21:7–9.

perhaps, Nicodemus experienced a twinge of conscience, for had not he been afraid to come in the light, and had he not chosen the dark hours for his visit? Our Lord's concluding words combined both instruction and reproof: "But he that doeth truth cometh to the light, that his deeds may be made manifest, that they are wrought in God."

The narrative of this interview between Nicodemus and the Christ constitutes one of our most instructive and precious scriptures relating to the absolute necessity of unreserved compliance with the laws and ordinances of the gospel, as the means indispensable to salvation. Faith in Jesus Christ as the Son of God, through whom alone men may gain eternal life; the forsaking of sin by resolute turning away from the gross darkness of evil to the saving light of righteousness; the unqualified requirement of a new birth through baptism in water, and this of necessity by the mode of immersion, since otherwise the figure of a birth would be meaningless; and the completion of the new birth through baptism by the Spirit—all these principles are taught herein in such simplicity and plainness as to make plausible no man's excuse for ignorance.

If Jesus and Nicodemus were the only persons present at the interview, John, the writer, must have been informed thereof by one of the two. As John was one of the early disciples, afterward one of the apostles, and as he was distinguished in the apostolic company by his close personal companionship with the Lord, it is highly probable that he heard the account from the lips of Jesus. It was evidently John's purpose to record the great lesson of the occasion rather than to tell the circumstantial story. The record begins and ends with equal abruptness; unimportant incidents are omitted; every line is of significance; the writer fully realized the deep import of his subject and treated it accordingly. Later mention of Nicodemus tends to confirm the estimate of the man as he appears in this meeting with Jesus—that of one who was conscious of a belief in the Christ, but whose belief was never developed into such genuine and virile faith as would impel to acceptance and compliance irrespective of cost or consequence.[z]

---

[z] Note 8, end of chapter. See *Articles of Faith*. pp. 96–100.

FROM CITY TO COUNTRY

Leaving Jerusalem, Jesus and His disciples went into the rural parts of Judea, and there tarried, doubtless preaching as opportunity was found or made; and those who believed on Him were baptized.[aa] The prominent note of His early public utterances was that of His forerunner in the wilderness: "Repent: for the kingdom of heaven is at hand."[bb] The Baptist continued his labors; though doubtless, since his recognition of the Greater One for whose coming he had been sent to prepare, he considered the baptism he administered as of somewhat different significance. He had at first baptized in preparation for One who was to come; now he baptized repentant believers unto Him who had come.

Disputation had arisen between some of John's zealous adherents and one or more Jews[cc] concerning the doctrine of purifying. The context[dd] leaves little room for doubt that a question was involved as to the relative merits of John's baptism and that administered by the disciples of Jesus. With excusable ardor and well-intended zeal for their master, the disciples of John, who had been embroiled in the dispute, came to him saying: "Rabbi, he that was with thee beyond Jordan, to whom thou bearest witness, behold, the same baptizeth, and all men come to him." John's supporters were concerned at the success of One whom they regarded in some measure as a rival to their beloved teacher. Had not John given to Jesus His first attestation? "He to whom thou bearest witness" said they, not deigning even to designate Jesus by name. Following the example of Andrew, and of John the future apostle, the people were leaving the Baptist and gathering about the Christ. John's reply to his ardent followers constitutes a sublime instance of self-abnegation. His answer was to this effect: A man receives only as God gives unto him. It is not given to me to do the work of Christ. Ye yourselves are witnesses that I disclaimed being the Christ, and that I said I was one sent before Him. He is as the Bridegroom; I am only as the friend of the bridegroom,[ee] His servant;

---

aa John 3:22; compare 4:2.

bb Matt. 4:17; compare Mark 1:15.

cc Note 9, end of chapter.

dd John 3:25–36.

ee Note 10, end of chapter.

and I rejoice greatly in being thus near Him; His voice gives me happiness; and thus my joy is fulfilled. He of whom you speak stands at the beginning of His ministry; I near the end of mine. He must increase but I must decrease. He came from heaven and therefore is superior to all things of earth; nevertheless men refuse to receive His testimony. To such a One, the Spirit of God is not apportioned; it is His in full measure. The Father loveth Him, the Son, and hath given all things into His hand, and: "He that believeth on the Son hath everlasting life: and he that believeth not the Son shall not see life; but the wrath of God abideth on him."[ff]

In such a reply, under the existent conditions, is to be found the spirit of true greatness, and of a humility that could rest only on a conviction of divine assurance to the Baptist as to himself and the Christ. In more than one sense was John great among all who are born of women.[gg] He had entered upon his work when sent of God so to do;[hh] he realized that his work had been in a measure superseded, and he patiently awaited his release, in the meantime continuing in the ministry, directing souls to his Master. The beginning of the end was near. He was soon seized and thrown into a dungeon; where, as shall be shown, he was beheaded to sate the vengeance of a corrupt woman whose sins he had boldly denounced.[ii]

The Pharisees observed with increasing apprehension the growing popularity of Jesus, evidenced by the fact that even more followed after Him and accepted baptism at the hands of His disciples than had responded to the Baptist's call. Open opposition was threatened; and as Jesus desired to avert the hindrance to His work which such persecution at that time would entail, He withdrew from Judea and retired to Galilee, journeying by way of Samaria. This return to the northern province was effected after the Baptist had been cast into prison.[jj]

[ff] John 3:27–36.
[gg] Matt. 11:11.
[hh] Luke 3:2, 3.
[ii] Matt. 14:3–12.
[jj] Matt. 4:12.

NOTES TO CHAPTER 12

1. Sea of Galilee.—This, the largest body of fresh water in Palestine, is somewhat pear-shape in outline and measures approximately thirteen miles in extreme length on a northerly-southerly line and between six and seven miles in greatest width. The river Jordan enters it at the northeast extremity and flows out at the southwest; the lake may be regarded, therefore, as a great expansion of the river, though the water-filled depression is about two hundred feet in depth. The outflowing Jordan connects the sea of Galilee with the Dead Sea, the latter a body of intensely saline water, which in its abundance of dissolved salts and in the consequent density of its brine is comparable to the Great Salt Lake in Utah, though the chemical composition of the waters is materially different. The sea of Galilee is referred to by Luke, in accordance with its more appropriate classification, as a lake (Luke 5:1, 2; 8:22, 23, 33). Adjoining the lake on the northwest is a plain, which in earlier times was highly cultivated: this was known as the land of Gennesaret (Matt. 14:34; Mark 6:53); and the water body came to be known as the sea or lake of Gennesaret (Luke 5:1). From the prominence of one of the cities on its western shore, it was known also as the sea of Tiberias (John 6:1, 23; 21:1). In the Old Testament it is called the sea of Chinnereth (Num. 34:11) or Chinneroth (Josh. 12:3) after the name of a contiguous city (Josh. 19:35). The surface of the lake or sea is several hundred feet below normal sea level, 681 feet lower than the Mediterranean according to Zenos, or 700 feet as stated by some others. This low-lying position gives to the region a semitropical climate. Zenos, in the *Standard Bible Dictionary*, says: "The waters of the lake are noted for abundant fish. The industry of fishing was accordingly one of the most stable resources of the country round about. . . . Another feature of the sea of Galilee is its susceptibility to sudden storms. These are occasioned partly by its lying so much lower than the surrounding tableland (a fact that creates a difference of temperature and consequent disturbances in the atmosphere), and partly by the rushing of gusts of wind down the Jordan valley from the heights of Hermon. The event recorded in Matt. 8:24 is no extraordinary case. Those who ply boats on the lake are obliged to exercise great care to avoid peril from such storms. The shores of the sea of Galilee as well as the lake itself were the scenes of many of the most remarkable events recorded in the Gospels."

2. The Four Gospels.—All careful students of the New Testament must have observed that the books of Matthew, Mark, and Luke, treat the events of the Savior's sayings and doings in Galilee with greater fulness than they accord to His work in Judea; the book or Gospel of John, on the other hand, treats particularly the incidents of our Lord's Judean ministry, without excluding, however, important events that occurred in Galilee. In style of writing and method of treatment, the authors of the first three Gospels (evangelists as they and John are collectively styled in theologic literature) differ more markedly from the author of the fourth Gospel than among themselves. The events recorded by the first three can be more readily classified, collated, or arranged, and in consequence the Gospels written by Matthew, Mark, and Luke are now commonly known as the Synoptics, or Synoptic Gospels.

3. Thirty Years of Age.—According to Luke (3:23) Jesus was about thirty years of age at the time of His baptism, and we find that soon thereafter, He entered publicly upon the work of His ministry. The law provided that at the age of thirty years the Levites were required to enter upon their special service (Num. 4:3). Clarke, *Bible Commentary*, treating the passage in Luke 3:23 says: "This was the age required by the law to which the priests must arrive before they could be installed in their office." Jesus may possibly have had regard for what had become a custom of the time, in waiting until He had attained that age before entering publicly on the labors of a Teacher among the people. Not being of Levitical descent He was not eligible to priestly ordination in the Aaronic order, and therefore, certainly did not wait for such before beginning His ministry. To have taught in public at an earlier age would have been to arouse criticism, and objection, which might have resulted in serious handicap or hindrance at the outset.

4. Throngs and Confusion at the Passover Festival.—While it is admittedly impossible that even a reasonably large fraction of the Jewish people could be present at the annual Passover gatherings at Jerusalem, and in consequence provision was made for local observance of the feast, the usual attendance at the temple celebration in the days of Jesus was undoubtedly enormous. Josephus calls the Passover throngs "an innumerable multitude" (*Wars*, ii, 1:3), and in another place (*Wars*, vi, 9:3) states that the attendance reached the enormous aggregate of three millions of souls; such is the record, though many modern writers treat the statement as an exaggeration. Josephus says that for the purpose of giving the emperor Nero information as to the numerical strength of the Jewish people, particularly in Palestine, the chief priests were asked by Cestius to count the number of lambs slain at the feast, and the number reported was 256,500 which on the basis of between ten and eleven persons to each paschal table would indicate the presence, he says, of at least 2,700,200 not including visitors other than Jews, and such of the people of Israel as were debarred from participation in the paschal meal because of ceremonial unfitness.

The scenes of confusion, inevitable under the conditions then prevailing, are admirably summarized by Geikie (*Life and Words of Christ*, chap. 30), who cites many earlier authorities for his statements: "The streets were blocked by the crowds from all parts, who had to make their way to the Temple, past flocks of sheep, and droves of cattle, pressing on in the sunken middle part of each street reserved for them, to prevent contact and defilement. Sellers of all possible wares beset the pilgrims, for the great feasts were, as has been said, the harvest time of all trades at Jerusalem, just as, at Mecca, even at this day, the time of the great concourse of worshippers at the tomb of the Prophet, is that of the busiest trade among the merchant pilgrims, who form the caravans from all parts of the Mohammedan world.

"Inside the Temple space, the noise and pressure were, if possible, worse. Directions were posted up to keep to the right or the left, as in the densest thoroughfares of London. The outer court, which others than Jews might enter, and which was, therefore, known as the Court of the Heathen, was in part covered with pens for sheep, goats, and cattle, for the feast and the thank offerings. Sellers shouted the merits of their beasts, sheep bleated, and oxen lowed. It was, in fact, the great yearly fair of Jerusalem, and the crowds added to the din and tumult, till the services in the neighboring courts were sadly disturbed. Sellers of doves, for poor women coming for purification from all parts of the country, and for others, had a space set apart for them. Indeed, the sale of doves was, in great measure, secretly, in the hands of the priests themselves: Hannas, the high priest, especially, gaining great profits from his dove cotes on Mount Olivet. The rents of the sheep and cattle pens, and the profits on the doves, had led the priests to sanction the incongruity of thus turning the Temple itself into a noisy market. Nor was this all. Potters pressed on the pilgrims their clay dishes and ovens for the Passover lamb; hundreds of traders recommended their wares aloud; shops for wine, oil, salt, and all else needed for sacrifices, invited customers; and, in addition, persons going across the city, with all kinds of burdens, shortened their journey by crossing the Temple grounds. The provision for paying the tribute, levied on all, for the support of the Temple, added to the distraction. On both sides of the east Temple gate, stalls had for generations been permitted for changing foreign money. From the fifteenth of the preceding month money changers had been allowed to set up their tables in the city, and from the twenty-first,—or twenty days before the Passover,—to ply their trade in the Temple itself. Purchasers of materials for offerings paid the amount at special stalls, to an officer of the Temple, and received a leaden cheque for which they got what they had bought, from the seller. Large sums, moreover, were changed, to be cast, as free offerings, into one of the thirteen chests which formed the Temple treasury. Every Jew, no matter how poor, was, in addition, required to pay yearly a half-shekel— about eighteen pence—as atonement money for his soul, and for the support of the Temple. As this would not be received except in a native coin, called the Temple shekel, which was not generally current, strangers had to change their Roman, Greek, or Eastern money, at the stalls of the money changers, to get the coin required. The trade gave ready means for fraud, which was only too common. Five per cent exchange was charged, but this was indefinitely increased by tricks and chicanery, for which the class had everywhere earned so bad a name that, like the publicans, their witness would not be taken before a court."

Touching the matter of the defilement to which the temple courts had been subjected by traffickers acting under priestly license, Farrar (*Life of Christ*, p. 152) gives us the following: "And this was the entrance-court to the Temple of the Most High! The court which was a witness that that house should be a House of Prayer for all nations had been degraded into a place which, for foulness, was more like shambles, and for bustling commerce more like a densely crowded bazaar; while the lowing of oxen, the bleating of sheep, the Babel of many languages, the huckstering and wrangling, and the clinking of money and of balances (perhaps not always just), might be heard in the adjoining courts, disturbing the chant of the Levites and the prayers of priests!"

5. The Servility of the Jews in the Presence of Jesus.—The record of the achievement of Jesus, in ridding the temple courts of those who had made the House of the Lord a market place, contains nothing to suggest the inference that He exercised superhuman strength or more than manly vigor. He employed a whip of His own making, and drove all before Him. They fled helter-skelter. None are said to have voiced an objection until the expulsion had been made complete. Why did not some among the multitude object? The submission appears to have been abject and servile in the extreme. Farrar, (*Life of Christ*, pp. 151, 152) raises the question and answers it with excellent reasoning and in eloquent lines: "Why did not this multitude of ignorant pilgrims resist? Why did these greedy chafferers content themselves with dark scowls and muttered maledictions, while they suffered their oxen and sheep to be chased into the streets and themselves ejected, and their money flung rolling on the floor by one who was then young and unknown, and in the garb of despised Galilee? Why, in the same way we might ask, did Saul suffer Samuel to beard him in the very presence of his army? Why did David abjectly obey the orders of Joab? Why did Ahab not dare to arrest Elijah at the door of Naboth's vineyard? Because sin is weakness; because there is in the world nothing so abject as a guilty conscience, nothing so invincible as the sweeping tide of a Godlike indignation against all that is base and wrong. How could these paltry sacrilegious buyers and sellers, conscious of wrongdoing, oppose that scathing rebuke, or face the lightnings of those eyes that were enkindled by an outraged holiness? When Phinehas the priest was zealous for the Lord of Hosts, and drove through the bodies of the prince of Simeon and the Midianitish woman with one glorious thrust of his indignant spear, why did not guilty Israel avenge that splendid murder? Why did not every man of the tribe of Simeon become a Goel to the dauntless assassin? Because Vice cannot stand for one moment before Virtue's uplifted arm. Base and grovelling as they were, these money-mongering Jews felt, in all that remnant of their souls which was not yet eaten away by infidelity and avarice, that the Son of Man was right.

"Nay, even the Priests and Pharisees, and Scribes and Levites, devoured as they were by pride and formalism, could not condemn an act which might have been performed by a Nehemiah or a Judas Maccabaeus, and which agreed with all that was purest and best in their traditions. But when they had heard of this deed, or witnessed it, and had time to recover from the breathless mixture of admiration, disgust, and astonishment which it inspired, they came to Jesus, and though they did not dare to condemn what He had done, yet half indignantly asked Him for some sign that He had a right to act thus."

6. Jewish Regard for the Temple.—The Jews professed high regard for the temple. "An utterance of the Savior, construed by the dark-minded as an aspersion upon the temple, was used against Him as one of the chief accusations on which His death was demanded. When the Jews clamored for a sign of His authority He predicted His own death and subsequent Resurrection, saying, 'Destroy this temple, and in three days I will raise it up.' (John 2:19–22; see also Matt. 26:61; 27:40; Mark 14:58; 15:29). They blindly regarded this remark as a disrespectful allusion to their temple, a structure built by human hands, and they refused to forget or forgive. That this veneration continued after the crucifixion of our Lord is evident from accusations brought against Stephen, and still later against Paul. In their murderous rage the people accused Stephen of disrespect for the temple, and brought false witnesses who uttered perjured testimony saying, 'This man ceaseth not to speak blasphemous words against this holy place.' (Acts 6:13.) And Stephen was numbered with the martyrs. When it was claimed that Paul had brought with him into the temple precincts, a Gentile, the whole city was aroused, and the infuriated mob dragged Paul from the place and sought to kill him. (Acts 21:26–31.)"— *The House of the Lord*, pp. 60, 61.

7. Some of the "Chief Rulers" Believed.—Nicodemus was not the only one among the ruling classes who believed in Jesus; but of most of these we learn nothing to indicate that they had sufficient courage to come even by night to make independent and personal inquiry. They feared the result in loss of popularity and standing. We read in John 12:42, 43: "Nevertheless among the chief rulers also many believed on him; but because of the Pharisees they did not confess him, lest they should be put out of the synagogue: for they loved the praise of men more than the praise of God." Note also the instance of the scribe who proffered to become a professed disciple, but, probably because of some degree of insincerity or unfitness, was rather discouraged than approved by Jesus. (Matt. 8:19, 20.)

8. Nicodemus.—The course followed by this man evidences at once that he really believed in Jesus as one sent of God, and that his belief failed of development into a condition of true faith, which, had it but been realized, might have led to a life of devoted service in the Master's cause. When at a later stage than that of his interview with Christ the chief priests and Pharisees upbraided the officers whom they had sent to take Jesus into custody and who returned to report their failure, Nicodemus, one of the council, ventured to mildly expostulate against the murderous determination of the rulers, by stating a general proposition in interrogative form: "Doth our law judge any man before it hear him and know what he doeth?" He was answered by his colleagues with contempt, and appears to have abandoned his well-intended effort (John 7:50–53; read preceding verses 30–49). We next hear of him bringing a costly contribution of myrrh and aloes, about a hundred-weight, to be used in the burial of Christ's then crucified body; but even in this deed of liberality and devotion, in which his sincerity of purpose cannot well be questioned, he had been preceded by Joseph of Arimathea, a man of rank, who boldly asked for and secured the body for reverent burial (John 19:38–42).

Nevertheless Nicodemus did more than did most of his believing associates among the noble and great ones; and to him let all due credit be given; he will not fail of his reward.

9. "The Jews" or "A Jew."—We read that "there arose a question between some of John's disciples and the Jews about purifying" (John 3:25). Bearing in mind that the expression "the Jews" is very commonly used by the author of the fourth Gospel to designate the officials or rulers among the people, the passage quoted may be understood to mean that the Baptist's disciples were engaged in disputation with the priestly rulers. It is held, however, by Biblical scholars generally, that "the Jew" in this passage is a mistranslation, and that the true rendering is "a Jew." The disputation concerning purifying appears to have arisen between some of the Baptist's followers and a single opponent; and the passage as it appears in the King James version of the Bible is an instance of scripture not translated correctly.

10. Friend of the Bridegroom.—Judean marriage customs in the days of Christ required the appointing of a chief groomsman, who attended to all the preliminaries and made arrangements for the marriage feast, in behalf of the bridegroom. He was distinctively known as the friend of the bridegroom. When the ceremonial requirements had been complied with, and the bride had been legally and formally given unto her spouse, the joy of the bridegroom's friend was fulfilled inasmuch as his appointed duties had been successfully discharged. (John 3:29.) According to Edersheim (*Life and Times of Jesus the Messiah*, vol. 1, p. 148), by the simpler customs prevalent in Galilee a "friend of the bridegroom" was not often chosen; and (pp. 663–64) the expression "children of the bridechamber" (Matt. 9:15; Mark 2:19; Luke 5:34, in all of which citations the expression is used by Jesus), was applied collectively to all the invited guests at a wedding festival. He says: "As the institution of 'friends of the bridegroom' prevailed in Judea, but not in Galilee, this marked distinction of the 'friend of the bridegroom' in the mouth of the Judean John, and 'sons (children) of the bridechamber' in that of the Galilean Jesus, is itself evidential of historic accuracy."

11. The Atonement Money.—In the course of the exodus, the Lord required of every male in Israel who was twenty years old or older at the time of a census the payment of a ransom, amounting to half a shekel (Ex. 30:12–16). As to the use to which this money was to be put, the Lord thus directed Moses: "And thou shalt take the atonement money of the children of Israel, and shalt appoint it for the service of the tabernacle of the congregation; that it may be a memorial unto the children of Israel before the Lord, to make an atonement for your souls" (Ex. 30:16; see also 38:25–31). In time, the tax of half a shekel, equivalent to a bekah (Ex. 38:26), was collected annually, though for this exaction no scriptural authority is of record. This tax must not be confused with the redemption money, amounting to five shekels for every firstborn male, the payment of which exempted the individual from service in the labors of the sanctuary. In place of the firstborn sons in all the tribes, the Lord designated the Levites for this special ministry; nevertheless He continued to hold the firstborn males as peculiarly His own, and required the payment of a ransom as a mark of their redemption from the duties of exclusive service. See Ex. 13:2, 13–15; Num. 3:13, 40–51; 8:15–18; 18:15, 16.

CHAPTER 13

HONORED BY STRANGERS, REJECTED BY HIS OWN

JESUS AND THE SAMARITAN WOMAN

The direct route from Judea to Galilee lay through Samaria; but many Jews, particularly Galileans, chose to follow an indirect though longer way rather than traverse the country of a people so despised by them as were the Samaritans. The ill-feeling between Jews and Samaritans had been growing for centuries, and at the time of our Lord's earthly ministry had developed into most intense hatred.[a] The inhabitants of Samaria were a mixed people, in whom the blood of Israel was mingled with that of the Assyrians and other nations; and one cause of the animosity existing between them and their neighbors both on the north and the south was the Samaritans' claim for recognition as Israelites; it was their boast that Jacob was their father; but this the Jews denied. The Samaritans had a version of the Pentateuch, which they revered as the law, but they rejected all the prophetical writings of what is now the Old Testament, because they considered themselves treated with insufficient respect therein.

To the orthodox Jew of the time a Samaritan was more unclean than a Gentile of any other nationality. It is interesting to note the extreme and even absurd restrictions then in force in the matter of regulating unavoidable relations between the two peoples. The testimony of a Samaritan could not be heard before a Jewish tribunal. For a Jew to eat food prepared by a Samaritan was at one time regarded by rabbinical authority as an offense as great as that of eating the flesh of

[a] Note 1, end of chapter.

swine. While it was admitted that produce from a field in Samaria was not unclean, inasmuch as it sprang directly from the soil, such produce became unclean if subjected to any treatment at Samaritan hands. Thus, grapes and grain might be purchased from Samaritans, but neither wine nor flour manufactured therefrom by Samaritan labor. On one occasion the epithet "Samaritan" was hurled at Christ as an intended insult. "Say we not well that thou art a Samaritan, and hast a devil?"[b] The Samaritan conception of the mission of the expected Messiah was somewhat better founded than was that of the Jews, for the Samaritans gave greater prominence to the spiritual kingdom the Messiah would establish, and were less exclusive in their views as to whom the Messianic blessings would be extended.

In His journey to Galilee Jesus took the shorter course, through Samaria; and doubtless His choice was guided by purpose, for we read that "He must needs go" that way.[c] The road led through or by the town called Sychar,[d] "near to the parcel of ground that Jacob gave to his son Joseph."[e] There was Jacob's well, which was held in high esteem, not only for its intrinsic worth as an unfailing source of water, but also because of its association with the great patriarch's life. Jesus, travel-worn and weary, rested at the well, while His disciples went to the town to buy food. A woman came to fill her water jar, and Jesus said to her: "Give me to drink." By the rules of oriental hospitality then prevailing, a request for water was one that should never be denied if possible to grant; yet the woman hesitated, for she was amazed that a Jew should ask a favor of a Samaritan, however great the need. She expressed her surprise in the question: "How is it that thou, being a Jew, askest drink of me, which am a woman of Samaria? for the Jews have no dealings with the Samaritans." Jesus, seemingly forgetful of thirst in His desire to teach, answered her by saying: "If thou knewest the gift of God, and who it is that saith to thee, Give me to drink; thou wouldest have asked of him, and he would have given thee living water." The woman reminded Him that He had no

[b] John 8:48.

[c] John 4:4; for incidents following, see verses 5–43.

[d] Note 2, end of chapter.

[e] Gen. 33: 19; and Josh. 24:32.

bucket or cord with which to draw from the deep well, and inquired further as to His meaning, adding: "Art thou greater than our father Jacob, which gave us the well, and drank thereof himself, and his children, and his cattle?"

Jesus found in the woman's words a spirit similar to that with which the scholarly Nicodemus had received His teachings; each failed alike to perceive the spiritual lesson He would impart. He explained to her that water from the well would be of but temporary benefit; to one who drank of it thirst would return. "But," he added, "whosoever drinketh of the water that I shall give him shall never thirst; but the water that I shall give him shall be in him a well of water springing up into everlasting life." The woman's interest was keenly aroused, either from curiosity or as an emotion of deeper concern, for she now became the petitioner, and, addressing Him by a title of respect, said: "Sir, give me this water, that I thirst not, neither come hither to draw." She could see nothing beyond the material advantage attaching to water that would once and for all quench thirst. The result of the draught she had in mind would be to give her immunity from one bodily need, and save her the labor of coming to draw from the well.

The subject of the conversation was abruptly changed by Jesus bidding her to go, call her husband, and return. To her reply that she had no husband Jesus revealed to her His superhuman powers of discernment, by telling her she had spoken truthfully, inasmuch as she had had five husbands, while the man with whom she was then living was not her husband. Surely no ordinary being could have so read the unpleasing story of her life; she impulsively confessed her conviction, saying: "Sir, I perceive that thou art a prophet." She desired to turn the conversation, and, pointing to Mount Gerizim, upon which the sacrilegious priest Manasseh had erected a Samaritan temple, she remarked with little pertinence to what had been said before: "Our fathers worshipped in this mountain; and ye say, that in Jerusalem is the place where men ought to worship." Jesus replied in yet deeper vein, telling her that the time was near when neither that mountain nor Jerusalem would be preeminently a place of worship; and He clearly rebuked her presumption that the traditional belief of the Samaritans was equally good with that of the Jews; for, said

He: "Ye worship ye know not what: we know what we worship: for salvation is of the Jews." Changed and corrupted as the Jewish religion had become, it was better than that of her people; for the Jews did accept the prophets, and through Judah the Messiah had come. But, as Jesus expounded the matter to her, the place of worship was of lesser importance than the spirit of the worshiper." God is a Spirit: and they that worship him must worship him in spirit and in truth."

Unable or unwilling to understand Christ's meaning, the woman sought to terminate the lesson by a remark that probably was to her but casual: "I know that Messias cometh, which is called Christ: when he is come, he will tell us all things." Then, to her profound amazement, Jesus rejoined with the awe-inspiring declaration: "I that speak unto thee am he." The language was unequivocal, the assertion one that required no elucidation. The woman must regard Him thereafter as either an impostor or the Messiah. She left her pitcher at the well, and hastening to the town told of her experience, saying: "Come, see a man, which told me all things that ever I did: is not this the Christ?"

Near the conclusion of the interview between Jesus and the woman, the returning disciples arrived with the provisions they had gone to procure. They marveled at finding the Master in conversation with a woman, and a Samaritan woman at that, yet none of them asked of Him an explanation. His manner must have impressed them with the seriousness and solemnity of the occasion. When they urged Him to eat He said: "I have meat to eat that ye know not of." To them His words had no significance beyond the literal sense, and they queried among themselves as to whether someone had brought Him food during their absence; but He enlightened them in this way: "My meat is to do the will of him that sent me, and to finish his work."

A crowd of Samaritans appeared, coming from the city. Looking upon them and upon the grain fields nearby, Jesus continued. "Say not ye, There are yet four months, and then cometh harvest? behold, I say unto you, Lift up your eyes, and look on the fields; for they are white and already to harvest." The import of the saying seems to be that while months would elapse before the wheat and the barley were ready for the sickle, the harvest of souls, exemplified by the approaching crowd, was even then ready; and that from what He had sown the disciples might reap, to their inestimable advantage, since they would have wages for their hire and would gather the fruits of other labor than their own.

Many of the Samaritans believed on Christ, at first on the strength of the woman's testimony, then because of their own conviction; and they said to the woman at whose behest they had at first gone to meet Him: "Now we believe, not because of thy saying: for we have heard him ourselves, and know that this is indeed the Christ, the Saviour of the world." Graciously He acceded to their request to remain, and tarried with them two days. It is beyond question that Jesus did not share in the national prejudice of the Jews against the people of Samaria; an honest soul was acceptable to Him come whence he may. Probably the seed sown during this brief stay of our Lord among the despised people of Samaria was that from which so rich a harvest was reaped by the apostles in after years.[f]

JESUS AGAIN IN GALILEE: AT CANA AND NAZARETH

Following the two days' sojourn among the Samaritans, Jesus, accompanied by the disciples who had traveled with Him from Judea, resumed the journey northward into Galilee, from which province He had been absent several months. Realizing that the people of Nazareth, the town in which He had been brought up, would be probably loath to acknowledge Him as other than the carpenter, or, as He stated, knowing that "a prophet hath no honour in his own country,"[g] He went first to Cana. The people of that section, and indeed the Galileans generally, received Him gladly; for many of them had attended the last Passover and probably had been personal witnesses of the wonders He had wrought in Judea. While at Cana He was visited by a nobleman, most likely a high official of the province, who entreated Him to proceed to Capernaum and heal his son, who was then lying at the point of death. With the probable design of showing the man the true condition of his mind, for we cannot doubt that Jesus could read his thoughts, our Lord said to him: "Except ye see signs and wonders, ye will not believe."[h] As

[f] Acts 8:5; 9:31; 15:3.

[g] John 4:44; compare Matt. 13:57; Mark 6:4; Luke 4:24.

[h] John 4:48.

observed in earlier instances, notably in the refusal of Jesus to commit Himself to the professing believers at Jerusalem, whose belief rested solely on their wonder at the things He did,[i] our Lord would not regard miracles, though wrought by Himself, as a sufficient and secure foundation for faith. The entreating nobleman, in anguish over the precarious state of his son, in no way resented the rebuke such as a captious mind may have found in the Lord's reply; but with sincere humility, which showed his belief that Jesus could heal the boy, he renewed and emphasized his plea: "Sir, come down ere my child die."

Probably the man had never paused to reason as to the direct means or process by which death might be averted and healing be insured through the words of any being; but in his heart he believed in Christ's power, and with pathetic earnestness besought our Lord to intervene in behalf of his dying son. He seemed to consider it necessary that the Healer be present, and his great fear was that the boy would not live until Jesus could arrive. 'Jesus saith unto him, Go thy way; thy son liveth. And the man believed the word that Jesus had spoken unto him, and he went his way." The genuineness of the man's trust is shown by his grateful acceptance of the Lord's assurance, and by the contentment that he forthwith manifested. Capernaum, where his son lay, was about twenty miles away; had he been still solicitous and doubtful he would probably have tried to return home that day, for it was one o'clock in the afternoon when Jesus spoke the words that had given him such relief; but he journeyed leisurely, for on the following day he was still on the road, and was met by some of his servants who had been sent to cheer him with the glad word of his son's recovery. He inquired when the boy had begun to amend, and was told that at the seventh hour on the yesterday the fever had left him. That was the time at which Christ had said, "Thy son liveth." The man's belief ripened fast, and both he and his household accepted the gospel.[j] This was the second miracle wrought by Jesus when in Cana, though in this instance the subject of the blessing was in Capernaum.

Our Lord's fame spread through all the region round about. During a period not definitely stated, He taught in the synagogs of

---

[i] John 2:23, 24.

[j] Note 3, end of chapter.

the towns and was received with favor, being "glorified of all."[k] He then returned to Nazareth, His former home, and, as was His custom, attended the synagog service on the Sabbath day. Many times as a boy and man He had sat in that house of worship, listening to the reading of the law and the prophets and to the commentaries or Targums[l] relating thereto, as delivered by appointed readers; but now, as a recognized teacher of legal age He was eligible to take the reader's place. On this occasion He stood up to read, when the service had reached the stage at which extracts from the prophetical books were to be read to the congregation. The minister in charge handed Him the roll, or book, or Isaiah; He turned to the part known to us as the beginning of the sixty-first chapter, and read: "The Spirit of the Lord is upon me, because he hath anointed me to preach the gospel to the poor; he hath sent me to heal the broken-hearted, to preach deliverance to the captives, and recovering of sight to the blind, to set at liberty them that are bruised, to preach the acceptable year of the Lord."[m] Handing the book to the minister, He sat down. It was allowable for the reader in the service of the Jewish synagog to make comments in explanation of what had been read; but to do so he must sit. When Jesus took His seat the people knew that He was about to expound the text, and "the eyes of all them that were in the synagogue were fastened on him." The scripture He had quoted was one recognized by all classes as specifically referring to the Messiah, for whose coming the nation waited. The first sentence of our Lord's commentary was startling; it involved no labored analysis, no scholastic interpretation, but a direct and unambiguous application: "This day is this scripture fulfilled in your ears." There was such graciousness in His words that all wondered, and they said, "Is not this Joseph's son?"[n]

Jesus knew their thoughts even if He heard not their words, and, forestalling their criticism, He said: "Ye will surely say unto me this proverb, Physician, heal thyself: whatsoever we have heard done in Capernaum, do also here in thy country. And he said, Verily I say

[k] Luke 4:14, 15; read verses 16–32.

[l] Note 4, end of chapter.

[m] Luke 4:18, 19; compare Isa. 61:1, 2.

[n] Luke 4:22; compare Matt. 13:55–57; Mark 6:3; John 6:42.

unto you, No prophet is accepted in his own country." In their hearts the people were eager for a sign, a wonder, a miracle. They knew that Jesus had wrought such in Cana, and a boy in Capernaum had been healed by His word; at Jerusalem too He had astonished the people with mighty works. Were they, His townsmen, to be slighted? Why would He not treat them to some entertaining exhibition of His powers? He continued His address, reminding them that in the days of Elijah, when for three years and a half no rain had fallen, and famine had reigned, the prophet had been sent to but one of the many widows, and she a woman of Sarepta in Sidon, a Gentile, not a daughter of Israel. And again, though there had been many lepers in Israel in the days of Elisha, but one leper, and he a Syrian, not an Israelite, had been cleansed through the prophet's ministration, for Naaman alone had manifested the requisite faith.

Then great was their wrath. Did He dare to class them with Gentiles and lepers? Were they to be likened unto despised unbelievers, and that too by the son of the village carpenter, who had grown from childhood in their community? Victims of diabolical rage, they seized the Lord and took Him to the brow of the hill on the slopes of which the town was built, determined to avenge their wounded feelings by hurling Him from the rocky cliffs. Thus early in His ministry did the forces of opposition attain murderous intensity. But our Lord's time to die had not yet come. The infuriated mob was powerless to go one step farther than their supposed victim would permit. "But he passing through the midst of them went his way." Whether they were over-awed by the grace of His presence, silenced by the power of His words, or stayed by some more appalling intervention, we are not informed. He departed from the unbelieving Nazarenes, and thenceforth Nazareth was no longer His home.

IN CAPERNAUM

Jesus wended His way to Capernaum,° which became to Him as nearly a place of abode as any He had in Galilee. There He taught, particularly on Sabbath days; and the people were astonished at His

---

° Note 5, end of chapter.

doctrine, for He spoke with authority and power.[P] In the synagog, on one of these occasions, was a man who was a victim of possession, and subject to the ravages of an evil spirit, or, as the text so forcefully states, one who "had a spirit of an unclean devil." It is significant that this wicked spirit, which had gained such power over the man as to control his actions and utterances, was terrified before our Lord and cried out with a loud voice, though pleadingly: "Let us alone; what have we to do with thee, thou Jesus of Nazareth? art thou come to destroy us? I know thee who thou art; the Holy One of God." Jesus rebuked the unclean spirit, commanding him to be silent, and to leave the man; the demon obeyed the Master, and after throwing the victim into violent though harmless paroxysm, left him. Such a miracle caused the beholders to wonder the more, and they exclaimed: "What a word is this! for with authority and power he commandeth the unclean spirits, and they come out. And the fame of him went out into every place of the country round about."[q]

In the evening of the same day, when the sun had set, and therefore after the Sabbath had passed,[r] the people flocked about Him, bringing their afflicted friends and kindred; and these Jesus healed of their divers maladies whether of body or of mind. Among those so relieved were many who had been possessed of devils, and these cried out, testifying perforce of the Master's divine authority. "Thou art Christ the Son of God."[s]

On these as on other occasions, we find evil spirits voicing through the mouths of their victims their knowledge that Jesus was the Christ; and in all such instances the Lord silenced them with a word; for He wanted no such testimony as theirs to attest the fact of His Godship. Those spirits were of the devil's following, members of the rebellious and defeated hosts that had been cast down through the power of the very Being whose authority and power they now acknowledged in their demoniac frenzy. Together with Satan himself, their vanquished chief, they remained unembodied, for to all of them

[P] Luke 4:32; compare Matt. 7:28, 29; 13:54; Mark 1:22.
[q] Luke 4:33–37; and Mark 1:23–28. Note 6, end of chapter.
[r] The Jews' Sabbath began at sunset Friday and ended with the setting of the sun on Saturday.
[s] Luke 4:41; compare Mark 1:34; 3:11, 12; 5:1–18; Matt. 8:28–34.

the privileges of the second or mortal estate had been denied;[t] their remembrance of the scenes that had culminated in their expulsion from heaven was quickened by the presence of the Christ, though He stood in a body of flesh.

Many modern writers have attempted to explain the phenomenon of demoniacal possession; and beside these there are not a few who deny the possibility of actual domination of the victim by spirit personages. Yet the scriptures are explicit in showing the contrary. Our Lord distinguished between this form of affliction and that of simple bodily disease in His instructions to the Twelve: "Heal the sick, cleanse the lepers, raise the dead, cast out devils."[u] In the account of the incidents under consideration, the evangelist Mark observes the same distinction, thus: "They brought unto him all that were diseased, and them that were possessed with devils." In several instances, Christ, in rebuking demons, addressed them as individuals distinct from the human being afflicted,[v] and in one such instance commanded the demon to "come out of him, and enter no more into him."[w]

In this matter as in others the simplest explanation is the pertinent truth; theory raised on other than scriptural foundation is unstable. Christ unequivocally associated demons with Satan, specifically in His comment on the report of the Seventy whom He authorized and sent forth, and who testified with joy on their return that even the devils had been subject unto them through His name; and to those faithful servants He said: "I beheld Satan as lightning fall from heaven."[x] The demons that take possession of men, overruling their agency and compelling them to obey Satanic bidding, are the unembodied angels of the devil, whose triumph it is to afflict mortals, and if possible to impel them to sin. To gain for themselves the transitory gratification of tenanting a body of flesh, these demons are eager to enter even into the bodies of beasts.[y]

[t] Pages 7–9

[u] Matt. 10:8; see verse 1; compare 4:24; Mark 1:32; 16:17, 18; Luke 9:1.

[v] Matt. 8:32; Mark 1:25; Luke 4:35.

[w] Mark 9:25.

[x] Luke 10:17, 18; compare Rev. 12:7–9.

[y] Matt. 8:29–33; Mark 5:11–14; Luke 8:32–34.

Possibly it was during the interval between the rebuking of the evil spirit in the synagog and the miracles of healing and casting out devils in the evening of that Sabbath, that Jesus went to the house of Simon, whom He had before named Peter, and there found the mother-in-law of His disciple lying ill of fever. Acceding to the request of faith He rebuked the disease; the woman was healed forthwith, rose from her bed, and ministered the hospitality of her home unto Jesus and those who were with Him.[z]

NOTES TO CHAPTER 13

1. Animosity Between Jews and Samaritans.—In any consideration of the Samaritans, it must be kept in mind that a certain city and the district or province in which it was situated were both known as Samaria. The principal facts pertaining to the origin of the Samaritans and the explanation of the mutual animosity existing between the people and the Jews in the time of Christ, have been admirably summarized by Geikie (*Life and Words of Christ*, vol. 1, pp. 495–6). Omitting his citation of authorities, we quote: "After the deportation of the Ten Tribes to Assyria, Samaria had been repeopled by heathen colonists from various provinces of the Assyrian empire, by fugitives from the authorities of Judea, and by stragglers of one or other of the Ten Tribes, who found their way home again. The first heathen settlers, terrified at the increase of wild animals, especially lions, and attributing it to their not knowing the proper worship of the God of the country, sent for one of the exiled priests, and, under his instructions, added the worship of Jehovah to that of their idols—an incident in their history from which later Jewish hatred and derision taunted them as 'proselytes of the lions,' as it branded them, from their Assyrian origin, with the name of Cuthites. Ultimately, however, they became even more rigidly attached to the Law of Moses than the Jews themselves. Anxious to be recognized as Israelites, they set their hearts on joining the Two Tribes, on their return from captivity, but the stern puritanism of Ezra and Nehemiah admitted no alliance between the pure blood of Jerusalem and the tainted race of the north. Resentment at this affront was natural, and excited resentment in return, till, in Christ's day, centuries of strife and mutual injury, intensified by theological hatred on both sides, had made them implacable enemies. The Samaritans had built a temple on Mount Gerizim, to rival that of Jerusalem, but it had been destroyed by John Hyrcanus, who had also levelled Samaria to the ground. They claimed for their mountain a greater holiness than that of Moriah; accused the Jews of adding to the word of God, by receiving the writings of the prophets, and prided themselves on owning only the Pentateuch as inspired; favoured Herod because the Jews hated

---

[z] Matt. 8:14, 15; Mark 1:29–31; Luke 4:38, 39.

him, and were loyal to him and equally hated Romans; had kindled false lights on the hills, to vitiate the Jewish reckoning by the new moons, and thus throw their feasts into confusion, and, in the early youth of Jesus, had even defiled the very Temple itself, by strewing human bones in it, at the Passover.

"Nor had hatred slumbered on the side of the Jews. They knew the Samaritans only as Cuthites, or heathens from Cuth. 'The race that I hate is no race,' says the son of Sirach. It was held that a people who once had worshipped five gods could have no part in Jehovah. The claim of the Samaritans that Moses had buried the Tabernacle and its vessels on the top of Gerizim, was laughed to scorn. It was said that they had dedicated their temple, under Antiochus Epiphanes, to the Greek Jupiter. Their keeping the commands of Moses even more strictly than the Jews, that it might seem they were really of Israel, was not denied; but their heathenism, it was said, had been proved by the discovery of a brazen dove, which they worshipped, on the top of Gerizim. It would have been enough that they boasted of Herod as their good king, who had married a daughter of their people; that he had been free to follow, in their country, his Roman tastes, so hated in Judea; that they had remained quiet, after his death, when Judea and Galilee were in uproar, and that for their peacefulness a fourth of their taxes had been remitted and added to the burdens of Judea. Their friendliness to the Romans was an additional provocation. While the Jews were kept quiet only by the sternest severity, and strove to the utmost against the introduction of anything foreign, the Samaritans rejoiced in the new importance which their loyalty to the empire had given them. Shechem flourished: close by, in Caesarea, the procurator held his court: a division of cavalry, in barracks at Sebaste—the old Samaria—had been raised in the territory. The Roman strangers were more than welcome to while away the summer in their umbrageous valleys.

"The illimitable hatred, rising from so many sources, found vent in the tradition that a special curse had been uttered against the Samaritans, by Ezra, Zerubbabel, and Joshua. It was said that these great ones assembled the whole congregation of Israel in the Temple, and that three hundred priests, with three hundred trumpets, and three hundred books of the Law, and three hundred scholars of the Law, had been employed to repeat, amidst the most solemn ceremonial, all the curses of the Law against the Samaritans. They had been subjected to every form of excommunication; by the incommunicable name of Jehovah; by the Tables of the Law, and by the heavenly and earthly synagogues. The very name became a reproach. 'We know that Thou art a Samaritan, and hast a devil,' said the Jews, to Jesus, in Jerusalem. . . . A Samaritan egg, as the hen laid it, could not be unclean, but what of a boiled egg? Yet interest and convenience strove, by subtle casuistry, to invent excuses for what intercourse was unavoidable. The country of the Cuthites was clean, so that a Jew might, without scruple, gather and eat its produce. The waters of Samaria were clean, so that a Jew might drink them or wash in them. Their dwellings were clean, so that he might enter them, and eat or lodge in them. Their roads were clean, so that the dust of them did not defile a Jew's feet. The Rabbis even went so far in their contradictory utterances, as to say that the victuals of the Cuthites were allowed, if none of their wine or vinegar were mixed with them, and even their unleavened bread was to be reckoned fit for use at the Passover. Opinions thus wavered, but, as a rule, harsher feeling prevailed."

That the hostile sentiment has continued unto this day, at least on the part of the Jews, is affirmed by Frankl and others. Thus, as quoted by Farrar (p. 166 note): "'Are you a Jew?' asked Salameh Cohen, the Samaritan high priest, of Dr. Frankl; 'and do you come to us, the Samaritans, who are despised by the Jews?' (*Jews in the East*, 2, 329). He added that they would willingly live in friendship with the Jews, but that the Jews avoided all intercourse with them. Soon after, visiting Sepharedish Jews of Nablous, Dr. Frankl asked one of that sect, 'if he had any intercourse with the Samaritans?' The women retreated with a cry of horror, and one of them said, 'Have you been among the worshipers of the pigeons?' I said that I had. The women again fell back with the same expression of repugnance and one of them said, 'Take a purifying bath!'" (idem, p. 334). Canon Farrar adds, "I had the pleasure of spending a day among the Samaritans encamped on Mount Gerizim, for their annual passover, and neither in their habits nor apparent character could I see any cause for all this horror and hatred."

2. Sychar.—The town where dwelt the Samaritan woman with whom Jesus conversed at Jacob's well, is named Sychar in John 4:5; the name occurs nowhere else in the Bible. Attempts have been made to identify the place with Shechem, a city dear to the Jewish heart because of its prominence in connection with the lives of the early patriarchs. It is now generally admitted, however, that Sychar was a small village on the site of the present Askar, which is, says Zenos, "a village with a spring and some ancient rock-hewn tombs, about five eighths of a mile north of Jacob's well."

3. The Nobleman of Capernaum.—The name of the nobleman whose son was healed by the word of Jesus is not given. Attempts to identify him with Chuza, the steward of Herod Antipas, are based on unreliable tradition. The family of the nobleman accepted the teachings of Christ. "Joanna the wife of Chuza Herod's steward" (Luke 8:3) was among the grateful and honorable women who had been recipients of our Lord's healing ministry, and who contributed of their substance for the furtherance of His work. Unconfirmed tradition should not be confounded with authentic history.

4. The Targums are ancient Jewish paraphrases on the scriptures, which were delivered in the synagogs in the languages of the common people. In the time of Christ the language spoken by the Jews was not Hebrew, but an Aramaic dialect. Edersheim states that pure Hebrew was the language of scholars and of the synagog, and that the public readings from the scriptures had to be rendered by an interpreter. "In earliest times indeed," says he, "it was forbidden to the Methurgeman [interpreter] to read his translation, or to write down a Targum, lest the paraphrase should be regarded as of equal authority with the original." The use of written targums was "authoritatively sanctioned before the end of the second century after Christ. This is the origin of our two oldest extant Targumim—that of Onkelos (as it is called) on the Pentateuch; and that on the Prophets, attributed to Jonathan the son of Uzziel. These names do not indeed, accurately represent the authorship of the oldest Targumim, which may more correctly be regarded as later and authoritative recensions of what, in some form, had existed before. But although these works had their origin in Palestine, it is noteworthy that in the form in which at present we possess them, they are the outcome of the schools of Babylon." (*Life and Times of Jesus the Messiah*, vol. 1, pp. 10, 11.)

5. Capernaum.—"The name Capernaum signifies, according to some authorities, 'the Village of Nahum,' according to others, 'the Village of Consolation.' As we follow the history of Jesus we shall discover that many of His mighty works were wrought, and many of His most impressive words were spoken in Capernaum. The infidelity of the inhabitants, after all the discourses and wonderful works which He had done among them, brought out the saying of Jesus, 'And thou, Capernaum, which art exalted unto heaven, shalt be cast down to hell.' (Matt. 11:23.) So thoroughly has this prediction been fulfilled that no trace of the city remains, and the very site which it occupied is now a matter of conjecture, there being even no ecclesiastical tradition of the locality. At the present day two spots have claims which are urged, each with such arguments of probability as to make the whole question the most difficult in sacred topography. . . . We shall probably never be able to know the exact fact. Jesus damned it to oblivion, and there it lies. We shall content ourselves with the New Testament notices as bearing on the work of Jesus.

"We learn that it was somewhere on the borders of Zabulun and Nephthalim, on the western shore of the Sea of Galilee (compare Matt. 4:13, with John 6:24). It was near or in 'the land of Gennesaret' (compare Matt. 14:34, with John 6:17, 20, 24), a plain about three miles long and one mile wide, which we learn from Josephus was one of the most prosperous and crowded districts of Palestine. It was probably on the great road leading from Damascus to the south, 'by the way of the sea.' (Matt. 4:15.) There was great wisdom in selecting this as a place to open a great public ministry. It was full of a busy population. The exceeding richness of the wonderful plain of Gennesaret supported the mass of inhabitants it attracted. Josephus (B. J., iii, 10:8) gives a glowing description of this land."—Deems, *Light of the Nations*, pp. 167, 168.

6. Knowledge Does Not Insure Salvation.—James of old chided his brethren for certain empty professions (James 2:19). Said he in effect: You take pride and satisfaction in declaring your belief in God; you boast of being distinguished from the idolaters and the heathen because you accept one God; you do well to so profess, and so believe; but, remember, others do likewise; even the devils believe; and, we may add, so firmly that they tremble at the thought of the fate which that belief makes sure. Those confessions of the devils, that Christ was the Son of God, were founded on knowledge; yet their knowledge of the great truth did not change their evil natures. How different was their acknowledgment of the Savior from that of Peter, who, to the Master's question "Whom say ye that I am?" replied in practically the words used by the unclean spirits before cited, "Thou art the Christ, the Son of the living God" (Matt. 16:15–16; see also Mark 8:29; Luke 9:20). Peter's faith had already shown its vital power; it had caused him to forsake much that had been dear, to follow his Lord through persecution and suffering, and to put away worldliness with all its fascinations, the sacrificing godliness which his faith made so desirable. His knowledge of God as the Father, and of the Son as the Redeemer, was perhaps no greater than that of the unclean spirits; but while to them that knowledge was but an added cause of condemnation, to him it was a means of salvation. —Abridged from *The Articles of Faith*, pp. 97–98.

CHAPTER 14

CONTINUATION OF OUR LORD'S MINISTRY IN GALILEE

A LEPER MADE CLEAN

Early in the morning following that eventful Sabbath in Capernaum, our Lord arose "a great while before day" and went in quest of seclusion beyond the town. In a solitary place He gave Himself to prayer, thus demonstrating the fact that, Messiah though He was, He was profoundly conscious of His dependence upon the Father, whose work He had come to do. Simon Peter and other disciples found the place of His retirement, and told Him of the eager crowds who sought Him. Soon the people gathered about Him, and urged that He remain with them; but "he said unto them, I must preach the kingdom of God to other cities also: for therefore am I sent."[a] And to the disciples He said: "Let us go into the next towns, that I may preach there also: for therefore came I forth."[b] Thence He departed, accompanied by the few whom He had already closely associated with Himself, and ministered in many towns of Galilee, preaching in the synagogs, healing the sick, and casting out devils.

Among the afflicted seeking the aid that He alone could give came a leper,[c] who knelt before Him, or bowed with his face to the ground, and humbly professed his faith, saying: "If thou wilt, thou canst make me clean." The petition implied in the words of this poor creature was pathetic; the confidence he expressed is inspiring. The question in his mind was not—Can Jesus heal me? but—Will he

[a]Luke 4:42–44.

[b]Mark 1:38.

[c] Mark 1:40–45; Matt. 8:2–4; Luke 5:12–15.

heal me? In compassionate mercy Jesus laid His hand upon the sufferer, unclean though he was, both ceremonially and physically, for leprosy is a loathsome affliction, and we know that this man was far advanced in the disease since we are told that he was "full of leprosy." Then the Lord said: "I will: be thou clean." The leper was immediately healed. Jesus instructed him to show himself to the priest, and make the offerings prescribed in the law of Moses for such cases as his.[d]

In this instruction we see that Christ had not come to destroy the law, but, as He affirmed at another time, to fulfil it;[e] and at this stage of His work the fulfillment was incomplete. Moreover, had the legal requirements been disregarded in as serious a matter as that of restoring an outcast leper to the society of the community from which he had been debarred, priestly opposition, already waxing strong and threatening against Jesus, would have been augmented, and further hindrance to the Lord's work might have resulted. There was to be no delay in the man's compliance with the Master's instruction; Jesus "straitly charged him, and forthwith sent him away." Furthermore He explicitly directed the man to tell nobody of the manner of his healing. There was perhaps good reason for this injunction of silence, aside from the very general course of our Lord in discountenancing undesirable notoriety; for, had word of the miracle preceded the man's appearing before the priest, obstacles might have been thrown in the way of his Levitical recognition as one who was clean. The man, however, could not keep the good word to himself, but went about "and began to publish it much, and to blaze abroad the matter, insomuch that Jesus could no more openly enter into the city, but was without in desert places: and they came to him from every quarter."[f]

A PALSIED MAN HEALED AND FORGIVEN

It must be borne in mind that no one of the evangelists attempts to give a detailed history of all the doings of Jesus, nor do all follow

[d] Lev. 14:2–10. Note 1, end of chapter.

[e] Matt. 5:17.

[f] Mark 1:45.

the same order in relating the incidents with which they associate the great lessons of the Master's teachings. There is much uncertainty as to the actual sequence of events.

"Some days" after the healing of the leper, Jesus was again in Capernaum. The details of His employment during the interval are not specified; but, we may be sure that His work continued, for His characteristic occupation was that of going about doing good.[g] His place of abode in Capernaum was well known, and word was soon noised about that He was in the house.[h] A great throng gathered, so that there was no room to receive them; even the doorway was crowded, and later comers could not get near the Master. To all who were within hearing Jesus preached the gospel. A little party of four approached the house bearing a litter or pallet on which lay a man afflicted with palsy, a species of paralysis which deprived the subject of the power of voluntary motion and usually of speech; the man was helpless. His friends, disappointed at finding themselves unable to reach Jesus because of the press, resorted to an unusual expedient, which exhibited in an unmistakable way their faith in the Lord as One who could rebuke and stay disease, and their determination to seek the desired blessing at His hands.

By some means they carried the afflicted man to the flat roof of the house, probably by an outside stairway or by the use of a ladder, possibly by entering an adjoining house, ascending the stairs to its roof and crossing therefrom to the house within which Jesus was teaching. They broke away part of the roof, making an opening, or enlarging that of the trapdoor such as the houses of that place and time were usually provided with; and, to the surprise of the assembled crowd, they then let down through the tiling the portable couch upon which the palsied sufferer lay. Jesus was deeply impressed by the faith and works[i] of those who had thus labored to place a helpless paralytic before Him; doubtless, too, He knew of the trusting faith in the heart of the sufferer; and, looking compassionately upon the man, He said: "Son, thy sins be forgiven thee."

---

[g] Acts 10:38.

[h] Mark 2:1–12; compare Matt. 9:2–8; Luke 5:17–24.

[i] Compare James 2:14–18.

Among the people there assembled were scribes, Pharisees, and doctors of the law, not only representatives of the local synagog but some who had come from distant towns in Galilee, and some from Judea, and even from Jerusalem. The official class had opposed our Lord and His works on earlier occasions, and their presence in the house at this time boded further unfriendly criticism and possible obstruction. They heard the words spoken to the paralytic, and were angered thereat. In their hearts they accused Jesus of the awful offense of blasphemy, which consists essentially in claiming for human or demon power the prerogatives of God, or in dishonoring God by ascribing to Him attributes short of perfection.[j] These unbelieving scholars, who incessantly wrote and talked of the coming of the Messiah, yet rejected Him when He was there present, murmured in silence, saying to themselves: "Who can forgive sins but God only?" Jesus knew their inmost thoughts,[k] and made reply thereto, saying: "Why reason ye these things in your hearts? Whether is it easier to say to the sick of the palsy, Thy sins be forgiven thee; or to say, Arise, and take up thy bed, and walk?" And then to emphasize, and to put beyond question His possession of divine authority, He added: "But that ye may know that the Son of man hath power on earth to forgive sins, (he saith to the sick of the palsy,) I say unto thee, Arise, and take up thy bed, and go thy way into thine house." The man arose, fully restored; and, taking up the mattress upon which he had been brought, walked out before them. The amazement of the people was mingled with reverence, and many glorified God, of whose power they were witnesses.

The incident demands our further study. According to one of the accounts, the Lord's first words to the afflicted one were: "Son, be of good cheer"; followed directly by the comforting and authoritative assurance: "Thy sins be forgiven thee."[l] The man was probably in a state of fear; he may have known that his ailment was the result of wicked indulgences; nevertheless, though he may have considered the possibility of hearing only condemnation for his transgression, he had faith to be

---

[j] Note 2, end of chapter.

[k] See another instance of our Lord reading unuttered thoughts, Luke 7:39–50.

[l] Matt. 9:2. Note 5, end of chapter.

brought. In this man's condition there was plainly a close connection between his past sins and his present affliction; and in this particular his case is not unique, for we read that Christ admonished another, whom He healed, to sin no more lest a worse thing befall him.[m] We are not warranted, however, in assuming that all bodily ills are the result of culpable sin; and against such a conception stands the Lord's combined instruction and rebuke to those who, in the case of a man born blind, asked who had sinned, the man or his parents to bring so grievous an affliction upon him, to which inquiry our Lord replied that the man's blindness was due neither to his own sin nor to that of his parents.[n]

In many instances, however, disease is the direct result of individual sin. Whatever may have been the measure of past offense on the part of the man suffering from palsy, Christ recognized his repentance together with the faith that accompanied it, and it was the Lord's rightful prerogative to decide upon the man's fitness to receive remission of his sins and relief from his bodily affliction. The interrogative response of Jesus to the unuttered criticism of the scribes, Pharisees, and doctors, has been interpreted in many ways. He inquired which was easier, to say, "Thy sins be forgiven thee," or to say, "Arise, and take up thy bed, and walk." Is it not a rational explanation that, when spoken authoritatively by Him, the two expressions were of allied meaning? The circumstance should have been a sufficient demonstration to all who heard, that He, the Son of Man, claimed and possessed the right and the power to remit both physical and spiritual penalties, to heal the body of visible disease, and to purge the spirit of the no less real malady of sin. In the presence of people of all classes Jesus thus openly asserted His divinity, and affirmed the same by a miraculous manifestation of power.

The charge of blasphemy, which the rabbinical critics formulated in their minds against the Christ, was not to end as a mental conception of theirs, nor to be nullified by our Lord's later remarks. It was through perjured testimony that He finally received unrighteous condemnation and was sent to His death.[o] Already, in that house at Capernaum, the shadow of the cross had fallen athwart the course of His life.

[m] John 5:14.

[n] John 9:1–3.

[o] Compare John 10:33; 5:18; Matt. 26:65, 66.

PUBLICANS AND SINNERS

From the house Jesus repaired to the seaside, whither the people followed Him; there He taught them again. At the close of His discourse He walked farther and saw a man named Levi, one of the publicans[p] or official collectors of taxes, sitting at the customhouse where the tariff levied under Roman law had to be paid. This man was known also as Matthew, a name less distinctively Jewish than is Levi.[q] He afterward became one of the Twelve and the author of the first of the evangelical Gospels. To him Jesus said, "Follow me." Matthew left his place and followed the Lord. Some time later the new disciple provided a great feast at his house, in honor of the Master; and other disciples were present. So obnoxious to the Jews was the power of Rome to which they were subject, that they regarded with aversion all officials in Roman employ. Particularly humiliating to them was the system of compulsory taxation, by which they, the people of Israel, had to pay tribute to an alien nation, which in their estimation was wholly pagan and heathen.

Naturally, the collectors of these taxes were abhorred; and they, known as publicans, probably resented the discourteous treatment by inconsiderate enforcement of the tax requirements, and, as affirmed by historians, often inflicted unlawful extortion upon the people. If publicans in general were detested, we can readily understand how bitter would be the contempt in which the Jews would hold one of their own nation who had accepted appointment as such an official. In this unenviable status was Matthew when Jesus called him. The publicans formed a distinct social class, for from the community in general they were practically ostracized. All who associated with them were made to share in the popular odium, and "publicans and sinners" became a common designation for the degraded caste. To Matthew's feast many of his friends and some of his fellow officials were invited, so that the gathering was largely made up of these despised "publicans and sinners." And to such an assemblage went Jesus with His disciples.

The scribes and Pharisees could not let pass such an opportunity for faultfinding and caustic criticism. They hesitated to address themselves directly to Jesus, but of the disciples they asked in disdain:

---

[p] Note 3, end of chapter.

[q] Matt. 9:9–13; Mark 2:13–17; Luke 5:27–32.

"Why eateth your Master with publicans and sinners?" The Master heard, and replied with edifying incisiveness mingled with splendid irony. Citing one of the common aphorisms of the day, He said; "They that be whole need not a physician, but they that are sick." To this He added: "I am not come to call the righteous, but sinners to repentance." The hypercritical Pharisees were left to make their own application of the rejoinder, which some may have understood to mean that their self-righteousness was arraigned and their claims to superiority derided. Aside from the veiled sarcasm in the Master's words, they ought to have perceived the wisdom enshrined in His answer and to have profited thereby. Is not the physician's place among the afflicted ones? Would he be justified in keeping aloof from the sick and the suffering? His profession is that of combating disease, preventing when possible, curing when necessary, to the full extent of his ability. If the festive assembly at Matthew's house really did comprise a number of sinners, was not the occasion one of rare opportunity for the ministrations of the Physician of Souls? The righteous need no call to repentance; but are the sinners to be left in sin, because those who profess to be spiritual teachers will not condescend to extend a helping hand?

THE OLD AND THE NEW

Shortly after the entertainment provided by Matthew, the Pharisees were ready with another criticism, and in this they were associated with some of the Baptist's adherents. John was in prison; but many of those who had been drawn to his baptism, and had professed discipleship to him, still clung to his teachings, and failed to see that the Greater One of whom he had testified was then ministering amongst them. The Baptist had been a scrupulous observer of the law; his strict asceticism vied with the rigor of Pharisaic profession. His nonprogressive disciples, now left without a leader, naturally fell in with the Pharisees. Some of John's disciples came to Jesus, and questioned Him concerning His seeming indifference in the matter of fasting. They propounded a plain question: "Why do the disciples of John and of the Pharisees fast, but thy disciples fast not?"[r] To the

---

[r] Mark 2:18–22; Matt. 9:14–17; Luke 5:33–39.

friends of the now imprisoned Baptist our Lord's reply must have brought memories of their beloved leader's words, when he had compared himself to the Bridegroom's friend, and had plainly told them who was the real Bridegroom.[s] "Jesus said unto them, Can the children of the bridechamber fast, while the bridegroom is with them? as long as they have the bridegroom with them, they cannot fast. But the days will come, when the bridegroom shall be taken away from them, and then shall they fast in those days."[t]

If the questioners were able to comprehend the true import of this reply, they could not fail to find therein an implied abrogation of purely ceremonial observances comprised in the code of rabbinical rules and the numerous traditions associated with the law. But to make the subject clearer to their biased minds, Jesus gave them illustrations, which may be classed as parabolic. "No man also," said He, "seweth a piece of new cloth on an old garment: else the new piece that filled it up taketh away from the old, and the rent is made worse. And no man putteth new wine into old bottles: else the new wine doth burst the bottles, and the wine is spilled, and the bottles will be marred: but new wine must be put into new bottles."[u]

In such wise did our Lord proclaim the newness and completeness of His gospel. It was in no sense a patching up of Judaism. He had not come to mend old and torn garments; the cloth He provided was new, and to sew it on the old would be but to tear afresh the threadbare fabric and leave a more unsightly rent than at first. Or to change the figure, new wine could not safely be entrusted to old bottles. The bottles here referred to were really bags, made of the skins of animals, and of course they deteriorated with age. Just as old leather splits or tears under even slight strain, so the old bottle-skins would burst from the pressure of fermenting juice, and the good wine would be lost. The gospel taught by Christ was a new revelation, superseding the past, and marking the fulfillment of the law; it was no mere addendum, nor was it a reenactment of past requirements; it embodied a new and an everlasting covenant. Attempts to patch the

[s] Page 156.

[t] Mark 2:19, 20.

[u] Mark 2:21, 22.

Judaistic robe of traditionalism with the new fabric of the covenant could result in nothing more sightly than a rending of the fabric. The new wine of the gospel could not be held in the old time-worn containers of Mosaic libations. Judaism would be belittled and Christianity perverted by any such incongruous association.[v]

FISHERS OF MEN

It is improbable that the disciples who followed Jesus in the early months of His ministry had remained with Him continuously down to the time now under consideration. We find that some of those who were later called to the apostleship were following their vocation as fishermen even while Jesus was actively engaged as a Teacher in their own neighborhood. One day, as the Lord stood by the lake or sea of Galilee, the people pressed about Him in great numbers, eager to hear more of the wondrous words He was wont to speak.[w] Near the place were two fishing boats drawn in upon the beach; the owners were close by, washing and mending their nets. One of the boats belonged to Simon Peter, who had already become identified with the Master's work; this boat Jesus entered, and then asked Simon to thrust out a little from the land. Seating Himself, as teachers of that time usually did in delivering discourses, the Lord preached from this floating pulpit to the multitude on shore. The subject of the address is not given us.

When the sermon was ended, Jesus directed Simon to launch out into deep water and then let down the nets for a draught. Presumably Andrew was with his brother and possibly other assistants were in the boat. Simon replied to Jesus: "Master, we have toiled all the night, and have taken nothing: nevertheless at thy word I will let down the net." It was soon filled with fishes; so great was the haul that the net began to break, and the busy fishermen signalled to those in the other boat to come to their assistance. The catch filled both boats so that they appeared to be in danger of sinking. Simon Peter was overcome with this new evidence of the Master's power, and, falling at the feet of Jesus, he exclaimed: "Depart from me; for I am a sinful man, O

[v] See *The Great Apostasy,* chap. 7, para. 5.
[w] Luke 5:1–11; compare Matt. 4:18–22; Mark 1:16–20.

Lord." Jesus answered graciously and with promise: "Fear not; from henceforth thou shalt catch men."[x] The occupants of the second boat were Zebedee and his two sons James and John, the last named being he who with Andrew had left the Baptist to follow Jesus at the Jordan. Zebedee and his sons were partners with Simon in the fishing business. When the two boats were brought to land, the brothers Simon and Andrew, and Zebedee's two sons James and John, left their boats and accompanied Jesus.

The foregoing treatment is based on Luke's record; the briefer and less circumstantial accounts given by Matthew and Mark omit the incident of the miraculous draught of fishes, and emphasize the calling of the fishermen. To Simon and Andrew Jesus said: "Come ye after me, and I will make you to become fishers of men." The contrast thus presented between their former vocation and their new calling is strikingly forceful. Theretofore they had caught fish, and the fate of the fish was death; thereafter they were to draw men—to a life eternal. To James and John the call was no less definite; and they too left their all to follow the Master.

NOTES TO CHAPTER 14

1. **Leprosy.**—In Biblical usage this name is applied to several diseases, all, however, having some symptoms in common, at least in the earlier stages of the malady. The real leprosy is a scourge and a plague in many oriental lands today. Zenos, in *Standard Bible Dict.,* says: "True leprosy, as known in modern times, is an affection characterized by the appearance of nodules in the eyebrows, the cheeks, the nose, and the lobes of the ears, also in the hands and feet, where the disease eats into the joints, causing the falling off of fingers and toes. If nodules do not appear, their place is taken by spots of blanched or discolored skin (Mascular leprosy). Both forms are based upon a functional degeneration of the nerves of the skin. Its cause was discovered by Hansen in 1871 to be a specific bacillus. Defective diet, however, seems to serve as a favorable condition for the culture of the bacillus. Leprosy was one of the few abnormal conditions of the body which the Levitical law declared unclean. Elaborate provision was therefore made for testing its existence and for the purification of those who were cured of it."

Deems, *Light of the Nations,* p. 185, summing up the conditions incident to the advanced stages of the dread disease, writes: "The symptoms and the effects of

[x] Note 4, end of chapter.

this disease are very loathsome. There comes a white swelling or scab, with a change of the color of the hair on the part from its natural hue to yellow; then the appearance of a taint going deeper than the skin, or raw flesh appearing in the swelling. Then it spreads and attacks the cartilaginous portions of the body. The nails loosen and drop off, the gums are absorbed, and the teeth decay and fall out; the breath is a stench, the nose decays; fingers, hands, feet, may be lost, or the eyes eaten out. The human beauty has gone into corruption, and the patient feels that he is being eaten as by a fiend, who consumes him slowly in a long remorseless meal that will not end until he be destroyed. He is shut out from his fellows. As they approach he must cry, 'Unclean! unclean!' that all humanity may be warned from his precincts. He must abandon wife and child. He must go to live with other lepers, in disheartening view of miseries similar to his own. He must dwell in dismantled houses or in the tombs. He is, as Trench says, a dreadful parable of death. By the laws of Moses (Lev. 13:45; Num. 6:9; Ezek. 24:17) he was compelled, as if he were mourning for his own decease, to bear about him the emblems of death, the rent garments; he was to keep his head bare and his lip covered, as was the custom with those who were in communion with the dead. When the Crusaders brought the leprosy from the East, it was usual to clothe the leper in a shroud, and to say for him the masses for the dead. . . . In all ages this indescribably horrible malady has been considered incurable. The Jews believed that it was inflicted by Jehovah directly, as a punishment for some extraordinary perversity or some transcendent act of sinfulness, and that only God could heal it. When Naaman was cured, and his flesh came back like that of a little child, he said 'Now I know that there is no God in all the earth but in Israel.' (2 Kgs. 5:14, 15.)

The fact that leprosy is not ordinarily communicable by mere outward contact is accentuated by Trench, *Notes on the Miracles,* pp. 165–168, and the isolation of lepers required by the Mosaic law is regarded by him as an intended object lesson and figure to illustrate spiritual uncleanness. He says: "I refer to the mistaken assumption that leprosy was catching from one person to another; and that the lepers were so carefully secluded from their fellowmen lest they might communicate the disease to others, as in like manner that the torn garment, the covered lip, the cry, 'Unclean, unclean' (Lev. 13:45) were warnings to all that they should keep aloof, lest unawares touching a leper, or drawing unto too great a nearness, they should become partakers of this disease. So far from any danger of the kind existing, nearly all who have looked closest into the matter agree that the sickness was incommunicable by ordinary contact from one person to another. A leper might transmit it to his children, or the mother of a leper's children might take it from him; but it was by no ordinary contact communicable from one person to another. All the notices in the Old Testament, as well as in other Jewish books, confirm the statement that we have here something very much higher than a mere sanitary regulation. Thus, when the law of Moses was not observed, no such exclusion necessarily found place; Naaman the leper commanded the armies of Syria (2 Kgs. 5:1); Gehazi, with his leprosy that never should be cleansed (2 Kgs. 5:27); talked familiarly with the king of apostate Israel (2 Kgs. 8:5). . . . How, moreover, should the Levitical priests, had the disease been this creeping infection, have ever themselves escaped it, obliged as they were by their very office to submit the leper to actual handling and closest examination? . . . Leprosy was nothing short of a living death, a corrupting of all the humors, a poisoning of the very springs, of life; a dissolution, little by little, of the whole body, so that one limb after another actually decayed and fell away. Aaron exactly describes the appearance which the leper presented to the eyes of the beholders, when, pleading for Miriam, he says, 'Let her not be as one dead, of whom the flesh is half consumed when he cometh out of his mother's womb.' (Num. 12:12.) The disease, moreover, was incurable by the art and skill of man; not that the leper might not return to health; for, however rare, such cases are contemplated in the Levitical law. . . . The leper, thus fearfully bearing about the body the outward and visible tokens of sin in the soul, was treated throughout as a sinner, as one in whom sin had reached its climax, as one dead in trespasses and sins. He was himself a dreadful parable of death. He bore about him the emblems of death (Lev. 13:45); the rent garments, mourning for himself as one dead; the head bare as they were wont to have it who were defiled by communion with the dead (Num. 6:9; Ezek. 24:27); and the lip covered (Ezek. 24:17). . . . But the leper was as one dead, and as such was shut out of the camp (Lev. 13:46; Num. 5:2–4), and the city (2 Kgs. 7:3), this law being so strictly enforced that even the sister of Moses might not be exempted from it (Num. 12:14, 15); and kings themselves, as Uzziah (2 Chr. 26:21; 2 Kgs. 15:5) must submit to it; men being by this exclusion taught that what here took place in a figure, should take place in the reality with every one who was found in the death of sin."

For the elaborate ceremonies incident to the cleansing of a recovered leper see Lev., chap. 14.

2. Blasphemy.—The essence of the deep sin of blasphemy lies not, as many suppose, in profanity alone, but as Dr. Kelso, *Stand. Bible Dict.*, summarizes: "Every improper use of the divine name (Lev. 24:11), speech derogatory to the Majesty of God (Matt. 26:65), and sins with a high hand—i.e. premeditated transgressions of the basal principles of the theocracy (Num. 9:13; 15:30; Ex. 31:14)—were regarded as blasphemy; the penalty was death by stoning (Lev. 24:16)." *Smith's Bible Dictionary* states: "Blasphemy, in its technical English sense, signifies the speaking evil of God, and in this sense it is found in Ps. 74:18; Isa. 52:5; Rom. 2:24, etc. . . . On this charge both our Lord and Stephen were condemned to death by the Jews. When a person heard blasphemy he laid his hand on the head of the offender, to symbolize his sole responsibility for the guilt, and rising on his feet, tore his robe, which might never again be mended." (See Matt. 26:65.)

3. Publican.—"A word originally meaning a contractor for public works or supplies, or a farmer of public lands, but later applied to Romans who bought from the government the right to collect taxes in a given territory. These buyers, always knights (senators were excluded by their rank), became capitalists and formed powerful stock companies, whose members received a percentage on the capital invested. Provincial capitalists could not buy taxes, which were sold in Rome to the highest bidders, who to recoup themselves sublet their territory (at a great advance on the price paid the government) to the native (local) publicans, who in their turn had to make a profit on their purchase money, and being assessors of property as well as collectors of taxes, had abundant opportunities for oppressing the people, who hated them both for that reason and also because the tax itself was the mark of their subjection to foreigners."—J. R. Sterrett in *Stand. Bible Dict.*

4. Fishers of Men.—"Follow me, and I will make you fishers of men," said Jesus to fishermen who afterward became His apostles (Matt. 4:19). Mark's version is nearly the same (1:17), while that of Luke (5:10) reads: "From henceforth thou shalt catch men." The correct translation is, as commentators practically agree, "From henceforth thou shalt take men alive." This reading emphasizes the contrast given in the text— that between capturing fish to kill them and winning men to save them. Consider in this connection the Lord's prediction through Jeremiah (16:16), that in reaching scattered Israel, "Behold, I will send for many fishers, saith the Lord, and they shall fish them"; etc.

5. "Thy Sins Be Forgiven Thee."—The following commentary by Edersheim (*Life and Times of Jesus the Messiah,* vol. 1, pp. 505, 506) on the incident under consideration is instructive: "In this forgiveness of sins He presented His person and authority as divine, and He proved it such by the miracle of healing which immediately followed. Had the two been inverted, [i.e. had Christ first healed the man and afterward told him that his sins were forgiven] there would have been evidence, indeed, of His power, but not of His divine personality, nor of His having authority to forgive sins; and this, not the doing of miracles, was the object of His teaching and mission, of which the miracles were only secondary evidence. Thus the inward reasoning of the scribes, which was open and known to Him who readeth all thoughts, issued in quite the opposite of what they could have expected. Most unwarranted, indeed, was the feeling of contempt which we trace in their unspoken words, whether we read them: 'Why does this one thus speak blasphemies?' or, according to a more correct transcript of them: 'Why does this one speak thus? He blasphemeth!' Yet from their point of view they were right, for God alone can forgive sins; nor has that power ever been given or delegated to man. But was He a mere man, like even the most honored of God's servants? Man, indeed; but 'the Son of Man.' . . . It seemed easy to say: 'Thy sins have been forgiven.' But to Him, who had authority to do so on earth, it was neither more easy nor more difficult than to say: 'Rise, take up thy bed, and walk.' Yet this latter, assuredly, proved the former, and gave it in the sight of all men unquestioned reality. And so it was the thoughts of these scribes, which, as applied to Christ, were 'evil'—since they imputed to Him blasphemy—that gave occasion for offering real evidence of what they would have impugned and denied. In no other manner could the object alike of miracles and of this special miracle have been so attained as by the 'evil thoughts' of these scribes, when, miraculously brought to light, they spoke out the inmost possible doubt, and pointed to the highest of all questions concerning the Christ. And so it was once more the wrath of man which praised Him."

CHAPTER 15

THE LORD OF THE SABBATH

THE SABBATH DISTINCTIVELY SACRED TO ISRAEL

The observance of the Sabbath as a holy day was prominent among the Lord's requirements of His people, Israel, from a very early period in their history as a nation. Indeed, the keeping of the Sabbath as a day of surcease from ordinary toil was a national characteristic, by which the Israelites were distinguished from pagan peoples, and rightly so, for the holiness of the Sabbath was made a mark of the covenant between the chosen people and their God. The sanctity of the Sabbath had been prefigured in the account of the creation, antedating the placing of man upon the earth, as shown by the fact that God rested after the six periods or days of creative work, and blessed the seventh day and hallowed it.[a] In the course of Israel's exodus, the seventh day was set apart as one of rest, upon which it was not allowed to bake, seethe, or otherwise cook food. A double supply of manna had to be gathered on the sixth day, while on other days the laying-by of a surplus of this daily bread sent from heaven was expressly forbidden. The Lord observed the sacredness of the holy day by giving no manna thereon.[b]

The commandment to celebrate the Sabbath in strictness was made definite and explicit in the decalog, written by the hand of God amidst the awful glory of Sinai; and the injunction was kept before the people through frequent proclamation.[c] It was unlawful to kindle

---

[a] Gen. 2:3.

[b] Ex. 16:16–31.

[c] Ex. 20:8–11; 23:12; 31:13–15; 34:21; Lev. 19:3; 23:3; Deut. 5:12–14.

a fire on that day; and record is made of a man who was put to death for gathering sticks on the seventh day.[d] Under the administration of later prophets, the holiness of the Sabbath, the blessings promised to those who sanctified the day unto themselves, and the sin of Sabbath desecration were reiterated in words of inspired forcefulness.[e] Nehemiah admonished and reproved in the matter, and attributed the affliction of the nation to the forfeiture of Jehovah's favor through Sabbath violation.[f] By the mouth of Ezekiel the Lord affirmed that the institution of the Sabbath was a sign of the covenant between Himself and the people of Israel; and with stern severity He upbraided those who heeded not the day.[g] To the separate branch of the Israelitish nation that had been colonized on the western hemisphere, regard for the sanctity of the Sabbath was no less an imperative requirement.[h]

The observance demanded, however, was the very opposite of affliction and burden; the Sabbath was consecrated to rest and righteous enjoyment, and was to be a day of spiritual feasting before the Lord. It was not established as a day of abstinence; all might eat, but both mistress and maid were to be relieved from the work of preparing food; neither master nor man was to plow, dig or otherwise toil; and the weekly day of rest was as much the boon of the cattle as of their owners.

In addition to the weekly Sabbath, the Lord in mercy prescribed also a sabbatic year; in every seventh year the land was to rest, and thereby its fertility was enhanced.[i] After seven times seven years had passed, the fiftieth was to be celebrated throughout as a year of jubilee, during which the people should live on the accumulated increase of the preceding seasons of plenty, and rejoice in liberality by granting to one another redemption from mortgage and bond, forgiveness of debt, and general relief from burdens—all of which had to be done in mercy and justice.[j] The Sabbaths established by the

---

[d] Ex. 35:3; Num. 15:32–36.

[e] Isa. 56:2; 58:13; Jer. 17:21–24.

[f] Neh. 8:9–12; 13:15–22.

[g] Ezek. 20:12–24.

[h] Jar. 1:5; Mosiah 13:16-19; 18:23.

[i] Lev. 25:1–8; compare 26:34, 35.

[j] Lev. 25:10–55.

Lord, whether of days, of years, or of weeks of years, were to be times of refreshing, relief, blessing, bounty, and worship.

To the many who profess to regard the necessity of toil as a part of the curse evoked through Adam's fall, the Sabbath should appeal as a day of temporary reprieve, a time of exemption from labor, and as affording blessed opportunity of closer approach to the Presence from which mankind has been shut out through sin. And to those who take the higher view of life, and find in work both happiness and material blessing, the periodical relief brings refreshment and gives renewed zest for the days that follow.

But long before the advent of Christ, the original purpose of the Sabbath had come to be largely ignored in Israel; and the spirit of its observance had been smothered under the weight of rabbinical injunction and the formalism of restraint. In the time of the Lord's ministry, the technicalities prescribed as rules appended to the law were almost innumerable; and the burden thus forced upon the people had become well nigh unbearable. Among the many wholesome requirements of the Mosaic law, which the teachers and spiritual rulers of the Jews had made thus burdensome, that of Sabbath observance was especially prominent. The "hedge," which by unwarranted assumption they professedly set about the law,[k] was particularly thorny in the sections devoted to the Jewish Sabbath. Even trifling infractions of traditional rules were severely punished, and the capital penalty was held before the eyes of the people as a supreme threat for extreme desecration.[l]

THE HEALING OF A CRIPPLE ON THE SABBATH

In view of these conditions, we are not surprised to find our Lord confronted with charges of Sabbath violation relatively early in the course of His public work. An instance attended with many great developments is recorded by John,[m] whose narrative covers the incident of a very impressive miracle. Jesus was again in Jerusalem, at the time of one of the Jewish festivals.[n] There was a pool of water, called Bethesda, near the

[k] Page 61.

[l] Note 1, end of chapter.

[m] John 5.

[n] Note 2, end of chapter.

sheep market in the city. From the recorded description, we may understand this to have been a natural spring; possibly the water was rich in dissolved solids or gases, or both, making it such as we would call today a mineral spring; for we find that the water was reputed to possess curative virtues, and many afflicted folk came to bathe therein. The spring was of the pulsating variety; at intervals its waters rose with bubbling disturbance, and then receded to the normal level. Mineral springs of this kind are known today in many parts of the world. Some believed that the periodical upwelling of the Bethesda waters was the result of supernatural agency; and it was said that "whosoever then first after the troubling of the water stepped in was made whole of whatsoever disease he had." The Bethesda pool was wholly or partly enclosed; and five porches had been built for the shelter of those who waited at the spring for the intermittent bubbling up of the water.

On a certain Sabbath day, Jesus visited the pool and saw many afflicted folk thus waiting. Among them lay a man who for thirty-eight years had been grievously afflicted. From the man's statement of his helplessness we may infer that his malady was paralysis, or possibly an extreme form of rheumatism; whatever his affliction, it was so disabling as to give him little chance of getting into the pool at the critical time, for others less crippled crowded him away; and, according to the legends regarding the curative properties of the spring, only the first to enter the pool after the agitation of the water might expect to be healed.

Jesus recognized in the man a fit subject for blessing, and said to him: "Wilt thou be made whole?" The question was so simple as almost to appear superfluous. Of course the man wanted to be made well, and on the small chance of being able to reach the water at the right moment was patiently yet eagerly waiting. There was purpose, however, in these as in all other words of the Master. The man's attention was drawn to Him, fixed upon Him; the question aroused in the sufferer's heart renewed yearning for the health and strength of which he had been bereft since the days of his youth. His answer was pitiful, and revealed his almost hopeless state of mind; he thought only of the rumored virtues of Bethesda pool, as he said: "Sir, I have no man, when the water is troubled, to put me into the pool: but while I am coming, another steppeth down before me." Then spake Jesus: "Rise, take up thy bed, and walk." Immediately strength returned to the man, who for nearly four decades had been a helpless invalid; he obeyed the Master, and, taking up the little mattress or pallet on which he had rested, walked away.

He had not gone far, before the Jews, that is to say, some of the official class, for so the evangelist John employs the term, saw him carrying his bed; and it was the Sabbath day. To their peremptory reprimand he replied out of the gratitude and honest simplicity of his heart, that He who had healed him had told him to take up his bed and walk. The interest of the inquisitors was instantly turned from the man toward Him who had wrought the miracle; but the erstwhile cripple could not name his Benefactor, as he had lost sight of Jesus in the crowd before he had found opportunity for question or thanks. The man who had been healed went to the temple, possibly impelled by a desire to express in prayer his gratitude and joy. There Jesus found him, and said unto him: "Behold, thou art made whole: sin no more, lest a worse thing come unto thee."° The man had probably brought about his affliction through his own sinful habits. The Lord decided that he had suffered enough in body, and terminated his physical suffering with the subsequent admonition to sin no more.

The man went and told the rulers who it was that had healed him. This he may have done with a desire to honor and glorify the Giver of his boon; we are not justified in ascribing to him any unworthy purpose, though by his act he was instrumental in augmenting the persecution of his Lord. So intense was the hatred of the priestly faction that the rulers sought a means of putting Jesus to death, under the specious pretense of His being a Sabbath-breaker. We may well ask for what act they could possibly have hoped to convict Him, even under the strictest application of their rules. There was no proscription against speaking on the Sabbath; and Jesus had but spoken to heal. He had not carried the man's bed, nor had He attempted even the lightest physical labor. By their own interpretation of the law they had no case against Him.

° See another instance, pages 225–232.

OUR LORD'S REPLY TO THE ACCUSING JEWS

Nevertheless, the Jewish officials confronted Jesus with accusations. Whether the interview took place within the temple walls, on the open street, at the market place, or in the judgment hall, matters not. His reply to their charges is not confined to the question of Sabbath observance; it stands as the most comprehensive sermon in scripture on the vital subject of the relationship between the Eternal Father and His Son, Jesus Christ.

His first sentence added to the already intense anger of the Jews. Referring to the work He had done on the holy day, He said: "My Father worketh hitherto, and I work." This remark they construed to be a blasphemy.ᵖ "Therefore the Jews sought the more to kill him, because he not only had broken the Sabbath, but said also that God was his Father, making himself equal with God." To their spoken or unuttered protest, Jesus replied, that He, the Son, was not acting independently, and in fact could do nothing except what was in accordance with the Father's will, and what He had seen the Father do; that the Father so loved the Son as to show unto Him the Father's works.

Be it observed that Jesus in no way attempted to explain away their construction of His words; on the contrary He confirmed their deductions as correct. He did associate Himself with the Father, even in a closer and more exalted relationship than they had conceived. The authority given to Him by the Father was not limited to the healing of bodily infirmities; He had power even to raise the dead— "For as the Father raiseth up the dead, and quickeneth them; even so the Son quickeneth whom he will." Moreover, the judgment of men had been committed unto Him; and no one could honor the Father except by honoring the Son. Then followed this incisive declaration: "Verily, verily, I say unto you, He that heareth my word, and believeth on him that sent me, hath everlasting life, and shall not come into condemnation; but is passed from death unto life."

Christ's realm was not bounded by the grave; even the dead were wholly dependent upon Him for their salvation; and to the terrified ears of His dumbfounded accusers He proclaimed the solemn truth,

---

ᵖ For further justification of this act of healing on the Sabbath, see John 7:21–24.

that even then the hour was near in which the dead should hear the voice of the Son of God. Ponder His profound affirmation: "Verily, verily, I say unto you, The hour is coming, and now is, when the dead shall hear the voice of the Son of God: and they that hear shall live." The murderous rage of the Jews was rebuffed by the declaration that without His submission they could not take His life: "For as the Father hath life in himself; so hath he given to the Son to have life in himself." Another utterance was equally portentous: "And hath given him authority to execute judgment also, because he is the Son of man." He, the Son of the exalted and glorified Man of Holiness and now Himself a mortal Man,[q] was to be the judge of men.

No wonder they marveled; such doctrine they had never before heard nor read; it was not of the scribes nor of the rabbis, of neither the Pharisaic nor Saducean schools. But He reproved their amazement, saying: "Marvel not at this: for the hour is coming, in the which all that are in the graves shall hear his voice, And shall come forth; they that have done good, unto the resurrection of life; and they that have done evil, unto the resurrection of damnation."[r]

This enunciation of the resurrection, so plainly made that the most unlettered could understand, must have offended any Sadducees present, for they emphatically denied the actuality of the resurrection. The universality of a resurrection is here unquestionably affirmed; not only the righteous but even those who merit condemnation are to come forth from their graves in their bodies of flesh and bones.[s]

Then, renewing His solemn asseveration of the unity of His Father's will and His own, Christ discussed the matter of witnesses to His work. He admitted what was a recognized tenet of the time, that no man's unsupported witness of himself was sufficient; but, He added: "There is another that beareth witness of me; and I know that the witness which he witnesseth of me is true." He cites John the Baptist, and reminds them that they had sent a delegation to him, and that John had answered them by bearing testimony of the Messiah; and John had been a burning and a shining light, in whose

[q] Page 137
[r] Compare D&C 76:16, 17.
[s] Pages 22–25.

illuminating ministry many had temporarily rejoiced. The hostile Jews were left to see that the witness of John was valid under their strictest construction of the rules of evidence; "But," He continued, "I receive not testimony from man . . . But I have greater witness than that of John: for the works which the Father hath given me to finish, the same works that I do, bear witness of me, that the Father hath sent me. And the Father himself, which hath sent me, hath borne witness of me."

Then in terms of unqualified condemnation, He told them they were devoid of the Father's word, for they refused to accept Himself whom the Father had sent. With humiliating directness He admonished these learned men of the law, these interpreters of the prophets, these professional expounders of sacred writ, to betake themselves to reading and study. "Search the scriptures," said He, "for in them ye think ye have eternal life: and they are they which testify of me." Convictingly He continued—that they who admitted and taught that in the scriptures lay the way to eternal life, refused to come to Him, of whom those same scriptures testified, though by coming they might obtain eternal life. "I receive not honour from men," He added, "But I know you, that ye have not the love of God in you." They knew that they sought for honor among men, received honors from one another, were made rabbis and doctors, scribes and teachers, by the bestowal of titles and degrees—all of men; but they rejected Him who came in the name of One infinitely greater than all their schools or societies—He had come in the supreme name of the Father. The cause of their spiritual ignorance was pointed out—they relied upon the honors of men, and sought not the honor of real service in the cause of God.

He had spoken of the authority of judgment that had been committed to Himself; now He explained that they should not think He would accuse them before the Father; a lesser one than He would accuse, even Moses, another of His witnesses in whom they professed such trust—Moses whom they all were said to believe—and, driving home the full effect of His powerful arraignment, the Lord continued: "For had ye believed Moses, ye would have believed me: for he wrote of me. But if ye believe not his writings, how shall ye believe my words?" Such was the illuminating instruction combined with burning denunciation that these men had called forth by their futile attempt to convict Jesus on the charge of Sabbath desecration. This was but one of many evil machinations by which they so determinedly plotted, and strove to attach the stigma and invoke the penalty of Sabbath-breaking upon the very One who had ordained the Sabbath and was in truth and verity the one and only Lord thereof.

THE DISCIPLES CHARGED WITH SABBATH-BREAKING

We may profitably consider in this connection other instances of good work done by our Lord on Sabbath days; and this we may do without undue regard to the order of the events in time. We again find Jesus in Galilee, whether prior to or after His visit to Jerusalem at the time of the unidentified feast, on which occasion He wrought the miracle of healing at the Bethesda pool, matters not. On a certain Sabbath, He and the disciples walked through a field of grain,[t] and, being hungry, the disciples began to pluck some of the ripening ears; rubbing out the kernels between their hands, they ate. There was no element of theft in what they did, for the Mosaic law provided that in passing through another's vineyard or corn field one might pluck grapes or corn to relieve hunger; but it was forbidden to use a sickle in the field, or to carry away any of the grapes in a vessel.[u] The permission extended only to the relief of present need. When the disciples of Jesus availed themselves of this lawful privilege, there were Pharisees on the watch, and these came at once to the Master, saying: "Behold, thy disciples do that which is not lawful to do upon the sabbath day." The accusers doubtless had in mind the rabbinical dictum that rubbing out an ear of grain in the hands was a species of threshing; that blowing away the chaff was winnowing; and that it was unlawful to thresh or winnow on the Sabbath. Indeed, some learned rabbis had held it to be a sin to walk on grass during the Sabbath, inasmuch as the grass might be in seed, and the treading out of the seed would be as the threshing of grain.

Jesus defended the disciples by citing a precedent applicable to the case, and of much greater import. The instance was that of David,

[t] Matt. 12:1–8; compare Mark 2:23–28; Luke 6:1–5.
[u] Deut. 23:24, 25.

who with a small company of men had asked bread of the priest Ahimelech; for they were hungry and in haste. The priest had none but consecrated bread, the loaves of shewbread which were placed in the sanctuary at intervals, and which none but the priests were allowed to eat. In view of the condition of urgent need the priest had given the shewbread to the hungry men.[v] Jesus also reminded the critical Pharisees that the priests in the temple regularly did much work on the Sabbath in the slaughtering of sacrificial victims and in altar service generally, yet were held blameless because of the higher requirements of worship which rendered such labor necessary; and added with solemn emphasis: "But I say unto you, That in this place is one greater than the temple." He cited the word of God spoken through Hosea, "I will have mercy, and not sacrifice,"[w] and reproved at once their ignorance and their unrighteous zeal by telling them that had they known what that scripture meant they would not have condemned the guiltless. Be it remembered, "The sabbath was made for man, and not man for the sabbath."[x]

His reproof was followed by the affirmation of His personal supremacy: "*For the Son of man is Lord even of the sabbath day.*" What can we gather from the declaration but that He, Jesus, there present in the flesh, was the Being through whom the Sabbath had been ordained, that it was He who had given and written in stone the decalog, including "Remember the sabbath day, to keep it holy," and, "the seventh day is the sabbath of the Lord thy God"?

A PHARISAICAL PLOT

Again on a Sabbath, Jesus went into a synagog, and saw in the congregation a man whose right hand was withered.[y] There were Pharisees present, and they watched to see whether Jesus would heal the man, their purpose being to accuse Him if He did so. The Pharisees asked: "Is it lawful to heal on the sabbath days?" Our Lord countered their poorly veiled purpose by asking: "Is it lawful to do good on the sabbath days?" and extended the question, "or to do evil? to save life, or

[v] Note 3, end of chapter.

[w] Hos. 6:6; compare Micah 6:6–9.

[x] Mark 2:27. Note 4, end of chapter.

[y] Matt. 12:10–13; Mark 3:1–6; Luke 6:6–8.

to kill?" They held their peace, for the question was double-edged. To reply in the affirmative would have been to justify the work of healing; a negative answer would have stultified them. He put another question: "What man shall there be among you, that shall have one sheep, and if it fall into a pit on the sabbath day, will he not lay hold on it, and lift it out? How much then is a man better than a sheep?"

As the Pharisees could not or would not reply, He summed up the whole matter thus: "Wherefore it is lawful to do well on the sabbath days." He called upon the man with the withered hand to stand forth before the congregation. Grief and anger were mingled in His penetrating and sweeping glance; but, turning with compassion toward the afflicted one, He commanded him to stretch forth his hand; the man obeyed, and lo! the hand "was restored whole, like as the other."

The discomfited Pharisees were furious, "filled with madness" Luke says; and they went out to plot anew against the Lord. So bitter was their hatred that they allied themselves with the Herodians, a political party generally unpopular among the Jews. The rulers of the people were ready to enter into any intrigue or alliance to accomplish their avowed purpose of bringing about the death of the Lord Jesus. Aware of the wicked determination against Him, Jesus withdrew Himself from the locality. Other accusations of Sabbath-breaking, brought against Christ by Jewish casuists, will be considered later.[z]

NOTES TO CHAPTER 15

1. Rabbinical Requirements Concerning Sabbath Observance.—"No feature of the Jewish system was so marked as their extraordinary strictness in the outward observance of the Sabbath, as a day of entire rest. The Scribes had elaborated from the command of Moses, a vast array of prohibitions and injunctions, covering the whole of social, individual, and public life, and carried it to the extreme of ridiculous caricature. Lengthened rules were prescribed as to the kinds of knots which might legally be tied on the Sabbath. The camel driver's knot and the sailor's were unlawful, and it was equally illegal to tie or to loose them. A knot which could be untied with one hand might be undone. A shoe or sandal, a woman's cup, a wine or oilskin, or a flesh-pot might be tied. A pitcher at a spring might be tied to the body-sash, but not with a cord. . . . To kindle or extinguish a fire on the Sabbath was a great desecration of the day, nor was even sickness allowed to violate Rabbinical

[z] For instances, see Luke 13:14–16; 14:3–6; John 9:14–16.

rules. It was forbidden to give an emetic on the Sabbath—to set a broken bone, or put back a dislocated joint, though some Rabbis, more liberal, held that whatever endangered life made the Sabbath law void, 'for the commands were given to Israel only that they might live by them.' One who was buried under ruins on the Sabbath, might be dug for and taken out, if alive, but, if dead, he was to be left where he was, till the Sabbath was over."—Geikie, *Life and Words of Christ,* chap. 38.

2. The Unnamed Feast.—There has been no little discussion as to the particular festival referred to in John 5:1, at the time of which Jesus healed the cripple at the pool of Bethesda. Many writers hold that it was the Passover, others that it was the feast of Purim, or some other Jewish celebration. The only semblance of importance attaching to the question is the possibility of learning from the fact, if it could be proved, something of the chronological order of events at this period of our Lord's life. We are not told which feast this was, neither the year nor the time of the year when it occurred. The miracle wrought on the occasion, and the doctrinal discourse delivered as a result thereof, depend for their value in no degree on the determination of date.

3. Shewbread.—The name means "bread of the presence," signifying that it was placed in the presence of Jehovah. The bread so sanctified consisted of twelve loaves, made without leaven. They were to be deposited in the Holy Place in two columns of six loaves each. Zenos, in *Stand. Bible Dict.* writes: "They were allowed to remain there for a whole week, at the end of which period they were removed, and eaten by the priest upon holy ground, i.e. within the precincts of the sanctuary. For other persons than priests to eat of the loaves of the shewbread was regarded as sacrilegious, for they were "holy." See Ex. 25:30; Lev. 24:5–9; 1 Sam. 21:1–6.

4. The Sabbath Was Made for Man and Not Man for the Sabbath.—Edersheim (vol. 1, pp. 57, 58) says: "When on his flight from Saul, David had, 'when an hungered,' eaten of the shewbread and given it to his followers, although, by the letter of the Levitical law, it was only to be eaten by the priests, Jewish tradition vindicated his conduct on the plea that 'danger to life superseded the Sabbath law,' and hence, all laws connected with it. . . . In truth, the reason why David was blameless in eating the shewbread was the same as that which made the Sabbath labor of the priests lawful. The Sabbath law was not one merely of rest, but of rest for worship. The service of the Lord was the object in view. The priests worked on the Sabbath, because this service was the object of the Sabbath; and David was allowed to eat of the shewbread, not [solely] because there was danger to life from starvation, but because he pleaded that he was on the service of the Lord, and needed this provision. The disciples, when following the Lord, were similarly on the service of the Lord; ministering to Him was more than ministering in the temple, for He was greater than the temple. If the Pharisees had believed this, they would not have questioned their conduct, nor in so doing have themselves infringed that higher law which enjoined mercy, not sacrifice."

CHAPTER 16

The Chosen Twelve

THEIR CALL AND ORDINATION[a]

The night preceding the morn on which the Twelve Apostles were called and ordained was spent by the Lord in solitary seclusion; He had "continued all night in prayer to God."[b] Then, when day had come, and while many people were gathering to hear more of the new and wonderful gospel of the kingdom, He called to come closer some who had theretofore been devotedly associated together as His disciples or followers, and from among them He chose twelve, whom he ordained and named apostles.[c] Prior to that time none of these had been distinguished by any special delegation of authority or appointment; they had been numbered with the disciples in general, though, as we have seen, seven had received a preliminary call, and had promptly responded thereto by abandoning wholly or in part their business affairs, and had followed the Master. These were Andrew, John, Simon Peter, Philip, Nathanael, James, and Levi Matthew. Prior to this eventful day, however, none of the Twelve had been ordained or set apart to their sacred office.

The three Gospel-writers who make record of the organization of the Twelve place Simon Peter first and Judas Iscariot last in the category; they agree also in the relative position of some but not of all the others. Following the order given by Mark, and this may be the most convenient since he names as the first three those who later became

[a] Matt. 10:1–4; Mark 3:13–19; Luke 6:12–16.

[b] Luke 6:12.

[c] Luke 3:13; compare John 15:16; see also Acts 1:22.

most prominent, we have the following list: Simon Peter, James (son of Zebedee), John (brother of the last-named), Andrew (brother of Simon Peter), Philip, Bartholomew (or Nathanael), Matthew, Thomas, James (son of Alpheus), Judas (also known as Lebbeus or Thaddeus), Simon (distinguished by his surname Zelotes, also known as the Canaanite), and Judas Iscariot.

THE TWELVE CONSIDERED INDIVIDUALLY

Simon, named as the first apostle, is more commonly known as *Peter*—the appellation given him by the Lord on the occasion of their first meeting, and afterward confirmed.[d] He was the son of Jona, or Jonas, and by vocation was a fisherman. He and his brother Andrew were partners with James and John, the sons of Zebedee; and apparently the fishing business was a prosperous one with them, for they owned their boats and gave employment to other men.[e] Peter's early home had been at the little fishery town of Bethsaida[f] on the west shore of the Sea of Galilee; but about the time of his first association with Jesus, or soon thereafter, he, with others of his family, removed to Capernaum, where he appears to have become an independent householder.[g] Simon Peter was a married man before his call to the ministry. He was well to do in a material way; and when he once spoke of having left all to follow Jesus, the Lord did not deny that Peter's sacrifice of temporal possessions was as great as had been implied. We are not justified in regarding him as unlettered or ignorant. True, both he and John were designated by the council of rulers as "unlearned and ignorant men,"[h] but this was spoken of them as indicating their lack of training in the schools of the rabbis; and it is worthy of note, that the members of that same council were amazed at the wisdom and power manifested by the two apostles, whom they professed to despise.

In temperament Peter was impulsive and stern, and, until trained by severe experience, was lacking in firmness. He had many human

[d] John 1:42; compare Matt. 16:18.

[e] Mark 1:16–20; Luke 5:10.

[f] John 1:44; 12:21.

[g] Matt. 8:14; Mark 1:29; Luke 4:38.

[h] Acts 4:13.

weaknesses, yet in spite of them all he eventually overcame the temptations of Satan and the frailties of the flesh, and served his Lord as the appointed and acknowledged leader of the Twelve. Of the time and place of his death the scriptures do not speak; but the manner thereof was prefigured by the resurrected Lord,[i] and in part was foreseen by Peter himself.[j] Tradition, originating in the writings of the early Christian historians other than the apostles, states that Peter met death by crucifixion as a martyr during the persecution incident to the reign of Nero, probably between A.D. 64 and 68. Origen states that the apostle was crucified with his head downward. Peter, with James and John, his associates in the presidency of the Twelve, has ministered as a resurrected being in the present dispensation, in restoring to earth the Melchizedek Priesthood, including the Holy Apostleship, which had been taken away because of the apostasy and unbelief of men.[k]

James and *John*, brothers by birth, partners in business as fishermen, brethren in the ministry, were associated together and with Peter in the apostolic calling. The Lord bestowed upon the pair a title in common—Boanerges, or Sons of Thunder[l]—possibly with reference to the zeal they developed in His service, which, indeed, at times had to be restrained, as when they would have had fire called from heaven to destroy the Samaritan villagers who had refused hospitality to the Master.[m] They and their mother aspired to the highest honors of the kingdom, and asked that the two be given places, one on the right the other on the left of Christ in His glory. This ambition was gently reproved by the Lord, and the request gave offense to the other apostles.[n] With Peter these two brothers were witnesses of many of the most important incidents in the life of Jesus; thus, the three were the only apostles admitted to witness the raising of the daughter of Jairus from death to life;[o] they were the only members of

[i] John 21:18, 19.

[j] 2 Pet. 1:14.

[k] D&C 27:12.

[l] Mark 3:17.

[m] Luke 9:54. See also Mark 9:38, for instance of John's impulsive zeal.

[n] Mark 10:35–41; compare Matt. 20:20–24.

[o] Mark 5:37; Luke 8:51.

the Twelve present at the transfiguration of Christ;[p] they were nearest the Lord during the period of His mortal agony in Gethsemane;[q] and, as heretofore told, they have ministered in these modern days in the restoration of the Holy Apostleship with all its ancient authority and power of blessing.[r] James is commonly designated in theological literature as James I, to distinguish him from the other apostle bearing the same name. James, the son of Zebedee, was the first of the apostles to meet a martyr's violent death; he was beheaded by order of the king, Herod Agrippa.[s] John had been a disciple of the Baptist, and had demonstrated his confidence in the latter's testimony of Jesus by promptly turning from the forerunner and following the Lord.[t] He became a devoted servant, and repeatedly refers to himself as the disciple "whom Jesus loved."[u] At the last supper John sat next to Jesus leaning his head upon the Master's breast;[v] and next day as he stood beneath the cross he received from the dying Christ the special charge to care for the Lord's mother;[w] and to this he promptly responded by conducting the weeping Mary to his own house. He was the first to recognize the risen Lord on the shores of Galilee, and received from His immortal lips encouragement of his hope that his life would be continued in the body, in order that he might minister among men until the Christ shall come in His glory.[x] The realization of that hope has been attested by revelation in modern days.[y]

Andrew, son of Jona and brother of Simon Peter, is mentioned less frequently than the three already considered. He had been one of the Baptist's followers, and with John, the son of Zebedee, left the Baptist

p Matt. 17:1–2; Luke 9:28–29.

q Matt. 26:36, 37.

r D&C 27:12.

s Acts 12:1, 2.

t John 1:35–40.

u John 13:23; 19:26; 20:2.

v John 13:23, 25.

w John 19:25–27.

x John 21:7, 21–23.

y D&C 7; compare 3 Ne. 28:1–12.

to learn from Jesus; and having learned he went in search of Peter, solemnly averred to him that the Messiah had been found, and brought his brother to the Savior's feet.[z] He shared with Peter in the honor of the call of the Lord on the sea shore, and in the promise "I will make you fishers of men."[aa] In one instance we read of Andrew as present with Peter, James and John, in a private interview with the Lord;[bb] and he is mentioned in connection with the miraculous feeding of the five thousand,[cc] and as associated with Philip in arranging an interview between certain inquiring Greeks and Jesus.[dd] He is named with others in connection with our Lord's ascension.[ee] Tradition is rife with stories about this man, but of the extent of his ministry, the duration of his life, and the circumstances of his death, we have no authentic record.

Philip may have been the first to receive the authoritative call "Follow me" from the lips of Jesus, and we find him immediately testifying that Jesus was the long expected Messiah. His home was in Bethsaida, the town of Peter, Andrew, James, and John. It is said that Jesus found him,[ff] whereas the others concerned in that early affiliation seem to have come of themselves severally to Christ. We find brief mention of him at the time the five thousand were fed, on which occasion Jesus asked him "Whence shall we buy bread, that these may eat?" This was done to test and prove him, for Jesus knew what would be done. Philip's reply was based on a statement of the small amount of money at hand, and showed no expectation of miraculous intervention.[gg] It was to him the Greeks applied when they sought a meeting with Jesus as noted in connection with Andrew. He was mildly reproved for his misunderstanding when he asked Jesus to show to him and the others the Father—"Have I been

[z] John 1:35–40.
[aa] Matt. 4:18, 19.
[bb] Mark 13:3.
[cc] John 6:8.
[dd] John 12:20–22.
[ee] Acts 1:13.
[ff] John 1:43–45.
[gg] John 6:5–7.

so long time with you, and yet hast thou not known me, Philip?"[hh] Aside from incidental mention of his presence as one of the Eleven after the ascension, the scriptures tell us nothing more concerning him.

Bartholomew is mentioned in scripture by this name only in connection with his ordination to the apostleship, and as one of the Eleven after the ascension. The name means son of Tolmai. It is practically certain, however, that he is the man called Nathanael in John's Gospel—the one whom Christ designated as "an Israelite indeed, in whom is no guile."[ii] He is named again as among those who went fishing with Peter after the Resurrection of Christ.[jj] His home was in Cana of Galilee. The reasons for assuming that Bartholomew and Nathanael are the same person are these: Bartholomew is named in each of the three synoptic Gospels as an apostle, but Nathanael is not mentioned. Nathanael is named twice in John's Gospel, and Bartholomew not at all; Bartholomew and Philip, or Nathanael and Philip, are mentioned together.

Matthew, or *Levi,* son of Alpheus, was one of the seven who received a call to follow Christ before the ordination of the Twelve. He it was who gave a feast, for attending which Jesus and the disciples were severely criticized by the Pharisees,[kk] on the charge that it was unseemly for Him to eat with publicans and sinners, Matthew was a publican; he so designates himself in the Gospel he wrote;[ll] but the other evangelists omit the mention when including him with the Twelve. His Hebrew name, Levi, is understood by many as an indication of priestly lineage. Of his ministry we have no detailed account; though he is the author of the first Gospel, he refrains from special mention of himself except in connection with his call and ordination. He is spoken of by other than scriptural writers as one of the most active of the apostles after Christ's death, and as operating in lands far from Palestine.

---

hh John 14:8, 9.

ii John 1:45–51.

jj John 21:2, 3.

kk Pages 186–87.

ll Matt. 10:3.

Thomas, also known as Didymus, the Greek equivalent of his Hebrew name, meaning "a twin," is mentioned as a witness of the raising of Lazarus. His devotion to Jesus is shown by his desire to accompany the Lord to Bethany, though persecution in that region was almost certain. To his fellow apostles Thomas said: "Let us also go, that we may die with him."[mm] Even as late in his experience as the night before the Crucifixion, Thomas had failed to comprehend the impending necessity of the Savior's sacrifice; and when Jesus referred to going away and leaving the others to follow, Thomas asked how they could know the way. For his lack of understanding he stood reproved.[nn] He was absent when the resurrected Christ appeared to the assembled disciples in the evening of the day of His rising; and on being informed by the others that they had seen the Lord, he forcefully expressed his doubt, and declared he would not believe unless he could see and feel for himself the wounds in the crucified body. Eight days later the Lord visited the apostles again, when, as on the earlier occasion, they were within closed doors; and to Thomas the Lord said: "Reach hither thy finger, and behold my hands; and reach hither thy hand, and thrust it into my side." Then Thomas, no longer doubting but with love and reverence filling his soul, exclaimed "My Lord and my God." The Lord said unto him: "Thomas, because thou hast seen me, thou hast believed: blessed are they that have not seen, and yet have believed."[oo] Of Thomas no further record appears in the New Testament aside from that of his presence with his fellows after the ascension.

James, son of Alpheus, is mentioned in the Gospels only in the matter of his ordination to the apostleship; and but once elsewhere in the New Testament by the appellation "Son of Alpheus."[pp] In writings other than scriptural he is sometimes designated as James II to avoid confusing him with James the son of Zebedee. There is acknowledged uncertainty concerning the identity of James the son of Alpheus as the James or one of the Jameses referred to in the Acts and the Epistles;[qq]

[mm] John 11:16.

[nn] John 14:1–7.

[oo] John 20:24–29.

[pp] Acts 1:13. Note 3, end of chapter.

[qq] Acts 12:17; 15:13–21; 21:18; 1 Cor. 15:7; Gal. 1:19; 2:9, 12; and the Epistle of James.

and a plenitude of controversial literature on the subject is extant.[rr]

Judas is called *Lebbeus Thaddeus* by Matthew, *Thaddeus* by Mark, and *Judas the brother of James* by Luke.[ss] The only other specific reference to this apostle is made by John, and is incident to the last long interview between Jesus and the apostles, when this Judas, "not Iscariot," asked how or why Jesus would manifest Himself to His chosen servants and not to the world at large. The man's question shows that the really distinguishing character of the apostleship was not fully comprehended by him at that time.

Simon Zelotes, so designated in Acts,[tt] and as *Simon called Zelotes* in Luke's Gospel, is distinguished by both Matthew and Mark as the *Canaanite*. The last designation has no reference to the town of Cana, nor to the land of Canaan, neither is it in any sense of geographical signification; it is the Syro-Chaldaic equivalent of the Greek word which is rendered in the English translation "Zelotes." The two names, therefore, have the same fundamental meaning, and each refers to the Zealots, a Jewish sect or faction, known for its zeal in maintaining the Mosaic ritual. Doubtless Simon had learned moderation and toleration from the teachings of Christ; otherwise he would scarcely have been suited to the apostolic ministry. His zealous earnestness, properly directed, may have developed into a most serviceable trait of character. This apostle is nowhere in the scriptures named apart from his colleagues.

[rr] Concerning the James's mentioned in the New Testament, the opinion of Bible scholars is divided, the question being as to whether two or three individuals are indicated. Those who hold that there were three men of this name distinguish them as follows: (1) James the son of Zebedee and brother of John the apostle; all scriptural references to him are explicit; (2) James the son of Alpheus; and (3) James the brother of the Lord (Matt. 13:55; Mark 6:3; Gal. 1:19). If we accept this classification, the references given in footnote qq on the previous page apply to James the Lord's brother. Both the Oxford and Bagster Bible "Helps" treat James the son of Alpheus and James the Lord's brother as one person, the expression "son of" being understood in a general sense only. The Bagster designation is: "James II, apostle, son of Alpheus, brother or cousin to Jesus." (See Note 3, end of chapter.) The Nave "Student's Bible" states (pate 1327) that the question as to whether James the Lord's brother "is identical with James the son of Alpheus is one of the most difficult questions in the biographical history of the Gospels." Fausset (in his *Cyclopedia Critical and Expository*) supports the contention that but one James is meant; and other acknowledged authorities treat the two as one. For detailed consideration of the subject the reader is referred to special works.

[ss] Note 1, end of chapter.

[tt] Acts 1:13; compare Luke 6:15.

Judas Iscariot is the only Judean named among the Twelve; all the others were Galileans. He is generally understood to have been a resident of Kerioth, a small town in the southerly part of Judea, but a few miles west from the Dead Sea, though for this tradition, as also for the signification of his surname, we lack direct authority. So too we are uninformed as to his lineage, except that his father's name was Simon.ᵘᵘ He served as treasurer or agent of the apostolic company, receiving and disbursing such offerings as were made by disciples and friends, and purchasing supplies as required.ᵛᵛ That he was unprincipled and dishonest in the discharge of this trust is attested by John. His avaricious and complaining nature revealed itself in his murmuring against what he called a waste of costly spikenard, in the anointing of the Lord by Mary but a few days before the Crucifixion; he hypocritically suggested that the precious ointment could have been sold and the proceeds given to the poor.ʷʷ The crowning deed of perfidy in the career of Iscariot was his deliberate betrayal of his Master to death; and this the infamous creature did for a price, and accomplished the foul deed with a kiss. He brought his guilty life to a close by a revolting suicide and his spirit went to the awful fate reserved for the sons of perdition.ˣˣ

GENERAL CHARACTERISTICS OF THE TWELVE

A survey of the general characteristics and qualifications of this body of twelve men reveals some interesting facts. Before their selection as apostles they had all become close disciples of the Lord; they believed in Him; several of them, possibly all, had openly confessed that He was the Son of God; and yet it is doubtful that any one of them fully understood the real significance of the Savior's work. It is evident by the later remarks of many of them, and by the instructions and rebuke they called forth from the Master, that the common Jewish expectation of a Messiah who would reign in splendor as an earthly sovereign after He had subdued all other nations, had a place even in

uu John 6:71; 12:4; 13:26.

vv John 12:6; 13:29.

ww John 12:1–7; compare Matt. 26:6–13; Mark 14:3–9.

xx Matt. 27:5; compare Acts 1:18; see also John 17:12; D&C 76:31–48; 132:27.

the hearts of these chosen ones. After long experience, Peter's concern was: "Behold, we have forsaken all, and followed thee; what shall we have therefore?"*yy* They were as children to be trained and taught; but they were mostly willing pupils, receptive of soul, and imbued with a sincere eagerness to serve. To Jesus they were His little ones, His children, His servants, and His friends, as they merited.*zz* They were all of the common people, not rabbis, scholars, nor priestly officials. Their inner natures, not their outward accomplishments, were taken into prime account in the Lord's choosing. The Master chose them; they did not choose themselves; by Him they were ordained,*aaa* and they could in consequence rely the more implicitly upon His guidance and support. To them much was given; much of them was required. With the one black exception they all became shining lights in the kingdom of God, and vindicated the Master's selection. He recognized in each the characteristics of fitness developed in the primeval world of spirits.*bbb*

DISCIPLES AND APOSTLES

Discipleship is general; any follower of a man or devotee to a principle may be called a disciple, The Holy Apostleship is an office and calling belonging to the Higher or Melchizedek Priesthood, at once exalted and specific, comprising as a distinguishing function that of personal and special witness to the divinity of Jesus Christ as the one and only Redeemer and Savior of mankind.*ccc* The apostleship is an individual bestowal, and as such is conferred only through ordination. That the Twelve did constitute a council or "quorum" having authority in the Church established by Jesus Christ is shown by their ministrations after the Lord's Resurrection and ascension. Their first official act was that of filling the vacancy in their organization occasioned by the apostasy and death of Judas Iscariot; and in connection with this procedure, the presiding apostle, Peter, set forth the essential qualifications of the one who would be chosen and ordained, which

yy Matt. 19:27.

zz Matt. 10:42; John 21:5; 13: 16, compare verse 13; 15:14, 15.

aaa John 15:16.

bbb Pages 9 and 17

ccc D&C 18:27–33; 20:38–44; 107:1–9, 23, 24, 39.

comprised such knowledge of Jesus, His life, death, and Resurrection, as would make the new apostle one with the Eleven as special witnesses of the Lord's work.[ddd]

The ordination of the Twelve Apostles marked the inauguration of an advanced epoch in the earthly ministry of Jesus, an epoch characterized by the organization of a body of men invested with the authority of the Holy Priesthood, upon whom would rest, more particularly after the Lord's departure, the duty and responsibility of continuing the work He had begun, and of building up the Church established by Him.

The word "apostle" is an Anglicized form derived from the Greek *apostolos*, meaning literally "one who is sent," and connoting an envoy or official messenger, who speaks and acts by the authority of one superior to himself. In this sense Paul afterward applied the title to Christ as one specially sent and commissioned of the Father.[eee]

The Lord's purpose in choosing and ordaining the Twelve is thus enunciated by Mark: "And he ordained twelve, that they should be with him, and that he might send them forth to preach, and to have power to heal sicknesses, and to cast out devils."[fff] For a season following their ordination the apostles remained with Jesus, being specially trained and instructed by Him for the work then before them; afterward they were specifically charged and sent forth to preach and to administer in the authority of their priesthood, as shall be hereafter considered.

NOTES TO CHAPTER 16

1. Judas Lebbeus Thaddeus.—This Judas (not Iscariot) is designated in the authorized version of Luke 6:16, and Acts 1:13, as "*the brother* of James." That the words "the brother" are an addition to the original text is indicated by italics. The revised version of these passages reads in each instance "the son of James," with italics of corresponding significance. The original reads "Judas of James." We are uninformed as to which James is referred to, and as to whether the Judas here mentioned was the son, the brother, or some other relative of the unidentified James.

[ddd] Acts 1:15–26.

[eee] Heb. 3:1; see Note 2, end of chapter.

[fff] Mark 3:14, 15.

2. The Meaning of "Apostle."—"The title 'Apostle' is likewise one of special significance and sanctity; it has been given of God, and belongs only to those who have been called and ordained as 'special witnesses of the name of Christ in all the world, thus differing from other officers in the Church in the duties of their calling' (D&C 107:23). By derivation the word 'apostle' is the English equivalent of the Greek *apostolos,* indicating a messenger, an ambassador, or literally 'one who is sent.' It signifies that he who is rightly so called, speaks and acts not of himself, but as the representative of a higher power whence his commission issued; and in this sense the title is that of a servant, rather than that of a superior. Even the Christ, however, is called an Apostle with reference to His ministry in the flesh (Hebrews 3:1), and this appellation is justified by His repeated declaration that He came to earth to do not His own will but that of the Father by whom *He was sent.*

"Though an apostle is thus seen to be essentially an envoy, or ambassador, his authority is great, as is also the responsibility associated therewith, for he speaks in the name of a power greater than his own—the name of Him whose special witness he is. When one of the Twelve is sent to minister in any stake, mission or other division of the Church, or to labor in regions where no Church organization has been effected, he acts as the representative of the First Presidency, and has the right to use his authority in doing whatever is requisite for the furtherance of the work of God. His duty is to preach the Gospel, administer the ordinances thereof, and set in order the affairs of the Church, wherever he is sent. So great is the sanctity of this special calling, that the title 'Apostle' should not be used lightly as the common or ordinary form of address applied to living men called to this office. The quorum or council of the Twelve Apostles as existent in the Church today may better be spoken of as the 'Quorum of the Twelve,' the 'Council of the Twelve,' or simply as the 'Twelve,' than as the 'Twelve Apostles,' except as particular occasion may warrant the use of the more sacred term. It is advised that the title 'Apostle' be not applied as a prefix to the name of any member of the Council of the Twelve; but that such a one be addressed or spoken of as 'Brother _____,' or 'Elder _____,' and when necessary or desirable, as in announcing his presence in a public assembly, an explanatory clause may be added, thus, 'Elder _____, one of the Council of the Twelve.'"—From "The Honor and Dignity of Priesthood," by the author, *Improvement Era,* vol. 17, no. 5, pp. 409–410.

3. "Of Alpheus," or "Son of Alpheus."—In all Bible passages specifying "James *son* of Alpheus" (Matt. 10:3; Mark 3:18; Luke 6:15; Acts 1:13) the word *son* has been supplied by the translators, and therefore properly appears in *italics.* The phrase in the Greek reads "James of Alpheus." This fact must not be given undue weight in support of the thought that the James spoken of was not the son of Alpheus; for the word *son* has been similarly added in the translation of other passages, in all of which *italics* are used to indicate the words supplied, e.g. "James *the son* of Zebedee" (Matt. 10:2; see Mark 3:17). Read in connection Note 1 on the previous page.

CHAPTER 17

THE SERMON ON THE MOUNT

At some time very near that of the ordination of the Twelve, Jesus delivered a remarkable discourse, which, in reference to the place where it was given, has come to be known as the Sermon on the Mount. Matthew presents an extended account occupying three chapters of the first Gospel; Luke gives a briefer synopsis.[a] Circumstantial variations appearing in the two records are of minor importance;[b] it is the sermon itself to which we may profitably devote attention. Luke introduces in different parts of his writings many of the precious precepts given as parts of the sermon recorded as a continuous discourse in the Gospel written by Matthew. In our present study we shall be guided principally by Matthew's account. Some portions of this comprehensive address were expressly directed to the disciples, who had been or would be called to the apostleship and in consequence be required to renounce all their worldly interests for the labors of the ministry; other parts were and are of general application. Jesus had ascended the mountain side, probably to escape the crowds that thronged Him in or near the towns.[c] The disciples gathered about Him, and there He sat and taught them.[d]

---

[a] Matt. 5, 6, 7; Luke 6:20–49. See also the version of the Sermon as delivered by Jesus Christ after His Resurrection, to the Nephites on the western continent; 3 Ne. 12, 13, 14. See also chapter 39 herein.

[b] Note 1, end of chapter.

[c] Matt. 4:23–25; read these verses in connection with 5:1; see also Luke 6:17–19.

[d] Note 1, end of chapter.

THE BEATITUDES [e]

The opening sentences are rich in blessing, and the first section of the discourse is devoted to an explanation of what constitutes genuine blessedness; the lesson, moreover, was made simple and unambiguous by specific application, each of the blessed being assured of recompense and reward in the enjoyment of conditions directly opposite to those under which he had suffered. The blessings particularized by the Lord on this occasion have been designated in literature of later time as the Beatitudes. The poor in spirit are to be made rich as rightful heirs to the kingdom of heaven; the mourner shall be comforted for he shall see the divine purpose in his grief, and shall again associate with the beloved ones of whom he has been bereft; the meek, who suffer spoliation rather than jeopardize their souls in contention, shall inherit the earth; those that hunger and thirst for the truth shall be fed in rich abundance; they that show mercy shall be judged mercifully; the pure in heart shall be admitted to the very presence of God; the peacemakers, who try to save themselves and their fellows from strife, shall be numbered among the children of God; they that suffer persecution for the sake of righteousness shall inherit the riches of the eternal kingdom. To the disciples the Lord spake directly, saying: "Blessed are ye, when men shall revile you, and persecute you, and shall say all manner of evil against you falsely, for my sake. Rejoice, and be exceeding glad: for great is your reward in heaven: for so persecuted they the prophets which were before you."[f]

It is evident that the specified blessings and the happiness comprised therein are to be realized in their fulness only beyond the grave; though the joy that comes from the consciousness of right living brings, even in this world, a rich return. An important element in this splendid elucidation of the truly blessed state is the implied distinction between pleasure and happiness.[g] Mere pleasure is at best but fleeting; happiness is abiding, for in the recollection thereof is joy renewed. Supreme happiness is not an earthly attainment; the

[e] Matt. 5:3–12; compare Luke 6:20–26; and 3 Ne. 12:1–12.

[f] Matt. 5:11, 12; compare Luke 6:26; 3 Ne. 12:11, 12.

[g] Note 2, end of chapter.

promised "fulness of joy" lies beyond death and the resurrection.[h] While man exists in this mortal state he needs some of the things of the world; he must have food and clothing and provision for shelter; and besides these bare necessities he may righteously desire the facilities of education, the incidentals of advancing civilization, and the things that are conducive to refinement and culture; yet all of these are but aids to achievement, not the end to attain which man was made mortal.

The Beatitudes are directed to the duties of mortal life as a preparation for a greater existence yet future. In the kingdom of heaven, twice named in this part of the Lord's discourse, are true riches and unfailing happiness to be found. The kingdom of heaven was the all-comprising text of this wonderful sermon; the means of reaching the kingdom and the glories of eternal citizenship therein are the main divisions of the treatise.

DIGNITY AND RESPONSIBILITY IN THE MINISTRY[i]

The Master next proceeded to instruct with particular directness those upon whom would devolve the responsibility of the ministry as His commissioned representatives. "Ye are the salt of the earth," said He. Salt is the great preservative; as such it has had practical use since very ancient times. Salt was prescribed as an essential addition to every meat offering under the Mosaic law.[j] Long before the time of Christ, the use of salt had been accorded a symbolism of fidelity, hospitality, and covenant.[k] To be of use salt must be pure; to be of any saving virtue as salt, it must be salt indeed, and not the product of chemical alteration or of earthy admixture, whereby its saltiness or "savor" would be lost;[l] and, as worthless stuff, it would be fit only to be thrown away. Against such change of faith, against such admixture with the sophistries, so-called philosophies, and heresies of the times, the disciples were especially warned. Then, changing the figure, Jesus likened them to the

---

[h] D&C 93:33.

[i] Matt. 5:13–20; compare Luke 14:34–35; 3 Ne. 12:13–20.

[j] Lev. 2:13; compare Ezra 6:9; Ezek. 43:24.

[k] Note the expression "covenant of salt," indicating the covenant between Jehovah and Israel, Lev. 2:13; Num. 8:19; compare 2 Chr. 13:5.

[l] Note 3, end of chapter.

light of the world, and enjoined upon them the duty of keeping their light before the people, as prominently as stands a city built upon a hill, to be seen from all directions, a city that cannot be hid. Of what service would a lighted candle be if hidden under a tub or a box? "Let your light so shine before men," said He, "that they may see your good works, and glorify your Father which is in heaven."

That they should make no error as to the relationship of the ancient law and the gospel of the kingdom which He was elucidating, Jesus assured them that He had not come to destroy the law nor to nullify the teachings and predictions of the prophets, but to fulfill such and to establish that for which the developments of the centuries gone had been but preparatory. The gospel may be said to have destroyed the Mosaic law only as the seed is destroyed in the growth of the new plant, only as the bud is destroyed by the bursting forth of the rich, full, and fragrant flowers, only as infancy and youth pass forever as the maturity of years develops. Not a jot or a tittle of the law was to be void. A more effective analogy than the last could scarcely have been conceived; the jot or yod, and the tittle, were small literary marks in the Hebrew script; for present purposes we may regard them as equivalent to the dot of an "i" or the cross of a "t"; with the first, the jot, our English word "iota," signifying a trifle, is related. Not even the least commandment could be violated without penalty; but the disciples were admonished to take heed that their keeping of the commandments was not after the manner of the scribes and Pharisees, whose observance was that of ceremonial externalism, lacking the essentials of genuine devotion; for they were assured that by such an insincere course they could "in no case enter into the kingdom of heaven."

THE LAW SUPERSEDED BY THE GOSPEL[m]

The next section of the sermon deals with the superiority of the gospel of Christ over the law of Moses, and contrasts the requirements of the two in particular instances. Whereas the law forbade murder, and provided a just penalty for the crime, Christ taught that one's

[m] Matt. 5:21–48; Luke 6:27–36; compare 3 Ne. 12:21–48.

giving way to anger, which might possibly lead to violence or even murder, was of itself a sin. To maliciously use an offensive epithet such as "Raca" laid one liable to punishment under the decree of the council, and to call another a fool placed one "in danger of hell fire." These objectionable designations were regarded at that time as especially opprobrious and were therefore expressive of hateful intent. The murderer's hand is impelled by the hatred in his heart. The law provided penalty for the deed; the gospel rebuked the evil passion in its incipiency. To emphasize this principle, the Master showed that hatred was not to be atoned by a material sacrifice; and that if one came to make an offering at the altar, and remembered that he was at enmity with his brother, he should first go to that brother and be reconciled, even though such a course involved the interruption of the ceremonial, which was a particularly grievous incident according to the judgment of the priests. Differences and contentions were to be adjusted without delay.

The law forbade the awful sin of adultery; Christ said that the sin began in the lustful glance, the sensual thought; and He added that it was better to become blind than to look with evil eye; better to lose a hand than to work iniquity therewith. Touching the matter of divorcement, in which great laxity prevailed in that day, Jesus declared that except for the most serious offense of infidelity to marriage vows, no man could divorce his wife without becoming himself an offender, in that she, marrying again while still a wife not righteously divorced, would be guilty of sin, and so would be the man to whom she was so married.

Of old it had been forbidden to swear or take oaths except in solemn covenant before the Lord; but in the gospel dispensation the Lord forbade that men swear at all; and the heinousness of wanton oaths was expounded. Grievously sinful indeed it was and is to swear by heaven, which is the abode of God; or by earth, which is His creation and by Him called His footstool; or by Jerusalem, which was regarded by those who swore as the city of the great King; or by one's own head, which is part of the body God has created. Moderation in speech, decision and simplicity were enjoined, to the exclusion of expletives, profanity and oaths.

Of old the principle of retaliation had been tolerated, by which one who had suffered injury could exact or inflict a penalty of the same nature as the offense. Thus an eye was demanded for the loss of an eye, a tooth for a tooth, a life for a life.[n] In contrast, Christ taught that men should rather suffer than do evil, even to the extent of submission without resistance under certain implied conditions. His forceful illustrations—that if one were smitten on one cheek he should turn the other to the smiter; that if a man took another's coat by process of law, the loser should allow his cloak to be taken also; that if one was pressed into service to carry another's burden a mile, he should willingly go two miles; that one should readily give or lend as asked—are not to be construed as commanding abject subservience to unjust demands, nor as an abrogation of the principle of self-protection. These instructions were directed primarily to the apostles, who would be professedly devoted to the work of the kingdom to the exclusion of all other interests. In their ministry it would be better to suffer material loss or personal indignity and imposition at the hands of wicked oppressors, than to bring about an impairment of efficiency and a hindrance in work through resistance and contention. To such as these the Beatitudes were particularly applicable—Blessed are the meek, the peacemakers, and they that are persecuted for righteousness' sake.

Of old it had been said: "Love thy neighbour, and hate thine enemy";[o] but the Lord now taught: "Love your enemies, bless them that curse you, do good to them that hate you, and pray for them which despitefully use you, and persecute you." This was a new doctrine. Never before had Israel been required to love their foes. Friendship for enemies had found no place in the Mosaic code: indeed the people had grown to look upon Israel's enemies as God's enemies; and now Jesus required that tolerance, mercy, and even love be meted out to such! He supplemented the requirement by an explanation—through the course indicated by Him men may become children of God, like unto their Heavenly Father to the extent of their obedience; for the Father is kind, long-suffering and tolerant, causing His sun to shine on the evil and on the good, and sending rain for the sustenance of both just and unjust.[p] And further, what excellence has the man

[n] Ex. 21:23–25; Lev. 24:17–22; Deut. 19:21.

[o] Compare Lev. 19:18; Deut. 23:6; Ps. 41:10.

[p] Compare the lesson taught in the Parable of the Tares, Matt. 13:24–30.

who gives only as he receives, acknowledges only those who salute him with respect, loves only as he is loved? Even the publicans[q] did that much. Of the disciples of Christ much more was expected. The admonition closing this division of the discourse is an effective and comprehensive summary of all that had preceded: *"Be ye therefore perfect, even as your Father which is in heaven is perfect."* [r]

SINCERITY OF PURPOSE [s]

In the matter of almsgiving the Master warned against, and inferentially denounced, ostentation and hypocritical display. To give to the needy is praiseworthy; but to give for the purpose of winning the praise of men is rank hypocrisy. The tossing of alms to a beggar, the pouring of offerings into the temple treasure chests, to be seen of men,[t] and similar displays of affected liberality, were fashionable among certain classes in the time of Christ; and the same Spirit is manifest today. Some there be now who cause a trumpet to be sounded, through the columns of the press perchance, or by other means of publicity, to call attention to their giving, that they may have glory of men—to win political favor, to increase their trade or influence, to get what in their estimation is worth more than that from which they part. With logical incisiveness the Master demonstrated that such givers have their reward. They have received what they bid for; what more can such men demand or consistently expect? *"But,"* said the Lord, *"when thou doest alms, let not thy left hand know what thy right hand doeth: That thine alms may be in secret: and thy Father which seeth in secret himself shall reward thee openly."*

In the same spirit did the Preacher denounce hypocritical prayers—the saying of prayers in place of praying. There were many who sought places of public resort, in the synagogs, and even on the street-corners, that they might be seen and heard of men when saying their prayers. They secured the publicity they sought; what more

[q] Note 4, end of chapter.

[r] Note 5, end of chapter.

[s] Matt. 6:1–18; compare Luke 11:2–4; 3 Ne. 13:1–18.

[t] Consider the incident of the gifts of the rich and the widow's mite, Mark 12:41–44; Luke 21:1–4.

could they ask? "Verily I say unto you, They have their reward." He who would really pray—pray as nearly as possible as Christ prayed, pray in actual communion with God to whom the prayer is addressed—will seek privacy, seclusion, isolation; if opportunity permits he will retire to his chamber, and will shut the door, that none may intrude; there he may pray indeed, if the spirit of prayer be in his heart; and this course was commended by the Lord. Wordy supplications, made up largely of iterations and repetitions such as the heathen use, thinking that their idol deities will be pleased with their much speaking, were forbidden.

It is well to know that prayer is not compounded of words, words that may fail to express what one desires to say, words that so often cloak inconsistencies, words that may have no deeper source than the physical organs of speech, words that may be spoken to impress mortal ears. The dumb may pray, and that too with the eloquence that prevails in heaven. Prayer is made up of heart throbs and the righteous yearnings of the soul, of supplication based on the realization of need, of contrition and pure desire. If there lives a man who has never really prayed, that man is a being apart from the order of the divine in human nature, a stranger in the family of God's children. Prayer is for the uplifting of the suppliant. God without our prayers would be God; but we without prayer cannot be admitted to the kingdom of God. So did Christ instruct: "Your Father knoweth what things ye have need of, before ye ask him."

Then gave He unto those who sought wisdom at His feet, a model prayer, saying: "After this manner therefore pray ye:

"Our Father which art in heaven, Hallowed be thy name." In this we acknowledge the relation we bear to our Heavenly Father, and while reverencing His great and holy Name, we avail ourselves of the inestimable privilege of approaching Him, less with the thought of His infinite glory as the Creator of all that is, the Supreme Being above all creation, than with the loving realization that He is Father, and that we are His children. This is the earliest Biblical scripture giving instruction, permission, or warrant, for addressing God directly as "Our Father." Therein is expressed the reconciliation which the human family, estranged through sin, may attain by the means provided through the well beloved Son. This instruction is equally

definite in demonstrating the brotherhood between Christ and humanity. As He prayed so pray we to the same Father, we as brethren and Christ as our Elder Brother.

"Thy kingdom come. Thy will be done in earth, as it is in heaven." The kingdom of God is to be a kingdom of order, in which toleration and the recognition of individual rights shall prevail. One who really prays that this kingdom come will strive to hasten its coming by living according to the law of God. His effort will be to keep himself in harmony with the order of the kingdom, to subject the flesh to the spirit, selfishness to altruism, and to learn to love the things that God loves. To make the will of God supreme on earth as it is in heaven is to be allied with God in the affairs of life. There are many who profess belief that as God is omnipotent, all that is is according to His will. Such a supposition is unscriptural, unreasonable, and untrue.[u] Wickedness is not in harmony with His will; falsehood, hypocrisy, vice and crime are not God's gifts to man. By His will these monstrosities that have developed as hideous deformities in human nature and life shall be abolished, and this blessed consummation shall be reached when by choice, without surrender or abrogation of their free agency, men shall do the will of God.

"Give us this day our daily bread." Food is indispensable to life. As we need it we should ask for it. True, the Father knows our need before we ask, but by asking we acknowledge Him as the Giver, and are made humble, grateful, contrite, and reliant by the request. Though the sun shines and the rain falls alike upon the just and the unjust, the righteous man is grateful for these blessings; the ungodly man receives the benefits as a matter of course with a soul incapable of gratitude. The capacity to be grateful is a blessing, for the possession of which we should be further grateful. We are taught to pray day by day for the food we need, not for a great store to be laid by for the distant future. Israel in the desert received manna as a daily supply,[v] and were kept in mind of their reliance upon Him who gave. The man with much finds it easier to forget his dependence than he who must ask with each succeeding day of need.

[u] Page 18.
[v] Ex. 16:16–21.

"And forgive us our debts, as we forgive our debtors." He who can thus pray with full intent and unmixed purpose merits forgiveness. In this specification of personal supplication we are taught to expect only as we deserve. The selfish and sinful would rejoice in exemption from their lawful debts, but being selfish and sinful would exact the last farthing from those who owe them.[w] Forgiveness is too precious a pearl to be cast at the feet of the unforgiving;[x] and, without the sincerity that springs from a contrite heart, no man may justly claim mercy. If others owe us, either in actual money or goods as suggested by debts and debtors, or through some infringement upon our rights included under the broader designation as a trespass, our mode of dealing with them will be taken into righteous account in the judgment of our own offenses.

"And lead us not into temptation, but deliver us from evil." The first part of this petition has occasioned comment and question. We are not to understand that God would ever lead a man into temptation except, perhaps, by way of wise permission, to test and prove him, thereby affording him opportunity of overcoming and so of gaining spiritual strength, which is the only true advancement in man's eternal course of progress. The one purpose of providing bodies for the preexistent spirits of the race, and of advancing them to the mortal state, was to "prove them herewith, to see if they will do all things whatsoever the Lord their God shall command them."[y] The plan of mortality involved the certainty of temptation. The intent of the supplication appears to be that we be preserved from temptation beyond our weak powers to withstand; that we be not abandoned to temptation without the divine support that shall be as full a measure of protection as our exercise of choice will allow.

How inconsistent then to go, as many do, into the places where the temptations to which we are most susceptible are strongest; for the man beset with a passion for strong drink to so pray and then resort to the dramshop; for the man whose desires are lustful to voice such a prayer and then go where lust is kindled; for the dishonest man, though he say

---

[w] Note the lesson of the parable of the Unmerciful Servant, Matt. 18:23–25.

[x] Compare Matt. 7:6.

[y] Abr. 3:25.

the prayer, to then place himself where he knows the opportunity to steal will be found! Can such souls as these be other than hypocrites in asking God to deliver them from the evils they have sought? Temptation will fall in our way without our seeking, and evil will present itself even when We desire most to do right; for deliverance from such we may pray with righteous expectation and assurance.

"For thine is the kingdom, and the Power, and the glory, for ever. Amen." Herein we acknowledge the supremacy of the Being whom we addressed at the beginning as Father. He is the Almighty in whom and through whose provision we live and move and have our existence.[z] To assert independence of God is both sacrilege and blasphemy; to acknowledge Him is a filial duty and a just confession of His majesty and dominion. The Lord's Prayer is closed with a solemn "Amen," set as a seal to the document of the supplication, attesting its genuineness as the true expression of the suppliant's soul; gathering within the compass of a word the meaning of all that has been uttered or thought. *So let it be* is the literal signification of *Amen.*

From the subject of prayer the Master turned to that of fasting, and emphasized the important truth that to be of avail fasting must be a matter between the man and his God, not between man and his kind. It was a common thing in the Master's day to see men parading the fact of their abstinence as an advertisement of their assumed piety.[aa] That they might appear haggard and faint, this class of hypocrites disfigured their faces, went with unkempt hair, gazed about with sad countenances. Of these also the Lord said, "Verily I say unto you, They have their reward." Believers were admonished to fast secretly, with no outward display, and to fast unto God, who could see in secret and would heed their sacrifice and prayer.

TREASURES OF EARTH AND OF HEAVEN [bb]

The transitory character of worldly wealth was next contrasted with the enduring riches of eternity. Many there were and many there

[z] Acts 17:28.

[aa] Compare the instance connected with the parable of the Pharisee and the Publican, Luke 18:10–14.

[bb] Matt. 6:19–34; compare Luke 12:24–34; 16:13; 18:22; 3 Ne. 13:19–34.

are whose principal effort in life has been that of amassing treasures of earth, the mere possession of which entails responsibility, care, and disturbing anxiety. Some kinds of wealth are endangered by the ravages of moths, such as silks and velvets, satins and furs; some are destroyed by corrosion and rust—silver and copper and steel; while these and others are not infrequently made the booty of thieves. Infinitely more precious are the treasures of a life well spent, the wealth of good deeds, the account of which is kept in heaven, where the riches of righteous achievement are safe from moth, rust, and robbers. Then followed the trenchant lesson: *"For where your treasure is, there will your heart be also."*

Spiritual light is shown to be greater than any product of physical illuminants. What does the brightest light avail the man who is blind? It is the bodily eye that discerns the light of the candle, the lamp, or the sun; and the spiritual eye sees by spiritual light; if then man's spiritual eye be single, that is, pure and undimmed by sin, he is filled with the light that shall show him the way to God; whereas if his Soul's eye be evil, he will be as one full of darkness. Solemn caution is expressed in the summary, "If therefore the light that is in thee be darkness, how great is that darkness!" Those whom the Master was addressing had received of the light of God; the degree of belief they had already professed was proof of that. Should they turn from the great emprise on which they had embarked, the light would be lost, and the succeeding darkness would be denser than that from which they had been relieved.[cc] There was to be no indecision among the disciples. No one of them could serve two masters; if he professed so to do he would be an untrue servant to the one or the other. Then followed another profound generalization: *"Ye cannot serve God and mammon."*[dd]

They were told to trust the Father for what they needed, taking no thought of food, drink, clothing, or even of life itself, for all these were to be supplied by means above their power to control. With the wisdom of a Teacher of teachers, the Master appealed to their hearts and their understanding by citing the lessons of nature, in language of such simple yet forceful eloquence that to amplify or condense it is but to mar.

[cc] Luke 11:34–36.

[dd] Compare Gal. 1:10; 1 Tim. 6:17; James 4:4; 1 John 2:15.

"Behold the fowls of the air: for they sow not, neither do they reap, nor gather into barns; yet your heavenly Father feedeth them. Are ye not much better than they? Which of you by taking thought can add one cubit unto his stature? And why take ye thought for raiment? Consider the lilies of the field, how they grow; they toil not, neither do they spin: And yet I say unto you, That even Solomon in all his glory was not arrayed like one of these."

The weakness of faith was reproved in the reminder that the Father who cared even for the grass of the field, which one day flourishes and on the next is gathered up to be burned, would not fail to remember His own. Therefore the Master added: *"Seek ye first the kingdom of God, and his righteousness; and all these things shall be added unto you."*

HYPOCRISY FURTHER CONDEMNED [ee]

Men are prone to judge their fellows and to praise or censure without due consideration of fact or circumstance. On prejudiced or unsupported judgment the Master set His disapproval. "Judge not, that ye be not judged," He admonished, for, according to one's own standard of judging others, shall he himself be judged. The man who is always ready to correct his brother's faults, to remove the mote from his neighbor's eye so that that neighbor may see things as the interested and interfering friend would have him see, was denounced as a hypocrite. What was the speck in his neighbor's vision to the obscuring beam in his own eye? Have the centuries between the days of Christ and our own time made us less eager to cure the defective vision of those who cannot or will not assume our point of view, and see things as we see them?

These disciples, some of whom were soon to minister in the authority of the Holy Apostleship, were cautioned against the indiscreet and indiscriminate scattering of the sacred truths and precepts committed to them. Their duty would be to discern the spirits of those whom they essayed to teach, and to impart unto them in wisdom. The words of the Master were strong: "Give not that which is holy unto the dogs, neither cast ye your pearls before swine, lest they trample them under their feet, and turn again and rend you."[ff]

[ee] Matt. 7:1–5; Luke 6:37, 38, 41, 42; compare 3 Ne. 14:1–5.
[ff] Matt. 7:6; compare 3 Ne. 14:6.

PROMISE AND REASSURANCE ᵍᵍ

That their supplications would be heard and answered followed as a rich promise. They were to ask and they would receive; they were to knock and the door would be opened. Surely the Heavenly Father would not be less considerate than a human parent; and what father would answer his son's plea for bread by giving him a stone, or who would give a serpent when a fish was desired? With greater certainty would God bestow good gifts upon those who asked according to their need, in faith. *"Therefore all things whatsoever ye would that men should do to you, do ye even so to them: for this is the law and the Prophets."*

The straight and narrow way by which man may walk in Godliness was compared with the broad highway leading to destruction. False prophets were to be shunned, such as were then among the people, comparable in their pretense to sheep, and in their reality to ravening wolves. These were to be recognized by their works and the results thereof, even as a tree is to be judged as good or bad according to its fruit. A thorn bush does not produce grapes, nor can thistles bear figs. Conversely, it is as truly impossible for a good tree to produce evil fruit as for a useless and corrupt tree to bring forth good fruit.

Religion is more than the confession and profession of the lips. Jesus averred that in the day of judgment many would pretend allegiance to Him, saying: "Lord, Lord, have we not prophesied in thy name? and in thy name have cast out devils? and in thy name done many wonderful works? And then will I profess unto them, I never knew you: depart from me, ye that work iniquity." Only by doing the will of the Father is the saving grace of the Son obtainable. To assume to speak and act in the name of the Lord without the bestowal of authority, such as the Lord alone can give, is to add sacrilege to hypocrisy. Even miracles wrought will be no vindication of the claims of those who pretend to minister in the ordinances of the gospel while devoid of the authority of the Holy Priesthood.ʰʰ

ᵍᵍ Matt. 7:7–23; Luke 6:43–44; 11:9–13; 13:24–30; compare 3 Ne. 14:7–23.

ʰʰ *Articles of Faith,* pp. 179–89; 198–211.

HEARING AND DOING [ii]

The Sermon on the Mount has stood through all the years since its delivery without another to be compared with it. No mortal man has ever since preached a discourse of its kind. The spirit of the address is throughout that of sincerity and action, as opposed to empty profession and neglect. In the closing sentences the Lord showed the uselessness of hearing alone, as contrasted with the efficacy of doing. The man who hears and acts is likened unto the wise builder who set the foundation of his house upon a rock; and in spite of rain and hurricane and flood, the house stood. He that hears and obeys not is likened unto the foolish man who built his house upon the sand; and when rain fell, or winds blew, or floods came, behold it fell, and great was the fall thereof.

Such doctrines as these astonished the people. For His distinctive teachings the Preacher had cited no authority but His own. His address was free from any array of rabbinical precedents; the law was superseded by the gospel: *"For he taught them as one having authority, and not as the scribes."*

NOTES TO CHAPTER 17

1. **Time and Place of the Sermon on the Mount.**—Matthew gives the address early mention, placing it even before the record of his own call from the seat of custom—which call certainly preceded the ordination of the Twelve as a body—and before his account of many sayings and doings of the Lord already considered in these pages. Luke's partial summary of the sermon follows his record of the ordination of the apostles. Matthew tells us that Jesus had gone up the mountain and that He sat while speaking; Luke's account suggests the inference that Jesus and the Twelve first descended from the mountain heights to a plain, where they were met by the multitude, and that Jesus preached unto them, standing. Critics who rejoice in trifles, often to the neglect of weightier matters, have tried to make much of these seeming variations. Is it not probable that Jesus spoke at length on the mountainside to the disciples then present, and from whom He had chosen the Twelve, and that after finishing His discourse to them He descended with them to the plain where a multitude had assembled, and that to these He repeated parts of what He had before spoken? The relative fulness of Matthew's report may be due to the fact that he, as one of the Twelve, was present at the first and more extended delivery.

ii Matt. 7:24–29; Luke 6:46–49; compare 3 Ne. 14:24–27.

2. Pleasure Versus Happiness.—"The present is an age of pleasure-seeking, and men are losing their sanity in the mad rush for sensations that do but excite and disappoint. In this day of counterfeits, adulterations, and base imitations, the devil is busier than he has ever been in the course of human history, in the manufacture of pleasures, both old and new; and these he offers for sale in most attractive fashion, falsely labeled, *Happiness*. In this soul-destroying craft he is without a peer; he has had centuries of experience and practice, and by his skill he controls the market. He has learned the tricks of the trade, and knows well how to catch the eye and arouse the desire of his customers. He puts up the stuff in bright-colored packages, tied with tinsel string and tassel; and crowds flock to his bargain counters, hustling and crushing one another in their frenzy to buy.

"Follow one of the purchasers as he goes off gloatingly with his gaudy packet, and watch him as he opens it. What finds he inside the gilded wrapping? He has expected fragrant happiness, but uncovers only an inferior brand of pleasure, the stench of which is nauseating.

"Happiness includes all that is really desirable and of true worth in pleasure, and much besides. Happiness is genuine gold, pleasure but guilded brass, which corrodes in the hand, and is soon converted into poisonous verdigris. Happiness is as the genuine diamond, which, rough or polished, shines with its own inimitable luster; pleasure is as the paste imitation that glows only when artificially embellished. Happiness is as the ruby, red as the heart's blood, hard and enduring; pleasure, as stained glass, soft, brittle, and of but transitory beauty.

"Happiness is true food, wholesome, nutritious and sweet; it builds up the body and generates energy for action, physical, mental and spiritual; pleasure is but a deceiving stimulant which, like spiritous drink, makes one think he is strong when in reality enfeebled; makes him fancy he is well when in fact stricken with deadly malady.

"Happiness leaves no bad after-taste, it is followed by no depressing reaction; it calls for no repentance, brings no regret, entails no remorse; pleasure too often makes necessary repentance, contrition, and suffering; and, if indulged to the extreme, it brings degradation and destruction.

"True happiness is lived over and over again in memory, always with a renewal of the original good; a moment of unholy pleasure may leave a barbed sting, which, like a thorn in the flesh, is an everpresent source of anguish.

"Happiness is not akin with levity, nor is it one with light-minded mirth. It springs from the deeper fountains of the soul, and is not infrequently accompanied by tears. Have you never been so happy that you have had to weep? I have."— Article by the author, *Improvement Era,* vol. 17, no. 2, pp. 172–73.

3. Salt of the Earth.—Dummelow's *Commentary,* on Matt. 5:13, states: "Salt in Palestine, being gathered in an impure state, often undergoes chemical changes by which its flavor is destroyed while its appearance remains." Perhaps a reasonable interpretation of the expression, "if the salt have lost his savour," may be suggested by the fact that salt mixed with insoluble impurities may be dissolved out by moisture, leaving the insoluble residue but slightly salty. The lesson of the Lord's illustration is that spoiled salt is of no use as a preservative. The corresponding passage in the sermon delivered by Jesus to the Nephites after His Resurrection reads: "Verily, verily, I say unto you, I give unto you to be the salt of the earth; but if the salt shall lose its savor, wherewith shall the earth be salted? The salt shall be thenceforth good for nothing, but to be cast out, and to be trodden under foot of men." (3 Ne. 12:13.)

4. Reference to Publicans.—Observe that Matthew, who had been a publican, frankly records this reference (5:46, 47) to his despised class. Luke writes "sinners," instead of "publicans" (6:32–34). Of course, if the accounts of the two writers refer to separate addresses (see Note 1, above), both may be accurate. But we find Matthew's designation of himself as a publican in his list of the apostles (10:3) and the considerate omission of the unenviable title by the other evangelists (Mark 3:18; Luke 6:15).

5. Relative Perfection.—Our Lord's admonition to men to become perfect, even as the Father is perfect (Matt. 5:48) cannot rationally be construed otherwise than as implying the possibility of such achievement. Plainly, however, man cannot become perfect in mortality in the sense in which God is perfect as a supremely glorified Being. It is possible, though, for man to be perfect in his sphere in a sense analogous to that in which superior intelligences are perfect in their several spheres; yet the relative perfection of the lower is infinitely inferior to that of the higher. A college student in his freshman or sophomore year may be perfect as freshman or sophomore; his record may possibly be a hundred percent on the scale of efficiency and achievement; yet the honors of the upper classman are beyond him, and the attainment of graduation is to him remote, but of assured possibility, if he do but continue faithful and devoted to the end.

CHAPTER 18

As One Having Authority

Matthew's account of the invaluable address, known to us as the Sermon on the Mount, is closed with a forceful sentence of his own, referring to the effect of the Master's words upon the people: "For he taught them as one having authority, and not as the scribes."[a] A striking characteristic of Christ's ministry was the entire absence of any claim of human authorization for His words or deeds; the commission He professed to have was that of the Father who sent Him. His addresses, whether delivered to multitudes or spoken in relative privacy to few, were free from the labored citations in which the teachers of the day delighted. His authoritative "I say unto you" took the place of invocation of authority and exceeded any possible array of precedent commandment or deduction. In this His words differed essentially from the erudite utterances of scribes, Pharisees and rabbis. Throughout His ministry, inherent power and authority were manifest over matter and the forces of nature, over men and demons, over life and death. It now becomes our purpose to consider a number of instances in which the Lord's power was demonstrated in divers mighty works.

THE CENTURION'S SERVANT HEALED [b]

From the Mount of Beatitudes Jesus returned to Capernaum, whether directly or by a longer way marked by other works of power and mercy is of little importance. There was at that time a Roman

---

[a] Matt. 7:29; compare Luke 4:32; John 7:46.

[b] Luke 7:1–10; compare Matt. 8:5–13.

garrison in the city. A military officer, a centurion or captain of a hundred men, was stationed there. Attached to the household of this officer was an esteemed servant, who was ill, "and ready to die." The centurion had faith that Christ could heal his servant, and invoked the intercession of the Jewish elders to beg of the Master the boon desired. These elders implored Jesus most earnestly, and urged the worthiness of the man, who, though a Gentile, loved the people of Israel and out of his munificence had built for them a synagog in the town. Jesus went with the elders, but the centurion, probably learning of the approach of the little company, hastily sent other envoys to say that he did not consider himself worthy to have Jesus enter his home, from which sense of unworthiness he had not ventured to make his request in person.[c] "But," ran the message of supplication, "say in a word, and my servant shall be healed." We may well contrast this man's conception of Christ's power with that of the nobleman of the same town, who had requested Jesus to hasten in person to the side of his dying son.[d]

The centurion seems to have reasoned in this way: He himself was a man of authority, though under the direction of superior officers. To his subordinates he gave orders which were obeyed. He did not find it necessary to personally attend to the carrying out of his instructions. Surely One who had such power as Jesus possessed could command and be obeyed. Moreover, the man may have heard of the marvelous restoration of the nobleman's dying son, in accomplishing which the Lord spoke the effective word when miles away from the sufferer's bed. That the centurion's trust and confidence, his belief and faith, were genuine, is not to be doubted, since Jesus expressly commended the same.[e] The afflicted one was healed. Jesus is said to have marveled at the centurion's manifestation of faith, and, turning to the people who followed, He thus spake: "I say unto you, I have not found so great faith, no, not in Israel." This remark may have caused some of the listeners to wonder; the Jews were unaccustomed to hear the faith of a Gentile so extolled, for, according to the traditionalism of the day, a

[c] Note 1, end of chapter.

[d] John 4:46–53.

[e] Note 2, end of chapter.

Gentile, even though an earnest proselyte to Judaism, was accounted essentially inferior to even the least worthy of the chosen people. Our Lord's comment plainly indicated that Gentiles would be preferred in the kingdom of God if they excelled in worthiness. Turning to Matthew's record we find this additional teaching, introduced as usual with "I say unto you"—"That many shall come from the east and west, and shall sit down with Abraham, and Isaac, and Jacob, in the kingdom of heaven. But the children of the kingdom shall be cast out into outer darkness: there shall be weeping and gnashing of teeth."[f] This lesson, that the supremacy of Israel can be attained only through excellence in righteousness, is reiterated and enlarged upon in the Lord's teachings, as we shall see.

A YOUNG MAN OF NAIN RAISED FROM THE DEAD [g]

On the day after that of the miracle last considered, Jesus went to the little town of Nain, and, as usual, many people accompanied Him. This day witnessed what in human estimation was a wonder greater than any before wrought by Him. He had already healed many, sometimes by a word spoken to afflicted ones present, and again when He was far from the subject of His beneficent power; bodily diseases had been overcome, and demons had been rebuked at His command; but, though the sick who were nigh unto death had been saved from the grave, we have no earlier record of our Lord having commanded dread death itself to give back one it had claimed.[h] As Jesus and His followers approached the town, they met a funeral cortege of many people; the only son of a widow was being borne to the tomb; the body was carried according to the custom of the day on an open bier. Our Lord looked with compassion upon the sorrowing mother, now bereft of both husband and son; and, feeling in Himself [i] the pain of her grief, He said in gentle tone, "Weep not." He touched the stretcher upon which the dead man lay, and the bearers stood still. Then addressing the corpse He said: "Young man, I

[f] Matt. 8:11, 12; see also Luke 13:28, 29; compare Acts 10:45.

[g] Luke 7:11–17.

[h] Note 3, end of chapter.

[i] Matt. 8:17; compare Isa. 53:4.

say unto thee, Arise." And the dead heard the voice of Him who is Lord of all[j] and immediately sat up and spoke. Graciously Jesus delivered the young man to his mother. We read without wonder that there came a fear on all who were present, and that they glorified God, testifying that a great prophet was amongst them and that God has visited His people. Reports of this miracle were carried throughout the land, and even reached the ears of John the Baptist, who was confined in the prison of Herod. The effect of the information conveyed to John concerning this and other mighty works of Christ now claims our attention.

JOHN BAPTIST'S MESSAGE TO JESUS

Even before Jesus had returned to Galilee after His baptism and the forty days of solitude in the wilderness, John the Baptist had been imprisoned by order of Herod Antipas, tetrarch of Galilee and Perea.[k] During the subsequent months of our Lord's activities, in preaching the gospel, teaching the true significance of the kingdom, reproving sin, healing the afflicted, rebuking evil spirits and even raising the dead to life, His forerunner, the Godfearing, valiant John, had lain a prisoner in the dungeons of Machaerus, one of the strongest of Herod's citadels.[l]

The tetrarch had some regard for John, having found him to be a holy man; and many things had Herod done on the direct advice of the Baptist or because of the influence of the latter's general teaching. Indeed, Herod had listened to John gladly, and had imprisoned him through a reluctant yielding to the importunities of Herodias, whom Herod claimed as a wife under cover of an illegal marriage. Herodias had been and legally was still the wife of Herod's brother Philip, from whom she had never been lawfully divorced; and her pretended marriage to Herod Antipas was both adulterous and incestuous under Jewish law. The Baptist had fearlessly denounced this sinful association; to Herod he had said: "It is not lawful for thee to have thy brother's wife." Though Herod might possibly have ignored this stern rebuke,

---

[j] Luke 20:36, 38; compare Acts 10:42; 2 Tim. 4:1; 1 Pet. 4:5; Rom. 14:9.

[k] Matt. 4:12; Mark 1:14; Luke 3:19, 20; see Note 2, chap. 9; Note 4, end of chapter.

[l] Note 5, end of chapter.

or at least might have allowed it to pass without punishment, Herodias would not condone. It was she, not the tetrarch, who most hated John; she "had a quarrel against him," and succeeded in inducing Herod to have the Baptist seized and incarcerated as a step toward the consummation of her vengeful plan of having him put to death.[m] Moreover, Herod feared an uprising of the people in the event of John being slain by his order.[n]

In the course of his long imprisonment John had heard much of the marvelous preaching and works of Christ; these things must have been reported to him by some of his disciples and friends who were allowed to visit him.[o] Particularly was he informed of the miraculous raising of the young man at Nain;[p] and forthwith he commissioned two of his disciples to bear a message of inquiry to Jesus.[q] These came to Christ and reported the purpose of their visit thus: "John Baptist hath sent us unto thee, saying, Art thou he that should come? or look we for another?" The messengers found Jesus engaged in beneficent ministrations; and, instead of giving an immediate reply in words, He continued His labor, relieving in that same hour many who were afflicted by blindness or infirmities, or who were troubled by evil spirits. Then, turning to the two who had communicated the Baptist's question, Jesus said: "Go your way, and tell John what things ye have seen and heard; how that the blind see, the lame walk, the lepers are cleansed, the deaf hear, the dead are raised, to the poor the gospel is preached. And blessed is he, whosoever shall not be offended in me."

The words of John's inquiring disciples were answered by wondrous deeds of beneficence and mercy. When the reply was reported to John, the imprisoned prophet could scarcely have failed to remember the predictions of Isaiah, that by those very tokens of miracle and blessing should the Messiah be known;[r] and the reproof must have been convincing and convicting as he called to mind his

[m] Mark 6:17–20.

[n] Matt. 14:5.

[o] Matt. 11:2. Note a similar liberty allowed to Paul when in durance, Acts 24:23.

[p] Luke 7:18; Matt. 11:2.

[q] Matt. 11:2–6; Luke 7:18–23.

[r] Isa. 35:5, 6.

own citations of Isaiah's prophecies, when he had proclaimed in fiery, withering eloquence the fulfillment of those earlier predictions in his own mission and in that of the Mightier One to whom he had borne personal testimony.[s]

The concluding sentence of our Lord's answer to John was the climax of what had preceded, and a further though yet gentle rebuke of the Baptist's defective comprehension of the Messiah's mission. "Blessed is he, whosoever shall not be offended in me," said the Lord. Misunderstanding is the prelude to offense. Gaged by the standard of the then current conception of what the Messiah would be, the work of Christ must have appeared to many as failure; and those who were looking for some sudden manifestation of His power in the conquest of Israel's oppressors and the rehabilitation of the house of David in worldly splendor, grew impatient, then doubtful; afterward they took offense and were in danger of turning in open rebellion against their Lord. Christ has been an offender to many because they, being out of harmony with His words and works, have of themselves taken offense.[t]

John's situation must be righteously considered by all who assume to render judgment as to his purpose in sending to inquire of Christ, "Art thou he that should come?" John thoroughly understood that his own work was that of preparation; he had so testified and had openly borne witness that Jesus was the One for whom he had been sent to prepare. With the inauguration of Christ's ministry, John's influence had waned, and for many months he had been shut up in a cell, chafing under his enforced inactivity, doubtless yearning for the freedom of the open, and for the locusts and wild honey of the desert. Jesus was increasing while he decreased in popularity, influence, and opportunity; and he had affirmed that such condition was inevitable.[u]

But, left in prison, he may have become despondent, and may have permitted himself to wonder whether that Mightier One had forgotten him. He knew that were Jesus to speak the word of command the prison of Machaerus could no longer hold him; nevertheless Jesus seemed to have abandoned him to his fate, which comprised not only

[s] Matt. 3:3; compare Isa. 40:3; Matt. 3:7; compare Isa. 59:5; Luke 3:6; compare Isa. 52:10.

[t] Matt. 13:57; 24:10; 26:31; Mark 6:3; 14:27; John 6:61. Note 6, end of chapter.

[u] John 3:30.

confinement but other indignities, and physical torture.ᵛ It may have been a part of John's purpose to call Christ's attention to his pitiable plight; and in this respect his message was rather a reminder than a plain inquiry based on actual doubt. Indeed, we have good grounds for inference that John's purpose in sending disciples to inquire of Christ was partly, and perhaps largely, designed to confirm in those disciples an abiding faith in the Christ. The commission with which they were charged brought them into direct communication with the Lord, whose supremacy they could not well fail to comprehend. They were personal witnesses of His power and authority.

Our Lord's commentary on John's message indicated that the Baptist had no full understanding of what the spiritual kingdom of God comprised. After the envoys had departed, Jesus addressed Himself to the people who had witnessed the interview. He would not have them underrate the importance of the Baptist's service.ʷ He reminded them of the time of John's popularity, when some of those then present, and multitudes of others, had gone into the wilderness to hear the prophet's stern admonition; and they had found him to be no reed, shaken by the wind, but a firm and unbending oak. They had not gone to see a man in fashionable attire; those who wore soft raiment were to be looked for in the court of the king, not in the wilderness, nor in the dungeon where John now lay. They had found in John a prophet indeed, yea, more than a prophet; "For," affirmed the Lord, "I say unto you, Among those that are born of women there is not a greater prophet than John the Baptist: but he that is least in the kingdom of God is greater than he."ˣ What stronger testimony of the Baptist's integrity is needed? Other prophets had told of the Messiah's coming, but John had seen Him, had baptized Him, and had been to Jesus as a body servant to his master. Nevertheless from the day of John's preaching to the time at which Christ then spoke, the kingdom of

---

ᵛ Note that Jesus compared the sufferings of John while in prison as in part comparable to those He would Himself have to endure, in that they did unto John "whatsoever they listed" (Matt. 17:12; Mark 9:13).

ʷ Luke 7:24–30; see also Matt. 11:7–14; compare Christ's testimony of John the Baptist delivered at Jerusalem, John 5:33–35.

ˣ Luke 7:28; See Note 7, end of chapter.

heaven had been rejected with violence, and this even though all the prophets and even the fundamental law had told of its coming, and though both John and Christ had been abundantly predicted.

Concerning John, the Lord continued: "And if ye will receive it, this is Elias, which was for to come. He that hath ears to hear, let him hear."[y] It is important to know that the designation, Elias, here applied by Jesus to the Baptist, is a title rather than a personal name, and that it has no reference to Elijah, the ancient prophet called the Tishbite.[z] Many of those who heard the Lord's eulogy on the Baptist rejoiced, for they had accepted John, and had turned from him to Jesus as from the lesser to the Greater, as from the priest to the great High Priest, as from the herald to the King. But Pharisees and lawyers were present, those of the class that John had so vehemently denounced as of a generation of vipers, and those who had rejected the counsel of God in refusing to heed the Baptist's call to repentance.[aa]

At this point the Master resorted to analogy to make His meaning clearer. He compared the unbelieving and dissatisfied generation to fickle children at play, disagreeing among themselves. Some wanted to enact the pageantry of a mock wedding, and though they piped the rest would not dance; then they changed to a funeral procession and essayed the part of mourners, but the others would not weep as the rules of the game required. Ever critical, ever skeptical, by nature fault-finders and defamers, hard of hearing and of heart, they grumbled. John the Baptist had come amongst them like the eremitic prophets of old, as strict as any Nazarite, refusing to eat with the merry-makers or drink with the convivial, and they had said "He hath a devil." Now came the Son of Man,[bb] without austerity or hermit ways, eating and drinking as a normal man would do, a guest at the houses of the people, a participant in the festivities of a marriage party, mingling alike with the publicans and the Pharisees—and they complained again, saying: "Behold a gluttonous man, and a winebibber, a friend of publicans and sinners!" The Master explained that such inconsistency,

[y] Matt. 11:12–15; compare 17:12; Luke 1:17.

[z] Note 8, end of chapter.

[aa] Matt. 3:7; Luke 7:30.

[bb] Pages 136–138.

such wicked trifling with matters most sacred, such determined opposition to truth, would surely be revealed in their true light, and the worthlessness of boasted learning would appear. "But," said He, "wisdom is justified of all her children."

From reproof for unbelieving individuals He turned to unappreciative communities, and upbraided the cities in which He had wrought so many mighty works, and wherein the people repented not: "Woe unto thee, Chorazin! woe unto thee, Bethsaida! for if the mighty works, which were done in you, had been done in Tyre and Sidon, they would have repented long ago in sackcloth and ashes. But I say unto you, It shall be more tolerable for Tyre and Sidon at the day of judgment, than for you. And thou, Capernaum, which art exalted unto heaven, shalt be brought down to hell: for if the mighty works, which have been done in thee, had been done in Sodom, it would have remained until this day. But I say unto you, That it shall be more tolerable for the land of Sodom in the day of judgment, than for thee."[cc]

Seemingly faint at heart over the unbelief of the people, Jesus sought strength in prayer.[dd] With the eloquence of soul for which one looks in vain save in the anguish-laden communion of Christ with His Father, He voiced His reverent gratitude that God had imparted a testimony of the truth to the humble and simple rather than to the learned and great; though misunderstood by men He was known for what He really was by the Father. Turning again to the people, He urged anew their acceptance of Him and His gospel, and His invitation is one of the grandest outpourings of spiritual emotion known to man: "Come unto me, all ye that labour and are heavy laden, and I will give you rest. Take my yoke upon you, and learn of me; for I am meek and lowly in heart: and ye shall find rest unto your souls. For my yoke is easy, and my burden is light."[ee] He invited them from drudgery to pleasant service; from the well-nigh unbearable burdens of ecclesiastical exactions and traditional formalism, to the liberty of truly spiritual worship; from slavery to freedom; but they would not.

[cc] Matt. 11:20–24; compare Luke 10:13–15.

[dd] Matt. 11:25–27; compare Luke 10:21, 22.

[ee] Matt. 11:28–30.

The gospel He offered them was the embodiment of liberty, but not of license; it entailed obedience and submission; but even if such could be likened unto a yoke, what was its burden in comparison with the incubus under which they groaned?

DEATH OF JOHN THE BAPTIST

Reverting to John Baptist in his dungeon solitude, we are left without information as to how he received and understood the reply to his inquiry, as brought by his messengers. His captivity was destined soon to end, though not by restoration to liberty on earth. The hatred of Herodias increased against him. An opportunity for carrying into effect her fiendish plots against his life soon appeared.[ff] The king celebrated his birthday by a great feast, to which his lords, high captains, and the principal officials of Galilee were bidden. To grace the occasion, Salome, daughter of Herodias though not of Herod, came in and danced before the company. So enchanted were Herod and his guests that the king bade the damsel ask whatever she would, and he swore he would give it unto her, even though the gift were half of his kingdom.

She retired to consult her mother as to what she should ask, and, being instructed, returned with the appalling demand: "I will that thou give me by and by in a charger the head of John the Baptist." The king was astounded; his amazement was followed by sorrow and regret; nevertheless he dreaded the humiliation that would follow a violation of the oath he had sworn in the presence of his court; so, summoning an executioner, he immediately gave the fatal order; and John was forthwith beheaded in the dungeon. The headsman returned, carrying a dish in which lay the ghastly trophy of the corrupt queen's vengeance. The bloody gift was delivered to Salome, who carried it with inhuman triumph to her mother. Some of John's disciples came, secured the corpse, laid it in a tomb; and bore the tidings of his death to Jesus. Herod was sorely troubled over the murder he had ordered; and when, later, the marvels wrought by Jesus were reported to him, he was afraid, and said: "That John the Baptist

---

[ff] Mark 6:21–29.

was risen from the dead, and therefore mighty works do shew forth themselves in him." To those who dissented, the terrified king replied: "It is John, whom I beheaded: he is risen from the dead."[gg]

So ended the life of the prophet-priest, the direct precursor of the Christ; thus was stilled the mortal voice of him who had cried so mightily in the wilderness: "Prepare ye the way of the Lord." After many centuries his voice has been heard again, as the voice of one redeemed and resurrected; and the touch of his hand has again been felt, in this the dispensation of restoration and fulness. In May, 1829, a resurrected personage appeared to Joseph Smith and Oliver Cowdery, announced himself as John, known of old as the Baptist, laid his hands upon the two young men, and conferred upon them the priesthood of Aaron, which comprises authority to preach and minister the gospel of repentance and of baptism by immersion for the remission of sins.[hh]

IN THE HOUSE OF SIMON THE PHARISEE

"And one of the Pharisees desired him that he would eat with him. And he went into the Pharisee's house, and sat down to meat."[ii]

From the place of this incident in Luke's narration of events, it appears that it may have occurred on the day of the visit of John's messengers. Jesus accepted the Pharisee's invitation, as He had accepted the invitations of others, including even publicans, and those called by the rabbis, sinners. His reception at Simon's house appears to have been somewhat lacking in warmth, hospitality and honorable attendance. The narrative suggests an attitude of condescension on the part of the host. It was the custom of the times to treat a distinguished guest with marked attention; to receive him with a kiss of welcome, to provide water for washing the dust from his feet, and oil for anointing the hair of the head and the beard. All these courteous attentions were omitted by Simon. Jesus took His place, probably on one of the divans or couches on which it was usual to partly sit, partly recline, while eating.[jj] Such an attitude would place the feet of the

---

[gg] Mark 6:14–16.

[hh] *Articles of Faith*, pp. 187–88.

[ii] Luke 7:36; see further, verses 37–50.

[jj] Note 9, end of chapter.

person outward from the table. In addition to these facts relating to the usages of the time it should be further remembered that dwellings were not protected against intrusion by such amenities of privacy as now prevail. It was not unusual at that time in Palestine for visitors and even strangers, usually men however, to enter a house at meal time, observe the procedure and even speak to the guests, all without bidding or invitation.

Among those who entered Simon's house while the meal was in progress, was a woman; and the presence of a woman, though somewhat unusual, was not strictly a social impropriety and could not well be forbidden on such an occasion. But this woman was one of the fallen class, a woman who had been unvirtuous, and who had to bear, as part of the penalty for her sins, outward scorn and practical ostracism from those who professed to be morally superior. She approached Jesus from behind, and bent low to kiss His feet as a mark of humility on her part and of respectful homage to Him. She may have been one of those who had heard His gracious words, spoken possibly that day: "Come unto me, all ye that labour and are heavy laden, and I will give you rest." Whatever her motive in coming, she had certainly come in a repentant and deeply contrite state. As she leaned over the feet of Jesus her tears rained upon them. Seemingly oblivious of her surroundings and of disapproving eyes watching her movements, she shook out her tresses and wiped the Lord's feet with her hair. Then, opening an alabaster box of ointment, she anointed them, as a slave might do to his master. Jesus graciously permitted the woman to proceed unrebuked and uninterrupted in her humble service inspired by contrition and reverent love.

Simon had observed the whole proceeding; by some means he had knowledge as to the class to which this woman belonged; and though not aloud, within himself he said: "This man, if he were a prophet, would have known who and what manner of woman this is that toucheth him: for she is a sinner." Jesus read the man's thoughts, and thus spake: "Simon, I have somewhat to say unto thee," to which the Pharisee replied, "Master, say on." Jesus continued, "There was a certain creditor which had two debtors: the one owed five hundred pence, and the other fifty. And when they had nothing to pay, he frankly forgave them both. Tell me therefore, which of them will love him most?" But one answer could be given with reason, and that Simon gave, though apparently with some hesitation or reserve. He possibly feared that he might involve himself. "I suppose," he ventured, "that he, to whom he forgave most." Jesus said, "Thou hast rightly judged," and proceeded: "Seest thou this woman? I entered into thine house, thou gavest me no water for my feet; but she hath washed my feet with tears, and wiped them with the hairs of her head. Thou gavest me no kiss: but this woman since the time I came in hath not ceased to kiss my feet. My head with oil thou didst not anoint: but this woman hath anointed my feet with ointment."

The Pharisee could not fail to note so direct a reminder of his having omitted the ordinary rites of respect to a specially invited guest. The lesson of the story had found its application in him, even as Nathan's parable had drawn from David the king a self-convicting answer.[kk] "Wherefore," Jesus continued, "I say unto thee, Her sins, which are many, are forgiven; for she loved much: but to whom little is forgiven, the same loveth little." Then to the woman He spake the words of blessed relief: "Thy sins are forgiven." Simon and the others at table murmured within themselves, "Who is this that forgiveth sins also?" Understanding their unspoken protest, Christ addressed the woman again, saying, "Thy faith hath saved thee; go in peace."

The latter part of the narrative brings to mind another occasion on which Christ granted remission of sins, and because of opposition in the minds of some hearers, opposition none the less real because unvoiced, had supplemented His authoritative utterance by another pronouncement.[ll]

The name of the woman who thus came to Christ, and whose repentance was so sincere as to bring to her grateful and contrite soul the assurance of remission, is not recorded. There is no evidence that she figures in any other incident recorded in scripture. By certain writers she has been represented as the Mary of Bethany who, shortly before Christ's betrayal, anointed the head of Jesus with spikenard;[mm]

kk 2 Sam. 12:1–7.
ll Matt. 9:2–6; Mark 2:5–7.
mm Matt. 26:6, 7; Mark 14:3; John 11:2.

but the assumption of identity is wholly unfounded,[nn] and constitutes an unjustifiable reflection upon the earlier life of Mary, the devoted and loving sister of Martha and Lazarus. Equally wrong is the attempt made by others to identify this repentant and forgiven sinner with Mary Magdalene, no period of whose life was marked by the sin of unchastity so far as the scriptures aver. The importance of guarding against mistakes in the identity of these women renders advisable the following addition to the foregoing treatment.

In the chapter following that in which are recorded the incidents last considered, Luke[oo] states that Jesus went throughout the region, visiting every city and village, preaching the gospel of the kingdom and showing the glad tidings thereof. With Him on this tour were the Twelve, and also "certain women, which had been healed of evil spirits and infirmities, Mary called Magdalene, out of whom went seven devils, and Joanna the wife of Chuza Herod's steward, and Susanna, and many others, which ministered unto him of their substance." Further reference is made to some or all of these honorable women in connection with the death, burial, and Resurrection of our Lord, and of Mary Magdalene particular mention appears.[pp] Mary Magdalene, whose second name is probably derived from her home town, Magdala, had been healed through the ministrations of Jesus from both physical and mental maladies, the latter having been associated with possession by evil spirits. Out of her we are told Christ had cast seven devils,[qq] but even such grievous affliction affords no warrant for the assertion that the woman was unvirtuous or unchaste.

Mary Magdalene became one of the closest friends Christ had among women; her devotion to Him as her Healer and as the One whom she adored as the Christ was unswerving; she stood close by the cross while other women tarried afar off in the time of His mortal agony; she was among the first at the sepulchre on the Resurrection morning, and was the first mortal to look upon and recognize a resurrected

---

[nn] Note 10, end of chapter.

[oo] Luke 8:1–3.

[pp] Matt. 27:55, 56, 61; 28:1, 5; Mark 15:40, 47; 16:1, 9; Luke 23:49, 55; 24:10, 22; John 19:25; 20:1, 13, 18.

[qq] Mark 16:9; Luke 8:2.

Being—the Lord whom she had loved with all the fervor of spiritual adoration. To say that this woman, chosen from among women as deserving of such distinctive honors, was once a fallen creature, her soul seared by the heat of unhallowed lust, is to contribute to the perpetuating of an error for which there is no excuse. Nevertheless the false tradition, arising from early and unjustifiable assumption, that this noble woman, distinctively a friend of the Lord, is the same who, admittedly a sinner, washed and anointed the Savior's feet in the house of Simon the Pharisee and gained the boon of forgiveness through contrition, has so tenaciously held its place in the popular mind through the centuries, that the name, Magdalene, has come to be a generic designation for women who fall from virtue and afterward repent. We are not considering whether the mercy of Christ could have been extended to such a sinner as Mary of Magdala is wrongly reputed to have been; man cannot measure the bounds nor fathom the depths of divine forgiveness; and if it were so that this Mary and the repentant sinner who ministered to Jesus as He sat at the Pharisee's table were one and the same, the question would stand affirmatively answered, for that woman who had been a sinner was forgiven. We are dealing with the scriptural record as a history, and nothing said therein warrants the really repellent though common imputation of unchastity to the devoted soul of Mary Magdalene.

CHRIST'S AUTHORITY ASCRIBED TO BEELZEBUB [rr]

At the time of our Lord's earthly ministry, the curing of the blind, deaf, or dumb was regarded as among the greatest possible achievements of medical science or spiritual treatment; and the subjection or casting out of demons was ranked among the attainments impossible to rabbinical exorcism. Demonstrations of the Lord's power to heal and restore, even in cases universally considered as incurable, had the effect of intensifying the hostility of the sacerdotal classes; and they, represented by the Pharisaic party, evolved the wholly inconsistent and ridiculous suggestion that miracles were wrought by Jesus through the power of the prince of devils, with whom He was in league.[ss]

[rr] Matt. 12:24, 25; compare 9:33, 34; see also Mark 3:22–30; Luke 11:14–26.
[ss] Matt. 9:34.

While the Lord was making His second missionary tour through Galilee, going about through "all the cities and villages, teaching in their synagogues, and preaching the gospel of the kingdom, and healing every sickness and every disease among the people,^{tt} the absurd theory that Christ was Himself a victim of demoniacal possession, and that He operated by the power of the devil, was urged and enlarged upon until it became the generally accepted explanation among the Pharisees and their kind. Jesus had withdrawn Himself for a time from the more populous centers, where He was constantly watched by emissaries, whom the ruling classes had sent from Jerusalem into Galilee; for the Pharisees were in conspiracy against Him, seeking excuse and opportunity to take His life; but even in the smaller towns and rural districts He was followed and beset by great multitudes, to whom He ministered for both physical and spiritual ailments.^{uu}

He urged the people to refrain from spreading His fame; and this He may have done for the reason that at that stage of His work an open rupture with the Jewish hierarchy would have been a serious hindrance; or possibly He desired to leave the rulers, who were plotting against Him, time and opportunity to brew their bitter enmity and fill to the brim the flagons of their determined iniquity. Matthew sees in the Lord's injunctions against publicity a fulfillment of Isaiah's prophecy that the chosen Messiah would not strive nor cry out on the street to attract attention, nor would He use His mighty power to crush even a bruised reed, or to quench even the smoking flax; He would not fail nor be discouraged, but would victoriously establish just judgment upon the earth for the Gentiles, as well as, by implication, for Israel.^{vv} The figure of the bruised reed and the smoking flax is strikingly expressive of the tender care with which Christ treated even the weakest manifestation of faith and genuine desire to learn the truth, whether exhibited by Jew or Gentile.

Soon after His return from the missionary tour referred to, an excuse for the Pharisees to assail Him was found in His healing of a man who was under the influence of a demon, and was both blind

^{tt} Matt. 9:35.
^{uu} Matt. 12:14–15.
^{vv} Matt. 12:17–20; compare Isa. 42:1.

and dumb. This combination of sore afflictions, affecting body, mind, and spirit, was rebuked, and the sightless, speechless demoniac was relieved of his threefold burden.[ww] At this triumph over the powers of evil the people were the more amazed and said: "Is not this the son of David?" in other words, Can this be any other than the Christ we have been so long expecting? The popular judgment so voiced maddened the Pharisees, and they told the almost adoring people: "This fellow doth not cast out devils, but by Beelzebub the prince of devils." Jesus took up the malicious charge and replied thereto, not in anger but in terms of calm reason and sound logic. He laid the foundation of His defense by stating the evident truth that a kingdom divided against itself cannot endure but must surely suffer disruption. If their assumption were in the least degree founded on truth, Satan through Jesus would be opposing Satan. Then, referring to the superstitious practices and exorcisms of the time, by which some such effects as we class today under mind cures were obtained, He asked: "If I by Beelzebub cast out devils, by whom do your children cast them out? therefore they shall be your judges." And to make the demonstration plainer by contrast, He continued: "But if I cast out devils by the Spirit of God, then the kingdom of God is come unto you." By the acceptance of either proposition, and surely one was true, for the fact that Jesus did cast out devils was known throughout the land and was conceded in the very terms of the charge now brought against Him, the accusing Pharisees stood defeated and condemned.

But the illustration went further. Jesus continued: "Or else how can one enter into a strong man's house, and spoil his goods, except he first bind the strong man? and then he will spoil his house." Christ had attacked the stronghold of Satan, had driven his evil spirits from the human tabernacles of which they had unwarrantably taken possession; how could Christ have done this had He not first subdued the "strong man," the master of devils, Satan himself? And yet those ignorant scholars dared to say in the face of such self-evident refutation of their own premises, that the powers of Satan were subdued by Satanic agency. There could be no agreement, no truce nor armistice between

---

[ww] Matt. 12:22, 23.

the contending powers of Christ and Satan. Offering a suggestion of self judgment to His accusers, that they might severally decide on which side they were aligned, Jesus added: "He that is not with me is against me; and he that gathereth not with me scattereth abroad."

Then, the demonstration being complete, and the absurdity of His opponents' assumption proved, Christ directed their thoughts to the heinous sin of condemning the power and authority by which Satan was overcome. He had proved to them on the basis of their own proposition that He, having subdued Satan, was the embodiment of the Spirit of God, and that through Him the kingdom of God was brought to them. They rejected the Spirit of God, and sought to destroy the Christ through whom that Spirit was made manifest. What blasphemy could be greater? Speaking as one having authority, with the solemn affirmation "I say unto you," He continued: "All manner of sin and blasphemy shall be forgiven unto men: but the blasphemy against the Holy Ghost shall not be forgiven unto men. And whosoever speaketh a word against the Son of man, it shall be forgiven him: but whosoever speaketh against the Holy Ghost, it shall not be forgiven him, neither in this world, neither in the world to come."

Who among men can word a more solemn and awful warning against the danger of committing the dread unpardonable sin?[xx] Jesus was merciful in His assurance that words spoken against Himself as a Man, might be forgiven; but to speak against the authority He possessed, and particularly to ascribe that power and authority to Satan, was very near to blasphemy against the Holy Ghost, for which sin there could be no forgiveness. Then, in stronger terms, which developed into cutting invective, He told them to be consistent—if they admitted that the result of His labors was good, as the casting out of devils surely was, to be likened unto good fruit—why did they not acknowledge that the power by which such results were attained, in other words that the tree itself, was good? "Either make the tree good, and his fruit good; or else make the tree corrupt, and his fruit corrupt: for the tree is known by his fruit." With burning words of certain conviction He continued: "O generation of vipers, how can

[xx] Note 11, end of chapter.

ye, being evil, speak good things? for out of the abundance of the heart the mouth speaketh." By the truths He had made so plain it was evident that their accusing words were drawn from hearts stored with evil treasure. Moreover their words were shown to be not only malicious but foolish, idle and vain, and therefore doubly saturated with sin. Another authoritative declaration followed: "But I say unto you, That every idle word that men shall speak, they shall give account thereof in the day of judgment."

SEEKERS AFTER SIGNS[yy]

The Master's lesson, enforced though it was by illustration and analogy, by direct application, and by authoritative avowal, fell on ears that were practically deaf to spiritual truth, and found no place in hearts already stuffed with great stores of evil. To the profound wisdom and saving instruction of the word of God to which they had listened, they responded with a flippant request: "Master, we would see a sign from thee." Had they not already seen signs in profusion? Had not the blind and the deaf, the dumb and the infirm, the palsied and the dropsical, and people afflicted with all manner of diseases, been healed in their houses, on their streets, and in their synagogs; had not devils been cast out and their foul utterances been silenced by His word; and had not the dead been raised, and all by Him whom they now importuned for a sign? They would have some surpassing wonder wrought, to satisfy curiosity, or perhaps to afford them further excuse for action against Him—they wanted signs to waste on their lust.[zz] Small wonder, that "he sighed deeply in his spirit" when such demands were made.[aaa] To the scribes and Pharisees who had shown such inattention to His words, He replied: "An evil and adulterous generation[bbb] seeketh after a sign; and there shall no sign be given to it, but the sign of the prophet Jonas."

The sign of Jonas (or Jonah) was that for three days he had been in the belly of the fish and then had been restored to liberty; so would

[yy] Matt. 12:38–45; compare 16:1; Mark 8:11; Luke 11:16, 29; John 2:18; 1 Cor. 1:22.

[zz] D&C 46:9; compare 63:7–12.

[aaa] Mark 8:12.

[bbb] Note 12, end of chapter.

the Son of Man be immured in the tomb, after which He would rise again. That was the only sign He would give them, and by that would they stand condemned. Against them and their generation would the men of Nineveh rise in judgment, for they, wicked as they were, had repented at the preaching of Jonas; and behold a greater than Jonas was among them.[ccc] The queen of Sheba would rise in judgment against them, for she had journeyed far to avail herself of Solomon's wisdom; and behold a greater than Solomon stood before them.[ddd]

Then, reverting to the matter of unclean and evil spirits, in connection with which they had spread the accusation that He was one of the devil's own, He told them, that when a demon is cast out, he tries after a season of loneliness to return to the house or body from which he had been expelled and, finding that house in order, sweet and clean since his filthy self had been forced to vacate it, he calls other spirits more wicked than himself, and they take possession of the man, and make his state worse than it was at first.[eee] In this weird example is typified the condition of those who have received the truth, and thereby have been freed from the unclean influences of error and sin, so that in mind and spirit and body they are as a house swept and garnished and set in cleanly order, but who afterward renounce the good, open their souls to the demons of falsehood and deceit, and become more corrupt than before. "Even so," declared the Lord, "shall it be also unto this wicked generation."

Though the scribes and Pharisees were mostly unconvinced, if at all really impressed by His teachings, our Lord was not entirely without appreciative listeners. A woman in the company raised her voice in an invocation of blessing on the mother who had given birth to such a Son, and on the breasts that had suckled Him. While not rejecting this tribute of reverence, which applied to both mother and Son, Jesus answered: "Yea rather, blessed are they that hear the word of God, and keep it."[fff]

[ccc] Jonah 1–4.

[ddd] 1 Kgs. 10:1; 2 Chr. 9:1; compare Luke 11:31.

[eee] Matt. 12:43–45; Luke 11:24–26.

[fff] Luke 11:27–28.

CHRIST'S MOTHER AND BRETHREN COME TO SEE HIM[ggg]

While Jesus was engaged with the scribes and Pharisees, and a great number of others, possibly at or near the conclusion of the teachings last considered, word was passed to Him that His mother and His brethren were present and desired to speak with Him. On account of the press of people they had been unable to reach His side. Making use of the circumstance to impress upon all the fact that His work took precedence over the claims of family and kinship, and thereby explaining that He could not meet His relatives at that moment, He asked, "Who is my mother? and who are my brethren?" Answering His own question and expressing in the answer the deeper thought in His mind, He said, pointing toward His disciples: "Behold my mother and my brethren! For whosoever shall do the will of my Father which is in heaven, the same is my brother, and sister, and mother."

The incident reminds one of the answer He made to His mother, when she and Joseph had found Him in the temple after their long and anxious search: "How is it that ye sought me? wist ye not that I must be about my Father's business?"[hhh] In that business He was engaged when His mother and brethren desired to speak with Him as He sat amidst the crowd. The superior claims of His Father's work caused Him to let all minor matters wait. We are not justified in construing these remarks as evidence of disrespect, far less of filial and family disloyalty. Devotion, similar in kind at least, was expected by Him of the apostles, who were called to devote without reserve their time and talents to the ministry.[iii] The purpose on which the relatives of Jesus had come to see Him is not made known; we may infer, therefore, that it was of no great importance beyond the family circle.[jjj]

NOTES TO CHAPTER 18

1. **The Two Accounts of the Miracle.**—In the commentary on the miraculous healing of the centurion's servant, as given in the text, we have followed in the main

[ggg] Matt. 12:46–50; Mark 3:31–35; Luke 8:19–21.
[hhh] Luke 2:49.
[iii] Matt. 10:37; compare Luke 14:26.
[jjj] Note 13, end of chapter.

Luke's more circumstantial account. Matthew's briefer statement of the officer's petition, and the Lord's gracious compliance therewith, represents the man as coming in person to Jesus; while Luke refers to the elders of the local synagog as presenting the request. There is here no real discrepancy. It was then allowable, as in our time it is, to speak of one who causes something to be done as doing that thing himself. One may properly be said to notify another, when he sends the notification by a third party. A man may say he has built a house, when in reality others did the work of building though at his instance. An architect may with propriety be said to have constructed a building, when as a matter of fact he made the design, and directed others who actually reared the structure.

2. Jesus Marveled.—Both Matthew and Luke tell us that Jesus marveled at the faith shown by the centurion, who begged that his beloved servant be healed (Matt. 8:10; Luke 7:9). Some have queried how Christ, whom they consider to have been omniscient during His life in the flesh, could have marveled at anything. The meaning of the passage is evident in the sense that when the fact of the centurion's faith was brought to His attention, He pondered over it, and contemplated it, probably as a refreshing contrast to the absence of faith He so generally encountered. In similar way, though with sorrow in place of joy, He is said to have marveled at the people's unbelief (Mark 6:6).

3. Sequence of the Miracles of Raising the Dead.—As stated and reiterated in the text the chronology of the events in our Lord's ministry, as recorded by the Gospel-writers, is uncertain. Literature on the subject embodies much disputation and demonstrates absence of any near approach to agreement among Biblical scholars. We have record of three instances of miraculous restoration of the dead to life at the word of Jesus—the raising of the son of the widow of Nain, the raising of the daughter of Jairus, and the raising of Lazarus; and on the sequence of two of these there is difference of opinion. Of course the placing of the raising of Lazarus as the latest of the three is based on certainty. Dr. Richard C. Trench, in his scholarly and very valuable *Notes on the Miracles of Our Lord* definitely asserts that the raising of the daughter of Jairus is the first of the three works of restoration to life. Dr. John Laidlaw, in *The Miracles of Our Lord,* treats this first among the miracles of its class though without affirming its chronological precedence; many other writers make it the second of the three. The incentive to arrange the three miracles of this group in the sequence indicated may, perhaps, be found in the desire to present them in the increasing order of apparent greatness—the raising of the damsel being an instance of recalling to life one who had but just died, ("hardly dead" as some wrongly describe her condition), the raising of the young man of Nain being the restoration of one on the way to the tomb, and the raising of Lazarus an instance of recalling to life one who had lain four days in the sepulchre. We cannot consistently conceive of these cases as offering grades of greater or lesser difficulty to the power of Christ; in each case His word of authority was sufficient to reunite the spirit and body of the dead person. Luke, the sole recorder of the miracle at Nain, places the event before that of the raising of the daughter of Jairus, with many incidents between. The great preponderance of evidence is in favor of considering the three miracles in the order followed herein, (1) the raising of the young man of Nain, (2) that of the daughter of Jairus, and (3) that of Lazarus.

4. Tetrarch.—This title by derivation of the term and as originally used was applied to the ruler of a fourth part, or one of four divisions of a region that had formerly been one country. Later it came to be the designation of any ruler or governor over a part of a divided country, irrespective of the number or extent of the fractions. Herod Antipas is distinctively called the tetrarch in Matt. 14:1; Luke 3:1, 19; 9:7; and Acts 13:1; and is referred to as king in Matt. 14:9; Mark 6:14, 22, 25, 26.

5. Machaerus.—According to the historian Josephus (*Antiquities* xviii, 5:2), the prison to which John the Baptist was consigned by Herod Antipas was the strong fortress Machaerus.

6. Christ an Offender to Many.—The concluding part of our Lord's message to the imprisoned Baptist, in answer to the latter's inquiry, was, "Blessed is he whosoever is not offended in me." In passing it may be well to observe that whatever of reproof or rebuke these words may connote, the lesson was given in the gentlest way and in the form most easy to understand. As Deems has written, "Instead of saying 'Woe to him who is offended in me,' He puts it in the softer way 'Blessed is he who is not offended.'" In our English version of the Holy Bible the word "offend" and its cognates are used in place of several different expressions which occur in the original Greek. Thus, actual infractions of the law, sin, and wickedness in general are all called offenses and the perpetrators of such are guilty offenders who deserve punishment. In other instances even the works of righteousness are construed as causes of offense to the wicked; but this is so, not because the good works were in any way offenses against law or right, but because the lawbreaker takes offense thereat. The convicted felon, if unrepentant and still of evil mind, is offended and angry at the law by which he has been brought to justice; to him the law is a cause of offense. In a very significant sense Jesus Christ stands as the greatest offender in history; for all who reject His gospel, take offense thereat. On the night of His betrayal Jesus told the apostles that they would be offended because of Him (Matt. 26:31; see also verse 33). The Lord's personal ministry gave offense not alone to Pharisees and priestly opponents, but to many who had professed belief in Him (John 6:61; compare 16:1). The gospel of Jesus Christ is designated by Peter as "a stone of stumbling and a rock of offense, even to them which stumble at the words, being disobedient" (1 Pet. 2:8; compare Paul's words, Rom. 9:33). Indeed blessed is he to whom the gospel is welcome, and who finds therein no cause for offense.

7. The Greatness of the Baptist's Mission.—The exalted nature of the mission of John the Baptist was thus testified to by Jesus: "Verily I say unto you, Among them that are born of women there hath not risen a greater than John the Baptist: notwithstanding he that is least in the kingdom of heaven is greater than he" (Matt. 11:11; compare Luke 7:28). In elucidation of the first part of this testimony, the prophet Joseph Smith said, in the course of a sermon delivered May 24, 1843 (*History of the Church*, under date named): "It could not have been on account of the miracles John performed, for he did no miracles; but it was—First, because he was trusted with a divine mission of preparing the way before the face of the Lord. Who was trusted with such a mission before or since? No man. Second, he was trusted and it was required at his hands to baptize the Son of Man. Who ever did that? Who ever had so great a privilege or glory? Who ever led the Son of God into the waters of baptism, beholding the Holy Ghost descend upon Him in the sign of a dove? No man. Third, John at that time was the only legal administrator holding the keys of power there was on earth. The keys, the kingdom, the power, the glory had departed from the Jews; and John, the son of Zacharias, by the holy anointing and decree of heaven, held the keys of power at that time."

The latter part of our Lord's statement—"notwithstanding he that is least in the kingdom of heaven is greater than he" (John), has given rise to diverse interpretations and comment. The true meaning may be, that surpassingly great as was John's distinction among the prophets, he had not learned, at the time of the incident under consideration, the full purpose of the Messiah's mission, and such he would surely have to learn before he became eligible for admission into the kingdom of heaven; therefore, the least of those who, through knowledge gained and obedience rendered, would be prepared for a place in the kingdom of which Jesus taught, was greater than was John the Baptist at that time. Through latter-day inspiration we learn that "it is impossible for a man to be saved in ignorance" (D&C 131:6), and that "The glory of God is intelligence, or, in other words, light and truth" (D&C 93:36). The Baptist's inquiry showed that he was then lacking in knowledge, imperfectly enlightened and unable to comprehend the whole truth of the Savior's appointed death and subsequent Resurrection as the Redeemer of the world. But we must not lose sight of the fact that Jesus in no wise intimated that John would remain less than the least in the kingdom of heaven. As he increased in knowledge of the vital truths of the kingdom, and rendered obedience thereto, he would surely advance, and become great in the kingdom of heaven as he was great among the prophets of earth.

8. John the Baptist the Elias that Was to Come.—In the days of Christ the people clung to the traditional belief that the ancient prophet Elijah was to return in person. Concerning this tradition the Dummelow *Commentary* says, on Matt. 11:14: "It was supposed that his [Elijah's] peculiar activity would consist in settling ceremonial and ritual questions, doubts and difficulties and that he would restore to Israel (1) the golden pot of manna, (2) the vessel containing the anointing oil,

(3) the vessel containing the waters of purification, (4) Aaron's rod that budded and bore fruit." For this belief there was no scriptural affirmation. That John was to go before the Messiah in the spirit and power of Elias was declared by the angel Gabriel in his announcement to Zacharias (Luke 1:17); and our Lord made plain the fact that John was the predicted Elias. "Elias" is both a name and a title of office. Through revelation in the present dispensation we learn of the separate individuality of Elias and Elijah, each of whom appeared in person and committed to modern prophets the particular powers pertaining to his respective office (D&C 110:12, 13). We learn that the office of Elias is that of restoration (D&C 27:6, 7; 76:100; 77:9, 14). Under date of March 10, 1844, the following is recorded (*History of the Church*) as the testimony of the prophet Joseph Smith:—

"The spirit of Elias is to prepare the way for a greater revelation of God, which is the Priesthood of Elias, or the Priesthood that Aaron was ordained unto. And when God sends a man into the world to prepare for a greater work, holding the keys of the power of Elias, it was called the doctrine of Elias, even from the early ages of the world.

"John's mission was limited to preaching and baptizing; but what he did was legal; and when Jesus Christ came to any of John's disciples, He baptized then with fire and the Holy Ghost.

"We find the apostles endowed with greater power than John: their office was more under the spirit and power of Elijah than Elias.

"In the case of Philip when he went down to Samaria, when he was under the spirit of Elias, he baptized both men and women. When Peter and John heard of it, they went down and laid hands upon them, and they received the Holy Ghost. This shows the distinction between the two powers.

"When Paul came to certain disciples, he asked if they had received the Holy Ghost? They said, No. Who baptized you, then? We were baptized unto John's baptism. No, you were not baptized unto John's baptism, or you would have been baptized by John. And so Paul went and baptized them, for he knew what the true doctrine was, and he knew that John had not baptized them. And these principles are strange to me, that men who have read the Scriptures of the New Testament are so far from it.

"What I want to impress upon your minds is the difference of power in the different parts of the Priesthood, so that when any man comes among you, saying, 'I have the spirit of Elias,' you can know whether he be true or false; for any man that comes, having the spirit and power of Elias, he will not transcend his bounds.

"John did not transcend his bounds, but faithfully performed that part belonging to his office; and every portion of the great building should be prepared right and assigned to its proper place; and it is necessary to know who holds the keys of power, and who does not, or we may be likely to be deceived.

"That person who holds the keys of Elias hath a preparatory work. . . .

"This is the Elias spoken of in the last days, and here is the rock upon which many split, thinking the time was past in the days of John and Christ, and no more to be. But the spirit of Elias was revealed to me, and I know it is true; therefore I speak with boldness, for I know verily my doctrine is true."

9. At the Pharisee's Table.—The expression "sat at meat," as in Luke 7:37 and in other instances, is stated by good authority to be a mistranslation; it should be rendered "lay" or "reclined" (see Smith's *Comp. Dictionary of the Bible,* article "Meals"). That sitting was the early Hebrew posture at meals is not questioned (Gen. 27:19; Judg. 19:6; 1 Sam. 16:11; 20:5, 18, 24; 1 Kgs. 13:20); but the custom of reclining on couches set around the table seems to date back long before the days of Jesus (Amos 3:12; 6:4). The Roman usage of arranging the tables and adjoining couches along three sides of a square, leaving the fourth side open for the passage of the attendants who served the diners was common in Palestine. Tables and couches so placed constituted the *triclinium.* In reference to the ceremonial of the Pharisees in the matter of prescribed washing of articles used in eating, Mark (7:4) specifies "tables"; this mention is conceded to be a mistranslation, as couches or literally beds, are meant by the Greek expression. (See marginal reading, "beds" in Oxford Bible, and others.) A person reclining at table would have the feet directed outward. Thus it was a simple matter for the contrite woman to approach Jesus from behind and anoint His feet without causing disturbance to others at the table.

10. The Woman's Identity not Specified.—The attempt to identify the contrite sinner who anointed the feet of Jesus in the house of Simon the Pharisee with Mary of Bethany is thus strongly condemned by Farrar (p. 228, note): "Those who identify this feast at the house of Simon the Pharisee, in Galilee, with the long-subsequent feast at the house of Simon the leper, at Bethany, and the anointing of the feet by 'a woman that was a sinner' in the city, with the anointing of the head by Mary the sister of Martha, adopt principles of criticism so reckless and arbitrary that their general acceptance would rob the Gospels of all credibility, and make them hardly worth study as truthful narratives. As for the names Simon and Judas, which have led to so many identifications of different persons and different incidents, they were at least as common among the Jews of that day as Smith and Jones among ourselves. There are five or six Judes and nine Simons mentioned in the New Testament, and two Judes and two Simons among the Apostles alone; Josephus speaks of some ten Judes and twenty Simons in his writings, and there must, therefore, have been thousands of others who at this period had one of these two names. The incident (of anointing with ointment) is one quite in accordance with the customs of the time and country, and there is not the least improbability in its repetition under different circumstances. (Eccl. 9:8; Cant. 4:10; Amos 6:6.) The custom still continues.

The learned canon is fully justified in his vigorous criticism; nevertheless he endorses the commonly accepted identification of the woman mentioned in connection with the meal in the house of Simon the Pharisee with Mary Magdalene, although he admits that the foundation of the assumed identification is "an ancient tradition,—especially prevalent in the Western Church, and followed by the translation of our English version" (p. 233). As stated in our text, there is an entire absence of trustworthy evidence that Mary Magdalene was ever tainted with the sin for which the repentant woman in the Pharisee's house was so graciously pardoned by our Lord.

11. The Unpardonable Sin.—The nature of the awful sin against the Holy Ghost, against which the Lord warned the Pharisaic accusers who sought to ascribe His divine power to Satan, is more fully explained, and its dread results are more explicitly set forth in modern revelation. Concerning them and their dreadful fate, the Almighty has said:—"I say that it had been better for them never to have been born, for they are vessels of wrath, doomed to suffer the wrath of God, with the devil and his angels in eternity; concerning whom I have said there is no forgiveness in this world nor in the world to come. . . . They shall go away into everlasting punishment, which is endless punishment, which is eternal punishment, to reign with the devil and his angels in eternity, where their worm dieth not, and the fire is not quenched, which is their torment; and the end thereof, neither the place thereof, nor their torment, no man knows, neither was it revealed, neither is, neither will be revealed unto man, except to them who are made partakers thereof: nevertheless I, the Lord, show it by vision unto many, but straightway shut it up again; wherefore the end, the width, the height, the depth, and the misery thereof, they understand not, neither any man except them who are ordained unto this condemnation." (D&C 76:31–48; see also Heb. 6:4–6; Alma 39:6.)

12. An Adulterous Generation Seeking after Signs.—Our Lord's reply to those who clamored for a sign, that "An evil and adulterous generation seeketh after a sign" (Matt. 12:39; see also 16:4; Mark 8:38) could only be interpreted by the Jews as a supreme reproof. That the descriptive designation "adulterous" was literally applicable to the widespread immorality of the time, they all knew. Adam Clarke in his commentary on Matt. 12:39, says of this phase of our topic: "There is the utmost proof from their [the Jews'] own writings, that in the time of our Lord, they were most literally an adulterous race of people; for at this very time Rabbi Jachanan ben Zacchi abrogated the trial by the bitter waters of jealousy, because so many were found to be thus criminal." For the information concerning the trial of the accused by the bitter waters, see Num. 5:11–31. Although Jesus designated the generation in which He lived as adulterous, we find no record that the Jewish rulers, who by their demand for a sign had given occasion for the accusation, ventured to deny or attempt to repel the charge. The sin of adultery was included among capital offenses (Deut. 22:22–25). The severity of the accusation as applied by Jesus, however, was intensified by the fact that the older scriptures represented the covenant between Jehovah and Israel as a marriage bond (Isa. 54:5–7; Jer. 3:14; 31:32; Hosea 2:19, 20); even as the later scriptures typify the Church as a bride, and Christ as the husband (2 Cor. 11:2; compare Rev. 21:2). To be spiritually adulterous, as the rabbis construed the utterances of the prophets, was to be false to the covenant by which the Jewish nations claimed distinction, as the worshipers of Jehovah, and to be wholly recreant and reprobate. Convicted on such a charge those sign-seeking Pharisees and scribes understood that Jesus classed them as worse than the idolatrous heathen. The words "adultery" and "idolatry" are of related origin, each connoting the act of unfaithfulness and the turning away after false objects of affection or worship.

13. The Mother and the Brethren of Jesus.—The attempt of Mary and some members of her family to speak with Jesus on the occasion referred to in the text has been construed by many writers to mean that the mother and sons had come to protest against the energy and zeal with which Jesus was pursuing His work. Some indeed have gone so far as to say that the visiting members of the family had come to put Him under restraint, and to stem, if they could, the tide of popular interest, criticism, and offense, which surged about Him. The scriptural record furnishes no foundation for even a tentative conception of the kind. The purpose of the desired visit is not intimated. It is a fact as will be shown in pages to follow, that some members of Mary's household had failed to understand the great import of the work in which Jesus was so assiduously engaged; and we are told that some of His friends (marginal rendering, "kinsmen,") on one occasion set out with the purpose of laying hold on Him and stopping His public activities by physical force, for they said "He is beside himself." (Mark 3:21); furthermore we learn that His brethren did not believe on Him (John 7:5). These facts, however, scarcely warrant the assumption that the desire of Mary and her sons to speak with him on the occasion referred to was other than peaceful. And to assume that Mary, His mother, had so far forgotten the wondrous scenes of the angelic annunciation, the miraculous conception, the heavenly accompaniments of the birth, the more than human wisdom and power exhibited in youth and manhood, as to believe her divine Son an unbalanced enthusiast, whom she ought to restrain, is to assume responsibility for injustice to the character of one whom the angel Gabriel declared was blessed among women, and highly favored of the Lord.

The statement that the brethren of Jesus did not believe on Him at the time referred to by the recorder (John 7:5) is no proof that some or even all of those same brethren did not later believe on their divine Brother. Immediately after the Lord's ascension, Mary, the mother of Jesus, and His brethren were engaged in worship and supplication with the Eleven and other disciples (Acts 1:14). The attested fact of Christ's Resurrection converted many who had before declined to accept Him as the Son of God. Paul records special manifestation of the resurrected Christ to James (1 Cor. 15:7) and the James here referred to may be the same person elsewhere designated as "the Lord's brother" (Gal. 1:19); compare Matt. 13:55; Mark 6:3. It appears that "brethren of the Lord" were engaged in the work of the ministry in the days of Paul's active service (1 Cor. 9:5). The specific family relationship of our Lord to James, Joses, Simon, Judas and the sisters referred to by Matthew (13:55, 56), and Mark (6:3), has been questioned; and several theories have been invented in support of divergent views. Thus, the eastern or Epiphanian hypothesis holds, on no firmer basis than assumption, that the brethren of Jesus were children of Joseph of Nazareth by a former wife, and not the children of Mary the Lord's mother. The Levirate theory assumes that Joseph of Nazareth and Clopas (the latter name, it is interesting to note, is regarded as the equivalent of Alpheus), were brothers; and that, after the death of Clopas or Alpheus, Joseph married his brother's widow according to the levirate law. The Hieronymian hypothesis is based on the belief that the persons referred to as brethren and sisters of Jesus were children of Clopas (Alpheus) and Mary the sister of the Lord's mother, and therefore cousins to Jesus. (See Matt. 27:56; Mark 15:40; John 19:25.) It is beyond reasonable doubt that Jesus was regarded by those who were acquainted with the family of Joseph and Mary as a close blood relative of other sons and daughters belonging to the household. If these others were children of Joseph and Mary, they were all juniors to Jesus, for He was undoubtedly His mother's firstborn child. The acceptance of this relationship between Jesus and His "brethren" and "sisters" mentioned by the synoptists constitutes what is known in theological literature as the Helvidian view.

CHAPTER 19

"HE SPAKE MANY THINGS UNTO THEM IN PARABLES"

Throughout with which we have thus far dealt, His fame had continuously increased, because of the authority with which He spoke and of the many mighty works He did. His popularity had become such that whenever He moved abroad great multitudes followed Him. At times the people so thronged as to impede His movements, some with a desire to hear more of the new doctrine, others to plead at His feet for relief from physical or other ills; and many there were who had faith that could they but reach Him, or even touch the border of His robe, they would be healed.[a] One effect of the people's eagerness, which led them to press and crowd around Him, was to render difficult if not impossible at times the effective delivery of any discourse. His usual place for open air teaching while He tarried in the vicinity of the sea, or lake, of Galilee was the shore; and thither flocked the crowds to hear Him. At His request the disciples had provided a "small ship," which was kept in readiness on the beach;[b] and it was usual with Him to sit in the boat a short distance off shore, and preach to the people, as He had done when in the earlier days He called the chosen fishermen to leave their nets and follow Him.[c]

On one such occasion He employed a means of instruction, which, prior to that time, had not been characteristic of His teaching; this consisted in the use of parables,[d] or simple stories to illustrate His

[a] Mark 3: 10; compare Matt. 9:20, 21; 14:36; Mark 6:56; Luke 6:19.
[b] Mark 3:9.
[c] Luke 5:10.
[d] Note 1, end of chapter.

doctrines. Some of these we shall here consider briefly, in the order most advantageous for treatment, and, as best we know, in what may have been the sequence in which they were given.

"A SOWER WENT FORTH TO SOW"

First in the order of delivery is the Parable of the Sower. It is a splendid type of our Lord's parables in general, and is particularly valuable for its great intrinsic worth and because we possess a comprehensive interpretation of it by the divine Author. This is the story:

> Behold, a sower went forth to sow; and when he sowed, some seeds fell by the way side, and the fowls came and devoured them up: some fell upon stony places, where they had not much earth: and forthwith they sprung up, because they had no deepness of earth: and when the sun was up, they were scorched; and because they had no root, they withered away. And some fell among thorns; and the thorns sprung up, and choked them: but other fell into good ground, and brought forth fruit, some an hundredfold, some sixtyfold, some thirty-fold. Who hath ears to hear, let him hear.^e

This new way of teaching, this departure from the Master's earlier method of doctrinal exposition, caused even the most devoted of the disciples to marvel. The Twelve and a few others came to Jesus when He was apart from the multitude, and asked why He had spoken to the people in this manner, and what was the meaning of this particular parable. Our Lord's reply to the first part of the inquiry we shall consider presently; concerning the second He asked "Know ye not this parable? and how then will ye know all parables?"^f Thus did He indicate the simplicity of this the first of His parables, together with its typical and fundamental character, and at the same time intimate that other parables would follow in the course of His teaching. Then He gave the interpretation:

^e Matt. 13:3–9; compare Mark 4:3–9; Luke 8:5–8.
^f Mark 4:13.

Hear ye therefore the parable of the sower. When any one heareth the word of the kingdom, and understandeth it not, then cometh the wicked one, and catcheth away that which was sown in his heart. This is he which received seed by the way side. But he that received the seed into stony places, the same is he that heareth the word, and anon with joy receiveth it; yet hath he not root in himself, but dureth for a while: for when tribulation or persecution ariseth because of the word, by and by he is offended. He also that received seed among the thorns is he that heareth the word; and the care of this world, and the deceitfulness of riches, choke the word, and he becometh unfruitful. But he that received seed into the good ground is he that heareth the word, and understandeth it; which also beareth fruit, and bringeth forth, some an hundredfold, some sixty, some thirty.[g]

Further exposition may appear superfluous; some suggestion as to the individual application of the contained lessons may be in place, however. Observe that the prominent feature of the story is that of the prepared or unprepared condition of the soil. The seed was the same, whether it fell on good ground or bad, on mellow mold or among stones and thistles. The primitive method of sowing, still followed in many countries, consisted in the sower throwing the grain by handfuls against the wind, thus securing a widespread scattering. Running through the Galilean fields were pathways, hard trodden by feet of men and beasts. Though seed should fall on such tracts, it could not grow; birds would pick up the living kernels lying unrooted and uncovered and some of the grains would be crushed and trodden down. So with the seed of truth falling upon the hardened heart; ordinarily it cannot take root, and Satan, as a marauding crow, steals it away, lest a grain of it perchance find a crack in the trampled ground, send down its rootlet, and possibly develop.

Seed falling in shallow soil, underlain by a floor of unbroken stone or hard-pan, may strike root and flourish for a brief season; but

[g] Matt. 13:18–23; compare Mark 4:13–20; Luke 8:11–15.

as the descending rootlets reach the impenetrable stratum they shrivel, and the plant withers and dies, for the nutritive juices are insufficient where there is no depth of earth.[h] So with the man whose earnestness is but superficial, whose energy ceases when obstacles are encountered or opposition met; though he manifest enthusiasm for a time persecution deters him; he is offended,[i] and endures not. Grain sown where thorns and thistles abound is soon killed out by their smothering growth; even so with a human heart set on riches and the allurements of pleasure—though it receive the living seed of the gospel it will produce no harvest of good grain, but instead, a rank tangle of noxious weeds. The abundant yield of thorny thistles demonstrates the fitness of the soil for a better crop, were it only free from the cumbering weeds. The seed that falls in good deep soil, free from weeds and prepared for the sowing, strikes root and grows; the sun's heat scorches it not, but gives it thrift; it matures and yields to the harvester according to the richness of the soil, some fields producing thirty, others sixty, and a few even a hundred times as much grain as was sown.

Even according to literary canons, and as judged by the recognized standards of rhetorical construction and logical arrangement of its parts, this parable holds first place among productions of its class. Though commonly known to us as the Parable of the Sower, the story could be expressively designated as the Parable of the Four Kinds of Soil. It is the ground upon which the seed is cast, to which the story most strongly directs our attention, and which so aptly is made to symbolize the softened or the hardened heart, the clean or the thorn-infested soil. Observe the grades of soil, given in the increasing order of their fertility: (1) the compacted highway, the wayside path, on which, save by a combination of fortuitous circumstances practically amounting to a miracle, no seed can possibly strike root or grow; (2) the thin layer of soil covering an impenetrable bedrock, wherein seed may sprout yet can never mature; (3) the weed-encumbered field, capable of producing a rich crop but for the jungle of thistles and thorns; and (4) the clean rich mold receptive and fertile. Yet even soils classed as good are of varying

[h] Note 2, end of chapter.
[i] Pages 242, 259.

degrees of productiveness, yielding an increase of thirty, sixty, or even a hundred fold, with many inter-gradations.

Some Bible expositors have professed to find in this splendid parable evidence of decisive fatalism in the lives of individuals, so that those whose spiritual state is comparable to the hardened pathway or wayside ground, to the shallow soil on stony floor, or to the neglected, thorn-ridden tract, are hopelessly and irredeemably bad; while the souls who may be likened unto good soil are safe against deterioration and will be inevitably productive of good fruit. Let it not be forgotten that a parable is but a sketch, not a picture finished in detail; and that the expressed or implied similitude in parabolic teaching cannot logically and consistently be carried beyond the limits of the illustrative story. In the parable we are considering, the Teacher depicted the varied grades of spiritual receptivity existing among men, and characterized with incisive brevity each of the specified grades. He neither said nor intimated that the hard-baked soil of the wayside might not be plowed, harrowed, fertilized, and so be rendered productive; nor that the stony impediment to growth might not be broken up and removed, or an increase of good soil be made by actual addition; nor that the thorns could never be uprooted, and their former habitat be rendered fit to support good plants. The parable is to be studied in the spirit of its purpose; and strained inferences or extensions are unwarranted. A strong metaphor, a striking simile, or any other expressive figure of speech, is of service only when rationally applied; if carried beyond the bounds of reasonable intent, the best of such may become meaningless or even absurd.

THE WHEAT AND THE TARES

Another parable, somewhat closely related to the foregoing as to the actual story, dealing again with seed and sowing, and, like the first, accompanied by an interpretation, was delivered by the Master as follows:

The kingdom of heaven is likened unto a man which sowed good seed in his field: but while men slept, his enemy came and sowed tares among the wheat, and went his way. But when the blade was sprung up, and brought forth fruit, then appeared the tares also. So the servants of the householder came and said unto him, Sir, didst not thou sow good seed in thy field? from whence then hath it tares? He said unto them, An enemy hath done this. The servants said unto him, Wilt thou then that we go and gather them up? But he said, Nay; lest while ye gather up the tares, ye root up also the wheat with them. Let both grow together until the harvest: and in the time of harvest I will say to the reapers, Gather ye together first the tares, and bind them in bundles to burn them: but gather the wheat into my barn.[j]

When Jesus had retired to the house in which He lodged, the disciples came, saying: "Declare unto us the parable of the tares of the field."

He answered and said unto them, He that soweth the good seed is the Son of man; the field is the world; the good seed are the children of the kingdom; but the tares are the children of the wicked one; the enemy that sowed them is the devil; the harvest is the end of the world; and the reapers are the angels. As therefore the tares are gathered and burned in the fire; so shall it be in the end of this world. The Son of man shall send forth his angels, and they shall gather out of his kingdom all things that offend, and them which do iniquity; and shall cast them into a furnace of fire: there shall be wailing and gnashing of teeth. Then shall the righteous shine forth as the sun in the kingdom of their Father. Who hath ears to hear, let him hear.[k]

By the Author's explication, the sower was Himself, the Son of Man; and, as the condition of wheat and tares growing together was one that shall continue until "the end of the world," those who were ordained to carry on the ministry after Him are by direct implication also sowers. The seed as here represented is not, as in the last parable, the gospel itself, but the children of men, the good seed typifying the honest in heart, righteous-minded children of the kingdom; while

[j] Matt. 13:24–30.
[k] Verses 36–43.

the tares are those souls who have given themselves up to evil and are counted as children of the wicked one. Inspired by zeal for their Master's profit, the servants would have forcibly rooted up the tares, but were restrained, for their unwise though well-intended course would have endangered the wheat while yet tender, since in the early stages of growth it would have been difficult to distinguish the one from the other, and the intertwining of the roots would have caused much destruction of the precious grain.

One cardinal lesson of the parable, apart from the representation of actual conditions present and future, is that of patience, long-suffering, and toleration—each an attribute of Deity and a trait of character that all men should cultivate. The tares mentioned in the story may be considered as any kind of noxious weed, particularly such as in early growth resembles the wholesome grain.[l] Over-sowing with the seed of weeds in a field already sown with grain is a species of malignant outrage not unknown even in the present day.[m] The certainty of a time of separation, when the wheat shall be garnered in the store-house of the Lord, and the tares be burned, that their poisonous seed may reproduce no more, is placed beyond question by the Lord's own exposition.

So important is the lesson embodied in this parable, and so assured is the literal fulfillment of its contained predictions, that the Lord has given a further explication through revelation in the current dispensation, a period in which the application is direct and immediate. Speaking through Joseph Smith the Prophet in 1832, Jesus Christ said:

But behold, in the last days, even now while the Lord is beginning to bring forth the word, and the blade is springing up and is yet tender. Behold, verily I say unto you, the angels are crying unto the Lord day and night, who are ready and waiting to be sent forth to reap down the fields; but the Lord saith unto them, pluck not up the tares while the blade is yet tender, (for verily your faith is weak,) lest you destroy the wheat also. Therefore let the wheat and the tares grow

[l] Note 3, end of chapter.
[m] Note 4, end of chapter.

together until the harvest is fully ripe, then ye shall first gather out the wheat from among the tares, and after the gathering of the wheat, behold and lo! the tares are bound in bundles, and the field remaineth to be burned.[n]

THE SEED GROWING SECRETLY

Matthew records the Parable of the Tares as immediately following that of the Sower; Mark places in the same position of sequence a parable found in his writings alone. It is presented in outline form, and by critical expositors would be classed rather as a simple analogy than a typical parable. Read it:

And he said, So is the kingdom of God, as if a man should cast seed into the ground; and should sleep, and rise night and day, and the seed should spring and grow up, he knoweth not how. For the earth bringeth forth fruit of herself; first the blade, then the ear, after that the full corn in the ear. But when the fruit is brought forth, immediately he putteth in the sickle, because the harvest is come.[o]

We have no record of the disciples asking nor of the Master giving any interpretation of this, or of any later parable.[p] In this story we find effectively illustrated the fact of the vitality of the seed of truth, though the secret processes of its growth be a mystery to all save God alone. A man having planted seed must needs leave it alone. He may tend the field, removing weeds, protecting the plants as best he may, but the growth itself is dependent upon conditions and forces beyond his power to ultimately control. Though it were Paul who planted and Apollos who watered, none but God could insure the increase.[q] The one who sowed may go about his other affairs, for the field does not demand continuous or exclusive attention; nevertheless, under the influences of sunshine and shower, of breeze

[n] D&C 86:4–7; read the entire section.

[o] Mark 4:26–29.

[p] Note 5, end of chapter.

[q] 1 Cor. 3:6.

and dew, the blade develops, then the ear, and in due time the full corn in the ear. When the grain is ripe the man gladly harvests his crop.

The sower in this story is the authorized preacher of the word of God; he implants the seed of the gospel in the hearts of men, knowing not what the issue shall be. Passing on to similar or other ministry elsewhere, attending to his appointed duties in other fields, he, with faith and hope, leaves with God the result of his planting. In the harvest of souls converted through his labor, he is enriched and made to rejoice.[r] This parable was probably directed more particularly to the apostles and the most devoted of the other disciples, rather than to the multitude at large; the lesson is one for teachers, for workers in the Lord's fields, for the chosen sowers and reapers. It is of perennial value, as truly applicable today as when first spoken. Let the seed be sown, even though the sower be straightway called to other fields or other duties; in the gladsome harvest he shall find his recompense.

THE MUSTARD SEED

Another parable put he forth unto them, saying, The kingdom of heaven is like to a grain of mustard seed, which a man took, and sowed in his field: which indeed is the least of all seeds: but when it is grown, it is the greatest among herbs, and becometh a tree, so that the birds of the air come and lodge in the branches thereof.[s]

This little story, addressed to the assembled multitude, must have set many thinking, because of the simplicity of the incident related and the thoroughly un-Jewish application made of it. To the mind taught by teachers of the time the kingdom was to be great and glorious from its beginning; it was to be ushered in by blare of trumpets and tramp of armies, with King Messiah at the head; yet this new Teacher spoke of it as having so small a beginning as to be comparable to a mustard seed. To make the illustration more effective He specified that the seed spoken of was "the least of all seeds." This superlative

[r] Read the Lord's early promise of souls as the hire of the appointed harvesters: John 4:35–38; see also Matt. 9:37, 38; Luke 10:2.

[s] Matt. 13:31, 32; compare Mark 4:30–32; Luke 13:18, 19.

expression was made in a relative sense; for there were and are smaller seeds than the mustard, even among garden plants, among which rue and poppy have been named; but each of these plants is very small in maturity, while the well-cultivated mustard plant is one of the greatest among common herbs, and presents a strong contrast of growth from tiny seed to spreading shrub.

Moreover, the comparison "as small as a mustard seed" was in every-day use among the Jews of the time. The comparison employed by Jesus on another occasion evidences the common usage, as when He said: "If ye have faith as a grain of mustard seed . . . nothing shall be impossible unto you."[t] It should be known that the mustard plant attains in Palestine a larger growth than in more northerly climes.[u] The lesson of the parable is easy to read. The seed is a living entity. When rightly planted it absorbs and assimilates the nutritive matters of soil and atmosphere, grows, and in time is capable of affording lodgment and food to the birds. So the seed of truth is vital, living, and capable of such development as to furnish spiritual food and shelter to all who come seeking. In both conceptions, the plant at maturity produces seed in abundance, and so from a single grain a whole field may be covered.

THE LEAVEN

Another parable spake he unto them; The kingdom of heaven is like unto leaven, which a woman took, and hid in three measures of meal, till the whole was leavened.[v]

Points of both similarity and contrast between this parable and the last are easily discerned. In each the inherent vitality and capacity for development, so essentially characteristic of the kingdom of God, are illustrated. The mustard seed, however, typifies the effect of vital growth in gathering the substance of value from without; while the leaven or yeast disseminates and diffuses outward its influence throughout the mass of otherwise dense and sodden dough. Each of

[t] Matt. 17:20; compare Luke 17:6.

[u] Note 6, end of chapter.

[v] Matt. 13:33; compare Luke 13:20, 21.

the processes represents a means whereby the Spirit of Truth is made effective. Yeast is no less truly a living organism than a mustard seed. As the microscopic yeast plant develops and multiplies within the dough, its myriad living cells permeate the lump, and every bit of the leavened mass is capable of affecting likewise another batch of properly prepared meal. The process of leavening, or causing dough "to rise," by the fermentation of the yeast placed in the mass, is a slow one, and moreover as quiet and seemingly secret as that of the planted seed growing without the sower's further attention or concern.[w]

THE HIDDEN TREASURE

Again, the kingdom of heaven is like unto treasure hid in a field; the which when a man hath found, he hideth, and for joy thereof goeth and selleth all that he hath, and buyeth that field.[x]

This and the two parables following are recorded by Matthew only; and the place assigned them in his narrative indicates that they were spoken to the disciples alone, in the house, after the multitude had departed. The quest for treasure-trove is always fascinating. Instances of finding buried valuables were not uncommon in the time of which we speak, since the practice of so concealing treasure was usual with people exposed to bandit incursions and hostile invasion. Observe that the fortunate and happy man is represented as finding the treasure seemingly by accident rather than as a result of diligent search. He gladly sold all that he possessed to make possible his purchase of the field. The hidden treasure is the kingdom of heaven; when a man finds that, he ought to be ready to sacrifice all that he has, if by so doing he may gain possession. His joy in the new acquisition will be unbounded; and, if he but remain a worthy holder, the riches thereof shall be his beyond the grave.[y]

Casuists have raised the question of propriety as to the man's course of action in the story, inasmuch as he concealed the fact of his discovery from the owner of the field, to whom the treasure, they say,

[w] Note 7, end of chapter.

[x] Matt. 13:44.

[y] Compare Matt. 6:19, 20.

rightly belonged. Whatever opinion one may hold as to the ethics of the man's procedure, his act was not illegal, since there was an express provision in Jewish law that the purchaser of land became the legal owner of everything the ground contained.[z] Assuredly Jesus commended no dishonest course; and had not the story been in every detail probable, its effect as a parable would have been lost. The Master taught by this illustration that when once the treasure of the kingdom is found, the finder should lose no time nor shrink from any sacrifice needful to insure his title thereto.

THE PEARL OF GREAT PRICE

Again, the kingdom of heaven is like unto a merchant man, seeking goodly pearls: who, when he had found one pearl of great price, went and sold all that he had, and bought it.[aa]

Pearls have always held high place among gems, and long before, as indeed ever since, the time of Christ, pearl-merchants have been active and diligent in seeking the largest and richest to be had. Unlike the man in the last parable, who found a hidden treasure with little or no search, the merchant in this story devoted his whole energy to the quest for goodly pearls, to find and secure which was his business. When at last he beheld the pearl that excelled all others, though it was, as of right it ought to have been, held at high cost, he gladly sold all his other gems; indeed he sacrificed "all that he had"—gems and other possessions—and purchased the pearl of great price. Seekers after truth may acquire much that is good and desirable, and not find the greatest truth of all, the truth that shall save them. Yet, if they seek persistently and with right intent, if they are really in quest of pearls and not of imitations, they shall find. Men who by search and research discover the truths of the kingdom of heaven may have to abandon many of their cherished traditions, and even their theories of imperfect philosophy and "science falsely so called,"[bb] if they would possess themselves of the pearl of great price. Observe that in this

[z] Note 8, end of chapter.

[aa] Matt. 13:45, 46.

[bb] 1 Tim. 6:20.

parable as in that of the hidden treasure, the price of possession is one's all. No man can become a citizen of the kingdom by partial surrender of his earlier allegiances; he must renounce everything foreign to the kingdom or he can never be numbered therein. If he willingly sacrifices all that he has, he shall find that he has enough. The cost of the hidden treasure, and of the pearl, is not a fixed amount, alike for all; it is all one has. Even the poorest may come into enduring possession; his all is a sufficient purchase price.

THE GOSPEL NET

Again, the kingdom of heaven is like unto a net, that was cast into the sea, and gathered of every kind: which, when it was full, they drew to shore, and sat down, and gathered the good into vessels, but cast the bad away. So shall it be at the end of the world: the angels shall come forth, and sever the wicked from among the just, and shall cast them into the furnace of fire: there shall be wailing and gnashing of teeth.[cc]

Men of many minds, men good and bad, all nationalities and races, are affected by the gospel of the kingdom. The "fishers of men"[dd] are skilful, active, and comprehensive in their haul. The sorting takes place after the net is brought to shore; and, as the fisherman discards every bad fish while he saves the good, so shall the angels who do the bidding of the Son of Man separate the just and the wicked, preserving the one kind to life eternal, consigning the other to destruction. Unwise efforts to carry the application of the parable beyond the Author's intent have suggested the criticism that whether the fish be good or bad they die. The good, however, die to usefulness, the bad to utter waste. Though all men die, they die not alike; some pass to rest, and shall come forth in the resurrection of the just; others go to a state of sorrow and disquiet there to anxiously and with dread await the resurrection of the wicked.[ee] Similarity of application in the present parable as in that of the tares is apparent in the emphasis

[cc] Matt. 13:47–50.
[dd] Matt. 4:19; Mark 1:17; Luke 5:10.
[ee] John 5:29; see also Alma 40:11–14; and the author, *Articles of Faith,* pp. 387–92.

given to the decreed separation of the just from the unjust, and in the awful fate of those who are fit subjects for condemnation. A further parallelism is noticed in the postponement of the judgment until the "end of the world," by which expression we may understand the consummation of the Redeemer's work, subsequent to the Millennium and the final resurrection of all who have had existence on earth.[ff]

Following His delivery of this, the last of the group of parables recorded in the thirteenth chapter of Matthew, Jesus asked the disciples, "Have ye understood all these things?" They answered, "Yea, Lord." He impressed upon them that they should be ready, like well-taught teachers, to bring, from the store-house of their souls, treasures of truth both old and new, for the edification of the world.[gg]

CHRIST'S PURPOSE IN USING PARABLES

As before stated, the Twelve and other disciples were surprised at the Lord's innovation of parabolic instruction. Prior to that time His doctrines had been set forth in unveiled plainness, as witness the explicit teachings in the Sermon on the Mount. It is noticeable that the introduction of parables occurred when opposition to Jesus was strong, and when scribes, Pharisees, and rabbis were alert in maintaining a close watch upon His movements and His works, ever ready to make Him an offender for a word. The use of parables was common among Jewish teachers; and in adopting this mode of instruction Jesus was really following a custom of the time; though between the parables He spake and those of the scholars there is possible no comparison except that of most pronounced contrast.[hh]

To the chosen and devoted followers who came asking the Master why He had changed from direct exposition to parables, He explained[ii] that while it was their privilege to receive and understand the deeper truths of the gospel, "the mysteries of the kingdom of heaven" as He expressed it, with people in general, who were unreceptive and unprepared, such fulness of understanding was impossible. To the

---

[ff] See chapter 42.

[gg] Matt. 13:51, 52.

[hh] Note 9, end of chapter.

[ii] Matt. 13:10–17; compare Mark 4:10–13; Luke 8:9, 10.

disciples who had already gladly accepted the first principles of the gospel of Christ, more should be given; while from those who had rejected the proffered boon, even what they had theretofore possessed should be taken away.[jj] Therefore," said He, "speak I to them in parables: because they seeing see not; and hearing they hear not, neither do they understand." That the state of spiritual darkness then existing among the Jews had been foreseen was instanced by a citation of Isaiah's words, in which the ancient prophet had told of the people becoming blind, deaf, and hard of heart respecting the things of God, whereby though they would both hear and see in a physical sense yet should they not understand.[kk]

There is plainly shown an element of mercy in the parabolic mode of instruction adopted by our Lord under the conditions prevailing at the time. Had He always taught in explicit declaration, such as required no interpretation, many among His hearers would have come under condemnation, inasmuch as they were too weak in faith and unprepared in heart to break the bonds of traditionalism and the prejudice engendered by sin, so as to accept and obey the saving word. Their inability to comprehend the requirements of the gospel would in righteous measure give Mercy some claim upon them, while had they rejected the truth with full understanding, stern Justice would surely demand their condemnation.[ll]

That the lesson of the parables was comprehensible through study, prayer and search was intimated in the Teacher's admonishment: "Who hath ears to hear, let him hear."[mm] To the more studious inquirers, the Master added: "Take heed what ye hear: with what measure ye mete, it shall be measured to you: and unto you that hear shall more be given. For he that hath, to him shall be given: and he that hath not, from him shall be taken even that which he hath."[nn] Two men may hear the same words; one of them listens in indolence and indifference, the other with active mind intent on

---

jj Matt. 13:12; compare 25:29; Mark 4:25; Luke 8:18; 19:26.

kk Isa. 6:9; see also 42:20; 43:8; Ezek. 12:2; John 12:40; Acts 28:26, 27.

ll See the author's *Articles of Faith,* pp. 59–60; 2 Ne. 9:25–27; Rom 2:12; D&C 45:54; 76:72.

mm Matt. 13:9, 43; see also 11:15; Mark 4:9.

nn Mark 4:24, 25.

learning all that the words can possibly convey; and, having heard, the diligent man goes straightway to do the things commended to him, while the careless one neglects and forgets. The one is wise, the other foolish; the one has heard to his eternal profit, the other to his everlasting condemnation.⁰⁰

Another example of the merciful adaptation of the word of truth to the varied capacities of the people who heard the parables is found in the psychological fact, that the incidents of an impressive though simple story will live, even in minds which for the time being are incapable of comprehending any meaning beyond that of the commonplace story itself. Many a peasant who had heard the little incident of the sower and the four kinds of soil, of the tares sown by an enemy at night, of the seed that grew though the planter had temporarily forgotten it, would be reminded by the recurring circumstances of his daily work; the gardener would recollect the story of the mustard seed whenever he planted afresh, or when he looked upon the umbrageous plant with birds nesting in its branches; the housewife would be impressed anew by the story of the leaven as she mixed and kneaded and baked; the fisherman at his nets would think again of the good fish and the bad and compare the sorting of his catch with the judgment to come. And then, when time and experience, including suffering perhaps, had prepared them for deeper thought, they would find the living kernel of gospel truth within the husk of the simple tale.

PARABLES IN GENERAL

The essential feature of a parable is that of comparison or similitude, by which some ordinary, well-understood incident is used to illustrate a fact or principle not directly expressed in the story. The popular thought that a parable necessarily rests on a fictitious incident is incorrect; for, inasmuch as the story or circumstance of the parable must be simple and indeed common-place, it may be real. There is no fiction in the parables we have thus far studied; the fundamental stories are true to life and the given circumstances are facts of experience. The narrative or incident

---

⁰⁰ Read again Matt. 7:24–27; Luke 6:46–49.

upon which a parable is constructed may be an actual occurrence or fiction; but, if fictitious, the story must be consistent and probable, with no admixture of the unusual or miraculous. In this respect the parable differs from the fable, the latter being imaginative, exaggerated and improbable as to fact; moreover, the intent is unlike in the two, since the parable is designed to convey some great spiritual truth, while the so-called moral of the fable is at best suggestive only of worldly achievement and personal advantage. Stories of trees, animals and inanimate things talking together or with men are wholly fanciful; they are fables or apologues whether the outcome be depicted as good or bad; to the parable these show contrast, not similarity. The avowed purpose of the fable is rather to amuse than to teach. The parable may embody a narrative as in the instances of the sower and the tares, or merely an isolated incident, as in those of the mustard seed and the leaven.

Allegories are distinguished from parables by greater length and detail of the story, and by the intimate admixture of the narrative with the lesson it is designed to teach; these are kept distinctly separate in the parable. Myths are fictitious stories, sometimes with historic basis of fact, but without symbolism of spiritual worth. A proverb is a short, sententious saying, in the nature of a maxim, connoting a definite truth or suggestion by comparison. Proverbs and parables are closely related, and in the Bible the terms are sometimes used interchangeably.[pp] The Old Testament contains two parables, a few fables and allegories, and numerous proverbs; of the last-named we possess an entire book.[qq] Nathan the prophet reproved King David by the parable of the poor man's ewe lamb, and so effective was the story that the king decreed punishment for the wealthy offender, and was overcome by sorrow and contrition when the prophet made application of his parable by the fateful words, "Thou art the man."[rr] The story of the vineyard, which though fenced and well-tended yet brought forth only wild, useless fruit, was used by Isaiah to portray the sinful state of Israel in his attempt to awaken the people to lives of righteousness.[ss]

pp Note 10, end of chapter.

qq Note 11, end of chapter.

rr 2 Sam. 12:1–7, 13.

ss Isa. 5:1–7.

The parables of the New Testament, spoken by the Teacher of teachers, are of such beauty, simplicity, and effectiveness, as to stand unparalleled in literature.

NOTES TO CHAPTER 19

1. The First Group of Parables.—Many Bible scholars hold that the seven parables recorded in the thirteenth chapter of Matthew were spoken at different times and to different people, and that the writer of the first Gospel grouped them for convenience in recording and with prime consideration of their subjective interest. Some color is found for this claim in Luke's mention of some of these parables in different relations of both time and place; thus, the Parables of the Mustard Seed and the Leaven are given (Luke 13:18, 21) as directly following the healing of the infirm woman in the synagog, and the rebuke to the hypocritical ruler. While we must admit that Matthew may have grouped with the parables spoken on that particular day some of other dates, it is probable that Jesus repeated some of His parables, as He certainly did other teachings, and thus presented the same lesson on more occasions than one. As a matter of fact each parable is a lesson in itself, and holds its high intrinsic value whether considered as an isolated story or in connection with related teachings. Let us give heed to the lesson of each whatever opinions men may promulgate as to the circumstances of its first delivery.

2. Local Setting for the Parable of the Sower.—Dr. R. C. Trench, in his excellent work *Notes on the Parables of Our Lord* (p. 57, note), quotes Dean Stanley's description of existing conditions in the place where the Parable of the Sower was given by Jesus; and as there is reason to believe that the environment has changed but little since the days of Christ, the account is here reproduced: "A slight recess in the hillside close upon the plain disclosed at once in detail, and with a conjunction which I remember nowhere else in Palestine, every feature of the great parable. There was the undulating corn-field descending to the water's edge. There was the trodden pathway running through the midst of it, with no fence or hedge to prevent the seed falling here or there on either side of it, or upon it—itself hard with the constant tramp of horse and mule and human feet. There was the 'good' rich soil, which distinguishes the whole of that plain and its neighborhood from the bare hills elsewhere, descending into the lake, and which, where there is no interruption, produces one vast mass of corn. There was the rocky ground of the hillside protruding here and there through the corn-fields, as elsewhere, through the grassy slopes. There were the large bushes of thorn, the 'nabk'. . . springing up, like the fruit-trees of the more inland parts, in the very midst of the waving wheat."

3. Tares.—This term occurs nowhere within the Bible except in this instance of the parable. Plainly any kind of weed, particularly a poisonous sort, such as would seriously depreciate the garnered crop, would serve the Master's purpose in the illustration. The traditional belief commonly held is that the plant referred to in the parable is the darnel weed, known to botanists as *Lolium temulentum*, a species of bearded rye-grass. This plant closely resembles wheat in the early period of growth, and exists as a pest to the farmers in Palestine today; it is called by the Arabians "Zowan" or "Zawan" which name, says Arnot, citing Thompson, "bears some resemblance to the original word in the Greek text." The writer of the article "Tares" in Smith's Dictionary says: "Critics and expositors are agreed that the Greek plural *zizania*, A. V. 'tares,' of the parable (Matt. 13:25) denotes the weed called 'bearded darnel' (*Lolium temulentum*), a widely distributed grass, and the only species of the order that has deleterious properties. The bearded darnel before it comes into ear is very similar in appearance to wheat, and the roots of the two are often intertwined; hence the command that the 'tares' should be left till the harvest, lest while men plucked up the tares 'they should root up also the wheat with them.' This darnel is easily distinguishable from the wheat and barley when headed out, but when both are less developed, 'the closest scrutiny will often fail to detect it. Even the farmers, who in this country generally weed their fields, do not attempt to separate the one from the other. . . . The taste is bitter, and, when eaten separately, or even when diffused in ordinary bread, it causes dizziness, and often acts as a violent emetic.'" The secondary quotation is from Thompson's *The Land and the Book*, ii, 111, 112. It has been asserted that the darnel is a degenerated kind of wheat; and attempts have been made to give additional significance to our Lord's instructive parable by injecting this thought; there is no scientific warrant for the strained conception, however, and earnest students will not be misled thereby.

4. The Wickedness of the Sower of Tares.—Attempts have been made to disparage the Parable of the Tares on the ground that it rests on an unusual if not unknown practice. Trench thus meets the criticism (*Notes on the Parables*, pp. 72, 73): "Our Lord did not imagine here a form of malice without example, but adduced one which may have been familiar enough to His hearers, one so easy of execution, involving so little risk, and yet effecting so great and lasting a mischief, that it is not strange, where cowardice and malice meet, that this should have been often the shape in which they displayed themselves. We meet traces of it in many quarters. In Roman law the possibility of this form of injury is contemplated; and a modern writer, illustrating Scripture from the manners and habits of the East, with which he had become familiar through a sojourn there, affirms the same to be now practiced in India." In a subjoined note the author adds: "We are not without this form of malice nearer home. Thus in Ireland I have known an outgoing tenant, in spite at his eviction, to sow wild oats in the fields which he was leaving. These, like the tares in the parable, ripening and seeding themselves before the crops in which they were mingled, it became next to impossible to extirpate."

5. The Parable of the Seed Growing Secretly.—This parable has given rise to much discussion among expositors, the question being as to who is meant by the man who cast seed into the ground. If, as in the parables of the Sower and the Tares, the Lord Jesus be the planter, then, some ask, how can it be said "that the seed should spring and grow up, he knoweth not how," when all things are known unto Him? If on the other hand the planter represents the authorized teacher or preacher of the gospel, how can it be said that at the harvest time "he putteth in the sickle," since the final harvesting of souls is the prerogative of God? The perplexities of the critics arise from their attempt to find in the parable a literalism never intended by the Author. Whether the seed be planted by the Lord Himself, as when He taught in Person, or by any one of His authorized servants, the seed is alive and will grow. Time is required; the blade appears first and is followed by the ear, and the ear ripens in season, without the constant attention which a shaping of several parts by hand would require. The man who figures in the parable is presented as an ordinary farmer, who plants, and waits, and in due time reaps. The lesson imparted is the vitality of the seed as a living thing, endowed by its Creator with the capacity to both grow and develop.

6. The Mustard Plant.—The wild mustard, which in the temperate zone seldom attains a height of more than three or four feet, reaches in semitropical lands the height of a horse and its rider (Thompson, *The Land and the Book,* ii, 100). Those who heard the parable evidently understood the contrast between size of seed and that of the fully developed plant. Arnot (*The Parables*, p. 102), aptly says: "This plant obviously was chosen by the Lord, not on account of its absolute magnitude, but because it was, and was recognized to be, a striking instance of increase from very small to very great. It seems to have been in Palestine, at that time, the smallest seed from which so large a plant was known to grow. There were, perhaps, smaller seeds, but the plants which sprung from them were not so great; and there were greater plants, but the seeds from which they sprung were not so small." Edersheim (1, p. 593) states that the diminutive size of the mustard seed was commonly used in comparison by the rabbis, "to indicate the smallest amount such as the least drop of blood, the least defilement, etc." The same author continues, in speaking of the grown plant: "Indeed, it looks no longer like a large garden-herb or shrub, but 'becomes' or rather appears like 'a tree'—as St. Luke puts it, 'a great tree,' of course, not in comparison with other trees, but with garden-shrubs. Such growth of mustard seed was also a fact well known at the time, and, indeed, still observed in the East. . . . And the general meaning would the more easily be apprehended, that a tree, whose wide-spreading branches afforded lodgment to the birds of heaven, was a familiar Old Testament figure for a mighty kingdom that gave shelter to the nations (Ezek. 31:6, 12; Dan. 4:12, 14, 21, 22). Indeed, it is specifically used as an illustration of the Messianic Kingdom (Ezek. 17:23)."

7. The Symbolism of Leaven.—In the parable, the kingdom of heaven is likened unto leaven. In other scriptures leaven is figuratively mentioned as representing evil, thus, "the leaven of the Pharisees and of the Sadducees" (Matt. 16:6, see also Luke 12:1), "the leaven of Herod" (Mark 8:15). These instances, and others (1 Cor. 5:7, 8) are illustrative of the contagion of evil. In the incident of the woman using leaven in the ordinary process of bread-making, the spreading, penetrating, vital effect of truth is symbolized by the leaven. The same thing in different aspects may very properly be used to represent good in one instance and evil in another.

8. Treasure Belonging to the Finder.—As to the justification of the man who found a treasure hidden in another's field and then, concealing the fact of his discovery, bought the field that he might possess the treasure, Edersheim (1, pp. 595–96) says: "Some difficulty has been expressed in regard to the morality of such a transaction. In reply it may be observed, that it was, at least, in entire accordance with Jewish law. If a man had found a treasure in loose coins among the corn it would certainly be his if he bought the corn. If he had found it on the ground, or in the soil, it would equally certainly belong to him if he could claim ownership of the soil, and even if the field were not his own, unless others could prove their right to it. The law went so far as to adjudge to the purchaser of fruits anything found among these fruits. This will suffice to vindicate a question of detail, which, in any case, should not be too closely pressed in a parabolic history."

9. Superiority of Our Lord's Parables.—"Perhaps no other mode of teaching was so common among the Jews as that by parables. Only in their case, they were almost entirely illustrations of what had been said or taught; while in the case of Christ, they served as the foundation for His teaching. . . . In the one case it was intended to make spiritual teaching appear Jewish and national, in the other to convey spiritual teaching in a form adapted to the stand-point of the hearers. This distinction will be found to hold true, even in instances where there seems the closest parallelism between a Rabbinic and an Evangelic parable. . . . It need scarcely be said that comparison between such parables, as regards their spirit, is scarcely possible, except by way of contrast" (Edersheim, 1, pp. 580–81). Geikie tersely says: "Others have uttered parables, but Jesus so far transcends them, that He may justly be called the creator of this mode of instruction" (2, p. 145).

10. Parables and Other Forms of Analogy.—"The parable is also clearly distinguishable from the proverb, though it is true that, in a certain degree, the words are used interchangeably in the New Testament, and as equivalent the one to the other. Thus 'Physician, heal thyself' (Luke 4:23) is termed a parable, being more strictly a proverb; so again, when the Lord had used that proverb, probably already familiar to His hearers 'If the blind lead the blind, both shall fall into the ditch'; Peter said 'Declare unto us this parable' (Matt. 15:14, 15); and Luke 5:36 is a proverb or proverbial expression, rather than a parable, which name it bears. . . . So, upon the other hand, those are called 'proverbs' in St. John, which if not strictly parables, yet claim much closer affinity to the parable than to the proverb, being in fact allegories;

thus Christ's setting forth of His relations to His people under those of a shepherd to his sheep is termed a 'proverb,' though our translators, holding fast to the sense rather than to the letter, have rendered it a 'parable' (John 10:6; compare 16:25, 29). It is easy to account for this interchange of words. Partly it arose from one word in Hebrew signifying both parable and proverb."—Trench, *Notes on the Parables*, pp. 9, 10.

For the convenience of readers who may not have a dictionary at hand as they read, the following definitions are given:

Allegory.—The setting forth of a subject under the guise of some other subject or aptly suggestive likeness.

Apologue.—A fable or moral tale, especially one in which animals or inanimate things speak or act, and by which a useful lesson is suggested or taught.

Fable.—A brief story or tale feigned or invented to embody a moral, and introducing animals and sometimes even inanimate things as rational speakers and actors; a legend or myth.

Myth.—A fictitious or conjectural narrative presented as historical, but without any basis of fact.

Parable.—A brief narrative or descriptive allegory founded on real scenes or events such as occur in nature and human life, and usually with a moral or religious application.

Proverb.—A brief, pithy saying, condensing in witty or striking form the wisdom of experience; a familiar and widely known popular saying in epigrammatic form.

11. Old Testament Parables, etc.—"Of parables in the strictest sense the Old Testament contains only two" (2 Sam. 12:1–; and Isa. 5:1–). "Other stories, such as that of the trees assembled to elect a king (Judg. 9:8), and of the thistle and cedar (2 Kgs. 14:9), are more strictly fables. Still others, such as Ezekiel's account of the two eagles and the vine (17:2–), and of the caldron (24:3–) are allegories. The small number of parabolic narratives to be found in the Old Testament must not, however, be taken as an indication of indifference toward this literary form as suitable for moral instruction. The number is only apparently small. In reality, similitudes, which, though not explicitly couched in the terms of fictitious narrative, suggest and furnish the materials for such narrative, are abundant."—Zenos, *Standard Bible Dictionary*, article "Parables."

By applying the term "parable" in its broadest sense, to include all ordinary forms of analogy, we may list the following as the most impressive parables of the Old Testament. Trees electing a king (Judg. 9:7–15); the poor man's ewe lamb (2 Sam. 12:1–6); the contending brothers and the avengers (2 Sam. 14:1–20); story of the escaped captive (1 Kgs. 20:35–43); the thistle and the cedar (2 Kgs. 14:9); the vineyard and its wild grapes (Isa. 5:1–); the eagles and the vine (Ezek. 17:3–10); the lion's whelps (Ezek. 19:2–9); the seething pot (Ezek. 24:3–5).

CHAPTER 20

"PEACE, BE STILL"

INCIDENTS PRELIMINARY TO THE VOYAGE

Near the close of the day on which Jesus had taught the multitudes for the first time by parables, He said to the disciples, "Let us pass over unto the other side."[a] The destination so indicated is the east side of the sea of Galilee. While the boat was being made ready, a certain scribe came to Jesus and said: "Master, I will follow thee whithersoever thou goest." Prior to that time, few men belonging to the titled or ruling class had offered to openly ally themselves with Jesus. Had the Master been mindful of policy and desirous of securing official recognition, this opportunity to attach to Himself as influential a person as a scribe would have received careful consideration if not immediate acceptance; but He, who could read the minds and know the hearts of men, chose rather than accepted. He had called men who were to be thenceforth His own, from their fishing boats and nets, and had numbered one of the ostracized publicans among the Twelve; but He knew them, every one, and chose accordingly. The gospel was offered freely to all; but authority to officiate as a minister thereof was not to be had for the asking; for that sacred labor, one must be called of God.[b]

In this instance, Christ knew the character of the man, and, without wounding his feelings by curt rejection, pointed out the sacrifice required of one who would follow whithersoever the Lord went, saying: "The foxes have holes, and the birds of the air have nests; but the Son of man hath not where to lay his head." As Jesus

[a] Mark 4:35.
[b] *Articles of Faith*, pp. 179–89.

had no fixed place of abode, but went wherever His duty called Him, so was it necessary that they who represented Him, men ordained or set apart to His service, be ready to deny themselves the enjoyment of their homes and the comfort of family associations, if the duties of their calling so demanded. We do not read that the aspiring scribe pressed his offer.

Another man indicated his willingness to follow the Lord, but asked first for time to go and bury his father; to him Jesus said: "Follow me; and let the dead bury their dead." Some readers have felt that this injunction was harsh, though such an inference is scarcely justified. While it would be manifestly unfilial for a son to absent himself from his father's funeral under ordinary conditions, nevertheless, if that son had been set apart to service of importance transcending all personal or family obligations, his ministerial duty would of right take precedence. Moreover, the requirement expressed by Jesus was no greater than that made of every priest during his term of active service, nor was it more afflicting than the obligation of the Nazarite vow,[c] under which many voluntarily placed themselves. The duties of ministry in the kingdom pertained to spiritual life; one dedicated thereto might well allow those who were negligent of spiritual things, and figuratively speaking, spiritually dead, to bury their dead.

A third instance is presented; a man who wanted to be a disciple of the Lord asked that, before entering upon his duties, he be permitted to go home and bid farewell to his family and friends. The reply of Jesus has become an aphorism in life and literature: "No man, having put his hand to the plough, and looking back, is fit for the kingdom of God."[d]

From Matthew's record we draw the inference that the first two of these candidates for discipleship offered themselves to our Lord as He stood on the shore or in the boat ready to begin the evening voyage across the lake. Luke places the instances in a different connection, and adds to the offers of the scribe and the man who would first bury his father, that of the one who wished to go home and then return to Christ. The three incidents may be profitably considered together,

[c] Page 84.

[d] Luke 9:57–62; see also Matt. 8:19–22.

whether all occurred in the evening of that same eventful day or at different times.

STILLING THE STORM [e]

The instruction to launch forth and cross to the opposite side of the lake was given by Jesus, who probably desired a respite after the arduous labors of the day. No time had been lost in unnecessary preparation; "they took him, even as he was, into the ship," and set out without delay. Even on the water some of the eager people tried to follow; for a number of small boats, "little ships" as Mark styles them, accompanied the vessel on which Jesus was embarked; but these lesser craft may have turned back, possibly on account of the approaching storm; anyway, we do not hear of them further.

Jesus found a resting place near the stern of the ship and soon fell asleep. A great storm arose;[f] and still He slept. The circumstance is instructive as it evidences at once the reality of the physical attributes of Christ, and the healthy, normal condition of His body. He was subject to fatigue and bodily exhaustion from other causes, as are all men; without food He grew hungry; without drink He thirsted; by labor He became weary. The fact that after a day of strenuous effort He could calmly sleep, even amidst the turmoil of a tempest, indicates an unimpaired nervous system and a good state of health. Nowhere do we find record of Jesus having been ill. He lived according to the laws of health, yet never allowed the body to rule the spirit; and His daily activities, which were of a kind to make heavy demands on both physical and mental energy, were met with no symptoms of nervous collapse nor of functional disturbance. Sleep after toil is natural and necessary. The day's work done, Jesus slept.

Meanwhile the storm increased in fury; the wind rendered the boat unmanageable; waves beat over the side; so much water was shipped that the vessel seemed about to founder. The disciples were terror-stricken; yet through it all Jesus rested peacefully. In their extremity of fear, the disciples awakened Him, crying out, according to the several independent accounts, "Master, Master, we perish"; "Lord,

[e] Matt. 8:23–27; Mark 4:35–41; Luke 8:22–25.

[f] Note 1, end of chapter.

save us: we perish"; and, "Master, carest thou not that we perish?" They were abjectly frightened, and at least partly forgetful that there was with them One whose voice even death had to obey. Their terrified appeal was not wholly devoid of hope nor barren of faith: "Lord, save us" they cried. Calmly He replied to their piteous call, "Why are ye fearful, O ye of little faith?"

Then He arose; and out through the darkness of that fearsome night, into the roaring wind, over the storm-lashed sea, went the voice of the Lord as He "rebuked the wind, and said unto the sea, Peace, be still. And the wind ceased, and there was a great calm." Turning to the disciples, He asked in tones of gentle yet unmistakable reproof: "Where is your faith?" and "How is it that ye have no faith?" Gratitude for rescue from what but a moment before had seemed impending death was superseded by amazement and fear. "What manner of man is this," they asked one of another, "that even the wind and the sea obey him?"

Among the recorded miracles of Christ, none has elicited greater diversity in comment and in attempt at elucidation than has this marvelous instance of control over the forces of nature. Science ventures no explanation. The Lord of earth, air, and sea spoke and was obeyed. He it was who, amidst the black chaos of creation's earliest stages, had commanded with immediate effect—Let there be light; Let there be a firmament in the midst of the waters; Let the dry land appear—and, as He had decreed, so it was. The dominion of the Creator over the created is real and absolute. A small part of that dominion has been committed to man[g] as the offspring of God, tabernacled in the very image of his divine Father. But man exercises that delegated control through secondary agencies, and by means of complicated mechanism. Man's power over the objects to his own devising is limited. It is according to the curse evoked by Adam's fall, which came through transgression, that by the strain of his muscles, by the sweat of his brow, and by stress of his mind, shall he achieve. His word of command is but a sound-wave in air, except as it is followed by labor. Through the Spirit that emanates from the very

[g] Gen. 1:28; Moses 2:26; 5:1.

Person of Deity, and which pervades all space, the command of God is immediately operative.

Not man alone, but also the earth and all the elemental forces pertaining thereto came under the Adamic curse;[h] and as the soil no longer brought forth only good and useful fruits, but gave of its substance to nurture thorns and thistles, so the several forces of nature ceased to be obedient to man as agents subject to his direct control. What we call natural forces—heat, light, electricity, chemical affinity—are but a few of the manifestations of eternal energy through which the Creator's purposes are subserved; and these few, man is able to direct and utilize only through mechanical contrivance and physical adjustment. But the earth shall yet be "renewed and receive its paradisaical glory"; then soil, water, air, and the forces acting upon them, shall directly respond to the command of glorified man, as now they obey the word of the Creator.[i]

QUIETING THE DEMONS [j]

Jesus and the disciples with Him landed on the eastern or Perean side of the lake, in a region known as the country of the Gadarenes or Gergesenes. The precise spot has not been identified, but it was evidently a country district apart from the towns.[k] As the party left the boat, two maniacs, who were sorely tormented by evil spirits, approached. Matthew states there were two; the other writers speak of but one; it is possible that one of the afflicted pair was in a condition so much worse than that of his companion that to him is accorded greater prominence in the narrative; or, one may have run away while the other remained. The demoniac was in a pitiful plight. His frenzy had become so violent and the physical strength incident to his mania so great that all attempts to hold him in captivity had failed. He had been bound in chains and fetters, but these he had broken asunder by the aid of demon power; and he had fled to the mountains, to the caverns that served as tombs, and there he had

[h] Gen. 3: 17–19.

[i] Note 2, end of chapter.

[j] Matt. 8:28–34; Mark 5:1–19; Luke 8:26–39.

[k] Note 3, end of chapter.

lived more like a wild beast than a man. Night and day his weird, terrifying shrieks had been heard, and through dread of meeting him people traveled by other ways rather than pass near his haunts. He wandered about naked, and in his madness often gashed his flesh with sharp stones.

Seeing Jesus, the poor creature ran toward Him, and, impelled by the power of his demon control, prostrated himself before Christ, the while crying out with a loud voice: "What have I to do with thee, Jesus, thou Son of the most high God?" As Jesus commanded the evil spirits to leave, one or more of them through the voice of the man, pleaded to be left alone, and with blasphemous presumption exclaimed: "I adjure thee by God, that thou torment me not." Matthew records the further question addressed to Jesus: "Art thou come hither to torment us before the time?" The demons, by whom the man was possessed and controlled, recognized the Master, whom they knew they had to obey; but they pleaded to be left alone until the decreed time of their final punishment would come.[l]

Jesus asked, "What is thy name?" and the demons within the man answered, "My name is Legion, for we are many." The fact of the man's dual consciousness or multi-personality is here apparent. So complete was his possession by wicked spirits that he could no longer distinguish between his individual personality and theirs. The devils implored that Jesus would not banish them from that country; or as Luke records in words of awful import, "that he would not command them to go out into the deep."[m] In their wretched plight, and out of diabolical eagerness to find abode in bodies of flesh even though of beasts, they begged that, being compelled to leave the man they be allowed to enter a herd of hogs feeding nearby. Jesus gave permission; the unclean demons entered the swine; and the whole herd, numbering about two thousand, went wild, stampeded in terror, ran violently down a steep place into the sea, and were drowned. The swineherds were frightened, and, hastening to the town, told what had happened to the hogs. People came out in crowds to see for themselves; and all were astounded to behold the

---

[l] Compare Rev. 20:3.

[m] Revised version, "abyss" instead of "deep."

once wild man of whom they had all been afraid, now clothed, and restored to a normal state of mind, sitting quietly and reverently at the feet of Jesus. They were afraid of One who could work such wonders, and, conscious of their sinful unworthiness, begged Him to leave their country.[n]

The man who had been rid of the demons feared not; in his heart love and gratitude superseded all other feeling; and as Jesus returned to the boat he prayed that he might go also. But Jesus forbade, saying. "Go home to thy friends, and tell them how great things the Lord hath done for thee, and hath had compassion on thee." The man became a missionary, not alone in his home town but throughout Decapolis, the region of the ten cities; wherever he went he told of the marvelous change Jesus had wrought on him.

The testimony of wicked and unclean spirits to the divinity of Christ as the Son of God is not confined to this instance. We have already considered the case of the demoniac in the synagog at Capernaum;[o] and another instance appeared, when Jesus, withdrawing from the towns in Galilee, betook Himself to the sea shore, and was followed by a great multitude comprizing Galileans and Judeans, and people from Jerusalem and Idumea, and from beyond Jordan (i.e. from Perea), and inhabitants of Tyre and Sidon, amongst whom He had healed many of divers diseases; and those who were in bondage to unclean spirits had fallen down and worshiped Him; while the demons cried out: "Thou art the Son of God."[p]

In the course of the short journey considered in this chapter, the power of Jesus as Master of earth, men and devils, was manifest in miraculous works of the most impressive kind. We cannot classify the Lord's miracles as small and great, nor as easy and difficult of accomplishment; what one may consider the least is to another of profound import. The Lord's word was sufficient in every instance. To the wind and the waves, and to the demon-ridden mind of the man possessed, He had but to speak and be obeyed. "Peace, be still."

---

[n] Note 4, end of chapter.

[o] Mark 1:24; Luke 4:34, also verse 41.

[p] Mark 3:7–11; compare Luke 6:17–19.

THE RAISING OF THE DAUGHTER OF JAIRUS q

Jesus and His attendants recrossed the lake from the land of Gadara to the vicinity of Capernaum, where He was received with acclamation by a multitude of people, "for they were all waiting for him." Immediately after landing, Jesus was approached by Jairus, one of the rulers of the local synagog, who "besought him greatly, saying, My little daughter lieth at the point of death: I pray thee, come and lay thy hands on her, that she may be healed; and she shall live."

The fact of this man's coming to Jesus, with the spirit of faith and supplication, is an evidence of the deep impression the ministry of Christ had made even in priestly and ecclesiastical circles. Many of the Jews, rulers and officials as well as the people in common, believed in Jesus;[r] though few belonging to the upper classes were willing to sacrifice prestige and popularity by acknowledging their discipleship. That Jairus, one of the rulers of the synagog, came only when impelled by grief over the impending death of his only daughter, a girl of twelve years, is no evidence that he had not before become a believer; certainly at this time his faith was genuine and his trust sincere, as the circumstances of the narrative prove. He approached Jesus with the reverence due One whom he considered able to grant what he asked, and fell at the Lord's feet, or as Matthew says, worshiped Him. When the man had started from his home to seek aid of Jesus, the maiden was at the point of death; he feared lest she had died in the interval. In the very brief account given in the first Gospel, he is reported as saying to Jesus: "My daughter is even now dead: but come and lay thy hand upon her and she shall live."[s] Jesus went with the imploring father, and many followed.

On the way to the house an incident occurred to hinder progress. A sorely afflicted woman was healed, under circumstances of peculiar interest; this occurrence we shall consider presently. No intimation is given that Jairus showed impatience or displeasure over the delay; he had placed trust in the Master and awaited His time and pleasure; and while Christ was engaged in the matter of the suffering woman,

q Mark 5:22–24, 35–43; Luke 8:41, 42, 49–56; Matt. 9:18, 19, 23–26.
r John 11:45; compare 8:30; 10:42.
s Note 5, end of chapter.

messengers came from the ruler's house with the saddening word that the girl was dead. We may infer that even these dread tidings of certainty failed to destroy the man's faith; he seems to have still looked to the Lord for help, and those who had brought the message asked, "Why troublest thou the Master any further—?" Jesus heard what was said, and sustained the man's sorely taxed faith by the encouraging behest: "Be not afraid, only believe." Jesus permitted none of His followers save three of the apostles to enter the house with Himself and the bereaved but trusting father. Peter and the two brothers James and John were admitted.

The house was no place of such respectful silence or subdued quiet as we now consider appropriate to the time and place of death; on the contrary it was a scene of tumult, but that condition was customary in the orthodox observances of mourning at the time.[t] Professional mourners, including singers of weird dirges, and minstrels who made great noise with flutes and other instruments, had already been summoned to the house. To all such Jesus said, on entering: "Why make ye this ado, and weep? the damsel is not dead but sleepeth." It was in effect a repetition of His command uttered on a then recent occasion—Peace, be still. His words drew scorn and ridicule from those who were paid for the noise they made, and who, if what He said proved true, would lose this opportunity of professional service. Moreover, they knew the maid was dead; preparations for the funeral, which custom required should follow death as speedily as possible, were already in progress. Jesus ordered these people out, and restored peace to the house.[u] He then entered the death chamber, accompanied only by the three apostles and the parents of the girl. Taking the dead maiden by the hand He "said unto her, Talitha cumi; which is, being interpreted, Damsel, I say unto thee, arise." To the astonishment of all but the Lord, the girl arose, left her bed, and walked. Jesus directed that food be given her, as bodily needs, suspended by death, had returned with the girl's renewal of life.

The Lord imposed an obligation of secrecy, charging all present to refrain from telling what they had seen. The reasons for this injunction

[t] Note 6, end of chapter.

[u] Note 7, end of chapter.

are not stated. In some other instances a similar instruction was given to those who had been blessed by Christ's ministrations; while on many occasions of healing no such instructions are recorded, and in one case at least the man who had been relieved of demons was told to go and tell how great a thing had been done for him.[v] In His own wisdom Christ knew when to prudently forbid and when to permit publication of His doings. Though the grateful parents, the girl herself, and the three apostles who had been witnesses of the restoration, may all have been loyal to the Lord's injunction of silence, the fact that the maiden had been raised to life could not be kept secret, and the means by which so great a wonder had been wrought would certainly be inquired into. The minstrels and the wailers who had been expelled from the place while it was yet a house of mourning, and who had scornfully laughed at the Master's assertion that the maiden was asleep and not dead as they thought, would undoubtedly spread reports. It is not surprising, therefore, to read in Matthew's short version of the history, that the fame of the miracle "went abroad into all that land."

RESTORATION TO LIFE AND RESURRECTION

The vital distinction between a restoration of the dead to a resumption of mortal life, and the resurrection of the body from death to a state of immortality, must be thoughtfully heeded. In each of the instances thus far considered—that of the raising of the dead man of Nain,[w] and that of the daughter of Jairus, as also in the raising of Lazarus to be studied later—the miracle consisted in reuniting the spirit and the body in a continuation of the interrupted course of mortal existence. That the subject of each of these miracles had to subsequently die is certain. Jesus Christ was the first of all men who have lived on earth to come forth from the tomb an immortalized Being; He is therefore properly designated as "the first fruits of them that slept."[x]

Though both Elijah and Elisha, many centuries prior to the time of Christ, were instrumental in restoring life to the dead, the former

[v] Mark 5:19–20; Luke 8:39.

[w] Pages 239–240.

[x] 1 Cor. 15:20, 23; see also Acts 26:23; Col. 1:18; Rev. 1:5; and Articles of Faith, pp. 387–90.

to the widow's son in Zareptha, the latter to the child of the Shunammite woman,[y] in these earlier miracles the restoration was to mortal existence, not to immortality. It is instructive to observe the difference in the procedure of each of the Old Testament prophets mentioned as compared with that of Christ in analogous miracles. By both Elijah and Elisha the wonderful change was brought about only after long and labored ministrations, and earnest invocation of the power and intervention of Jehovah; but Jehovah, embodied in flesh as Jesus Christ, did nothing outwardly but command, and the bonds of death were immediately broken. He spoke in His own name and by inherent authority, for by the power with which He was invested He held control of both life and death.

A REMARKABLE HEALING BY THE WAY[z]

While Jesus was walking to the house of Jairus with a great crowd of people thronging about Him, the progress of the company was arrested by another case of suffering. In the throng was a woman who for twelve years had been afflicted with a serious ailment involving frequent hemorrhage. She had spent in medical treatment all she had owned, and "had suffered many things of many physicians," but had steadily grown worse. She worked her way through the crowd, and, approaching Jesus from behind, touched His robe; "For she said, If I may touch but his clothes I shall be whole." The effect was more than magical; immediately she felt the thrill of health throughout her body, and knew that she had been healed of her affliction. Her object attained, the blessing she sought being now secured, she tried to escape notice by hastily dropping back into the crowd. But her touch was not unheeded by the Lord. He turned to look over the throng and asked, "Who touched my clothes?" or as Luke puts it, "Who touched me?" As the people denied, the impetuous Peter speaking for himself and the others said: "Master, the multitude throng thee and press thee, and sayest thou, Who touched me?" But Jesus answered: "Somebody hath touched me: for I perceive that virtue is gone out of me."

[y] 1 Kgs. 17:17–24; 2 Kgs. 4:31–37.
[z] Mark 5:25–34; Matt. 9:20–22; Luke 8:43–48.

The woman, finding that she could not escape identification, came tremblingly forward, and, kneeling before the Lord, confessed what she had done, her reason for so doing, and the beneficent result. If she had expected censure her fears were promptly set at rest, for Jesus, addressing her by a term of respect and kindness, said: "Daughter, be of good comfort: thy faith hath made thee whole; go in peace," and as Mark adds, "be whole of thy plague."

This woman's faith was sincere and free from guile, nevertheless it was in a sense defective. She believed that the influence of Christ's person, and even that attaching to His raiment, was a remedial agency, ample to cure her malady; but she did not realize that the power to heal was an inherent attribute to be exercised at His will, and as the influence of faith might call it forth. True, her faith had already been in part rewarded, but of greater worth to her than the physical cure of illness would be the assurance that the divine Healer had granted the desire of her heart, and that the faith she had manifested was accepted by Him. To correct her misapprehension and to confirm her faith, Jesus gently subjected her to the necessary ordeal of confession, which must have been made easier through her consciousness of the great relief already experienced. He confirmed the healing and let her depart with the comforting assurance that her recovery was permanent.

In contrast with the many cases of healing in connection with which the Lord charged the beneficiaries that they should tell none how or by whom they had been relieved, we see here that publicity was made sure by His own action, and that too, when secrecy was desired by the recipient of the blessing. The purposes and motives of Jesus may be but poorly understood by man; but in this woman's case we see the possibility of stories strange and untrue getting afloat, and it appears to have been the wiser course to make plain the truth then and there. Moreover the spiritual worth of the miracle was greatly enhanced by the woman's confession and by the Lord's gracious assurance.

Observe the significant assertion, "Thy faith hath made thee whole." Faith is of itself a principle of power;[aa] and by its presence or absence, by its fulness or paucity, even the Lord was and is influenced,

---

[aa] *Articles of Faith*, pp. 102–5.

and in great measure controlled, in the bestowal or withholding of blessings; for He ministers according to law, and not with caprice or uncertainty. We read that at a certain time and place Jesus "could there do no mighty work" because of the people's unbelief.[bb] Modern revelation specifies that faith to be healed is one of the gifts of the Spirit, analogous to the manifestations of faith in the work of healing others through the exercise of the power of the Holy Priesthood.[cc]

Our Lord's inquiry as to who had touched Him in the throng affords us another example of His asking questions in pursuance of a purpose, when He could readily have determined the facts directly and without aid from others. There was a special purpose in the question, as every teacher finds a means of instruction in questioning his pupils.[dd] But there is in Christ's question, "Who touched me?" a deeper significance than could inhere in a simple inquiry as to the identity of an individual; and this is implied in the Lord's further words: "Somebody hath touched me: for I perceive that virtue is gone out of me." The usual external act by which His miracles were wrought was a word or a command, sometimes accompanied by the laying on of hands, or by some other physical ministration as in anointing the eyes of a blind man.[ee] That there was an actual giving of His own strength to the afflicted whom He healed is evident from the present instance. Passive belief on the part of a would-be recipient of blessing is insufficient; only when it is vitalized into active faith is it a power; so also of one who ministers in the authority given of God, mental and spiritual energy must be operative if the service is to be effective.

THE BLIND SEE AND DUMB SPEAK[ff]

Two other instances of miraculous healing are chronicled by Matthew as closely following the raising of the daughter of Jairus. As Jesus passed down the streets of Capernaum, presumably on His departure from the house of the ruler of the synagog, two blind men

[bb] Mark 6:5, 6; compare Matt. 13:58.
[cc] D&C 46:19; compare Matt. 8:10; 9:28; 29; Acts 14:9.
[dd] Note 8, end of chapter.
[ee] Matt. 8:3; Luke 4:40; 13:13; John 9:6; compare Mark 6:5; 7:33, 8:23.
[ff] Matt. 9:27–35.

followed Him, crying out: "Thou son of David, have mercy on us." This title of address was voiced by others at sundry times, and in no case do we find record of our Lord disclaiming it or objecting to its use.[gg] Jesus paused not to heed this call of the blind, and the two sightless men followed Him, even entering the house after Him. Then He spoke to them, asking: "Believe ye that I am able to do this?" And they replied, "Yea, Lord." Their persistency in following the Lord was evidence of their belief that in some way, though to them unknown and mysterious, He could help them; and they promptly and openly confessed that belief. Our Lord touched their eyes, saying: "According to your faith be it unto you." The effect was immediate; their eyes were opened. They were explicitly instructed to say nothing of the matter to others; but, rejoicing in the inestimable blessing of sight, they "spread abroad his fame in all that country." So far as we can unravel the uncertain threads of sequence in the works of Christ, this is the earliest instance, recorded with attendant details, of His giving sight to the blind. Many remarkable cases follow.[hh]

It is worthy of note that in blessing the sightless by the exercise of His healing power, Jesus usually ministered by some physical contact in addition to uttering the authoritative words of command or assurance. In this instance, as also in that of two blind men who sat by the wayside, He touched the sightless eyes; in the giving of sight to the blind indigent in Jerusalem He anointed the man's eyes with clay; to the eyes of another He applied saliva.[ii] An analogous circumstance is found in the healing of one who was deaf and defective of speech, in which instance the Lord put His fingers into the man's ears and touched his tongue.[jj] In no case can such treatment be regarded as medicinal or therapeutic. Christ was not a physician who relied upon curative substances, nor a surgeon to perform physical operations; His healings were the natural results of the application of a power of His own. It is conceivable that confidence, which is a stepping-stone to belief, as that in turn is to faith, may have been encouraged by these

gg Matt. 15:22; 20:30, 31; Mark 10:47, 48; Luke 18:38, 39.

hh Note 9, end of chapter.

ii Matt. 20:30–34; John 9:6; Mark 8:23.

jj Mark 7:32–37.

physical ministrations, strengthened, and advanced to a higher and more abiding trust in Christ, on the part of the afflicted who had not sight to look upon the Master's face and derive inspiration therefrom, nor hearing to hear His uplifting words. There is apparent not alone an entire absence of formula and formalism in His ministration, but a lack of uniformity of procedure quite as impressive.

As the two men, once sightless but now seeing, departed, others came, bringing a dumb friend whose affliction seems to have been primarily due to the malignant influence of an evil spirit rather than to any organic defect. Jesus rebuked the wicked spirit—cast out the demon that had obsessed the afflicted one and held him in the tyranny of speechlessness. The man's tongue was loosened, he was freed from the evil incubus, and was no longer dumb.[kk]

NOTES TO CHAPTER 20

1. Storms on the Lake of Galilee.—It is a matter of record that sudden and violent storms are common on the lake or sea of Galilee; and the tempest that was quieted by the Lord's word of command was of itself no unusual phenomenon, except perhaps in its intensity. Another incident connected with a storm on this small body of water is of scriptural record, and will be considered later in the text (Matt. 14:22–26; Mark 6:45–56; John 6:15–21). Dr. Thompson (*The Land and the Book*, 2.32) gives a description founded on his personal experience on the shores of the lake: "I spent a night in that Wady Shukaiyif, some three miles up it, to the left of us. The sun had scarcely set when the wind began to rush down toward the lake, and it continued all night long with constantly increasing violence, so that when we reached the shore next morning the face of the lake was a huge boiling caldron. The wind howled down every wady from the northeast and east with such fury that no efforts of rowers could have brought a boat to shore at any point along that coast. . . . To understand the causes of these sudden and violent tempests, we must remember that the lake lies low—six hundred feet lower than the ocean; that the vast and naked plateaus of the Jaulan rise to a great height, spreading backward to the wilds of the Hauran, and upward to snowy Hermon; and the water-courses have cut out profound ravines and wild gorges, converging to the head of this lake, and that these act like gigantic funnels to draw down the cold winds from the mountains."

2. The Earth Before and After Its Regeneration.—That the earth itself fell under the curse incident to the Fall of the first parents of the race, and that even as man

[kk] Matt. 9:32, 33. Note 10, end of chapter.

shall be redeemed so shall the earth be regenerated, is implied in Paul's words: "Because the creature itself also shall be delivered from the bondage of corruption into the glorious liberty of the children of God. For we know that the whole creation groaneth and travaileth in pain together until now. And not only they, but ourselves also, which have the firstfruits of the Spirit, even we ourselves groan within ourselves, waiting for the adoption, to wit, the redemption of our body" (Rom. 8:21–23). The present author has written elsewhere: "According to the scriptures, the earth has to undergo a change analogous to death, and to be regenerated in a manner comparable to a resurrection. References to the elements melting with heat, and to the earth being consumed and passing away, such as occur in many scriptures already cited, are suggestive of death; and the new earth, really the renewed or regenerated planet, which is to result, may be compared with a resurrected organism. The change has been likened unto a transfiguration (D&C 63:20, 21). Every created thing has been made for a purpose; and everything that fills the measure of its creation is to be advanced in the scale of progression, be it an atom or a world, an animalcule, or man—the direct and literal offspring of Deity. In speaking of the degrees of glory provided for His creations, and of the laws of regeneration and sanctification, the Lord, in a revelation dated 1832, speaks plainly of the approaching death and subsequent quickening of the earth. These are His words:—'And again, verily I say unto you, the earth abideth the law of a celestial kingdom, for it filleth the measure of its creation, and transgresseth not the law. Wherefore it shall be sanctified; yes, notwithstanding it shall die, it shall be quickened again, and shall abide the power by which it is quickened, and the righteous shall inherit it.' (D&C 88:25–26.)"

The vital Spirit that emanates from God and is coextensive with space may operate directly and with as positive effect upon inanimate things, and upon energy in its diverse manifestations known to us as the forces of nature, as upon organized intelligences, whether yet unembodied, in the flesh, or disembodied. Thus, the Lord may speak directly to the earth, the air, the sea, and be heard and obeyed, for the divine affluence, which is the sum of all energy and power may and does operate throughout the universe. In the course of a revelation from God to Enoch, the earth is personified, and her groans and lamentations over the wickedness of men were heard by the prophet: "And it came to pass that Enoch looked upon the earth; and he heard a voice from the bowels thereof, saying: Wo, wo is me, the mother of men; I am pained, I am weary, because of the wickedness of my children. When shall I rest, and be cleansed from the filthiness which is gone forth out of me? When will my Creator sanctify me, that I may rest, and righteousness for a season abide upon my face?" Enoch pleaded: "O Lord, wilt thou not have compassion upon the earth?" Following further revelation as to the then future course of mankind in sin and in the rejection of the Messiah who was to be sent, the prophet wept with anguish, and asked of God "When shall the earth rest?" It was then shown unto him that the crucified Christ shall return to earth and establish a millennial reign of peace: "And the Lord said unto Enoch: As I live, even so will I come in the last days, in the days of wickedness and vengeance, to fulfil the oath which I have made unto you concerning the children of Noah; and the day shall come that the earth shall rest, but before that day the heavens shall be darkened, and a veil of darkness shall cover the earth; and the heavens shall shake, and also the earth; and great tribulations shall be among the children of men." And the glorious assurance followed "that for the space of a thousand years the earth shall rest." (P. of G. P., Moses 7:48, 49, 58, 60, 61, 64.)

A partial description of the earth in its regenerated state has been given through the prophet Joseph Smith in the present dispensation: "This earth, in its sanctified and immortal state, will be made like unto crystal and will be a Urim and Thummim to the inhabitants who dwell thereon, whereby all things pertaining to an inferior kingdom, or all kingdoms of a lower order, will be manifest to those who dwell on it; and this earth will be Christ's." (D&C 130:9.)

That Jesus Christ, in the exercise of His powers of Godship, should speak directly to the wind or the sea and be obeyed, is no less truly in accord with the natural law of heaven, than that He should effectively command a man or an unembodied spirit. That through faith even mortal man may set in operation the forces that act upon matter and with assurance of stupendous results has been explicitly declared by Jesus Christ: "For verily I say unto you, If ye have faith as a grain of mustard seed, ye shall say unto this mountain, Remove hence to yonder place; and it shall remove; and nothing shall be impossible unto you" (Matt. 17:20; compare Mark 11:23; Luke 17:6).

3. **The Land of the Gergesenes.**—Attempts have been made to discredit the account of Christ's healing the demoniac in "the country of the Gadarenes" (Mark 5:1; Luke 8:26) on the claim that the ancient town of Gadara the capital of the district (see Josephus, *Wars*, iii, 7:1), was too far inland to make possible the precipitous dash of the swine into the sea from that place. Others lay stress on the fact that Matthew differs from the two other Gospel-historians, in specifying "the country of the Gergesenes" (8:28). As stated in the text, a whole region or section is referred to, not a town. The keepers of the swine ran off to the towns to report the disaster that had befallen their herd. In that district of Perea there were at the time towns named respectively Gadara, Gerasa, and Gergesa; the region in general, therefore, could properly be called the land of the Gadarenes or of the Gergesenes. Farrar (*Life of Christ*, p. 254 note) says: "After the researches of Dr. Thompson (*The Land and the Book*, 2:25), there can be no doubt that Gergesa . . . was the name of a little town nearly opposite Capernaum, the ruined site of which is still called Kerza or Gersa by the Bedawin. The existence of this little town was apparently known both to Origen, who first introduced the reading, and to Eusebius and Jerome; and in their day a steep declivity near it, where the hills approach to within a little distance from the lake, was pointed out as the scene of the miracle."

4. Jesus Entreated to Leave the Country.—The people were frightened over the power possessed by Jesus, as demonstrated in the cure of the demoniac, and in the destruction of the swine, which latter occurrence, however, was not in pursuance of His command. It was the fear that sinful men feel in the presence of the Righteous. They were not prepared for other manifestations of divine power, and they dreaded to think who among them might be directly affected thereby should it be exerted. We must judge the people mercifully, however, if at all. They were in part heathen, and had but superstitious conceptions of Deity. Their prayer that Jesus leave them brings to mind the ejaculation of Simon Peter in his witnessing one of Christ's miracles: "Depart from me: for I am a sinful man, O Lord" (Luke 5:8).

5. "Dead," or "At the point of Death."—According to Luke (8:42) the daughter of Jairus "lay a dying" when the grief-stricken father sought help of the Lord; Mark (5:23) reports the man as stating that the girl lay "at the point of death." These two accounts agree; but Matthew (9:18) represents the father as saying: "My daughter is even now dead." Unbelieving critics have dwelt at length on what they designate an inconsistency if not a contradiction in these versions; and yet both accounts embodied in the three records so plainly true. The maid was seemingly breathing her last, she was in the very throes of death, when the father hurried away. Before he met Jesus he felt that the end had probably come; nevertheless his faith endured. His words attest his trust, that even had his daughter actually died since he left her side, the Master could recall her to life. He was in a state of frenzied grief, and still his faith held true.

6. Mourning Customs Among Orientals—Observances that to us seem strange, weird, and out of place, prevailed from very early times among oriental peoples, some of which customs were common to the Jews in the days of Christ. Noise and tumult, including screeching lamentations by members of the bereaved family and by professional mourners, as also the din of instruments, were usual accompaniments of mourning. Geikie, citing Buxtorf's quotation from the Talmud, gives place to the following: "Even a poor Israelite was required to have not fewer than two flute players and one mourning woman at the death of his wife; but if he be rich all things are to be done according to his quality." In Smith's *Dictionary of the Bible,* we read: "The number of words (about eleven Hebrew and as many Greek) employed in scripture to express the various actions characteristic of mourning, shows in a great degree the nature of Jewish customs in this respect. They appear to have consisted chiefly in the following particulars: (1) Beating upon the breast or other parts of the body. (2) Weeping and screaming in an excessive degree. (3) Wearing sad-colored garments. (4) Songs of lamentation. (5) Funeral feasts. (6) Employment of persons, especially women, to lament. One marked feature of oriental mourning is what may be called its studied publicity, and the careful observance of prescribed ceremonies (Gen. 23:2; Job 1:20; 2:8; Isa. 15:3; etc.)."

7. "Not Dead, but Sleepeth."—That the daughter of Jairus was dead is placed beyond reasonable doubt by the scriptural record. Our Lord's statement to the noisy mourners that "the damsel is not dead but sleepeth" told that her sleep was to be of short duration. It was a rabbinical and common custom of the time to speak of death as a sleep, and those who laughed Jesus to scorn for His statement chose to construe His words in a sense of such literalism as the context scarcely warrants. It is noticeable that the Lord used a strictly equivalent expression with respect to the death of Lazarus. "Our friend Lazarus sleepeth," said He, "but I go that I may awake him out of sleep." The literal construction placed upon these words by the apostles evoked the plain declaration "Lazarus is dead" (John 11:11, 14). In the Talmud death is repeatedly designated as sleep—hundreds of times says Lightfoot, a recognized authority on Hebrew literature.

8. Why Did Jesus Make Inquiries?—We have already considered many instances of Christ's possession of what man would call superhuman knowledge, extending even to the reading of unuttered thoughts. Some people find difficulty in reconciling this superior quality with the fact that Jesus often asked questions even on matters of minor circumstance. We should realize that even complete knowledge may not preclude the propriety of making inquiries, and, moreover, that even omniscience does not imply ever-present consciousness of all that is. Undoubtedly through his paternal heritage of divine attributes, Jesus had the power of ascertaining for Himself, by means not possessed by others, any facts He might have desired to know; nevertheless we find Him repeatedly asking questions on circumstantial detail (Mark 9:21; 8:27; Matt. 16:13; Luke 8:45); and this He did even after His Resurrection (Luke 24:41; John 21:5; 3 Ne. 17:7).

That catechization is one of the most effective means of mind development is exampled in the methods followed by the best of human teachers. Trench (*Notes on the Miracles,* pp. 148–49), thus instructively points the lesson as illustrated by our Lord's question concerning the woman who was healed of her issue of blood: With little force "can it be urged that it would have been inconsistent with absolute truth for the Lord to profess ignorance, and to ask the question which He did ask, if all the while He perfectly knew what He thus seemed implicitly to say that He did not know. A father among his children, and demanding Who committed this fault? himself conscious, even while he asks, but at the same time willing to bring the culprit to a full confession, and so to put him in a pardonable state, can he be said, in any way to violate the law of the highest truth? The same offense might be found in Elisha's 'Whence comest thou, Gehazi?' (2 Kgs. 5:25) when his heart went with his servant all the way that he had gone; and even in the question of God Himself to Adam, 'Where art thou?' (Gen. 3:9), and to Cain, 'Where is Abel thy brother?' (Gen. 4:9). In every case there is a moral purpose in the question, an opportunity given even at the latest moment for making good at least a part of the error by its unreserved confession."

9. The Blind See.—In his treatment of the miraculous healing of the two blind men who had followed Jesus into the house, Trench (*Notes on the Miracles of Our Lord,* p. 152) says: "We have here the first of those many healings of the blind recorded (Matt. 12:22; 20:30; 21:14; John 9) or alluded to (Matt. 11:5) in the Gospels; each of them a literal fulfilment of that prophetic word of Isaiah concerning the days of Messiah: 'Then the eyes of the blind shall be opened' (35:5). Frequent as these miracles are, they yet will none of them be found without distinguishing features of their own. That they should be so numerous is nothing wonderful, whether we regard the fact from a natural or spiritual point of view. Regarded naturally they need not surprise us if we keep in mind how far commoner a calamity is blindness in the East than with us. Regarded from a spiritual point of view we have only to remember how commonly sin is contemplated in Scripture as a moral blindness (Deut. 28:29; Isa. 59:10; Job 12:25; Zeph. 1:17), and deliverance from sin as a removal of this blindness (Isa. 6:9, 10; 43:8; Eph. 1:18; Matt. 15:14); and we shall at once perceive how fit it was that He who was the 'light of the world' should often accomplish works which symbolized so well that higher work which He came into the world to accomplish."

10. Imputation of Satanic Agency.—Observe that in the matter of healing the dumb demoniac referred to in the text, Christ was charged with being in league with the devil. Although the people, impressed by the manifestation of divine power in the healing, exclaimed in reverence, "It was never so seen in Israel," the Pharisees, intent on counteracting the good effect of the Lord's miraculous ministration, said "He casteth out devils through the prince of the devils." (Matt. 9:32–34.) (For further treatment of this inconsistent and, strictly speaking blasphemous charge, see pages 251–255.)

CHAPTER 21

THE APOSTOLIC MISSION AND
EVENTS RELATED THERETO

JESUS AGAIN IN NAZARETH [a]

It will be remembered that, in the early days of His public ministry, Jesus had been rejected by the people of Nazareth, who thrust Him out from their synagog and tried to kill Him.[b] It appears that subsequent to the events noted in our last chapter, He returned to the town of His youth, and again raised His voice in the synagog, thus mercifully affording the people another opportunity to learn and accept the truth. The Nazarenes, as they had done before, now again openly expressed their astonishment at the words He spoke, and at the many miraculous works He had wrought; nevertheless they rejected Him anew, for He came not as they expected the Messiah to come; and they refused to know Him save as "the carpenter, the son of Mary, the brother of James, and Joses, and of Juda, and Simon"; all of whom were common folk as were also His sisters. "And they were offended at him."[c] Jesus reminded them of the proverb then current among the people, "A prophet is not without honour, but in his own country, and among his own kin, and in his own house." Their unbelief was so dense as to cause Him to marvel;[d] and because of their lack of faith He was unable to accomplish any great work except to heal a few exceptional believers upon whom He laid His hands. Leaving

---

[a] Matt. 13:53–58; Mark 6:1–6.

[b] Luke 4:28–30.

[c] Pages 242, 259.

[d] Note 2, chapter 18.

Nazareth, He entered upon His third tour of the Galilean towns and villages, preaching and teaching as He went.[e]

THE TWELVE CHARGED AND SENT[f]

About this time, also, Jesus inaugurated a notable expansion of the ministry of the kingdom, by sending forth the Twelve on assigned missions. Since their ordination the apostles had been with their Lord, learning from Him by public discourse and private exposition, and acquiring invaluable experience and training through that privileged and blessed companionship. The purpose of their ordination was specified—"that they should be with him, and that he might send them forth to preach."[g] They had been pupils under the Master's watchful guidance for many months; and now they were called to enter upon the duties of their calling as preachers of the gospel and individual witnesses of the Christ. By way of final preparation they were specifically and solemnly charged.[h] Some of the instructions given them on this occasion had particular reference to their first mission, from which they would in due time return and report; other directions and admonitions were to be of effect throughout their ministry, even after the Lord's ascension.

They were directed to confine their ministrations for the time being "to the lost sheep of the house of Israel," and not to open a propaganda among the Gentiles,[i] nor even in Samaritan cities. This was a temporary restriction, imposed in wisdom and prudence; later, as we shall see, they were directed to preach among all nations, with the world for their field.[j] The subject of their discourses was to be that upon which they had heard the Master preach—"the kingdom of heaven is at hand." They were to exercise the authority of the Holy Priesthood as conferred upon them by ordination; it was a specified part of their mission to "heal the sick, cleanse the lepers, raise the

[e] Note 1, end of chapter.

[f] Matt. 10:5–42; Mark 6:7–13; Luke 9:1–6.

[g] Mark 3:14.

[h] Matt. 10:5–42; Mark 6:7–13; Luke 9:1–6.

[i] Note 2, end of chapter.

[j] Matt. 28:19; Mark 16:15.

dead, cast out devils," as occasion presented itself; and they were commanded to give freely, even as they had freely received. Personal comfort and bodily needs they were not to provide for; the people were to be proved as to their willingness to receive and assist those who came in the name of the Lord; and the apostles themselves were to learn to rely upon a Provider more to be trusted than man; therefore money, extra clothing, and things of mere convenience were to be left behind. In the several towns they entered they were to seek entertainment and leave their blessing upon every worthy family into which they were received. If they found themselves rejected by a household or by a town as a whole, they were to shake the dust from their feet on leaving, as a testimony against the people;[k] and it was decreed that, in the day of judgment, the place so denounced would fare worse than wicked Sodom and Gomorrha upon which fire from heaven had descended.

The apostles were told to be prudent, to give no needless offense, but to be wise as serpents, and harmless as doves; for they were sent forth as sheep into the midst of wolves. They were not to recklessly entrust themselves to the power of men; for wicked men would persecute them, seek to arraign them before councils and courts, and to afflict them in the synagogs. Moreover they might expect to be brought before governors and kings, under which extreme conditions they were to rely upon divine inspiration as to what they should say, and not depend upon their own wisdom in preparation and premeditation; "For," said the Master, "it is not ye that speak, but the Spirit of your Father which speaketh in you."[l]

They were not to trust even the claims of kinship for protection, for families would be divided over the truth, brother against brother, children against parents, and the resulting strife would be deadly. These servants of Christ were told that they would be hated of all men, but were assured that their sufferings were to be for His name's sake, They were to withdraw from the cities that persecuted them, and go to others; and the Lord would follow them, even before they would be able to complete the circuit of the cities of Israel. They were

[k] Note 3, end of chapter.

[l] Matt. 10:18–20; compare Mark 13:9; Luke 12:10–12.

admonished to humility, and were always to remember that they were servants, who ought not to expect to escape when even their Master was assailed. Nevertheless they were to be fearless, hesitating not to preach the gospel in plainness; for the most their persecutors could do was to kill the body, which fate was as nothing compared to that of suffering destruction of the soul in hell.

Assurance of the Father's watchful care was impressed upon them by the simple reminder that though sparrows were sold two for a farthing, and yet not a sparrow could be sacrificed without the Father's concern, they, who were of more value than many sparrows, would not be forgotten. They were solemnly warned that whosoever would freely confess the Christ before men would be acknowledged by Him in the Father's presence, while they who denied Him before men would be denied in heaven. And again they were told that the gospel would bring strife, whereby households would be disrupted; for the doctrine the Lord had taught would be as a sword to cut and divide. The duties of their special ministry were to supersede the love for kindred; they must be willing to leave father, mother, son, or daughter, whatever the sacrifice; for, said Jesus "He that taketh not his cross, and followeth after me, is not worthy of me."

The significance of this figure must have been solemnly impressive, and actually terrifying; for the cross was a symbol of ignominy, extreme suffering, and death. However, should they lose their lives for His sake, they would find life eternal; while he who was not willing to die in the Lord's service should lose his life in a sense at once literal and awful. They were never to forget in whose name they were sent; and were comforted with the assurance that whoever received them would be rewarded as one who had received the Christ and His Father; and that though the gift were only that of a cup of cold water, the giver should in no wise lose his reward.

Thus charged and instructed, the twelve special witnesses of the Christ set out upon their mission, traveling in pairs,[m] while Jesus continued His personal ministry.

---

[m] Mark 6:7.

THE TWELVE RETURN

We are without definite information as to the duration of the apostles' first mission, and as to the extent of the field they traversed. The period of their absence was marked by many important developments in the individual labors of Jesus. It is probable that during this time our Lord visited Jerusalem, on the occasion mentioned by John as coincident with the unnamed feast of the Jews.[n] While the apostles were absent, Jesus was visited by the Baptist's disciples, as we have already seen,[o] and the return of the Twelve occurred near the time of the infamous execution of John the Baptist in prison.[p]

The missionary labors of the apostles greatly augmented the spread of the new doctrine of the kingdom, and the name and works of Jesus were proclaimed throughout the land. The people of Galilee were at that time in a state of discontent threatening open insurrection against the government; their unrest had been aggravated by the murder of the Baptist. Herod Antipas, who had given the fatal order, trembled in his palace. He heard, with fear due to inward conviction of guilt, of the marvelous work wrought by Jesus, and in terror averred that Christ could be none other than John Baptist returned from the tomb. His fawning courtiers essayed to allay his fears by saying that Jesus was Elijah, or some other of the prophets whose advent had been predicted; but the conscience-stricken Herod said: "It is John whom I beheaded: he is risen from the dead." Herod desired to see Jesus; perhaps through the fascination of fear, or with the faint hope that sight of the renowned Prophet of Nazareth might dispel his superstitious dread that the murdered John had returned to life.

Upon the completion of their missionary tour, the apostles rejoined the Master and reported to Him both what they had taught and what they had done by way of authoritative ministration. They had preached the gospel of repentance in all the cities, towns, and villages to which they had gone; they had anointed with oil many afflicted ones, and the power of their priesthood had been attested by

[n] John 5.
[o] Matt. 11:2–19; Luke 7:18–34.
[p] Pages 246-47.

consequent healings; even unclean spirits and devils had been subject
unto them.[q] They found Jesus attended by great multitudes; and they
had little opportunity of private conference with Him; "for there were
many coming and going, and they had no leisure so much as to eat."
The apostles must have heard in gladness the Lord's invitation: "Come
ye yourselves apart into a desert place, and rest awhile." In quest of
seclusion, Jesus and the Twelve withdrew from the throng, and privately
entered a boat in which they crossed to a rural spot adjacent to the city
of Bethsaida.[r] Their departure had not been unobserved, however, and
eager crowds hastened along the shore, and partly around the northerly
end of the lake, to join the party at the landing place. From John's
account we are led to infer that, before the arrival of great numbers,
Jesus and His companions had ascended the hillside near the shore,
where, for a short time they had rested. As the multitude gathered on
the lower slopes, our Lord looked upon them as upon sheep without a
shepherd; and, yielding to their desire and to His own emotions of
divine pity, He taught them many things, healed their afflicted ones,
and comforted their hearts with compassionate tenderness.

FIVE THOUSAND FED IN THE DESERTS [s]

So intent were the people on hearing the Lord's words, and so
concerned in the miraculous relief resulting from His healing ministrations, that they remained in the wilderness, oblivious to the passing
of the hours, until the evening approached. It was the springtime,
near the recurrence of the annual Passover festival, the season of grass
and flowers.[t] Jesus, realizing that the people were hungry, asked
Philip, one of the Twelve, "Whence shall we buy bread, that these
may eat?" The purpose of the question was to test the apostle's faith;
for the Lord had already determined as to what was to be done.
Philip's reply showed surprise at the question, and conveyed his

[q] Mark 6:12, 13; Luke 9:10. Note similar testimony of the Seventy, who were sent out at a
later time, and who returned rejoicing in the power that had been manifest in their ministry;
Luke 10:17.

[r] Note 4, end of chapter.

[s] John 6:5–14; compare Matt. 14:15–21; Mark 6:35–44; Luke 9:12–17.

[t] John 6:4; Matt. 14:19; Mark 6:39.

thought that the suggested undertaking was impossible. "Two hundred pennyworth of bread is not sufficient for them, that every one of them may take a little," said he. Andrew added that there was a lad present who had five barley loaves, and two small fishes, "But," said he, "what are they among so many?"

Such is John's account; the other writers state that the apostles reminded Jesus of the lateness of the hour, and urged that He send the people away to seek for themselves food and lodging in the nearest towns. It appears most probable that the conversation between Jesus and Philip occurred earlier in the afternoon;[u] and that as the hours sped, the Twelve became concerned and advised that the multitude be dismissed. The Master's reply to the apostles was: "They need not depart; give ye them to eat." In amazed wonder they replied: "We have here but five loaves and two fishes"; and Andrew's despairing comment is implied again—What are they among so many?

Jesus gave command, and the people seated themselves on the grass in orderly array; they were grouped in fifties and hundreds; and it was found that the multitude numbered about five thousand men, beside women and children. Taking the loaves and the fishes, Jesus looked toward heaven and pronounced a blessing upon the food; then, dividing the provisions, He gave to the apostles severally, and they in turn distributed to the multitude. The substance of both fish and bread increased under the Master's touch; and the multitude feasted there in the desert, until all were satisfied. To the disciples Jesus said: "Gather up the fragments that remain, that nothing be lost"; and twelve baskets were filled with the surplus.

As to the miracle itself, human knowledge is powerless to explain. Though wrought on so great a scale, it is no more nor less inexplicable than any other of the Lord's miraculous works. It was a manifestation of creative power, by which material elements were organized and compounded to serve a present and pressing need. The broken but unused portion exceeded in bulk and weight the whole of the original little store. Our Lord's direction to gather up the fragments was an impressive object lesson against waste; and it may have been to afford

---

[u] Note 5, end of chapter.

such lesson that an excess was supplied. The fare was simple, yet nourishing, wholesome and satisfying. Barley bread and fish constituted the usual food of the poorer classes of the region. The conversion of water into wine at Cana was a qualitative transmutation; the feeding of the multitude involved a quantitative increase; who can say that one, or which, of these miracles of provision was the more wonderful?

The multitude, now fed and filled, gave some consideration to the miracle. In Jesus, by whom so great a work had been wrought, they recognized One having superhuman powers. "This is of a truth the prophet that should come into the world," said they—the Prophet whose coming had been foretold by Moses and who should be like unto himself. Even as Israel had been miraculously fed during the time of Moses, so now was bread provided in the desert by this new Prophet. In their enthusiasm the people proposed to proclaim Him king, and forcibly compel Him to become their leader. Such was their gross conception of Messianic supremacy. Jesus directed His disciples to depart by boat, while He remained to dismiss the now excited multitude. The disciples hesitated to leave their Master; but He constrained them and they obeyed. His insistence, that the Twelve depart from both Himself and the multitude, may have been due to a desire to protect the chosen disciples against possible infection by the materialistic and unrighteous designs of the throng to make Him king. By means that are not detailed, He caused the people to disperse; and, as night came on, He found that for which He had come in quest, solitude and quiet. Ascending the hill, He chose a secluded place, and there remained in prayer during the greater part of the night.

"IT IS I; BE NOT AFRAID" ᵛ

The return by boat proved to be a memorable journey for the disciples. They encountered a boisterous headwind, which of course rendered impossible the use of sails; and though they toiled heavily at the oars the vessel became practically unmanageable and wallowed in the midst of the sea.ʷ Though they had labored through the night

---

ᵛ Matt. 14:22–33; compare Mark 6:45–52; John 6:15–21.
ʷ Page 302

they had progressed less than four miles on their course; to turn and run before the wind would have been to invite disastrous wreck; their sole hope lay in their holding the vessel to the wind by sheer power of muscle. Jesus, in His place of solitary retirement, was aware of their sad plight, and along in the fourth watch,[x] that is, between three and six o'clock in the morning, He came to their assistance, walking upon the storm-tossed water as though treading solid ground. When the voyagers caught sight of Him as He approached the ship in the faint light of the near-spent night, they were overcome by superstitious fears, and cried out in terror, thinking that they saw a ghostly apparition. "But straightway Jesus spake unto them, saying, Be of good cheer; it is I; be not afraid."

Relieved by these assuring words, Peter, impetuous and impulsive as usual, cried out: "Lord, if[y] it be thou, bid me come unto thee on the water." Jesus assenting, Peter descended from the ship and walked toward his Master; but as the wind smote him and the waves rose about him, his confidence wavered and he began to sink. Strong swimmer though he was,[z] he gave way to fright, and cried, "Lord, save me." Jesus caught him by the hand, saying: "O thou of little faith, wherefore didst thou doubt?"

From Peter's remarkable experience, we learn that the power by which Christ was able to walk the waves could be made operative in others, provided only their faith was enduring. It was on Peter's own request that he was permitted to attempt the feat. Had Jesus forbidden him, the man's faith might have suffered a check; his attempt, though attended by partial failure, was a demonstration of the efficacy of faith in the Lord, such as no verbal teaching could ever have conveyed. Jesus and Peter entered the vessel; immediately the wind ceased, and the boat soon reached the shore. The amazement of the apostles, at this latest manifestation of the Lord's control over the forces of nature, would have been more akin to worship and less like terrified consternation had they remembered the earlier wonders they

[x] Note 6, end of chapter.

[y] That is to say "since" or "inasmuch."

[z] Compare Peter's impetuous leap into the sea to reach the resurrected Lord on the shore, John 21:7.

had witnessed; but they had forgotten even the miracle of the loaves, and their hearts had hardened.[aa] Marveling at the power of One to whom the wind-lashed sea was a sustaining floor, the apostles bowed before the Lord in reverent worship, saying: "Of a truth thou art the Son of God."[bb]

Aside from the marvelous circumstances of its literal occurrence, the miracle is rich in symbolism and suggestion. By what law or principle the effect of gravitation was superseded, so that a human body could be supported upon the watery surface, man is unable to affirm. The phenomenon is a concrete demonstration of the great truth that faith is a principle of power, whereby natural forces may be conditioned and controlled.[cc] Into every adult human life come experiences like unto the battling of the storm-tossed voyagers with contrary winds and threatening seas; ofttimes the night of struggle and danger is far advanced before succor appears; and then, too frequently the saving aid is mistaken for a greater terror. As came unto Peter and his terrified companions in the midst of the turbulent waters, so comes to all who toil in faith, the voice of the Deliverer—"It is I; be not afraid."

IN THE LAND OF GENNESARET

The night voyage, in the course of which Jesus had reached the boat with its frightened occupants while "in the midst of the sea," ended at some point within the district known as the land of Gennesaret, which, as generally believed, embraced the rich and fertile region in the vicinity of Tiberias and Magdala. Of the natural beauties for which the region was famed much has been written.[dd] Word of our Lord's presence there spread rapidly, and, from "all that country round about" the people flocked to Him, bringing their afflicted to receive of His beneficence by word or touch. In the towns through which He walked, the sick were laid in the streets that the blessing of His passing might fall upon them; and many "besought

---

[aa] Mark 6:52.

[bb] Note that this is the first occurrence of this title in the Synoptic Gospels, as applied to Jesus by mortals; compare an earlier instance of its application by Nathanael, John 1:49.

[cc] *Articles of Faith*, pp. 102–5.

[dd] Josephus, *Wars*, iii, 10:7, 8.

him that they might touch if it were but the border of his garment; and as many as touched him were made whole."[ee] Bounteously did He impart of His healing virtue to all who came asking with faith and confidence. Thus, accompanied by the Twelve, He wended His way northerly to Capernaum, making the pathway bright by the plenitude of His mercies.

IN SEARCH OF LOAVES AND FISHES[ff]

The multitude who, on the yesterday, had partaken of His bounty on the other side of the lake, and who dispersed for the night after their ineffectual attempt to force upon Him the dignity of earthly kingship, were greatly surprised in the morning to discover that He had departed. They had seen the disciples leave in the only boat there present, while Jesus had remained on shore; and they knew that the night tempest had precluded the possibility of other boats reaching the place. Nevertheless their morning search for Him was futile; and they concluded that He must have returned by land round the end of the lake. As the day advanced some boats were sighted, bound for the western coast; these they hailed, and, securing passage, crossed to Capernaum.

Their difficulty in locating Jesus was at an end, for His presence was known throughout the town. Coming to Him, probably as He sat in the synagog, for on this day He taught there, some of the most intrusive of the crowd asked, brusquely and almost rudely, "Rabbi, when camest thou hither?" To this impertinent inquiry Jesus deigned no direct reply; in the miracle of the preceding night the people had no part, and no account of our Lord's movements was given them. In tone of impressive rebuke Jesus said unto them: "Verily, verily, I say unto you, Ye seek me, not because ye saw the miracles, but because ye did eat of the loaves, and were filled." Their concern was for the bread and fishes. One who could supply them with victuals as He had done must not be lost sight of.

The Master's rebuke was followed by admonition and instruction: "Labour not for the meat which perisheth, but for that meat which endureth unto everlasting life, which the Son of man shall give unto

[ee] Mark 6:53–56; compare Matt. 14:34–36. Note 7, end of chapter.
[ff] John 6:22–27.

you: for him hath God the Father sealed." This contrast between material and spiritual food they could not entirely fail to understand, and some of them asked what they should do to serve God as Jesus required. The answer was: "This is the work of God, that ye believe on him whom he hath sent." That Jesus was referring to Himself none could doubt; and straightway they demanded of Him further evidence of His divine commission; they would see greater signs. The miracle of the loaves and fishes was nearly a day old; and its impressiveness as evidence of Messianic attributes was waning. Moses had fed their fathers with manna in the desert, they said; and plainly they regarded a continued daily supply as a greater gift than a single meal of bread and fish, however much the latter may have been appreciated in the exigency of hunger. Moreover, the manna was heavenly food;[gg] whereas the bread He had given them was of earth, and only common barley bread at that. He must show them greater signs, and give them richer provender, before they would accept Him as the One whom they at first had taken Him to be and whom He now declared Himself to be.

CHRIST, THE BREAD OF LIFE [hh]

"Then Jesus said unto them, Verily, verily, I say unto you, Moses gave you not that bread from heaven; but my Father giveth you the true bread from heaven. For the bread of God is he which cometh down from heaven, and giveth life unto the world." They were mistaken in assuming that Moses had given them manna; and after all, the manna had been but ordinary food in that those who ate of it hungered again; but now the Father offered them bread from heaven such as would insure them life.

As the Samaritan woman at the well, on hearing the Lord speak of water that would satisfy once for all, had begged impulsively and with thought only of physical convenience, "Sir, give me this water, that I thirst not, neither come hither to draw,"[ii] so these people, eager to secure so satisfying a food as that of which Jesus spake, implored:

[gg] Note 8, end of chapter.
[hh] John 6:32–59.
[ii] John 4:13–15.

"Lord, evermore give us this bread." Perhaps this request was not wholly gross; there may have been in the hearts of some of them at least a genuine desire for spiritual nourishment. Jesus met their appeal with an explanation: "I am the bread of life: he that cometh to me shall never hunger; and he that believeth on me shall never thirst." He reminded them that though they had seen Him they believed not His words; and assured them that those who really accepted Him would do as the Father directed. Then, without metaphor or symbolism, He affirmed: "I came down from heaven, not to do mine own will, but the will of him that sent me." And the Father's will was that all who would accept the Son should have everlasting life.

There were present in the synagog some of the rulers— Pharisees, scribes, rabbis—and these, designated collectively as the Jews, criticized Jesus, and murmured against Him because He had said, "I am the bread which came down from heaven." They averred that He could do nothing more than any man could do; He was known to them as the son of Joseph, and as far as they knew was of ordinary earthly parentage, and yet He had the temerity to declare that He had come down from heaven. Chiefly to this class rather than to the promiscuous crowd who had hastened after Him, Jesus appears to have addressed the remainder of His discourse. He advised them to cease their murmurings; for it was a certainty that they could not apprehend His meaning, and therefore would not believe Him, unless they had been "taught of God" as the prophets had written;[jj] and none could come to Him in the sense of accepting His saving gospel unless the Father drew them to the Son; and none save those who were receptive, willing, and prepared, could be so drawn.[kk] Yet belief in the Son of God is an indispensable condition to salvation, as Jesus indicated in His affirmation: "Verily, verily, I say unto you, he that believeth on me hath everlasting life."

Then, reverting to the symbolism of the bread, He reiterated: "I am the bread of life." In further elucidation He explained that while their fathers did truly eat manna in the wilderness, yet they were dead; whereas the bread of life of which He spake would insure

---

[jj] Isa. 54:13; Jer. 31:34; Micah 4:2; compare Heb. 8:10; 10:16.
[kk] Note 9, end of chapter.

eternal life unto all who partook thereof. That bread, He averred, was His flesh. Against this solemn avowal the Jews complained anew, and disputed among themselves, some asking derisively: "How can this man give us his flesh to eat." Emphasizing the doctrine, Jesus continued: "Verily, verily, I say unto you, Except ye eat the flesh of the Son of man, and drink his blood, ye have no life in you. Whoso eateth my flesh, and drinketh my blood, hath eternal life; and I will raise him up at the last day. For my flesh is meat indeed, and my blood is drink indeed. He that eateth my flesh, and drinketh my blood, dwelleth in me, and I in him. As the living Father hath sent me, and I live by the Father: so he that eateth me, even he shall live by me. This is that bread which came down from heaven: not as your fathers did eat manna, and are dead: he that eateth of this bread shall live forever."

There was little excuse for the Jews pretending to understand that our Lord meant an actual eating and drinking of His material flesh and blood. The utterances to which they objected were far more readily understood by them than they are by us on first reading; for the representation of the law and of truth in general as bread, and the acceptance thereof as a process of eating and drinking, were figures in every-day use by the rabbis of that time.[ll] Their failure to comprehend the symbolism of Christ's doctrine was an act of will, not the natural consequence of innocent ignorance. To eat the flesh and drink the blood of Christ was and is to believe in and accept Him as the literal Son of God and Savior of the world, and to obey His commandments. By these means only may the Spirit of God become an abiding part of man's individual being, even as the substance of the food he eats is assimilated with the tissues of his body.

It is not sufficing to accept the precepts of Christ as we may adopt the doctrines of scientists, philosophers, and savants, however great the wisdom of these sages may be; for such acceptance is by mental assent or deliberate exercise of will, and has relation to the doctrine only as independent of the author. The teachings of Jesus Christ endure because of their intrinsic worth; and many men respect His aphorisms, proverbs, parables, and His profoundly philosophical

[ll] Note 10, end of chapter.

precepts, who yet reject Him as the Son of God, the Only Begotten in the flesh, the God-Man in whom were united the attributes of Deity with those of humanity, the chosen and foreordained Redeemer of mankind, through whom alone may salvation be attained. But the figure used by Jesus—that of eating His flesh and drinking His blood as typical of unqualified and absolute acceptance of Himself as the Savior of men, is of superlative import; for thereby are affirmed the divinity of His Person, and the fact of His pre-existent and eternal Godship. The sacrament of the Lord's supper, established by the Savior on the night of His betrayal, perpetuates the symbolism of eating His flesh and drinking His blood, by the partaking of bread and wine in remembrance of Him.[mm] Acceptance of Jesus as the Christ implies obedience to the laws and ordinances of His gospel; for to profess the One and refuse the other is but to convict ourselves of inconsistency, insincerity, and hypocrisy.

A CRUCIAL TEST—MANY TURN AWAY [nn]

The truth respecting Himself, as taught by the Lord in this, His last, discourse in the synagog at Capernaum, proved to be a test of faith through which many fell away. Not alone critical Jews of the official class, whose hostility was openly avowed, but those who had professed some measure of belief in Him were affected. "Many therefore of his disciples, when they had heard this, said, This is an hard saying; who can hear it?" Jesus, cognizant of their disaffection, asked: "Doth this offend you?" and added: "What and if ye shall see the Son of man ascend up where he was before?" His ascension, which was to follow His death and Resurrection, is here definitely implied. The spiritual significance of His teachings was put beyond question by the explanation that only through the Spirit could they comprehend; "Therefore," He added, "said I unto you, that no man can come unto me, except it were given unto him of my Father."

Many deserted Him, and from that time sought Him no more. The occasion was crucial; the effect was that of sifting and separation. The portentous prediction of the Baptist-prophet had entered upon

[mm] Matt. 26:26–28; Mark 14:22–25; Luke 22:19, 20.
[nn] John 6:59–71.

the stage of fulfillment: "One mightier than I cometh, . . . Whose fan is in his hand, and he will thoroughly purge his floor, and gather his wheat into the garner; but he will burn up the chaff with unquenchable fire."[oo] The fan was in operation, and much chaff was blown aside.

It appears that even the Twelve were unable to comprehend the deeper meaning of these latest teachings; they were puzzled, though none actually deserted. Nevertheless, the state of mind of some was such as to evoke from Jesus the question: "Will ye also go away?" Peter, speaking for himself and his brethren, answered with pathos and conviction: "Lord, to whom shall we go? thou hast the words of eternal life."[pp] The spirit of the Holy Apostleship was manifest in this confession. Though they were unable to comprehend in fulness the doctrine, they knew Jesus to be the Christ, and were faithful to Him while others turned away into the dark depths of apostasy.

While Peter spoke for the apostolic body as a whole, there was among them one who silently revolted; the treacherous Iscariot, who was in worse plight than an openly avowed apostate, was there. The Lord knew this man's heart, and said: "Have not I chosen you twelve, and one of you is a devil?" The historian adds: "He spake of Judas Iscariot the son of Simon: for he it was that should betray him, being one of the twelve."

NOTES TO CHAPTER 21

1. **Jesus at Nazareth.**—As no one of the Gospel writers records two occasions of our Lord's ministry in Nazareth, and as the separate accounts appearing in the synoptic Gospels closely resemble one another in a few particulars, some commentators hold that our Lord preached to His townsmen in Nazareth and was rejected by them but once. Luke's account (4:14–30) refers to an occasion immediately following the first return of Jesus to Galilee after His baptism and temptations, and directly preceding the preliminary call of the fishermen-disciples, who afterward were numbered among the apostles. Matthew (13:53–58) and Mark (6:1–6) chronicle a visit of Jesus to Nazareth later than the occasion of the first teaching in parables, and the events immediately following the same. We have good reason for accepting Luke's record as that of an early incident, and the accounts given by Matthew and Mark as those of a later visit.

[oo] Luke 3:16, 17; Matt. 3:11, 12.

[pp] Compare this confession (John 6:68, 69) with Peter's later testimony (Matt. 16:16). Note 11, end of chapter.

2. Gentiles.—In a general way the Jews designated all other peoples as Gentiles; though the same Hebrew word is rendered in the Old Testament variously, as "Gentiles" (Gen. 10:5; Judg. 4:2; 13, 16; Isa. 11:10; etc.), "nations" (Gen. 10:5, 20, 31, 32; 14:1, 9; etc.), and "heathen" (Neh. 5:8; Ps. 2:1, 8, etc.), the essential element of designation being that of foreigners. In Smith's *Dictionary of the Bible,* we read "It [the name 'Gentiles'] acquired an ethnographic and also an invidious meaning, as other nations were idolatrous, rude, hostile, etc., yet the Jews were able to use it in a purely technical, geographical sense, when it was usually translated 'nations.'" Dr. Edward E. Nourse, writing for the *Standard Bible Dictionary,* says: "In New Testament times, the Jew divided mankind into three classes, (1) Jews, (2) Greeks (Hellenes, made to include Romans, thus meaning the civilized peoples of the Roman Empire, often rendered 'Gentiles' in Authorized Version), and (3) barbarians (the uncivilized, Acts 28:4; Rom. 1:14; 1 Cor. 14:11)." The injunction laid by Jesus upon the Twelve—"Go not into the way of the Gentiles"—was to restrain them for the time being from attempting to make converts among the Romans and Greeks, and to confine their ministry to the people of Israel.

3. Shaking the Dust from the Feet.—To ceremonially shake the dust from one's feet as a testimony against another was understood by the Jews to symbolize a cessation of fellowship and a renunciation of all responsibility for consequences that might follow. It became an ordinance of accusation and testimony by the Lord's instructions to His apostles as cited in the text. In the current dispensation, the Lord has similarly directed His authorized servants to so testify against those who wilfully and maliciously oppose the truth when authoritatively presented (see D&C 24:15; 60:15; 75:20; 84:92; 99:4). The responsibility of testifying before the Lord by this accusing symbol is so great that the means may be employed only under unusual and extreme conditions, as the Spirit of the Lord may direct.

4. The Two Bethsaidas.—It is held by many Bible students that Bethsaida, in the desert region adjoining which Jesus and the Twelve sought rest and seclusion, was the town of that name in Perea, on the eastern side of the Jordan, and known more specifically as Bethsaida Julias to distinguish it from Bethsaida in Galilee, which latter was close to Capernaum. The Perean village of Bethsaida had been enlarged and raised to the rank of a town by the tetrarch, Philip, and by him had been named Julias in honor of Julia, daughter of the reigning emperor. The Gospel narratives of the voyage by which Jesus and His companions reached the place, and of the return therefrom, are conformable to the assumption that Bethsaida Julias in Perea and not Bethsaida in Galilee was the town to which the "desert place" referred to was an outlying district.

5. The Earlier and the Later Evening.—Matthew specifies two evenings of the day on which the five thousand were fed; thus "when it was evening" the disciples asked Jesus to send away the multitude; and later, after the miraculous feeding and after the disciples had left by boat, and after the crowds had departed, "when the evening was come" Jesus was alone on the mountain (Matt. 14:15, 23; compare Mark 6:35, 47). Trench, *Notes on the Miracles* (p. 217), says: "St. Matthew and St. Mark with him, makes two evenings to this day—one which had already commenced before the preparations for the feeding of the multitude had begun (verse 15), the other now, when the disciples had entered into the ship and set forth on their voyage (verse 23). And this was an ordinary way of speaking among the Jews, the first evening being very much our afternoon . . . the second evening being the twilight, or from six o'clock to twilight, on which absolute darkness followed." See Smith's *Dict.*, article "Chronology," from which the following excerpt is taken: "'Between the two evenings' (margin of Ex. 12:6; Num. 9:3; 28:4) is a natural division between the late afternoon when the sun is low, and the evening when his light has not wholly disappeared, the two evenings into which the natural evening would be cut by the commencement of the civil day if it began at sunset."

6. Watches of the Night.—During the greater part of Old Testament time, the people of Israel divided the night into three watches, each of four hours, such a period being that of individual sentinel duty. Before the beginning of the Christian era, however, the Jews had adopted the Roman order of four night watches, each lasting three hours. These were designated numerically, e.g. the fourth watch mentioned in the text (see Matt. 14:25), or as even, midnight, cock-crowing, and morning (see Mark 13:35). The fourth watch was the last of the three-hour periods between sunset and sunrise, or between 6 p.m. and 6 a.m. and therefore extended from 3 to 6 o'clock in the morning.

7. The Hem of the Garment.—The faith of those who believed that if they could but touch the border of the Lord's garment they would be healed is in line with that of the woman who was healed of her long-standing malady by so touching His robe (see Matt. 9:21; Mark 5:27, 28; Luke 8:44). The Jews regarded the border or hem of their outer robes as of particular importance, because of the requirement made of Israel in earlier days (Num. 15:38, 39) that the border be fringed and supplied with a band of blue, as a reminder to them of their obligations as the covenant people. The desire to touch the hem of Christ's robe may have been associated with this thought of sanctity attaching to the hem or border.

8. Traditions Concerning Manna.—The supplying of manna to the Israelites incident to the exodus and the long travel in the wilderness was rightly regarded as a work of surpassing wonder (Ex. 16:14–36; Num. 11:7–9; Deut. 8:3, 16; Josh. 5:12; Ps. 78:24, 25). Many traditions, some of them perniciously erroneous, gathered about the incident, and were transmitted with invented additions from generation to generation. In the time of Christ the rabbinical teaching was that the manna on which the fathers had fed was literally the food of the angels, sent down from heaven; and that it was of diverse taste and flavor to suit all ages, conditions, or desires; to one it tasted like honey, to another as bread, etc.; but in all Gentile mouths it was bitter. Moreover it was said that the Messiah would give an unfailing supply of manna to Israel when He came amongst them. These erroneous conceptions in part explain the demand of those who had been fed on barley loaves and fishes, for a sign that would surpass the giving of manna in the olden days, as evidence of the Messiahship of Jesus.

9. Faith a Gift of God.—"Though within the reach of all who diligently strive to gain it, faith is nevertheless a divine gift, and can be obtained only from God (Matt. 16:17; John 6:44, 65; Eph. 2:8; 1 Cor. 12:9; Rom. 12:3; Moro. 10:11). As is fitting for so priceless a pearl, it is given to those only who show by their sincerity that they are worthy of it, and who give promise of abiding by its dictates. Although faith is called the first principle of the Gospel of Christ, though it be in fact the foundation of all religion, yet even faith is preceded by sincerity of disposition and humility of soul, whereby the word of God may make an impression upon the heart (Rom. 10:17). No compulsion is used in bringing men to a knowledge of God; yet, as fast as we open our hearts to the influences of righteousness, the faith that leads to life eternal will be given us of our Father."—*Articles of Faith*, p. 107.

10. Spiritual Symbolism of Eating.—"The idea of eating, as a metaphor for receiving spiritual benefit, was familiar to Christ's hearers, and was as readily understood as our expressions—'devouring a book,' or 'drinking in' instruction. In Isaiah 3:1, the words 'the whole stay of bread,' were explained by the rabbis as referring to their own teaching, and they laid it down as a rule, that wherever, in Ecclesiastes, allusion was made to food or drink, it meant study of the law, and the practice of good works. It was a saying among them—'In the time of the Messiah the Israelites will be fed by Him.' Nothing was more common in the schools and synagogs than the phrases of eating and drinking, in a metaphorical sense. 'Messiah is not likely to come to Israel,' said Hillel, 'for they have already eaten Him'—that is, greedily, received His words—'in the days of Hezekiah.' A current conventionalism in the synagogs was that the just would 'eat the Shekinah.' It was peculiar to the Jews to be taught in such metaphorical language. Their rabbis never spoke in plain words, and it is expressly said that Jesus submitted to the popular taste, for 'without a parable spake he not unto them' (Mark 4:34)."—Geikie, *Life and Words of Christ*, vol. 1, p. 184.

11. The Crucial Nature of the Discourse.—Commenting on the effect of our Lord's discourse (John 6:26–71), Edersheim (vol. 2, p. 36) says: "Here then we are at the parting of the two ways; and, just because it was the hour of decision, did Christ so clearly set forth the highest truths concerning Himself, in opposition to the views which the multitude entertained about the Messiah. The result was yet another and a sorer defection. Upon this many of His disciples went back, and walked no more with Him. Nay, the searching trial reached even unto the hearts of the Twelve. Would they also go away? It was an anticipation of Gethsemane—its first experience. But one thing kept them true. It was the experience of the past. This was the basis of their present faith and allegiance. They could not go back to their old past; they must cleave to Him. So Peter spake it in name of them all: Lord, to whom shall we go? Words of eternal life hast thou! Nay, and more than this, as the result of what they had learned: And we have believed and know that thou art the Holy One of God. It is thus, also, that many of us, whose thoughts may have been sorely tossed, and whose foundations terribly assailed, may have found our first resting-place in the assured, unassailable spiritual experience of the past. Whither can we go for Words of eternal life, if not to Christ? If He fails us, then all hope of the eternal is gone. But He has the words of eternal life—and we believed when they first came to us; nay, we know that He is the Holy One of God. And this conveys all that faith needs for further learning. The rest will He show when He is transfigured in our sight. But of these Twelve Christ knew one to be a devil—like that angel, fallen from highest height to lowest depth. The apostasy of Judas had already commenced in his heart. And the greater the popular expectancy and disappointment had been, the greater the reaction and the enmity that followed. The hour of decision was past, and the hand on the dial pointed to the hour of His death."

CHAPTER 22

A PERIOD OF DARKENING OPPOSITION

Our Lord's last recorded discourse in the synagog at Capernaum, which followed close upon the miracle of feeding the five thousand and that of walking upon the water, marked the beginning of another epoch in the development of His life's work. It was the season of an approaching Passover festival;[a] and at the next succeeding Passover, one year later, as shall be shown, Jesus would be betrayed to His death. At the time of which we now speak, therefore, He was entering upon the last year of His ministry in the flesh. But the significance of the event is other and greater than that of a chronological datum-plane. The circumstance marked the first stage of a turn in the tide of popular regard toward Jesus, which theretofore had been increasing, and which now began to ebb. True, He had been repeatedly criticized and openly assailed by complaining Jews on many earlier occasions; but these crafty and even venomous critics were mostly of the ruling classes; the common people had heard Him gladly, and indeed many of them continued so to do;[b] nevertheless His popularity, in Galilee at least, had begun to wane. The last year of His earthly ministry was inaugurated by a sifting of the people who professed to believe His word, and this process of test, trial, and separation, was to continue to the end.

We are without information as to Jesus having attended this Passover feast; and it is reasonable to infer that in view of the increasing hostility on the part of the rulers, He refrained from going

---

[a] John 6:4. Note 1, end of chapter.
[b] Mark 12:37.

to Jerusalem on the occasion. Conjecture as to whether any of the
Twelve went up to the festival is profitless; we are not told. Certain it
is that immediately after this time, the detectives and spies, who had
been sent from Jerusalem into Galilee to watch Jesus, became more
active than ever in their critical espionage. They dogged His footsteps,
noted every act, and every instance of omission of traditional or
customary observance, and were constantly on the alert to make Him
out an offender.

CEREMONIAL WASHINGS,
"AND MANY SUCH LIKE THINGS"[c]

Shortly after the Passover to which allusion has been made, and
probably in accordance with a plan decided upon by the Jewish
rulers, Jesus was visited by a delegation of Pharisees and scribes who
had come from Jerusalem, and who made protest against the disregard
of traditional requirements by His followers. It appears that the disciples,
and almost certainly the Master Himself, had so far transgressed "the
tradition of the elders" as to omit the ceremonial washing of hands
before eating; the Pharisaic critics found fault, and came demanding
explanation, and justification if such were possible. Mark tells us that
the disciples were charged with having eaten with "defiled," or, as the
marginal reading gives it, with "common" hands; and he interpolates
the following concise and lucid note concerning the custom which
the disciples were said to have ignored: "For the Pharisees, and all the
Jews, except they wash their hands oft, eat not, holding the tradition
of the elders. And when they come from the market, except they
wash, they eat not. And many other things there be, which they have
received to hold, as the washing of cups, and pots, brasen vessels, and
of tables."[d] It should be borne in mind that the offense charged
against the disciples was that of ceremonial uncleanness, not physical
uncleanliness or disregard of sanitary propriety; they were said to have
eaten with common or defiled hands, not specifically with dirty
fingers. In all the externals of their man-made religionism, the Jews

---

[c] Matt. 15:1–9; Mark 7:1–13.

[d] As the Oxford marginal note shows "beds" is a more literal rendering than "tables," the
couches upon which the eaters reclined at table being meant.

were insistent on scrupulous exactitude; every possibility of ceremonial defilement was to be carefully guarded against, and the effects thereof had to be counteracted by prescribed washings.[e]

To the question: "Why do thy disciples transgress the tradition of the elders? for they wash not their hands when they eat bread," Jesus gave no direct reply; but asked as rejoinder: "Why do ye also transgress the commandment of God by your tradition?" To the Pharisaic mind this must have been a very sharp rebuke; for rabbinism held that rigorous compliance with the traditions of the elders was more important than observance of the law itself; and Jesus in His counter-question put their cherished traditions as in direct conflict with the commandment of God. Adding to their discomfiture, He cited the prophecy of Isaiah, and applied to them whom He designated hypocrites, the prophet's words: "Well hath Esaias prophesied of you hypocrites, as it is written, This people honoureth me with their lips, but their heart is far from me. Howbeit in vain do they worship me, teaching for doctrines the commandments of men."[f] With deserved severity Jesus carried the lesson home to their consciences, declaring that they had laid aside the commandments of God in order that they might follow the traditions of men.

This accusing affirmation was followed by the citing of an undeniable instance: Moses had voiced the direct commandment of God in saying: "Honour thy father and thy mother," and had proclaimed the ordained penalty in extreme cases of unfilial conduct thus: "Whoso curseth father or mother, let him die";[g] but this law, though given of God direct to Israel, had been so completely superseded that any ungrateful and wicked son could find ready means, which their traditions had made lawful, of escaping all filial obligations, even though his parents were destitute. If a needy father or mother craved help of a son, he had but to say—What you ask of me is Corban—or in other words, an intended gift to God; and he was held to be legally exempt from all requirements to contribute of that substance to the

[e] Note 2, end of chapter.

[f] Mark 7:6, 7; see also Matt. 15:7–9; Isa. 29:13; compare the words of the resurrected Christ to the prophet Joseph Smith, in the present dispensation, Joseph Smith—History 1:19.

[g] Compare Ex. 20:12; Deut. 5:16; Ex. 21:17; Lev. 20:9.

support of his parents.[h] Other obligations could be similarly evaded. To declare that any article of property real or personal, or any part or proportion of one's possessions was "corban," was generally understood as an averment that the property so characterized was dedicated to the temple, or at least was intended to be devoted to ecclesiastical purposes, and would eventually be turned over to the officials, though the donor might continue to hold possession during a specified period, extending even to the end of his life. Property was often declared to be "corban" for other purposes than dedication to ecclesiastical use. The result of such established though utterly unlawful and pernicious traditions was, as Jesus emphatically stated to the Pharisees and scribes, to make the word of God of none effect, and, He added, "Many such like things do ye."

Turning from His titled visitors, He called the people together and proclaimed unto them the truth, as follows: "Hearken unto me every one of you, and understand: There is nothing from without a man, that entering into him can defile him: but the things which come out of him, those are they that defile the man. If any man have ears to hear, let him hear." This was directly in conflict with rabbinical precept and practice; the Pharisees were offended, for they had said that to eat with hands that had not been ritualistically cleansed was to defile the food touched, and in turn to become yet more defiled from the food thus rendered unclean.

The apostles were not sure that they understood the Master's lesson; though couched in plain, non-figurative language, it was to some of them very like a parable, and Peter asked an exposition. The Lord explained that the food one eats is but temporarily part of his body; having served its purpose of nourishing the tissues and supplying energy to the organism, it is eliminated; therefore the food that enters the body through the mouth is of small and transient importance compared with the utterances that issue from the mouth, for these, if evil, are truly defiling. As Jesus set forth: "Those things which proceed out of the mouth come forth from the heart; and they defile the man. For out of the heart proceed evil thoughts, murders,

[h] Note 3, end of chapter.

adulteries, fornications, thefts, false witness, blasphemies: these are the things which defile a man; but to eat with unwashen hands defileth not a man."[i]

Some of the disciples asked Jesus whether He knew that the Pharisees had taken offense at His saying; His answer was a further denunciation of Pharisaism: "Every plant, which my heavenly Father hath not planted, shall be rooted up. Let them alone: they be blind leaders of the blind. And if the blind lead the blind, both shall fall into the ditch." There could be no compromise between His doctrine of the kingdom and the corrupt Judaism of the time. The rulers were plotting against His life; if their emissaries chose to take offense at His words, let them be offended and stand the consequences; but blessed would they be if they were not offended because of Him.[j] He had no conciliatory measures to offer those whose inability to understand His meaning was the result of willful obstinacy, or darkness of mind produced by persistence in sin.

WITHIN THE BORDERS OF TYRE AND SIDON [k]

Unable to find in Galilee rest, seclusion, or adequate opportunity of instructing the Twelve as He desired to do, Jesus departed with them northward, and journeyed into the coasts or borders of Phenicia, a district commonly known by the names of its prominent cities, Tyre and Sidon. In one of the little towns near the border, the party took lodgings; but the attempt to secure privacy was futile, for the Master's presence "could not be hid." His fame had preceded Him beyond the boundaries of the land of Israel. On earlier occasions, people from the region of Tyre and Sidon had been among His listeners, and some of them had been blessed by His healing mercies.[l]

A woman, hearing of His presence within her own land, came asking a boon. Mark tells us she was a Greek, or more literally a Gentile [m] who spoke Greek, and by nationality a Syro-Phenician;

---

[i] Matt. 15:10–20; compare Mark 7:14–23.

[j] Matt. 11:6; Luke 7:23.

[k] Matt. 15:21–28; Mark 7:24–30.

[l] Mark 3:8; Luke 6:17.

[m] See marginal reading in Oxford and Bagster Bibles; see also Note 2, chapter 21.

Matthew says she was "a woman of Canaan"; these statements are in harmony, since the Phenicians were of Canaanite descent. The Gospel-historians make clear the fact that this woman was of pagan or heathen birth; and we know that among the peoples so classed the Canaanites were held in particular disrepute by the Jews. The woman cried aloud to Jesus, saying: "Have mercy on me, O Lord, thou son of David; my daughter is grievously vexed with a devil." Her words expressed at once faith in the Lord's power, and a fulness of mother-love, for she implored as though she were the afflicted sufferer. The fact that she addressed Jesus as Son of David demonstrates her belief that He was the Messiah of Israel. At first Jesus refrained from answering her. Undeterred, she pleaded the more, until the disciples besought the Lord saying: "Send her away; for she crieth after us." Their intervention was probably an intercession in her behalf; she could be quieted by the granting of her request; as it was, she was making an undesirable scene, probably on the street, and the Twelve knew well that their Master sought quietude. To them Jesus said: "I am not sent but unto the lost sheep of the house of Israel," and the remark must have reminded them of the restriction under which they had been sent out.[n]

The woman, with importunate desire came near, possibly entering the house; she fell at the Lord's feet and worshiped Him, pleading pitifully, "Lord, help me." To her Jesus said, "It is not meet to take the children's bread, and to cast it to dogs." The words, harsh as they may sound to us, were understood by her in the spirit of the Lord's intent. The original term here translated "dogs" connoted, as the narrative shows, not the vagrant and despised curs elsewhere spoken of in the Bible as typical of a degraded state, or of positive badness,[o] but literally the "little dogs" or domestic pets, such as were allowed in the house and under the table. Certainly the woman took no offense at the comparison, and found therein no objectionable epithet. Instantly she adopted the analogy, and applied it in combined argument and supplication.[p] "Truth, Lord: yet the dogs eat of the crumbs which

---

[n] Matt. 10:5, 6.

[o] Deut. 23:18; 1 Sam. 17:43; 24:14; 2 Sam. 3:8; 16:9; Job 30:1; Matt. 7:6; Philip 3:2; Rev. 22: 15.

[p] Note 4, end of chapter.

fall from their masters' table"; or, in the words of Mark's version: "Yes, Lord: yet the dogs under the table eat of the children's crumbs." Her prayer was immediately granted; for Jesus said unto her, "O woman, great is thy faith: be it unto thee even as thou wilt. And her daughter was made whole from that very hour." Mark emphasizes the special recognition of her final plea, and adds: "And when she was come to her house, she found the devil gone out, and her daughter laid upon the bed." The woman's commendable persistency was based on the faith that overcomes apparent obstacles and endures even under discouragement. Her case reminds one of the lesson taught by the Lord on another occasion through the story of the importunate widow.[q]

Many have queried as to why Jesus delayed the blessing. We may not be able to fathom His purposes; but we see that, by the course He adopted, the woman's faith was demonstrated and the disciples were instructed. Jesus impressed upon her that she was not of the chosen people, to whom He had been sent; but His words prefigured the giving of the gospel to all, both Jew and Gentile: "Let the children *first* be filled" He had said. The resurrected Christ was to be made known to every nation;[r] but His personal ministry as a mortal, as also that of the apostles while He was with them in the flesh, was directed to the house of Israel.[s]

IN THE COASTS OF DECAPOLIS [t]

We are not told how long Jesus and the Twelve tarried in the land of Tyre and Sidon, nor which portions of the district they traversed. They went thence into the region adjoining the sea of Galilee on the east, "through the midst of the coasts of Decapolis."[u] Though still among semi-pagan peoples, our Lord was greeted by great crowds, amongst whom were many lame, blind, dumb, maimed, and otherwise afflicted; and them He healed. Great was the astonishment of these aliens, "when they saw the dumb to speak, the maimed to be

[q] Luke 18:1–8.

[r] Acts 3:25, 26; 13:46–48; Rom. 15:8.

[s] Matt. 28:19; Mark 16:15.

[t] Mark 7:31–37; compare Matt. 15:29–31.

[u] Note 5, end of chapter.

whole, the lame to walk, and the blind to see: and they glorified the God of Israel."

Among the many who were healed was one of whom special mention is made. He was deaf and defective in speech. The people asked the Lord to lay His hands upon the man; but Jesus led him away from the multitude, put His fingers in the man's ears, spat, and touched the man's tongue; then looking upward in prayer, and sighing the while, He uttered a word of command in Aramaic, "Ephphatha, that is, Be opened. And straightway his ears were opened, and the string of his tongue was loosed, and he spake plain." The manner of effecting this cure was different again from the usual mode of our Lord's healing ministrations. It may be that by the finger-touch to the closed ears and to the bound tongue, the man's faith was strengthened and his confidence in the Master's power increased. The people were forbidden to tell abroad what they had witnessed; but the more they were charged the more they published the news. Their conclusion as to Jesus and His works was: "He hath done all things well: he maketh both the deaf to hear, and the dumb to speak."

ANOTHER MEAL IN THE DESERT; OVER FOUR THOUSAND FED [v]

For three days the glad crowds remained with Jesus and the apostles. Camping out at that season and in that region entailed no great hardship incident to exposure. Their supply of food, however, had become exhausted; and many of them were far from home. Jesus had compassion upon the people, and was loath to send them away fasting, lest they would faint by the way. When He spoke to the disciples on the matter they intimated the impossibility of feeding so great a number, for the entire stock of food at hand comprised but seven loaves and a few little fishes. Had they forgotten the former occasion on which a greater multitude had been fed and filled with but five loaves and two small fishes? Rather let us believe that the disciples remembered well, yet deemed it beyond their duty or privilege

[v] Matt. 15:32–39; Mark 8:1–9.

to suggest a repetition of the miracle. But the Master commanded; and the people seated themselves on the ground. Blessing and dividing the small provision as before, He gave to the disciples and they distributed to the multitude. Four thousand men, beside women and children, were abundantly fed; and of the broken but uneaten food there remained enough to fill seven baskets. With no semblance of the turbulent enthusiasm that had followed the feeding of the five thousand, this multitude dispersed quietly and returned to their homes, grateful and doubly blessed.

AGAIN BESET BY SIGN-SEEKERS[w]

Jesus and the apostles returned by boat to the western shore of the lake, and landed near Magdala and Dalmanutha. These towns are understood to have been so close together as to virtually make the latter a suburb of the other. Here the party was met by the ever-vigilant Pharisees, who on this occasion were accompanied by their usually unfriendly rivals, the Sadducees. That the two parties had temporarily laid aside their mutual differences, and had combined their forces in the common cause of opposition to Christ, is a demonstration of the determined purpose of the ecclesiastical authorities to find occasion against Him, and, if possible, destroy Him. Their immediate object was to further alienate the common people, and to counteract the influence of His former teachings with the masses. They set anew the old-time snare of demanding from Him a supernatural sign of His Messiahship, though thrice already had they or others of their kind so attempted to entrap Him, and thrice had they been foiled.[x] Before them, Satan in person had similarly tried and failed.[y] To their present impertinent and impious demand He gave a brief and definite refusal coupled with an exposure of their hypocrisy. This was His reply: "When it is evening, ye say, It will be fair weather: for the sky is red. And in the morning, It will be foul weather today: for the sky is red and lowring. O ye hypocrites, ye can discern the face of the sky; but can ye not discern the signs of the times? A wicked and adulterous

[w] Matt. 15:29; 16:1–5; Mark 8:10–13.

[x] John 2:18; 6:30; Matt. 12:38.

[y] Matt. 4:6, 7; Luke 4:9–12.

generation seeketh after a sign; and there shall no sign be given unto it, but the sign of the prophet Jonas. And he left them, and departed."ᶻ

THE LEAVEN OF THE PHARISEES
AND OF THE SADDUCEES ᵃᵃ

Again with the Twelve upon the water, since on the Galilean coast neither peace nor opportunity for effective teaching was found, Jesus directed the vessel's course toward the north-easterly shore. When well out from land, He said to His companions: "Take heed and beware of the leaven of the Pharisees and of the Sadducees," and, as Mark adds, "and of the leaven of Herod." In their hasty departure the disciples had forgotten to take a supply of food; they had with them but a single loaf. They construed His words respecting leaven as a reference to bread, and possibly as a reproof for their neglect. Jesus chided them as of little faith for thinking then of material bread, and refreshed their recollection of the miracles by which the multitudes had been fed, so that their lack of loaves would not further trouble them. Finally they were made to understand that the Master's warning was directed against the false doctrines of the Pharisees and those of the Sadducees, and against the political aspirations of the scheming Herodians.ᵇᵇ

The party left the boat near the site of the first miraculous feeding of the multitude, and made their way to Bethsaida Julias. A blind man was brought, and Jesus was asked to touch him. He took the sightless one by the hand, led him outside the town, applied saliva to his eyes, laid hands upon him in a ministration, and asked him if he could see. The man answered that he saw dimly, but was unable to distinguish men from trees. Applying His hands to the man's eyes, Jesus told him to look up; the man did so and saw clearly. Bidding him not to enter the town, nor to tell of his deliverance from blindness to any in the place, the Lord sent him away rejoicing. This miracle presents the unique feature of Jesus healing a person by stages; the result of the first ministration was but a partial recovery. No explanation of the exceptional circumstance is given.

ᶻ Matt. 16:2–4; compare 12:38–41.
ᵃᵃ Matt. 16:6–12; Mark 8:14–21; compare Luke 12:1.
ᵇᵇ Page 64–65.

"THOU ART THE CHRIST"[cc]

Accompanied by the Twelve, Jesus continued His way northward to the neighborhood or "coasts" of Caesarea Philippi, an inland city situated near the eastern and principal source of the Jordan, and near the foot of Mount Hermon.[dd] The journey afforded opportunity for special and confidential instruction to the apostles. Of them Jesus asked: "Whom do men say that I the Son of man am?" In reply they reported the rumors and popular fancies that had come to their notice. Some people, sharing the superstitious fears of the conscience-stricken Herod Antipas, said that Jesus was John the Baptist returned to life, though such a belief could not have been entertained seriously by many, as John and Jesus were known to have been contemporaries; others said He was Elias, or more exactly, Elijah; still others suggested He was Jeremiah or some other one of the ancient prophets of Israel. It is significant that among all the conceptions of the people as to the identity of Jesus there was no intimation of belief that He was the Messiah. Neither by word nor deed had He measured up to the popular and traditional standard of the expected Deliverer and King of Israel. Fleeting manifestations of evanescent hope that He might prove to be the looked-for Prophet, like unto Moses, had not been lacking; but all such incipient conceptions had been neutralized by the hostile activity of the Pharisees and their kind. To them it was a matter of supreme though evil determination to maintain in the minds of the people the thought of a yet future, not a present, Messiah.

With deep solemnity, and as a soul-searching test for which the Twelve had been in unconscious preparation through many months of close and privileged companionship with their Lord, Jesus asked of them: "But whom say ye that I am?" Answering for all, but more particularly testifying as to his own conviction, Peter, with all the fervor of his soul, voiced the great confession: "Thou art the Christ, the Son of the living God." This was no avowal of mere belief, no expression of a result at which he had arrived by mental process, no solution of a problem laboriously worked out, no verdict based on the weighing of evidence; he spoke in the sure knowledge that knows no question and

---

[cc] Matt. 16:13–20; Mark 8:27–30; Luke 9:18–21. Note 10, end of chapter.
[dd] Note 6, end of chapter.

from which doubt and reservations are as far removed as is the sky from the ground.

"And Jesus answered and said unto him, Blessed art thou, Simon Barjona: for flesh and blood hath not revealed it unto thee, but my Father which is in heaven." Peter's knowledge, which was also that of his brethren, was of a kind apart from all that man may find out for himself; it was a divine bestowal, in comparison with which human wisdom is foolishness and the treasure of earth but dross. Addressing Himself further to the first of the apostles, Jesus continued: "And I say also unto thee, That thou art Peter, and upon this rock I will build my church; and the gates of hell shall not prevail against it. And I will give unto thee the keys of the kingdom of heaven: and whatsoever thou shalt bind on earth shall be bound in heaven: and whatsoever thou shalt loose on earth shall be loosed in heaven."

Through direct revelation from God Peter knew that Jesus was the Christ; and upon revelation, as a rock of secure foundation, the Church of Christ was to be built.[ee] Though torrents should fall, floods roll, winds rage, and all beat together upon that structure, it would not, could not, fall, for it was founded upon a rock,[ff] and even the powers of hell would be impotent to prevail against it. By revelation alone could or can the Church of Jesus Christ be builded and maintained; and revelation of necessity implies revelators, through whom the will of God may be made known respecting His Church. As a gift from God comes the testimony of Jesus into the heart of man. This principle was comprised in the Master's teachings at Capernaum, that none could come to Him save such as the Father would bring.[gg] The Lord's promise, that unto Peter He would give "the keys of the kingdom of heaven," embodies the principle of divine authority in the Holy Priesthood, and of the commission of presidency. Allusion to keys as symbolical of power and authority is not uncommon in Jewish literature, as was well understood in that period and is generally current today.[hh] So also the analogies of

---

[ee] Note 7, end of chapter.

[ff] Compare Matt. 7:24, 25.

[gg] John 6:46; compare verses 37, 39, 40.

[hh] See Isa. 22:22; Luke 11:52; Rev. 1:18; 3:7; compare D&C 6:28; 7:7; 27:5, 6, 9; 28:7; 42:69; 84:26.

binding and loosing as indicative of official acts were then usual, as they are now, particularly in connection with judicial functions. Peter's presidency among the apostles was abundantly manifest and generally recognized after the close of our Lord's mortal life. Thus, it was he who spoke in behalf of the Eleven, in the council meeting at which a successor to the traitor Iscariot was chosen; he was the spokesman of his brethren on the occasion of the Pentecostal conversion; it was he who opened the doors of the Church to the Gentiles;[ii] and his office of leadership is apparent throughout the apostolic period.

The confession by which the apostles avowed their acceptance of Jesus as the Christ, the Son of the living God, was evidence of their actual possession of the spirit of the Holy Apostleship, by which they were made particular witnesses of their Lord. The time for a general proclamation of their testimony had not arrived, however; nor did it come until after Christ had emerged from the tomb a resurrected, immortalized Personage. For the time being they were charged "that they should tell no man that he was Jesus the Christ." Proclamation of Jesus as the Messiah, particularly if made by the apostles who were publicly known as His most intimate disciples and associates, or open assumption of the Messianic title by Himself, would have aggravated the hostility of the rulers, which had already become a grave interference if not an actual menace to the Savior's ministry; and seditious uprisings against the political government of Rome might easily have resulted. A yet deeper reason for the secrecy enjoined upon the Twelve appears in the fact that the Jewish nation was not prepared to accept their Lord; and to ignore Him through lack of certain knowledge involved a lesser degree of culpability than would have attached to an unpalliated rejection. The particular mission of the apostles at the time then future was to proclaim to all nations Jesus, the crucified and resurrected Christ.

From the time of Peter's confession, however, Jesus instructed the Twelve more plainly and with greater intimacy concerning the future developments of His mission, and particularly as touching His appointed death. On earlier occasions He had referred in their hearing to the cross, and to His approaching death, burial, and ascension; but

---

[ii] Acts 1:15–26; 2:14–40; chap. 10, compare with 15:7.

the mention in each case was in a measure figurative, and they had apprehended but imperfectly if at all. Now, however, He began to show, and often afterward made plain unto them, "how that he must go unto Jerusalem, and suffer many things of the elders and chief priests and scribes, and be killed, and be raised again the third day."

Peter was shocked at this unqualified declaration, and, yielding to impulse, remonstrated with Jesus, or, as two of the evangelists state, "began to rebuke him," even going so far as to say: "This shall not be unto thee."ᶦ The Lord turned upon him with this sharp reproof: "Get thee behind me, Satan: thou art an offence unto me: for thou savourest not the things that be of God, but those that be of men." Peter's words constituted an appeal to the human element in Christ's nature; and the sensitive feelings of Jesus were wounded by this suggestion of unfaithfulness to His trust, coming from the man whom He had so signally honored but a few moments before. Peter saw mainly as men see, understanding but imperfectly the deeper purposes of God. Though deserved, the rebuke he received was severe. The adjuration, "Get thee behind me, Satan," was identical with that used against the arch-tempter himself, who had sought to beguile Jesus from the path upon which He had entered,ᵏᵏ and the provocation in the two instances was in some respects similar—the temptation to evade sacrifice and suffering, though such was the world's ransom, and to follow a more comfortable way.ᶦᶦ The forceful words of Jesus show the deep emotion that Peter's ill-considered attempt to counsel if not to tempt his Lord had evoked.

Beside the Twelve, who were immediately about the Lord's person, others were nearby; it appears that even in those remote parts, far removed from the borders of Galilee—the habitat of a heathen population, with whom, however, many Jews were intermixed—the people gathered around the Master. These He now called together, and to them and the disciples said: "If any man will come after me, let him deny himself, and take up his cross, and follow me." Here the frightful figure of the cross was again made prominent. There was left

ᶦ Matt. 16:22, 23; Mark 8:32, 33.
ᵏᵏ Luke 4:8.
ᶦᶦ Note 8, end of chapter.

no shadow of excuse for the thought that devotion to Christ would not mean denial and privation. He who would save his life at the cost of duty, as Peter had just suggested that Christ should do, would surely lose it in a sense worse than that of physical death; whereas he who stood willing to lose all, even life itself, should find the life that is eternal.

As evincing the soundness of His teachings, Jesus uttered what has since become an inspiring aphorism of life: "For what is a man profited, if he shall gain the whole world, and lose his own soul? or what shall a man give in exchange for his soul?" Whosoever is ashamed of Christ because of His lowly estate, or through offense at His teachings, shall yet find that the Son of Man, when He comes in the glory of the Father, with attending cohorts of angels, will be ashamed of that man. The record of this memorable day in the Savior's life closes with His blessed promise: "Verily I say unto you, There be some standing here, which shall not taste of death, till they see the Son of man coming in his kingdom."[mm]

NOTES TO CHAPTER 22

1. Passover Celebrations Comprised within the Period of Our Lord's Public Ministry.—The dates on which specific acts occurred in the ministry of Jesus are difficult if not impossible to fix, except in few instances; and as heretofore stated and reiterated, even the order of events is often found to be uncertain. It will be remembered that Jesus was in Jerusalem at the time of the Passover soon after His baptism, and that on the visit referred to He forcibly cleared the temple courts of traffickers and their property. This is known as the *first* Passover during the public life of Jesus. If the unnamed "feast of the Jews" referred to by John (5:1) was a Passover, as many Bible students hold, it marked the close of the year following the cleansing the temple; it is commonly spoken of and written about as the *second* Passover in the course of our Lord's ministry. Then the Passover near which Jesus fed the five thousand (John 6:4) would be the *third*, and would mark the expiration of two years and a fraction since the baptism of Jesus; it certainly marks the beginning of the last year of the Savior's life on earth.

2. Ceremonial Ablutions.—The numerous washings required by Jewish custom in the time of Christ were admittedly incident to rabbinism and "the tradition of the elders" and not in compliance with the Mosaic law. Under certain conditions,

[mm] Note 9, end of chapter.

successive washings were prescribed, in connection with which we find mention of "first," "second" and "other" waters, the "second water" being necessary to wash away the "first water," which had become defiled by contact with the "common" hands; and so further with the later waters. Sometimes the hands had to be dipped or immersed; at other times they were to be cleansed by pouring, it being necessary that the water be allowed to run to the wrist or the elbow according to the degree of supposed defilement; then again, as the disciples of Rabbi Shammai held, only the finger tips, or the fingers up to the knuckles, needed to be wetted under particular circumstances. Rules for the cleansing of vessels and furniture were detailed and exacting; distinct methods applied respectively to vessels of clay, wood, and metal. Fear of unwittingly defiling the hands led to many extreme precautions. It being known that the Roll of the Law, the Roll of the Prophets, and other scriptures, when laid away were sometimes touched, scratched, or even gnawed by mice, there was issued a rabbinical decree, that the Holy Scriptures, or any part thereof comprising as many as eighty-five letters (the shortest section in the law having just that number), defiled the hands by mere contact. Thus the hands had to be ceremonially cleansed after touching a copy of the scriptures, or even a written passage therefrom.

Emancipation from these and "many such like things" must have been relief indeed. Escape from this thraldom Jesus freely offered, saying: "Come unto me, all ye that labour and are heavy laden, and I will give you rest. Take my yoke upon you, and learn of me; for I am meek and lowly in heart; and ye shall find rest unto your souls. For my yoke is easy, and my burden is light." (Matt. 11:28–30.)

3. "Corban," a Gift.—The law of Moses prescribed rules relating to vows (Lev. 27; Num. 30). "Upon these rules," says the writer in Smith's *Bible Dict.*, "the traditionalists enlarged, and laid down that a man might interdict himself by vow, not only from using for himself, but from giving to another or receiving from him, some particular object whether of food or any other kind whatsoever. The thing thus interdicted was considered as corban. A person might thus exempt himself from any inconvenient obligation under plea of corban. Our Lord denounced practices of this sort (Matt. 15:5; Mark 7:11), as annulling the spirit of the law."

The revised version, Matt. 15:5 is made to read "But ye say, whosoever shall say to his father or his mother, That wherewith thou mightest have been profited by me is given to God; he shall not honor his father (or, his mother)." The following account of this pernicious custom appears in the *Commentary on The Holy Bible* edited by Dummelow, "'Corban,' meaning originally a sacrifice or a gift to God, was used in New Testament times as a mere word of vowing, without implying that the thing vowed would actually be offered or given, to God. Thus a man would say 'Corban to me is wine for such a time,' meaning that he took a vow to abstain from wine. Or a man would say to a friend 'Corban to me for such a time is whatsoever I might be profited by thee,' meaning that for such a time he vowed that he would receive neither hospitality nor any other benefit from his friend. Similarly, if a son said to his father or mother, 'Corban is whatsoever thou mightest have profited by me' he took a vow not to assist his father or mother in any way, however much they might require it. A vow of this kind was held by the scribes to excuse a man from the duty of supporting his parents, and thus by their tradition they made void the word of God."

4. The "Dogs" that Eat of the Crumbs.—The woman's fervid rejoinder, "Truth, Lord: yet the dogs eat of the crumbs which fall from their masters' table," (Matt. 15:27), is thus commented upon and paraphrased by Trench (*Notes on the Miracles*, p. 271): "The rendering of her answer in our translation is not, however, altogether satisfactory. For, indeed, she accepts the Lord's declaration, not immediately to make exception against the conclusion which He draws from it, but to show how in that very declaration is involved the granting of her petition. 'Saidest thou dogs? It is well; I accept the title and the place; for the dogs have a portion of the meal,—not the first, not the children's portion, but a portion still,—the crumbs which fall from the master's table. In this very putting of the case, Thou bringest us heathen, Thou bringest me, within the circle of the blessings which God, the Great Householder, is ever dispensing to His family. We also belong to His household, though we occupy but the lowest place therein.'"

The Dummelow *Commentary*, on Matt. 15:26, reads in part as follows: "The rabbis often spoke of the Gentiles as dogs, e.g. 'He who eats with an idolater is like one who eats with a dog.'. . . 'The nations of the world are compared to dogs.' 'The holy convocation belongs to you, not to the dogs.' Yet Jesus in adopting the contemptuous expression slightly softens it. He says not 'dogs,' but 'little dogs,' i.e. household, favorite, dogs; and the woman cleverly catches at the expression, arguing that if the Gentiles are household dogs, then it is only right that they should be fed with the crumbs that fall from their masters' table." Edersheim, referring to the original text, says: "The term means 'little dogs,' or 'house dogs.'"

5. Decapolis.—The name means "the ten cities," and was applied to a region of indefinite boundaries lying mostly on the east of Jordan and southerly from the sea of Galilee. Scythopolis, which Josephus (*Wars of the Jews*, iii, 9:7) refers to as the largest of the ten cities, was on the west side of the river. There is lack of agreement among historians as to the cities comprised under the name. Biblical mention (Matt. 4:25; Mark 5:20; 7:31) implies a general region rather than a definite area.

6. The Coasts of Caesarea Philippi.—The term "coast" as it appears in the Bible (authorized, or King James version), is used to connote boundary, limit, or border, and not distinctively a seashore. (For examples see Ex. 10:4, 14, 19; Josh. 15:1, 4; Judg. 11:20; Matt. 2:16, etc.) It is applied therefore to inland areas, and frequently occurs as indicating a vicinity or neighborhood.

Caesarea Philippi, a town located, as stated in the text, near Mount Hermon at the source of the Jordan, had been enlarged and beautified by Philip the tetrarch, and by him was named Caesarea in honor of the Roman emperor. It was called Caesarea Philippi to distinguish it from the already existing Caesarea, which was situated on the Mediterranean shore of Samaria, and which in later literature came to be known as Caesarea Palestina. Caesarea Philippi is believed to be identical with the ancient Baal Gad (Josh. 11:17) and Baal Hermon (Judg. 3:3). It was known as a place of idolatrous worship, and while under Greek sovereignty was called Paneas in recognition of the mythological deity Pan. See Josephus, Ant. xviii, 2:1; this designation persists in the present Arabic name of the place, Banias.

7. Simon Peter and the "Rock" of Revelation.—Simon the son of Jonas, on the occasion of his first recorded interview with Jesus had received from the Lord's lips the distinguishing name-title "Peter," or in the Aramaic tongue "Cephas," the English equivalent of which is "a rock" or "a stone" (John 1:42). The name was confirmed upon the apostle on the occasion now under consideration (Matt. 16:18). Jesus said to him "thou art Peter," adding, "and upon this rock I will build my church." In the course of the general apostasy subsequent to the ancient apostolic ministry, the Bishop of Rome laid claim to supreme authority as the alleged lineal successor to Peter; and an erroneous doctrine gained currency to the effect that Peter was the "rock" upon which the Church of Christ was founded. Detailed consideration of this inconsistent and infamous claim cannot be undertaken here; it is sufficient to say that a church founded or dependent upon Peter or any other man would be Peter's or the other man's church, and not the Church of Jesus Christ. (See *The Great Apostasy*, chap. 9; also 3 Ne. 27:1–8; also chapter 40 herein). That upon Peter rested the responsibility of presidency in the ministry, after the ascension of the resurrected Christ, is not questioned; but that he was, even typically, the foundation upon which the Church was built, is at once unscriptural and untrue. The Church of Jesus Christ must authoritatively bear His name, and guided by revelation, direct and continuous, as the conditions of its building require. Revelation from God to His servants invested with the Holy Priesthood through authorized ordination as was Peter is the impregnable "rock" upon which the Church is built. (See *Articles of Faith*, chapter 16.)

8. Christ's Rebuke to Peter.—In addressing Peter as "Satan," Jesus was obviously using a forceful figure of speech, and not a literal designation; for Satan is a distinct personage, Lucifer, that fallen, unembodied son of the morning; and certainly Peter was not he. In his remonstrance or "rebuke" addressed to Jesus, Peter was really counseling what Satan had before attempted to induce Christ to do, or tempting, as Satan himself had tempted. The command, "Get thee behind me, Satan," as directed to Peter, is rendered in English by some authorities "Get thee behind me, tempter." The essential meaning attached to both Hebrew and Greek originals for our word "Satan" is that of an adversary, or "one who places himself in another's way and thus opposes him." (Zenos.) The expression "Thou art an offense unto me" is admittedly a less literal translation than "Thou art a stumbling-block unto me." The man whom Jesus had addressed as Peter—"the rock," was now likened to a stone in the path, over which the unwary might stumble.

9. Some to Live Until Christ Returns.—The Savior's declaration to the apostles and others in the neighborhood of Caesarea Philippi, "Verily I say unto you, There be some standing here which shall not taste of death, till they see the Son of man coming in his kingdom," (Matt. 16:28; compare Mark 9:1; Luke 9:27), has occasioned great and diverse comment. The event referred to, that of the Son of Man coming in the glory of His Father attended by the angels, is yet future. At least a partial fulfillment of the prediction is presented in the prolongation of the life of John the apostle, who was there present, and who yet lives in the flesh according to his desire (John 21:20–24; see further 3 Ne. 28:1–6; D&C 7).

10. "Thou Art the Christ."—Peter's solemn and soulful confession of Jesus as the Christ is worded differently by each of the three synoptists. To many the most expressive version is that of Luke: "The Christ of God." On earlier occasions, some or all of the Twelve had acknowledged Jesus Christ to be the Son of God, e.g. following the miracle of walking upon the sea (Matt. 14:33), and again, after the crucial sermon at Capernaum (John 6:69); but it is evident that Peter's upwelling and reverential confession in answer to the Lord's question "But whom say ye that I am?" had a significance, greater in assurance and more exalted in kind, that had any prior expression of his conception concerning his Lord. Yet even the conviction given through direct revelation (Matt. 16:17) did not at the time comprise a comprehensive knowledge of the Savior's mission. Indeed, a fullness of understanding and assurance came to the apostles after the Lord's Resurrection (compare Romans 1:4). Nevertheless, Peter's testimony in the land of Caesarea Philippi evidences a very exalted attainment. At that stage of the Savior's ministry, the public proclamation of His divine status would have been as the casting of pearls before swine (Matt. 7:6); therefore the Lord instructed the apostles that at that time "they should tell no man that he was Jesus Christ."

CHAPTER 23
THE TRANSFIGURATION

Of the week following the events last considered, no record is found in the Gospels. We may safely assume that the time was devoted, in part at least, to the further instruction of the Twelve respecting the rapidly approaching consummation of the Savior's mission on earth, the awful circumstances of which the apostles were loath to believe possible. When the week had passed[a] Jesus took Peter, James, and John[b] and with them ascended a high mountain, where they would be reasonably safe from human intrusion.[c] There the three apostles witnessed a heavenly manifestation, which stands without parallel in history; in our Bible captions it is known as the Transfiguration of Christ.[d]

One purpose of the Lord's retirement was that of prayer, and a transcendent investiture of glory came upon Him as He prayed. The apostles had fallen asleep, but were awakened by the surpassing splendor of the scene, and gazed with reverent awe upon their glorified Lord. "The fashion of his countenance was altered, and his raiment was white and glistering." His garments, though made of earth-woven fabric, "became shining, exceeding white as snow; so as no fuller on earth can white them"; "and his face did shine as the sun." Thus was Jesus transfigured before the three privileged witnesses.

With Him were two other personages, who also were in a state of glorified radiance, and who conversed with the Lord. These, as the

[a] Note 1, end of chapter.
[b] Note 2, end of chapter.
[c] Note 3, end of chapter.
[d] Matt. 17:1–8; Mark 9:2–8; Luke 9:28–36.

apostles learned, by means not stated though probably as gathered from the conversation in progress, were Moses and Elias, or more literally to us, Elijah; and the subject of their conference with Christ was "his decease which he should accomplish at Jerusalem." As the prophet visitants were about to depart, "Peter said unto Jesus, Master, it is good for us to be here: and let us make three tabernacles; one for thee, and one for Moses, and one for Elias: not knowing what he said." Undoubtedly Peter and his fellow apostles were bewildered, "sore afraid" indeed; and this condition may explain the suggestion respecting the three tabernacles. "He wist not what to say"; yet, though his remark appears confused and obscure, it becomes somewhat plainer when we remember that, at the annual feast of Tabernacles, it was customary to erect a little bower, or booth of wattled boughs, for each individual worshiper, into which he might retire for devotion. So far as there was a purpose in Peter's proposition, it seems to have been that of delaying the departure of the visitants.

The sublime and awful solemnity of the occasion had not yet reached its climax. Even as Peter spake, "behold, a bright cloud overshadowed them: and behold a voice out of the cloud, which said, This is my beloved Son, in whom I am well pleased; hear ye him." It was Elohim,ᵉ the Eternal Father, who spake; and at the sound of that voice of supreme Majesty, the apostles fell prostrate. Jesus came and touched them, saying, "Arise, and be not afraid." When they looked they saw that again they were alone with Him.

The impression made upon the three apostles by this manifestation was one never to be forgotten; but they were expressly charged to speak of it to no man until after the Savior had risen from the dead. They were puzzled as to the significance of the Lord's reference to His prospective rising from the dead. They had heard with great sorrow, and reluctantly they were being brought to understand it to be an awful certainty, that their beloved Master was to "suffer many things, and be rejected of the elders, and of the chief priests, and scribes, and be killed."ᶠ Such had been declared to them before, in language devoid of ambiguity and admitting of no figurative construction; and

---

ᵉ Page 34–36.

ᶠ Mark 8:31. Note 6, end of chapter.

with equal plainness they had been told that Jesus would rise again; but of this latter eventuality they had but dim comprehension. The present reiteration of these teachings seems to have left the three with no clearer understanding of their Lord's Resurrection from the dead than they had before. They seem to have had no definite conception as to what was meant by a resurrection; "And they kept that saying with themselves, questioning one with another what the rising from the dead should mean."g

The comprehensiveness of the Lord's injunction, that until after His rising from the dead they tell no man of their experiences on the mount, prohibited them from informing even their fellows of the Twelve. Later, after the Lord had ascended to His glory, Peter testified to the Church of the wondrous experience, in this forceful way: "For we have not followed cunningly devised fables, when we made known unto you the power and coming of our Lord Jesus Christ, but were eyewitnesses of his majesty. For he received from God the Father honour and glory, when there came such a voice to him from the excellent glory, This is my beloved Son, in whom I am well pleased. And this voice which came from heaven we heard, when we were with him in the holy mount."h And John, reverently confessing before the world the divinity of the Word, the Son of God who had been made flesh to dwell among men, solemnly affirmed: "And we beheld his glory, the glory as of the only begotten of the Father, full of grace and truth."i

The divine purpose as shown forth in the Transfiguration may be as incomprehensible to the human mind as is a full conception of the attendant splendor from verbal description; some features of the results achieved are apparent, however. Unto Christ the manifestation was strengthening and encouraging. The prospect of the experiences immediately ahead must naturally have been depressing and disheartening in the extreme. In faithfully treading the path of His life's work, He had reached the verge of the valley of the shadow of death; and the human part of His nature called for refreshing. As angels had been sent to minister unto Him after the trying scenes of the forty

g Mark 9:10.
h 2 Pet. 1:16–18.
i John 1:14.

days' fast and the direct temptation of Satan,[j] and as, in the agonizing hour of His bloody sweat, He was to be sustained anew by angelic ministry,[k] so at this critical and crucial period, the beginning of the end, visitants from the unseen world came to comfort and support Him. What of actual communication passed in the conference of Jesus with Moses and Elijah is not of full record in the New Testament Gospels.

The voice of His Father, to whom He was the Firstborn in the spirit-world, and the Only Begotten in the flesh, was of supreme assurance; yet that voice had been addressed to the three apostles rather than to Jesus, who had already received the Father's acknowledgment and attestation on the occasion of His baptism. The fullest version of the Father's words to Peter, James, and John is that recorded by Matthew: "This is my beloved Son, in whom I am well pleased; hear ye him." Aside from the proclamation of the Son's divine nature, the Father's words were otherwise decisive and portentous. Moses, the promulgator of the law, and Elijah the representative of the prophets and especially distinguished among them as the one who had not died,[l] had been seen ministering unto Jesus and subservient to Him. The fulfillment of the law and the superseding of the prophets by the Messiah was attested in the command—Hear ye *Him.* A new dispensation had been established, that of the gospel, for which the law and the prophets had been but preparatory. The apostles were to be guided neither by Moses nor Elijah, but by *Him,* their Lord, Jesus the Christ.

The three selected apostles, "the Man of Rock and the Sons of Thunder" had seen the Lord in glory; and they marveled that such a thing could be at that time, since as they had interpreted the scriptures, it had been predicted that Elijah should precede the Messiah's triumphal advent. As they wended their way down the mountain-side, they asked the Master:[m] "Why then say the scribes that Elias must first come?" Jesus confirmed the prophecy that Elias should first come, that is, before the Lord's advent in glory, which event they had

[j] Matt. 4:11; Mark 1:13.
[k] Luke 22:43; compare John 12:27–28.
[l] 2 Kings 2:11.
[m] Matt. 17:10–13; Mark 9:11–13.

in mind: "But," He added, "I say unto you, That Elias is come already, and they knew him not, but have done unto him whatsoever they listed. Likewise shall also the Son of man suffer of them. Then the disciples understood that he spake unto them of John the Baptist." That John the Baptist would officiate "in the spirit and power of Elias," as the forerunner of the Christ, had been announced by the angel Gabriel to Zacharias,[n] before the Baptist's birth; and that John was *that* particular Elias had been shown by Jesus in His memorable tribute to the Baptist's fidelity and greatness. That His words would not be generally accepted with understanding is evidenced by the context; Jesus, on that occasion, had said: "And if ye will receive it, this is Elias, which was for to come."[o]

It is not possible that Jesus could have meant that John was the same individual as Elijah; nor could the people have so understood His words, since the false doctrine of transmigration or reincarnation of spirits was repudiated by the Jews.[p] The seeming difficulty is removed when we consider that, as the name appears in the New Testament, "Elias" is used for "Elijah,"[q] with no attempt at distinction between Elijah the Tishbite, and any other person known as Elias. Gabriel's declaration that the then unborn John should manifest "the spirit and power of Elias" indicates that "Elias" is a title of office; every restorer, forerunner, or one sent of God to prepare the way for greater developments in the gospel plan, is an Elias. The appellative "Elias" is in fact both a personal name and a title.

In the present dispensation both the ancient Elias, who belonged to the Abrahamic dispensation and in the spirit of whose office man have officiated in different periods, and also the prophet Elijah, have appeared in person and have conferred their particular and separate authority upon latter-day bearers of the Holy Priesthood, and the keys of the powers exercised by them while on earth are today inherent in the restored Church of Jesus Christ. The authority of Elias is inferior to that of Elijah, the first being a function of the

[n] Luke 1:17.

[o] Matt. 11:14.

[p] Edersheim, *Life and Times of Jesus,* vol. 2, p. 79.

[q] Note 4, end of chapter.

Lesser or Aaronic order of Priesthood, while the latter belongs to the Higher or Melchizedek Priesthood. Malachi's prediction, that before "the great and dreadful day of the Lord" Elijah the prophet would be sent to earth to "turn the heart of the fathers to the children, and the heart of the children to their fathers,"[r] did not reach fulfillment in the mission of John the Baptist, nor in that of any other "Elias";[s] its complete realization was inaugurated on the third day of April, 1836, when Elijah appeared in the temple at Kirtland, Ohio, and committed to Joseph Smith and Oliver Cowdery the keys of the authority theretofore vested in himself. "The great and dreadful day of the Lord" was not the meridian of time; that awful though blessed period of consummation is yet future, but "near, even at the doors."[t]

NOTES TO CHAPTER 23

1. Interval Between Time of Peter's Confession and that of the Transfiguration.—Both Matthew (17:1) and Mark (9:2) state that the Transfiguration occurred "after six days" following the time of Peter's great confession that Jesus was the Christ; while Luke (9:28) notes an interval of "about an eight days." It is probable that the six-day period was meant to be exclusive of the day on which the earlier events had occurred and of that on which Jesus and the three apostles retired to the mountain; and that Luke's "about an eight days" was made to include these two days. There is here no ground for a claim of discrepancy.

2. Peter, James and John, who were selected from among the Twelve as the only earthly witnesses of the transfiguration of Christ, had been similarly chosen as witnesses of a special manifestation, that of the raising of the daughter of Jairus (Mark 5:37; Luke 8:51); and, later, the same three were the sole witnesses of our Lord's night agony in Gethsemane (Matt. 26:37; Mark 14:33).

3. Place of the Transfiguration.—The mountain on which the Transfiguration occurred is neither named nor otherwise indicated by the Gospel-writers in such a way as to admit of its positive identification. Mount Tabor, in Galilee, has long been held by tradition as the site, and in the sixth century three churches were erected on its plateau-like summit, possibly in commemoration of Peter's desire to make three tabernacles or booths, one each for Jesus, Moses, and Elijah. Later a

[r] Mal. 4:5,6.

[s] Note 5, end of chapter.

[t] D&C 110:13–16. See chapter 41, herein.

monastery was built there. Nevertheless, Mt. Tabor is now rejected by investigators, and Mt. Hermon is generally regarded as the place. Hermon stands near the northerly limits of Palestine, just beyond Caesarea Philippi, where Jesus is known to have been a week before the Transfiguration. Mark (9:30) distinctly tells us that after His descent from the mount, Jesus and the apostles departed and went through Galilee. Weight of evidence is in favor of Hermon as the Mount of Transfiguration, though nothing that may be called decisive is known in the matter.

4. The Names "Elias" and "Elijah."—The following statement which appears in Smith's *Bible Dictionary* is supported by authorities in general: "'Elias'" is "the Greek and Latin form of 'Elijah' given in the Authorized Version of Apocrypha and New Testament."

5. "The Spirit and Power of Elias."—That John the Baptist, in his capacity as a restorer, a forerunner, or as one sent to prepare the way for a work greater than his own, did officiate as an "Elias" is attested by both ancient and latter-day scripture. Through him water baptism for the remission of sins was preached and administered, and the higher baptism, that of the Spirit, was made possible. True to his mission, he has come in the last dispensation, and has restored by ordination the Priesthood of Aaron, which has authority to baptize. He thus prepared the way for the vicarious labor of baptism for the dead, the authority for which was restored by Elijah, and which is preeminently the work by which the children and the fathers shall be united in an eternal bond.

On the 10th of March, 1844, the Prophet Joseph Smith gave the following exposition of the power of Elias as compared with higher authority: "The spirit of Elias is first, Elijah second, and Messiah last. Elias is a forerunner to prepare the way, and the spirit and power of Elijah is to come after, holding the keys of power, building the temple to the capstone, placing the seals of the Melchizedek Priesthood upon the house of Israel, and making all things ready; then Messiah comes to His temple, which is last of all.

"Messiah is above the spirit and power of Elijah, for He made the world, and was that spiritual rock unto Moses in the wilderness. Elijah was to come and prepare the way and build up the kingdom before the coming of the great day of the Lord, although the spirit of Elias might begin it."—*Hist. of the Church*, under date named.

6. Mention of the Lord's Approaching "Decease."—Of the three synoptists, Luke alone makes even brief mention of the matter upon which Moses and Elijah conversed with the Lord at the Transfiguration. The record states that the visitants, who appeared in glory, "spake of his decease which he should accomplish at Jerusalem" (Luke 9:3 1). It is significant that the *decease*, which the Lord should *accomplish*, not the *death* that He should *suffer* or *die*, was the subject of that exalted communion. The Greek word of which "decease" appears as the English equivalent in many of the MSS. of the Gospels is one connoting "exodus" or "departure," and the word occurring in other early versions signifies "glory." So also the Greek original of "accomplish," in the account of the Transfiguration, connotes the successful filling out or completion of a specific undertaking, and not distinctively the act of dying. Both the letter of the record and the spirit in which the recorder wrote indicate that Moses and Elijah conversed with their Lord on the glorious consummation of His mission in mortality—a consummation recognized in the law (personified in Moses) and the prophets (represented by Elijah)—and an event of supreme import, determining the fulfillment of both the law and the prophets, and the glorious inauguration of a new and higher order as part of the divine plan. The *decease* that the Savior was then so soon to *accomplish* was the voluntary surrender of His life in fulfillment of a purpose at once exalted and foreordained, not a *death* by which He would passively *die* through conditions beyond His control.

CHAPTER 24

FROM SUNSHINE TO SHADOW

Our Lord's descent from the holy heights[a] of the Mount of Transfiguration was more than a physical return from greater to lesser altitudes; it was a passing from sunshine into shadow, from the effulgent glory of heaven to the mists of worldly passions and human unbelief; it was the beginning of His rapid descent into the valley of humiliation. From lofty converse with divinely-appointed ministers, from supreme communion with His Father and God, Jesus came down to a scene of disheartening confusion and a spectacle of demonized dominion before which even His apostles stood in impotent despair. To His sensitive and sinless soul the contrast must have brought superhuman anguish; even to us who read the brief account thereof it is appalling.

HEALING OF YOUTHFUL DEMONIAC

Jesus and the three apostles returned from the mount on the morrow following the Transfiguration;[b] this fact suggests the assumption that the glorious manifestation had occurred during the night. At or near the base of the mountain the party found the other apostles, and with them a multitude of people, including some scribes or rabbis.[c] There was evidence of disputation and disturbance amongst the crowd; and plainly the apostles were on the defensive. At the unexpected approach of Jesus many of the people ran to meet Him with respectful salutations. Of the contentious scribes He asked: "What

[a] Compare 2 Pet. 1:18.

[b] Luke 9:37.

[c] Matt. 17:14–21; Mark 9:14–29; Luke 9:37–42.

question ye with them?" thus assuming the burden of the dispute, whatever it might be, and so relieving the distressed disciples from further active participation. The scribes remained silent; their courage had vanished when the Master appeared. A man, "one of the multitude," gave, though indirectly, the answer. "Master," said he, kneeling at the feet of Christ, "I have brought unto thee my son, which hath a dumb spirit; and wheresoever he taketh him, he teareth him: and he foameth, and gnasheth with his teeth, and pineth away: and I spake to thy disciples that they should cast him out; and they could not."

The disciples' failure to heal the stricken youth had evidently brought upon them hostile criticism, taunts and ridicule from the unbelieving scribes; and their discomfiture must have been intensified by the thought that through them doubt had been cast upon the authority and power of their Lord. Pained in spirit at this—another instance of dearth of faith and consequent lack of power among His chosen and ordained servants—Jesus uttered an exclamation of intense sorrow: "O faithless generation, how long shall I be with you? how long shall I suffer you?" These words in which there is evident reproof, however mild and pitying it may be, were addressed primarily to the apostles; whether exclusively so or to them and others is of minor importance. As Jesus directed, the afflicted lad was brought nearer; and the tormenting demon, finding himself in the Master's presence, threw his youthful victim into a terrible paroxysm, so that the boy fell to the ground and wallowed in convulsions, the while frothing and foaming at the mouth. With calm deliberation, which contrasted strongly with the eager impatience of the distracted parent, Jesus inquired as to when the malady had first befallen the lad. "Of a child," answered the father, adding, "And ofttimes it hath cast him into the fire, and into the waters, to destroy him." With pathetic eagerness he implored, "If thou canst do anything, have compassion on us and help us." The man spoke of his son's affliction as though shared by himself. "Help us," was his prayer.

To this qualifying expression "If thou canst do anything," which implied a measure of uncertainty as to the ability of the Master to grant what he asked, and this perhaps as in part a result of the failure of the apostles, Jesus replied: "If thou canst believe"; and added, "all things are possible to him that believeth." The man's understanding was enlightened; up to that moment he had thought that all depended upon Jesus; he now saw that the issue rested largely with himself. It is noteworthy that the Lord specified belief rather than faith as the condition essential to the case. The man was evidently trustful, and assuredly fervent in his hope that Jesus could help; but it is doubtful that he knew what faith really meant. He was receptive and eagerly teachable, however, and the Lord strengthened his feeble and uncertain belief. The encouraging explanation of the real need stimulated him to a more abounding trust. Weeping in an agony of hope he cried out: "Lord, I believe"; and then, realizing the darkness of error from which he was just beginning to emerge, he added penitently "help thou mine unbelief."[d]

Looking compassionately upon the writhing sufferer at His feet, Jesus rebuked the demon, thus: "Thou dumb and deaf spirit, I charge thee, come out of him, and enter no more into him. And the spirit cried, and rent him sore, and came out of him: and he was as one dead; insomuch that many said, He is dead. But Jesus took him by the hand, and lifted him up; and he arose"; and as Luke adds, "and delivered him again to his father." The permanency of the cure was assured by the express command that the evil spirit enter no more into the lad;[e] it was no relief from that present attack alone; the healing was permanent.

The people were amazed at the power of God manifested in the miracle; and the apostles who had tried and failed to subdue the evil spirit were disturbed. While on their mission, though away from their Master's helpful presence, they had successfully rebuked and cast out evil spirits as they had received special power and commission to do;[f] but now, during His absence of a day they had found themselves unable. When they had retired to the house, they asked of Jesus, "Why could not we cast him out?" The reply was: "Because of your unbelief"; and in further explanation the Lord said, "Howbeit this kind goeth not out but by prayer and fasting."[g]

[d] Note 1, end of chapter.

[e] Compare Matt. 12:40–45.

[f] Mark 6:12, 13; compare verse 7; also 3:15; Matt. 10:1.

[g] Note 2, end of chapter.

Hereby we learn that the achievements possible to faith are limited or conditioned by the genuineness, the purity, the unmixed quality of that faith. "O ye of little faith"; "Where is your faith?" and "Wherefore didst thou doubt?"[h] are forms of admonitory reproof that had been repeatedly addressed to the apostles of the Lord. The possibilities of faith were now thus further affirmed: "Verily I say unto you, If ye have faith as a grain of mustard seed, ye shall say unto this mountain, Remove hence to yonder place; and it shall remove; and nothing shall be impossible unto you."[i] The comparison between effective faith and a grain of mustard seed is one of quality rather than of quantity; it connotes living, virile faith, like unto the seed, however small, from which a great plant may spring,[j] in contrast with a lifeless, artificial imitation, however prominent or demonstrative.

THE LORD'S DEATH AND
RESURRECTION AGAIN PREDICTED[k]

From the locality whereat the last miracle was wrought, Jesus departed with the Twelve, and passed through Galilee toward Capernaum. It is probable that they traveled by the less frequented roads, as He desired that His return should not be publicly known. He had gone into comparative retirement for a season, primarily it seems in quest of opportunity to more thoroughly instruct the apostles in their preparation for the work, which within a few months they would be left to carry on without His bodily companionship. They had solemnly testified that they knew Him to be the Christ; to them therefore He could impart much that the people in general were wholly unprepared to receive. The particular theme of His special and advanced instruction to the Twelve was that of His approaching death and Resurrection; and this was dwelt upon again and again, for they were slow or unwilling to comprehend.

"Let these sayings sink down into your ears" was His forceful prelude on this occasion, in Galilee. Then followed the reiterated

h Matt. 14:31; 16:8; Luke 8:25.

i Matt. 17:20; compare 21:21; Mark 11:23; Luke 17:6; also Note 3, end of chapter.

j Compare Parable of the Mustard Seed, chapter 19.

k Matt. 17:22–23; Mark 9:30–32; Luke 9:44, 45.

prediction, spoken in part in the present tense as though already begun in fulfillment: "The Son of man is delivered into the hands of men, and they shall kill him; and after that he is killed, he shall rise the third day." We read with some surprise that the apostles still failed to understand. Luke's comment is: "But they understood not this saying, and it was hid from them, that they perceived it not: and they feared to ask him of that saying." The thought of what the Lord's words might mean, even in its faintest outline, was terrifying to those devoted men; and their failure to comprehend was in part due to the fact that the human mind is loath to search deeply into anything it desires not to believe.

THE TRIBUTE MONEY—SUPPLIED BY A MIRACLE[l]

Jesus and His followers were again in Capernaum. There Peter was approached by a collector of the temple tax, who asked: "Doth not your Master pay tribute?"[m] Peter answered "Yes." It is interesting to find that the inquiry was made of Peter and not directly of Jesus; this circumstance may be indicative of the respect in which the Lord was held by the people at large, and may suggest the possibility of doubt in the collector's mind as to whether Jesus was amenable to the tax, since priests and rabbis generally claimed exemption.

The annual capitation tax here referred to amounted to half a shekel or a didrachma, corresponding to about thirty-three cents in our money; and this had been required of every male adult in Israel since the days of the exodus; though, during the period of captivity the requirement had been modified.[n] This tribute, as prescribed through Moses, was originally known as "atonement money," and its payment was in the nature of a sacrifice to accompany supplication for ransom from the effects of individual sin. At the time of Christ the annual contribution was usually collected between early March and the Passover. If Jesus was subject to this tax, He was at this time several weeks in arrears.

The conversation between Peter and the tax-collector had occurred outside the house. When Peter entered, and was about to inform the

[l] Matt. 17:24–27.

[m] Note 4, end of chapter.

[n] Ex. 30:13; 38:26.

Master concerning the interview, Jesus forestalled him, saying: "What thinkest thou, Simon? of whom do the kings of the earth take custom or tribute? of their own children, or of strangers? Peter saith unto him, Of strangers. Jesus saith unto him, Then are the children free."

Peter must have seen the inconsistency of expecting Jesus, the acknowledged Messiah, to pay atonement money, or a tax for temple maintenance, inasmuch as the temple was the House of God, and Jesus was the Son of God, and particularly since even earthly princes were exempted from capitation dues. Peter's embarrassment over his inconsiderate boldness, in pledging payment for his Master without first consulting Him, was relieved however by Jesus, who said: "Notwithstanding, lest we should offend them, go thou to the sea, and cast an hook, and take up the fish that first cometh up; and when thou hast opened his mouth, thou shalt find a piece of money: that take, and give unto them for me and thee."

The money was to be paid, not because it could be rightfully demanded of Jesus, but lest nonpayment give offense and furnish to His opponents further excuse for complaint. The "piece of money," which Jesus said Peter would find in the mouth of the first fish that took his bait, is more correctly designated by the literal translation "stater,"[o] indicating a silver coin equivalent to a shekel, or two didrachms, and therefore the exact amount of the tax for two persons. "That take, and give unto them for me and thee" said Jesus. It is notable that He did not say "for us." In His associations with men, even with the Twelve, who of all were nearest and dearest to Him, our Lord always maintained His separate and unique status, in every instance making the fact apparent that He was essentially different from other men. This is illustrated by His expressions "My Father and your Father," "My God and your God,"[p] instead of our Father and our God. He reverently acknowledged that He was the Son of God in a literal sense that did not apply to any other being.

While the circumstances of the finding of the stater in the fish are not detailed, and the actual accomplishment of the miracle is not positively recorded, we cannot doubt that what Jesus had promised

---

[o] See reading in revised version, and in margin of Oxford and Bagster Bibles.

[p] John 20:17.

was realized, as otherwise there would appear no reason for introducing the incident into the Gospel narrative. The miracle is without a parallel or even a remotely analogous instance. We need not assume that the stater was other than an ordinary coin that had fallen into the water, nor that it had been taken by the fish in any unusual way. Nevertheless, the knowledge that there was in the lake a fish having a coin in its gullet, that the coin was of the denomination specified, and that that particular fish would rise, and be the first to rise to Peter's hook, is as incomprehensible to man's finite understanding as are the means by which any of Christ's miracles were wrought. The Lord Jesus held and holds dominion over the earth, the sea, and all that in them is, for by His word and power were they made.

The Lord's purpose in so miraculously supplying the money should be studiously considered. The assumption that superhuman power had to be invoked because of a supposed condition of extreme poverty on the part of Jesus and Peter is unwarranted. Even if Jesus and His companions had been actually penniless, Peter and his fellow fishermen could easily have cast their net, and, with ordinary success have obtained fish enough to sell for the needed amount. Moreover, we find no instance of a miracle wrought by the Lord for personal gain or relief of His own need, however pressing. It appears probable, that by the means employed for obtaining the money, Jesus intentionally emphasized His exceptional reasons for redeeming Peter's pledge that the tax would be paid. The Jews, who did not know Jesus as the Messiah, but only as a Teacher of superior ability and a Man of unusual power, might have taken offense had He refused to pay the tribute required of every Jew. On the other hand, to the apostles and particularly to Peter who had been the mouth-piece of all in the great confession, the payment of the tax in ordinary course and without explanation by Jesus might have appeared as an admission that He was subject to the temple, and therefore less than He had claimed and less than they had confessed Him to be. His catechization of Peter had clearly demonstrated that He maintained His right as the King's Son, and yet would condescend to voluntarily give what could not be righteously demanded. Then, in conclusive demonstration of His exalted status, He provided the money by the utilization of knowledge such as no other man possessed.

AS A LITTLE CHILD[q]

On the way to Capernaum the apostles had questioned among themselves, as they supposed beyond the Master's hearing; questioning had led to argument, and argument to disputation. The matter about which they were so greatly concerned was as to who among them should be the greatest in the kingdom of heaven. The testimony they had received convinced them beyond all doubt, that Jesus was the long-awaited Christ, and this had been supplemented and confirmed by His unqualified acknowledgment of His Messianic dignity. With minds still tinctured by the traditional expectation of the Messiah as both spiritual Lord and temporal King, and remembering some of the Master's frequent references to His kingdom and the blessed state of those who belonged thereto, and furthermore realizing that His recent utterances indicated a near crisis or climax in His ministry, they surrendered themselves to the selfish contemplation of their prospective stations in the new kingdom, and the particular offices of trust, honor, and emolument each most desired. Who of them was to be prime minister; who would be chancellor, who the commander of the troops? Personal ambition had already engendered jealousy in their hearts.

When they were together with Jesus in the house at Capernaum, the subject was brought up again. Mark tells us that Jesus asked: "What was it that ye disputed among yourselves by the way?" and that they answered not, because, as may be inferred, they were ashamed. From Matthew's record it may be understood that the apostles submitted the question for the Master's decision. The apparent difference of circumstance is unimportant; both accounts are correct; Christ's question to them may have eventually brought out their questions to Him. Jesus, comprehending their thoughts and knowing their unenlightened state of mind on the matter that troubled them, gave them an illustrated lesson. Calling a little child, whom He lovingly took into His arms, He said: "Verily I say unto you, Except ye be converted, and become as little children, ye shall not enter into the kingdom of heaven. Whosoever therefore shall humble himself as this little child, the same is greatest in the kingdom of heaven. And whoso

[q] Matt. 18:1–11; Mark 9:33–37, 42; Luke 9:46–48.

shall receive one such little child in my name receiveth me. But whoso shall offend one of these little ones which believe in me, it were better for him that a millstone were hanged about his neck, and that he were drowned in the depth of the sea." With this lesson we may profitably associate a later teaching, that little children are typical of the kingdom of heaven.[r]

Even the apostles were in need of conversion;[s] respecting the matter at issue their hearts were turned, partly at least, from God and His kingdom. They had to learn that genuine humility is an attribute essential to citizenship in the community of the blessed; and that the degree of humility conditions whatsoever there is akin to rank in the kingdom; for therein the humblest shall be greatest.

Christ would not have had His chosen representatives become childish; far from it, they had to be men of courage, fortitude, and force; but He would have them become childlike. The distinction is important. Those who belong to Christ must become like little children in obedience, truthfulness, trustfulness, purity, humility, and faith. The child is an artless, natural, trusting believer; the childish one is careless, foolish, and neglectful. In contrasting these characteristics, note the counsel of Paul: "Brethren, be not children in understanding: howbeit in malice be ye children, but in understanding be men."[t] Children as such, and children as types of adults who are true believers, are closely associated in this lesson. Whosoever shall offend, that is cause to stumble or go astray, one such child of Christ, incurs guilt so great that it would have been better for him had he met death even by violence before he had so sinned.

Dwelling upon offenses, or causes of stumbling, the Lord continued: "Woe unto the world because of offences! for it must needs be that offences come; but woe to that man by whom the offence cometh!" Then, repeating some of the precious truths embodied in His memorable Sermon on the Mount,[u] He urged the overcoming of evil propensities whatever the sacrifice. As it is better that a man undergo

[r] Matt. 19:13–15; Mark 10:13–16; Luke 18:15–17.

[s] Compare Luke 22:32.

[t] 1 Cor. 14:20; compare 13:11; Matt. 11:25; Ps. 131:2.

[u] Page 219 and 238.

surgical treatment though he lose thereby a hand, a foot, or an eye, than that his whole body be involved and his life forfeited, so is it commended that he cut off, tear away, or root out from his soul the passions of evil, which, if suffered to remain shall surely bring him under condemnation. In that state his conscience shall gnaw as an undying worm, and his remorse shall be as a fire that cannot be quenched. Every human soul shall be tested as by fire; and as the flesh of the altar sacrifices had to be seasoned with salt, as a type of preservation from corruption,[v] so also the soul must receive the saving salt of the gospel; and that salt must be pure and potent, not a dirty mixture of inherited prejudice and unauthorized tradition that has lost whatever saltness it may once have had. "Have salt in yourselves, and have peace one with another," was the Lord's admonition to the disputing Twelve.[w]

As applicable to children of tender years, and to childlike believers young and old, the Savior gave to the apostles this solemn warning and profound statement of fact: "Take heed that ye despise not one of these little ones; for I say unto you, That in heaven their angels do always behold the face of my Father which is in heaven." The mission of the Christ was presented as that of saving those who are temporarily lost, and who, but for His aid would be lost forever. In elucidation of His meaning, the Teacher presented a parable which has found place among the literary treasures of the world.

THE PARABLE OF THE LOST SHEEP[x]

"How think ye? if a man have an hundred sheep, and one of them be gone astray, doth he not leave the ninety and nine, and goeth into the mountains, and seeketh that which is gone astray? And if so be that he find it, verily I say unto you, he rejoiceth more of that sheep, than of the ninety and nine which went not astray. Even so it is not the will of your Father which is in heaven, that one of these little ones should perish."

[v] Mark 9:49, 50; compare Lev. 2:13; Ezek. 43:24.

[w] Mark 9:43–50; compare Matt. 18:8, 9.

[x] Matt. 18:12–14; compare Luke 15:3–7 in which occurs a repetition of this impressive parable, as given on a later occasion to Pharisees and scribes at Jerusalem with a somewhat different application.

In this effective analogy the saving purpose of Christ's mission is made prominent. He is verily the Savior. The shepherd is portrayed as leaving the ninety and nine, pastured or folded in safety we cannot doubt, while he goes alone into the mountains to seek the one that has strayed. In finding and bringing back the wayward sheep, he has more joy than that of knowing the others are yet safe. In a later version of this splendid parable, as addressed to the murmuring Pharisees and scribes at Jerusalem, the Master said of the shepherd on his finding the lost sheep:

"And when he hath found it, he layeth it on his shoulders, rejoicing. And when he cometh home, he calleth together his friends and neighbours, saying unto them, Rejoice with me; for I have found my sheep which was lost. I say unto you, that likewise joy shall be in heaven over one sinner that repenteth, more than over ninety and nine just persons, which need no repentance."[y]

Many have marveled that there should be greater rejoicing over the recovery of one stray sheep, or the saving of a soul that had been as one lost, than over the many who have not been in such jeopardy. In the safe-folded ninety and nine the shepherd had continued joy; but to him came a new accession of happiness, brighter and stronger because of his recent grief, when the lost was brought back to the fold. To this parable in connection with others of analogous import we shall recur in a later chapter.

"IN MY NAME"[z]

In continuation of the lesson illustrated by the little child, Jesus said: "Whosoever shall receive this child in my name receiveth me: and whosoever shall receive me receiveth him that sent me: for he that is least among you all, the same shall be great." It may have been Christ's reference to deeds done in His name that prompted John to interject a remark at this point: "Master, we saw one casting out devils in thy name, and he followeth not us: and we forbad him, because he followeth not us. But Jesus said, Forbid him not: for there is no man which shall do a miracle in my name, that can lightly speak evil of

[y] Luke 15:1–7.

[z] Luke 9:48–50; Mark 9:37–41.

me. For he that is not against us is on our part." The young apostle had allowed his zeal for the Master's name to lead to intolerance. That the man who had attempted to do good in the name of Jesus was evidently sincere, and that his efforts were acceptable to the Lord we cannot doubt; his act was essentially different from the unrighteous assumptions for which some others were afterward rebuked;[aa] he was certainly a believer in Christ, and may have been one of the class from which the Lord was soon to select and commission special ministers and the Seventy.[bb] In the state of divided opinion then existing among the people concerning Jesus, it was fair to say that all who were not opposed to Him were at least tentatively on His side. On other occasions He asserted that those who were not with Him were against him.[cc]

MY BROTHER AND I[dd]

The proper method of adjusting differences between brethren and the fundamental principles of Church discipline were made subjects of instruction to the Twelve. The first step is thus prescribed: "Moreover if thy brother shall trespass against thee, go and tell him his fault between thee and him alone: if he shall hear thee, thou hast gained thy brother." The rule of the rabbis was that the offender must make the first advance; but Jesus taught that the injured one should not wait for his brother to come to him, but go himself, and seek to adjust the difficulty; by so doing he might be the means of saving his brother's soul. If the offender proved to be obdurate, the brother who had suffered the trespass was to take two or three others with him, and again try to bring the transgressor to repentant acknowledgment of his offense; such a course provided for witnesses, by whose presence later misrepresentation would be guarded against.

Extreme measures were to be adopted only after all gentler means had failed. Should the man persist in his obstinacy, the case was to be brought before the Church, and in the event of his neglect or refusal to heed the decision of the Church, he was to be deprived of

---

[aa] Contrast the instance of the sons of Sceva, Acts 19:13–17.

[bb] Compare Luke 9:52; 10:1.

[cc] Matt. 12:30; Luke 11:23.

[dd] Matt. 18:15–20; compare Luke 17:3, 4.

fellowship, thereby becoming in his relationship to his former associates "as an heathen man and a publican." In such state of nonmembership he would be a fit subject for missionary effort; but, until he became repentant and manifested willingness to make amends, he could claim no rights or privileges of communion in the Church. Continued association with the unrepentant sinner may involve the spread of his disaffection, and the contamination of others through his sin. Justice is not to be dethroned by Mercy. The revealed order of discipline in the restored Church is similar to that given to the apostles of old.[ee]

The authority of the Twelve to administer the affairs of Church government was attested by the Lord's confirming to them as a body the promise before addressed to Peter: "Verily I say unto you, Whatsoever ye shall bind on earth shall be bound in heaven: and whatsoever ye shall loose on earth shall be loosed in heaven."[ff] Through unity of purpose and unreserved sincerity they would have power with God, as witness the Master's further assurance: "Again I say unto you, That if two of you shall agree on earth as touching any thing that they shall ask, it shall be done for them of my Father which is in heaven. For where two or three are gathered together in my name, there am I in the midst of them." Peter here broke in with a question: "Lord, how oft shall my brother sin against me, and I forgive him? till seven times?" He would fain have some definite limit set, and he probably considered the tentative suggestion of seven times as a very liberal measure, inasmuch as the rabbis prescribed a triple forgiveness only.[gg] He may have chosen seven as the next number above three having a special Pharisaical significance. The Savior's answer was enlightening: "Jesus saith unto him, I say not unto thee, Until seven times: but, Until seventy times seven." This reply must have meant to Peter as it means to us, that to forgiveness man may set no bounds; the forgiveness, however, must

---

[ee] Compare D&C 20:80; 42:88–93; 98:39–48.

[ff] Matt. 18:18; compare 16:19, and John 20:23.

[gg] They based this limitation on Amos 1:3 and Job 33:29. In the latter passage, as it appears in the authorized version, the word "oftentimes" is an erroneous rendering of the original, which really signified "twice and thrice."

be merited by the recipient.[hh] The instruction was made memorable by the following story:

PARABLE OF THE UNMERCIFUL SERVANT

"Therefore is the kingdom of heaven likened unto a certain king, which would take account of his servants. And when he had begun to reckon, one was brought unto him, which owed him ten thousand talents. But forasmuch as he had not to pay, his lord commanded him to be sold, and his wife, and children, and all that he had, and payment to be made. The servant therefore fell down, and worshipped him, saying, Lord, have patience with me, and I will pay thee all. Then the lord of that servant was moved with compassion, and loosed him, and forgave him the debt. But the same servant went out, and found one of his fellowservants, which owed him an hundred pence: and he laid hands on him, and took him by the throat, saying, Pay me that thou owest. And his fellowservant fell down at his feet, and besought him, saying, Have patience with me, and I will pay thee all. And he would not: but went and cast him into prison, till he should pay the debt. So when his fellowservants saw what was done, they were very sorry, and came and told unto their lord all that was done. Then his lord, after that he had called him, said unto him. O thou wicked servant, I forgave thee all that debt, because thou desiredst me: Shouldest not thou also have had compassion on thy fellowservant, even as I had pity on thee? And his lord was wroth, and delivered him to the tormentors, till he should pay all that was due unto him. So likewise shall my heavenly Father do also unto you, if ye from your hearts forgive not every one his brother their trespasses."[ii]

Ten thousand talents are specified as expressive of a sum so great as to put the debtor beyond all reasonable possibility of paying. We may regard the man as a trusted official, one of the king's ministers, who had been charged with the custody of the royal revenues, or one of the chief treasurers of taxes; that he is called a servant introduces no inconsistency, as in an absolute monarchy all but the sovereign are subjects and servants. The selling of the debtor's wife and children and all that he had would

---

hh Compare Luke 17:3, 4.

ii Matt. 18:23–35.

not have been in violation of the law in the supposed case, which implies the legal recognition of slavery.[jj] The man was in arrears for debt. He did not come before his lord voluntarily but had to be brought. So in the affairs of our individual lives periodical reckonings are inevitable; and while some debtors report of their own accord, others have to be cited to appear. The messengers who serve the summons may be adversity, illness, the approach of death; but, whatever, whoever they are, they enforce a rendering of our accounts.

The contrast between ten thousand talents and a hundred pence is enormous.[kk] In his fellowservant's plea for time in which to pay the hundred pence, the greater debtor should have been reminded of the dire straits from which he had just been relieved; the words, "Have patience with me, and I will pay thee all," were identical with those of his own prayer to the king. The base ingratitude of the unmerciful servant justified the king in revoking the pardon once granted. The man came under condemnation, not primarily for defalcation and debt, but for lack of mercy after having received of mercy so abundantly. He, as an unjust plaintiff, had invoked the law; as a convicted transgressor he was to be dealt with according to the law. Mercy is for the merciful. As a heavenly jewel it is to be received with thankfulness and used with sanctity, not to be cast into the mire of undeservedness. Justice may demand retribution and punishment: "With what measure ye mete, it shall be measured to you again."[ll] The conditions under which we may confidently implore pardon are set forth in the form of prayer prescribed by the Lord: "Forgive us our debts, as we forgive our debtors."[mm]

NOTES TO CHAPTER 24

1. Faith in Behalf of Others.—The supplication of the agonized father for the benefit of his sorely afflicted son—"Have compassion on us, and help us" (Mark 9:22)—shows that he made the boy's case his own. In this we are reminded of the Canaanite woman who implored Jesus to have mercy on her, though her daughter was the afflicted one (Matt. 15:22). In these cases, faith was exercised in behalf of

---

[jj] Compare 2 Kgs. 4:1; Lev. 25:39.

[kk] Note 5, end of chapter.

[ll] Matt. 7:1; see also verse 6.

[mm] Matt. 6:12; compare Luke 11:4; 3 Ne. 13:11.

the sufferers by others; and the same is true of the centurion who pleaded for his servant and whose faith was specially commended by Jesus (Matt. 8:5–10), of Jairus whose daughter lay dead (Luke 8:41, 42, 49, 50), and of many who brought their helpless kindred or friends to Christ and pleaded for them. As heretofore shown, faith to be healed is as truly a gift of God as is faith to heal and, as the instances cited prove, faith may be exercised with effect in behalf of others. In connection with the ordinance of administering to the afflicted, by anointing with oil and the laying on of hands, as authoritatively established in the restored Church of Jesus Christ, the elders officiating should encourage the faith of all believers present, that such be exerted in behalf of the sufferer. In the case of infants and of persons who are unconscious, it is plainly useless to look for active manifestation of faith on their part, and the supporting faith of kindred and friends is all the more requisite.

2. Power Developed by Prayer and Fasting.—The Savior's statement concerning the evil spirit that the apostles were unable to subdue—"Howbeit this kind goeth not out but by prayer and fasting"—indicates gradation in the malignity and evil power of demons, and gradation also in the results of varying degrees of faith. The apostles who failed on the occasion referred to had been able to cast out demons at other times. Fasting, when practised in prudence, and genuine prayer are conducive to the development of faith with its accompanying power for good. Individual application of this principle may be made with profit. Have you some besetting weakness, some sinful indulgence that you have vainly tried to overcome? Like the malignant demon that Christ rebuked in the boy, your sin may be of a kind that goeth out only through prayer and fasting.

3. Nothing Impossible to Faith.—Many people have questioned the literal truth of the Lord's declaration that by faith mountains may be removed from their place. Plainly there would have to be a purpose in harmony with the divine mind and plan, in order that faith could be exerted at all in such an undertaking. Neither such a miracle nor any other is possible as a gratification of the yearning for curiosity, nor for display, nor for personal gain or selfish satisfaction. Christ wrought no miracle with any such motive; He persistently refused to show signs to mere signseekers. But to deny the possibility of a mountain being removed through faith, under conditions that would render such removal acceptable to God, is to deny the word of God, both as to this specific possibility, and as to the general assurance that "nothing shall be impossible" to him who hath faith adequate to the end desired. It is worthy of note, however, that the Jews in the days of Christ and since often spoke of removing mountains as a figurative expression for the overcoming of difficulties. According to Lightfoot and other authorities a man able to solve intricate problems, or of particular power in argument or acumen in judgment, was referred to as a "rooter up of mountains."

4. The Temple Tribute.—That the tribute money referred to in the text was a Jewish contribution to the temple and not a tax levied by the Roman government is apparent from the specification of the "didrachma," which in the authorized version is translated "tribute." This coin was equivalent to the half shekel, reckoned "after the shekel of the sanctuary," which was the fixed amount to be paid annually by every male "from twenty years old and above," with the provision that "the rich shall not give more and the poor shall not give less" (Ex. 30:13–15). A tax levied by the political powers would not be designated as the didrachma. Moreover, had the collector who approached Peter been one of the official publicans, he probably would have demanded the tax instead of inquiring as to whether or not the Master was to be counted among the contributors.

Among the many humiliations to which the Jews were subjected in later years, after the destruction of the temple, was the compulsory payment of what had been their temple tribute, to the Romans, who decreed it as a revenue to the pagan temple of Jupiter Capitolinus. Of the emperor Vespasian, Josephus (*Wars of the Jews*, vii, 6:6) says: That he also laid a tribute wheresoever they were, and enjoined every one of them to bring two drachmae every year into the capitol, as they used to pay the same to the temple at Jerusalem.

5. Talents and Pence.—It is evident that by specifying ten thousand talents as the debt due the king, and a hundred pence as that owed by the fellowservant, the Lord intended to present a case of great disparity and striking contrast. The actual amounts involved are of minor significance in the story. We are not told which variety of talent was meant; there were Attic talents, and both silver and gold talents of Hebrew reckoning; and each differed from the others in value. The Oxford marginal explanation is: "A talent is 750 ounces of silver, which after five shillings the ounce is 187 pounds, ten shillings." This would be in American money over nine and a quarter millions of dollars as the sum of the ten thousand talents. The same authority gives as the value of the penny (Roman) sevenpence halfpenny, or fifteen cents, making the second debt equivalent to about fifteen dollars. Comparison with talents mentioned elsewhere may be allowable. Trench says: "How vast a sum it was we can most vividly realize to ourselves by comparing it with other sums mentioned in Scripture. In the construction of the tabernacle, twenty-nine talents of gold were used (Ex. 38:24); David prepared for the temple three thousand talents of gold, and the princes five thousand (1 Chr. 29:4–7); the queen of Sheba presented to Solomon one hundred and twenty talents (1 Kgs. 10:10); the king of Assyria laid upon Hezekiah thirty talents of gold (2 Kgs. 18:14); and in the extreme impoverishment to which the land was brought at the last, one talent of gold was laid upon it, after the death of Josiah, by the king of Egypt (2 Chr. 36:3)." Farrar estimates the debt owed to the king as 1,250,000 times that owed by the lesser to the greater debtor.

6. An Assumed Approval of Slavery.—Some readers have assumed that they find in the parable of the Unmerciful Servant an implied approval of the institution of slavery. The greater debtor, who figures in the story, was to be sold, together with his wife and children and all that he had. A rational consideration of the story as a whole is likely to find at most, in the particular incident of the king's command that the debtor and his family be sold, that the system of buying and selling bondservants, serfs, or slaves, was legally recognized at the time. The purpose of the parable was not even remotely to endorse or condemn slavery or any other social institution. The Mosaic law is explicit in matters relating to bondservants. The "angel of the Lord" who brought to Hagar a message of encouragement and blessing respected the authority of her mistress (Gen. 16:8, 9). In the apostolic epoch, instruction was directed toward right living under the secular law, not rebellion against the system (Eph. 6:5; Col. 3:22; 1 Tim. 6:1–3; 1 Pet. 2:18). Recognition of established customs, institutions, and laws, and proper obedience thereto, do not necessarily imply individual approval. The gospel of Jesus Christ, which shall yet regenerate the world, is to prevail—not by revolutionary assaults upon existing governments, nor through anarchy and violence—but by the teaching of individual duty and by the spread of the spirit of love. When the love of God shall be given a place in the hearts of mankind, when men shall unselfishly love their neighbors, then social systems and governments shall be formed and operated to the securing of the greatest good to the greatest number. Until men open their hearts to the reception of the gospel of Jesus Christ, injustice and oppression, servitude and slavery, in some form or other, are sure to exist. Attempts to extirpate social conditions that spring from individual selfishness cannot be otherwise than futile so long as selfishness is left to thrive and propagate.

CHAPTER 25

JESUS AGAIN IN JERUSALEM

DEPARTURE FROM GALILEE[a]

Of our Lord's labors during His brief sojourn in Galilee following His return from the region of Caesarea Philippi we have no record aside from that of His instructions to the apostles. His Galilean ministry, so far as the people in general were concerned, had practically ended with the discourse at Capernaum on His return thither after the miracles of feeding the five thousand and walking upon the sea. At Capernaum many of the disciples had turned away from the Master,[b] and now, after another short visit, He prepared to leave the land in which so great a part of His public work had been accomplished.

It was autumn; about six months had passed since the return of the apostles from their missionary tour; and the Feast of Tabernacles was near at hand. Some of the kinsmen of Jesus came to Him, and proposed that He go to Jerusalem and take advantage of the opportunity offered by the great national festival to declare Himself more openly than He had theretofore done. His brethren, as the visiting relatives are called, urged that He seek a broader and more prominent field than Galilee for the display of His powers, arguing that it was inconsistent for any man to keep himself in comparative obscurity when he wanted to be widely known. "Shew thyself to the world," said they. Whatever their motives may have been, these brethren of His did not advise more extended publicity through any zeal for His divine mission; indeed, we are expressly told that they did not believe in

[a] John 7:1–10.
[b] Page 323–24.

Him.[c] Jesus replied to their presumptuous advice: "My time is not yet come: but your time is always ready. The world cannot hate you; but me it hateth, because I testify of it, that the works thereof are evil. Go ye up unto this feast: I go not up yet unto this feast; for my time is not yet full come." It was not their prerogative to direct His movements, not to say when He should do even what He intended to do eventually.[d] He made it plain that between their status and His there was essential difference; they were of the world, which they loved as the world loved them; but the world hated Him because of His testimony.

This colloquy between Jesus and His brethren took place in Galilee. They soon started for Jerusalem leaving Him behind. He had not said that He would not go to the feast; but only "I go not up yet unto this feast; for my time is not yet full come." Some time after their departure He followed, traveling "not openly, but as it were in secret." Whether He went alone, or accompanied by any or all of the Twelve, we are not told.

AT THE FEAST OF TABERNACLES[e]

The agitated state of the public mind respecting Jesus is shown by the interest manifest in Jerusalem as to the probability of His presence at the feast. His brethren, who probably were questioned, could give no definite information as to His coming. He was sought for in the crowds; there was much discussion and some disputation concerning Him. Many people expressed their conviction that He was a good man, while others contradicted on the claim that He was a deceiver. There was little open discussion, however, for the people were afraid of incurring the displeasure of the rulers.

As originally established, the Feast of Tabernacles was a seven day festival, followed by a holy convocation on the eighth day. Each day was marked by special and in some respects distinctive services, all characterized by ceremonies of thanksgiving and praise.[f] "Now about the midst of the feast," probably on the third or fourth day, "Jesus

---

[c] John 7:5; compare Mark 3:21 in which "friends" is an inaccurate rendition for "kinsmen."

[d] Compare Christ's answer to His mother, John 2:4; see also 7:30; 8:20.

[e] John 7:11–53.

[f] Note 1, end of chapter.

went up into the temple, and taught." The first part of His discourse is not recorded, but its scriptural soundness is intimated in the surprise of the Jewish teachers, who asked among themselves: "How knoweth this man letters, having never learned?" He was no graduate of their schools; He had never sat at the feet of their rabbis; He had not been officially accredited by them nor licensed to teach. Whence came His wisdom, before which all their academic attainments were as nothing? Jesus answered their troubled queries, saying: My doctrine is not mine, but his that sent me. If any man will do his will, he shall know of the doctrine, whether it be of God, or whether I speak of myself." His Teacher, greater even than Himself, was the Eternal Father, whose will He proclaimed. The test proposed to determine the truth of His doctrine was in every way fair, and withal simple; anyone who would earnestly seek to do the will of the Father should know of himself whether Jesus spoke truth or error.[g] The Master proceeded to show that a man who speaks on his own authority alone seeks to aggrandize himself. Jesus did not so; He honored His Teacher, His Father, His God, not Himself; and therefore was He free from the taint of selfish pride or unrighteousness. Moses had given them the law, and yet, as Jesus affirmed, none of them kept the law.

Then, with startling abruptness, He challenged them with the question, "Why go ye about to kill me?" On many occasions had they held dark counsel with one another as to how they could get Him into their power and put Him to death; but they thought that the murderous secret was hidden within their own circle. The people had heard the seducing assertions of the ruling classes, that Jesus was possessed by a demon, and that He wrought wonders through the power of Beelzebub; and in the spirit of this blasphemous slander, they cried out: "Thou hast a devil: who goeth about to kill thee?"

Jesus knew that the two specifications of alleged guilt on which the rulers were striving most assiduously to convict Him in the popular mind, and so turn the people against Him, were those of Sabbath-breaking and blasphemy. On an earlier visit to Jerusalem He had healed an afflicted man on the Sabbath, and had utterly

---

[g] Note 2, end of chapter.

disconcerted the hypercritical accusers who even then had sought to compass His death.[h] To this act of mercy and power Jesus now referred, saying: "I have done one work, and ye all marvel." Seemingly they were still of unsettled mind, in doubt as to accepting Him because of the miracle or denouncing Him because He had done it on the Sabbath. Then He showed the inconsistency of charging Him with Sabbath-desecration for such a merciful deed, when the law of Moses expressly allowed acts of mercy, and even required that the mandatory rite of circumcision should not be deferred because of the Sabbath. "Judge not according to the appearance, but judge righteous judgment," said He.

The masses were still divided in their estimate of Jesus, and were moreover puzzled over the indecision of the rulers. Some of the Jerusalem Jews knew of the plan to arrest Him, and if possible to bring Him to death, and the people queried why nothing was done when He was there teaching publicly within reach of the officials. They wondered whether the rulers had not at least come to believe that Jesus was indeed the Messiah. The thought, however, was brushed aside when they remembered that all knew whence He came; He was a Galilean, and from Nazareth, whereas as they had been taught, however wrongly, the advent of the Christ was to be mysterious so that none would know whence He came. Strange it was, indeed, that men should reject Him because of a lack of mystery and miracle in His advent; when, had they known the truth, they would have seen in His birth a miracle without precedent or parallel in the annals of time. Jesus directly answered their weak and faulty reasoning. Crying aloud within the temple courts, He assured them that while they knew whence He came as one of their number, yet they did not know that He had come from God, neither did they know God who had sent Him: "But," He added, "I know him: for I am from him, and he hath sent me." At this reiterated testimony of His divine origin, the Jews were the more enraged, and they determined anew to take Him by force; nevertheless none laid hands upon him "because his hour was not yet come."

[h] John 5.

Many of the people believed in their hearts that He was of God, and ventured to ask among themselves whether Christ would do greater works than Jesus had done. The Pharisees and chief priests feared a possible demonstration in favor of Jesus, and forthwith sent officers to arrest Him and bring him before the Sanhedrin.[i] The presence of the temple police caused no interruption to the Master's discourse, though we may reasonably infer that He knew the purpose of their errand. He spoke on, saying that He would be with the people but a little while; and that after He had returned to the Father, they would seek Him vainly, for where He would then be they could not come. This remark evoked more bitter discussion. Some of the Jews wondered whether He intended to leave the borders of the land and go among the Gentiles to teach them and the dispersed Israelites.

As part of the temple service incident to the feast, the people went in procession to the Pool of Siloam[j] where a priest filled a golden ewer, which he then carried to the altar and there poured out the water to the accompaniment of trumpet blasts and the acclamations of the assembled hosts.[k] According to authorities on Jewish customs, this feature was omitted on the closing day of the feast. On this last or "great day," which was marked by ceremonies of unusual solemnity and rejoicing, Jesus was again in the temple. It may have been with reference to the bringing of water from the pool, or to the omission of the ceremony from the ritualistic procedure of the great day, that Jesus cried aloud, His voice resounding through the courts and arcades of the temple: "If any man thirst, let him come unto me, and drink. He that believeth on me, as the scripture hath said, out of his belly shall flow rivers of living water."[l]

John, the recorder, remarks parenthetically that this promise had reference to the bestowal of the Holy Ghost, which at that time had not been granted, nor was it to be until after the ascension of the risen Lord.[m]

---

[i] Page 66–67.

[j] Note 3, end of chapter.

[k] This was regarded as a literal fulfillment of Isa. 12:3.

[l] John 7:37, 38; compare with the assurance respecting "living water" given to the Samaritan woman, 4:10–15.

[m] John 7:39; compare 14:16, 17, 26; 15:26; 16:7; Luke 24:49; Acts 2:4.

Again many of the people were so impressed that they declared Jesus could be none other than the Messiah; but others objected, saying that the Christ must come from Bethlehem of Judea and Jesus was known to have come from Galilee.[n] So there was further dissension; and though some wanted Him apprehended, not a man was found who would venture to lay hold on Him.

The police officers returned without their intended prisoner. To the angry demand of the chief priests and Pharisees as to why they had not brought Him, they acknowledged that they had been so affected by His teachings as to be unable to make the arrest. "Never man spake like this man," they said. Their haughty masters were furious. "Are ye also deceived?" they demanded; and further, "Have any of the rulers or of the Pharisees believed on him?" What was the opinion of the common people worth? They had never learned the law, and were therefore accursed and of no concern. Yet with all this show of proud disdain, the chief priests and Pharisees were afraid of the common people, and were again halted in their wicked course.

One voice of mild protest was heard in the assembly. Nicodemus, a member of the Sanhedrin, and the same who had come to Jesus by night to inquire into the new teaching,[o] mustered courage enough to ask: "Doth our law judge any man, before it hear him, and know what he doeth?" The answer was insulting. Maddened with bigotry and bloodthirsty fanaticism, some of his colleagues turned upon him with the savage demand: "Art thou also of Galilee?" meaning, Art thou also a disciple of this Galilean whom we hate? Nicodemus was curtly told to study the scriptures, and he would fail to find any prediction of a prophet arising in Galilee. The anger of these learned bigots had blinded them even to their own vaunted knowledge, for several of the ancient prophets were regarded as Galileans;[p] if, however they had meant to refer only to that Prophet of whom Moses had spoken, the Messiah, they were correct, since all predictions pointed to Bethlehem in Judea as His

[n] Note 4, end of chapter.

[o] John 3.

[p] According to many excellent authorities, Jonah, Nahum, and Hosea were all of Galilee; and it is further believed that Elijah also was of Galilean nativity.

birthplace. It is evident that Jesus was thought of as a native of Nazareth, and that the circumstances of His birth were not of public knowledge.

"GO, AND SIN NO MORE"[q]

After the festivities were over, Jesus went to the temple one morning early; and as He sat, probably in the Court of the Women, which was the usual place of public resort, many gathered about Him and He proceeded to teach them as was His custom. His discourse was interrupted by the arrival of a party of scribes and Pharisees with a woman in charge, who, they said, was guilty of adultery. To Jesus they presented this statement and question: "Now Moses in the law commanded us, that such should be stoned; but what sayest thou?" The submitting of the case to Jesus was a prearranged snare, a deliberate attempt to find or make a cause for accusing Him. Though it was not unusual for Jewish officials to consult rabbis of recognized wisdom and experience when difficult cases were to be decided, the case in point involved no legal complications. The woman's guilt seems to have been unquestioned, though the witnesses required by the statutes are not mentioned as appearing unless the accusing scribes and Pharisees are to be so considered; the law was explicit, and the custom of the times in dealing with such offenders was well known. While it is true that the law of Moses had decreed death by stoning as the penalty for adultery, the infliction of the extreme punishment had lapsed long before the time of Christ. One may reasonably ask why the woman's partner in the crime was not brought for sentence, since the law so zealously cited by the officious accusers provided for the punishment of both parties to the offense.[r]

The question of the scribes and Pharisees, "But what sayest thou?" may have intimated their expectation that Jesus would declare the law obsolete; perhaps they had heard of the Sermon on the Mount, in which many requirements in advance of the Mosaic code had been proclaimed.[s] Had Jesus decided that the wretched

[q] John 8:1–11.
[r] Deut. 22:22–27.
[s] Matt. 5:21–48.

woman ought to suffer death, her accusers might have said that he was defying the existing authorities; and possibly the charge of opposition to the Roman government might have been formulated, since power to inflict the death penalty had been taken from all Jewish tribunals; and moreover, the crime with which this woman was charged was not a capital offense under Roman law. Had He said that the woman should go unpunished or suffer only minor infliction, the crafty Jews could have charged Him with disrespect for the law of Moses. To these scribes and Pharisees Jesus at first gave little heed. Stooping down He traced with His finger on the ground; but as He wrote they continued to question Him. Lifting Himself up He answered them, in a terse sentence that has become proverbial: "He that is without sin among you, let him first cast a stone at her." Such was the law; the accusers on whose testimony the death penalty was pronounced were to be the first to begin the work of execution.[t]

Having spoken, Jesus again stooped and wrote upon the ground. The woman's accusers were "convicted by their own conscience"; shamed and in disgrace they slunk away, all of them from the eldest to the youngest. They knew themselves to be unfit to appear either as accusers or judges.[u] What cowards doth conscience make! "When Jesus had lifted up himself, and saw none but the woman, he said unto her, Woman, where are those thine accusers? hath no man condemned thee? She said, No man, Lord. And Jesus said unto her, Neither do I condemn thee: go and sin no more."[v]

The woman was repentant; she remained humbly awaiting the Master's decision, even after her accusers had gone. Jesus did not expressly condone; He declined to condemn; but He sent the sinner away with a solemn adjuration to a better life.[w]

[t] Deut. 17:6, 7; also 13:9.

[u] Compare Rom. 2:1, 22; Matt. 7:1, 2; Luke 6:37; 2 Sam. 12:5–7.

[v] John 8:10, 11; compare 5:14. Consider another instance of mercy granted through contrition, Luke 7:36–50.

[w] Note 5, end of chapter.

THE LIGHT OF THE WORLD[x]

Sitting within the temple enclosure in the division known as the Treasury, which was connected with the Court of the Women,[y] our Lord continued His teaching, saying: "I am the light of the world: he that followeth me shall not walk in darkness, but shall have the light of life."[z] The great lamps set up in the court as a feature of the joyful celebration just ended gave point to our Lord's avowal of Himself as the Light of the World. It was another proclamation of His divinity as God and the Son of God. The Pharisees challenged His testimony, declaring it of no worth because He bore record of Himself. Jesus admitted that He testified of Himself, but affirmed nevertheless that what He said was true, for He knew whereof He spoke, whence He came and whither He would go, while they spoke in ignorance. They thought, talked, and judged after the ways of men and the frailties of the flesh; He was not sitting in judgment, but should He choose to judge, then His judgment would be just, for He was guided by the Father who sent Him. Their law required the testimony of two witnesses for the legal determination of any question of fact;[aa] and Jesus cited Himself and His Father as witnesses in support of His affirmation. His opponents then asked with contemptuous or sarcastic intent, "Where is thy Father?" The reply was in lofty tone: "Ye neither know me, nor my Father: if ye had known me, ye should have known my Father also." Enraged at their own discomfiture, the Pharisees would have seized Him, but found themselves impotent. "No man laid hands on him; for his hour was not yet come."

THE TRUTH SHALL MAKE YOU FREE[bb]

Again addressing the mixed assemblage, which probably comprised Pharisees, scribes, rabbis, priests, Levites, and lay people,

[x] John 8:12–20.

[y] Note 6, end of chapter.

[z] John 8:12; compare 1:4, 5, 9; 3:19; 9:5; 12:35, 36, 46. See also D&C 6:21; 10:58, 70; 11:11; 14:9; 84:45,46; 88:6–13.

[aa] Deut. 17:6; 19:15; Num. 35:30; Matt. 18:16.

[bb] John 8:21–59.

Jesus repeated His former assertion that soon He would leave them, and that whither He went they could not follow; and added the fateful assurance that they would seek Him in vain and would die in their sins. His solemn portent was treated with light concern if not contempt. Some of them asked querulously, "Will he kill himself?" the implication being that in such case they surely would not follow Him; for according to their dogma, Gehenna was the place of suicides, and they, being of the chosen people, were bound for heaven not hell. The Lord's dignified rejoinder was: "Ye are from beneath; I am from above: ye are of this world; I am not of this world. I said therefore unto you, that ye shall die in your sins: for if ye believe not that I am he, ye shall die in your sins."

This reiteration of His distinctive supremacy brought forth the challenging question, "Who art thou?" Jesus replied, "Even the same that I said unto you from the beginning." The many matters on which He might have judged them He refrained from mentioning, but testified anew of the Father, saying: "He that sent me is true; and I speak to the world those things which I have heard of him." Explicit as His earlier explanations had been, the Jews in their gross prejudice "understood not that he spake to them of the Father." To His Father Jesus ascribed all honor and glory, and repeatedly declared Himself as sent to do the Father's will. "Then said Jesus unto them, When ye have lifted up the Son of man, then shall ye know that I am he, and that I do nothing of myself; but as my Father hath taught me, I speak these things. And he that sent me is with me: the Father hath not left me alone; for I do always those things that please him."

The evident earnestness and profound conviction with which Jesus spoke caused many of His hearers to believe on Him; and these He addressed with the promise that if they continued in that belief, and shaped their lives according to His word, they should be His disciples indeed. A further promise followed: "And ye shall know the truth, and the truth shall make you free." At these words, so rich in blessing, so full of comfort for the believing soul, the people were stirred to angry demonstrations; their Jewish temper was immediately ablaze. To promise them freedom was to imply that they were not already free. "We be Abraham's seed, and were never in bondage to any man: how sayest thou, Ye shall be made free?" In their unbridled fanaticism they had forgotten the bondage of Egypt, the captivity of Babylon, and were oblivious of their existing state of vassalage to Rome. To say that Israel had never been in bondage was not only to convict themselves of falsehood but to stultify themselves wretchedly.

Jesus made it clear that He had not referred to freedom in its physical or political sense alone, though to this conception their false disavowal had been directed; the liberty He proclaimed was spiritual liberty; the grievous bondage from which He would deliver them was the serfdom of sin. To their vaunted boast that they were free men, not slaves, He replied: "Verily, verily, I say unto you, Whosoever committeth sin is the servant of sin." As a sinner, every one of them was in slavery. A bond-servant, Jesus reminded them, was allowed in the master's house by sufferance only; it was not his inherent right to remain there; his owner could send him away at any time, and might even sell him to another; but a son of the family had of his own right a place in his father's home. Now, if the Son of God made them free they would be free indeed. Though they were of Abrahamic lineage in the flesh, they were no heirs of Abraham in spirit or works. Our Lord's mention of His Father as distinct from their father drew forth the angry reiteration, "Abraham is our father," to which Jesus replied: "If ye were Abraham's children, ye would do the works of Abraham. But now ye seek to kill me, a man that hath told you the truth, which I have heard of God: this did not Abraham. Ye do the deeds of your father." In their blind anger they apparently construed this to imply that though they were children of Abraham's household some other man than Abraham was their actual progenitor, or that they were not of unmixed Israelitish blood. "We be not born of fornication" they cried, "we have one Father, even God. Jesus said unto them, If God were your Father, ye would love me: for I proceeded forth and came from God; neither came I of myself, but he sent me."

They failed to understand because of their stubborn refusal to listen dispassionately. With forceful accusation Jesus told them whose children they actually were, as evinced by the hereditary traits manifest in their lives: "Ye are of your father the devil, and the lusts of your father ye will do. He was a murderer from the beginning, and abode not in the truth, because there is no truth in him. When he speaketh a lie, he speaketh of his own: for he is a liar, and the father of it.ᶜᶜ And because I tell you the truth, ye believe me not." He challenged them to find sin in Him; and then asked why, if He spake the truth, they so persistently refused to believe Him. Answering His own question, He told them that they were not of God and therefore they understood not the words of God. The Master was unimpeachable; His terse, cogent assertions were unanswerable. In impotent rage the discomfited Jews resorted to invective and calumny. "Say we not well that thou art a Samaritan, and hast a devil?" they shrieked. They had before called Him a Galilean; that appellative was but mildly depreciatory, and moreover was a truthful designation according to their knowledge; but the epithet "Samaritan" was inspired by hate,ᵈᵈ and by its application they meant to disown Him as a Jew.

The charge that He was a demoniac was but a repetition of earlier slanders. "Jesus answered, I have not a devil; but I honour my Father, and ye do dishonour me." Reverting to the eternal riches offered by His gospel, the Master said: "Verily, verily, I say unto you, If a man keep my saying, he shall never see death." This rendered them the more infuriate: "Now we know that thou hast a devil" they cried, and as evidence of what they professed to regard as His insanity, they cited the fact that great as were Abraham and the prophets they were dead, yet Jesus dared to say that all who kept His sayings should be exempt from death. Did He pretend to exalt Himself above Abraham and the prophets? "Whom makest thou thyself?" they demanded. The Lord's reply was a disclaimer of all self-aggrandizement; His honor was not of His own seeking, but was the gift of His Father, whom He knew; and were He to deny that He knew the Father He would be a liar like unto themselves. Touching the relationship between Himself and the great patriarch of their race, Jesus thus affirmed and emphasized His own supremacy: "Your father Abraham rejoiced to see my day: and he saw it, and was glad." Not only angered but puzzled, the Jews demanded further explanation. Construing the last declaration as applying to the mortal state only, they said: "Thou art not yet fifty years old, and hast thou seen Abraham?" Jesus answered, "Verily, verily, I say unto you, Before Abraham was, I am."

ᶜᶜ Compare Moses 4:4; 5:24; 2 Ne. 2:18; D&C 10:25; 93:25.
ᵈᵈ Pages 165–66 and 175–77.

This was an unequivocal and unambiguous declaration of our Lord's eternal Godship. By the awful title I AM He had made Himself known to Moses and thereafter was so known in Israel.[ee] As already shown, it is the equivalent of "Yahveh," or "Jahveh" now rendered "Jehovah," and signifies "The Self-existent One" "The Eternal" "The First and the Last."[ff] Jewish traditionalism forbade the utterance of the sacred Name; yet Jesus claimed it as His own. In an orgy of self-righteous indignation, the Jews seized upon the stones that lay in the unfinished courts, and would have crushed their Lord, but the hour of His death had not yet come, and unseen of them He passed through the crowd and departed from the temple.

His seniority to Abraham plainly referred to the status of each in the antemortal or preexistent state; Jesus was as literally the Firstborn in the spirit-world, as He was the Only Begotten in the flesh. Christ is as truly the Elder Brother of Abraham and Adam as of the last-born child of earth.[gg]

BODILY AND SPIRITUAL BLINDNESS—
SIGHT GIVEN TO A MAN ON THE SABBATH[hh]

At Jerusalem Jesus mercifully gave sight to a man who had been blind from his birth.[ii] The miracle is an instance of Sabbath-day healing, of more than ordinary interest because of its attendant incidents. It is recorded by John alone, and, as usual with that writer, his narrative is given with descriptive detail. Jesus and His disciples saw the sightless one upon the street. The poor man lived by begging. The disciples, eager to learn, asked: "Master, who did sin, this man, or his parents, that he was born blind?" The Lord's reply was: "Neither hath this man sinned, nor his parents: but that the works of God should be

---

[ee] Ex. 3:14; compare 6:3.

[ff] Compare Isa. 44:6; Rev. 1:4, 8; see also John 17:5, 24; Col. 1:17.

[gg] Page 13–14

[hh] John 9.

[ii] Whether this incident occurred in immediate sequence to the events last considered, or at a later time after the return of Jesus to Jerusalem following an unrecorded departure therefrom, is not stated in the scriptural record. The value of the lesson is not affected by its place in the catalog of our Lord's works.

made manifest in him." The disciples' question implied their belief in a state of moral agency and choice antedating mortality; else, how could they have thought of the man having sinned so as to bring upon himself congenital blindness? We are expressly told that he was born blind. That he might have been a sufferer from the sins of his parents was conceivable.[jj] The disciples evidently had been taught the great truth of an antemortal existence. It is further to be seen that they looked upon bodily affliction as the result of personal sin. Their generalization was too broad; for, while as shown by instances heretofore cited,[kk] individual wickedness may and does bring physical ills in its train, man is liable to err in his judgment as to the ultimate cause of affliction. The Lord's reply was sufficing; the man's blindness would be turned to account in bringing about a manifestation of divine power. As Jesus explained respecting His own ministry, it was necessary that He do the Father's work in the season appointed, for His time was short. With impressive pertinency as relating to the state of the man who had been in darkness all his days, our Lord repeated the affirmation before made in the temple, "I am the light of the world."

The outward ministration to the blind man was different from the usual course followed by Jesus. "He spat on the ground, and made clay of the spittle, and he anointed the eyes of the blind man with the clay"; and then directed him to go to the pool of Siloam and wash in its waters.[ll] The man went, washed, and came seeing. He was evidently a well-known character; many had seen him in his accustomed place begging alms, and the fact that he had been blind from birth was also of common knowledge. When, therefore, it was noised about that he could see, there was much excitement and comment. Some doubted that the man they questioned was the once sightless beggar; but he assured them of his identity, and told how he had been made to see. They brought the man to the Pharisees, who questioned him rigorously; and, having heard his account of the miracle, tried to undermine his faith by telling him that Jesus who had healed him could not be a man of God since He had done the deed on the Sabbath. Some of those who

jj Ex. 20:5; 34:7; Lev. 26:39; Num. 14:18; 1 Kgs. 21:29; compare Ezek. chap. 18.
kk Pages 185 and 197-99.
ll Note 3, end of chapter.

heard demurred to the Pharisaic deduction, and asked: "How can a man that is a sinner do such miracles?" The man was questioned as to his personal opinion of Jesus, and promptly answered: "He is a prophet." The man knew his Benefactor to be more than any ordinary being; as yet, however, he had no knowledge of Him as the Christ.

The inquisitorial Jews were afraid of the result of such a wondrous healing, in that the people would support Jesus whom the rulers were determined to destroy. They assumed it to be possible that the man had not been really blind; so they summoned his parents, who answered their interrogatories by affirming that he was their son, and they knew him to have been born blind; but as to how he had received sight, or through whose ministration, they refused to commit themselves, knowing the rulers had decreed that any one who confessed Jesus to be the Christ should be cast out from the community of the synagog, or, as we would say today, excommunicated from the Church. With pardonable astuteness the parents said of their son: "He is of age; ask him: he shall speak for himself."

Compelled to acknowledge, to themselves at least, that the fact and the manner of the man's restoration to sight were supported by irrefutable evidence, the crafty Jews called the man again, and insinuatingly said unto him: "Give God the praise: we know that this man is a sinner." He replied fearlessly, and with such pertinent logic as to completely offset their skill as cross-examiners: "Whether he be a sinner or no, I know not: one thing I know, that, whereas I was blind, now I see." He very properly declined to enter into a discussion with his learned questioners as to what constituted sin under their construction of the law; of what he was ignorant he declined to speak; but on one matter he was happily and gratefully certain, that whereas he had been blind, now he could see.

The Pharisaical inquisitors next tried to get the man to repeat his story of the means employed in the healing, probably with the subtle purpose of leading him into inconsistent or contradictory statements; but he replied with emphasis, and possibly with some show of impatience, "I have told you already, and ye did not hear:^mm wherefore would ye hear it again? will ye also be his disciples?" They retorted

---

^mm That is, "heed" or "believe."

with anger, and reviled the man; the ironical insinuation that they perchance wished to become disciples of Jesus was an insult they would not brook. "Thou art his disciple," said they, "but we are Moses' disciples. We know that God spake unto Moses: as for this fellow, we know not from whence he is." They were enraged that this unlettered mendicant should answer so boldly in their scholarly presence; but the man was more than a match for all of them. His rejoinder was maddening because it flouted their vaunted wisdom, and withal was unanswerable. "Why herein is a marvellous thing," said he, "that ye know not from whence he is, and yet he hath opened mine eyes. Now we know that God heareth not sinners: but if any man be a worshipper of God, and doeth his will, him he heareth. Since the world began was it not heard that any man opened the eyes of one that was born blind. If this man were not of God, he could do nothing."

For such an affront from a layman there was no precedent in all the lore of rabbis or scribes. "Thou wast altogether born in sins, and dost thou teach us?" was their denunciatory though weak and inadequate rejoinder. Unable to cope with the sometime sightless beggar in argument or demonstration, they could at least exercise their official authority, however unjustly, by excommunicating him; and this they promptly did. "Jesus heard that they had cast him out; and when he had found him, he said unto him, Dost thou believe on the Son of God? he answered and said, Who is he, Lord, that I might believe on him? And Jesus said unto him, Thou hast both seen him, and it is he that talketh with thee. And he said, Lord, I believe. And he worshipped him."

In commenting upon the matter Jesus was heard to say that one purpose of His coming into the world was "that they which see not might see; and that they which see might be made blind." Some of the Pharisees caught the remark, and asked in pride: "Are we blind also?" The Lord's reply was a condemnation: "If ye were blind, ye should have no sin: but now ye say, We see; therefore your sin remaineth."

SHEPHERD AND SHEEP-HERDER[nn]

"Verily, verily, I say unto you, He that entereth not by the door

[nn] John 10:1–21.

into the sheepfold, but climbeth up some other way, the same is a thief and a robber. But he that entereth in by the door is the shepherd of the sheep." With these words Jesus prefaced one of His most impressive discourses. The mention of shepherd and sheep must have brought to the minds of His hearers many of the oft-quoted passages from prophets and psalms.[oo] The figure is an effective one, and all the more so when we consider the circumstances under which it was used by the Master. Pastoral conditions prevailed in Palestine, and the dignity of the shepherd's vocation was very generally recognized. By specific prophecy a Shepherd had been promised to Israel. David, the king of whom all Israelites were proud, had been taken directly from the sheepfold, and had come with a shepherd's crook in his hand to the anointing that made him royal.

As the Teacher showed, a shepherd has free access to the sheep. When they are folded within the enclosure of safety, he enters at the gate; he neither climbs over nor creeps in.[pp] He, the owner of the sheep loves them; they know his voice and follow him as he leads from fold to pasture, for he goes before the flock; while the stranger, though he be the herder, they know not; he must needs drive, for he cannot lead. Continuing the allegory, which the recorder speaks of as a parable, Jesus designated Himself as the door to the sheepfold, and made plain that only through Him could the undershepherds rightly enter. True, there were some who sought by avoiding the portal and climbing over the fence to reach the folded flock; but these were robbers, trying to get at the sheep as prey; their selfish and malignant purpose was to kill and carry off.

Changing the figure, Christ proclaimed: "I am the good shepherd." He then further showed, and with eloquent exactness, the difference between a shepherd and a hireling herder. The one has personal interest in and love for his flock, and knows each sheep by name, the other knows them only as a flock, the value of which is gaged by number; to the hireling they are only as so many or so much. While the shepherd is ready to fight in defense of his own, and if necessary even imperil his

---

[oo] Note the promise of a Shepherd to Israel, Isa. 40:11; 49:9, 10; Ezek. 34:23; 37:24; compare Jer. 3:15; 23:4; Heb. 13:20; 1 Pet. 2:25; 5:4; Rev. 7:17. Read studiously Psalm 23.
[pp] Note 7, end of chapter.

life for his sheep, the hireling flees when the wolf approaches, leaving the way open for the ravening beast to scatter, rend, and kill.

Never has been written or spoken a stronger arraignment of false pastors, unauthorized teachers, self-seeking hirelings who teach for pelf and divine for dollars, deceivers who pose as shepherds yet avoid the door and climb over "some other way," prophets in the devil's employ, who to achieve their master's purpose, hesitate not to robe themselves in the garments of assumed sanctity, and appear in sheep's clothing, while inwardly they are ravening wolves.[qq]

With effective repetition Jesus continued: "I am the good shepherd, and know my sheep, and am known of mine. As the Father knoweth me, even so know I the Father: and I lay down my life for the sheep." For this cause was Jesus the Father's Beloved Son—that He was ready to lay down His life for the sake of the sheep. That the sacrifice He was soon to render was in fact voluntary, and not a forfeiture under compulsion, is solemnly affirmed in the Savior's words: "Therefore doth my Father love me, because I lay down my life, that I might take it again. No man taketh it from me, but I lay it down of myself. I have power to lay it down, and I have power to take it again. This commandment have I received of my Father." The certainty of His death and of His subsequent Resurrection are here reiterated. A natural effect of His immortal origin, as the earth-born Son of an immortal Sire, was that He was immune to death except as He surrendered thereto. The life of Jesus the Christ could not be taken save as He willed and allowed. The power to lay down His life was inherent in Himself, as was the power to take up His slain body in an immortalized state.[rr] These teachings caused further division among the Jews. Some pretended to dispose of the matter by voicing anew the foolish assumption that Jesus was but an insane demoniac, and that therefore His words were not worthy of attention. Others with consistency said "These are not the words of him that hath a devil. Can a devil open the eyes of the blind?" So it was that a few believed, many doubted though partly convinced, and some condemned.

[qq] Matt. 7:15; compare 24:4, 5, 11, 24; Mark 13:22; Rom. 16:17, 18; Eph. 5:6; Col. 2:8; 2 Pet. 2:1–3; 1 Jn. 4:1; Acts 20:29.

[rr] Pages 20–23 and 78–79.

As part of this profound discourse, Jesus said: "And other sheep I have, which are not of this fold: them also I must bring, and they shall hear my voice; and there shall be one fold, and one shepherd."[ss] The "other sheep" here referred to constituted the separated flock or remnant of the house of Joseph, who, six centuries prior to the birth of Christ, had been miraculously detached from the Jewish fold in Palestine, and had been taken beyond the great deep to the American continent. When to them the resurrected Christ appeared He thus spake: "And verily, I say unto you, that ye are they of whom I said, other sheep I have which are not of this fold; them also I must bring, and they shall hear my voice; and there shall be one fold, and one shepherd."[tt] The Jews had vaguely understood Christ's reference to other sheep as meaning in some obscure way, the Gentile nations; and because of their unbelief and consequent inability to rightly comprehend, Jesus had withheld any plainer exposition of His meaning, for so, He informed the Nephites, had the Father directed. "This much did the Father command me," He explained, "that I should tell unto them, That other sheep I have, which are not of this fold; them also I must bring, and they shall hear my voice; and there shall be one fold, and one shepherd." On the same occasion the Lord declared that there were yet other sheep, those of the Lost, or Ten, Tribes, to whom He was then about to go, and who would eventually be brought forth from their place of exile, and become part of the one blessed fold under the governance of the one supreme Shepherd and King.[uu]

NOTES TO CHAPTER 25

1. **The Feast of Tabernacles.**—In the order of yearly occurrence this was the third of the great festivals, the observance of which was among the national characteristics of the people of Israel; the others were the Passover, and the feast of weeks or Pentecost; at each of the three all the males in Israel were required to appear before the Lord in formal celebration of the respective feast (Ex. 23:17). The feast of Tabernacles was also known as the "feast of ingathering" (Ex. 23:16); it was both a memorial and a

---

[ss] John 10:16; compare as to "one fold and one shepherd," Ezek. 37:22; Isa. 11:13; Jer. 3:18; 50:4. See *Articles of Faith,* chapter 18.

[tt] 3 Ne. 15:21; read verses 12–24; see chapter 39 herein.

[uu] 3 Ne. 16:1–5.

current harvest celebration. In commemoration of their long journeying in the wilderness following their deliverance from Egypt, in the course of which journey they had to live in tents and improvised booths, the people of Israel were required to observe annually a festival lasting seven days, with an added day of holy convocation. During the week the people lived in booths, bowers, or tabernacles, made of the branches or "boughs of goodly trees" wattled with willows from the brook (Lev. 23:34–43; Num. 29:12–38; Deut. 16:13–15; 31:10–13). The festival lasted from the 15th to the 22nd of the month Tizri, the seventh in the Hebrew calendar, corresponding to parts of our September and October. It was made to follow soon after the annual Day of Atonement which was a time of penitence and affliction of the soul in sorrow for sin (Lev. 23:26–32). The altar sacrifices at the feast of Tabernacles exceeded those prescribed for other festivals, and comprised a daily offering of two rams, fourteen lambs, and a kid as a sin offering, and in addition a varying number of young bullocks, thirteen of which were sacrificed on the first day, twelve on the second, eleven on the third, and so on to the seventh day, on which seven were offered, making in all seventy bullocks (Num. 29:12–38). Rabbinism invested this number, seventy, and the graded diminution in the number of altar victims, with much symbolical significance not set forth in the law.

At the time of Christ, tradition had greatly embellished many of the prescribed observances. Thus the "boughs of goodly trees," more literally rendered "fruit" (Lev. 23:40), had come to be understood as the citron fruit; and this every orthodox Jew carried in one hand while, in the other he bore a leafy branch or a bunch of twigs, known as the "lulab," when he repaired to the temple for the morning sacrifice, and in the joyous processions of the day. The ceremonial carrying of water from the spring of Siloam to the altar of sacrifice was a prominent feature of the service. This water was mingled with wine at the altar and the mixture was poured upon the sacrificial offering. Many authorities hold that the bringing of water from the pool was omitted on the last or great day of the feast, and it is inferred that Jesus had in mind the circumstance of the omission when He cried: "If any man thirst, let him come unto me, and drink." At night, during the progress of the feast, great lamps were kept burning in the temple courts, and this incident Christ may have used as an objective illustration in his proclamation: "I am the light of the world."

For fuller account see any reliable and comprehensive Bible dictionary, and Josephus, Ant. viii, 4:1, xv, 3:3, etc. The following is an excerpt from Edersheim, *Life and Times of Jesus the Messiah*, vol. ii, pp. 158–160: "When the Temple-procession had reached the Pool of Siloam, the priest filled his golden pitcher from its waters. Then they went back to the Temple, so timing it that they should arrive just as they were laying the pieces of the sacrifice on the great altar of burnt-offering, towards the close of the ordinary morning-sacrifice service. A threefold blast of the priests' trumpets welcomed the arrival of the priest as he entered through the Water Gate, which obtained its name from this ceremony, and passed straight into the Court of the Priests. . . . Immediately after the 'pouring of the water,' the great 'Hallel,' consisting of Psalms 113 to 118 inclusive, was chanted antiphonally, or rather, with responses, to the accompaniment of the flute. . . . In further symbolism of this Feast, as pointing to the ingathering of the heathen nations, the public services closed with a procession round the altar by the priests. . . . But on 'the last, the Great Day of the Feast,' this procession of priests made the circuit of the altar, not only once, but seven times, as if they were again compassing, but now with prayer, the Gentile Jericho which barred their possession of the promised land."

2. The Test of Our Lord's Doctrine.—Any man may know for himself whether the doctrine of Christ is of God or not by simply doing the will of the Father (John 7:17). Surely it is a more convincing course than that of relying upon another's word. The writer was once approached by an incredulous student in college, who stated that he could not accept as true the published results of a certain chemical analysis, since the specified amounts of some of the ingredients were so infinitesimally small that he could not believe it possible to determine such minute quantities. The student was but a beginner in chemistry; and with his little knowledge he had undertaken to judge as to the possibilities of the science. He was told to do the things his instructor prescribed, and he should some day know for himself whether the results were true or false. In the senior year of his course, he received for laboratory analysis a portion of the very substance whose composition he had once questioned. With the skill attained by faithful devotion he successfully completed the analysis, and reported results similar to those, which in his inexperience he had thought impossible to obtain. He was manly enough to acknowledge as unfounded his earlier skepticism and rejoice in the fact that he had been able to demonstrate the truth for himself.

3. The Pool of Siloam.—"The names 'Shiloah' ('Shelah,' Neh. 3:15, 'Siloah' in authorized version) and 'Siloam' are the exact equivalent in Hebrew and Greek, respectively, of 'Silwan' in the modern Arabic name ('Ain Silwan') of the pool at the mouth of El-Wad. All the ancient references agree with this identification (compare Neh. 3:15; Josephus, *Wars of the Jews*, v, 4:1, 2; 6:1; 9:4; 12:2; ii, 16:2; vi, 7:2; 8:5). In spite of its modern designation as an 'ain' (spring), Siloam is not a spring, but is fed by a tunnel cut through the rock from the Gihon, or Virgin's Fountain."—L. B. Paton, in article, "Jerusalem," *Standard Bible Dictionary*.

4. Whence was the Messiah to Come?—Many stifled their inward promptings to a belief in Jesus as the Messiah, by the objection that all prophecies relating to His coming pointed to Bethlehem as His birthplace, and Jesus was of Galilee. Others rejected Him because they had been taught that no man was to know whence the Messiah came and they all knew Jesus came from Galilee. The seeming inconsistency is thus explained: The city of David, or Bethlehem in Judea, was beyond question the foreappointed place of the Messiah's birth; but the rabbis had erroneously taught that soon after birth the Christ Child would be caught away, and after a time would appear as a Man, and that no one would know whence or how He had returned. Geikie (2, p. 274), citing Lightfoot in part, thus states the popular criticism:

"'Do not the rabbis tell us' said some, 'that the Messiah will be born at Bethlehem, but that He will be snatched away by spirits and tempests soon after His birth, and that when He returns the second time no one will know from whence He has come?' But we know this man comes from Nazareth."

5. The Record Relating to the Woman Taken in Adultery.—Some modern critics claim that the verses John 7:53 and 8:1–11 inclusive are out of place as they appear in the authorized or King James version of the Bible, on the grounds that the incident therein recorded does not appear in certain of the ancient manuscript copies of John's Gospel, and that the style of the narrative is distinctive. In some manuscripts it appears at the end of the book. Other manuscripts contain the account as it appears in the English Bible. Canon Farrar pertinently asks (p. 404, note), why, if the incident is out of place or not of John's authorship, so many important manuscripts give place to it as we have it?

6. The Treasury, and Court of the Women.—"Part of the space within the inner courts was open to Israelites of both sexes, and was known distinctively as the Court of the Women. This was a colonnaded enclosure, and constituted the place of general assembly in the prescribed course of public worship. Chambers used for ceremonial purposes occupied the four corners of this court; and between these and the houses at the gates, were other buildings, of which one series constituted the Treasury wherein were set trumpet-shaped receptacles for gifts." (See Mark 12:41–44.)—*The House of the Lord*, pp. 57–58.

7. The Sheepfold.—Dummelow's *Commentary* says, on John 10:2: "To understand the imagery, it must be remembered that Eastern folds are large open enclosures, into which several flocks are driven at the approach of night. There is only one door, which a single shepherd guards, while the others go home to rest. In the morning the shepherds return, are recognized by the doorkeeper, call their flocks round them, and lead them forth to pasture."

CHAPTER 26

Our Lord's Ministry in Perea and Judea

When or under what attendant circumstances our Lord departed from Jerusalem after the Feast of Tabernacles, in the last autumn of His earthly life, we are not told. The writers of the synoptic Gospels have recorded numerous discourses, parables, and miracles, as incidents of a journey toward Jerusalem, in the course of which, Jesus, accompanied by the apostles, traversed parts of Samaria and Perea, and the outlying sections of Judea. We read of Christ's presence in Jerusalem at the Feast of Dedication,[a] between two and three months after the Feast of Tabernacles; and it is probable that some of the events now to be considered occurred during that interval.[b] That Jesus left Jerusalem soon after the Feast of Tabernacles is certain; whether He returned to Galilee, or went only into Perea, possibly with a short detour across the border into Samaria, is not conclusively stated. We shall here as heretofore devote our study primarily to His words and works, with but minor regard to place, time, or sequence.

As the time of His foreknown betrayal and Crucifixion drew near, "he stedfastly set his face to go to Jerusalem"[c] though, as we shall find, He turned northward on two occasions, once when He retired to the region of Bethabara, and again to Ephraim.[d]

[a] John 10:22.
[b] Note 1, end of chapter.
[c] Luke 9:51.
[d] John 10:40; 11:54.

HIS REJECTION IN SAMARIA[e]

Jesus sent messengers ahead to announce His coming and to prepare for His reception. In one of the Samaritan villages He was refused entertainment and a hearing "because his face was as though he would go to Jerusalem." Racial prejudice had superseded the obligations of hospitality. This repulse is in unfavorable contrast with the circumstances of His earlier visit among the Samaritans, when He had been received with gladness and entreated to remain, but on that occasion He was journeying not toward but farther from Jerusalem.[f]

The disrespect shown by the Samaritans was more than the disciples could endure without protest. James and John, those Sons of Thunder, were so resentful as to yearn for vengeance. Said they: "Lord, wilt thou that we command fire to come down from heaven, and consume them, even as Elias did?"[g] Jesus rebuked His uncharitable servants thus: "Ye know not what manner of spirit ye are of. For the Son of man is not come to destroy men's lives, but to save them." Repulsed in this village the little company went to another, as the Twelve had been instructed to do under like circumstances.[h] This was but one of the impressive lessons given to the apostles in the matter of tolerance, forbearance, charity, patience, and long-suffering.

Luke gives next place to the incident of three men who were desirous or willing to become disciples of Christ; one of them seems to have been discouraged at the prospect of hardship such as the ministry entailed; the others wished to be temporarily excused from service, one that he might attend the burial of his father, the other that he might first bid his loved ones farewell. This, or a similar occurrence, is recorded by Matthew in another connection, and has already received attention in these pages.[i]

THE SEVENTY CHARGED AND SENT

The supreme importance of our Lord's ministry, and the shortness of the time remaining to Him in the flesh, demanded more missionary

[e] Luke 9:51–56.
[f] John 4:4–42.
[g] Luke 9:54; compare 2 Kgs. 1:10, 12.
[h] Matt. 10:23.
[i] Luke 9:57–62.

laborers. The Twelve were to remain with Him to the end; every hour of possible instruction and training had to be utilized in their further preparation for the great responsibilities that would rest upon them after the Master's departure. As assistants in the ministry, He called and commissioned the Seventy, and straightway sent them forth,[j] "two and two before his face into every city and place, whither he himself would come." The need of their service was explained in the introduction to the impressive charge by which they were instructed in the duties of their calling. "Therefore said he unto them, The harvest truly is great, but the labourers are few: pray ye therefore the Lord of the harvest, that he would send forth labourers into his harvest."[k]

Many matters on which the Twelve had been instructed prior to their missionary tour were now repeated to the Seventy. They were told that they must expect unfriendly and even hostile treatment; their situation would be as that of lambs among wolves. They were to travel without purse or scrip, and thus necessarily to depend upon the provision that God would make through those to whom they came. As their mission was urgent, they were not to stop on the way to make or renew personal acquaintanceships. On entering a house they were to invoke peace upon it; if the household deserved the gift peace would rest therein, but otherwise the Lord's servants would feel that their invocation was void.[l] To any family by whom they were received they were to impart blessing—healing the afflicted, and proclaiming that the kingdom of God had come nigh unto that house. They were not to go from one house to another seeking better entertainment, nor should they expect or desire to be feasted, but they should accept what was offered, eating that which was set before them, thus sharing with the family. If rejected in any city, they were to depart therefrom, leaving, however, their solemn testimony that the city had turned away from the kingdom of God, which had been brought to its doors, and attesting the same by ridding themselves of the dust of

---

[j] Luke 10:1–12.

[k] Compare Matt. 9:37, 38; see also John 4:35.

[l] Edersheim (vol. 2, p. 138) says: "The expression 'if the son of peace be there' is a Hebraism, equivalent to 'if the house be worthy' (compare Matt. 10:13) and refers to the character of the head of the house and the tone of the household."

that place.[m] It was not for them to pronounce anathema or curse, but the Lord assured them that such a city would bring upon itself a fate worse than the doom of Sodom.[n] He reminded them that they were His servants, and therefore whoever heard or refused to hear them would be judged as having so treated Him.

They were not restrained, as the Twelve had been, from entering Samaritan towns or the lands of the Gentiles. This difference is consistent with the changed conditions, for now the prospective itinerary of Jesus would take Him into non-Jewish territory, where His fame had already spread; and furthermore, His plan provided for an extension of the gospel propaganda, which was to be ultimately world-wide. The narrow Jewish prejudice against Gentiles in general and Samaritans in particular was to be discountenanced; and proof of this intent could not be better given than by sending authorized ministers among those peoples. We must keep in mind the progressiveness of the Lord's work. At first the field of gospel preaching was confined to the land of Israel,[o] but the beginning of its extension was inaugurated during our Lord's life, and was expressly enjoined upon the apostles after His Resurrection.[p] Duly instructed, the Seventy set out upon their mission.[q]

Mention of the condemnation that would follow willful rejection of the authorized servants of God aroused in our Lord's mind sad memories of the repulses He had suffered, and of the many unrepentant souls, in the cities wherein He had accomplished so many mighty works. In profound sorrow He predicted the woes then impending over Chorazin, Bethsaida, and Capernaum.[r]

m Compare Matt. 10:14.

n Compare the charge given the Seventy with that of the Twelve, Matt. 10:5–42; Mark 6:7–11; Luke 9:1–5.

o Matt. 10:5, 6; 15:24.

p Matt. 28:19; Mark 16:15.

q D&C 107:25; 124:137–140; see also *Articles of Faith,* pp. 207, 211. The special office of the Seventy has been reestablished in the restored Church; and in this, the last dispensation, many quorums of Seventy are maintained for the work of the ministry. The office of the Seventy is one belonging to the Higher or Melchizedek Priesthood.

r Luke 10:13–15; compare Matt. 11:20–24.

THE SEVENTY RETURN

Considerable time may have elapsed, weeks or possibly months, between the departure of the Seventy and their return. We are not told when or where they rejoined the Master; but this we know, that the authority and power of Christ had been abundantly manifest in their ministry; and that they had rejoiced in the realization. "Lord," said they, "even the devils are subject unto us through thy name."[s] This testimony was followed by the Lord's solemn statement: "I beheld Satan as lightning fall from heaven." This was said with reference to the expulsion of the rebellious son of the morning, after his defeat by Michael and the heavenly hosts.[t] Commending the Seventy for their faithful labors, the Lord gave them assurance of further power, on the implied condition of their continued worthiness: "I give unto you power to tread on serpents and scorpions, and over all the power of the enemy: and nothing shall by any means hurt you."[u] The promise that they should tread on serpents and scorpions included immunity from injury by venomous creatures if encountered in the path of duty [v] and power to prevail over the wicked spirits that serve the devil, who is elsewhere expressly called the serpent.[w] Great as was the power and authority thus imparted, these disciples were told not to rejoice in such, nor primarily in the fact that evil spirits were subject unto them, but rather because they were accepted of the Lord, and that their names were written in heaven.[x]

The righteous joy of His servants and His contemplation of their faithfulness caused Jesus to rejoice. His happiness found its most appropriate expression in prayer, and thus He prayed: "I thank thee, O Father, Lord of heaven and earth, that thou hast hid these things from the wise and prudent, and hast revealed them unto babes: even so, Father; for so it seemed good in thy sight." Compared with the learned men of the time, such as the rabbis and scribes, whose knowledge

---

[s] Luke 10:17.

[t] Rev. 9:1; 12:8, 9.

[u] Luke 10:19; read verses 20–24.

[v] Compare Mark 16:18; Acts 28:5.

[w] Rev. 12:9; 20:2; compare Gen. 3:1–4, 14, 15.

[x] Compare Rev. 13:8; 20:12; 21;27.

served but to harden their hearts against the truth, these devoted servants were as babes in humility, trust, and faith. Such children were and are among the nobles of the kingdom. As in the hours of darkest sorrow, so in this moment of righteous exultation over the faithfulness of His followers, Jesus communed with the Father, to do whose will was His sole purpose.

Our Lord's joy on this occasion is comparable to that which He experienced when Peter had burst forth with the confession of his soul: "Thou art the Christ, the Son of the living God." In solemn discourse Jesus said: "All things are delivered to me of my Father: and no man knoweth who the Son is, but the Father; and who the Father is, but the Son, and he to whom the Son will reveal him." Then in more intimate communion with the disciples He added: "Blessed are the eyes which see the things that ye see: For I tell you, that many prophets and kings have desired to see those things which ye see, and have not seen them; and to hear those things which ye hear, and have not heard them."

WHO IS MY NEIGHBOR?

We have seen that the Pharisees and their kind were constantly on the alert to annoy and if possible disconcert Jesus on questions of law and doctrine, and to provoke Him to some overt utterance or deed.[y] It may be such an attempt that is recorded by Luke in immediate sequence to his account of the joyous return of the Seventy,[z] for he tells us that the "certain lawyer," of whom he speaks, put a question to tempt Jesus. Viewing the questioner's motive with all possible charity, for the basal meaning of the verb which appears in our version of the Bible as "to tempt" is that of putting to test or trial and not necessarily and solely to allure into evil,[aa] though the element of entrapping or ensnaring is connoted, we may assume that he wished to test the knowledge and wisdom of the famous Teacher, probably for the purpose of embarrassing Him. Certainly his purpose was not that of sincere search for truth.

[y] Compare Mark 12:13; see also Luke 11:53, 54.
[z] Luke 10:25–37.
[aa] Compare Gen. 22:1.

This lawyer, standing up among the people who had gathered to hear Jesus, asked: "Master, what shall I do to inherit eternal life?"[bb] Jesus replied by a counter question, in which was plainly intimated that if this man, who was professedly learned in the law, had read and studied properly, he should know without asking what he ought to do. "What is written in the law? how readest thou?" The man replied with an admirable summary of the commandments: "Thou shalt love the Lord thy God with all thy heart, and with all thy soul, and with all thy strength, and with all thy mind; and thy neighbour as thyself."[cc] The answer was approved. "This do, and thou shalt live" said Jesus. These simple words conveyed a rebuke, as the lawyer must have realized; they indicated the contrast between knowing and doing. Having thus failed in his plan to confound the Master, and probably realizing that he, a lawyer, had made no creditable display of his erudition by asking so simple a question and then answering it himself, he tamely sought to justify himself by inquiring further: "And who is my neighbour?" We may well be grateful for the lawyer's question; for it served to draw from the Master's inexhaustible store of wisdom one of His most appreciated parables.

The story is known as the *Parable of the Good Samaritan*; it runs as follows:

"A certain man went down from Jerusalem to Jericho, and fell among thieves, which stripped him of his raiment, and wounded him, and departed, leaving him half dead. And by chance there came down a certain priest that way: and when he saw him, he passed by on the other side. And likewise a Levite, when he was at the place, came and looked on him, and passed by on the other side. But a certain Samaritan, as he journeyed, came where he was: and when he saw him, he had compassion on him, and went to him, and bound up his wounds, pouring in oil and wine, and set him on his own beast, and brought him to an inn, and took care of him. And on the morrow when he departed, he took out two pence, and gave them to the host, and said unto him, Take care of him; and whatsoever thou spendest more, when I come again, I will repay thee."

[bb] Compare Matt. 19:16; Mark 10:17; Luke 18:18.

[cc] Luke 10:27; compare Deut. 6:5, and Lev. 19:18; see also Matt. 22:35–40.

Then of the lawyer Jesus asked: "Which now of these three, thinkest thou, was neighbour unto him that fell among the thieves? And he said, He that shewed mercy on him. Then said Jesus unto him, Go, and do thou likewise."[dd]

Whatever of motive there may have been in the lawyer's query, "Who is my neighbour?" aside from that of self-justification and a desire to retreat in the best form possible from an embarrassing situation, we may conceive to lie in the wish to find a limitation in the application of the law, beyond which he would not be bound to go. If he had to love his neighbors as he loved himself, he wanted to have as few neighbors as possible. His desire may have been somewhat akin to that of Peter, who was eager to learn just how many times he was required to forgive an offending brother.[ee]

The parable with which our Lord replied to the lawyer's question is rich in interest as a story alone, and particularly so as an embodiment of precious lessons. It was withal so true to existing conditions, that, like the story of the sower who went forth to sow, and other parables given by the Lord Jesus, it may be true history as well as parable. The road between Jerusalem and Jericho was known to be infested by highway robbers; indeed a section of the thoroughfare was called the Red Path or Bloody Way because of the frequent atrocities committed thereon. Jericho was prominent as a residence place for priests and Levites. A priest, who, out of respect to his office, if for none other cause, should have been willing and prompt in acts of mercy, caught sight of the wounded traveler and passed by on the far side of the road. A Levite followed; he paused to look, then passed on. These ought to have remembered the specified requirement of the law—that if one saw an ass or an ox fall down by the way, he should not hide himself, but should surely help the owner to lift the creature up again.[ff] If such was their duty toward a brother's beast, much greater was their obligation when a brother himself was in so extreme a plight.

Doubtless priest as well as Levite salved his conscience with ample excuse for his inhumane conduct; he may have been in a hurry, or was

dd Luke 10:30–37.

ee Matt. 18:21, 22; compare Luke 17:4.

ff Deut. 22:4; compare Ex. 23:5.

fearful, perhaps, that the robbers would return and make him also a victim of their outrage. Excuses are easy to find; they spring up as readily and plentifully as weeds by the wayside. When the Samaritan came along and saw the wretched state of the wounded man, he had no excuse for he wanted none. Having done what he could by way of emergency treatment as recognized in the medical practice of the day, he placed the injured one upon his own beast, probably a mule or an ass, and took him to the nearest inn, where he tended him personally and made arrangements for his further care. The essential difference between the Samaritan and the others was that the one had a compassionate heart, while they were unloving and selfish. Though not definitely stated, the victim of the robbers was almost certainly a Jew; the point of the parable requires it to be so. That the merciful one was a Samaritan, showed that the people called heretic and despised by the Jews could excel in good works. To a Jew, none but Jews were neighbors. We are not justified in regarding priest, Levite, or Samaritan as the type of his class; doubtless there were many kind and charitable Jews, and many heartless Samaritans; but the Master's lesson was admirably illustrated by the characters in the parable; and the words of His application were pungent in their simplicity and appropriateness.

MARTHA AND MARY[gg]

On one of His visits to Bethany, a small town about two miles from Jerusalem, Jesus was received at the home where dwelt two sisters, Martha and Mary. Martha was housekeeper, and therefore she assumed responsibility for the proper treatment of the distinguished Guest. While she busied herself with preparations and "was cumbered about much serving," well intended for the comfort and entertainment of Jesus, Mary sat at the Master's feet, listening with reverent attention to His words. Martha grew fretful in her bustling anxiety, and came in, saying: "Lord, dost thou not care that my sister hath left me to serve alone? bid her therefore that she help me." She was talking to Jesus but really at Mary. For the moment she had lost her calmness in undue worry over incidental details. It is reasonable to infer that Jesus was on terms of familiarity in the

[gg] Luke 10:38–42. Note 2, end of chapter.

household, else the good woman would scarcely have appealed to Him in a little matter of domestic concern. He replied to her complaining words with marked tenderness: "Martha, Martha, thou art careful and troubled about many things: but one thing is needful: and Mary hath chosen that good part, which shall not be taken away from her."

There was no reproof of Martha's desire to provide well; nor any sanction of possible neglect on Mary's part. We must suppose that Mary had been a willing helper before the Master's arrival; but now that He had come, she chose to remain with Him. Had she been culpably neglectful of her duty, Jesus would not have commended her course. He desired not well-served meals and material comforts only, but the company of the sisters, and above all their receptive attention to what He had to say. He had more to give them than they could possibly provide for Him. Jesus loved the two sisters and their brother as well.[hh] Both these women were devoted to Jesus, and each expressed herself in her own way. Martha was of a practical turn, concerned in material service; she was by nature hospitable and self-denying. Mary, contemplative and more spiritually inclined, showed her devotion through the service of companionship and appreciation.[ii]

By inattention to household duties, the little touches that make or mar the family peace, many a woman has reduced her home to a comfortless house; and many another has eliminated the essential elements of home by her self-assumed and persistent drudgery, in which she denies to her dear ones the cheer of her loving companionship. One-sided service, however devoted, may become neglect. There is a time for labor inside the home as in the open; in every family time should be found for cultivating that better part, that one thing needful—true, spiritual development.

ASK, AND IT SHALL BE GIVEN YOU[jj]

"And it came to pass, that, as he was praying in a certain place, when he ceased, one of his disciples said unto him, Lord, teach us to pray." Our Lord's example and the spirit of prayer manifest in His

[hh] John 11:5.

[ii] Compare John 12:2, 3.

[jj] Luke 11:1–13.

daily life moved the disciples to ask for instruction as to how they should pray. No form of private prayer was given in the law, but formal prayers had been prescribed by the Jewish authorities, and John the Baptist had instructed his followers in the mode or manner of prayer. Responding to the disciples' request, Jesus repeated that brief epitome of soulful adoration and supplication which we call the Lord's Prayer. This He had before given in connection with the Sermon on the Mount.[kk] On this occasion of its repetition, the Lord supplemented the prayer by explaining the imperative necessity of earnestness and enduring persistency in praying.

The lesson was made plain by the *Parable of the Friend at Midnight:*

"And he said unto them, Which of you shall have a friend, and shall go unto him at midnight, and say unto him, Friend, lend me three loaves; For a friend of mine in his journey is come to me, and I have nothing to set before him? And he from within shall answer and say, Trouble me not: the door is now shut, and my children are with me in bed; I cannot rise and give thee. I say unto you, Though he will not rise and give him, because he is his friend, yet because of his importunity he will rise and give him as many as he needeth."

The man to whose home a friend had come at midnight could not let his belated and weary guest go hungry, yet there was no bread in the house. He made his visitor's wants his own, and pleaded at his neighbor's door as though asking for himself. The neighbor was loath to leave his comfortable bed and disturb his household to accommodate another; but, finding that the man at the door was importunate, he at last arose and gave him what he asked, so as to get rid of him and be able to sleep in peace. The Master added by way of comment and instruction: *Ask, and it shall be given you; seek, and ye shall find; knock, and it shall be opened unto you.*"

The hospitable man in the parable had refused to be repulsed; he kept on knocking until the door was opened; and as a result received what he wanted, found what he had set out to obtain. The parable is regarded by some as a difficult one to apply, since it deals with the selfish and comfort-loving element of human nature, and apparently

[kk] Pages 225–29.

uses this to symbolize God's deliberate delay. The explanation, however, is clear when the context is duly considered. The Lord's lesson was, that if man, with all his selfishness and disinclination to give, will nevertheless grant what his neighbor with proper purpose asks and continues to ask in spite of objection and temporary refusal, with assured certainty will God grant what is persistently asked in faith and with righteous intent. No parallelism lies between man's selfish refusal and God's wise and beneficent waiting. There must be a consciousness of real need for prayer, and real trust in God, to make prayer effective; and in mercy the Father sometimes delays the granting that the asking may be more fervent. But in the words of Jesus: "If ye then, being evil, know how to give good gifts unto your children: how much more shall your heavenly Father give the Holy Spirit to them that ask him?"

Sometime later Jesus spake another parable, the moral of which is so closely akin to that of the story of the midnight visitor, as to suggest the study of the later lesson here. It is known as the *Parable of the Unjust Judge*, or of the *Importunate Widow*:

"There was in a city a judge, which feared not God, neither regarded man: And there was a widow in that city; and she came unto him, saying, Avenge me of mine adversary. And he would not for a while: but afterward he said within himself, Though I fear not God, nor regard man; Yet because this widow troubleth me, I will avenge her, lest by her continual coming she weary me."[ll]

The judge was of wicked character; he denied justice to the widow, who could obtain redress from none other. He was moved to action by the desire to escape the woman's importunity. Let us beware of the error of comparing his selfish action with the ways of God. Jesus did not indicate that as the wicked judge finally yielded to supplication so would God do; but He pointed out that if even such a being as this judge, who "feared not God, neither regarded man," would at last hear and grant the widow's plea, no one should doubt that God, the Just and Merciful, will hear and answer. The judge's obduracy, though wholly wicked on his part, may have been ultimately

---

[ll] Luke 18:2–5; read verses 1, and 6–8. See also D&C 101:81–94.

advantageous to the widow. Had she easily obtained redress she might have become again unwary, and perchance a worse adversary than the first might have oppressed her. The Lord's purpose in giving the parable is specifically stated; it was "to this end, that men ought always to pray, and not to faint."mm

CRITICISM ON PHARISEES AND LAWYERSnn

Varied comment as to the source of our Lord's superhuman powers was aroused afresh by His merciful act of expelling a demon from a man, who, in consequence of this evil possession had been dumb. The old Pharisaic theory, that He cast out devils through the power of "Beelzebub, the chief of the devils," was revived. The utter foolishness of such a conception was demonstrated, as it had been on an earlier occasion to which we have given attention.oo The spiritual darkness, in which evil men grope for signs, the disappointment and condemnation that await them, and other precious precepts, Jesus elucidated in further discourse.pp

Then, by invitation He went to the house of a certain Pharisee to dine. Other Pharisees, as also lawyers and scribes, were present. Jesus intentionally omitted the ceremonial washing of hands, which all others in the company scrupulously performed before taking their places at table. The omission caused a murmur of disapproval if not an open expression of fault-finding. Jesus utilized the occasion by voicing a pungent criticism of Pharisaic externalism, which He likened to the cleansing of cups and platters on the outside, while the inside is left filthy. "Fools" said He, "did not he that made that which is without make that which is within also?" In another form we may ask, Did not God who established the outward observances of the law, ordain the inward and spiritual requirements of the gospel also? In response to a question by one of the lawyers, Jesus included them in His sweeping reproof. Pharisees and scribes resented the censure to which they had been subjected, and "began to urge him vehemently, and to

mm Luke 18:1; compare 21:36; Rom. 12:12; Eph. 6:18; Col. 4:2; 1 Thes. 5:17.

nn Luke 11:37–54.

oo Luke 11:14–28.

pp Luke 11:29–36.

provoke him to speak of many things: laying wait for him, and seeking to catch something out of his mouth, that they might accuse him." As our Lord's recorded utterances on this occasion appear also in His final denunciation of Pharisaism, later delivered at the temple, we may well defer further consideration of the matter until we take up in order that notable occurrence.[qq]

THE DISCIPLES ADMONISHED AND ENCOURAGED[rr]

Popular interest in our Lord's movements was strong in the region beyond Jordan, as it had been in Galilee. We read of Him surrounded by "an innumerable multitude of people, insomuch that they trode one upon another." Addressing the multitude, and more particularly His disciples, Jesus warned them of the leaven of the Pharisees, which He characterized as hypocrisy.[ss] The recent scene at the table of a Pharisee gave special significance to the warning. Some of the precepts recorded in connection with His Galilean ministry were here repeated, and particular stress was laid upon the superiority of the soul to the body, and of eternal life as contrasted with the brief duration of mortal existence.

One man in the company, intent on selfish interests and unable to see beyond the material affairs of life, spoke out saying, "Master, speak to my brother, that he divide the inheritance with me." Jesus promptly refused to act as mediator or judge in the matter. "Man, who made me a judge or a divider over you?" was the Master's rejoinder. The wisdom underlying His refusal to interfere is apparent. As in the case of the guilty woman who had been brought before Him for judgment,[tt] so in this instance, He refrained from intervention in matters of legal administration. An opposite course would have probably involved Him in useless disputation, and might have given color to a complaint that He was arrogating to Himself the functions of the legally established tribunals. The man's appeal, however, was made the nucleus of valuable instruction; his clamor for a share in the family inheritance caused Jesus to say: "Take heed, and beware of

[qq] Matt. 23; see chapter 31 herein.
[rr] Luke 12:1–12.
[ss] Page 338.
[tt] Page 381–82.

covetousness: for a man's life consisteth not in the abundance of the things which he possesseth."

This combined admonition and profound statement of truth was emphasized by the *Parable of the Foolish Rich Man*. Thus runs the story:

"The ground of a certain rich man brought forth plentifully: And he thought within himself, saying, What shall I do, because I have no room where to bestow my fruits? And he said, This will I do: I will pull down my barns, and build greater; and there will I bestow all my fruits and my goods. And I will say to my soul, Soul, thou hast much goods laid up for many years; take thine ease, eat, drink, and be merry. But God said unto him, Thou fool, this night thy soul shall be required of thee: then whose shall those things be, which thou hast provided? So is he that layeth up treasure for himself, and is not rich toward God."[uu]

The man's abundance had been accumulated through labor and thrift; neglected or poorly-tilled fields do not yield plentifully. He is not represented as one in possession of wealth not rightfully his own. His plans for the proper care of his fruits and goods were not of themselves evil, though he might have considered better ways of distributing his surplus, as for the relief of the needy. His sin was twofold; first, he regarded his great store chiefly as the means of securing personal ease and sensuous indulgence; secondly, in his material prosperity he failed to acknowledge God, and even counted the years as his own. In the hour of his selfish jubilation he was smitten. Whether the voice of God came to him as a fearsome presentiment of impending death, or by angel messenger, or how otherwise, we are not informed; but the voice spoke his doom: "Thou fool, this night thy soul shall be required of thee."[vv] He had used his time and his powers of body and mind to sow, reap and garner—all for himself. And what came of it all? Whose should be the wealth, to amass which he had jeopardized his soul? Had he been other than a fool he might have realized as Solomon had done,

---

[uu] Luke 12:14–21.

[vv] Compare the fate that overtook Nebuchadnezzar, while the words of boastful pride were yet in his mouth (Dan. 4:24–33); and that of Belshazzar, before whose eyes appeared the hand of destiny in the midst of his riotous feast; in that night was the king's soul required of him. (Dan. 5.)

the vanity of hoarding wealth for another, and he perhaps of uncertain character, to possess.ᵂᵂ

Turning to the disciples Jesus reiterated some of the glorious truths He had uttered when preaching on the mount,ˣˣ and pointed to the birds of the air, the lilies and grass of the field, as examples of the Father's watchful care; He admonished His hearers to seek the kingdom of God, and, doing so, they should find all needful things added. "Fear not, little flock," He added in tone of affectionate and paternal regard, "for it is your Father's good pleasure to give you the kingdom." They were urged to store their wealth in bags that wax not old,ʸʸ containers suited to the heavenly treasure which, unlike the goods of the foolish rich man, shall not be left behind when the soul is summoned. The man whose treasure is of earth leaves it all at death; he whose wealth is in heaven goes to his own, and death is but the portal to his treasury.

The disciples were admonished to be ever ready, waiting as servants wait at night with lights burning, for their master's return; and, inasmuch as the lord of the household comes at his will, in the early or later watches, if when he comes he finds his faithful servants ready to open immediately to his knock he will honor them as they deserve. So is the Son of Man to come, perhaps when least expected. To a question interjected by Peter as to whether "this parable" was spoken to the Twelve only or to all, Jesus made no direct reply; the answer, however, was conveyed in the continuation of the allegory of contrast between faithful and wicked servants.ᶻᶻ "Who then is that faithful and wise steward, whom his lord shall make ruler over his household, to give them their portion of meat in due season?" The faithful steward is a good type of the apostles, individually or as a body. As stewards they were charged with the care of the other servants, and of the household; and as to them more had been given than to the others, so of them more would be required; and they would be held to strict accountability for their stewardship.

ᵂᵂ Eccl. 2:18, 19; compare succeeding verses; see also Ps. 39:6; 49:6–20; Job 27:16,17.

ˣˣ Luke 12:22–31; compare Matt. 6:25–34.

ʸʸ Compare Matt. 6:20.

ᶻᶻ Luke 12:35–48.

The Lord then referred feelingly to His own mission, and especially to the dreadful experiences then soon to befall Him, saying: "I have a baptism to be baptized with; and how am I straitened till it be accomplished!" He told again of the strife and dissension that would follow the preaching of His gospel, and dwelt upon the significance of then current events. To those who, ever ready to interpret the signs of the weather yet remained willfully blind to the important developments of the times, He applied the caustic epithet, hypocrites![aaa]

"EXCEPT YE REPENT YE SHALL ALL LIKEWISE PERISH"[bbb]

Some of the people who had been listening to our Lord's discourse reported to Him the circumstances of a tragical event that had taken place, probably but a short time before, inside the temple walls. A number of Galileans had been slain by Roman soldiers, at the base of the altar, so that their blood had mingled with that of the sacrificial victims. It is probable that the slaughter of these Galileans was incident to some violent demonstration of Jewish resentment against Roman authority, which the procurator, Pilate, construed as an incipient insurrection, to be promptly and forcibly quelled. Such outbursts were not uncommon, and the Roman tower or fortress of Antonia had been erected in a commanding position overlooking the temple grounds, and connected therewith by a wide flight of steps, so that soldiers could have ready access to the enclosure at the first indication of turmoil. The purpose of the informants who brought this matter to the attention of Jesus is not stated; but we find probability in the thought that His reference to the signs of the times had reminded them of the tragedy, and that they were inclined to speculate as to the deeper significance of the occurrence. Some may have wondered as to whether the fate of the Galilean victims had befallen them as a merited retribution. Anyway, to some such conception as this Jesus directed His reply. By question and answer He assured them that those who had so been slain were not to be considered as sinners above other Galileans; "But," said He, "except ye repent, ye shall all likewise perish."

[aaa] Luke 12:49–57. Compare Matt. 10:34–37.
[bbb] Luke 13:1–5.

Then, referring on His own initiative to another catastrophe, He cited the instance of eighteen persons who had been killed by the fall of a tower at Siloam, and affirmed that these were not to be counted greater sinners than other Jerusalemites. "But," came the reiteration, "except ye repent, ye shall all likewise perish." There were perhaps some who believed that the men upon whom the tower had fallen had deserved their fate; and this conception is the more probable if the generally accepted assumption be correct, that the calamity came upon the men while they were engaged under Roman employ in work on the aqueduct, for the construction of which Pilate had used the "corban" or sacred treasure, given by vow to the temple.[ccc]

It is not man's prerogative to pass upon the purposes and designs of God, nor to judge by human reason alone that this person or that suffers disaster as a direct result of individual sin.[ddd] Nevertheless men have ever been prone to so judge. There are many inheritors of the spirit of Job's friends, who assumed his guilt as certain because of the great misfortunes and sufferings that had come upon him.[eee] Even while Jesus spake, calamity dark and dire was impending over temple, city and nation; and unless the people would repent and accept the Messiah then in their midst, the decree of destruction would be carried to its dread fulfilment. Hence, as Jesus said, except the people repented they should perish. The imperative need of reformation was illustrated by the *Parable of the Barren Fig Tree.*

"A certain man had a fig tree planted in his vineyard; and he came and sought fruit thereon, and found none. Then said he unto the dresser of his vineyard, Behold, these three years I come seeking fruit on this fig tree, and find none: cut it down; why cumbereth it the ground? And he answering said unto him, Lord, let it alone this year also, till I shall dig about it, and dung it: And if it bear fruit, well: and if not, then after that thou shalt cut it down."[fff]

In Jewish literature, particularly in rabbinical lore, the fig tree is of frequent mention as a symbol of the nation. The warning conveyed in

[ccc] Josephus, *Wars,* ii, 9:4.
[ddd] Compare John 9:2, 3.
[eee] Job 4:7; 8:2–14, 20; 22:5.
[fff] Luke 13:6–9.

the parable is plain; the element of possible escape is no less evident. If the fig tree represents the covenant people, then the vineyard is naturally the world at large, and the dresser of the vineyard is the Son of God, who by personal ministry and solicitous care makes intercession for the barren tree, in the hope that it may yet bear fruit. The parable is of universal application; but so far as it had special bearing upon the Jewish "fig tree" of that time, it was attended by an awful sequel. The Baptist had cried out in warning that the ax was even then in readiness, and every unfruitful tree would be hewn down.^{ggg}

A WOMAN HEALED ON THE SABBATH ^{hhh}

On a certain Sabbath Jesus was teaching in a synagog, of what place we are not told, though it was probably in one of the towns of Perea. There was present a woman who for eighteen years had been suffering from an infirmity that had so drawn and atrophied the muscles as to bend her body so that she could in no wise straighten herself. Jesus called her to Him, and without waiting for petition or request, said simply, "Woman, thou art loosed from thine infirmity." These words He accompanied by the laying-on of hands, a feature of His healing ministrations not always performed. She was healed forthwith and stood erect; and, acknowledging the source of the power by which she had been released from her bonds, glorified God in a fervent prayer of thanksgiving. Doubtless many of the beholders rejoiced with her; but there was one whose soul was stirred by indignation only; and he, the ruler of the synagog. Instead of addressing himself to Jesus, of whose power he may have been afraid, he vented his ill feeling upon the people, by telling them there were six days in which men ought to work, and that on those days they who wished to be healed should come, but not on the Sabbath. The rebuke was ostensibly directed to the people, especially to the woman who had received the blessing, but in reality against Jesus; for if there were any element of work in the healing it had been done by Him, not by the woman nor by others. Upon the ruler of the synagog the Lord turned with direct address: "Thou hypocrite, doth not each one of you on

^{ggg} Luke 3:9.
^{hhh} Luke 13:11–17.

the sabbath loose his ox or his ass from the stall, and lead him away to watering? And ought not this woman, being a daughter of Abraham, whom Satan hath bound, lo, these eighteen years, be loosed from this bond on the sabbath day?"

It may be inferred that the woman's affliction had been more deeply seated than in the muscles; for Luke who was himself a physician ⁱⁱⁱ tells us she "had a spirit of infirmity," and records the significant words of the Lord to the effect that Satan had held her bound for eighteen years. But whatever her ailment, whether wholly physical or in part mental and spiritual, she was freed from her bonds. Again was the Christ triumphant; His adversaries were shamed into silence, while the believers rejoiced. The rebuke to the ruler of the synagog was followed by a brief discourse in which Jesus gave to these people some of the teachings before delivered in Galilee; these included the parables of the mustard seed and the leaven.^{jjj}

WILL MANY OR FEW BE SAVED?^{kkk}

Continuing His journey toward Jerusalem, Jesus taught in many of the cities and towns of Perea. His coming had probably been announced by the Seventy, who had been sent to prepare the people for His ministry. One of those who had been impressed by His doctrines submitted this question: "Lord, are there few that be saved?" Jesus replied: "Strive to enter in at the strait gate: for many, I say unto you, will seek to enter in, and shall not be able."^{lll} The counsel was enlarged upon to show that neglect or procrastination in obeying the requirements for salvation may result in the soul's loss. When the door is shut in judgment many will come knocking, and some will plead that they had known the Lord, having eaten and drunk in His company, and that He had taught upon their streets; but to them who had failed to accept the truth when offered the Lord shall say: "I tell you, I know you not whence ye are; depart from me, all ye workers of iniquity." The people were warned that their

---

iii Col. 4:14.

jjj Luke 13:19–21.

kkk Luke 13:23–30. Note 3, end of chapter.

lll Compare Matt. 7:13.

Israelitish lineage would in no wise save them, for many who were not of the covenant people would believe and be saved, while unworthy Israelites would be thrust out.[mmm] So is it that "There are last which shall be first, and there are first which shall be last."

JESUS WARNED OF HEROD'S DESIGN [nnn]

On the day of the discourse last noted, certain Pharisees came to Jesus with this warning and advice: "Get thee out, and depart hence: for Herod will kill thee."[ooo] We have heretofore found the Pharisees in open hostility to the Lord, or secretly plotting against Him; and some commentators regard this warning as another evidence of Pharisaic cunning—possibly intended to rid the province of Christ's presence, or designed to drive Him toward Jerusalem, where He would be again within easy reach of the supreme tribunal. Ought we not to be liberal and charitable in our judgment as to the intent of others? Doubtless there were good men in the fraternity of Pharisees,[ppp] and those who came informing Christ of a plot against His life were possibly impelled by humane motives, and may even have been believers at heart. That Herod had designs against our Lord's liberty or life appears most probable in the answer Jesus made. He received the information in all seriousness, and His comment thereon is one of the strongest of His utterances against an individual. "Go ye," said He, "and tell that fox, Behold, I cast out devils, and I do cures to day and to morrow, and the third day I shall be perfected." The specifying of today, tomorrow, and the third day, was a means of expressing the present in which the Lord was then acting, the immediate future, in which he would continue to minister, since, as He knew, the day of His death was yet several months distant, and the time at which his earthly work would be finished and He be perfected. He placed beyond doubt the fact that He did not intend to hasten His steps, neither cut short His journey nor cease His labors through fear of Herod Antipas, who for craft and cunning was best typified by a sly and murderous fox. Nevertheless it

---

[mmm] Compare Matt. 7:23; 8:11, 12; 19:30; Mark 10:31.

[nnn] Luke 13:31–33.

[ooo] In the revised version the last clause reads "for Herod would fain kill thee."

[ppp] Paul the apostle had been a Pharisee of the most pronounced type (Acts 23:6; 26:5).

was Christ's intention to go on, and soon in ordinary course He would leave Perea, which was part of Herod's domain, and enter Judea; and at the foreknown time would make His final entry into Jerusalem, for in that city was He to accomplish his sacrifice. "It cannot be," He explained, "that a prophet perish out of Jerusalem."

The awful reality that He, the Christ, would be slain in the chief city of Israel wrung from Him the pathetic apostrophe over Jerusalem, which was repeated when for the last time His voice was heard within the temple walls.[qqq]

NOTES TO CHAPTER 26

1. **Christ's Ministry Following His Final Withdrawal from Galilee.**—John tells us that when Jesus went from Galilee to Jerusalem to attend the Feast of Tabernacles, He went "not openly, but as it were in secret" (7:10). It appears improbable that the numerous works recorded by the synoptic writers as features of our Lord's ministry, which extended from Galilee through Perea, into Samaria and parts of Judea, could have attended that special and, as it were, secret, journey, at the time of the Feast of Tabernacles. The lack of agreement among writers as to the sequence of events in Christ's life is wide. A comparison of the "Harmonies" published in the most prominent Bible Helps (see e.g. Oxford and Bagster "Helps") exemplifies these divergent views. The subject matter of our Lord's teachings maintains its own intrinsic worth irrespective of merely circumstantial incidents. The following excerpt from Farrar (*Life of Christ*, chap. 42) will be of assistance to the student, who should bear in mind, however, that it is professedly but a tentative or possible arrangement. "It is well known that the whole of one great section in St. Luke—from 9:51 to 18:30—forms an episode in the Gospel narrative of which many incidents are narrated by this Evangelist alone, and in which the few identifications of time and place all point to one slow and solemn progress from Galilee to Jerusalem (9:51; 13:22; 17:11; 10:38). Now after the Feast of Dedication our Lord retired into Perea, until He was summoned thence by the death of Lazarus (John 10:40, 42; 11:1–46); after the resurrection [raising] of Lazarus, He fled to Ephraim (11:54); and He did not leave His retirement at Ephraim until He went to Bethany, six days before His final Passover (12:1).

"This great journey, therefore, from Galilee to Jerusalem, so rich in occasions which called forth some of His most memorable utterances, must have been either a journey to the Feast of Tabernacles or to the Feast of Dedication. That it could not have been the former may be regarded as settled, not only on other grounds, but decisively because that was a rapid and secret journey, this an eminently public and leisurely one.

"Almost every inquirer seems to differ to a greater or less degree as to the exact

[qqq] Luke 13:34, 35; compare Matt. 23:37–39.

sequence and chronology of the events which follow. Without entering into minute and tedious disquisitions where absolute certainty is impossible, I will narrate this period of our Lord's life in the order which, after repeated study of the Gospels, appears to me to be the most probable, and in the separate details of which I have found myself again and again confirmed by the conclusions of other independent inquirers. And here I will only premise my conviction—

"1. That the episode of St. Luke up to 18:30, mainly refers to a single journey, although unity of subject, or other causes, may have led the sacred writer to weave into his narrative some events or utterances which belong to an earlier or later epoch.

"2. That the order of the facts narrated even by St. Luke alone is not, and does not in any way claim to be, strictly chronological; so that the place of any event in the narrative by no means necessarily indicates its true position in the order of time.

"3. That this journey is identical with that which is partially recorded in Matt. 18:1; 20:16; Mark 10:1–31.

"4. That (as seems obvious from internal evidence) the events narrated in Matt. 20:17–28; Mark 10:32–45; Luke 18:31–34, belong not to this journey but to the last which Jesus ever took—the journey from Ephraim to Bethany and Jerusalem."

2. Jesus at the Home in Bethany.—Some writers (e.g. Edersheim) place this incident as having occurred in the course of our Lord's journey to Jerusalem to attend the Feast of Tabernacles; others (e.g. Geikie) assume that it took place immediately after that feast; and yet others (e.g. Farrar) assign it to the eve of the Feast of Dedication, nearly three months later. The place given it in the text is that in which it appears in the scriptural record.

3. Shall but Few Be Saved?—Through latter-day revelation we learn that graded conditions await us in the hereafter, and that beyond salvation are the high glories of exaltation. The specified kingdoms or glories of the redeemed, excepting the sons of perdition, are the Celestial, the Terrestrial, and the Telestial. Those who obtain place in the Telestial, the lowest of the three, are shown to be "as innumerable as the stars in the firmament of heaven, or as the sand upon the seashore." And these shall not be equal, "For they shall be judged according to their works, and every man shall receive according to his own works, his own dominion, in the mansions which are prepared. And they shall be servants of the Most High, but where God and Christ dwell they cannot come, worlds without end." See D&C 76:111, 112; read the entire section; see also *The Articles of Faith*, pp. 404–11.

CHAPTER 27

CONTINUATION OF THE PEREAN
AND JUDEAN MINISTRY

IN THE HOUSE OF ONE OF THE CHIEF PHARISEES[a]
On a certain Sabbath Jesus was a guest at the house of a prominent
Pharisee. A man afflicted with dropsy was there; he may have come
with the hope of receiving a blessing, or possibly his presence had
been planned by the host or others as a means of tempting Jesus to
work a miracle on the holy day. The exercise of our Lord's healing
power was at least thought of if not openly intimated or suggested,
for we read that "Jesus answering spake unto the lawyers and
Pharisees, saying, Is it lawful to heal on the sabbath day?"[b] No one
ventured to reply. Jesus forthwith healed the man; then He turned to
the assembled company and asked: "Which of you shall have an ass
or an ox fallen into a pit, and will not straightway pull him out on
the sabbath day?"[c] The learned expositors of the law remained
prudently silent.

Observing the eager activity of the Pharisee's guests in securing
for themselves prominent places at table, Jesus instructed them in a
matter of good manners, pointing out not only the propriety but the
advantage of decent self-restraint. An invited guest should not select for
himself the seat of honor, for someone more distinguished than he may
come, and the host would say: "Give this man place." Better is it to
take a lower seat, then possibly the lord of the feast may say: "Friend, go

---

[a] Luke 14:1–24.

[b] The question is identical with that asked of Jesus in the synagog at Capernaum preliminary to the healing of the man with the withered hand (Matt. 12:10).

[c] Ex. 23:5; Deut. 22:4; Luke 13:15.

up higher." The moral follows: "For whosoever exalteth himself shall be abased; and he that humbleth himself shall be exalted."[d]

This festive gathering at the house of the chief Pharisee included persons of prominence and note, rich men and officials, leading Pharisees, renowned scholars, famous rabbis and the like. Looking over the distinguished company, Jesus said: "When thou makest a dinner or a supper, call not thy friends, nor thy brethren, neither thy kinsmen, nor thy rich neighbours; lest they also bid thee again, and a recompense be made thee. But when thou makest a feast, call the poor, the maimed, the lame, the blind: And thou shalt be blessed; for they cannot recompense thee: for thou shalt be recompensed at the resurrection of the just." This bit of wholesome advice was construed as a reproof; and someone attempted to relieve the embarrassing situation by exclaiming: "Blessed is he that shall eat bread in the kingdom of God."[e] The remark was an allusion to the great festival, which according to Jewish traditionalism was to be a feature of signal importance in the Messianic dispensation. Jesus promptly turned the circumstance to good account by basing thereon the profoundly significant *Parable of the Great Supper*:

"A certain man made a great supper, and bade many: And sent his servant at supper time to say to them that were bidden, Come; for all things are now ready. And they all with one consent began to make excuse. The first said unto him, I have bought a piece of ground, and I must needs go and see it: I pray thee have me excused. And another said, I have bought five yoke of oxen, and I go to prove them: I pray thee have me excused. And another said, I have married a wife, and therefore I cannot come. So that servant came, and shewed his lord these things. Then the master of the house being angry said to his servant, Go out quickly into the streets and lanes of the city, and bring in hither the poor, and the maimed, and the halt, and the blind. And the servant said, Lord, it is done as thou hast commanded, and yet there is room. And the lord said unto the servant, Go out into the highways and hedges, and compel them to come in, that my house

---

[d] Compare Matt. 23:12; Luke 1:52; 18:14; James 4:6; 1 Pet. 5:5.

[e] Compare Matt. 8:11; Rev. 19:9. The expression "eat bread" is a Hebraism, signifying eating in full as at a feast rather than partaking of bread only.

may be filled. For I say unto you, That none of those men which were bidden shall taste of my supper."[f]

The story implies that invitations had been given sufficiently early to the chosen and prospective guests; then on the day of the feast a messenger was sent to notify them again, as was the custom of the time. Though called a supper, the meal was to be a sumptuous one; moreover, the principal meal of the day was commonly spoken of as supper. One man after another declined to attend, one saying: "I pray thee have me excused"; another: "I cannot come." The matters that engaged the time and attention of those who had been bidden, or as we would say, invited, to the feast, were not of themselves discreditable, far less sinful; but to arbitrarily allow personal affairs to annul an honorable engagement once accepted was to manifest discourtesy, disrespect and practical insult toward the provider of the feast. The man who had bought a field could have deferred the inspection; he who had just purchased cattle could have waited a day to try them under the yoke; and the newly married man could have left his bride and his friends for the period of the supper that he had promised to attend. Plainly none of these people wanted to be present. The master of the house was justly angry. His command to bring in the poor and the maimed, the halt and the blind from the city streets must have appealed to those who listened to our Lord's recital as reminiscence of His counsel given a few minutes before, concerning the kind of guests a rich man could invite with profit to his soul. The second sending out of the servant, this time into the highways and hedges outside the city walls, to bring in even the country poor, indicated boundless benevolence and firm determination on the householder's part.

Explication of the parable was left to the learned men to whom the story was addressed. Surely some of them would fathom its meaning, in part at least. The covenant people, Israel, were the specially invited guests. They had been bidden long enough aforetime, and by their own profession as the Lord's own had agreed to be partakers of the feast. When all was ready, on the appointed day, they were severally

---

[f] Luke 14:16–24. Compare the parable relating to the marriage of the king's son (Matt. 22:2–10); study points of resemblance and difference between the two and the distinctive lessons of each.

summoned by the Messenger who had been sent by the Father; He was even then in their midst. But the cares of riches, the allurement of material things, and the pleasures of social and domestic life had engrossed them; and they prayed to be excused or irreverently declared they could not or would not come. Then the gladsome invitation was to be carried to the Gentiles, who were looked upon as spiritually poor, maimed, halt, and blind. And later, even the pagans beyond the walls, strangers in the gates of the holy city, would be bidden to the supper. These, surprised at the unexpected summons, would hesitate, until by gentle urging and effective assurance that they were really included among the bidden guests, they would feel themselves constrained or compelled to come. The possibility of some of the discourteous ones arriving later, after they had attended to their more absorbing affairs, is indicated in the Lord's closing words: "For I say unto you, That none of those men which were bidden shall taste of my supper."

COUNTING THE COST[g]

As had been in Galilee, so was it in Perea and Judea—great multitudes attended the Master whenever He appeared in public. When once a scribe had presented himself as a disciple, offering to follow wherever the Master led, Jesus had indicated the self-denial, privation and suffering incident to devoted service, with the result that the man's enthusiasm was soon spent.[h] So now to the eager multitude Jesus applied a test of sincerity. He would have only genuine disciples, not enthusiasts of a day, ready to desert His cause when effort and sacrifice were most needed. Thus did He sift the people: "If any man come to me, and hate not his father, and mother, and wife, and children, and brethren, and sisters, yea, and his own life also, he cannot be my disciple. And whosoever doth not bear his cross, and come after me, cannot be my disciple." Literal hatred toward one's family was not specified as a condition of discipleship; indeed a man who indulges hatred or any other evil passion is a subject for repentance and reformation. The preeminence of duty

[g] Luke 14:25–35.
[h] Matt. 8:19, 20; compare Luke 9:57, 58.

toward God over personal or family demands on the part of one who had assumed the obligations of a disciple was the precept.[i]

As Jesus pointed out, it is good common-sense to count well the cost before one enters upon a great undertaking, even in ordinary affairs. A man who wishes to build, say a tower or a house, tries to determine, before he begins the work, what the expense will be; otherwise he may be able to do no more than lay the foundation; then, not only will he find himself a loser, for the unfinished structure will be of no service, but people may laugh at his lack of prudent forethought. So also a king, finding his realm menaced by hostile invaders, does not rush into battle recklessly; he first tries to ascertain the strength of the enemy's forces; and then, if the odds against him be too great, he sends an embassage to treat for peace. "So likewise," said Jesus to the people around Him, "whosoever he be of you that forsaketh not all that he hath, he cannot be my disciple." All who entered His service would be expected to maintain their self-sacrificing devotion. He wanted no disciples who would become like salt that had spoiled, unsavory and useless. "He that hath ears to hear, let him hear."[j]

SALVATION FOR "PUBLICANS AND SINNERS"— ILLUSTRATIVE PARABLES[k]

The Pharisees in Galilee had intolerantly criticized Jesus because of His friendly and helpful ministry among the publicans and their associates, who were disparagingly classed together as "publicans and sinners."[l] He had replied to these uncharitable aspersions by saying that a physician is most needed by them that are sick, and that He had come to call sinners to repentance. The Judean Pharisees raised a similar complaint, and were particularly virulent when they saw that "all the publicans and sinners" drew near to hear Him. He met their murmurs by presenting a number of parables, designed to show the incumbent duty of trying to recover the lost, and the joy of success in

---

[i] Compare the requirement under the Mosaic administration, Deut. 13:6–11; and note the application of the principle to the apostles; Matt. 10:37–39.

[j] Compare Matt. 5:13; Mark 9:50.

[k] Luke 15.

[l] Matt. 9:10–13; Mark 2:15–17; Luke 5:29–32.

such God-like endeavor. The first of the series of parables was that of the *Lost Sheep*; this we have considered in connection with its earlier delivery in the course of instruction to the disciples in Galilee.[m] Its application in the present instance, however, is somewhat different from that of its former presentation. The lesson on this later occasion was directed to the self-seeking Pharisees and scribes who personified the theocracy, and whose bounden duty it should have been to care for the strayed and the lost. If the "publicans and sinners," whom these ecclesiasts so generally contemned, were nearly as bad as they were represented to be, if they were men who had broken through the close-hedged path of the law and had become in a measure apostate, they were the ones toward whom the helping hand of missionary service could be best extended. In no instance of Pharisaic slur upon, or open denunciation of, these "publicans and sinners," do we find Jesus defending their alleged evil ways; His attitude toward these spiritually sick folk was that of a devoted physician: His concern over these strayed sheep was that of a loving shepherd whose chief desire was to find them out and bring them back to the fold. This neither the theocracy as a system nor its officials as individual ministers even attempted to do. The shepherd, on finding the sheep that was lost, thinks not at the time of reprimand or punishment; on the contrary, "when he hath found it, he layeth it on his shoulders, rejoicing. And when he cometh home, he calleth together his friends and neighbours, saying unto them: Rejoice with me; for I have found my sheep which was lost."

A direct application of the parable appears in the Lord's concise address to the Pharisees and scribes: "I say unto you, that likewise joy shall be in heaven over one sinner that repenteth, more than over ninety and nine just persons, which need no repentance." Were they the ninety and nine, who, by self-estimation had strayed not, being "just persons, which need no repentance?" Some readers say they catch this note of just sarcasm in the Master's concluding words. In the earlier part of the story, the Lord Himself appears as the solicitous Shepherd, and by plain implication His example is such as the theocratic leaders ought to emulate. Such a conception puts the Pharisees

---

[m] Matt. 18:12–14.

and scribes in the position of shepherds rather than of sheep. Both explications are tenable; and each is of value as portraying the status and duty of professing servants of the Master in all ages.

Without break in the narrative, the Lord passed from the story of the lost sheep to the *Parable of the Lost Coin.*

"Either what woman having ten pieces of silver, if she lose one piece, doth not light a candle, and sweep the house, and seek diligently till she find it? And when she hath found it, she calleth her friends and her neighbours together, saying, Rejoice with me; for I have found the piece which I had lost. Likewise, I say unto you, there is joy in the presence of the angels of God over one sinner that repenteth."

Between this parable and that of the lost sheep there are certain notable differences, though the lesson in each is in general the same. The sheep had strayed by its own volition; the coin[n] had been dropped, and so was lost as a result of inattention or culpable carelessness on the part of its owner. The woman, discovering her loss institutes a diligent search; she sweeps the house, and perhaps learns of dirty corners, dusty recesses, cobwebby nooks, to which she had been oblivious in her self-complacency as an outwardly clean and conventional housewife. Her search is rewarded by the recovery of the lost piece, and is incidentally beneficial in the cleansing of her house. Her joy is like that of the shepherd wending his way homeward with the sheep upon his shoulders—once lost but now regained.

The woman who by lack of care lost the precious piece may be taken to represent the theocracy of the time, and the Church as an institution in any dispensational period; then the pieces of silver, every one a genuine coin of the realm, bearing the image of the great King, are the souls committed to the care of the Church; and the lost piece symbolizes the souls that are neglected and, for a time at least, lost sight of, by the authorized ministers of the Gospel of Christ. These cogent illustrations were followed by one yet richer in imagery and more impressively elaborate in detail. It is the never to be forgotten *Parable of the Prodigal Son.*[o]

---

[n] That the lost piece of silver was a coin, and not a piece of unstamped bullion nor an ornament, is apparent from the original, "drachma," a silver coin.

[o] Luke 15:11–32.

"And he said, A certain man had two sons: And the younger of them said to his father, Father, give me the portion of goods that falleth to me. And he divided unto them his living. And not many days after the younger son gathered all together, and took his journey into a far country, and there wasted his substance with riotous living. And when he had spent all, there arose a mighty famine in that land; and he began to be in want. And he went and joined himself to a citizen of that country; and he sent him into his fields to feed swine. And he would fain have filled his belly with the husks that the swine did eat: and no man gave unto him. And when he came to himself, he said, How many hired servants of my father's have bread enough and to spare, and I perish with hunger! I will arise and go to my father, and will say unto him, Father, I have sinned against heaven, and before thee, And am no more worthy to be called thy son: make me as one of thy hired servants. And he arose, and came to his father. But when he was yet a great way off, his father saw him, and had compassion, and ran, and fell on his neck, and kissed him. And the son said unto him, Father, I have sinned against heaven, and in thy sight, and am no more worthy to be called thy son. But the father said to his servants, Bring forth the best robe, and put it on him; and put a ring on his hand, and shoes on his feet: And bring hither the fatted calf, and kill it; and let us eat, and be merry: For this my son was dead, and is alive again; he was lost, and is found. And they began to be merry. Now his elder son was in the field: and as he came and drew nigh to the house, he heard musick and dancing. And he called one of the servants, and asked what these things meant. And he said unto him, Thy brother is come; and thy father hath killed the fatted calf, because he hath received him safe and sound. And he was angry, and would not go in: therefore came his father out, and intreated him. And he answering said to his father, Lo, these many years do I serve thee, neither transgressed I at any time thy commandment: and yet thou never gavest me a kid, that I might make merry with my friends: But as soon as this thy son was come, which hath devoured thy living with harlots, thou hast killed for him the fatted calf. And he said unto him, Son, thou art ever with me, and all that I have is thine. It was meet that we should make merry, and be glad: for this thy brother was dead, and is alive again; and was lost, and is found."

The demand of the younger son for a portion of the patrimony, even during his father's lifetime, is an instance of deliberate and unfilial desertion; the duties of family cooperation had grown distasteful to him, and the wholesome discipline of the home had become irksome. He was determined to break away from all home ties, forgetful of what home had done for him and the debt of gratitude and duty by which he was morally bound. He went into a far country, and, as he thought, beyond the reach of the father's directing influence. He had his season of riotous living, of unrestrained indulgence and evil pleasure, through it all wasting his strength of body and mind, and squandering his father's substance; for what he had received had been given as a concession and not as the granting of any legal or just demand. Adversity came upon him, and proved to be a more effective minister for good than pleasure had been. He was reduced to the lowest and most menial service, that of herding swine, which occupation, to a Jew, was the extreme of degradation. Suffering brought him to himself. He, the son of honorable parentage, was feeding pigs and eating with them, while even the hired servants at home had good food in plenty and to spare. He realized not alone his abject foolishness in leaving his father's well-spread table to batten with hogs, but the unrighteousness of his selfish desertion; he was not only remorseful but repentant. He had sinned against his father and against God; he would return, confess his sin, and ask, not to be reinstated as a son, but to be allowed to work as a hired servant. Having resolved he delayed not, but immediately set out to find his long way back to home and father.

The father became aware of the prodigal's approach and hastened to meet him. Without a word of condemnation, the loving parent embraced and kissed the wayward but now penitent boy, who, overcome by this undeserved affection, humbly acknowledged his error, and sorrowfully confessed that he was not worthy to be known as his father's son. It is noteworthy that in his contrite confession he did not ask to be accepted as a hired servant as he had resolved to do; the father's joy was too sacred to be thus marred, he would please his father best by placing himself unreservedly at that father's disposal. The rough garb of poverty was discarded for the best robe; a ring was placed on his finger as a mark of reinstatement; shoes told of restored sonship, not of employment as a hired servant. The father's glad heart could express itself only in acts of abundant kindness; a feast was made ready, for was not the son, once counted as dead, now alive? Had not the lost been found again?

So far the story sustains a relation of close analogy to the two parables that preceded it in the same discourse; the part following introduces another important symbolism. No one had complained at the recovery of the stray sheep nor at the finding of the lost coin; friends had rejoiced with the finder in each case. But the father's happiness at the return of the prodigal was interrupted by the grumbling protest of the elder son. He, on approaching the house, had observed the evidences of festal joy; and, instead of entering as was his right, had inquired of one of the servants as to the cause of the unusual rejoicing. On learning that his brother had returned and that the father had prepared a festival in honor of the event, this elder son grew angry, and churlishly refused to enter the house even after his father had come out and entreated him. He cited his own faithfulness and devotion to the routine labor of the farm, to which claim of excellence the father did not demur; but the son and heir reproached his father for having failed to give him so much as a kid with which to make merry with his friends; while now that the wayward and spendthrift son had come back the father had killed for him even the fatted calf. There is significance in the elder one's designation of the penitent as "this thy son," rather than "my brother." The elder son, deafened by selfish anger, refused to hear aright the affectionate assurance: "Son, thou art ever with me, and all that I have is thine," and with heart hardened by unbrotherly resentment he stood unmoved by the emotional and loving outburst, "this thy brother was dead, and is alive again; and was lost, and is found."

We are not justified in extolling the virtue of repentance on the part of the prodigal above the faithful, plodding service of his brother, who had remained at home, true to the duties required of him. The devoted son was the heir; the father did not disparage his worth, nor deny his deserts. His displeasure over the rejoicing incident to the return of his wayward brother was an exhibition of illiberality and narrowness; but of the two brothers the elder was the more faithful, whatever his minor defects may have been. The particular point emphasized in the Lord's lesson, however, had to do with his uncharitable and selfish weaknesses.

Pharisees and scribes, to whom this masterpiece of illustrative incident was delivered, must have taken to themselves its personal application. They were typified by the elder son, laboriously attentive to routine, methodically plodding by rule and rote in the multifarious labors of the field, without interest except that of self, and all unwilling to welcome a repentant publican or a returned sinner. From all such they were estranged; such a one might be to the indulgent and forgiving Father, "this thy son," but never to them, a brother. They cared not who or how many were lost, so long as they were undisturbed in heirship and possession by the return of penitent prodigals. But the parable was not for them alone; it is a living perennial yielding the fruit of wholesome doctrine and soul-sustaining nourishment for all time. Not a word appears in condonation or excuse for the prodigal's sin; upon that the Father could not look with the least degree of allowance;[p] but over that sinner's repentance and contrition of soul, God and the household of heaven rejoiced.

The three parables, which appear in the scriptural record as parts of a continuous discourse, are as one in portraying the joy that abounds in heaven over the recovery of a soul once numbered among the lost, whether that soul be best symbolized by a sheep that had wandered afar, a coin that had dropped out of sight through the custodian's neglect, or a son who would deliberately sever himself from home and heaven. There is no justification for the inference that a repentant sinner is to be given precedence over a righteous soul who had resisted sin; were such the way of God, then Christ, the one sinless Man, would be surpassed in the Father's esteem by regenerate offenders. Unqualifiedly offensive as is sin, the sinner is yet precious in the Father's eyes, because of the possibility of his repentance and return to righteousness. The loss of a soul is a very real and a very great loss to God. He is pained and grieved thereby, for it is His will that not one should perish.[q]

THE DISCIPLES INSTRUCTED BY PARABLE

Addressing Himself more directly to the disciples present, who on this occasion probably comprised in addition to the apostles, many

[p] Compare D&C 1:31; Alma 45:16.
[q] Compare Matt. 18:14; Moses 1:39.

believers, including even some of the publicans, Jesus spake the *Parable of the Unrighteous Steward.*[r]

"And he said also unto his disciples, There was a certain rich man, which had a steward; and the same was accused unto him that he had wasted his goods. And he called him, and said unto him, How is it that I hear this of thee? give an account of thy stewardship: for thou mayest be no longer steward. Then the steward said within himself, What shall I do? for my lord taketh away from me the stewardship: I cannot dig; to beg I am ashamed. I am resolved what to do, that, when I am put out of the stewardship, they may receive me into their houses. So he called every one of his lord's debtors unto him, and said unto the first, How much owest thou unto my lord? And he said, An hundred measures of oil. And he said unto him, Take thy bill, and sit down quickly, and write fifty. Then said he to another, And how much owest thou? And he said, An hundred measures of wheat. And he said unto him, Take thy bill, and write fourscore. And the lord commended the unjust steward, because he had done wisely: for the children of this world are in their generation wiser than the children of light."

The three preceding parables show forth their lessons through the relationship of close analogy and intimate similarities; this one teaches rather by its contrast of situations. The steward in the story was the duly authorized agent of his employer, holding what we would call the power-of-attorney to act in his master's name.[s] He was called to account because a report of his wastefulness and lack of care had reached the master's ears. The steward did not deny his guilt, and forthwith he received notice of dismissal. Considerable time would be required for making up his accounts preparatory to turning the stewardship over to his successor. This interval, during which he remained in authority, he determined to use so far as possible to his own advantage, even though he wrought further injustice to his master's interests. He contemplated the condition of dependence in which he would soon find himself. Through unthrift and extravagance he had failed to lay by any store from his earnings; he had wasted his own

[r] Luke 16:1–8.

[s] Note 1, end of chapter.

and his lord's substance. He felt that he was unfit for hard manual labor; and he would be ashamed to beg, particularly in the community in which he had been a lavish spender and a man of influence. With the desire to put others under some obligation to himself so that when he was deposed he could the more effectively appeal to them, he called his lord's debtors and authorized them to change their bonds, bills of sale, or notes of hand, so as to show a greatly decreased indebtedness. Without doubt these acts were unrighteous; he defrauded his employer, and enriched the debtors through whom he hoped to be benefited. Most of us are surprised to know that the master, learning what his far-seeing though selfish and dishonest steward had done, condoned the offense and actually commended him for his foresight, "because he had done wisely" as our version reads, or "because he had done prudently," as many scholars aver to be the better rendering.

In pointing the moral of the parable Jesus said:[t] "For the children of this world are in their generation wiser than the children of light. And I say unto you, Make to yourselves friends of the mammon of unrighteousness; that, when ye fail, they may receive you into everlasting habitations." Our Lord's purpose was to show the contrast between the care, thoughtfulness, and devotion of men engaged in the money-making affairs of earth, and the half-hearted ways of many who are professedly striving after spiritual riches. Worldly-minded men do not neglect provision for their future years, and often are sinfully eager to amass plenty; while the "children of light," or those who believe spiritual wealth to be above all earthly possessions, are less energetic, prudent, or wise. By "mammon of unrighteousness" we may understand material wealth or worldly things. While far inferior to the treasures of heaven, money or that which it represents may be the means of accomplishing good, and of furthering the purposes of God. Our Lord's admonition was to utilize "mammon" in good works, while it lasted, for some day it shall fail, and only the results achieved through its use shall endure.[u] If the wicked steward, when cast out from his master's house because of unworthiness, might hope to be received into the homes of those whom he had favored, how much more

[t] Luke 16:9–13.
[u] Note 2, end of chapter.

confidently may they who are genuinely devoted to the right hope to be received into the everlasting mansions of God! Such seems to be part of the lesson.

It was not the steward's dishonesty that was extolled; his prudence and foresight were commended, however; for while he misapplied his master's substance, he gave relief to the debtors; and in so doing he did not exceed his legal powers, for he was still steward though he was morally guilty of malfeasance. The lesson may be summed up in this wise: Make such use of your wealth as shall insure you friends hereafter. Be diligent; for the day in which you can use your earthly riches will soon pass. Take a lesson from even the dishonest and the evil; if they are so prudent as to provide for the only future they think of, how much more should you, who believe in an eternal future, provide therefor! If you have not learned wisdom and prudence in the use of "unrighteous mammon," how can you be trusted with the more enduring riches? If you have not learned how to use properly the wealth of another, which has been committed to you as steward, how can you expect to be successful in the handling of great wealth should such be given you as your own? Emulate the unjust steward and the lovers of mammon, not in their dishonesty, cupidity, and miserly hoarding of the wealth that is at best but transitory, but in their zeal, forethought, and provision for the future. Moreover, let not wealth become your master; keep it to its place as a servant, for, "No servant can serve two masters: for either he will hate the one, and love the other; or else he will hold to the one, and despise the other. Ye cannot serve God and mammon."

DERISION OF THE PHARISEES MET;
ANOTHER ILLUSTRATIVE PARABLE [v]

The Pharisees, who were covetous, or more precisely stated, who were lovers of money,[w] overheard the foregoing instructions to the disciples, and openly scoffed at the Teacher and the lesson. What did this Galilean, who owned nothing but the clothes He wore, know about money or the best way of administering wealth? Our Lord's

[v] Luke 16:14–31.
[w] Note 2, end of chapter.

reply to their words of derision was a further condemnation. They knew all the tricks of the business-world, and could outdo the unrighteous steward in crafty manipulation; and yet so successfully could they justify themselves before men as to be outwardly honest and straightforward; furthermore, they made ostentatious display of a certain type of simplicity, plainness, and self-denial, in which external observances they asserted superiority over the luxury-loving Sadducees; they had grown arrogantly proud of their humility, but God knew their hearts, and the traits and practices they most esteemed were an abomination in His sight. They posed as custodians of the law and expounders of the prophets. The "law and the prophets" had been in force until the Baptist's time, since which the gospel of the kingdom had been preached, and people were eager to enter it[x] though the theocracy strove mightily to prevent. The law had not been invalidated; easier were it that heaven and earth pass away than that one tittle of the law fail of fulfilment;[y] yet those Pharisees and scribes had tried to nullify the law. In the matter of divorce, for example, they, by their unlawful additions and false interpretations, had condoned even the sin of adultery.

The Master gave as a further lesson the *Parable of the Rich Man and Lazarus*:

"There was a certain rich man, which was clothed in purple and fine linen, and fared sumptuously every day: And there was a certain beggar named Lazarus, which was laid at his gate, full of sores, And desiring to be fed with the crumbs which fell from the rich man's table: moreover the dogs came and licked his sores. And it came to pass, that the beggar died, and was carried by the angels into Abraham's bosom: the rich man also died, and was buried; And in hell he lift up his eyes, being in torments, and seeth Abraham afar off, and Lazarus in his bosom. And he cried and said, Father Abraham, have mercy on me, and send Lazarus, that he may dip the tip of his finger in water, and cool my tongue; for I am tormented in this flame. But Abraham said, Son, remember that thou in thy lifetime receivedst

[x] Revised version, Luke 16:16: "The law and the prophets were until John; from that time the gospel of the kingdom of God is preached, and every man entereth violently into it."

[y] Compare Matt. 5:18.

thy good things, and likewise Lazarus evil things: but now he is comforted, and thou art tormented. And beside all this, between us and you there is a great gulf fixed: so that they which would pass from hence to you cannot; neither can they pass to us, that would come from thence. Then he said, I pray thee therefore, father, that thou wouldest send him to my father's house: For I have five brethren; that he may testify unto them, lest they also come into this place of torment. Abraham saith unto him, They have Moses and the prophets; let them hear them. And he said, Nay, father Abraham; but if one went unto them from the dead, they will repent. And he said unto him, If they hear not Moses and the prophets, neither will they be persuaded, though one rose from the dead."[z]

The afflicted beggar is honored with a name; the other is designated simply as "a certain rich man."[aa] The two are presented as the extremes of contrast between wealth and destitution. The rich man was clothed in the costliest attire, purple and fine linen; and his everyday fare was a sumptuous feast. Lazarus had been brought to the gates of the rich man's palace, and there left, a helpless mendicant, his body covered with sores. The rich man was attended by servitors ready to gratify his slightest desire; the poor beggar at his gates had neither companions nor attendants except the dogs, which like himself waited for the refuse from the rich man's table. Such is the picture of the two in life. An abrupt change of scene brings into view the same two on the far side of the veil that hands between the here and the hereafter. Lazarus died; no mention is made of his funeral; his festering body was probably thrown into a pauper's grave; but angels bore his immortal spirit into Paradise, the resting place of the blessed and commonly known in the figurative lore of the rabbis as Abraham's bosom. The rich man also died; his burial was doubtless an elaborate affair, but we read not of any angelic escort receiving his spirit. In hell he lifted up his eyes and saw, afar, Lazarus at peace in the abode of Abraham.

As a Jew the man had often boasted of having Abraham for his father; and now the wretched spirit appealed to the patriarch of his race by the paternal address, "Father Abraham," and asked only the boon of

[z] Luke 16:19–31.
[aa] Note 3, end of chapter.

a single drop of water to be placed on his parched tongue; this he prayed that Lazarus, the erstwhile beggar, might bring. The reply throws light on certain conditions existing in the spirit world, though as in the use of parables generally, the presentation is largely figurative. Addressing the poor tormented spirit as "Son," Abraham reminded him of all the good things he had kept for himself on earth, whilst Lazarus had lain a suffering, neglected beggar at his gates; now by the operation of divine law, Lazarus had received recompense, and he, retribution. Moreover, to grant his pitiful request was impossible, for between the abode of the righteous where Lazarus rested and that of the wicked where he suffered "there is a great gulf fixed," and passage between the two is interdicted. The next request of the miserable sufferer was not wholly selfish; in his anguish he remembered those from whom he had been separated by death, fain would he save his brothers from the fate he had met; and he prayed that Lazarus be sent back to earth to visit the ancestral home, and warn those selfish, pleasure-seeking, and yet mortal brothers, of the awful doom awaiting them except they would repent and reform. There may have been in this petition an insinuation that had he been sufficiently warned he would have done better, and would have escaped the torment. To the reminder that they had the words of Moses and the prophets, which they should obey, he replied that if one went to them from the dead they would surely repent. Abraham answered that if they would not heed Moses and the prophets neither would "they be persuaded, though one rose from the dead."

In any attempt to interpret the parable as a whole or definitely apply any of its parts, we should bear in mind that it was addressed to the Pharisees as an instructive rebuke for the derision and scorn with which they had received the Lord's warning concerning the dangers attending servitude to mammon. Jesus employed Jewish metaphors, and the imagery of the parable is such as would most directly appeal to the official expounders of Moses and the prophets. While as a practice it would be critically unfair to deduce doctrinal principles from parabolic incidents, we cannot admit that Christ would teach falsely even in parable; and therefore we accept as true the portrayal of conditions in the world of the disembodied. That righteous and unrighteous dwell apart during the interval between death and resurrection is clear.

Paradise, or as the Jews like to designate that blessed abode, "Abraham's bosom," is not the place of final glory, any more than the hell to which the rich man's spirit was consigned is the final habitation of the condemned.[bb] To that preliminary or intermediate state, however, men's works do follow them;[cc] and the dead shall surely find that their abode is that for which they have qualified themselves while in the flesh.

The rich man's fate was not the effect of riches, nor was the rest into which Lazarus entered the resultant of poverty. Failure to use his wealth aright, and selfish satisfaction with the sensuous enjoyment of earthly things to the exclusion of all concern for the needs or privations of his fellows, brought the one under condemnation; while patience in suffering, faith in God and such righteous life as is implied though not expressed, insured happiness to the other. The proud self-sufficiency of the rich man, who lacked nothing that wealth could furnish and who kept aloof from the needy and suffering, was his besetting sin. The aloofness of the Pharisees, on which indeed they prided themselves, as their very name, signifying "separatists," expressed, was thus condemned. The parable teaches the continuation of individual existence after death, and the relation of cause to effect between the life one leads in mortality and the state awaiting him beyond.

UNPROFITABLE SERVANTS[dd]

From the Pharisees, Jesus turned to His disciples and admonished them to diligence. Having cautioned them against unguarded utterances or actions at which others might take offense, He proceeded to impress the absolute necessity of unselfish devotion, toleration and forgiveness. The apostles, realizing the whole-souled service required of them, implored the Lord, saying: "Increase our faith." They were shown that faith was less fitly reckoned in terms of quantity than by test of quality; and the analogy of the mustard seed was again invoked. "And the Lord said, If ye had faith as a grain of mustard seed, ye might say unto this sycamine tree, Be thou plucked up by the root, and be thou

[bb] Compare Alma 40:11–14; see *Articles of Faith,* chapter 21, Note 5.
[cc] Rev. 14:13.
[dd] Luke 17:1–10.

planted in the sea; and it should obey you."ᵉᵉ Their faith could best be gaged by obedience and untiring service.

This was emphasized by the *Parable of the Unprofitable Servants.*

"But which of you, having a servant plowing or feeding cattle, will say unto him by and by, when he is come from the held, Go and sit down to meat? And will not rather say unto him, Make ready wherewith I may sup, and gird thyself, and serve me, till I have eaten and drunken; and afterward thou shalt eat and drink? Doth he thank that servant because he did the things that were commanded him? I trow not. So likewise ye, when ye shall have done all those things which are commanded you, say, We are unprofitable servants: we have done that which was our duty to do."

The servant might well feel that after a day's work in the field he is entitled to rest; but on reaching the house he finds other demands made upon him. The master has a right to the servant's time and attention; such was among the conditions under which the servant had been engaged; and while his employer might thank him or give some substantial reward, the servant cannot demand such recompense. So the apostles, who had given themselves entirely up to their Master's service, were not to hesitate nor demur, whatever the effort or sacrifice required. The best they could do would be no more than their duty required; and, without regard to the Master's estimate of their worth, they were to account themselves as unprofitable servants.ᶠᶠ

TEN LEPERS HEALEDᵍᵍ

In the course of His journey toward Jerusalem Jesus "passed through the midst of Samaria and Galilee." Ten men afflicted with leprosy approached, probably they came as near as the law permitted, yet they were afar off. These men were of mixed nationality; the plague under which they suffered in common had made them companions in distress. They cried aloud "Jesus, Master, have mercy

---

ᵉᵉ Compare Matt. 17:20; 21:21; Mark 9:23; 11:23.

ᶠᶠ Compare Job 22:3; 35:7.

ᵍᵍ Luke 17:11–19. Many writers treat this ocurrence as having immediately followed the repulse of Jesus and the apostles in a certain Samaritan village (Luke 9:52–56). We give it place in the order followed by Luke, the sole recorder of the two incidents.

on us." The Lord answered: "Go shew yourselves unto the priests."[hh] This instruction implied their ultimate healing; obedience would be the test of their faith. None who had been leprous could be lawfully restored to community life until pronounced clean by a priest. The stricken ten hastened to obey the Lord's command, "and it came to pass, that, as they went, they were cleansed."[ii] One of the ten turned back, and with loud voice glorified God; then he prostrated himself at the feet of Christ, giving thanks. We are told that the grateful one was a Samaritan, from which we infer that some or all of the others were Jews. Pained over the lack of gratitude on the part of the nine, Jesus exclaimed: "Were there not ten cleansed? but where are the nine? There are not found that return to give glory to God, save this stranger." And to the cleansed Samaritan, still worshiping at His feet, the Lord said: "Arise, go thy way: thy faith hath made thee whole." Doubtless the nine who came not back were obedient to the strict letter of the Lord's command; for He had told them to go to the priests; but their lack of gratitude and their failure to acknowledge the power of God in their restoration stand in unfavorable contrast with the spirit of the one; and he was a Samaritan. The occurrence must have impressed the apostles as another evidence of acceptability and possible excellence on the part of aliens, to the disparagement of Jewish claims of superiority irrespective of merit.

THE PHARISEE AND THE PUBLICAN[jj]

"And he spake this parable unto certain which trusted in themselves that they were righteous, and despised others: Two men went up into the temple to pray; the one a Pharisee, and the other a publican. The Pharisee stood and prayed thus with himself, God, I thank thee, that I am not as other men are, extortioners, unjust, adulterers, or even as this publican. I fast twice in the week, I give tithes of

---

[hh] Compare Lev. 13:2; 14:2.

[ii] Compare case of Naaman the Syrian, 2 Kgs. 5:14.

[jj] Luke 18:9–14. Luke's narrative, the order of which we have followed in the events succeeding Christ's departure from Jerusalem after the Feast of Tabernacles includes our Lord's reply to the Pharisee's question as to "when the kingdom of God should come," and additions thereto (17:20–37); these 4 matters were afterward treated with greater fulness in a discourse near Jerusalem (Matt. 24) and will be considered in connection with that later event.

all that I possess. And the publican, standing afar off, would not lift up so much as his eyes unto heaven, but smote upon his breast, saying, God be merciful to me a sinner. I tell you, this man went down to his house justified rather than the other: for every one that exalteth himself shall be abased; and he that humbleth himself shall be exalted."

We are expressly told that this parable was given for the benefit of certain ones who trusted in their self-righteousness as an assurance of justification before God. It was not addressed to the Pharisees nor to the publicans specifically. The two characters are types of widely separated classes. There may have been much of the Pharisaic spirit of self-complacency among the disciples and some of it even among the Twelve. A Pharisee and a publican went up to the temple to pray. The Pharisee prayed "with himself"; his words can hardly be construed as a prayer to God. That he stood while praying was not an impropriety, for the standing attitude was usual in prayer; the publican also stood. The Pharisee thanked God that he was so much better than other men; he was true to his class, a separatist who looked with disdain upon all who were not like him. That he was not like "this publican" was made a point of special thanksgiving. His boast, that he fasted twice a week and gave tithes of all that he possessed, was a specification of worthiness above what was required by the law as then administered; he thus implied that God was his debtor.[kk] The publican, standing afar off, was so oppressed by his consciousness of sin and his absolute need of divine help, that he cast down his eyes and smote upon his breast, craving mercy as a penitent sinner. The Pharisee departed, justified in his own conscience and before man, prouder than ever; the other went down to his house justified before God though still a despised publican. The parable is applicable to all men; its moral was summed up in a repetition of our Lord's words spoken in the house of the chief Pharisee: "For every one that exalteth himself shall be abased; and he that humbleth himself shall be exalted."[ll]

[kk] Note to what blasphemous extreme the doctrine of supererogation, or excess of merit, was carried by the papacy in the 13th century; see *The Great Apostasy,* pp. 913–15.

[ll] Compare Luke 14:11.

ON MARRIAGE AND DIVORCE[mm]

While wending His way by short stages toward Jerusalem, and while still "beyond" or on "the farther side" of Jordan, and therefore in Perean territory, Jesus was met by a body of Pharisees, who had come with the deliberate purpose of inciting Him to say or do something on which they could base an accusation. The question they had agreed to submit related to marriage and divorce, and no subject had been more vehemently contested in their own schools and among their own rabbis.[nn] The crafty questioners may have hoped that Jesus would denounce the adulterous state in which Herod Antipas was then living, and so bring upon Himself the fury of Herodias, to which the Baptist had already died a victim. "Is it lawful for a man to put away his wife for every cause?" they asked. Jesus cited the original and eternal law of God in the matter; and indicated the only rational conclusion to be drawn therefrom: "Have ye not read, that he which made them at the beginning made them male and female, and said, For this cause shall a man leave father and mother, and shall cleave to his wife: and they twain shall be one flesh? Wherefore they are no more twain, but one flesh. What therefore God hath joined together, let no man put asunder."[oo] God had provided for honorable marriage, and had made the relation between husband and wife paramount even to that of children to parents; the severing of such a union was an invention of man, not a command of God. The Pharisees had a ready rejoinder: "Why did Moses then command to give a writing of divorcement, and to put her away?" Be it remembered that Moses had not commanded divorce, but had required that in case a man should separate from his wife he give her a bill of divorcement.[pp] Jesus made this fact plain, saying: "Moses because of the hardness of your hearts suffered you to put away your wives: but from the beginning it was not so."

The higher requirement of the gospel followed: "And I say unto

---

[mm] Matt. 19:3–12; see also Mark 10:2–12. This subject is introduced by Matthew and Mark directly preceding that of Christ blessing little children; which latter is recorded by Luke next after the Parable of the Pharisee and the Publican. We therefore turn from Luke's record to the accounts given by the other synoptic writers.

[nn] Note 4, end of chapter.

[oo] Compare Gen. 1:27; 2:24; 5:2; Eph. 5:31.

[pp] Deut. 24:1–4.

you, Whosoever shall put away his wife, except it be for fornication, and shall marry another, committeth adultery: and whoso marrieth her which is put away doth commit adultery."[qq] The Mosaic provision had been but permissive, and was justified only because of existing unrighteousness. Strict compliance with the doctrine enunciated by Jesus Christ is the only means by which a perfect social order can be maintained. It is important to note, however, that in His reply to the casuistical Pharisees, Jesus announced no specific or binding rule as to legal divorces; the putting away of a wife, as contemplated under the Mosaic custom, involved no judicial investigation or action by an established court. In our Lord's day the prevailing laxity in the matter of marital obligation had produced a state of appalling corruption in Israel; and woman, who by the law of God had been made a companion and partner with man, had become his slave. The world's greatest champion of woman and womanhood is Jesus the Christ.[rr]

The Pharisees retired foiled in purpose and convicted in conscience. The Lord's strict construction of the marriage bond was startling even to some of the disciples; these came to Him privately, saying that if a man was so bound it would be better not to marry at all. Such a broad generalization the Lord disapproved except so far as it might apply in special cases. True, there were some who were physically incapacitated for marriage; others voluntarily devoted themselves to a celibate life, and some few adopted celibacy "for the kingdom of heaven's sake," that thereby they might be free to render all their time and energy to the Lord's service. But the disciples' conclusion that "it is not good to marry" was true only in the exceptional instances stated. Marriage is honorable;[ss] for neither man without woman nor woman without man can be perfect in the Lord's sight.[tt]

JESUS AND THE LITTLE ONES[uu]

The next event of record is one of surpassing sweetness, rich in precept

[qq] Compare Matt. 5:32; Luke 16:18; see also 1 Cor. 7:10–13.

[rr] Note 5, end of chapter.

[ss] Compare Heb. 13:4.

[tt] Compare 1 Cor. 11:11.

[uu] Mark 10:13–16; compare Matt. 19:13–15; Luke 18:15–17.

and invaluable in example. Mothers brought their little children to Jesus, reverently desiring that the lives of those little ones be brightened by a sight of the Master and be blessed by a touch of His hand or a word from His lips. The circumstance appears in appropriate sequence to that of the Lord's instructions concerning the sacredness of marriage and the sanctity of the home. The disciples, zealous that their Master be not troubled unnecessarily, and conscious of the continuous demands on His time and attention, rebuked those who had so ventured to trespass. Even the disciples seem to have been yet under the influence of the traditional conception that women and children were of inferior status, and that for such to seek the Lord's attention was an act of presumption. Jesus was displeased over the misdirected zeal of His followers, and rebuked them. Then He uttered that memorable sentence of infinite tenderness and divine affection: *"Suffer the little children to come unto me, and forbid them not: for of such is the kingdom of God."* Taking the children one by one into His arms, He laid His hands upon them and blessed them.[vv] Then said He: "Verily I say unto you, Whosoever shall not receive the kingdom of God as a little child, he shall not enter therein."[ww]

"ONE THING THOU LACKEST"[xx]

Jesus was accosted on the way by a young man, who came running to meet or overtake Him, and who knelt at His feet, inquiring: "Good Master, what shall I do that I may inherit eternal life?" The question was asked in earnestness; the questioner was in very different spirit from that of the lawyer who made a similar inquiry with the purpose of tempting the Master.[yy] Jesus said: "Why callest thou me good? there is none good but one, that is, God." This remark was no denial of sinlessness on the Savior's part; the young man had called Him "good" by way of polite compliment rather than in recognition of His Godship, and Jesus declined to acknowledge the distinction when applied in that sense. The Lord's remark must have deepened the young man's conception as to the seriousness of his question. Then said Jesus: "If thou

---

[vv] Compare 3 Ne. 17:11–25. Note 6, end of chapter.

[ww] Page 364–66.

[xx] Matt. 19:16–26; Mark 10:17–27; Luke 18:18–30.

[yy] Luke 10:25.

wilt enter into life, keep the commandments." To the further inquiry, as to which commandments were meant, Jesus cited the prohibitions against murder, adultery, theft, and the bearing of false witness, and the requirements as to honoring parents, and loving one's neighbor as one's self. In simplicity and without pride or sense of self-righteousness, the young man said: "All these things have I kept from my youth up: what lack I yet?" His evident sincerity appealed to Jesus, who looked upon him lovingly and said: "One thing thou lackest: go thy way, sell whatsoever thou hast, and give to the poor, and thou shalt have treasure in heaven: and come, take up the cross, and follow me."[zz]

The young man was disappointed and saddened. He had probably expected to hear the great Teacher prescribe some one special observance, by which excellence could be achieved. Luke tells us that the young man was a ruler; this may mean that he was a presiding official in the local synagog or possibly a Sanhedrist. He was well versed in the law, and had been strict in obedience thereto. He desired to advance in good works and make clear his title to an eternal heritage. But the Master prescribed what he had least expected; "And he was sad at that saying, and went away grieved: for he had great possessions." In his way, he yearned for the kingdom of God, yet more devotedly he loved his great possessions. To give up wealth, social position, and official distinction, was too great a sacrifice; and the necessary self-denial was a cross too heavy for him to bear, even though treasure in heaven and life eternal were offered him. Love of worldly things was this man's besetting weakness; Jesus diagnosed his case and prescribed a suitable remedy. We are not warranted in saying that the same treatment would be best in all cases of spiritual defection; but where the symptoms indicate the need, it may be employed with confidence as to the cure.

Gazing sorrowfully upon the retreating figure of the wealthy young ruler Jesus said to the disciples: "Verily I say unto you, That a rich man shall hardly enter into the kingdom of heaven." To impress the lesson more thoroughly He applied one of the figurative proverbs of the age, and said: "It is easier for a camel to go through the eye of a needle, than for a rich man to enter into the kingdom of God."[aaa] At

[zz] This is Mark's record (10:21), which is the most detailed of the three accounts.
[aaa] Note 7, end of chapter.

this statement the disciples were amazed. "Who then can be saved?" they wondered. Jesus understood their perplexity, and encouraged them with the assurance that with God all things are possible. Thus were they given to understand that while wealth is a means of temptation to which many succumb, it is no insuperable obstacle, no insurmountable barrier, in the way of entrance to the kingdom. Had the young ruler followed the advice called forth by his inquiry, his possession of riches would have made possible to him meritorious service such as few are able to render. Willingness to place the kingdom of God above all material possessions was the one thing he lacked.[bbb] Everyone of us may pertinently ask, What do I lack?

THE FIRST MAY BE LAST, AND THE LAST FIRST[ccc]

The sorrowful departure of the rich young ruler, whose great possessions were so much a part of his life that he could not give them up at the time, though we may hope that he afterward did, brought forth from Peter an abrupt question, which revealed the course of his thoughts and aspirations: "Behold, we have forsaken all, and followed thee; What shall we have therefore?" Whether he spoke for himself alone, or by his use of the plural "we" meant to include all the Twelve, is uncertain and unimportant. He was thinking of the home and family he had left, and a longing for them was pardonable; he was thinking also of boats and nets, hooks and lines, and the lucrative business for which such things stood. All these he had forsaken; what was to be his reward? Jesus answered: "Verily I say unto you, That ye which have followed me, in the regeneration when the Son of man shall sit in the throne of his glory, ye also shall sit upon twelve thrones, judging the twelve tribes of Israel." It is doubtful that Peter or any other of the Twelve had ever conceived of so great a distinction. The day of regeneration, when the Son of Man shall sit on the throne of His glory, as Judge and King, is even yet future; but in that day, those of the Lord's Twelve who endured to the end shall be enthroned as judges in Israel. The further assurance was given that "every one that

---

bbb Consider the lessons of the parables of the Hidden Treasure and the Pearl of Great Price, chapter 19.

ccc Matt. 19:27–30; Mark 10:28–31; Luke 18:28–30.

hath forsaken houses, or brethren, or sisters, or father, or mother, or wife, or children, or lands, for my names's sake, shall receive an hundredfold, and shall inherit everlasting life." Rewards of such transcendent worth could scarcely be reckoned or their meaning comprehended. Lest those to whom they were promised might count too surely upon successful attainment, to the neglect of effort, and become proud withal, the Lord added this profound precept of caution: "But many that are first shall be last; and the last shall be first."

It was the text of the sermon known to us as the *Parable of the Laborers.*[ddd] Hear it:

"For the kingdom of heaven is like unto a man that is an householder, which went out early in the morning to hire labourers into his vineyard. And when he had agreed with the labourers for a penny a day, he sent them into his vineyard. And he went out about the third hour, and saw others standing idle in the marketplace, and said unto them: Go ye also into the vineyard, and whatsoever is right I will give you. And they went their way. Again he went out about the sixth and ninth hour, and did likewise. And about the eleventh hour he went out, and found others standing idle, and saith unto them, Why stand ye here all the day idle? They say unto him, Because no man hath hired us. He saith unto them, Go ye also into the vineyard; and whatsoever is right, that shall ye receive. So when even was come, the lord of the vineyard saith unto his steward, Call the labourers, and give them their hire, beginning from the last unto the first. And when they came that were hired about the eleventh hour, they received every man a penny. But when the first came, they supposed that they should have received more; and they likewise received every man a penny. And when they had received it, they murmured against the goodman of the house, saying, These last have wrought but one hour, and thou hast made them equal unto us, which have borne the burden and heat of the day. But he answered one of them, and said, Friend, I do thee no wrong: didst not thou agree with me for a penny? Take that thine is, and go thy way: I will give unto this last,

---

[ddd] Matt. 20:1–16. The parable is the outgrowth of the events immediately preceding it. Matt. 19:27–30 should be read as part of the narrative continued in chapter 20. The existing division into chapters is unfortunate.

even as unto thee. Is it not lawful for me to do what I will with mine own? Is thine eye evil, because I am good? So the last shall be first, and the first last: for many be called, but few chosen."

The procedure of a householder going into the marketplace to hire laborers was common to the time and place, and is still an ordinary occurrence in many lands. The first to be hired in the course of the story made a definite bargain as to wages. Those who were employed at nine, twelve, and three o'clock respectively went willingly without agreement as to what they were to receive; so glad were they to find a chance to work that they lost no time in specifying terms. At five o'clock in the afternoon or evening, when but a single hour of the working day remained, the last band of laborers went to work, trusting to the master's word that whatever was right they should receive. That they had not found work earlier in the day was no fault of theirs; they had been ready and willing, and had waited at the place where employment was most likely to be secured. At the close of the day, the laborers came for their wages; this was in accordance with law and custom, for it had been established by statute in Israel that the employer should pay the servant, hired by the day, before the sun went down.[eee] Under instructions, the steward who acted as paymaster began with those who had been engaged at the eleventh hour; and to each of them he gave a denarius, or Roman penny, worth about fifteen cents in our money, and the usual wage for a day's work. This was the amount for which those who began earliest had severally bargained; and as these saw their fellow-workers, who had served but an hour, receive each a penny, they probably exulted in the expectation of receiving a wage proportionately larger, notwithstanding their stipulation. But each of them received a penny and no more. Then they complained; not because they had been underpaid, but because the others had received a full day's pay for but part of a day's work. The master answered in all kindness, reminding them of their agreement. Could he not be just to them and charitable to the rest if he so chose? His money was his own, and he could give of it as he liked. Were those grumblers justified in their evil displeasure because their master

[eee] Deut. 24:15.

was charitable and good?" So," said Jesus, passing directly from the story to one of the lessons it was designed to teach, "the last shall be first, and the first last: for many be called, but few chosen."ᶠᶠ

The parable was plainly intended for the edification of the Twelve. It was called out by Peter's question, "What shall we have therefore?" It stands as truly in force today as when it was delivered by the Master, as a rebuke of the bargaining spirit in the Lord's work. God needs workers, and such as will labor faithfully and effectively are welcomed into the vineyard. If, before beginning they insist on the stipulation of a wage, and this be agreed to, each shall receive his penny provided he has not lost his place through idleness or transgression. But those who diligently labor, knowing that the Master will give to them whatever is right, and with thought for the work rather than for the wage, shall find themselves more bountifully enriched. A man may work for wages and yet not be a hireling. Between the worthy hired servant and the hireling there is the difference that distinguishes the shepherd from the sheep herder. Was there not a suggestion of the hireling's spirit in the query of even the first of the apostles, "What shall we have therefore?" The Twelve had been called into service early in the Savior's ministry; they had responded to the call, without promise of even a penny; they were yet to feel the burden and heat of the day; but they were solemnly cautioned against attempt or desire to fix their reward. The Master shall judge as to the deserts of each servant; the wage at best is a free gift; for on the basis of strict accounting who of us is not in debt to God? The last called is as likely as the first to prove unworthy. No general reversal is implied whereby all the late comers shall be advanced and all the early workers demoted. "Many that are first shall be last" was the Lord's statement, and by implication we may understand that not all the last, though some of them, may be counted among the first. Of the many called or permitted to labor in the vineyard of the Lord, few may so excel as to be chosen for exaltation above their fellows. Even the call and ordination to the Holy Apostleship is no guarantee of eventual exaltation in the celestial kingdom. Iscariot was so called and placed among the first; now, verily he is far below the last in the kingdom of God.

ᶠᶠThe concluding clause, "for many be called but few chosen," is omitted from the revised version.

NOTES TO CHAPTER 27

1. Rich Men and Their Stewards.—"'A certain rich man had a steward.' We learn here, incidentally, how evenly balanced are the various conditions of life in a community, and how little of substantial advantage wealth can confer on its possessor. As your property increases, your personal control over it diminishes; the more you possess the more you must entrust to others. Those who do their own work are not troubled with disobedient servants; those who look after their own affairs, are not troubled with unfaithful overseers."—Arnot's *Parables of Our Lord*, p. 454.

2. The Mammon of Unrighteousness.—The revised version of Luke 16:9, reads: "And I say unto you, Make to yourself friends by means of the mammon of unrighteousness, that, when it shall fail, they may receive you into the eternal tabernacles." The Lord's counsel to the disciples was to so use worldly wealth as to accomplish good thereby, that when "it," i.e. all earthly possessions, fail, they would have friends to welcome them into "the eternal tabernacles" or heavenly mansions. In studying a parable based on contrasts, such as this one is, care must be exercised not to carry too far any one point of analogy. Thus, we cannot reasonably gather that Jesus intended even to intimate that the prerogative of receiving any soul into the "eternal tabernacles" or excluding therefrom, rests with those who on earth had been benefited or injured through that person's acts, except so far as their witness to his deeds may be taken into account in the final judgment. The whole parable is full of wisdom for him who is in search of such; to the hypercritical mind it may appear inconsistent, as so it did appear to the Pharisees who derided Jesus for the story He had told. Luke 16:14 is rendered in the revised version, "And the Pharisees, who were lovers of money, heard all these things; and they scoffed at him."

3. Lazarus and Dives.—Of all our Lord's recorded parables this is the only one in which a personal name is applied to any of the characters. The name "Lazarus" used in the parable was also the true name of a man whom Jesus loved, and who, subsequent to the delivery of this parable, was restored to life after he had lain for days in the tomb. The name, a Greek variant of Eleazar, signifies "God is my help." In many theological writings, the rich man of this parable is called Dives, but the name is not of scriptural usage. "Dives" is a Latin adjective meaning "rich." Lazarus the brother of Martha and Mary (John 11:1, 2, 5) is one of three men mentioned by name as subjects of our Lord's beneficent miracles; the other two are Bartimeus (Mark 10:46) and Malchus (John 18:10). Commenting on the fact that our Lord gave a name to the beggar but left the rich man nameless in the parable, Augustine (in Sermon xli) suggestively asks: "Seems He not to you to have been reading from that book where He found the name of the poor man written, but found not the name of the rich: for that book is the Book of Life?"

4. Divergent Views Concerning Divorce.—In relation to the different opinions upon this subject among Jewish authorities in the time of Christ, Geikie (vol. 2, pp. 347–8) says: "Among the questions of the day fiercely debated between the great rival schools of Hillel and Shammai, no one was more so than that of divorce. The school of Hillel contended that a man had a right to divorce his wife for any cause he might assign, if it were no more than his having ceased to love her, or his having seen one he liked better, or her having cooked a dinner badly. The school of Shammai, on the contrary, held that divorce could be issued only for the crime of adultery, and offences against chastity. If it were possible to get Jesus to pronounce in favor of either school, the hostility of the other would be roused, and, hence, it seemed a favorable chance for compromising Him." The following from Dummelow's Commentary, dealing with Matt. 5:32, is further illustrative: "Rabbi Akiba (Hillelite) said, 'If a man sees a woman handsomer than his own wife he may put her [his wife] away, because it is said, If she find not favor in his eyes.' The school of Hillel said 'If the wife cook her husband's food ill, by oversalting or overroasting it, she is to be put away.' On the other hand Rabbi Jochanan (a Shammaite) said 'The putting away of a wife is odious.' Both schools agreed that a divorced wife could not be taken back. . . . Rabbi Chananiah said 'God has not subscribed His name to divorces, except among Israelites, as if He had said: I have conceded to the Israelites the right of dismissing their wives; but to the Gentiles I have not conceded it.' Jesus retorts that it is not the privilege but the infamy and reproach of Israel, that Moses found it necessary to tolerate divorce."

5. Jesus the Ennobler of Woman.—Geikie thus paraphrases part of Christ's reply to the Pharisee's question concerning divorce, and comments thereon. "'I say, therefore, that whoever puts away his wife, except for fornication, which destroys the very essence of marriage by dissolving the oneness it had formed, and shall marry another, commits adultery; and whoever marries her who is put away for any other cause commits adultery, because the woman is still, in God's sight, wife of him who had divorced her.' This statement was of far deeper moment than the mere silencing of malignant spies. It was designed to set forth for all ages the law of His New Kingdom in the supreme matter of family life. It swept away for ever from His Society the conception of woman as a mere toy or slave of man, and based true relations of the sexes on the eternal foundation of truth, right, honor, and love. To ennoble the House and the Family by raising woman to her true position was essential to the future stability of His Kingdom, as one of purity and spiritual worth. By making marriage indissoluble, He proclaimed the equal rights of woman and man within the limits of the family, and, in this, gave their charter of nobility to the mothers of the world. For her nobler position in the Christian era, compared with that granted her in antiquity, woman is indebted to Jesus Christ."—*Life and Words of Christ*, vol. 2, p. 349.

6. The Blessing of Children.—When Christ, a resurrected Being, appeared among the Nephites on the western continent, He took the children, one by one, and blessed them; and the assembled multitude saw the little ones encircled as with fire, while angels ministered unto them. (3 Ne. 17:11–25.) Through modern revelation the Lord has directed that all children born in the Church be brought for blessing to those who are authorized to administer this ordinance of the Holy Priesthood. The commandment is as follows: "Every member of the church of Christ having children, is to bring them unto the elders before the church, who are to lay their hands upon them in the name of Jesus Christ, and bless them in His name." (D&C 20:70.) Accordingly, it is now the custom in the Church to bring the little ones to the Fast-day service in the several wards, at which they are received one by one into the arms of the elders, and blessed, names being given them at the same time. The father of the child, if he be an elder, is expected to participate in the ordinance.

The blessing of children is in no sense analogous to, far less is it a substitution for, the ordinance of baptism, which is to be administered only to those who have come to years of understanding, and who are capable of repentance. As the author has written elsewhere, "Some point to the incident of Christ blessing little children, and rebuking those who would forbid the little ones coming unto Him (Matt. 19:13; Mark 10:13; Luke 18:15), as an evidence in favor of infant baptism; but, as has been tersely said:—'From the action of Christ's blessing infants, to infer they are to be baptized, proves nothing so much as that there is a want of better argument; for the conclusion would with more probability be derived thus: Christ blessed infants, and so dismissed them, but baptized them not, therefore infants are not to be baptized.'"—The author, *Articles of Faith*, p. 126.

7. The Camel and the Needle's Eye.—In comparing the difficulty of a rich man entering the kingdom with that of a camel passing through the eye of a needle, Jesus used a rhetorical figure, which, strong and prohibitory as it appears in our translation, was of a type familiar to those who heard the remark. There was a "common Jewish proverb, that a man did not even in his dreams see an elephant pass through the eye of a needle" (Edersheim). Some interpreters insist that a rope, not a camel, was mentioned by Jesus, and these base their contention on the fact that the Greek word *kamelos* (camel) differs in but a single letter from *kamilos* (rope), and that the alleged error of substituting "camel" for "rope" in the scriptural text is chargeable to the early copyists. Farrar (p. 476) rejects this possible interpretation on the ground that proverbs involving comparisons of a kind with that of a camel passing through the eye of a needle are common in the Talmud.

It has been asserted that the term "needle's eye" was applied to a small door or wicket set in or alongside the great gates in the walls of cities; and the assumption has been raised that Jesus had such a wicket in mind when He spoke of the seeming impossibility of a camel passing through a needle's eye. It would be possible though very difficult for a camel to squeeze its way through the little gate, and it could in no wise do so except when relieved of its load and stripped of all its harness. If this conception be correct, we may find additional similitude between the fact that the camel must first be unloaded and stripped, however costly its burden or rich its accoutrement, and the necessity of the rich young ruler, and so of any man, divesting himself of the burden and trappings of wealth, if he would enter by the narrow way that leadeth into the kingdom. The Lord's exposition of His saying is all-sufficient for the purposes of the lesson: "With men this is impossible, but with God all things are possible." (Matt. 19:26.)

8. **Undue Concern as to wages in the Lord's Service.**—The instructive and inspiring Parable of the Laborers was called forth by Peter's question of self-interest—"What shall we have therefore?" In tender mercy the Lord refrained from directly rebuking His impulsive servant for undue concern as to the wage to be expected; but He turned the incident to excellent purpose by making it the text of a valuable lesson. The following treatment by Edersheim (vol. 2, p. 416) is worth consideration. "There was here deep danger to the disciples: danger of lapsing into feelings akin to those with which the Pharisees viewed the pardoned publicans, or the elder son in the parable his younger brother; danger of misunderstanding the right relations, and with it the very character of the kingdom, and of work in and for it. It is to this that the Parable of the Laborers in the Vineyard refers. The principle which Christ lays down is, that, while nothing done for Him shall lose its reward, yet, from one reason or another, no forecast can be made, no inferences of self-righteousness may be drawn. It does not by any means follow, that most work done—at least, to our seeing and judging—shall entail a greater reward. On the contrary, 'many that are first shall be last; and the last shall be first.' Not all, nor yet always and necessarily, but 'many.' And in such cases no wrong has been done; there exists no claim, even in view of the promises of due acknowledgment of work. Spiritual pride and self assertion can only be the outcome either of misunderstanding God's relation to us, or else of a wrong state of mind towards others—that is, it betokens mental or moral unfitness. Of this the parable of the Laborers is an illustration. . . . But, while illustrating how it may come that some who were first are last, and how utterly mistaken or wrong is the thought that they must necessarily receive more than others, who, seemingly, have done more—how, in short, work for Christ is not a ponderable quantity, so much for so much, nor yet we be the judges of when and why a worker has come—it also conveys much that is new, and, in many respects, most comforting."

CHAPTER 28

THE LAST WINTER

AT THE FEAST OF DEDICATION[a]
Jesus returned to Jerusalem in time to attend the Feast of Dedication
during the last winter of His earthly life. This feast, like that of
Tabernacles, was one of national rejoicing, and was celebrated annually
for a period of eight days beginning on the 25th of Chislev,[b] which
corresponds in part to our December. It was not one of the great feasts
prescribed by Mosaic statute but had been established in 164 or 163
B.C. at the time of the rededication of the Temple of Zerubbabel
following the rehabilitation of the sacred structure after its profane
desecration by Antiochus Epiphanes, the pagan king of Syria.[c] While
the festival was in progress, Jesus went to the temple and was seen
walking in the part of the enclosure known as Solomon's Porch.[d] His
presence soon became known to the Jews, who came crowding about
Him in unfriendly spirit, ostensibly to ask questions. Their inquiry
was: "How long dost thou make us to doubt? If thou be the Christ,
tell us plainly." The mere asking of such a question evidences the deep
and disturbing impression which the ministry of Christ had produced
among the official classes and the people generally; in their estimation,
the works he had wrought appeared as worthy of the Messiah.

The Lord's reply was indirect in form, though in substance and
effect incisive and unmistakable. He referred them to His former

[a] John 10:22–39.

[b] Also rendered Kislev, Chisleu, and Cisleu. See Zech. 7:1.

[c] Josephus, *Antiquities*, xii, 5:3–5. See Ezra 6:17, 18; also Note 1, end of chapter.

[d] Note 2, end of chapter.

utterances and to His continued works. "I told you," He said, "and ye believed not: the works that I do in my Father's name, they bear witness of me. But ye believe not, because ye are not of my sheep, as I said unto you. My sheep hear my voice, and I know them, and they follow me: And I give unto them eternal life; and they shall never perish, neither shall any man pluck them out of my hand. My Father, which gave them me, is greater than all; and no man is able to pluck them out of my Father's hand. I and my Father are one." The reference to what had been before told was a reminder of His teachings on the occasion of an earlier sojourn among them, when He had proclaimed Himself as the I AM, who was older and greater than Abraham, and of His other proclamation of Himself as the Good Shepherd.[e]

He could not well answer their inquiry by a simple unqualified affirmation, for by such He would have been understood as meaning that He claimed to be the Messiah according to their conception, the earthly king and conqueror for whom they professed to be looking. He was no such Christ as they had in mind; yet was He verily Shepherd and King to all who would hear His words and do His works; and to such He renewed the promise of eternal life and the assurance that no man could pluck them out of His own or the Father's hand. To this doctrine, both exalted and profound in scope, the casuistical Jews could offer no refutation, nor could they find therein the much desired excuse for open accusation; our Lord's concluding sentence, however, stirred the hostile throng to frenzy. "I and my Father are one" was His solemn declaration.[f] In their rage they scrambled for stones wherewith to crush Him. Owing to the unfinished state of the temple buildings, there were probably many blocks and broken fragments of rock at hand; and this was the second murderous attempt upon our Lord's life within the purlieus of His Father's House.[g]

Fearless, and with the compelling calmness of more than human majesty, Jesus said: "Many good works have I shewed you from my Father; for which of those works do ye stone me?" They angrily retorted: "For a good work we stone thee not; but for blasphemy; and because

[e] John 8:58; 10:11.
[f] Revised version gives "I and the Father." Note 3, end of chapter.
[g] John 8:59.

that thou, being a man, makest thyself God."[h] Plainly they had found no ambiguity in His words. He then cited to them the scriptures, wherein even judges empowered by divine authority are called gods,[i] and asked: "Is it not written in your law, I said, Ye are gods? If he called them gods, unto whom the word of God came, and the scripture cannot be broken: say ye of him, whom the Father hath sanctified, and sent into the world, Thou blasphemest; because I said, I am the Son of God?" Then, reverting to the first avouchment that His own commission was of the Father who is greater than all, He added: "If I do not the works of my Father, believe me not. But if I do, though ye believe not me, believe the works: that ye may know, and believe, that the Father is in me, and I in him."[j] Again the Jews sought to take Him, but were foiled by means not stated; He passed from their reach and departed from the temple.

OUR LORD'S RETIREMENT IN PEREA[k]

The violent hostility of the Jews in Jerusalem, the headquarters of the theocracy, was such that Jesus withdrew from the city and its neighborhood. The day for His sacrifice had not yet come, and while His enemies could not kill Him until He allowed Himself to be taken into their hands, His work would be retarded by further hostile disturbances. He retired to the place at which John the Baptist had begun his public ministry, which is probably also the place of our Lord's baptism. The exact location is not specified; it was certainly beyond Jordan and therefore in Perea. We read that Jesus abode there, and from this we gather that He remained in one general locality instead of traveling from town to town as had been His custom. People resorted to Him even there, however, and many believed on Him. The place was endeared to those who had gone to hear John and to be baptized by him;[l] and as these recalled the impassioned call

---

[h] Concerning blasphemy see pages 184, 254, and 584.

[i] Ps. 82, particularly verses 1 and 6. Note 8, end of chapter.

[j] A better rendering of the last verse is: "But if I do them [i.e. the Father's works], though ye believe not me, believe the works; that ye may know and understand that the Father is in me, and I in the Father." —Revised Version.

[k] John 10:40–42.

[l] Pages 117–120.

to repentance, the stirring proclamation of the kingdom by the now murdered and lamented Baptist, they remembered his affirmation of One mightier than himself, and saw in Jesus the realization of that testimony. "John," they said, "did no miracle: but all things that John spake of this man were true."

The duration of this sojourn in Perea is nowhere recorded in our scriptures. It could not have lasted more than a few weeks at most. Possibly some of the discourses, instructions, and parables already treated as following the Lord's departure from Jerusalem after the Feast of Tabernacles in the preceding autumn, may chronologically belong to this interval. From this retreat of comparative quiet, Jesus returned to Judea in response to an earnest appeal from some whom He loved. He left the Bethany of Perea for the Judean Bethany, where dwelt Martha and Mary.[m]

LAZARUS RESTORED TO LIFE[n]

Lazarus, the brother of Mary and Martha, lay ill in the family home at Bethany of Judea. His devoted sisters sent a messenger to Jesus, with the simple announcement, in which, however, we cannot fail to recognize a pitiful appeal: "Lord, behold, he whom thou lovest is sick." When Jesus received the message, He remarked: "This sickness is not unto death, but for the glory of God, that the Son of God might be glorified thereby." This was probably the word carried back to the sisters, whom Jesus loved. Lazarus had died in the interval; indeed he must have expired soon after the messenger had started with the tidings of the young man's illness. The Lord knew that Lazarus was dead; yet He tarried where He was for two days after receiving the word; then He surprised the disciples by saying: "Let us go into Judea again." They sought to dissuade the Master by reminding Him of the recent attempt upon His life at Jerusalem, and asked wonderingly, "Goest thou thither again?" Jesus made clear to them that He was not to be deterred from duty in the time thereof, nor should others be; for as He illustrated, the working day is twelve hours long; and during that period a man may walk without stumbling, for he walks in the light,

[m] Note 4, end of chapter.

[n] John 11:1–46.

but if he let the hours pass and then try to walk or work in darkness, he stumbles. It was then His day to work, and He was making no mistake in returning to Judea.

He added: "Our friend Lazarus sleepeth; but I go, that I may awake him out of sleep." The simile between death and sleep was as common among the Jews as with us;[o] but the disciples construed the saying literally, and remarked that if the sick man was sleeping it would be well with him. Jesus set them right. "Lazarus is dead," He said, and added, "And I am glad for your sakes that I was not there, to the intent ye may believe; nevertheless let us go unto him." It is evident that Jesus had already decided to restore Lazarus to life; and, as we shall see, the miracle was to be a testimony of our Lord's Messiahship, convincing to all who would accept it. A return to Judea at that time was viewed by at least some of the apostles with serious apprehension; they feared for their Master's safety, and thought that their own lives would be in peril; nevertheless they did not hesitate to go. Thomas boldly said to the others: "Let us also go, that we may die with him."

Arriving on the outskirts of Bethany, Jesus found that Lazarus "had lain in the grave four days already."[p] The bereaved sisters were at home, where had gathered, according to custom, friends to console them in their grief. Among these were many prominent people, some of whom had come from Jerusalem. Words of the Master's approach reached Martha first, and she hastened to meet Him. Her first words were: "Lord, if thou hadst been here, my brother had not died." It was an expression of anguish combined with faith; but, lest it appear as lacking in trust, she hastened to add: "But I know, that even now, whatsoever thou wilt ask of God, God will give it thee." Then said Jesus in words of assuring tenderness: "Thy brother shall rise again." Perhaps some of the Jews who had come to comfort her had said as much, for they, the Sadducees excepted, believed in a resurrection; and Martha failed to find in the Lord's promise anything more than a general assurance that her departed brother should be raised with the rest of the dead. In natural and seemingly casual assent she remarked:

[o] Compare Matt. 9:24; Mark 5:39; Luke 8:52; Job 14:12; 1 Thes. 4:14.
[p] Note 5, end of chapter.

"I know that he shall rise again in the resurrection at the last day." Then said Jesus: "I am the resurrection, and the life: he that believeth in me, though he were dead, yet shall he live: And whosoever liveth and believeth in me shall never die. Believest thou this?"

The sorrowing woman's faith had to be lifted and centered in the Lord of Life with whom she was speaking. She had before confessed her conviction that whatever Jesus asked of God would be granted; she had to learn that unto Jesus had already been committed power over life and death. She was hopefully expectant of some superhuman interposition by the Lord Jesus in her behalf, yet she knew not what that might be. Apparently at this time she had no well-defined thought or even hope that He would call her brother from the tomb. To the Lord's question as to whether she believed what He had just said, she answered with simple frankness; all of it she was not able to understand; but she believed in the Speaker even while unable to fully comprehend His words. "Yea, Lord," she said, "I believe that thou art the Christ, the Son of God, which should come into the world."

Then she returned to the home, and with precaution of secrecy on account of the presence of some whom she knew to be unfriendly to Jesus, said to Mary: "The Master is come, and calleth for thee." Mary left the house in haste. The Jews who had been with her thought that she had been impelled by a fresh resurgence of grief to go again to the grave, and they followed her. When she reached the Master, she knelt at His feet, and gave expression to her consuming sorrow in the very words Martha had used: "Lord, if thou hadst been here, my brother had not died." We cannot doubt that the conviction so voiced had been the burden of comment and lamentation between the two sisters—if only Jesus had been with them they would not have been bereft of their brother.

The sight of the two women so overcome by grief, and of the people wailing with them, caused Jesus to sorrow, so that He groaned in spirit and was deeply troubled. "Where have ye laid him?" He asked; and Jesus wept. As the sorrowing company went toward the tomb, some of the Jews, observing the Lord's emotion and tears, said: "Behold how he loved him!" but others, less sympathetic because of their prejudice against Christ, asked critically and reproachfully: "Could not this man, which opened the eyes of the blind, have caused that even this man should not have died?" The miracle by which a man blind from birth had been made to see was very generally known, largely because of the official investigation that had followed the healing.[q] The Jews had been compelled to admit the actuality of the astounding occurrence; and the question now raised as to whether or why One who could accomplish such a wonder could not have preserved from death a man stricken with an ordinary illness, and that man one whom He seemed to have dearly loved, was an innuendo that the power possessed by Jesus was after all limited, and of uncertain or capricious operation. This manifestation of malignant unbelief caused Jesus again to groan with sorrow if not indignation.[r]

The body of Lazarus had been interred in a cave, the entrance to which was closed by a great block of stone. Such burial-places were common in that country, natural caves or vaults hewn in the solid rock being used as sepulchres by the better classes of people. Jesus directed that the tomb be opened. Martha, still unprepared for what was to follow, ventured to remonstrate, reminding Jesus that the corpse had been four days immured, and that decomposition must have already set in.[s] Jesus thus met her objection: "Said I not unto thee, that, if thou wouldest believe, thou shouldest see the glory of God?" This may have had reference both to His promise spoken to Martha in person—that her brother should rise again—and to the message sent from Perea—that the illness of Lazarus was not unto final death at that time, but for the glory of God and that the Son of God might be glorified thereby.

The stone was removed. Standing before the open portal of the tomb, Jesus looked upward and prayed: "Father, I thank thee that thou hast heard me. And I knew that thou hearest me always: but because of the people which stand by I said it, that they may believe that thou hast sent me." He did not ask the Father for power or authority; such had already been given Him; but He gave thanks, and in the hearing of all who stood by acknowledged the Father and expressed the oneness of His own and the Father's purposes. Then, with a loud voice

[q] John 9.
[r] Note 6, end of chapter.
[s] Note 5, end of chapter.

He cried: "Lazarus, come forth." The dead man heard that voice of authoritative command; the spirit straightway reentered the tabernacle of flesh, the physical processes of life were resumed; and Lazarus, again alive, came forth. His freedom of motion was limited, for the grave clothes hampered his movements, and his face was still bound by the napkin by which the lifeless jaw had been held in place. To those who stood near, Jesus said: "Loose him, and let him go."

The procedure throughout was characterized by deep solemnity and by the entire absence of every element of unnecessary display. Jesus, who when miles away and without any ordinary means of receiving the information knew that Lazarus was dead, doubtless could have found the tomb; yet He inquired: "Where have ye laid him?" He who could still the waves of the sea by a word could have miraculously effected the removal of the stone that sealed the mouth of the sepulchre; yet He said: "Take ye away the stone." He who could reunite spirit and body could have loosened without hands the cerements by which the reanimated Lazarus was bound; yet He said: "Loose him, and let him go." All that human agency could do was left to man. In no instance do we find that Christ used unnecessarily the superhuman powers of His Godship; the divine energy was never wasted; even the material creation resulting from its exercise was conserved, as witness His instructions regarding the gathering up of the fragments of bread and fish after the multitudes had been miraculously fed.[t]

The raising of Lazarus stands as the third recorded instance of restoration to life by Jesus.[u] In each the miracle resulted in a resumption of mortal existence, and was in no sense a resurrection from death to immortality. In the raising of the daughter of Jairus, the spirit was recalled to its tenement within the hour of its quitting; the raising of the widow's son is an instance of restoration when the corpse was ready for the grave; the crowning miracle of the three was the calling of a spirit to reenter its body days after death, and when, by natural processes the corpse would be already in the early stages of decomposition. Lazarus was raised from the dead, not simply to assuage the grief of mourning relatives; myriads have had to mourn over death,

[t] John 6:12; Matt. 15:37.
[u] Matt. 9:23–25; Luke 7:11–17.

and so myriads more shall have to do. One of the Lord's purposes was that of demonstrating the actuality of the power of God as shown forth in the works of Jesus the Christ, and Lazarus was the accepted subject of the manifestation, just as the man afflicted with congenital blindness had been chosen to be the one through whom "the Works of God should be made manifest."[v]

That the Lord's act of restoring Lazarus to life was of effect in testifying to His Messiahship is explicitly stated.[w] All the circumstances leading up to final culmination in the miracle contributed to its attestation. No question as to the actual death of Lazarus could be raised, for his demise had been witnessed, his body had been prepared and buried in the usual way, and he had lain in the grave four days. At the tomb, when he was called forth, there were many witnesses, some of them prominent Jews, many of whom were unfriendly to Jesus and who would have readily denied the miracle had they been able. God was glorified and the divinity of the Son of Man was vindicated in the result.

THE HIERARCHY GREATLY AGITATED OVER THE MIRACLE[x]

As in connection with most of our Lord's public acts—while some of those who heard and saw were brought to believe in Him, others rejected the proffered lesson and reviled the Master—so with this mighty work—some were stirred to faith and others went their ways each with mind darkened and spirit more malignant than ever. Some of those who had seen the dead man raised to life went immediately and reported the matter to the rulers, whom they knew to be intensely hostile toward Jesus. In the parable we have recently studied, the spirit of the rich man pleaded from his place of anguish that Lazarus, the once pitiable beggar, be sent from paradise to earth, to warn others of the fate awaiting the wicked, to which appeal Abraham replied: "If they hear not Moses and the prophets, neither will they be persuaded, though one rose from the dead."[y] Now a Lazarus had been

[v] John 9:3.
[w] John 12:9–11,17.
[x] John 11:46–54.
[y] Luke 16:31.

in reality raised from the dead, and many of the Jews rejected the testimony of his return and refused to believe in Christ through whom alone death is overcome. The Jews tried to get Lazarus into their power that they might kill him and, as they hoped, silence forever his testimony of the Lord's power over death.[z]

The chief priests, who were mostly Sadducees, and the Pharisees with them assembled in council to consider the situation created by this latest of our Lord's great works. The question they discussed was: "What do we? for this man doeth many miracles. If we let him thus alone, all men will believe on him: and the Romans shall come and take away both our place and nation." As stated by themselves, there was no denying the fact of the many miracles wrought by Jesus; but instead of earnestly and prayerfully investigating as to whether these mighty works were not among the predicted characteristics of the Messiah, they thought only of the possible effect of Christ's influence in alienating the people from the established theocracy, and of the fear that the Romans, taking advantage of the situation, would deprive the hierarchs of their "place" and take from the nation what little semblance of distinct autonomy it still possessed. Caiaphas, the high priest,[aa] cut short the discussion by saying: "Ye know nothing at all." This sweeping assertion of ignorance was most likely addressed to the Pharisees of the Sanhedrin; Caiaphas was a Sadducee. His next utterance was of greater significance than he realized: "Nor consider that it is expedient for us, that one man should die for the people, and that the whole nation perish not." John solemnly avers that Caiaphas spake not of himself, but by the spirit of prophecy, which, in spite of his implied unworthiness, came upon him by virtue of his office, and that thus: "He prophesied that Jesus should die for that nation; and not for that nation only, but that also he should gather together in one the children of God that were scattered abroad." But a few years after Christ had been put to death, for the salvation of the Jews and of all other nations, the very calamities which Caiaphas and the Sanhedrin had hoped to avert befell in full measure; the hierarchy was overthrown, the temple destroyed, Jerusalem demolished and the nation disrupted.

[z] John 12:10.
[aa] Note 7, end of chapter.

From the day of that memorable session of the Sanhedrin, the rulers increased their efforts to bring about the death of Jesus, by whatever means they might find available. They issued a mandate that whosoever knew of His whereabouts should give the information to the officials, that they might promptly take Him into custody.[bb]

JESUS IN RETIREMENT AT EPHRAIM[cc]

The hostility of the ecclesiastical rulers became so great that Jesus once more sought retirement in a region sufficiently far from Jerusalem to afford Him security from the watchful and malignant eyes of His powerful and openly avowed enemies. But a few weeks of mortal life remained to Him, and the greater part of this brief period had to be devoted to the further instruction of the apostles. He prudently withdrew from the vicinity of Bethany and "went thence unto a country near to the wilderness, into a city called Ephraim, and there continued with his disciples." Thus did our Lord spend the rest of the winter and probably the early days of the succeeding spring. That His retreat was private if not practically secret is suggested by John's statement that "Jesus therefore walked no more openly among the Jews"; and further indication is found in the fact that although the chief priests and Pharisees had virtually set a price upon His head, no man gave information as to His whereabouts. The place of this last retirement is not definitely known; it is generally thought to be the locality elsewhere called Ephrain and Ephron,[dd] which lay a little less than twenty miles northerly from Jerusalem. Equally uncertain is the duration of our Lord's abode there. When He emerged again into public notice, it was to enter upon His solemn march toward Jerusalem and the cross.

NOTES TO CHAPTER 28

1. **Origin of the Feast of Dedication.**—Concerning the second temple, known as the Temple of Zerubbabel, the author has written elsewhere: "Of the later history of this temple the biblical record gives but few details; but from other sources we learn

[bb] John 11:57.
[cc] John 11:54.
[dd] 2 Chr. 13:19; Josh. 15:9.

of its vicissitudes. In connection with the Maccabean persecution the House of the Lord was profaned. A Syrian king, Antiochus Epiphanes, captured Jerusalem (168 to 165 B.C.) and perpetrated blasphemous outrage against the religion of the people. He plundered the temple and carried away its golden candlestick, its golden altar of incense, its table of shewbread, and even tore down the sacred veils, which were of fine linen and scarlet. His malignity was carried so far that he purposely desecrated the altar of sacrifice by offering swine thereon, and erected a heathen altar within the sacred enclosure. Not content with the violation of the temple, this wicked monarch had altars erected in the towns, and ordered the offering of unclean beasts upon them. The rite of circumcision was forbidden on pain of death, and the worship of Jehovah was declared a crime. As a result of this persecution many of the Jews apostatized, and declared that they belonged to the Medes and Persians—the nations from whose dominion they had been delivered by the power of God. . . . Then in the year 163 B.C. the House was rededicated; and the occasion was remembered in annual festival thereafter under the name of the Feast of Dedication."—*The House of the Lord,* pp. 51–53. According to Josephus (Ant. xii, 7:7) the festival came to be known as The Lights; and brilliant illumination, both of the temple and of dwellings, was a feature of the celebration. Traditional accounts say that eight days had been set as the duration of the feast, in commemoration of a legendary miracle by which the consecrated oil in the only jar found intact, and bearing the unbroken seal of the high priest, had been made to serve for temple purposes through eight days, which time was required for the ceremonial preparation of a new supply.

2. Solomon's Porch.—This name had been applied to the eastern colonnade or row of porticoes within the temple enclosure, in recognition of a tradition that the porch covered and included a portion of the original wall belonging to the Temple of Solomon. See *House of the Lord,* pp. 46–48.

3. The Oneness of Christ and the Father.—The revised version gives for John 10:30: "I and the Father are one" instead of "I and my Father are one." By "the Father" the Jews rightly understood the Eternal Father, God. In the original Greek "one" appears in the neuter gender, and therefore expresses oneness in attributes, power, or purpose, and not a oneness of personality which would have required the masculine form. For treatment of the unity of the Godhead, and the separate personality of each Member, see *Articles of Faith,* pp. 40–42.

4. The Place of Our Lord's Retirement.—Jesus went "beyond Jordan into the place where John at first baptized" (John 10:40). This was probably Bethabara (1:28), which is called Bethany in some of the earliest manuscripts and is so designated in the latest revised version. Care must be taken not to confuse this Perean Bethany with the Bethany in Judea, the home of Martha and Mary, which was within two miles of Jerusalem.

5. Lazarus in the Tomb Four Days.—On the very probable assumption that the journey from Bethany in Judea to the place where Jesus was, in Perea, would require one day, Lazarus must have died on the day of the messenger's departure; for this day and the two days that elapsed before Jesus started toward Judea, and the day required for the return, would no more than cover the four days specified. It was and still is the custom in Palestine as in other oriental countries to bury on the day of death.

It was the popular belief that on the fourth day after death the spirit had finally departed from the vicinity of the corpse, and that thereafter decomposition proceeded unhindered. This may explain Martha's impulsive though gentle objection to having the tomb of her brother opened four days after his death (John 11:39). It is possible that the consent of the next of kin was required for the lawful opening of a grave. Both Martha and Mary were present, and in the presence of many witnesses assented to the opening of the tomb in which their brother lay.

6. Jesus Groaned in Spirit.—The marginal readings for "he groaned in the spirit" (John 11:33) and "again groaning in himself" (v. 38), as given in the revised version, are "was moved with indignation in the spirit" and "being moved with indignation in himself." All philological authorities agree that the words in the original Greek express sorrowful indignation, or as some aver, anger, and not alone a sympathetic emotion of grief. Any indignation the Lord may have felt, as intimated in verse 33, may be attributed to disapproval of the customary wailing over death, which, as vented by the Jews on this occasion, profaned the real and soulful grief of Martha and Mary; and His indignation, expressed by groaning as mentioned in verse 38, may have been due to the carping criticism uttered by some of the Jews as recorded in verse 37.

7. Caiaphas, High Priest that Year.—John's statement that Caiaphas was high priest "that same year" must not be construed as meaning that the office of high priest was of a single year's tenure. Under Jewish law the presiding priest, who was known as the high priest, would remain in office indefinitely, but the Roman government had arrogated to itself the appointive power as applying to this office; and frequent changes were made. This Caiaphas, whose full name was Josephus Caiaphas, was high priest under Roman appointment during a period of eleven years. To such appointments the Jews had to submit, though they often recognized as the high priest under their law, some other than the "civil high priest" appointed by Roman authority. Thus we find both Annas and Caiaphas exercising the authority of the office at the time of our Lord's arrest and later. (John 18:13, 24; Acts 4:6; compare Luke 3:2.) Farrar (p. 484, note) says: "Some have seen an open irony in the expression of St. John (11:49) that Caiaphas was high priest 'that same year,' as though the Jews had got into this contemptuous way of speaking during the rapid succession of priests—mere phantoms set up and displaced by the Roman fiat—who had in recent years succeeded each other. There must have been at least five living high priests, and ex-high priests at this council—Annas, Ismael Ben Phabi, Eleazar Ben Haman,

Simon Ben Kamhith, and Caiaphas, who had gained his elevation by bribery."

8. Divinely Appointed Judges Called "Gods."—In Psalm 82:6, judges invested by divine appointment are called "gods." To this scripture the Savior referred in His reply to the Jews in Solomon's porch. Judges so authorized officiated as the representatives of God and are honored by the exalted title "gods." Compare the similar appellation applied to Moses (Ex. 4:16; 7:1). Jesus Christ possessed divine authorization, not through the word of God transmitted to Him by man, but as an inherent attribute. The inconsistency of calling human judges "gods," and of ascribing blasphemy to the Christ who called Himself the Son of God, would have been apparent to the Jews but for their sin-darkened minds.

CHAPTER 29

ON TO JERUSALEM

JESUS AGAIN FORETELLS
HIS DEATH AND RESURRECTION[a]

Each of the three synoptic writers has made record of this last journey to Jerusalem and of occurrences connected therewith. The deep solemnity of the developments now so near at hand, and of the fate He was setting out to meet so affected Jesus that even the apostles were amazed at His absorption and evident sadness; they fell behind in amazement and fear. Then He paused, called the Twelve about Him, and in language of absolute plainness, without metaphor or simile, He said: "Behold, we go up to Jerusalem, and all things that are written by the prophets concerning the Son of man shall be accomplished. For he shall be delivered unto the Gentiles, and shall be mocked, and spitefully entreated, and spitted on: And they shall scourge him, and put him to death: and the third day he shall rise again."

It is to us an astounding fact that the Twelve failed to comprehend His meaning; yet Luke unqualifiedly affirms: "And they understood none of these things: and this saying was hid from them, neither knew they the things which were spoken." This avouchment of the Savior's approaching death and Resurrection spoken in confidential certainty to the Twelve was the third of its kind; and still they could not bring themselves to accept the awful truth.[b] According to Matthew's

---

[a] Matt. 20:17–19; Mark 10:32–34; Luke 18:31–34.

[b] The earlier predictions were: (1) that spoken shortly before the Transfiguration (Matt. 16:21; Mark 8:31), and (2) that which followed, in Galilee (Matt. 17:22, 23; Mark 9:31; compare Luke 9:44).

account, they were told of the very manner by which the Lord should die—that the Gentiles should crucify Him; yet they understood not. To them there was some dreadful incongruity, some dire inconsistency or inexplicable contradiction in the sayings of their beloved Master. They knew Him to be the Christ, the Son of the living God; and how could such a One be brought into subjection and be slain? They could not fail to realize that some unprecedented development in His life was impending; this they may have vaguely conceived to be the crisis for which they had been waiting, the open proclamation of His Messianic dignity, His enthronement as Lord and King. And such indeed Was to be, though in a manner far different from their anticipations. The culminating prediction—that on the third day He would rise again—seems to have puzzled them the most; and, at the same time, this assurance of ultimate triumph may have made all intermediate occurrences appear as of but secondary and transitory import. They persistently repelled the thought that they were following their Lord to the cross and the sepulchre.

THE QUESTION OF PRECEDENCE AGAIN[c]

Notwithstanding all the instructions the apostles had received concerning humility, and though they had before them the supreme example of the Master's life and conduct, in which the fact that service was the only measure of true greatness was abundantly demonstrated, they continued to dream of rank and honor in the kingdom of the Messiah. Perhaps because of the imminence of the Master's triumph, with which they all were particularly impressed at this time though ignorant of its real significance, certain of the Twelve appealed to the Lord in the course of this journey with a most ambitious request. The petitioners were James and John, though according to Matthew's record their mother[d] was the first to ask. The request was that when Jesus came into possession of His kingdom, He would so singly honor the aspiring pair as to install them in seats of eminence, one on His right hand, the other on His left. Instead of sharply rebuking such presumption, Jesus gently but impressively asked: "Are

[c] Matt. 20:20–28; Mark 10:35–45.

[d] Note 1, end of chapter.

ye able to drink of the cup that I shall drink of, and to be baptized with the baptism that I am baptized with?" The answer was full of self-confidence inspired by ignorant misapprehension. "We are able," they replied. Then said Jesus: "Ye shall drink indeed of my cup, and be baptized with the baptism that I am baptized with: but to sit on my right hand, and on my left, is not mine to give, but it shall be given to them for whom it is prepared of my Father."

The ten apostles were indignant at the two brothers, possibly less through disapproval of the spirit that had prompted the petition than because the two had forestalled the others in applying for the chief posts of distinction. But Jesus, patiently tolerant of their human weaknesses, drew the Twelve around Him, and taught them as a loving father might instruct and admonish his contentious children. He showed them how earthly rulers, such as princes among the Gentiles, domineer over their subjects, manifesting lordship and arbitrarily exercising the authority of office. But it was not to be so among the Master's servants; whoever of them would be great must be a servant indeed, willingly ministering unto his fellows; the humblest and most willing servant would be the chief of the servants. "For even the Son of man came not to be ministered unto, but to minister, and to give his life a ransom for many."[e]

SIGHT RESTORED TO THE BLIND NEAR JERICHO[f]

In the course of His journey Jesus came to Jericho, at or near which city He again exerted His wondrous power in opening the eyes of the blind. Matthew states that two sightless men were made to see, and that the miracle was enacted as Jesus was leaving Jericho; Mark mentions but one blind man, whom he names Bartimeus or the son of Timeus, and agrees with Matthew in saying that the healing was effected when Jesus was departing from the city; Luke specifies but one subject of the Lord's healing mercy, "a certain blind man," and chronicles the miracle as an incident of Christ's approach to Jericho. These slight variations attest the independent authorship of each of the records, and the

[e] For earlier lessons on the greatness of humility, see pages 363 and 440–41. For the significance of the title Son of Man, see pages 136–38.

[f] Matt. 20:30–34; Mark 10:46–52; Luke 18:35–43.

apparent discrepancies have no direct bearing upon the main facts, nor
do they detract from the instructional value of the Lord's work. As we
have found to be the case on an earlier occasion, two men were
mentioned though but one figures in the circumstantial account.[g]

The man who is more particularly mentioned, Bartimeus, sat by the
wayside, asking alms. Jesus approached, accompanied by the apostles,
many other disciples, and a great multitude of people, probably made
up largely of travelers on their way to Jerusalem to attend the Passover
festival, the time for which was about a week ahead. Hearing the
tramp of so great a company the sightless beggar inquired what it all
meant, and was answered, "Jesus of Nazareth passeth by." Eager lest
the opportunity of gaining the Master's attention be lost, he immediately
cried in a loud voice: "Jesus, thou son of David, have mercy on me."
His appeal, and particularly his use of the title, Son of David, show
that he knew of the great Teacher, had confidence in His power to
heal and faith in Him as the promised King and Deliverer of Israel.[h]
Those who were in advance of Jesus in the company tried to silence
the man, but the more they rebuked him the louder and more
persistently did he cry: "Thou son of David, have mercy on me."
Jesus halted in His course and directed that the man be brought to
Him. Those who but a moment before would have stopped the blind
man's yearning appeal, now that the Master had noticed him were
eager to be of service. To the sightless one they brought the glad
word: "Be of good comfort, rise; he calleth thee"; and he, casting
aside his outer garment lest it hinder, came in haste to Christ. To
the Lord's question, "What wilt thou that I shall do unto thee?"
Bartimeus answered: "Lord, that I may receive my sight." Then Jesus
spake the simple words of power and blessing: "Receive thy sight:
thy faith hath saved thee." The man, full of gratitude and knowing
that nothing short of divine interposition could have opened his eyes,
followed his Benefactor, glorifying God in heartfelt prayers of thanksgiving, in which many of those who had witnessed the miracle
fervently joined.

---

[g] See account of the two demoniacs, Matt. 8:28, compare Mark 5:1; Luke 8:27.
[h] Compare Matt. 9:27; 15:22.

ZACCHEUS, THE CHIEF AMONG THE PUBLICANS[i]

Jericho was a city of considerable importance; among its resident officials was a staff of publicans, or collectors of customs, and of these the chief was Zaccheus,[j] who had grown rich from the revenues of office. He had doubtless heard of the great Galilean who hesitated not to mingle with publicans, detested though they were by the Jews in general; he may have known, also, that Jesus had placed one of this publican class among the most prominent of the disciples. That Zaccheus was a Jew is indicated by his name, which is a variant of "Zacharias," with a Greek or Latin termination; he must have been particularly obnoxious to his people on account of his advanced status among the publicans, all of whom were in Roman employ. He had a great desire to see Jesus; the feeling was not one of mere curiosity; he had been impressed and set thinking by the things he had heard about this Teacher from Nazareth. But Zaccheus was a little man, and could not ordinarily see over the heads of others; so he ran ahead of the company and climbed a tree alongside the road. When Jesus reached the place, to the great surprise of the man in the tree He looked up and said: "Zaccheus, make haste, and come down; for to day I must abide at thy house." Zaccheus came down with haste, and joyfully received the Lord as his guest. The multitude by whom Jesus had been accompanied appear to have been generally friendly toward Him; but at this turn of affairs they murmured and criticized, saying that the Master "was gone to be guest with a man that is a sinner"; for all publicans were sinners in Jewish eyes, and Zaccheus admitted that the opprobrium in his case was possibly deserved. But having seen and conversed with Jesus, this chief among the publicans believed and was converted. As proof of his change of heart Zaccheus then and there voluntarily vowed unto the Lord to make amends and restitution if it were found that he owed such. "Behold, Lord," he said, "the half of my goods I give to the poor; and if I have taken anything from any man by false accusation, I restore him fourfold." These were works meet for repentance. The man realized that he could not change his past; but he knew he could in part at least atone for some of his misdeeds.

[i] Luke 19:1–10.
[j] Note 2, end of chapter.

His pledge to restore in fourfold measure whatever he had wrongfully acquired was in line with the Mosaic law as to restitution, but far in excess of the recompense required.[k] Jesus accepted the man's profession of repentance, and said: "This day is salvation come to this house, forsomuch as he also is a son of Abraham." Another stray sheep had been returned to the fold; another lost treasure had been found; another wayward son had come back to the Father's house.[l] "For the Son of man is come to seek and to save that which was lost."

UNTO EVERY ONE THAT HATH SHALL BE GIVEN [m]

As the multitude approached Jerusalem, Jesus being in their midst, expectation ran high as to what the Lord would do when He reached the capital of the nation. Many of those with Him were looking for a proclamation of His royal authority and "they thought that the kingdom of God should immediately appear." Jesus told them a story; we call it the *Parable of the Pounds*:

"A certain nobleman went into a far country to receive for himself a kingdom, and to return. And he called his ten servants, and delivered them ten pounds, and said unto them, Occupy till I come. But his citizens hated him, and sent a message after him, saying, We will not have this man to reign over us. And it came to pass, that when he was returned, having received the kingdom, then he commanded these servants to be called unto him, to whom he had given the money, that he might know how much every man had gained by trading. Then came the first, saying, Lord, thy pound hath gained ten pounds. And he said unto him, Well done, thou good servant: because thou hast been faithful in a very little, have thou authority over ten cities. And the second came, saying, Lord, thy pound hath gained five pounds. And he said likewise to him, Be thou also over five cities. And another came, saying, Lord, behold, here is thy pound, which I have kept laid up in a napkin: For I feared thee, because thou art an austere man: thou takest up that thou layedst not down, and reapest that thou didst not sow. And he saith unto him, Out of thine own

[k] Ex. 22:1–9.

[l] Compare pages 366 and 425–431.

[m] Luke 19:11–27.

mouth will I judge thee, thou wicked servant. Thou knewest that I was an austere man, taking up that I laid not down, and reaping that I did not sow: Wherefore then gavest not thou my money into the bank, that at my coming I might have required mine own with usury? And he said unto them that stood by, Take from him the pound, and give it to him that hath ten pounds. (And they said unto him, Lord, he hath ten pounds.) For I say unto you, That unto every one which hath shall be given; and from him that hath not, even that he hath shall be taken away from him. But those mine enemies, which would not that I should reign over them, bring hither, and slay them before me."

Both the circumstances of the story and the application of the parable were more readily apparent to the Jewish multitude than they are to us. The departure of a certain nobleman from a vassal province to the court of the suzerain to seek investiture of kingly authority, and the protest of the citizens over whom he asserted the right to reign, were incidents of Jewish history still fresh in the minds of the people to whom Christ spoke.[n] The explication of the parable is this: The people were not to look for an immediate establishment of the kingdom in temporal power. He who would be king was pictured as having departed for a far country from which he would assuredly return. Before leaving he had given to each of his servants a definite sum of money; and by their success in using this he would judge of their fitness to serve in offices of trust. When he returned he called for an accounting, in the course of which the cases of three servants are specified as types. One had so used the pound as to gain ten pounds; he was commended and received a reward such as only a sovereign could give, the governorship of ten cities. The second servant, with equal capital had increased it only five fold; he was properly rewarded in proportion by appointment as governor over five cities. The third gave back what he had received, without increase, for he had failed to use it. He had no reason and only a very poor excuse to offer for his dereliction. In justice he was severely reprimanded, and the money was taken from him. When the king directed that the pound so

[n] Note 3, end of chapter.

forfeited by the unfaithful servant be given to him who already had ten, some surprise was manifest amongst those who stood by; but the king explained, that "unto every one that hath shall be given," for such a one uses to advantage the means entrusted to his care, while "from him that hath not, even that he hath shall be taken away from him"; for he has demonstrated his utter unfitness to possess and use aright. This part of the parable, while on general application, must have appealed to the apostles as particularly apt; for each of them had received in trust an equal endowment through ordination, and each would be required to account for his administration.

The fact is apparent that Christ was the nobleman who was to be invested with the authority of kingship, and who would return to require the accounting at the hands of His trusted servants.[o] But many of the citizens hated Him and would protest His investiture, saying they would not have Him to reign over them.[p] When He does return in power and authority, these rebellious citizens shall surely receive the punishment they deserve.[q]

IN THE HOUSE OF SIMON THE LEPER [r]

Six days before the Feast of the Passover, that is to say before the day on which the paschal lamb was to be eaten,[s] Jesus arrived at Bethany, the home town of Martha and Mary, and of Lazarus who had recently died and been restored to life. The chronology of events during the last week of our Lord's life supports the generally accepted belief that in this year, the fourteenth day of Nisan, on which the Passover festival began, fell on Thursday; and this being so, the day on which Jesus reached Bethany was the preceding Friday, the eve of the Jewish Sabbath. Jesus fully realized that this Sabbath was the last He would live to see in mortality. The Gospel-writers have drawn a veil of reverent silence over the events of that day. It appears that Jesus

o Compare Mark 13:34.

p Note 4, end of chapter.

q Comparison of similarities and differences between this parable and that of the Talents (Matt. 25:14–30) will be made in chapter 32, pages 538–542.

r John 12:1–8; Matt. 26:6–13; Mark 14:3–9.

s See Ex. 12:1–10.

passed His last Sabbath in retirement at Bethany. The journey afoot from Jericho had been no easy walk, for the road ascended to an altitude of nearly three thousand feet, and was withal otherwise a toilsome way.

On Saturday,[t] probably in the evening after the Sabbath had passed, a supper was spread for Jesus and the Twelve in the house of Simon the leper. No other mention of this man, Simon, appears in scripture. If he was living at the time our Lord was entertained in the house known by his name, and if he was present, he must have been previously healed of his leprosy, as otherwise he could not have been allowed within the town, far less to be one of a festal company. It is reasonable to think that the man had once been a victim of leprosy and had come to be currently known as Simon the leper, and that he was one among the many sufferers from this dread disease who had been healed through the Lord's ministrations.

Martha was in charge of the supper arrangements on this memorable occasion, and her sister Mary was with her, while Lazarus sat at table with Jesus. Many have assumed that the house of Simon the leper was the family home of the two sisters and Lazarus, in which case it is possible that Simon was the father of the three; but of such relationship we have no proof.[u] There was no attempt to secure unusual privacy at this supper. Such occasions were customarily marked by the presence of many uninvited lookers-on in that time; and we are not surprised to learn, therefore, that many people were there and that they had come "not for Jesus' sake only, but that they might see Lazarus also, whom he had raised from the dead." Lazarus was a subject of much interest and doubtless of curiosity among the people; and at the time of his privileged and intimate association with Jesus in Bethany, the chief priests were plotting to put him to death, on account of the effect his restoration had had upon the people, many of whom believed on Jesus because of the miracle.

That supper in Bethany was an event never to be forgotten. Mary, the more contemplative and spiritually minded of the two sisters, she who loved to sit at the feet of Jesus and listen to His words, and who had been commended for having so chosen the one needful thing, which

[t] Note 5, end of chapter.
[u] Note 6, end of chapter.

her more practical sister lacked,[v] brought from among her treasures an alabaster cruse containing a pound of costly spikenard ointment; she broke the sealed flask [w] and poured its fragrant contents upon the head and feet of her Lord, and wiped His feet with her loosened tresses.[x] To anoint the head of a guest with ordinary oil was to do him honor; to anoint his feet also was to show unusual and single regard; but the anointing of head and feet with spikenard, and in such abundance, was an act of reverential homage rarely rendered even to kings.[y] Mary's act was an expression of adoration; it was the fragrant outwelling of a heart overflowing with worship and affection.

But this splendid tribute of a devout woman's love was made the cause of disagreeable protest. Judas Iscariot, treasurer of the Twelve, but dishonest, avaricious, and small-souled in character, vented his grumbling complaint, saying: "Why was not this ointment sold for three hundred pence, and given to the poor?"[z] His seeming solicitude for the poor was all hypocrisy. He was a thief and lamented that he had not been given the precious ointment to sell, or that the price had not been turned into the bag of which he was the self-interested custodian. Mary's use of the costly unguent had been so lavish that others beside Judas had let their surprise grow into murmuring; but to him is attributed the distinction of being the chief complainer. Mary's sensitive nature was pained by the ungracious words of disapproval; but Jesus interposed, saying: "Why trouble ye the woman? for she hath wrought a good work upon me." Then in further rebuke and by way of solemn instruction He continued: "For ye have the poor always with you; but me ye have not always. For in that she hath poured this ointment on my body, she did it for my burial. Verily I say unto you, Wheresoever this gospel shall be preached in the whole world, there shall also this, that this woman hath done, be told for a memorial of her."

---

[v] Luke 10:40–42.

[w] The better rendering is "cruse" or "flask" instead of "box." See revised version.

[x] This occurrence must not be confused with that of an earlier anointing of Jesus by a penitent sinner in the house of Simon the Pharisee (Luke 7:36–50) in Galilee.

[y] Note 7, end of chapter.

[z] Three hundred pence or Roman denarii would be approximately equal in value to forty-five dollars.

We are left without certain information as to whether Mary knew that within a few days her beloved Lord would be in the tomb. She may have been so informed in view of the hallowed intimacy between Jesus and the family; or she may have gathered from the remarks of Christ to the apostles that the sacrifice of His life was impending; or perhaps by inspired intuition she was impelled to render the loving tribute by which her memory has been enshrined in the hearts of all who know and love the Christ. John has preserved to us this remark of Jesus in the rebuke called forth by the grumbling Iscariot: "Let her alone; against the day of my burying hath she kept this"; and Mark's version is likewise suggestive of definite and solemn purpose on Mary's part: "She is come aforehand to anoint my body to the burying."

CHRIST'S TRIUMPHAL ENTRY INTO JERUSALEM [aa]

While still in Bethany or in the neighboring village of Bethphage, and according to John's account on the next day after the supper at Simon's house, Jesus directed two of His disciples to go to a certain place, where, He told them, they would find an ass tied, and with her a colt on which no man had ever sat. These they were to bring to Him. If stopped or questioned they were to say the Lord had need of the animals. Matthew alone mentions both ass and colt; the other writers specify the latter only; most likely the mother followed as the foal was led away, and the presence of the dam probably served to keep the colt tractable. The disciples found all to be as the Lord had said. They brought the colt to Jesus, spread their coats on the gentle creature's back, and set the Master thereon. The company started toward Jerusalem, Jesus riding in their midst.

Now, as was usual, great numbers of people had come up to the city many days before the beginning of the Passover rites, in order that they might attend to matters of personal purification, and make good their arrears in the offering of prescribed sacrifices. Though the great day, on which the festival was to be inaugurated, was yet four days ahead, the city was thronged with pilgrim crowds; and among these much questioning had arisen as to whether Jesus would venture

---

[aa] Matt. 21:1–11. Mark 11:1–11; Luke 19:29–44; John 12:12–19.

to appear publicly in Jerusalem during the feast, in view of the well-known plans of the hierarchy to take Him into custody. The common people were interested in every act and movement of the Master; and word of His departure from Bethany sped ahead of Him; so that by the time He began the descent from the highest part of the road on the flank of the Mount of Olives, great crowds had gathered about Him. The people were jubilant over the spectacle of Jesus riding toward the holy city; they spread out their garments, and cast palm fronds and other foliage in His path, thus carpeting the way as for the passing of a king. For the time being He was their king, and they His adoring subjects. The voices of the multitude sounded in reverberating harmony: "Blessed be the King that cometh in the name of the Lord: peace in heaven, and glory in the highest"; and again: "Hosanna to the son of David: Blessed is he that cometh in the name of the Lord; Hosanna in the highest."[bb]

But amidst all this jubilation, Jesus was sad as He came in sight of the great city wherein stood the House of the Lord; and He wept, because of the wickedness of His people, and of their refusal to accept Him as the Son of God; moreover He foresaw the awful scenes of destruction before which both city and temple were soon to fall. In anguish and tears, He thus apostrophized the doomed city: "If thou hadst known, even thou, at least in this thy day, the things which belong unto thy peace! but now they are hid from thine eyes. For the days shall come upon thee, that thine enemies shall cast a trench about thee, and compass thee round, and keep thee in on every side, and shall lay thee even with the ground, and thy children within thee; and they shall not leave in thee one stone upon another; because thou knewest not the time of thy visitation." The multitude was increased by tributary crowds who fell in with the imposing procession at every crossway; and the shouts of praise and homage were heard inside the city while the advancing company was yet far from the walls. When the Lord rode through the massive portal and actually entered the capital of the Great King, the whole city was thrilled. To the inquiry of the uninformed, "Who is this?" the multitude shouted: "This is Jesus,

[bb] Note 8, end of chapter.

the prophet of Nazareth of Galilee." It may be that the Galilean pilgrims were first to answer and loudest in the gladsome proclamation; for the proud Judeans held Galilee in low esteem, and on this day, Jesus of Galilee was the most prominent personage in Jerusalem. The Pharisees, resentful of the honors thus shown to One whom they had long plotted to destroy, impotently condoled with one another over the failure of all their nefarious schemes, saying: "Perceive ye how ye prevail nothing? behold, the world is gone after him." Unable to check the surging enthusiasm of the multitudes, or to silence the joyous acclamations, some of the Pharisees made their way through the throngs until they reached Jesus, and to Him they appealed, saying: "Master, rebuke thy disciples." But the Lord, "answered and said unto them, I tell you that, if these should hold their peace, the stones would immediately cry out."[cc]

Dismounting, He entered afoot the temple enclosure; shouts of adulation greeted Him there. Chief priests, scribes, and Pharisees, the official representatives of the theocracy, the hierarchy of Judaism, were incensed; there was no denying the fact that the people were rendering Messianic honors to this troublesome Nazarene; and that too within the very purlieus of the temple of Jehovah.

The purpose of Christ in thus yielding Himself for the day to the desires of the people and accepting their homage with kingly grace may not be fully comprehended by us of finite mind. That the occasion was no accidental or fortuitous happening, of which He took advantage without preconceived intention, is evident. He knew beforehand what would be, and what He would do. It was no meaningless pageantry; but the actual advent of the King into His royal city, and His entry into the temple, the house of the King of kings. He came riding on an ass, in token of peace, acclaimed by the Hosanna shouts of multitudes; not on a caparisoned steed with the panoply of combat and the accompaniment of bugle blasts and fanfare of trumpets. That the joyous occasion was in no sense suggestive of physical hostility or of seditious disturbance is sufficiently demonstrated by the indulgent unconcern with which it was viewed by the Roman officials, who were usually prompt to send

[cc] Compare Hab. 2:11.

their legionnaires swooping down from the fortress of Antonia at the first evidence of an outbreak; and they were particularly vigilant in suppressing all Messianic pretenders, for false Messiahs had arisen already, and much blood had been shed in the forcible dispelling of their delusive claims. But the Romans saw nothing to fear, perhaps much to smile at, in the spectacle of a King mounted upon an ass, and attended by subjects, who, though numerous, brandished no weapons but waved instead palm branches and myrtle sprigs. The ass has been designated in literature as "the ancient symbol of Jewish royalty," and one riding upon an ass as the type of peaceful progress.

Such triumphal entry of Jesus into the chief city of the Jews would have been strikingly inconsistent with the general tenor of His ministry in its early stages. Even the intimation that He was the Christ had been made with guarded care, if at all; and every manifestation of popular regard in which He might have figured as a national leader had been suppressed. Now, however, the hour of the great consummation was near at hand; the public acceptance of the nation's homage, and the acknowledgment of both kingly and Messianic titles, constituted an open and official proclamation of His divine investiture. He had entered city and temple in such royal state as befitted the Prince of Peace. By the rulers of the nation He had been rejected and His claims derided. The manner of His entry should have appealed to the learned teachers of the law and the prophets; for Zechariah's impressive forecast, the fulfilment of which the evangelist, John, finds in the events of this memorable Sunday,[dd] was frequently cited among them: "Rejoice greatly, O daughter of Zion; shout, O daughter of Jerusalem: behold, thy King cometh unto thee: he is just, and having salvation; lowly, and riding upon an ass, and upon a colt the foal of an ass."[ee]

CERTAIN GREEKS VISIT CHRIST [ff]

Among the multitudes who came to Jerusalem at the time of the annual Passover were people of many nations. Some of these, though

---

[dd] The Sunday before Easter is annually celebrated by many Christian sects as Palm Sunday, in commemoration of our Lord's triumphal entry into Jerusalem.

[ee] Zech. 9:9.

[ff] John 12:20–26.

not of Jewish descent, had been converted to Judaism; they were admitted to the temple precincts, but were not allowed to pass beyond the court of the Gentiles.[gg] Sometime during our Lord's last week of mortal life, possibly on the day of His royal entry into the city,[hh] certain Greeks, who were evidently numbered among the proselytes since they had come "to worship at the feast," sought an interview with Jesus. Imbued with a becoming sense of decorum they hesitated to directly approach the Master, and applied instead to Philip, one of the apostles, saying: "Sir, we would see Jesus." Philip consulted with Andrew, and the two then informed Jesus, who, as we may reasonably infer from the context though the fact is not explicitly stated, graciously received the foreign visitors and imparted to them precepts of the utmost worth. It is evident that the desire of these Greeks to meet the Master was not grounded on curiosity or other unworthy impulse; they earnestly wished to see and hear the Teacher whose fame had reached their country, and whose doctrines had impressed them.

To them Jesus testified that the hour of His death was near at hand, the hour in which "the Son of man should be glorified." They were surprised and pained by the Lord's words, and possibly they inquired as to the necessity of such a sacrifice. Jesus explained by citing a striking illustration drawn from nature: "Verily, verily, I say unto you, Except a corn of wheat fall into the ground and die, it abideth alone: but if it die, it bringeth forth much fruit."[ii] The simile is an apt one, and at once impressively simple and beautiful. A farmer who neglects or refuses to cast his wheat into the earth, because he wants to keep it, can have no increase; but if he sow the wheat in good rich soil, each living grain may multiply itself many fold, though of necessity the seed must be sacrificed in the process. So, said the Lord, "He that loveth his life shall lose it; and he that hateth his life in this world shall keep it unto life eternal." The Master's meaning is clear; he that loves his life so well that he will not imperil it, or, if need be, give it

---

[gg] See *House of the Lord,* pp. 56, 57.

[hh] John records this event in immediate sequence to the Lord's triumphal entry, though without any specific indication of the time of its occurrence.

[ii] Compare 1 Cor. 15:36.

up, in the service of God, shall forfeit his opportunity to win the bounteous increase of eternal life; while he who esteems the call of God as so greatly superior to life that his love of life is as hatred in comparison, shall find the life he freely yields or is willing to yield, though for the time being it disappear like the grain buried in the soil; and he shall rejoice in the bounty of eternal development. If such be true of every man's existence, how transcendently so was it of the life of Him who came to die that men may live? Therefore was it necessary that He die, as He had said He was about to do; but His death, far from being life lost, was to be life glorified.

THE VOICE FROM HEAVEN [jj]

The realization of the harrowing experiences upon which He was about to enter, and particularly the contemplation of the state of sin, which made His sacrifice imperative, so weighed upon the Savior's mind that He sorrowed deeply. "Now is my soul troubled," He groaned; "and what shall I say?" He exclaimed in anguish. Should He say, "Father, save me from this hour" when as He knew "for this cause" had He come "unto this hour?" To His Father alone could He turn for comforting support, not to ask relief from, but strength to endure, what was to come; and He prayed: "Father, glorify thy name." It was the rising of a mighty Soul to meet a supreme issue, which for the moment had seemed to be overwhelming. To that prayer of renewed surrender to the Father's will, "Then came there a voice from heaven, saying, I have both glorified it, and will glorify it again."

The voice was real; it was no subjective whisper of comfort to the inner consciousness of Jesus, but an external, objective reality. People who were standing by heard the sound, and interpreted it variously; some said it was thunder; others, of better spiritual discernment, said: "An angel spake to him"; and some may have understood the words as had Jesus. Now fully emerged from the passing cloud of enveloping anguish, the Lord turned to the people, saying: "This voice came not because of me, but for your sakes." And then, with the consciousness of assured triumph over sin and death, He exclaimed in accents of

[jj] John 12:27–36.

divine jubilation, as though the cross and the sepulchre were already of the past: "Now is the judgment of this world: now shall the prince of this world be cast out." Satan, the prince of the world was doomed.[kk] "And I," the Lord continued, "if I be lifted up from the earth, will draw all men unto me." John assures us that this last utterance signified the manner of the Lord's death; the people so understood, and they asked an explanation of what seemed to them an inconsistency, in that the scriptures, as they had been taught to interpret the same, declared that the Christ was to abide forever,[ll] and now He who claimed to be the Messiah, the Son of Man, averred that He must be lifted up. "Who is this Son of man?" they asked. Mindful as ever not to cast pearls where they would not be appreciated, the Lord refrained from a direct avowal, but admonished them to walk in the light while the light was with them, for darkness would surely follow; and, as He reminded them, "he that walketh in darkness knoweth not whither he goeth." In conclusion the Lord admonished them thus: "While ye have light, believe in the light, that ye may be the children of light."[mm]

At the close of this discourse Jesus departed from the people "and did hide himself from them." The record of the first day of what has come to be known as the week of our Lord's passion[nn] is thus concluded by Mark: "And when he had looked round about upon all things, and now the eventide was come, he went out unto Bethany with the twelve."[oo]

NOTES TO CHAPTER 29

1. The Mother of James and John.—The mother of these two sons of Zebedee (Matt. 20:20; compare 4:21) is generally understood to have been the Salome mentioned as one of the women present at the Crucifixion (Mark 15:40; compare Matt. 27:56 in which "the mother of Zebedee's children" is mentioned, and the name "Salome" is omitted), and one of those who arrived first at the tomb on the morning of the Resurrection (Mark 16:1). From the fact that John mentions the mother of Jesus and "his mother's sister" (19:25) and omits mention of Salome by name, some

---

kk Compare John 14:30; 16:11.

ll See e.g. Isa. 9:7; Dan. 7:14, 27; Ezek. 37:25.

mm Compare John 1:9; 3:19; 8:12; 9:5; 12:46.

nn Acts 1:3.

oo Mark 11:11. Note 9, end of chapter.

expositors hold that Salome was the sister of Mary the mother of Jesus; and therefore the Savior's aunt. This relationship would make James and John cousins to Jesus. While the scriptural record does not disprove this alleged kinship, it certainly does not affirm the same.

2. Jericho.—This was an ancient city, lying north-easterly from Jerusalem, a little less than fifteen miles in a straight line. In the course of the exodus it was captured by the people of Israel through a miraculous interposition of divine power. (Josh. 6) The productiveness of the region is indicated by the descriptive appellation "city of palm trees" (Deut. 34:3; Judg. 1:16; 3:13; 2 Chr. 28:15). The name Jericho means "place of fragrance." Its climate was semi-tropical, a consequence of its low altitude. It lay in a valley several hundred feet below the level of the Mediterranean; this explains Luke's statement (19:28) that after Jesus had spoken the Parable of the Pounds when on the way from Jericho, "he went before, ascending up to Jerusalem." In the time of Christ, Jericho was an important city; and the abundance of its commercial products, particularly balsam and spices, led to the maintenance of a customs office there, over which Zaccheus seems to have presided.

3. The Nobleman and the Kingdom.—The local setting of the part of the Parable of the Pounds that relates to a certain nobleman going into a far country to receive for himself a kingdom had its parallel in history. Archelaus, who by the will of his father, Herod the Great, had been named king of the Jews, set out for Rome to ask of the emperor the confirmation of his royal status. He was opposed by a protest from the people. On the utilization of this circumstance in the parable, Farrar (p. 493, note) says: "'A nobleman going into a far country to receive a kingdom' would be utterly unintelligible, had we not fortunately known that this was done both by Archelaus and by Antipas (Jos. Ant. xvii, 9:4). And in the case of Archelaus the Jews had actually sent to Augustus a deputation of fifty to recount his cruelties and oppose his claims, which, though it failed at the time, was subsequently successful (Jos. Ant. xvii, 13:2). Philipus defended the property of Archelaus, during his absence, from the encroachments of the proconsul Sabinus. The magnificent palace which Archelaus had built at Jericho (Jos. Ant. xvii, 13:1) would naturally recall these circumstances to the mind of Jesus, and the parable is another striking example of the manner in which He utilized the most ordinary circumstances around Him, and made them the bases of His highest teachings. It is also another unsuspected indication of the authenticity and truthfulness of the Gospels."

4. "We Will Not Have this Man to Reign Over Us."—On this phase of the parable, Trench (*Miracles*, p. 390) very aptly remarks: "Twice before He had gone to receive His kingdom, this very declaration found formal utterance from their lips,—once when they cried to Pilate, 'we have no king but Caesar'; and again when they remonstrated with him, 'Write not, The King of the Jews' (John 19:15, 21; compare Acts 17:7). But the stricter fulfilment of these words is to be found in the demeanor of the Jews after His ascension, their fierce hostility to Christ in His infant Church (Acts 12:3; 13:45; 14:18; 17:5; 18:6; 22:22; 23:12; 2 Thes. 2:15)."

5. The Day of the Supper at Bethany.—John places this event as having occurred on the day following Christ's arrival in Bethany, for as we see from 12:12, the triumphal entry into Jerusalem took place on the next day after the supper, and, as stated in the text, Jesus most probably reached Bethany on Friday. The joyous processional into Jerusalem did not occur on the day following Friday, for that was the Jewish Sabbath. Matthew (26:2–13) and Mark (14:1–9) give place to the incident of the supper after the record of the triumphal entry and other events, from which some have drawn the inference that these two writers place the supper two days before the Passover. This inference lacks confirmation. In this matter the chronological order given by John appears to be the true one.

6. The Family Home at Bethany.—The home of Martha, Mary, and Lazarus appears to have been the usual abiding place of Jesus when He was in Bethany. Undoubtedly He was on terms of very close and affectionate acquaintanceship with all members of the family, even before the miraculous raising of Lazarus from the dead, and, and, this supremely blessed occurrence must have intensified into worshipful reverence the esteem in which our Lord had been held in that household. As to whether this home was identical with the house of Simon the leper, the scriptural record does not state. John, who gives a fairly detailed account of the supper served by Martha, makes no mention of Simon or his house. It is noticeable that the synoptic writers say very little about this home in Bethany. Farrar has aptly remarked (p. 483): "We seem to trace in the Synoptists a special reticence about the family at Bethany. The house in which they take a prominent position is called 'the house of Simon the leper'; Mary is called simply 'a woman' by St. Matthew and St. Mark (Matt. 26:6, 7; Mark 14:3); and St. Luke contents himself with calling Bethany 'a certain village' (Luke 10:38), although he was perfectly aware of the name (Luke 19:29)."

7. Spikenard Ointment.—This was among the most highly prized of oriental unguents. That with which Mary anointed Jesus is described by Matthew and Mark as "very precious," and by John as "very costly." In the original the adjective "pistic" appears; this is translated by some as meaning "liquid," but by others as signifying "genuine." There were many inferior imitations of the real spikenard, or nard; and we are left without a doubt that Mary's precious gift was of the best. The plant from which the fragrant extract is obtained is a species of bearded grass indigenous in India. Spikenard is mentioned in Song of Solomon 1:12; 4:13, 14.

8. Hosanna!—"Hosanna" is a Greek form of the Hebrew expression for "Save us now," or "Save, we pray," which occurs in the original of Ps. 118:25. It occurs nowhere in the English Bible except in the acclamations of the people at Christ's triumphal entry into Jerusalem, and in the joyous shouts of children in the temple

(Matt. 21:9, 15). Note the rendering of the "Hosanna Shout" in the restored Church of Christ in the current dispensation on occasions of particular rejoicing before the Lord (see *House of the Lord,* pp. 120, 150, 210). "Hallelujah," literally rendered, means "Praise ye Jehovah." It occurs in the Greek form "Alleluia" in Rev. 19:1, 3, 4, 6.

9. The First Day in Passion Week.—A comparison of the accounts of the Lord's triumphal entry into Jerusalem, and of certain events following, as recorded by the three synoptists, shows at least a possibility of discrepancy as to sequence. It appears certain that Jesus visited the temple grounds on the day of the royal advent into the city. From Matthew 21:12 and Luke 19:45 and the context preceding these passages, the inference has been drawn that the second clearing of the temple occurred on the day of the processional entry; while others interpret Mark 11:11 and 15 as meaning that the event took place on a later day. The question is admittedly an open one; and the order of presentation followed in the text is one of convenience of treatment based on rational probability.

CHAPTER 30

JESUS RETURNS TO THE TEMPLE DAILY

AN INSTRUCTIVE INCIDENT ON THE WAY[a]

On the morrow, which, as we reckon, was Monday, the second day of Passion week, Jesus and the Twelve returned to Jerusalem and spent the greater part of the day at the temple. The start from Bethany was an early one, and Jesus hungered by the way. Looking ahead He saw a fig tree that differed from the rest of the many fig trees of the region in that it was in full leaf though the season of fruit had not yet come.[b] It is well known that the fruit-buds of a fig tree appear earlier than do the leaves, and that by the time the tree is in full foliage the figs are well advanced toward maturity. Moreover, certain species of figs are edible while yet green; indeed the unripe fruit is relished in the Orient at the present time. It would be reasonable, therefore, for one to expect to find edible figs even in early April on a tree that was already covered with leaves. When Jesus and His party reached this particular tree, which had rightly been regarded as rich in promise of fruit, they found on it nothing but leaves; it was a showy, fruitless, barren tree. It was destitute even of old figs, those of the preceding season, some of which are often found in spring on fruitful trees. Jesus pronounced upon that tree the sentence of perpetual barrenness. "No man eat fruit of thee hereafter forever" He said according to Mark's account; or, as Matthew records the judgment, "Let no fruit grow on thee henceforward for ever." The latter writer tells us in immediate sequence that "presently the fig tree withered away"; but the former makes it appear

---

[a] Matt. 21:18–22; Mark 11:12–14, 20–26.

[b] Note 1, end of chapter.

that the effect of the curse was not observed until the following morning, when, as Jesus and the apostles were once again on the way between Bethany and Jerusalem, they saw that the fig tree had withered and dried from the roots up. Peter called attention to the blasted tree, and, addressing Jesus, exclaimed: "Master, behold, the fig tree which thou cursedst is withered away."

Applying the lesson of the occasion, Jesus said, "Have faith in God"; and then He repeated some of His former assurances as to the power of faith, by which even mountains may be removed, should there be need of such miraculous accomplishment, and through which, indeed, any necessary thing may be done. The blighting of a tree was shown to be small in comparison with the greater possibilities of achievement through faith and prayer. But to so achieve one must work and pray without reservation or doubt, as the Lord thus made plain: "Therefore I say unto you, What things soever ye desire, when ye pray, believe that ye receive them, and ye shall have them." Prayer must be acceptable unto God to be effective; and it follows that he who desires to accomplish any work through prayer and faith must be fit to present himself before the Lord in supplication; therefore Jesus again instructed the apostles saying: "And when ye stand praying, forgive, if ye have ought against any: that your Father also which is in heaven may forgive you your trespasses. But if ye do not forgive, neither will your Father which is in heaven forgive your trespasses."[c]

The blighting of the barren fig tree is regarded by many as unique among the recorded miracles of Christ, from the fact that while all the others were wrought for relief, blessing, and beneficent purposes generally, this one appears as an act of judgment and destructive execution. Nevertheless in this miracle the Lord's purpose is not hidden; and the result, while fatal to a tree, is of lasting blessing to all who would learn and profit by the works of God. If no more has been accomplished by the miracle than the presenting of so impressive an object lesson for the instructions that followed, that smitten tree has proved of greater service to humanity than have all

[c] Page 228.

the fig orchards of Bethphage.[d] To the apostles the act was another and an indisputable proof of the Lord's power over nature, His control of natural forces and all material things, His jurisdiction over life and death. He had healed multitudes; the wind and the waves had obeyed His words; on three occasions He had restored the dead to life; it was fitting that He should demonstrate His power to smite and to destroy. In manifesting His command over death, He had mercifully raised a maiden from the couch on which she had died, a young man from the bier on which he was being carried to the grave, another from the sepulchre in which he had been laid away a corpse; but in proof of His power to destroy by a word He chose a barren and worthless tree for His subject. Could any of the Twelve doubt, when, a few days later they saw Him in the hands of vindictive priests and heartless pagans, that did He so will He could smite His enemies by a word, even unto death? Yet not until after His glorious Resurrection did even the apostles realize how truly voluntary His sacrifice had been.

But the fate that befell the barren fig tree is instructive from another point of view. The incident is as much parable as miracle. That leafy tree was distinguished among fig trees; the others offered no invitation, gave no promise; "the time of figs was not yet"; they, in due season would bring forth fruit and leaves; but this precocious and leafy pretender waved its umbrageous limbs as in boastful assertion of superiority. For those who responded to its ostentatious invitation, for the hungering Christ who came seeking fruit, it had naught but leaves. Even for the purposes of the lesson involved, we cannot conceive of the tree being blighted primarily because it was fruitless, for at that season the other fig trees were bare of fruit also; it was made the object of the curse and the subject of the Lord's instructive discourse, because, having leaves, it was deceptively barren. Were it reasonable to regard the tree as possessed of moral agency, we would have to pronounce it a hypocrite; its utter barrenness coupled with its abundance of foliage made of it a type of human hypocrisy.

---

[d] "Bethphage," the name of a village close to Bethany, and therefore near to the Mount of Olives, means "house of figs." See mention, Matt. 21:1; Mark 11:1; Luke 19:29. "Bethany" signifies "house of dates." For "house" in the literal translation we may read "place."

The leafy, fruitless tree was a symbol of Judaism, which loudly proclaimed itself as the only true religion of the age, and condescendingly invited all the world to come and partake of its rich ripe fruit; when in truth it was but an unnatural growth of leaves, with no fruit of the season, nor even an edible bulb held over from earlier years, for such as it had of former fruitage was dried to worthlessness and made repulsive in its worm-eaten decay. The religion of Israel had degenerated into an artificial religionism, which in pretentious show and empty profession outclassed the abominations of heathendom. As already pointed out in these pages, the fig tree was a favorite type in rabbinical representation of the Jewish race, and the Lord had before adopted the symbolism in the Parable of the Barren Fig Tree, that worthless growth which did but cumber the ground.[e]

THE SECOND CLEARING OF THE TEMPLE [f]
Within the temple grounds Jesus was filled with indignation at the scene of tumult and desecration which the place presented. Three years before, at Passover time, He had been wrought up to a high state of righteous anger by a similar exhibition of sordid chaffering within the sacred precincts, and had driven out the sheep and oxen, and forcibly expelled the traders and the money changers and all who were using His Father's house as a house of merchandise.[g] That was near the beginning of His public labor, and the vigorous action was among the first of His works to attract general attention; now, within four days of the cross, He cleared the courts again by casting out all "them that sold and bought in the temple, and overthrew the tables of the money-changers, and the seats of them that sold doves"; nor would He suffer any to carry their buckets and baskets through the enclosure, as many were in the habit of doing and so making the way a common thoroughfare. "Is it not written," He demanded of them in wrath, "My house shall be called of all nations the house of prayer? but ye have made it a den of thieves." On the former occasion, before He had declared or even confessed His Messiahship, He had designated

[e] Luke 13:6–9.
[f] Matt. 21:12–13; Mark 11:15–17; Luke 19:45, 46.
[g] John 2:14–17.

the temple as "My Father's house"; now that He had openly avowed Himself to be the Christ, He called it "My house." The expressions are in a sense synonymous; He and the Father were and are one in possession and dominion. The means by which the later expulsion was accomplished are not stated; but it is plain that none could withstand His authoritative command; He acted in the strength of righteousness, before which the forces of evil had to give way.

His wrath of indignation was followed by the calmness of gentle ministry; there in the cleared courts of His house, blind and lame folk came limping and groping about Him, and He healed them. The anger of the chief priests and scribes was raging against Him; but it was impotent. They had decreed His death, and had made repeated efforts to take Him, and there He sat within the very area over which they claimed supreme jurisdiction, and they were afraid to touch Him because of the common people, whom they professed to despise yet heartily feared—"for all the people were very attentive to hear him."

The rage of the officials was further aggravated by a touching incident, which seems to have accompanied or to have immediately followed His merciful healing of the afflicted folk at the temple. Children saw what He did; with their innocent minds yet unsullied by the prejudice of tradition and their sight yet undarkened by sin, they perceived in Him the Christ, and burst forth into praise and worship in a hymn that was heard by the angels: "Hosanna to the Son of David." With ill-concealed anger the temple officials demanded of Him: "Hearest thou what these say?" They probably expected Him to disclaim the title, or possibly hoped that He would reassert His claim in a manner that would afford excuse for legal action against Him, for to most of them the Son of David was the Messiah, the promised King. Would He clear Himself of the blasphemy that attached to the unjustified acknowledgment of so awful a dignity? Jesus answered, with an implied rebuke for their ignorance of the scriptures: "Yea; have ye never read, Out of the mouth of babes and sucklings thou hast perfected praise?"[h]

It was now Monday evening; Jesus left the city and retired again to Bethany, where He lodged. This course was a prudent one, in view

[h] Matt. 21:16; compare Ps. 8:2; see also Matt. 11:25; 1 Cor. 1:27.

of the determination of the rulers to get Him into their power provided they could do so without arousing the people. This they could not accomplish by day, for wherever He appeared He was the center of a multitude; but had He remained in Jerusalem over night the vigilant emissaries of the hierarchy might have succeeded in taking Him, unless He withstood them by some miraculous action. Near as was His hour, it had not yet struck; and He would be made captive only as He permitted Himself, a voluntary victim, to be taken into the hands of His enemies.

CHRIST'S AUTHORITY CHALLENGED BY THE RULERS [i]

On the following day, that is on Tuesday, He returned to the temple with the Twelve, passing the withered fig tree on the way and impressing the moral of the combined miracle and parable as we have already seen. As He taught in the sacred place, preaching the gospel to all who would hear, the chief priests with a number of scribes and elders came upon Him in a body. They had been debating about Him over night, and had resolved on at least one step; they would challenge His authority for what He had done the day before. They were the guardians of the temple, both the material structure and the theocratic system for which the holy edifice stood; and this Galilean, who permitted Himself to be called the Christ and defended those who so acclaimed Him, had for the second time ignored their authority within the temple walls and in the presence of the common people over whom they lorded so arrogantly. So this official deputation, with plans matured, came to Him saying: "By what authority doest thou these things? and who gave thee this authority?" This action was doubtless a preliminary step in a preconcerted attempt to suppress the activities of Jesus, both of word and deed, within the temple precincts. It will be remembered that after the first cleansing of the temple, the Jews had angrily demanded of Jesus a sign by which they might judge the question of His divine commission;[j] and it is significant that on this latter occasion no sign was asked, but instead thereof, a specific avowal as to the authority He possessed and by whom it had been

[i] Matt. 21:23–27; Mark 11:27–33; Luke 20:1–8.
[j] John 2:18–21.

given Him. A three years' course of miracle and teaching was known to them; on the yesterday blind and lame had been healed inside the temple walls; and Lazarus, the living testimony of the Lord's power over death and the grave was before them. To ask a further sign would have been to flagrantly expose themselves to the ridicule of the people.

They knew what authority the Lord claimed; their question was of sinister purpose. Jesus did not condescend to voice an answer in which they could possibly find further excuse for antagonizing Him; but He availed Himself of a method very common among themselves—that of countering one question with another. "And Jesus answered and said unto them, I also will ask you one thing, which if ye tell me, I in like wise will tell you by what authority I do these things. The baptism of John, whence was it? from heaven, or of men?" They consulted among themselves as to what answer would best serve to extricate them from an embarrassing position; no mention is made of any attempt to ascertain the truth and reply accordingly; they were thoroughly nonplussed. Should they answer that John's baptism was of God, Jesus would probably demand of them why then they had not believed in the Baptist, and why they did not accept John's testimony concerning Himself. On the other hand, should they aver that John had no divine authority to preach and baptize, the people would turn against them, for the martyred Baptist was revered by the masses as a prophet. In spite of their boasted learning, they answered as puzzled schoolboys might do when they perceive hidden difficulties in what at first seemed but a simple problem. "We cannot tell" said they. Then Jesus replied, "Neither tell I you by what authority I do these things."

Chief priests, scribes, and elders of the people were outwitted and humiliated. The tables were completely turned upon them; Jesus, whom they had come to question, became the examiner; they a class of cowed and unwilling listeners, He the ready instructor, and the multitude interested observers. With little likelihood of immediate interruption the Master proceeded in calm deliberation to relate to them a series of three splendid stories, each of which they felt applied to themselves with incisive certainty. The first of the narrations we call the *Parable of the Two Sons.*

"But what think ye? A certain man had two sons; and he came to the first, and said, Son, go work today in my vineyard. He answered and said, I will not: but afterward he repented, and went. And he came to the second, and said likewise. And he answered and said, I go, sir: and went not. Whether of them twain did the will of his father? They say unto him, The first. Jesus saith unto them, Verily I say unto you, That the publicans and the harlots go into the kingdom of God before you. For John came unto you in the way of righteousness, and ye believed him not: but the publicans and the harlots believed him: and ye, when ye had seen it, repented not afterward, that ye might believe him."[k]

The opening sentence, "But what think ye?" was a call to close attention. It implied a question soon to follow; and that proved to be: Which of the two sons was the obedient one? There was but one consistent answer, and they had to give it, however loath. The application of the parable followed with convicting promptness. They, the chief priests, scribes, Pharisees and elders of the people, were typified by the second son, who, when told to labor in the vineyard answered so assuringly, but went not, though the vines were running to wild growth for want of pruning, and such poor fruit as might mature would be left to fall and rot upon the ground. The publicans and sinners upon whom they vented their contempt, whose touch was defilement, were like unto the first son, who in rude though frank refusal ignored the father's call, but afterward relented and set to work, repentantly hoping to make amends for the time he had lost and for the unfilial spirit he had shown.[l] Publicans and sinners, touched in their hearts by the clarion call to repentance, had flocked to the Baptist in the wilderness with the earnest inquiry: "Master, what shall we do?"[m] John's call had been to no particular class; but while self-confessed sinners had repented and sought baptism at his hands, those very Pharisees and elders of the people had rejected his testimony and had hypocritically sought to ensnare him.[n] Through the parable Jesus answered His own question as to whether the baptism of John was of God or of man. The Lord's affirmation, "Verily I say unto you,

---

[k] Matt. 21:28–32.

[l] Note 2, end of chapter.

[m] Luke 3:12; compare 7:29.

[n] Matt. 3:7.

That the publicans and the harlots go into the kingdom of God before you," was condemnatory of the corrupt though sanctimonious polity of the hierarchy throughout. It was not wholly without intimation of possible reformation, however. He did not say that the repentant sinners should enter, and the priestly hypocrites stand forever excluded; for the latter there was hope if they would but repent, though they would have to follow, not lead, in the glorious procession of the redeemed.

In a continuation of the same discourse the Lord presented the *Parable of the Wicked Husbandmen*, as follows:

"Hear another parable: There was a certain householder, which planted a vineyard, and hedged it round about, and digged a winepress in it, and built a tower, and let it out to husbandmen, and went into a far country: And when the time of the fruit drew near, he sent his servants to the husbandmen, that they might receive the fruits of it. And the husbandmen took his servants, and beat one, and killed another, and stoned another. Again, he sent other servants more than the first: and they did unto them likewise. But last of all he sent unto them his son, saying, They will reverence my son. But when the husbandmen saw the son, they said among themselves, This is the heir; come, let us kill him, and let us seize on his inheritance. And they caught him, and cast him out of the vineyard, and slew him. When the lord therefore of the vineyard cometh, what will he do unto those husbandmen? They say unto him, He will miserably destroy those wicked men, and will let out his vineyard unto other husbandmen, which shall render him the fruits in their seasons."°

Again the Jews were compelled to make answer to the great question with which the parable dealt, and again by their answer they pronounced judgment upon themselves. The vineyard, broadly speaking, was the human family, but more specifically the covenant people, Israel; the soil was good and capable of yielding in rich abundance; the vines were choice and had been set out with care; and the whole vineyard was amply protected with a hedge, and suitably furnished with winepress and tower.ᵖ The husbandmen could be none other than the priests and

---

° Matt. 21:33–41; compare Mark 12:1–9; Luke 20:9–16.

ᵖ Note 3, end of chapter.

teachers of Israel, including the ecclesiastical leaders who were then and there present in an official capacity. The Lord of the vineyard had sent among the people prophets authorized to speak in His name; and these the wicked tenants had rejected, maltreated, and, in many instances, cruelly slain.[q] In the more detailed reports of the parable we read that when the first servant came, the cruel husbandmen "beat him and sent him away empty"; the next they wounded "in the head, and sent him away shamefully handled"; another they murdered and all who came later were brutally mistreated, and some of them were killed. Those wicked men had used the vineyard of their Lord for personal gain, and had rendered no part of the vintage to the lawful Owner. When the Lord sent other messengers, "more than the first," or in other words, greater than the earlier ones, the most recent example being John the Baptist, the husbandmen rejected them with evil determination more pronounced than ever. At last the Son had come in person; His authority they feared as that of the lawful heir, and with malignity almost beyond belief, they determined to kill Him that they might perpetuate their unworthy possession of the vineyard and thenceforward hold it as their own.

Jesus carried the story without break from the criminal past to the yet more tragic and awful future, then but three days distant; and calmly related in prophetic imagery, as though already fulfilled, how those evil men cast the well beloved Son out of the vineyard and slew Him. Unable to evade the searching question as to what the Lord of the vineyard would naturally and righteously do to the wicked husbandmen, the Jewish rulers gave the only pertinent answer possible—that He would surely destroy those wretched sinners, and let out His vineyard to tenants who were more honest and worthy.

Suddenly changing the figure, "Jesus saith unto them, Did ye never read in the scriptures, The stone which the builders rejected, the same is become the head of the corner: this is the Lord's doing, and it is marvellous in our eyes? Therefore say I unto you, The kingdom of God shall be taken from you, and given to a nation bringing forth the fruits thereof. And whosoever shall fall on this stone shall be broken;

[q] Compare Luke 11:47, 48; Matt. 23:29–33.

but on whomsoever it shall fall, it will grind him to powder."ʳ There could be no misapprehension as to the Lord's meaning; the rejected Stone which was eventually to have chief place, "the head of the corner," in the edifice of salvation, was Himself, the Messiah. To some that Stone would be a cause of stumbling; wo unto them, for thereby would they be broken, and only through repentance and works of righteousness could they even in part recover; but upon others, those who would persist in their opposition, the Stone would fall in judgment; and wo, wo to them, for beneath it they would be destroyed as though ground to powder.ˢ From them, the leaders, and from the people who followed their unholy precepts and foul example, the kingdom of God was about to be taken, and would in time be given to the Gentiles, who, the Lord affirmed, would prove more worthy than Israel had been. We gather from Luke's account that in contemplation of this awful penalty, "they," whether priestly rulers or common people we are not told, exclaimed in despair, "God forbid!"

As the chief priests and Pharisees realized the completeness of their discomfiture and the extent of the humiliation to which they had been subjected in the eyes of the people, they were incensed beyond measure, and even attempted to lay hold on Jesus there in the temple; but the sympathies of the multitude were so unmistakably in His favor that the angry ecclesiasts desisted. The people in general, while not prepared to openly proclaim Him as the Christ, knew that He was a prophet of God, and their dread of official displeasure and possible penalty did not deter them from friendly demonstrations.

Jesus resumed His teaching by relating the *Parable of the Royal Marriage Feast.*

"And Jesus answered and spake unto them again by parables, and said, The kingdom of heaven is like unto a certain king, which made a marriage for his son, And sent forth his servants to call them that were bidden to the wedding: and they would not come. Again, he sent forth other servants, saying, Tell them which are bidden, Behold, I have prepared my dinner: my oxen and my fatlings are killed, and

---

ʳ Matt. 21:42–44; see also Mark 12:10, 11; Luke 20:17, 18; compare Ps. 118:22; Isa. 28:16; Acts 4:11; Eph. 2:20; 1 Pet. 2:6,7.

ˢ Compare Dan. 2:44, 45; Isa. 60:12.

all things are ready: come unto the marriage. But they made light of it, and went their ways, one to his farm, another to his merchandise: And the remnant took his servants, and entreated them spitefully, and slew them. But when the king heard thereof, he was wroth: and he sent forth his armies, and destroyed those murderers, and burned up their city. Then saith he to his servants, The wedding is ready, but they which were bidden were not worthy. Go ye therefore into the highways, and as many as ye shall find, bid to the marriage. So those servants went out into the highways and gathered together all as many as they found, both bad and good: and the wedding was furnished with guests."[t]

The invitation of a king to his subjects is equivalent to a command. The marriage feast was no surprise event, for the selected guests had been bidden long aforetime; and, in accordance with oriental custom were notified again on the opening day of the festivities,[u] which, according to Hebrew customs, would be understood as extending over a period of seven or fourteen days; in this case of a marriage in the royal family the greater duration would be assumed. Many of the bidden guests refused to come when formally summoned; and of the tolerant king's later and more pressing message they made light and went their ways, while the most wicked turned upon the servants who brought the royal summons, mistreated them cruelly, and some of them they killed. It is plainly evident that the refusal to attend the king's feast was a deliberate rebellion against the royal authority and a personal indignity against both the reigning sovereign and his son. It was as much a duty as an honor for loyal subjects to attend the marriage festival of the prince, whom we cannot err in regarding as the lawful heir to the throne, and therefore the one who might some day reign over them. The turning away by one man to his farm and by another to his merchandise is in part an evidence of their engrossment in material pursuits to the utter disregard of their sovereign's will; but it signifies further an effort to deaden their troubled consciences by some absorbing occupation; and possibly also a premeditated demonstration of the fact that they placed their personal

[t] Matt. 22:1–10.
[u] Note 4, end of chapter.

affairs above the call of their king. The monarch executed a terrible retribution upon his rebellious subjects. If the parable was intended to be an allegorical presentation of actual events, it passes at this point from the story of the past to that of the future, for the destruction of Jerusalem postdates by several decades the death of Christ. Finding the guests who had some claim on the royal invitation to be utterly unworthy, the king sent out his servants again, and these gathered in from the highways and crossroads, from the byways and the lanes, all they could find, irrespective of rank or station, whether rich or poor, good or bad; "and the wedding was furnished with guests."

The great feast by which the Messianic reign was to be ushered in was a favorite theme of jubilant exposition in both synagog and school; and exultation ran high in the rabbinical dictum that none but the children of Abraham would be among the blessed partakers. The king in the parable is God; the son whose marriage was the occasion of the feast is Jesus, the Son of God; the guests who were bidden early, yet who refused to come when the feast was ready, are the covenant people who rejected their Lord, the Christ; the later guests, who were brought in from the streets and the roads, are the Gentile nations, to whom the gospel has been carried since its rejection by the Jews; the marriage feast is symbolical of the glorious consummation of the Messiah's mission.[v]

All students of the subject must have noted the points of resemblance by which this parable is related to that of the great supper;[w] fewer perhaps have considered the differences between the two. The earlier story was told in the house of one of the chief Pharisees, probably in some town in Perea; the later one was related within the temple, after Pharisaic opposition to Christ had reached its height. The first is of simpler plot and of gentler climax. The neglect of the invited guests in the first story was accompanied by excuses in which some approach to polite apology appears; the refusal of those bidden in the second parable was markedly offensive, and was coupled with outrageous abuse and murder. The host in one instance was a wealthy though private citizen, in the other the giver of the feast was a king.

[v] Compare Matt. 25:10; 2 Cor. 11:2; Eph. 5:32; Rev. 19:7; 21:2, 9.
[w] Luke 14:16–24.

In the first, the occasion was one of ordinary though abundant entertainment; in the second, the determining time was that of the appointed marriage of the royal heir. Retribution in the first instance was limited to exclusion from the banquet; in the latter the individual punishment was death, which was followed by the punitive example of the city's destruction.

Our account of the royal marriage feast is not yet complete; the story already considered is supplemented by the following:

"And when the king came in to see the guests, he saw there a man which had not on a wedding garment: And he saith unto him, Friend, how camest thou in hither not having a wedding garment? And he was speechless. Then said the king to the servants, Bind him hand and foot, and take him away, and cast him into outer darkness; there shall be weeping and gnashing of teeth. For many are called, but few are chosen."

The lessons embodied in this section of the parable may be advantageously considered apart from those of the first division. As was befitting his dignity, the king came into the banquet hall after the guests had taken their places in orderly array. His immediate detection of one who was without the prescribed garment implies a personal scrutiny of the guests. One may be led to inquire, how, under the circumstances of hurried summoning, the several guests could have suitably attired themselves for the feast. The unity of the narrative requires that some provision had been made whereby each one who properly applied was given the garment prescribed by the king's command, and in keeping with the established custom at court. That the unrobed guest was guilty of neglect, intentional disrespect, or some more grievous offense, is plain from the context. The king at first was graciously considerate, inquiring only as to how the man had entered without a wedding garment. Had the guest been able to explain his exceptional appearance, or had he any reasonable excuse to offer, he surely would have spoken; but we are told that he remained speechless. The king's summons had been freely extended to all whom his servants had found; but each of them had to enter the royal palace by the door; and before reaching the banquet room, in which the king would appear in person, each would be properly attired; but the deficient one, by some means had entered by another way; and not having passed the attendant sentinels at the portal, he was an intruder, of a kind with the man to whom the Lord had before referred as a thief and a robber because, not entering by the door, he had climbed up some other way.[x] The king gave a command, and his ministers[y] bound the offender and cast him forth from the palace into outer darkness, where the anguish of remorse caused weeping and gnashing of teeth.

As summary and epilogue of the three great parables constituting this series, the Lord spake these words of solemn import: "For many are called, but few are chosen."[z] Each of the parables has its own wealth of wisdom; and the three are as one in declaring the great truth that even the children of the covenant will be rejected except they make good their title by godly works; while to the heathen and the sinners the portals of heaven shall open, if by repentance and compliance with the laws and ordinances of the gospel they shall merit salvation.

The story of the royal marriage feast was the last of our Lord's parables delivered publicly to a mixed audience. Two others were spoken to the apostles, as they sat in solemn converse with the Lord on the Mount of Olives after the public ministry of Christ had been brought to a close.

NOTES TO CHAPTER 30

1. **Fig Tree.**—"The fig tree is very common in Palestine (Deut. 8:8). Its fruit is a well known and highly esteemed article of food. In the East this is of three kinds: (1) the early fig, ripening about the end of June; (2) the summer fig, ripening in August; (3) the winter fig, larger and darker than No. 2, hanging and ripening late on the tree, even after the leaves were shed, and sometimes gathered in the spring. The blossoms of the fig tree are within the receptacle or so-called fruit, and not visible outwardly; and this fruit begins to develop before the leaves. Hence the fig tree which had leaves before the usual time might naturally have been expected to have also some figs on it (Mark 11:13); but it was not true to its pretensions." (Smith's *Comprehensive Bible Dictionary*.)

[x] Compare page 391.

[y] Note 5, end of chapter.

[z] Matt. 22:14; compare 20:16. Note 6, end of chapter.

2. The Two Sons in the Parable.—Although this excellent parable was addressed to the chief priests, scribes, and elders, who had come in hostile spirit to demand of Christ the credentials of His authority, its lesson is of universal application. The two sons are yet alive in every human community—the one openly boastful of his sin, the other a hypocritical pretender. Jesus did not commend the rough refusal of the first son of whom the father made a righteous demand for service; it was his subsequent repentance attended by works that made him superior to his brother who had made fair promise but had kept it not. There are many today who boast that they make no profession of religion, nor pretense of godly life. Their frankness will not mitigate their sins; it simply shows that a certain species of hypocrisy is not prominent among their numerous offenses; but that a man is innocent of one vice, say that of drunkenness, in no wise diminishes his measure of guilt if he be a liar, a thief, an adulterer, or a murderer. Both the sons in the parable were grievous sinners; but the one turned from his evil ways, which theretofore he had followed with flagrant openness, while the other continued in dark deeds of sin, which he sought to cover by a cloak of hypocrisy. Let no man think that because he becomes intoxicated at the public bar he is any the less a drunkard than is he who swallows the "beverage of hell" in comparative privacy, though the latter be both drunkard and hypocrite. For these sins, as for all others, genuine repentance is the only saving antidote.

3. Israel Symbolized by Vineyard and Vines.—The aptness of our Lord's representation of Israel as a vineyard could not have escaped the perception of the Jews, to whom Old Testament similes of analogous form were familiar figures. Notable among others is the striking picture presented by Isaiah (5:1–7), in which the well provided vineyard is shown as producing wild grapes only, for which grievous disappointment of his expectations the owner determined to break down the wall, remove the hedge, and leave the vineyard to its fate of abandonment. The explication of the parable voiced by Isaiah is thus given: "For the vineyard of the Lord of hosts is the house of Israel, and the men of Judah his pleasant plant: and he looked for judgment, but behold oppression; for righteousness, but behold a cry." The worthlessness of a vine save only for its fruit was set forth by the Lord through His prophet Ezekiel (15:2–5); and truly it is so, that the wood of the grape plant is fit for nothing but burning; the whole vine as wood is inferior to a branch from a forest tree (verse 3). And Israel is represented as such a vine, precious if but fruitful, otherwise nothing but fuel and that of poor quality. The psalmist sang of the vine that Jehovah had brought out of Egypt and which, planted with care and hedged about, had flourished even with goodly boughs; but the favor of the Lord had been turned from the vine, and it had been left desolate (Ps. 80:8–16). For further allusions see Isa. 27:2–6; Jer. 2:21; Ezek. 19:10–14; Hosea 10:1.

4. The Call to the Marriage Feast.—The calling of the guests who had been bidden aforetime is thus commented upon by Trench (*Parables*, pp. 175–6): "This summoning of those already bidden, was, and, as modern travellers attest, is still, quite in accordance with Eastern manners. Thus Esther invites Haman to a banquet on the morrow (Esth. 5:8), and when the time has actually arrived, the chamberlain comes to usher him to the banquet (6:14). There is, therefore, no slightest reason why we should make '*them that were bidden*' to mean them that were now *to be bidden*; such an interpretation not merely violating all laws of grammar, but the higher purpose with which the parable was spoken; for our Lord, assuming that the guests had been invited long ago, does thus remind His hearers that what He brought, if in one sense new, was in another a fulfilment of the old; that He claimed to be heard, not as one suddenly starting up, unconnected with aught which had gone before but as Himself 'the end of the law,' to which it had been ever tending, the birth with which the whole Jewish dispensation had been pregnant, and which alone should give a meaning to it all. In His words, '*them that were bidden*,' is involved the fact that there was nothing abrupt in the coming of His kingdom, that its rudiments had a long while before been laid, that all to which His adversaries clung as precious in their past history was prophetic of blessings now actually present to them in Him. The original invitation, which had now come to maturity reached back to the foundation of the Jewish commonwealth, was taken up and repeated by each succeeding prophet, as he prophesied of the crowning grace that should one day be brought to Israel (Luke 10:24; 1 Pet. 1:12), and summoned the people to hold themselves in a spiritual readiness to welcome their Lord and their King."

5. Servants and Ministers.—According to good philological authority, "ministers" or "ministering attendants" is a more literal rendering of the original than "servants" in Matt. 22:13. In the earlier verses 3, 4, 6, 8, 10, of the same chapter, "servants" or "servitors" best expresses the meaning of the original. The distinction is significant, as it implies an important difference of station between the servants who were sent out to bid the people to the feast, and the ministers in immediate attendance upon the king. The first are typical of God's servants who proclaim His word in the world; the latter symbolize the angels who shall execute His judgments on the wicked by gathering out from His kingdom all things that offend. Compare Matt. 13:30, 39, 41; D&C 86:5.

6. The Called and the Chosen.—Edersheim's reflections upon this subject follow in part (vol. 2, pp. 429, 430): "The King entered to see His guests, and among them he descried one who had not on a wedding garment. . . . As the guests had been travelers, and as the feast was in the King's palace, we cannot be mistaken in supposing that such garments were supplied in the palace to all who sought them. And with this agrees the circumstance, that the man so addressed 'was speechless.' His conduct argued utter insensibility as regarded that to which he had been called—ignorance of what was due the King, and what became such a feast. For, although no previous state of preparedness was required of the invited guests, all being bidden, whether good or bad, yet the fact remained that, if they were to take part in the feast they must put on a garment suited to the occasion. All are invited to the gospel feast; but they who will partake of it must put on the King's wedding garment of evangelical holiness. And whereas it is said in the parable that only one was descried without this garment, this is intended to teach, that the King will not only generally view His guests, but that each will be separately examined, and that no one—no, not a single individual—will be able to escape discovery amidst the mass of guests, if he has not the wedding garment. In short, in that day of trial, it is not scrutiny of churches, but of individuals in the Church. . . . The call comes to all; but it may be outwardly accepted, and a man may sit down to the feast, and yet he may not be chosen to partake of the feast, because he has not the wedding garment of converting, sanctifying grace. And so, one may be thrust even from the marriage board into the darkness without, with its sorrow and anguish. Thus, side by side, yet wide apart, are these two—God's call and God's choice. The connecting link between them is the wedding garment, freely given in the Palace. Yet, we must seek it, ask it, put it on. And as here also, we have, side by side, God's gift and man's activity. And still, to all time, and to all men, alike in its warning, teaching, and blessing, is it true: Many are called, but few chosen!" Many words of related meaning, both Hebrew and Greek, are translated "garment" in our English Bible. The Greek original in the mention of the wedding garment is enduma; this does not occur in other Bible passages as the original of "garment." The noun is related to the Greek verb *enduein*, "to put on, as a garment." Compare Luke 24:49, "until ye be endued with power from on high."

CHAPTER 31

THE CLOSE OF OUR LORD'S PUBLIC MINISTRY

A CONSPIRACY OF PHARISEES AND HERODIANS[a]
The Jewish authorities continued unceasingly active in their determined efforts to tempt or beguile Jesus into some act or utterance
on which they could base a charge of offense, under either their
own or Roman law. The Pharisees counseled together as to "how
they might entangle him in his talk"; and then, laying aside their
partisan prejudices, they conspired to this end with the Herodians,
a political faction whose chief characteristic was the purpose of
maintaining in power the family of the Herods,[b] which policy of
necessity entailed the upholding of the Roman power, upon which
the Herods depended for their delegated authority. The same incongruous association had been entered into before in an attempt to
provoke Jesus to overt speech or action in Galilee; and the Lord had
coupled the parties together in His warning to the disciples to
beware of the leaven of both.[c] So, on the last day of our Lord's
teaching in public, Pharisees and Herodians joined forces against
Him; the one watchful for the smallest technical infringement of
the Mosaic law, the other alert to seize upon the slightest excuse for
charging Him with disloyalty to the secular powers. Their plans
were conceived in treachery, and put into operation as the living
embodiment of a lie. Choosing some of their number who had not
before appeared in personal antagonism to Jesus, and who were

[a] Matt. 22:15–22; Mark 12:13–17; Luke 20:19–26.
[b] Page 64–65.
[c] Mark 3:6; 8:15.

supposed to be unknown to Him, the chief conspirators sent these with instructions to "feign themselves just men, that they might take hold of his words, that so they might deliver him unto the power and authority of the governor."

This delegation of hypocritical spies came asking a question, in pretended sincerity, as though they were troubled in conscience and desired counsel of the eminent Teacher. "Master," said they with fawning duplicity, "we know that thou art true, and teachest the way of God in truth, neither carest thou for any man: for thou regardest not the person of men." This studied tribute to our Lord's courage and independence of thought and action was truthful in every word; but as uttered by those fulsome dissemblers and in their nefarious intent, it was egregiously false. The honeyed address, however, by which the conspirators attempted to cajole the Lord into unwariness, indicated that the question they were about to submit was one requiring for its proper answer just such qualities of mind as they pretendingly attributed to Him.

"Tell us therefore," they continued, "What thinkest thou? Is it lawful to give tribute unto Caesar, or not?" The question had been chosen with diabolic craft; for of all acts attesting compulsory allegiance to Rome that of having to pay the poll-tax was most offensive to the Jews. Had Jesus answered "Yes," the guileful Pharisees might have inflamed the multitude against Him as a disloyal son of Abraham; had His answer been "No," the scheming Herodians could have denounced Him as a promoter of sedition against the Roman government. Moreover the question was unnecessary; the nation, both rulers and people had settled it, however grudgingly, for they accepted and circulated among themselves the Roman coinage as a common medium of exchange; and it was a criterion of recognition among the Jews that to make current the coins of any sovereign was to acknowledge his royal authority. "But Jesus perceived their wickedness, and said, Why tempt ye me, ye hypocrites?" All their artful expressions of false adulation were countered by the withering epithet "hypocrites." "Shew me the tribute money," He commanded, and they produced a penny—a Roman denarius bearing the effigy and name of Tiberius Caesar, emperor of Rome. "Whose is this image and superscription?" He asked. They answered "Caesar's." "Then saith he unto them,

Render therefore unto Caesar the things which are Caesar's; and unto God the things that are God's."[d]

The reply was a masterly one by whatever standard we gauge it; it has become an aphorism in literature and life. It swept away any lingering thought or expectation that in the mind of Him who had so recently ridden into Jerusalem as King of Israel and Prince of Peace, there was even the semblance of aspiration for earthly power or dominion. It established for all time the one righteous basis of relationship between spiritual and secular duties, between church and state. The apostles in later years builded upon this foundation and enjoined obedience to the laws of established governments.[e]

One may draw a lesson if he will, from the association of our Lord's words with the occurrence of Caesar's image on the coin. It was that effigy with its accompanying superscription that gave special point to His memorable instruction, "Render therefore unto Caesar the things which are Caesar's." This was followed by the further injunction: "and unto God the things that are God's." Every human soul is stamped with the image and superscription of God, however blurred and indistinct the line may have become through the corrosion or attrition of sin;[f] and as unto Caesar should be rendered the coins upon which his effigy appeared, so unto God should be given the souls that bear His image. Render unto the world the stamped pieces that are made legally current by the insignia of worldly powers, and give unto God and His service, yourselves—the divine mintage of His eternal realm.

Pharisees and Herodians were silenced by the unanswerable wisdom of the Lord's reply to their crafty question. Try as they would, they could not "take hold of his words," and they were put to shame before the people who were witnesses to their humiliation. Marveling at His answer, and unwilling to take the chance of further and possibly greater embarrassment, they "left him, and went their way." Nevertheless these perverted Jews persisted in their base and treacherous purpose, as appears nowhere more glaringly evident than in their

[d] Note 1, end of chapter.

[e] Note 2, end of chapter.

[f] Page 12–13.

utterly false accusation before Pilate—that Jesus was guilty of "forbidding to give tribute to Caesar, saying that he himself is Christ a King."[g]

SADDUCEES QUESTION ABOUT THE RESURRECTION[h]

Next, the Sadducees tried to discomfit Jesus by propounding what they regarded as an involved if not indeed a very difficult question. The Sadducees held that there could be no bodily resurrection, on which point of doctrine as on many others, they were the avowed opponents of the Pharisees.[i] The question submitted by the Sadducees on this occasion related directly to the resurrection, and was framed to discredit the doctrine by a most unfavorable and grossly exaggerated application thereof. "Master," said the spokesman of the party, "Moses said, If a man die, having no children, his brother shall marry his wife, and raise up seed unto his brother. Now there were with us seven brethren: and the first, when he had married a wife, deceased, and, having no issue, left his wife unto his brother: Likewise the second also, and the third unto the seventh. And last of all the woman died also. Therefore in the resurrection whose wife shall she be of the seven? for they all had her." It was beyond question that the Mosaic law authorized and required that the living brother of a deceased and childless husband should marry the widow with the purpose of rearing children to the name of the dead, whose family lineage would thus be legally continued.[j] Such a state of affairs as that presented by the casuistical Sadducees, in which seven brothers in succession had as wife and left as childless widow the same woman, was possible under the Mosaic code relating to levirate marriages; but it was a most improbable instance.

Jesus stopped not, however, to question the elements of the problem as presented to Him; whether the case was assumed or real mattered not, since the question "Whose wife shall she be?" was based on an utterly erroneous conception. "Jesus answered and said unto them, Ye do err, not knowing the scriptures, nor the power of God. For in the resurrection they neither marry, nor are given in marriage,

[g] Luke 23:2.

[h] Matt. 22:23–33; Mark 12:18–27; Luke 20:27–38.

[i] Pages 62–63 and 69.

[j] Deut. 25:5.

but are as the angels of God in heaven." The Lord's meaning was clear, that in the resurrected state there can be no question among the seven brothers as to whose wife for eternity the woman shall be, since all except the first had married her for the duration of mortal life only, and primarily for the purpose of perpetuating in mortality the name and family of the brother who first died. Luke records the Lord's words as follows in part: "But they which shall be accounted worthy to obtain that world, and the resurrection from the dead, neither marry, nor are given in marriage: Neither can they die any more: for they are equal unto the angels; and are the children of God, being the children of the resurrection." In the resurrection there will be no marrying nor giving in marriage; for all questions of marital status must be settled before that time, under the authority of the Holy Priesthood, which holds the power to seal in marriage for both time and eternity.[k]

From the case presented by His treacherous questioners, Jesus turned to the actuality of the resurrection, which was involved in and implied by the inquiry. "But as touching the resurrection of the dead," said He, "have ye not read that which was spoken unto you by God, saying, I am the God of Abraham, and the God of Isaac, and the God of Jacob? God is not the God of the dead, but of the living." This was a direct assault upon the Sadducean doctrine of negation concerning the literal resurrection of the dead. The Sadducees were distinctively the zealous upholders of the law, wherein Jehovah affirms Himself to be the God of Abraham, Isaac, and Jacob;[l] yet they denied the possible resurrection of these patriarchs, and made the exalted title, under which the Lord had revealed Himself to Moses, valid only during the brief mortal existence of the progenitors of the Israelitish nation. The declaration that Jehovah is not the God of the dead but of the living was an unanswerable denunciation of the Sadducean perversion of scripture; and with solemn finality the Lord added: "Ye therefore do greatly err." Certain of the scribes present were impressed by the incontrovertible demonstration of the truth, and exclaimed with approbation: "Master, thou hast well said." The proud Sadducees were confuted and silenced; "and after that they durst not ask him any question at all."

[k] Note 3, end of chapter.
[l] Gen. 28:13; Ex. 3:6, 15.

THE GREAT COMMANDMENT[m]

The Pharisees, covertly rejoicing over the discomfiture of their rivals, now summoned courage enough to plan another attack of their own. One of their number, a lawyer, by which title we may understand one of the scribes who was distinctively also a professor of ecclesiastical law, asked: "Which is the first commandment of all?" or, as Matthew states the question: "Master, which is the great commandment in the law?" The reply was prompt, incisive, and so comprehensive as to cover the requirements of the law in their entirety. With the imperative call to attention with which Moses had summoned Israel to hear and heed,[n] the very words of which were written on the phylacteries[o] which the Pharisees wore as frontlets between their eyes, Jesus answered: "Hear, O Israel; The Lord our God is one Lord: And thou shalt love the Lord thy God with all thy heart, and with all thy soul, and with all thy mind, and with all thy strength: this is the first commandment. And the second is like, namely this, Thou shalt love thy neighbour as thyself. There is none other commandment greater than these." Matthew's wording of the concluding declaration is: "On these two commandments hang all the law and the prophets."

The philosophic soundness of the Lord's profound generalization and comprehensive summarizing of the "law and the prophets"[p] will appeal to all students of human nature. It is a common tendency of man to reach after, or at least to inquire after and marvel about, the superlative. Who is the greatest poet, philosopher, scientist, preacher or statesman? Who stands first and foremost in the community, the nation, or even, as the apostles in their aspiring ignorance asked, in the kingdom of heaven? Which mountain overtops all the rest? Which river is the longest or the largest? Such queries are ever current. The Jews had divided and subdivided the commandments of the law, and had supplemented even the minutest subdivision with rules of their own contriving. Now came the Pharisee asking which of all

[m] Matt. 22:34–40; Mark 12:28–34.

[n] Deut. 6:4, 5.

[o] Note 5, end of chapter.

[p] Compare page 232.

these requirements was the greatest.[q] To love God with all one's heart and soul and mind is to serve Him and keep all his commandments. To love one's neighbor as one's self is to be a brother in the broadest and, at the same time, the most exacting sense of the term. Therefore the commandment to love God and man is the greatest, on the basis of the simple and mathematical truth that the whole is greater than any part. What need of the decalog could there be if mankind would obey this first and great and all-embracing commandment? The Lord's reply to the question was convincing even to the learned scribe who had acted as spokesman for his Pharisaic colleagues. The man was honest enough to admit the righteousness and wisdom on which the reply was grounded, and impulsively he voiced acceptance, saying, "Well, Master, thou hast said the truth: for there is one God; and there is none other but he: And to love him with all the heart, and with all the understanding, and with all the soul, and with all the strength, and to love his neighbour as himself, is more than all whole burnt offerings and sacrifices." Jesus was no whit less prompt than the well-intending scribe in acknowledging merit in the words of an opponent; and to the man He gave the encouraging assurance: "Thou art not far from the kingdom of God." As to whether the scribe remained firm in purpose and eventually gained entrance into that blessed abode, the scriptural record is silent.

JESUS TURNS QUESTIONER[r]

Sadducees, Herodians, Pharisees, lawyers, and scribes, all had in turn met discomfiture and defeat in their efforts to entangle Jesus on questions of doctrine or practice, and had utterly failed to incite Him to any act or utterance on which they could lawfully charge Him with offense. Having so effectually silenced all who had ventured to challenge Him to debate, either covertly or with open intent, that "no man after that durst ask him any question," Jesus in turn became the aggressive interrogator. Turning to the Pharisees, who had clustered together for greater facility in consultation, Jesus began a colloquy which proceeded as follows: "What think ye of Christ? whose son is he? They say unto him, The son

[q] Note 4, end of chapter.
[r] Matt. 22:41–46; Mark 12:35–37; Luke 20:41–44.

of David. He saith unto them, How then doth David in spirit call him Lord, saying, The Lord said unto my Lord, Sit thou on my right hand, till I make thine enemies thy footstool? If David then call him Lord, how is he his son?" The Lord's citation of David's jubilant and worshipful song of praise, which, as Mark avers, Jesus said was inspired by the Holy Ghost, had reference to the Messianic psalms[s] in which the royal singer affirmed his own reverent allegiance, and extolled the glorious reign of the promised King of kings, who is specifically called therein "a priest forever after the order of Melchizedek."[t] Puzzling as was the unexpected question to the erudite Jews, we fail to perceive in it any inexplicable difficulty, since to us, less prejudiced than they who lived in expectation of a Messiah who would be David's son only in the sense of family descent and royal succession in the splendor of temporal rule, the eternal Godship of the Messiah is a fact demonstrated and undeniable. Jesus the Christ is the Son of David in the physical way of lineage by which both Jesus and David are sons of Jacob, Isaac, Abraham, and Adam. But while Jesus was born in the flesh as late in the centuries as the "meridian of time"[u] He was Jehovah, Lord and God, before David, Abraham, or Adam was known on earth.[v]

WICKED SCRIBES AND PHARISEES DENOUNCED[w]

The humiliating defeat of the Pharisaic party was made all the more memorable and bitter by the Lord's final denunciation of the system, and His condemnation of its unworthy representatives. Addressing Himself primarily to the disciples, yet speaking in the hearing of the multitude, He directed the attention of all to the scribes and Pharisees, who, He pointed out, occupied the seat of Moses as doctrinal expounders and official administrators of the law, and who were therefore to be obeyed in their authoritative rule; but against their pernicious example the disciples were forcefully warned. "All therefore whatsoever they bid you observe, that observe and do," said

[s] Ps. 110.

[t] Ps. 110:4; compare Heb. 5:6; 6:20; 7:17, 21.

[u] Chapter 6.

[v] Chapters 4 and 5.

[w] Matt. 23; Mark 12:38–40; Luke 20:45–47; compare Luke 11:39–52.

the Lord, "but do not ye after their works; for they say, and do not." Distinction between due observance of official precept and the personal responsibility of following evil example, though it be that of men high in authority, could not have been made plainer. Disobedience to law was not to be excused because of corruption among the law's representatives, nor was wickedness in any individual to be condoned or palliated because of another's villainy.

In explanation of the caution He so openly blazoned against the vices of the rulers, the Lord continued: "For they bind heavy burdens and grievous to be borne, and lay them on men's shoulders; but they themselves will not move them with one of their fingers." Rabbinism had practically superseded the law in the substitution of multitudinous rules and exactions, with conditional penalties; the day was filled with traditional observances by which even the trivial affairs of life were encumbered; yet from bearing these and other grievous burdens hypocritical officials could find excuse for personal exemption.

Their inordinate vanity and their irreverent assumption of excessive piety were thus stigmatized: "But all their works they do for to be seen of men: they make broad their phylacteries,[x] and enlarge the borders of their garments, and love the uppermost rooms at feasts, and the chief seats in the synagogues, and greetings in the markets, and to be called of men, Rabbi, Rabbi." The high-sounding title, Rabbi, signifying Master, Teacher, or Doctor, had eclipsed the divinely recognized sanctity of priesthood; to be a rabbi of the Jews was regarded as vastly superior to being a priest of the Most High God.[y] "But be not ye called Rabbi," said Jesus to the apostles and the other disciples present, "for one is your Master, even Christ; and all ye are brethren. And call no man your father upon the earth: for one is your Father, which is in heaven. Neither be ye called masters: for one is your Master, even Christ."[z]

Those upon whom would rest the responsibility of building the Church He had founded were not to aspire to worldly titles nor the honors of men; for those chosen ones were brethren, and their sole purpose should be the rendering of the greatest possible service to

[x] Note 5, end of chapter.
[y] Pages 49 and 53–54.
[z] Note 6, end of chapter.

their one and only Master. As had been so strongly impressed on earlier occasions, excellence or supremacy in the apostolic calling, and similarly in the duties of discipleship or membership in the Church of Christ, was and is to be achieved through humble and devoted service alone; therefore said the Master again, "he that is greatest among you shall be your servant. And whosoever shall exalt himself shall be abased; and he that shall humble himself shall be exalted."

From the mixed multitude of disciples and unbelievers, comprising many of the common people who listened in glad eagerness to learn,[aa] Jesus turned to the already abashed yet angry rulers, and deluged them with a veritable torrent of righteous indignation, through which flashed the lightning of scorching invective, accompanied by thunder peals of divine anathema.

"But woe unto you, scribes and Pharisees, hypocrites! for ye shut up the kingdom of heaven against men: for ye neither go in yourselves, neither suffer ye them that are entering to go in." The Pharisaic standard of piety was the learning of the schools; one unversed in the technicalities of the law was accounted as unacceptable to God and veritably accursed.[bb] By their casuistry and perverted explications of scripture they confused and misled the "common people," and so stood as obstacles at the entrance to the kingdom of God, refusing to go in themselves and barring the way to others.

"Woe unto you, scribes and Pharisees, hypocrites! for ye devour widows' houses, and for a pretence make long prayer: therefore ye shall receive the greater damnation."[cc] The avarice of the Jewish hierarchy in our Lord's lifetime was an open scandal. By extortion and unlawful exaction under cover of religious duty the priestly rulers had amassed an enormous treasure,[dd] of which the contributions of the poor, and the confiscation of property, including even the houses of dependent widows, formed a considerable proportion; and the perfidy of the practice was made the blacker by the outward pretense of sanctity and the sacrilegious accompaniment of wordy prayer.

[aa] Mark 12:37.

[bb] John 7:49. Compare 9:34.

[cc] Note 7, end of chapter.

[dd] Note 8, end of chapter.

"Woe unto you, scribes and Pharisees, hypocrites! for ye compass sea and land to make one proselyte, and when he is made, ye make him twofold more the child of hell than yourselves." It is possible that this woe was directed more against the effort to secure proselytes to Pharisaism than that of converting aliens to Judaism; but as the latter was thoroughly degraded and the former disgustingly corrupt, the application of our Lord's denunciation to either or both is warranted. Of the Jews who strove to make proselytes it has been said that "out of a bad heathen they made a worse Jew." Many of their converts soon became perverts.

"Woe unto you, ye blind guides, which say, Whosoever shall swear by the temple, it is nothing; but whosoever shall swear by the gold of the temple, he is a debtor! Ye fools and blind: for whether is greater, the gold, or the temple that sanctifieth the gold? And, Whosoever shall swear by the altar, it is nothing; but whosoever sweareth by the gift that is upon it, he is guilty. Ye fools and blind: for whether is greater, the gift, or the altar that sanctifieth the gift? Whoso therefore shall swear by the altar, sweareth by it, and by all things thereon. And whoso shall swear by the temple, sweareth by it, and by him that dwelleth therein. And he that shall swear by heaven, sweareth by the throne of God, and by him that sitteth thereon." Thus did the Lord condemn the infamous enactments of the schools and the Sanhedrin concerning oaths and vows; for they had established or endorsed a code of rules, inconsistent and unjust, as to technical trifles by which a vow could be enforced or invalidated. If a man swore by the temple, the House of Jehovah, he could obtain an indulgence for breaking his oath; but if he vowed by the gold and treasure of the Holy House, he was bound by the unbreakable bonds of priestly dictum. Though one should swear by the altar of God, his oath could be annulled; but if he vowed by the corban gift or by the gold upon the altar;[ee] his obligation was imperative. To what depths of unreason and hopeless depravity had men fallen, how sinfully foolish and how willfully blind were they, who saw not that the temple was greater than its gold, and the altar than the gift that lay upon it! In the Sermon on the Mount the

[ee] Page 331.

Lord had said, "Swear not at all";[ff] but upon such as would not live according to that higher law, upon those who persisted in the use of oaths and vows, the lesser and evidently just requirement of strict fidelity to the terms of self-assumed obligations was to be enforced, without unrighteous quibble or inequitable discrimination.

"Woe unto you, scribes and Pharisees, hypocrites! for ye pay tithe of mint and anise and cummin, and have omitted the weightier matters of the law, judgment, mercy, and faith: these ought ye to have done, and not to leave the other undone. Ye blind guides, which strain at a gnat, and swallow a camel." The law of the tithe had been a characteristic feature of the theocratic requirements in Israel from the days of Moses; and the practice really long antedated the exodus. As literally construed, the law required the tithing of flocks and herds, fruit and grain,[gg] but by traditional extension all products of the soil had been included. The conscientious tithing of all one's possessions, even potherbs and other garden produce, was approved by the Lord; but He denounced as rank hypocrisy the observance of such requirements as an excuse for neglecting the other duties of true religion. The reference to "the weightier matters of the law" may have been an allusion to the rabbinical classification of "light" and "heavy" requirements under the law; though it is certain the Lord approved no such arbitrary distinctions. To omit the tithing of small things, such as mint leaves, and sprigs of anise and cummin, was to fall short in dutiful observance; but to ignore the claims of judgment, mercy, and faith, was to forfeit one's claim to blessing as a covenant child of God. By a strong simile, the Lord stigmatized such inconsistency as comparable to one's scrupulous straining at a gnat while figuratively willing to gulp down a camel.[hh]

"Woe unto you, scribes and Pharisees, hypocrites! for ye make clean the outside of the cup and of the platter, but within they are full of extortion and excess. Thou blind Pharisee, cleanse first that which is within the cup and platter, that the outside of them may be clean

---

ff Matt. 5:33–37.

gg Lev. 27:30; Num. 18:21; Deut. 12:6; 14:22–28. See also the author's *The Law of the Tithe*, 20 pp., 1914.

hh The revised version, generally admitted the more nearly correct, reads "strain out the gnat" instead of "strain at a gnat."

also."[ii] Pharisaic scrupulosity in the ceremonial cleansing of platters and cups, pots and brazen vessels, has been already alluded to. Cleanliness the Lord in no wise depreciated; His shafts of disapprobation were aimed at the hypocrisy of maintaining at once outward spotlessness and inward corruption. Cups and platters though cleansed to perfection were filthy before the Lord if their contents had been bought by the gold of extortion, or were to be used in pandering to gluttony, drunkenness or other excess.

"Woe unto you, scribes and Pharisees, hypocrites! for ye are like unto whited sepulchres, which indeed appear beautiful outward, but are within full of dead men's bones, and of all uncleanness. Even so ye also outwardly appear righteous unto men, but within ye are full of hypocrisy and iniquity." It was an awful figure, that of likening them to whitewashed tombs, full of dead bones and rotting flesh. As the dogmas of the rabbis made even the slightest contact with a corpse or its cerements, or with the bier upon which it was borne, or the grave in which it has been lain, a cause of personal defilement, which only ceremonial washing and the offering of sacrifices could remove, care was taken to make tombs conspicuously white, so that no person need by defiled through ignorance of proximity to such unclean places; and, moreover, the periodical whitening of sepulchres was regarded as a memorial act of honor to the dead. But even as no amount of care or degree of diligence in keeping bright the outside of a tomb could stay the putrescence going on within, so no externals of pretended righteousness could mitigate the revolting corruption of a heart reeking with iniquity. Jesus had before compared Pharisees with unmarked graves, over which men inadvertently walked and so became defiled though they knew it not;[jj] on the occasion now under consideration He denounced them as whitened tombs, flauntingly prominent, but sepulchres nevertheless.

"Woe unto you, scribes and Pharisees, hypocrites! because ye build the tombs of the prophets, and garnish the sepulchres of the righteous, And say, If we had been in the days of our fathers, we would not have been partakers with them in the blood of the prophets. Wherefore ye be witnesses unto yourselves, that ye are the children of them which

ii Compare Luke 11:39, 40; Mark 7:4.
jj Luke 11:44.

killed the prophets." National pride, not wholly unlike patriotism, had for centuries expressed itself in formal regard for the burial crypts of the ancient prophets, many of whom had been slain because of their righteous and fearless zeal. Those modern Jews were voluble to disavow all sympathy with the murderous deeds of their progenitors, who had martyred the prophets, and ostentatiously averred that if they had lived in the times of those martyrdoms they would have been no participators therein, yet by such avouchment they proclaimed themselves the offspring of those who had shed innocent blood.

With scorching maledictions the Lord thus consigned them to their fate: "Fill ye up then the measure of your fathers. Ye serpents, ye generation of vipers, how can ye escape the damnation of hell? Wherefore, behold, I send unto you prophets, and wise men, and scribes: and some of them ye shall kill and crucify; and some of them shall ye scourge in your synagogues, and persecute them from city to city: That upon you may come all the righteous blood shed upon the earth, from the blood of righteous Abel unto the blood of Zacharias son of Barachias, whom ye slew between the temple and the altar. Verily I say unto you, All these things shall come upon this generation." To their sanctimonious asseverations of superiority over their fathers who had slain Jehovah's envoys, Jehovah Himself replied by predicting that they would dye their hands in the blood of prophets, wise men, and righteous scribes, whom He would send amongst them; and thus would prove themselves literal sons of murderers, and murderers themselves, so that upon them should rest the burden of all the righteous blood that had been shed for a testimony of God, from righteous Abel to the martyred Zacharias.[kk] That dread fate, outlined with such awful realism, was to be no eventuality of the distant future; every one of the frightful woes the Lord had uttered was to be realized in that generation.

THE LORD'S LAMENTATION OVER JERUSALEM[ll]

Concerning scribes, Pharisees, and Pharisaism, Jesus had uttered His last word. Looking from the temple heights out over the city of the

---

[kk] Note 9, end of chapter.

[ll] Matt. 23:37–39; compare Luke 13:34, 35.

great King, soon to be abandoned to destruction, the Lord was obsessed by emotions of profound sorrow. With the undying eloquence of anguish He broke forth in such a lamentation as no mortal father ever voiced over the most unfilial and recreant of sons.

"O Jerusalem, Jerusalem, thou that killest the prophets, and stonest them which are sent unto thee, how often would I have gathered thy children together, even as a hen gathereth her chickens under her wings, and ye would not! Behold, your house is left unto you desolate. For I say unto you, Ye shall not see me henceforth, till ye shall say, Blessed is he that cometh in the name of the Lord." Had Israel but received her King, the world's history of post-meridian time would never have been what it is. The children of Israel had spurned the proffered safety of a protecting paternal wing; soon the Roman eagle would swoop down upon them and slay. The stupendous temple, which but a day before the Lord had called "My house," was now no longer specifically His; "Your house," said He, "is left unto you desolate." He was about to withdraw from both temple and nation; and by the Jews His face was not again to be seen, until, through the discipline of centuries of suffering they shall be prepared to acclaim in accents of abiding faith, as some of them had shouted but the Sunday before under the impulse of an erroneous conception, "Blessed is he that cometh in the name of the Lord."

A WIDOW'S GIFT[mm]

From the open courts Jesus moved over toward the colonnaded treasury of the temple, and there He sat, seemingly absorbed in a revery of sorrow. Within that space were thirteen chests, each provided with a trumpet-shaped receptacle; and into these the people dropped their contributions for the several purposes indicated by inscriptions on the boxes. Looking up, Jesus observed the lines of donors, of all ranks and degrees of affluence and poverty, some depositing their gifts with evident devoutness and sincerity of purpose, others ostentatiously casting in great sums of silver and gold, primarily to be seen of men. Among the many was a poor widow, who with probable effort to

[mm] Mark 12:41–44; Luke 21:1–4.

escape observation dropped into one of the treasure chests two small bronze coins known as mites; her contribution amounted to less than half a cent in American money. The Lord called His disciples about Him, directed their attention to the poverty-stricken widow and her deed, and said: "Verily I say unto you, That this poor widow hath cast more in, than all they which have cast into the treasury: For all they did cast in of their abundance; but she of her want did cast in all that she had, even all her living."

In the accounts kept by the recording angels, figured out according to the arithmetic of heaven, entries are made in terms of quality rather than of quantity, and values are determined on the basis of capability and intent. The rich gave much yet kept back more; the widow's gift was her all. It was not the smallness of her offering that made it especially acceptable, but the spirit of sacrifice and devout intent with which she gave. On the books of the heavenly accountants that widow's contribution was entered as a munificent gift, surpassing in worth the largess of kings. "For if there be first a willing mind, it is accepted according to that a man hath, and not according to that he hath not."[nn]

CHRIST'S FINAL WITHDRAWAL FROM THE TEMPLE

Our Lord's public discourses and the open colloquies in which He had participated with professionals and priestly officials, in the course of His daily visits to the temple during the first half of Passion week, had caused many of the Chief rulers, beside others, to believe on Him as the veritable Son of God; but the fear of Pharisaic persecution and the dread of excommunication from the synagog[oo] deterred them from confessing the allegiance they felt, and from accepting the means of salvation so freely offered. "They loved the praise of men more than the praise of God."[pp]

It may have been while Jesus directed His course for the last time toward the exit portal of the one-time holy place that He uttered the solemn testimony of His divinity recorded by John.[qq] Crying with a

[nn] 2 Cor. 8:12.

[oo] John 12:42; compare 7:13; 9:22.

[pp] John 12:43; compare 5:44.

[qq] John 12:44–50.

loud voice to priestly rulers and the multitude generally, He said: "He that believeth on me, believeth not on me, but on him that sent me. And he that seeth me seeth him that sent me." Allegiance to Himself was allegiance to God; the people were plainly told that to accept Him was in no degree a weakening of their adherence to Jehovah, but on the contrary a confirmation thereof. Repeating precepts of earlier utterance, He again proclaimed Himself the light of the world, by whose rays alone mankind might be delivered from the enveloping darkness of spiritual unbelief. The testimony He left with the people would be the means of judgment and condemnation to all who willfully rejected it. "For," said He in solemn finality, "I have not spoken of myself; but the Father which sent me, he gave me a commandment, what I should say, and what I should speak. And I know that his commandment is life everlasting; whatsoever I speak therefore, even as the Father said unto me, so I speak."

DESTRUCTION OF THE TEMPLE PREDICTED [rr]

As Jesus was departing from the enclosure wherein stood what once had been the House of the Lord, one or more of the disciples called His attention to the magnificent structures, the massive stones, the colossal columns, and the lavish and costly adornment of the several buildings. The Lord's answering comment was an unqualified prophecy of the utter destruction of the temple and everything pertaining to it. "Verily I say unto you, There shall not be left here one stone upon another, that shall not be thrown down." Such was the definite and dire prediction. Those who heard were dumbfounded; neither by question nor other response did they attempt to elicit more. The literal fulfilment of that awful portent was but an incident in the annihilation of the city less than forty years later.

With the Lord's final departure from the temple, which probably occurred in the afternoon of the Tuesday of that last week, His public ministry was brought to its solemn ending. Whatever of discourse, parable, or ordinance was to follow, would be directed only to the further instruction and investiture of the apostles.

[rr] Matt. 24:1, 2; Mark 13:1, 2; Luke 21:5, 6. Note 10, end of chapter.

NOTES TO CHAPTER 31

1. The Image on the Coin.—The Jews had an aversion for images or effigies in general, the use of which they professed to hold as a violation of the second commandment. Their scruples, however, did not deter them from accepting coins bearing the effigies of kings, even though these monarchs were pagans. Their own coins bore other devices, such as plants, fruit, etc., in place of a human head; and the Romans had condescendingly permitted the issue of a special coinage for Jewish use, each piece bearing the name but not the effigy of the monarch. The ordinary coinage of Rome was current in Palestine, however.

2. Submission to Secular Authority.—Governments are instituted of God, sometimes by His direct interposition, sometimes by His permission. When the Jews had been brought into subjection by Nebuchadnezzar, king of Babylon, the Lord commanded through the prophet Jeremiah (27:4–8) that the people render obedience to their conqueror, whom He called His servant; for verily the Lord had used the pagan king to chastise the recreant and unfaithful children of the covenant. The obedience so enjoined included the payment of taxes and extended to complete submission. After the death of Christ the apostles taught obedience to the powers that be, which powers, Paul declared "are ordained of God." See Rom. 13:1–7; Titus 3:1; 1 Tim. 2:1–3; see also 1 Pet. 2:13, 14. Through the medium of modern revelation, the Lord has required of His people in the present dispensation, obedience to and loyal support of the duly established and existing governments in all lands. See D&C 58:21–22; 98:4–6; and section 134 throughout. The restored Church proclaims as an essential part of its belief and practice: "We believe in being subject to kings, presidents, rulers, and magistrates, in obeying, honoring, and sustaining the law." See *Articles of Faith*, chap. 23.

3. Marriage for Eternity.—Divine revelation in the dispensation of the fulness of times has made plain the fact, that contracts of marriage, as indeed all other agreements between parties in mortality, are of no validity beyond the grave, except such contracts be ratified and validated by the duly established ordinances of the Holy Priesthood. Sealing in the marriage covenant for time and eternity, which has come to be known as celestial marriage, is an ordinance established by divine authority in the restored Church of Jesus Christ. See the author's treatment of this subject in *Articles of Faith*, pp. 442–49, and *House of the Lord*, under "Sealing in Marriage."

4. Divisions and Subdivisions of the Law.—"The Rabbinical schools, in their meddling, carnal, superficial spirit of word-weaving and letter-worship, had spun large accumulations of worthless subtlety all over the Mosaic law. Among other things they had wasted their idleness in fantastic attempts to count, and classify, and weigh, and measure all the separate commandments of the ceremonial and moral law. They had come to the sapient conclusion that there were 248 affirmative precepts, being as many as the members in the human body, and 365 negative precepts, being as many as the arteries and veins, or the days of the year: the total being 613, which was also the number of letters in the decalog. They arrived at the same result from the fact that the Jews were commanded (Num. 15:38) to wear fringes (*tsitsith*) on the corners of their *tallith*, bound with a thread of blue; and as each fringe had eight threads and five knots, and the letters of the word *tsitsith* make 600, the total number of commandments was, as before 613. Now surely, out of such a large number of precepts and prohibitions, all could not be of quite the same value; some were 'light' (*kal*), and some were 'heavy (*kobhed*). But which? and what was the greatest commandment of all? According to some Rabbis, the most important of all is that about the *tephillin* and the *tsitsith*, the fringes and phylacteries; and 'he who diligently observes it is regarded in the same light as if he had kept the whole Law.'

"Some thought the omission of ablutions as bad as homicide; some that the precepts of the Mishna were all 'heavy'; those of the Law were some 'heavy' and some 'light.' Others considered the third to be the greatest commandment. None of them had realized the great principle, that the wilful violation of one commandment is the transgression of all (James 2:10), because the object of the entire Law is the spirit of *obedience to God*. On the question proposed by the lawyer the Shammaites and Hillelites were in disaccord, and, as usual, both schools were wrong: the Shammaites, in thinking that mere trivial external observances were valuable, apart from the spirit in which they were performed, and the principle which they exemplified; the Hillelites, in thinking that *any* positive command could in itself be unimportant, and in not seeing that great principles are essential to the due performance of even the slightest duties."—Farrar, *Life of Christ*, chap. 52.

5. Phylacteries and Borders.—Through a traditional interpretation of Ex. 13:9 and Deut. 6:8, the Hebrews adopted the custom of wearing phylacteries, which consisted essentially of strips of parchment on which were inscribed in whole or in part the following texts: Ex. 13:2–10 and 11–17; Deut. 6:4–9, and 11:13–21. Phylacteries were worn on the head and arm. The parchment strips for the head were four, on each of which one of the texts cited above was written. These were placed in a cubical box of leather measuring from 1/2 inch to 1 1/2 inches along the edge; the box was divided into four compartments and one of the little parchment rolls was placed in each. Thongs held the box in place on the forehead between the eyes of the wearer. The arm phylactery comprised but a single roll of parchment on which the four prescribed texts were written; this was placed in a little box which was bound by thongs to the inside of the left arm so as to be brought close to the heart when the hands were placed together in the attitude of devotion. The Pharisees wore the arm phylactery above the elbow, while their rivals, the Sadducees, fastened it to the palm of the hand (see Ex. 13:9). The common people wore phylacteries only at prayer time; but the Pharisees were said to display them throughout the day. Our Lord's reference to the Pharisees' custom of making broad their phylacteries had reference to the enlarging of the containing box, particularly the frontlet. The size of the parchment strips was fixed by rigid rule.

The Lord had required of Israel through Moses (Num. 15:38) that the people attach to the border of their garment a fringe with a ribbon of blue. In ostentatious display of assumed piety, the scribes and Pharisees delighted to wear enlarged borders to attract public attention. It was another manifestation of hypocritical sanctimoniousness.

6. Ecclesiastical Titles.—Our Lord severely condemned the seeking after titles as insignia of rank in His service. Nevertheless He named the Twelve whom He chose, Apostles; and in the Church founded by Himself the offices of Evangelist, High Priest, Pastor, Elder, Bishop, Priest, Teacher, and Deacon were established (see *Articles of Faith,* pp. 198–99). It was the empty man-made title that attached to the individual, not the authorized title of office to which men were called through authoritative ordination, to which the Lord affixed the seal of His disapproval. Titles of office in the Holy Priesthood are of too sacred a character to be used as marks of distinction among men. In the restored Church in the current dispensation, men are ordained to the Priesthood and to the several offices comprised within both the Lesser or Aaronic, and the Higher or Melchizedek Priesthood; but though one be thus made an Elder, a Seventy, a High Priest, a Patriarch or an Apostle, he should not court the usage of the title as a mere embellishment of his name. (See "The Honor and Dignity of Priesthood" by the author in *Improvement Era,* Salt Lake City, March 1914.)

Chas F. Deems, in *The Light of the Nations,* pp. 583–84, says in speaking of the irreverent use of ecclesiastical titles: "The Pharisees loved also the highest places in the synagogs, and it gratified their vanity to be called Teacher, Doctor, Rabbi. Against these Jesus warned His disciples. They were not to love to be called Rabbi, a title which occurs in three forms, *Rab,* Teacher, Doctor; *Rabbi,* My Doctor or Teacher; *Rabboni,* My great Doctor. Nor were they to call any man 'Father,' in the sense of granting him any infallibility of judgment or power over their consciences. . . . 'Papa,' as the simple Moravians call their great man, Count Zinzendorf: 'Founder,' as Methodists denominate good John Wesley; 'Holy Father in God,' as bishops are sometimes called; 'Pope,' which is the same as 'Papa'; 'Doctor of Divinity,' the Christian equivalent of the Jewish 'Rabbi,' are all dangerous titles. But it is not the employment of a name which Jesus denounces, it is the spirit of vanity which animated the Pharisees, and the servile spirit which the employment of titles is apt to engender. Paul and Peter spoke of themselves as spiritual fathers. Jesus teaches that positions in the societies of his followers, such as should afterward be formed, were not to be regarded as dignities, but rather as services; that no man should seek them for the honor they might confer, but for the field of usefulness they might afford; and that no man should lead off a sect, there being but one leader; and that the whole body of believers are brethren, of whom God is the Father."

The writer last quoted very properly disparages aspirations, stimulated by vanity and self-righteous assumption, to the use of the title "Reverend" as applied to men.

7. Seven or Eight Woes?—Some of the early Mss. of the Gospels omit verse 14 from Matt. 23. Such omission reduces the number of specific utterances beginning "woe unto you" from eight to seven. There is no question as to the appearance in the original of the passages in Mark 12:40 and Luke 20:47, which are one in meaning with Matthew 23:14.

8. The Temple Treasure.—In connection with the incident of the widow's mites, Edersheim (vol. 2, pp. 387–88) writes: "Some might come with appearance of self-righteousness, some even with ostentation, some as cheerfully performing a happy duty. 'Many that were rich cast in much'—yes, very much, for such was the tendency that a law had to be enacted forbidding the gift to the Temple of more than a certain proportion of one's possessions. And the amount of such contributions may be inferred by recalling the circumstance, that at the time of Pompey and Crassus, the Temple treasury, after having lavishly defrayed every possible expenditure, contained in money nearly half a million, and precious vessels to the value of nearly two millions sterling." See also Josephus, *Antiquities* xiv, 4:4; 7:1, 2.

9. Zacharias the Martyr.—In referring to the martyrs of ante-meridian time the Lord is recorded as having used the expression "from the blood of righteous Abel unto the blood of Zacharias son of Barachias, whom ye slew between the temple and the altar" (Matt. 23:35). The Old Testament as at present compiled, contains no mention of a martyr named Zacharias son of Barachias, but does chronicle the martyrdom of Zechariah son of Jehoiada (2 Chr. 24: 20–22). "Zechariah" and "Zacharias" are equivalent names. It is the opinion of most Bible scholars that the Zacharias referred to in Matthew's record is Zechariah son of Jehoiada. In the Jewish compilation of Old Testament scriptures, the murder of Zechariah appears as the last recorded martyrdom; and the Lord's reference to the righteous men who had been slain, from Abel to Zechariah or Zacharias, may have been a sweeping inclusion of all the martyrs down to that time, from first to last. However, we have a record of Zechariah son of Berechiah (Zech. 1:1, 7), and this Berechiah was the son of Iddo. Then again, Zechariah son of Iddo is mentioned (Ezra 5:1); but, as is elsewhere found in the older scriptures, the grandson is called the son. The Old Testament does not number this Zechariah among the martyrs, but traditional accounts (Whitby's citation of the Targum) say that he was killed "in the day of propitiation." That the Lord referred to a late and probably the latest of the recorded martyrdoms is probable; and it is equally evident that the case was well known among the Jews. It is likely that a fuller account appeared in scriptures current among the Jews at the time of Christ but since lost. See Note 4, chapter 9.

10. Destruction of the Temple.—"For thirty or more years after the death of Christ, the Jews continued the work of adding to and embellishing the temple buildings. The elaborate design conceived and projected by Herod had been practically completed; the Temple was well-nigh finished, and, as soon afterward appeared, was ready for destruction. Its fate had been definitely foretold by the Savior Himself. Commenting on a remark by one of the disciples concerning the great stones and the splendid buildings on the Temple hill, Jesus had said, 'Seest thou these great buildings? There shall not be left one stone upon another, that shall not be thrown down.' (Mark 13:1, 2; see also Matt. 24:1, 2; Luke 21:5, 6.) This dire prediction soon found its literal fulfilment. In the great conflict with the Roman legions under Titus, many of the Jews had taken refuge within the Temple courts, seemingly hoping that there the Lord would again fight the battles of His people and give them victory. But the protecting presence of Jehovah had long since departed therefrom and Israel was left a prey to the foe. Though Titus would have spared the Temple, his legionnaires, maddened by the lust of conflict, started the conflagration and everything that could be burned was burned. The slaughter of the Jews was appalling; thousands of men, women and children were ruthlessly butchered within the walls, and the temple courts were literally flooded with human blood. This event occurred in the year A.D. 70; and according to Josephus, in the same month and on the same day of the month as that on which the once glorious Temple of Solomon had fallen a prey to the flames kindled by the king of Babylon. (Josephus, *Wars of the Jews*, vi, 4:5, 8. For a detailed and graphic account of the destruction of the Temple see chapters 4 and 5 in their entirety.) Of the Temple furniture the golden candlestick and the table of shewbread from the Holy Place were carried by Titus to Rome as trophies of war; and representations of these sacred pieces are to be seen on the arch erected to the name of the victorious general. Since the destruction of the splendid Temple of Herod no other structure of the kind, no Temple, no House of the Lord as the terms are used distinctively, has been reared on the eastern hemisphere."—*The House of the Lord*, pp. 61–62.

Josephus ascribes the destruction of the Temple of Herod to the anger of God, and states that the devouring flames "took their rise from the Jews themselves, and were occasioned by them." The soldier who applied the torch to the Holy House, which had remained intact while fire raged in the courts, is regarded by the historian as an instrument of divine vengeance. We read (*Wars*, vi, 4:5): "One of the soldiers, without staying for any orders, and without any concern or dread upon him at so great an undertaking, and being hurried on by a certain divine fury, snatched somewhat out of the materials that were on fire, and being lifted up by another soldier, he set fire to a golden window, through which there was a passage to the rooms that were round the Holy House, on the north side of it. As the flames went upward, the Jews made a great clamor, such as so mighty an affliction required."

CHAPTER 32

FURTHER INSTRUCTION TO THE APOSTLES

PROPHECIES RELATING TO THE DESTRUCTION OF JERUSALEM AND THE LORD'S FUTURE ADVENT [a]

In the course of His last walk from Jerusalem back to the beloved home at Bethany, Jesus rested at a convenient spot on the Mount of Olives, from which the great city and the magnificent temple were to be seen in fullest splendor, illumined by the declining sun in the late afternoon of that eventful April day. As He sat in thoughtful revery He was approached by Peter and James, John and Andrew, of the Twelve, and to them certainly, though probably to all the apostles, He gave instruction, embodying further prophecy concerning the future of Jerusalem, Israel, and the world at large. His fateful prediction—that of the temple buildings not one stone would be left upon another—had caused the apostles to marvel and fear; so they came privately requesting explanation. "Tell us," said they, "when shall these things be? and what shall be the sign of thy coming, and of the end of the world?" The compound character of the question indicates an understanding of the fact that the destruction of which the Lord had spoken was to be apart from and precedent to the signs that were to immediately herald His glorious advent and the yet later ushering in of the consummation commonly spoken of then and now as"the end of the world." An assumption that the events would follow in close succession is implied by the form in which the question was put.

The inquiry referred specifically to time—when were these things to

---

[a] Matt. 24:3–51; Mark 13:3–37; Luke 21:5–36. Compare JS–M 1.

be? The reply dealt not with dates, but with events; and the spirit of the subsequent discourse was that of warning against misapprehension, and admonition to ceaseless vigilance. "Take heed that no man deceive you" was the first and all-important caution; for within the lives of most of those apostles, many blaspheming imposters would arise, each claiming to be the Messiah. The return of Christ to earth as Lord and Judge was more remote than any of the Twelve realized. Before that glorious event, many wonderful and appalling developments would be witnessed, among the earliest of which would be wars and rumors of wars, caused by nation rising against nation and kingdom against kingdom, to the dread accompaniment of famines, pestilences, and earthquakes in many places; yet all these would be but the beginning of the sorrow or travail to follow.

They, the apostles, were told to expect persecution, not only at the hands of irresponsible individuals, but at the instance of the officials such as they who were at that moment intent on taking the life of the Lord Himself, and who would scourge them in the synagogs, deliver them up to hostile tribunals, cite them before rulers and kings, and even put some of them to death—all because of their testimony of the Christ. As they had been promised before, so again were they assured, that when they would stand before councils, magistrates, or kings, the words they should speak would be given them in the hour of their trial, and therefore they were told to take no premeditative thought as to what they should say or how they should meet the issues confronting them; "for," said the Master, "it is not ye that speak, but the Holy Ghost."[b] Even though they found themselves despised and hated of men, and though they were to suffer ignominy, torture, and death, yet as to their eternal welfare they were promised such security that by comparison they would lose not so much as a hair of their heads. In consoling encouragement the Lord bade them possess their souls in patience.[c] In face of all trials and even the direst persecution, it was incumbent upon them to persevere in their ministry, for the divine plan provided and required that the gospel of the kingdom be preached amongst all nations. Their labors would be complicated and opposed by the revolutionary propaganda of many false prophets, and differences of creed would disrupt families, and engender such bitterness

[b] Mark 13:11; compare Matt. 10:19,20; Luke 12:11, 12; 21:14, 15.
[c] Luke 21:19; compare D&C 101:38.

that brothers would betray one another, and children would rise against their parents, accusing them of heresies and delivering them up to death. Even among those who had professed discipleship to Christ many would be offended and hatred would abound; love for the gospel would wax cold, and iniquity would be rampant among men; and only those who would endure to the end of their lives could be saved.

From this circumstantial forecast of conditions then directly impending, the Lord passed to other developments that would immediately precede the destruction of Jerusalem and the total disruption of the Jewish nation. "When ye therefore shall see the abomination of desolation, spoken of by Daniel the prophet, stand in the holy place," said He, according to Matthew's account, and virtually so also as stated by Mark, or "when ye shall see Jerusalem compassed with armies" as Luke writes, "then know that the desolation thereof is nigh." This was a specific sign that none could misunderstand. Daniel the prophet had foreseen the desolation and the abominations thereof, which comprised the forcible cessation of temple rites, and the desecration of Israel's shrine by pagan conquerors.[d]

The realization of Daniel's prophetic vision was to be heralded by the encompassing of Jerusalem by armies. Then all who would escape should make haste; from Judea they should flee to the mountains; he who was on the housetop would have no time to take his goods, but should hasten down by the outer steps and flee; he who was in the field would better leave without first returning to his house even for his clothes. Terrible, indeed, would that day be for women hampered by the conditions incident to approaching maternity, or the responsibility of caring for their suckling babes. All would do well to pray that their flight be not forced upon them in winter time; nor on the Sabbath, lest regard for the restrictions as to Sabbath-day travel, or the usual closing of the city gates on that day, should diminish the chances of escape. The tribulations of the time then foreshadowed would prove to be unprecedented in horror and would never be paralleled in all their awful details in Israel's history; but in mercy God had decreed that the dreadful period should be shortened for the sake of the elect believers, otherwise no flesh of Israel

[d] Dan. 9:27.

would be saved alive. Multitudes were to fall by the sword; other hosts were to be led away captive, and so be scattered amongst all nations; and Jerusalem, the pride and boast of degenerate Israel, should be "trodden down of the Gentiles, until the times of the Gentiles be fulfilled." In every frightful detail was the Lord's prediction brought to pass, as history avouches.[e]

After the passing of those terrible times, and thence onward for a period of unspecified duration, Satan would deceive the world through false doctrines, spread by evil men masquerading as ministers of God, who would continue to cry "Lo, here is Christ; or, lo, he is there"; but against all such the Twelve were put on their guard, and through them and other teachers, whom they would call and ordain, would the world be warned. Deceiving prophets, emissaries of the devil, would be active, some alluring people into the deserts, and impelling them to hermit lives of pernicious asceticism, others insisting that Christ could be found in the secret chambers of monastic seclusion; and some of them showing forth through the power of Satan, such signs and wonders as "to seduce, if it were possible, even the elect"; but of all such scheming of the prince of evil, the Lord admonished His own: "Believe it not"; and added, "take ye heed; behold I have foretold you all things."[f]

In the day of the Lord's advent in glory and vengeance, no man shall be in doubt; there shall be no chance of conflicting claims by contending sects, "For as the lightning cometh out of the east, and shineth even unto the west; so shall also the coming of the Son of man be."[g] The gathering of Israel in the last days was pictured as the flocking of eagles to the place where the body of the Church would be established.[h]

---

[e] Note 1, end of chapter.

[f] Note 2, end of chapter.

[g] Matt. 24:27; compare Luke 17:22–24.

[h] The "body," as that of the Church, is rendered "carcase" in both authorized and revised versions. For the application of the figure—of eagles gathering about a carcase — to the assembling of scattered Israel, see JS–M 1:27, where we read: "so likewise shall mine elect be gathered from the four quarters of the earth." Among Bible scholars, a favorite interpretation of the passage, "For wheresoever the carcase is, there will the eagles be gathered together," is that Christ was likening unto eagles (revised version "vultures") the angels that shall come with Him to execute judgment upon mankind, and unto a carcase the corruption of sin. See Matt. 24:28; compare Luke 17:37.

The chronological order of the predicted occurrences so far considered in this wonderful discourse on things to come, is clear; first there was to be a period of virulent persecution of the apostles and the Church of which they would be in charge; then the destruction of Jerusalem, with all the horrors of merciless warfare was to follow; and this in turn was to be succeeded by a long period of priestcraft and apostasy with bitter sectarian dissension and cruel persecution of the righteous. The brief reference to the nonlocalized, universal phenomena, by which His advent is to be signalized, is a parenthetical demonstration of the false claims as to where Christ would be found; later the Lord passed to distinctive and unquestionable reference to the circumstances of His then and yet future advent. Following the age of man-made creeds, and unauthorized ministry characteristic of the great apostasy, marvelous occurrences are to be manifested through the forces of nature, and the sign of the Son of Man shall ultimately appear, one accompanying feature of which shall be the completion of the gathering of the elect from all parts of the earth to the places appointed.

The duty that Jesus enjoined upon the apostles as of first importance throughout all the coming scenes of sorrow, suffering and turmoil, was that of vigilance. They were to pray, watch, and work, diligently and with unwavering faith. The lesson was, illustrated by a masterly analogy, which, under the broadest classification, may be called a parable. Directing their attention to the fig tree and other trees which flourished on the sunny slopes of Olivet, the Master said: "Behold the fig tree, and all the trees; when they now shoot forth, ye see and know of your own selves that summer is now nigh at hand. So likewise ye, when ye see these things come to pass, know ye that the kingdom of God is nigh at hand." Of the fig tree in particular the Lord remarked: "When his branch is yet tender, and putteth forth leaves, ye know that summer is nigh." This sign of events near at hand was equally applicable to the premonitory conditions which were to herald the fall of Jerusalem and the termination of the Jewish autonomy, and to the developments by which the Lord's second advent shall be immediately preceded.

The next declaration in the order of the evangelical record reads: "Verily I say unto you, This generation shall not pass, till all these things be fulfilled." This may be understood as applying to the generation in which the portentous happenings before described would be realized. So far as the predictions related to the overthrow of Jerusalem, they were literally fulfilled within the natural lifetime of several of the apostles and of multitudes of their contemporaries; such of the Lord's prophecies as pertain to the heralding of His Second Coming are to be brought to pass within the duration of the generation of some who witness the inauguration of their fulfilment. The certainty of fulfilment was emphasized by the Lord in the profound affirmation: "Heaven and earth shall pass away, but my words shall not pass away."[i]

All speculation concerning the time of the Lord's appearing, whether based on assumption, deduction, or calculation of dates, was forestalled by Christ's averment: "But of that day and that hour knoweth no man, no, not the angels which are in heaven, neither the Son, but the Father."[j] That His advent in power and glory is to be sudden and unexpected to the unobserving and sinful world, but in immediate sequence to the signs which the vigilant and devout may read and understand, was made plain by comparison with the prevailing social conditions of Noah's time, when in spite of prophecy and warning the people had continued in their feasting and merry-making, in marrying and giving in marriage, until the very day of Noah's entrance into the ark, "And knew not until the flood came, and took them all away; so shall also the coming of the Son of man be."

In the last stages of the gathering of the elect, the ties of companionship shall be quickly severed; of two men laboring in the field, or of two women engaged side by side in household duties, the faithful one shall be taken and the sinner left. "Watch therefore," was the solemn behest, "for ye know not what hour your Lord doth come." In explication of this admonishment, the Lord condescended to compare the suddenness and secrecy of His coming to the movements of a night-prowling thief; and pointed out, that if a householder had certain knowledge as to the time of a burglar's predetermined visit, he would

---

[i] Matt. 24:35; compare 5:18; Mark 13:31; Luke 21:33; compare 16:17; see also Heb. 1:10, 11; 2 Pet. 3:7–10; Rev. 21:1. Note 5, end of chapter.

[j] This is Mark's version; in the parallel passage Matt. 24:36, the words "neither the Son" are not found in the King James text, but do appear in the revised version. Note 3, end of chapter.

remain on vigilant watch; but because of uncertainty he may be found off his guard, and the thief may enter and despoil the home.

Again likening the apostles to duly appointed stewards in a great household,[k] the Lord spoke of Himself as the householder, saying: "The Son of man is as a man taking a far journey, who left his house, and gave authority to his servants, and to every man his work, and commanded the porter to watch. Watch ye therefore: for ye know not when the master of the house cometh, at even, or at midnight, or at the cockcrowing, or in the morning: Lest coming suddenly he find you sleeping. And what I say unto you I say unto all, Watch." But if the steward grow negligent because of his master's long absence, and give himself up to feasting and unlicensed pleasure, or become autocratic and unjust toward his fellow-servants, his lord shall come in an hour when least expected, and shall consign that wicked servant to a place among the hypocrites, where he shall weep bitter tears of remorse, and gnash his teeth in impotent despair.[l]

THE NEED OF WATCHFULNESS AND DILIGENCE ILLUSTRATED BY PARABLES

To more indelibly impress upon the apostles, and, through their subsequent ministry, upon the world, the absolute need of unceasing watchfulness and unwavering diligence in preparation for the coming of the Lord in judgment, Jesus depicted in parables the prospective condition of mankind in the last times. The first of these illustrative portrayals is the *Parable of the Ten Virgins*. The only report of it we have is that given by Matthew,[m] as follows:

"Then shall the kingdom of heaven be likened unto ten virgins, which took their lamps, and went forth to meet the bridegroom. And five of them were wise, and five were foolish. They that were foolish took their lamps, and took no oil with them: but the wise took oil in their vessels with their lamps. While the bridegroom tarried, they all slumbered and slept. And at midnight there was a cry made, Behold, the bridegroom cometh; go ye out to meet him. Then all those virgins

[k] Page 412.

[l] Matt. 24:45–51; Mark 13:34–37; Luke 21:34–36, compare 12:35–48.

[m] Matt. 25:1–13.

arose, and trimmed their lamps. And the foolish said unto the wise, Give us of your oil; for our lamps are gone out. But the wise answered, saying, Not so; lest there be not enough for us and you: but go ye rather to them that sell, and buy for yourselves. And while they went to buy, the bridegroom came; and they that were ready went in with him to the marriage: and the door was shut. Afterward came also the other virgins, saying, Lord, Lord, open to us. But he answered and said, Verily I say unto you, I know you not. Watch therefore, for ye know neither the day nor the hour wherein the Son of man cometh."

The story itself is based on oriental marriage customs, with which the Lord's attentive listeners were familiar. It was and yet is common in those lands, particularly in connection with marriage festivities among the wealthy classes, for the bridegroom to go to the home of the bride, accompanied by his friends in processional array, and later to conduct the bride to her new home with a larger body of attendants composed of groomsmen, bridesmaids, relatives and friends. As the bridal party progressed, to the accompaniment of gladsome music, it was increased by little groups who had gathered in waiting at convenient places along the route, and particularly near the end of the course where organized companies came forth to meet the advancing procession. Wedding ceremonies were appointed for the evening and night hours; and the necessary use of torches and lamps gave brilliancy and added beauty to the scene.

In the parable ten maidens were waiting to welcome and join in with the bridal company, the time of whose arrival was uncertain. Each had her lamp attached to the end of a rod so as to be held aloft in the festal march; but of the ten virgins five had wisely carried an extra supply of oil, while the other five, probably counting on no great delay, or assuming that they would be able to borrow from others, or perchance having negligently given no thought at all to the matter, had no oil except the one filling with which their lamps had been supplied at starting. The bridegroom tarried, and the waiting maidens grew drowsy and fell asleep. At midnight, the forerunners of the marriage party loudly proclaimed the bridegroom's approach, and cried in haste: "Go ye out to meet him." The ten maidens, no longer sleepy, but eagerly active, set to work to trim their lamps; then the wise ones found use for the oil in their flasks, while the thoughtless five bewailed their destitute condition, for their lamps were empty and they had no oil for replenishment. They appealed to their wiser sisters, asking a share of their oil; but these declined; for, in a time of such exigency, to give of their store would have been to render themselves unfit, inasmuch as there was oil enough for their own lamps only. Instead of oil they could impart only advice to their unfortunate sisters, whom they directed to go to the nearest shop and buy for themselves. While the foolish virgins were away in quest of oil, the wedding party passed into the house wherein the feast was provided, and the door was shut against all tardy comers. In time the unwise maidens, too late to participate in the processional entry, called from without, pleading for admittance; but the bridegroom refused their request, and disclaimed all acquaintanceship with them, since they had not been numbered among his attendants or those of the bride.

The Bridegroom is the Lord Jesus; the marriage feast symbolizes His coming in glory, to receive unto Himself the Church on earth as His bride.[n] The virgins typify those who profess a belief in Christ, and who, therefore, confidently expect to be included among the blessed participants at the feast. The lighted lamp, which each of the maidens carried, is the outward profession of Christian belief and practice; and in the oil reserves of the wiser ones we may see the spiritual strength and abundance which diligence and devotion in God's service alone can insure. The lack of sufficient oil on the part of the unwise virgins is analogous to the dearth of soil in the stony field, wherein the seed readily sprouted but soon withered away.[o] The Bridegroom's coming was sudden; yet the waiting virgins were not held blamable for their surprise at the abrupt announcement, but the unwise five suffered the natural results of their unpreparedness. The refusal of the wise virgins to give of their oil at such a critical time must not be regarded as uncharitable; the circumstance typifies the fact that in the day of judgment every soul must answer for himself; there is no way by which the righteousness of one can be credited to another's account; the doctrine of supererogation is wholly false.[p] The Bridegroom's

[n] Compare Rev. 21:2, 9; 22:17; see also Matt. 9:15; John 3:29.

[o] See Parable of the Sower, Matt. 13:5, 6, 20, 21.

[p] Note 4, end of chapter.

condemnatory disclaimer, "I know you not," was equivalent to a declaration that the imploring but neglectful ones, who had been found unready and unprepared, did not know Him.[q]

The application of the parable and its wealth of splendid suggestion are summarized in a masterly manner by the Lord's impressive adjuration: "Watch therefore, for ye know neither the day nor the hour wherein the Son of man cometh." The fulfilment of the predictions enshrined in this precious parable is yet future, but near. In 1831 the Lord Jesus Christ revealed anew the indications by which the imminence of His glorious advent may be perceived. Through the mouth of His prophet Joseph Smith he thus spake: "And at that day, when I shall come in my glory, shall the parable be fulfilled which I spake concerning the ten virgins: for they that are wise and have received the truth, and have taken the Holy Spirit for their guide, and have not been deceived; verily I say unto you, they shall not be hewn down and cast into the fire, but shall abide the day, and the earth shall be given unto them for an inheritance; and they shall multiply and wax strong, and their children shall grow up without sin unto salvation, for the Lord shall be in their midst, and his glory shall be upon them, and he will be their King and their Lawgiver."[r]

Still discoursing in solemn earnestness to the apostles as the evening shadows gathered about the Mount of Olives, the Lord delivered the last of His recorded parables. We call it the *Parable of the Entrusted Talents.*[s]

"For the kingdom of heaven is as a man travelling into a far country, who called his own servants, and delivered unto them his goods. And unto one he gave five talents, to another two, and to another one; to every man according to his several ability; and straightway took his journey. Then he that had received the five talents went and traded with the same, and made them other five talents. And likewise he that had received two, he also gained other two. But he that had received one went and digged in the earth, and hid his lord's money. After a long time the lord of those servants cometh, and

[q] Compare John 10:14.
[r] D&C 45:56–59; see also 63:53, 54.
[s] Matt. 25:14–30.

reckoneth with them. And so he that had received five talents came and brought other five talents, saying, Lord, thou deliveredst unto me five talents: behold, I have gained beside them five talents more. His lord said unto him, Well done, thou good and faithful servant: thou hast been faithful over a few things, I will make thee ruler over many things: enter thou into the joy of thy lord. He also that had received two talents came and said, Lord, thou deliveredst unto me two talents: behold, I have gained two other talents beside them. His lord said unto him, Well done, good and faithful servant; thou hast been faithful over a few things, I will make thee ruler over many things: enter thou into the joy of thy lord. Then he which had received the one talent came and said, Lord, I knew thee that thou art an hard man, reaping where thou hast not sown, and gathering where thou hast not strawed: And I was afraid, and went and hid thy talent in the earth: lo, there thou hast that is thine. His lord answered and said unto him, Thou wicked and slothful servant, thou knewest that I reap where I sowed not, and gather where I have not strawed: Thou oughtest therefore to have put my money to the exchangers, and then at my coming I should have received mine own with usury. Take therefore the talent from him, and give it unto him which hath ten talents. For unto every one that hath shall be given, and he shall have abundance: but from him that hath not shall be taken away even that which he hath. And cast ye the unprofitable servant into outer darkness: there shall be weeping and gnashing of teeth."

Some of the resemblances between this parable and that of the Pounds[t] appear on even a casual reading; significant differences are discovered by comparison and study. The earlier parable was spoken to a mixed multitude in the course of our Lord's last journey from Jericho to Jerusalem; the later one was given in privacy to the most intimate of His disciples in the closing hours of the last day of His public preaching. The two should be studied together. In the story of the Pounds, an equal amount of capital is given to each of the servants, and men's diverse ability to use and apply, with commensurate results in reward or penalty, is demonstrated; in that of the Entrusted

[t] Luke 19:12–27.

Talents, the servants receive different amounts, "every man according to his several ability"; and equal diligence, though shown in one instance by great gain and in the other by small but proportionate increase, is equally rewarded. Unfaithfulness and negligence are condemned and punished in both.

In the parable now under consideration, the master is presented as delivering his wealth into the hands of his own servants, literally, bondservants;[u] they, as well as the possessions held by them in trust, were his. Those servants had no rights of actual ownership, nor title of permanent proprietorship in the treasure committed to their care; all they had, the time and opportunity to use their talents, and they themselves, belonged to their lord. We cannot fail to perceive even in the early incidents of the story that the Master of the servants was the Lord Jesus; the servants, therefore, were the disciples and more particularly the apostles, who, while of equal authority through ordination in the Holy Priesthood, as specifically illustrated by the earlier parable of the Pounds, were of varied ability, of diverse personality, and unequal generally in nature and in such accomplishments as would be called into service throughout their ministry. The Lord was about to depart; He would return only "after a long time"; the significance of this latter circumstance is in line with that expressed through the parable of the Ten Virgins in the statement that the Bridegroom tarried.

At the time of reckoning, the servants who had done well, the one with his five talents, the other with his two, reported gladly, conscious as they were of having at least striven to do their best. The unfaithful servant prefaced his report with a grumbling excuse, which involved the imputation of unrighteousness in the Master. The honest, diligent, faithful servants saw and reverenced in their Lord the perfection of the good qualities which they possessed in measured degree; the lazy and unprofitable serf, afflicted by distorted vision, professed to see in the Master his own base defects. The story in this particular, as in the other features relating to human acts and tendencies, is psychologically true; in a peculiar sense men are prone to conceive of the attributes of God as comprising in augmented degree the dominant traits of their own nature.

---

[u] Margin, revised version.

Both the servant who had been entrusted with five talents and he who had received but two were equally commended, and, as far as we are told, were equally recompensed. The talents bestowed upon each were the gift of his Lord, who knew well whether that servant was capable of using to better advantage one, two, or five. Let no one conclude that good work of relatively small scope is less necessary or acceptable than like service of wider range. Many a man who has succeeded well in business with small capital would have failed in the administration of vast sums; so also in spiritual achievements "there are diversities of gifts, but the same Spirit."[v] Of the man endowed with many talents greater returns were expected; of the one-talented man relatively little was required, yet in that little he failed.[w] At the least he could have delivered the money to the bank, through which it would have been kept in circulation to the benefit of the community, and would have earned interest meanwhile. Likewise, in the spiritual application, a man possessed of any good gift, such as musical ability, eloquence, skill in handicraft, or the like, ought to use that gift to the full, that he or others may be profited thereby; but should he be too neglectful to exercise his powers in independent service, he may assist others to profitable effort, by encouragement if by nothing more.

Who can doubt in the spirit of the Lord's teaching, that had the man been able to report the doubling of his single talent, he would have been as cordially commended and as richly recompensed as were his more highly endowed and faithful fellows? It is notable that to the charge of unrighteousness made by the unfaithful servant, the Lord deigns no refutation; the spirit of the reply was the same as that expressed in the earlier parable: "Out of thine own mouth will I judge thee, thou wicked servant."[x] The unworthy man sought to excuse himself by the despicable but all too common subterfuge of presumptuously charging culpability in another, and in this instance, that other was his Lord. Talents are not given to be buried, and then to be dug up and offered back unimproved, reeking with the smell of earth and dulled by the corrosion of disuse. The unused talent was justly taken from him

[v] 1 Cor. 12:4; study the entire chapter.

[w] Luke 12:48.

[x] Luke 19:22; compare Matt. 12:37.

who had counted it as of so little worth, and was given to one, who, although possessing much, would use the additional gift to his own profit, to the betterment of his fellows, and to the glory of his Lord.

THE INEVITABLE JUDGMENT[y]

The Lord had uttered His last parable. In words of plainness, though suffused with the beauty of effective simile, He impressed upon the listening disciples the certainty of judgment by which the world shall be visited in the day of His appearing. Then shall the wheat be segregated from the tares,[z] and the sheep divided from the goats. "When the Son of man shall come in his glory, and all the holy angels with him, then shall he sit upon the throne of his glory: And before him shall be gathered all nations: and he shall separate them one from another, as a shepherd divideth his sheep from the goats: And he shall set the sheep on his right hand, but the goats on the left." Unto those on His right hand the King shall give commendation and blessing, bestowing a rich recompense for their good works, as attested by the hungry they had fed, the thirsty to whom they had given drink, the stranger they had lodged, the naked they had clothed, the sick to whom they had ministered, the prisoners they had visited and encouraged, all of which mercies are accredited to them as having been rendered to their Lord in person. The blessed company, overwhelmed by the plenitude of the King's bounty, of which they regard themselves as undeserving, will fain disclaim the merit attributed to them; "And the King shall answer and say unto them, Verily I say unto you, Inasmuch as ye have done it unto one of the least of these my brethren, ye have done it unto me."

Unto them who wait on the left in terrified expectancy, the King shall recount their several deficiencies, in that they had given Him neither food nor drink, shelter nor clothing despite His need; neither had they visited Him though ill, nor ministered unto His wants when He lay in a prison cell. In the desperation of anguish these shall ask when and where they had had such opportunity of comforting Him, and He shall answer, "Verily I say unto you, Inasmuch as ye did it not

[y] Matt. 25:31–46.
[z] Matt. 13:24–30.

to one of the least of these, ye did it not to me." The righteous shall be welcomed with "Come ye blessed of my Father"; the wicked shall hear the awful sentence, "Depart from me ye cursed." Eternal life is the inestimable reward; everlasting punishment the unfathomable doom.[aa]

Viewing as one discourse the two parables and the teaching that directly followed, we find in it such unity of subject and thoroughness of treatment as to give to the whole both beauty and worth beyond the sum of these qualities exhibited in the several parts. Vigilant waiting in the Lord's cause, and the dangers of unreadiness are exemplified in the story of the virgins; diligence in work and the calamitous results of sloth are prominent features of the tale of the talents. These two phases of service are of reciprocal and complementary import; it is as necessary at times to wait as at others to work. The lapse of a long period, as while the Bridegroom tarried, and as during the Master's absence in "a far country,"[bb] is made plain throughout as intervening between the Lord's departure and His return in glory. The absolute certainty of the Christ coming to execute judgment upon the earth, in the which every soul shall receive according to his deserts, is the sublime summary of this unparalleled discourse.

ANOTHER SPECIFIC PREDICTION OF THE LORD'S DEATH

Following the instructions to the apostles at the resting place on Olivet, and probably in the course of the continued walk toward Bethany that evening, Jesus reminded the Twelve of the awful fate awaiting Him, and specified the time of His betrayal and the manner of His death. "Ye know," He said, "that after two days is the feast of the passover, and the Son of man is betrayed to be crucified."[cc]

NOTES TO CHAPTER 32

1. **Early Fulfilment of the Lord's Prophecies.**—As to the literal fulfilment of the Lord's predictions relating to the times immediately following His ascension and down to the destruction of Jerusalem, the student must be referred to scriptural and other history. Only a brief summary of the most notable events can be attempted here.

[aa] Page 272–73.
[bb] The revised version reads "another country" instead of "a far country," in Matt. 25:14.
[cc] Matt. 26:2.

On the matter of wars and rumors or threats of wars, see Josephus, *Antiquities* xviii, ch. 9, and *Wars*, ii, ch. 10. The latter reference is to the account of the decree issued by Caligula that his statue be set up and duly reverenced in the temple, in consequence of which the Jews protested so strenuously that war was declared against them, but was averted by the death of the emperor. Concerning the death of Caligula, Josephus remarks that it "happened most happily for our nation in particular, which would have almost utterly perished, if he had not been suddenly slain." Other threats of war against the Jews were severally made by the emperors Claudius and Nero.

Nation rose against nation, as for example, in the assault of Greeks and Syrians upon the Jews, in the course of which 50,000 Jews were slain at Selucia on the Tigris, and 20,000 at Caesarea, 13,000 at Scythopolis, and 2,500 at Ascalon. Famine and its attendant pestilence prevailed during the reign of Claudius, (A.D. 41–54) and such had been specifically predicted by inspiration, through Agabus (Acts 11:28). The famine was very severe in Palestine (Josephus, *Antiquities*, xx, ch. 2). Earthquakes were of alarming frequency and of unusual severity, between the death of Christ and the destruction of Jerusalem, particularly in Syria, Macedonia, Campania, and Achia. See Tacitus, *Annals*, books xii and xiv; and for account of violent seismic disturbances at Rome, see Suetonius in his *Life of Galba*. Josephus (*Wars* iv, ch. 4) records a particularly severe earthquake that disrupted parts of Judea, and was accompanied by "amazing concussions and bellowings of the earth— a manifest indication that some destruction was coming upon men." The portent of "fearful sights and great signs" from heaven, as recorded by Luke was realized in the phenomenal events chronicled by Josephus (Preface to *Wars*).

Of the persecution that befell the apostles and others, and of their arraignment before rulers, Dr. Adam Clarke, in his commentary on passages in Matt. 24, says: "We need go no farther than the Acts of the Apostles for the completion of these particulars. Some were delivered to councils, as Peter and John (Acts 4:5). Some were brought before rulers and kings, as Paul before Gallio (18:12); before Felix (ch. 24); before Festus and Agrippa (ch. 25). Some had utterance and wisdom which their adversaries were not able to resist; so Stephen (6:10), and Paul who made even Felix himself tremble (24:25). Some were imprisoned, as Peter and John (4:3). Some were beaten, as Paul and Silas (16:23). Some were put to death, as Stephen (7:59); and James the brother of John (12:2). But if we look beyond the book of the Acts of the Apostles, to the bloody persecutions under Nero, we shall find these predictions still more amply fulfilled; in these, numberless Christians fell, besides those two champions of the faith, Peter and Paul. And it was, as says Tertullian, a war against the very name of Christ; for he who was called Christian had committed crime enough in bearing the name to be put to death. So true were our Savior's words that they should be hated of all men for His Name's sake."

Among the false prophets, and men who claimed to be the duly accredited ministers of Christ, were Simon Magus who drew many people after him (Acts 8:9, 13, 18–24; see also *The Great Apostasy*, 7:1, 2), Menander, Dositheus, and Theudas, and the false apostles referred to by Paul (2 Cor. 11:13) and others, such as Hymeneus and Philetus (2 Tim. 2:17, 18). Dummelow's *Commentary* applies here the record by Josephus concerning "a body of wicked men, who deceived and deluded the people under pretense of divine inspiration, who prevailed with the multitude to act like madmen, and went before them into the wilderness, pretending that God would there show them the signals of victory." Compare 2 Pet. 2:1; 1 Jn. 2:18; 4:1. That the love of many did wax cold, both before and after the destruction of Jerusalem, is attested by the facts of the worldwide apostasy, which was the result of corruption within and persecution from without the Church (see *The Great Apostasy*, chaps. 3–9).

The preaching of the gospel of the kingdom "in all the world" was no less truly an essential characteristic of the apostolic period than it is of the current or last dispensation. The rapid spread of the gospel and the phenomenal growth of the Church under the direction of the apostles of old, is recorded as one of the marvels of history (*Great Apostasy*, 1:21, and citation of Eusebius). Paul, writing about thirty years after Christ's ascension, affirms that the gospel had already been carried to every nation, and "preached to every creature under heaven" (Col. 1:23, compare verse 6).

The "abomination of desolation" cited by the Lord from the prophecy by Daniel was strictly fulfilled in the investment of Jerusalem by the Roman army (compare Luke 21:20, 21). To the Jews the ensigns and images of the Romans were a disgusting abomination. Josephus (*Wars* vi, ch. 6) states that the Roman ensigns were set up inside the temple and that the soldiery offered sacrifices before them.

The warning to all to flee from Jerusalem and Judea to the mountains when the armies would begin to surround the city was so generally heeded by members of the Church, that according to the early Church writers not one Christian perished in the awful siege (see Eusebius, *Eccls. Hist.*, book iii, ch. 5). The first siege by Gallus was unexpectedly raised, and then, before the armies of Vespasian arrived at the walls, all Jews who had faith in the warning given by Christ to the apostles, and by these to the people, fled beyond Jordan, and congregated mostly at Pella (compare Josephus, *Wars* ii, ch. 19).

As to the unprecedented horrors of the siege, which culminated in the utter destruction of Jerusalem and the temple, see Josephus, *Wars* vi, chaps. 3 and 4. That historian estimates the number slain in Jerusalem alone as 1,100,000 and in other cities and rural parts a third as many more. For details see Josephus, *Wars* ii, chaps. 18,20; iii, 2, 7, 8, 9; iv, 1, 2, 7, 8, 9; vii, 6, 9, 11. Many tens of thousands were taken captive, to be afterward sold into slavery, or to be slain by wild beasts, or in gladiatorial combat in the arena for the amusement of Roman spectators.

In the course of the siege, a wall was constructed about the entire city, thus fulfilling the Lord's prediction (Luke 19:43), "thine enemies shall cast a trench about thee," in which, by the admittedly better translation, "bank," or "palisade" should appear instead of "trench." In September A.D. 70 the city fell into the hands of the Romans; and its destruction was afterward made so thorough that its site was plowed up. Jerusalem was "trodden down of the Gentiles," and ever since has been under Gentile dominion, and so shall continue to be "until the times of the Gentiles be fulfilled." (Luke 21:24.)

2. In the Deserts and in Secret Chambers.—The 24th chapter of Matthew, and its parallel scriptures in Mark 13 and Luke 21, may be the more easily understood if we bear in mind that the Lord therein speaks of two distinct events, each a consummation of long ages of preparation, and the first a prototype of the second. Many of the specific predictions are applicable both to the time preceding or at the destruction of Jerusalem, and to developments of succeeding time down to the Second Coming of Christ. The passage in Matthew 24:26 may be given this two-fold application. Josephus tells of men leading others away into the desert, saying under pretended inspiration that there should they find God; and the same historian mentions a false prophet who led many into the secret chambers of the temple during the Roman assault, promising them that there would the Lord give them deliverance. Men, women, and children followed this fanatical leader, and were caught in the holocaust of destruction, so that 6,000 of them perished in the flames (Josephus, *Wars* vi, ch. 5). Concerning an application of the Lord's precepts to later times and conditions, the author has elsewhere written (*The Great Apostasy*, 7:22–25): One of the heresies of early origin and rapid growth in the Church was the doctrine of antagonism between body and spirit, whereby the former was regarded as an incubus and a curse. From what has been said this will be recognized as one of the perversions derived from the alliance of Gnosticism with Christianity. A result of this grafting in of heathen doctrines was an abundant growth of hermit practices, by which men sought to weaken, torture, and subdue their bodies, that their spirits or "souls" might gain greater freedom. Many who adopted this unnatural view of human existence retired to the solitude of the desert, and there spent their time in practices of stern self-denial and in acts of frenzied self-torture. Others shut themselves up as voluntary prisoners, seeking glory in privation and self-imposed penance. It was this unnatural view of life that gave rise to the several orders of recluses, hermits, and monks.

Think you not that the Savior had such practices in mind, when, warning the disciples of the false claims to sanctity that would characterize the times then soon to follow, He said: "Wherefore if they shall say unto you, Behold he [Christ] is in the desert, go not forth: behold, he is in the secret chambers, believe it not"?

3. The Time of Christ's Advent Not Known.—The Lord's statement that the time of His advent in glory was unknown to man, and that the angels knew it not, "neither the Son," but that it was known to the Father only, appears plain and unambiguous, notwithstanding many and conflicting commentaries thereon. Jesus repeatedly affirmed that His mission was to do the will of the Father; and it is evident that the Father's will was revealed to Him from time to time. While in the flesh He laid no claim to omniscience; though whatever He willed to know He learned through the medium of communication with the Father. Christ had not asked to know what the Father had not intimated His readiness to reveal, which, in this instance, was the day and hour of the Son's appointed return to earth as a glorified, resurrected Being. We need not hesitate to believe that at the time Jesus delivered to the apostles the discourse under consideration, He was uninformed on the matter; for He so states. In the last interview between Christ and the apostles immediately before His ascension (Acts 1:6, 7) they asked, "Lord, wilt thou at this time restore again the kingdom to Israel? And he said unto them, It is not for you to know the times or the seasons, which the Father hath put in his own power." Nor has the date of the Messianic consummation been since revealed to any man; though even now, the fig tree is rapidly putting forth its leaves, and he who hath eyes to see and a heart to understand knows that the summer of the Lord's purpose is near at hand.

4. The False Doctrine of Supererogation.—Among the pernicious fallacies promulgated as authorized dogmas by the apostate church during the long period of spiritual darkness following the close of the apostolic ministry, was the awful enormity known as the doctrine of supererogation. As stated by Mosheim (*Eccl. Hist.* Cent. xii, part ii, ch. 3:4) the dreadful doctrine was formulated in the thirteenth century as follows: "That there actually existed an immense treasure of *merit*, composed of the pious deeds and virtuous actions which the saints had performed *beyond what was necessary for their own salvation*, and which were therefore applicable to the benefit of others; that the guardian and dispenser of this precious treasure was the Roman pontiff, and that of consequence he was empowered to assign to such as he thought proper a portion of this inexhaustible source of merit, suitable to their respective guilt, and sufficient to deliver them from the punishment due to their crimes." Concerning the fallacy of this doctrine the author has written (*The Great Apostasy*, 9:15), in this wise: "This doctrine of supererogation is as unreasonable as it is unscriptural and untrue. Man's individual responsibility for his acts is as surely a fact as is his agency to act for himself. He will be saved through the merits and by the atoning sacrifice of our Redeemer and Lord; and his claim upon the salvation provided is strictly dependent on his compliance with the principles and ordinances of the gospel as established by Jesus Christ. Remission of sins and the eventual salvation of the human soul are provided for; but these gifts of God are not to be purchased with money. Compare the awful fallacies of supererogation and the blasphemous practice of assuming to remit the sins of one man in consideration of the merits of another, with the declaration of the one and only Savior of mankind: 'But I say unto you that every idle word that men shall speak, they shall give an account thereof in the day of judgment.'" If conclusions as to doctrine may be drawn from our Lord's parables, the parable of the Ten Virgins affords refutation of the Satanic suggestion that one man's sin may be neutralized by another's righteousness. We know no supererogation but that of the Lord Jesus Christ, through whose merits salvation is placed within the reach of all men.

5. "This Generation."—Consult any reliable unabridged dictionary of the English language for evidence of the fact that the term "generation," as connoting a period of time, has many meanings, among which are "race, kind, class." The term is not confined to a body of people living at one time. Fausett's *Bible Cyclopedia, Critical and Expository*, after citing many meanings attached to the word, says: "In Matthew

24:34 'this generation shall not pass (viz. the Jewish race, of which the generation in Christ's days was a sample in character: compare Christ's address to the "generation," 23:35, 36, in proof that "generation" means at times the whole Jewish race) till all these things be fulfilled'—a prophecy that the Jews shall be a distinct people still when He shall come again."

CHAPTER 33

THE LAST SUPPER AND THE BETRAYAL

THE PRIESTLY CONSPIRATORS AND THE TRAITOR

As the time for the annual Feast of the Passover approached, and particularly during the two days immediately preceding the beginning of the festival, the chief priests, scribes, and elders of the people, in short the Sanhedrin and the entire priestly party, conspired persistently together as to the best manner of taking Jesus into custody and putting Him to death. At one of these gatherings of evil counsel, which was held at the palace of the high priest, Caiaphas,[a] it was decided that Jesus should be taken by subtlety if possible, as the probable effect of an open arrest would be an uprising of the people. The rulers feared especially an outbreak by the Galileans, who had a provincial pride in the prominence of Jesus as one of their countrymen, and many of whom were then in Jerusalem. It was further concluded and for the same reasons, that the Jewish custom of making impressive examples of notable offenders by executing public punishment upon them at times of great general assemblages, be set aside in the case of Jesus; therefore the conspirators said: "Not on the feast day, lest there be an uproar among the people."[b]

On earlier occasions they had made futile attempts to get Jesus into their hands;[c] and they were naturally dubious as to the outcome of their later machinations. At this juncture they were encouraged and

---

[a] Matt. 26:3–5; see also Mark 14:1; Luke 22:1, 2.

[b] Revised version of Matt. 26:5 reads: "Not during the feast, lest there be a tumult among the people."

[c] John 7:30, 44; 45:53; 11:47–57.

gladdened in their wicked plots by the appearance of an unexpected ally. Judas Iscariot, one of the Twelve, sought an audience with these rulers of the Jews, and infamously offered to betray his Lord into their hands.[d] Under the impulse of diabolic avarice, which, however, was probably but a secondary element in the real cause of his perfidious treachery, he bargained to sell his Master for money, and chaffered with the priestly purchasers over the price of the Savior's blood. "What will ye give me?" he asked; "and they covenanted with him for thirty pieces of silver."[e] This amount, approximately seventeen dollars in our money, but of many times greater purchasing power with the Jews in that day than now with us, was the price fixed by the law as that of a slave; it was also the foreseen sum of the blood-money to be paid for the Lord's betrayal.[f] That the silver was actually paid to Judas, either at this first interview or at some later meeting between the traitor and the priests, is demonstrated by after events.[g]

He had pledged himself to the blackest deed of treachery of which man is capable, and from that hour he sought the opportunity of superseding his infamous promise by its more villainous fulfilment. We are yet to be afflicted by other glimpses of the evil-hearted Iscariot in the course of this dread chronicle of tragedy and perdition; for the present let it be said that before Judas sold Christ to the Jews, he had sold himself to the devil; he had become Satan's serf, and did his master's bidding.

THE LAST SUPPER

The day preceding the eating of the passover lamb had come to be known among the Jews as the first day of the feast of unleavened bread,[h] since on that day all leaven had to be removed from their dwellings, and thereafter for a period of eight days the eating of anything containing leaven was unlawful. On the afternoon of this day, the paschal lambs were slain within the temple court, by the

[d] Matt. 26:14–16; Mark 14:10, 11; Luke 22:3–6.
[e] Matt. 26:15. The revised version reads: "And they weighed unto him thirty pieces of silver." Compare Zech. 11:12.
[f] Ex. 21:32; Zech. 11:12, 13.
[g] Matt. 27:3–10.
[h] Matt. 26:17.

representatives of families or companies who were to eat together; and a portion of the blood of each lamb was sprinkled at the foot of the altar of sacrifice by one of the numerous priests on duty for the day. The slain lamb, then said to have been sacrificed, was borne away to the appointed gathering place of those by whom it was to be eaten. During the first of the days of unleavened bread, which in the year of our Lord's death appears to have fallen on Thursday,[i] some of the Twelve inquired of Jesus where they should make preparations for the paschal meal.[j] He instructed Peter and John to return to Jerusalem, and added: "Behold, when ye are entered into the city, there shall a man meet you, bearing a pitcher of water; follow him into the house where he entereth in. And ye shall say unto the goodman of the house, The Master saith unto thee, Where is the guest chamber, where I shall eat the passover with my disciples? And he shall shew you a large upper room furnished: there make ready. And they went, and found as he had said unto them: and they made ready the passover."

In the evening, Thursday evening as we reckon time, but the beginning of Friday according to the Jewish calendar,[k] Jesus came with the Twelve, and together they sat down to the last meal of which the Lord would partake before His death. Under strain of profound emotion, "He said unto them, With desire I have desired to eat this passover with you before I suffer: for I say unto you, I will not any more eat thereof, until it be fulfilled in the kingdom of God. And he took the cup, and gave thanks, and said, Take this, and divide it among yourselves: for I say unto you, I will not drink of the fruit of the vine, until the kingdom of God shall come." The pronouncing of a blessing by the host upon a cup of wine, which was afterward passed round the table to each participant in turn, was the customary manner of beginning the Passover supper. At this solemn meal Jesus appears to have observed the essentials of the Passover procedure; but we have no record of His compliance with the many supernumerary requirements with which the divinely established memorial of Israel's

[i] Note 1, end of chapter.
[j] Matt. 26:17–19; Mark 14:12–16; Luke 22:7–13.
[k] It should be remembered that the Jews counted their days as beginning at sunset, not, as with us, at midnight.

deliverance from bondage had been invested by traditional custom and rabbinical prescription. As we shall see, the evening's proceedings in that upper room comprised much beside the ordinary observance of an annual festival.

The supper proceeded under conditions of tense sadness. As they ate, the Lord sorrowfully remarked: "Verily I say unto you, One of you which eateth with me shall betray me." Most of the apostles fell into a state of introspection; and one after another exclaimed: "Is it I?" "Lord, is it I?" It is pleasing to note that each of those who so inquired was more concerned with the dread thought that possibly he was an offender, however inadvertently so, than as to whether his brother was about to prove himself a traitor. Jesus answered that it was one of the Twelve, then and there eating with Him from the common dish, and continued with the terrifying pronouncement: "The Son of man indeed goeth, as it is written of him: but woe to that man by whom the Son of man is betrayed! good were it for that man if he had never been born." Then Judas Iscariot, who had already covenanted to sell his Master for money, and who at this moment probably feared that silence might arouse suspicion against himself, asked with a brazen audacity that was veritably devilish: "Master, is it I?" With cutting promptness the Lord replied: "Thou hast said."[l]

There was further cause of sorrow to Jesus at the supper. Some of the Twelve had fallen into muttering dispute among themselves over the matter of individual precedence,[m] possibly as to the order in which they should take their places at table, over which triviality scribes and Pharisees as well as the Gentiles often quarreled;[n] and again the Lord had to remind the apostles that the greatest of them all was he who most willingly served his fellows. They had been taught before; yet now, at this late and solemn hour, they were suffused with vain and selfish ambition. In sorrowful earnestness the Lord pleaded with them, asking who is greater, he that sits at the table, or he that serves? And the obvious reply He supplemented by the statement: "But I am among you as he that serveth." With loving pathos He

[l] Note 2, end of chapter.
[m] Luke 22:24–30.
[n] Luke 14:7–11.

added: "Ye are they which have continued with me in my temptations;"[o] and then He assured them that they should lack neither honor nor glory in the kingdom of God, for if they proved faithful they should be appointed to thrones as the judges of Israel. For those of His chosen ones who were true to Him, the Lord had no feeling less than that of love, and of yearning for their victory over Satan and sin.

THE ORDINANCE OF THE WASHING OF FEET [p]

Leaving the table, the Lord laid aside His outer garments and girded Himself with a towel as an apron; then having provided Himself with a basin and a supply of water, He knelt before each of the Twelve in turn, washed his feet, and wiped them with the towel. When He reached Peter, that impulsive apostle protested, saying: "Lord, dost thou wash my feet?" That the proceeding was something more than mere service for personal comfort, and more than an object-lesson of humility, appears in the Lord's words to Peter—"What I do thou knowest not now; but thou shalt know hereafter." Peter, failing to understand, objected yet more vehemently; "Thou shalt never wash my feet," he exclaimed. Jesus answered: "If I wash thee not, thou hast no part with me." Then, with even greater impetuosity than before, Peter implored as he stretched forth both feet and hands, "Lord, not my feet only, but also my hands and my head." He had gone to the other extreme, insisting, though ignorantly and unthinkingly, that things be done his way, and failing yet to see that the ordinance had to be administered as the Lord willed. Again correcting His well-intending though presumptuous servant, Jesus said to him: "He that is washed needeth not save to wash his feet, but is clean every whit: and ye are clean, but not all." Each of them had been immersed at baptism; the washing of feet was an ordinance pertaining to the Holy Priesthood, the full import of which they had yet to learn.[q]

Having resumed His garments and returned to His place at the table, Jesus impressed the significance of what he had done, saying: "Ye call me Master and Lord: and ye say well; for so I am. If I then,

[o] Luke 22:28.

[p] John 13:1–20.

[q] Note 3, end of chapter.

your Lord and Master, have washed your feet; ye also ought to wash one another's feet. For I have given you an example, that ye should do as I have done to you. Verily, verily, I say unto you, The servant is not greater than his lord; neither he that is sent greater than he that sent him. If ye know these things, happy are ye if ye do them."[r]

THE SACRAMENT OF THE LORD'S SUPPER [s]

While Jesus with the Twelve still sat at table, He took a loaf or cake of bread, and having reverently given thanks and by blessing sanctified it, He gave a portion to each of the apostles, saying: "Take, eat; this is my body"; or, according to the more extended account, "This is my body which is given for you: this do in remembrance of me." Then, taking a cup of wine, He gave thanks and blessed it, and gave it unto them with the command: "Drink ye all of it; for this is my blood of the new testament, which is shed for many for the remission of sins. But I say unto you, I will not drink henceforth of this fruit of the vine, until that day when I drink it new with you in my Father's kingdom."[t] In this simple but impressive manner was instituted the ordinance, since known as the Sacrament of the Lord's Supper. The bread and wine, duly consecrated by prayer, become emblems of the Lord's body and blood, to be eaten and drunk reverently, and in remembrance of Him.

The proceedings at the institution of this sacred rite were afterward revealed to Paul the apostle, whose recorded testimony as to its establishment and sanctity is in accord with the accounts given by the Gospel-writers.[u] As shall be hereinafter shown, the ordinance was instituted by the Lord among the Nephites, on the western continent, and has been reestablished in the present dispensation.[v] During the dark ages of apostasy, unauthorized changes in the administration of

---

[r] The Lord's expression "neither he that is sent greater than he that sent him" (John 13:16) is more correctly rendered "neither the apostle than he that sent him" (revised version, margin).

[s] Matt. 26:26–29; Mark 14:22–25; Luke 22:19, 20.

[t] In the revised version we read "covenant" instead of "testament" in Matt. 26:28, and in parallel passages.

[u] 1 Cor. 11:23–34.

[v] 3 Ne. 18:6–11; D&C 20:75; see also *The Articles of Faith*, chapter 9.

the Sacrament were introduced, and many false doctrines as to its meaning and effect were promulgated.[w]

THE BETRAYER GOES OUT INTO THE NIGHT [x]

In saying to the Twelve, whose feet He had washed, "Ye are clean," the Lord had specified an exception by His after remark, "but not all." John the recorder, takes care to explain that Jesus had in mind the traitor, and, "therefore said he, Ye are not all clean." The guilty Iscariot had received without protest the Lord's service in the washing of his recreant feet, though after the ablution he was spiritually more filthy than before. When Jesus had again sat down, the burden of His knowledge concerning the treacherous heart of Judas again found expression. "I speak not of you all," He said, "I know whom I have chosen: but that the scripture may be fulfilled, He that eateth bread with me hath lifted up his heel against me."[y] The Lord was intent on impressing the fact of His foreknowledge as to what was to come, so that when the terrible development was an accomplished fact, the apostles would realize that thereby the scriptures had been fulfilled. Troubled in spirit, He reiterated the dreadful assertion that one of those present would betray Him. Peter made signs to John, who occupied the place next to Jesus and was at that moment leaning his head on the Lord's breast, that he asked which of them was the traitor. To John's whispered inquiry the Lord replied: "He it is, to whom I shall give a sop, when I have dipped it."

There was nothing unusual for a person at table, particularly the host, to dip a piece of bread into the dish of gravy or savory mixture, and hand it to another. Such action on the part of Jesus attracted no general attention. He dipped the morsel of bread and gave it to Judas Iscariot, with the words: "That thou doest, do quickly." The others understood the Lord's remark as an instruction to Judas to attend to some duty or go upon some errand of ordinary kind, perhaps to purchase something for the further celebration of the Passover, or to carry gifts to some of the poor, for Judas was the treasurer of the party and "had

[w] See The Great Apostasy, 8:15–19.

[x] John 13:18–30.

[y] Compare Ps. 41:9.

the bag." But Iscariot understood. His heart was all the more hardened by the discovery that Jesus knew of his infamous plans, and he
was maddened by the humiliation he felt in the Master's presence.
After the sop, which he had opened his mouth to receive from the Lord's
hand, "Satan entered into him" and asserted malignant mastership.
Judas went out immediately, abandoning forever the blessed company
of his brethren and the Lord. John chronicles the traitor's departure
with the terse and ominous remark, "and it was night."

DISCOURSE FOLLOWING THE SUPPER

The departure of Judas Iscariot appears to have dissipated to some
degree the cloud of utter sadness by which the little company had
been depressed; and our Lord Himself was visibly relieved. As soon as
the door had closed upon the retreating deserter, Jesus exclaimed, as
though His victory over death had been already accomplished: "Now
is the Son of man glorified, and God is glorified in him." Addressing
the Eleven in terms of parental affection, He said: "Little children, yet
a little while I am with you. Ye shall seek me: and as I said unto the
Jews, Whither I go, ye cannot come; so now I say to you. A new
commandment I give unto you, That ye love one another; as I have
loved you, that ye also love one another. By this shall all men know
that ye are my disciples, if ye have love one to another."[z] The law of
Moses enjoined mutual love among friends and neighbors;[aa] but the
new commandment, by which the apostles were to be governed,
embodied love of a higher order. They were to love one another as Christ
loved them; and their brotherly affection was to be a distinguishing
mark of their apostleship, by which the world would recognize them
as men set apart.

The Lord's reference to His impending separation from them
troubled the brethren. Peter put the question, "Lord, whither goest
thou?" Jesus answered: "Whither I go, thou canst not follow me now;
but thou shalt follow me afterwards. Peter said unto him, Lord, why
cannot I follow thee now? I will lay down my life for thy sake." Peter
seems to have realized that his Master was going to His death; yet,

[z] John 13:31–34.
[aa] Lev. 19:18.

undeterred, he asserted his readiness to follow even that dark way rather than be separated from his Lord. We cannot doubt the earnestness of Peter's purpose nor the sincerity of his desire at that moment. In his bold avowal, however, he had reckoned with the willingness of his spirit only, and had failed to take into full account the weakness of his flesh. Jesus, who knew Peter better than the man knew himself, thus tenderly reproved his excess of self-confidence: "Simon, Simon, behold, Satan hath desired to have you, that he may sift you as wheat: but I have prayed for thee, that thy faith fail not: and when thou art converted, strengthen thy brethren." The first of the apostles, the Man of Rock, yet had to be converted, or as more precisely rendered, "turned again";[bb] for as the Lord foresaw, Peter would soon be overcome, even to the extent of denying his acquaintanceship with Christ. When Peter stoutly declared again his readiness to go with Jesus, even into prison or to death, the Lord silenced him with the remark: "I tell thee, Peter, the cock shall not crow this day, before that thou shalt thrice deny that thou knowest me."

The apostles had to be prepared to meet a new order of things, new conditions and new exigencies; persecution awaited them, and they were soon to be bereft of the Master's sustaining presence. Jesus asked of them: "When I sent you without purse, and scrip, and shoes, lacked ye anything? And they said, Nothing. Then said he unto them, But now, he that hath a purse, let him take it, and likewise his scrip: and he that hath no sword, let him sell his garment, and buy one. For I say unto you, that this that is written must yet be accomplished in me, And he was reckoned among the transgressors: for the things concerning me have an end." The Lord was soon to be numbered among the transgressors, as had been foreseen;[cc] and His disciples would be regarded as the devotees of an executed criminal. In the mention of purse, scrip, shoes, and sword, some of the brethren caught at the literal meaning, and said, "Lord, behold, here are two swords." Jesus answered with curt finality, "It is enough," or as we might say, "Enough of this." He had not intimated any immediate need of weapons, and most assuredly not for His own defense. Again

---

[bb] So reads the revised version of Luke 22:32.

[cc] Isa. 53:12; compare Mark 15:28.

they had failed to fathom His meaning; but experience would later teach them.[dd]

For such information as we have concerning the last discourse delivered by Jesus to the apostles before His Crucifixion, we are indebted to John alone among the Gospel writers; and every reader is advised to study with care the three chapters in which these sublime utterances are preserved for the enlightenment of mankind.[ee] Observing the sorrowful state of the Eleven, the Master bade them be of good cheer, grounding their encouragement and hope on faith in Himself. "Let not your heart be troubled," He said, "ye believe in God, believe also in me." Then, as though drawing aside the veil between the earthly and the heavenly state and giving His faithful servants a glimpse of conditions beyond, He continued: "In my Father's house are many mansions: if it were not so, I would have told you. I go to prepare a place for you. And if I go and prepare a place for you, I will come again, and receive you unto myself; that where I am, there ye may be also. And whither I go ye know, and the way ye know."[ff] Thus in language simple and plain the Lord declared the fact of graded conditions in the hereafter, of variety of occupations and degrees of glory, of place and station in the eternal worlds.[gg] He had affirmed His own inherent Godship, and through their trust in Him and obedience to His requirements would they find the way to follow whither He was about to precede them. Thomas, that loving, brave, though somewhat skeptical soul, desiring more definite information ventured to say: "Lord, we know not whither thou goest; and how can we know the way?" The Lord's answer was a reaffirmation of His divinity; "I am the way, the truth, and the life: no man cometh unto the Father, but by me. If ye had known me, ye should have known my Father also: and from henceforth ye know him, and have seen him."

At this point Philip interposed with the request, "Lord, shew us the Father, and it sufficeth us." Jesus answered with pathetic and mild reproof: "Have I been so long time with you, and yet hast thou not

---

[dd] Read John 13:36–38; Luke 22:31–38; compare Matt. 26:31–35; Mark 14:27–31.

[ee] John 14, 15, 16.

[ff] John 14:1–4.

[gg] See *The Articles of Faith*, pp. 91–93 and 407–11

known me, Philip? he that hath seen me hath seen the Father; and how sayest thou then, Shew us the Father?" He was grieved by the thought that His nearest and dearest friends on earth, those upon whom He had conferred the authority of the Holy Priesthood, should be yet ignorant of His absolute oneness with the Father in purpose and action. Had the Eternal Father stood amongst them, in Person, under the conditions there existing, He would have done as did the Well Beloved and Only Begotten Son, whom they knew as Jesus, their Lord and Master. So absolutely were the Father and the Son of one heart and mind, that to know either was to know both; nevertheless the Father could be reached only through the Son. So far as the apostles had faith in Christ, and did His will, should they be able to do the works that Christ in the flesh had done, and even greater things, for His mortal mission was of but a few hours further duration, and the unfolding of the divine plan of the ages would call for yet greater miracles than those wrought by Jesus in the brief period of His ministry.

For the first time the Lord directed His disciples to pray in his name to the Father, and assurance of success in righteous supplication was given in these words: "And whatsoever ye shall ask in my name, that will I do, that the Father may be glorified in the Son. If ye shall ask any thing in my name, I will do it."[hh] The name of Jesus Christ was to be thenceforth the divinely established talisman by which the powers of heaven could be invoked to operate in any righteous undertaking.

The Holy Ghost was promised to the apostles; He would be sent through Christ's intercession, to be to them "another Comforter," or as rendered in later translations, "another Advocate" or "Helper," even the Spirit of Truth, who, though the world would reject Him as they had rejected the Christ, should dwell with the disciples, and in them even as Christ then dwelt in them and the Father in Him. "I will not leave you comfortless," Jesus assured the brethren, "I will come to you. Yet a little while, and the world seeth me no more; but ye see me: because I live, ye shall live also. At that day ye shall know that I am in my Father, and ye in me, and I in you."[ii] This was followed by the assurance

hh John 14:13, 14; compare 16:24.
ii John 14:15–20; compare verse 26, and 15:26.

that Christ though unknown by the world would manifest Himself to those who loved Him and kept His commandments.

Judas Thaddeus, otherwise known as Lebbeus,[jj] "not Iscariot," as the recorder is careful to particularize, was puzzled over the untraditional and un-Jewish thought of a Messiah who would be known but to the chosen few and not to Israel at large; and he asked: "Lord, how is it that thou wilt manifest thyself unto us, and not unto the world?" Jesus explained that His and the Father's companionship was attainable only by the faithful. He further cheered the apostles by the promise that when the Comforter, the Holy Ghost, whom the Father would send in the name of the Son, would come to them, He would teach them further, and would bring to their remembrance the teachings they had received from the Christ. The distinct personality of each member of the Godhead, Father, Son, and Holy Ghost, is here again plainly shown.[kk] Comforting the yet troubled disciples, Jesus said: "Peace I leave with you, my peace I give unto you"; and that they might realize that this meant more than the conventional salutation of the times, for "Peace be with you" was an every-day greeting among the Jews, the Lord affirmed that He gave that invocation in a higher sense, and "not as the world giveth." Again bidding them put aside their grief and be not afraid, Jesus added: "Ye have heard how I said unto you, I go away, and come again unto you. If ye loved me, ye would rejoice, because I said, I go unto the Father: for my Father is greater than I." The Lord made clear to His servants that He had told them these things beforehand, so that when the predicted events came to pass the apostles would be confirmed in their faith in Him, the Christ. He had time to say but little more, for the next hour would witness the beginning of the supreme struggle; "the prince of this world cometh," He said, and with triumphal joy added, "and hath nothing in me."[ll]

In superb allegory the Lord thus proceeded to illustrate the vital relationship between the apostles and Himself, and between Himself and the Father, by the figure of a vinegrower, a vine, and its

---

[jj] Matt. 10:3, and Luke 6:16.

[kk] See *The Articles of Faith*, pp. 41–42.

[ll] John 14:22–31.

branches:[mm] "I am the true vine, and my Father is the husbandman. Every branch in me that beareth not fruit he taketh away: and every branch that beareth fruit, he purgeth it,[nn] that it may bring forth more fruit." A grander analogy is not to be found in the world's literature. Those ordained servants of the Lord were as helpless and useless without Him as is a bough severed from the tree. As the branch is made fruitful only by virtue of the nourishing sap it receives from the rooted trunk, and if cut away or broken off withers, dries, and becomes utterly worthless except as fuel for the burning, so those men, though ordained to the Holy Apostleship, would find themselves strong and fruitful in good works, only as they remained in steadfast communion with the Lord. Without Christ what were they, but unschooled Galileans, some of them fishermen, one a publican, the rest of undistinguished attainments, and all of them weak mortals? As branches of the Vine they were at that hour clean and healthful, through the instructions and authoritative ordinances with which they had been blessed, and by the reverent obedience they had manifested.

"Abide in me," was the Lord's forceful admonition, else they would become but withered boughs. "I am the vine," He added in explication of the allegory; "ye are the branches: He that abideth in me, and I in him, the same bringeth forth much fruit: for without me ye can do nothing. If a man abide not in me, he is cast forth as a branch, and is withered; and men gather them, and cast them into the fire, and they are burned. If ye abide in me, and my words abide in you, ye shall ask what ye will, and it shall be done unto you. Herein is my Father glorified, that ye bear much fruit: so shall ye be my disciples." Their love for one another was again specified as an essential to their continued love for Christ.[oo] In that love would they find joy. Christ had been to them an exemplar of righteous love from the day of their first meeting; and He was about to give the supreme proof of His affection, as foreshadowed in His words, "Greater love hath no man than this, that a man lay down his life for his friends." And that those men were the Lord's friends was thus graciously affirmed; "Ye are my

[mm] John 15:1–8.
[nn] Revised version "cleanseth it."
[oo] John 15:9–17.

friends, if ye do whatsoever I command you. Henceforth I call you not servants; for the servant knoweth not what his lord doeth: but I have called you friends; for all things that I have heard of my Father I have made known unto you." This intimate relationship in no sense modified the position of Christ as their Lord and Master, for by Him they had been chosen and ordained; and it was His will that they should so live that whatever they asked in the name of the holy friendship which He acknowledged should be granted them of the Father.

They were again told of the persecutions that awaited them, and of their apostolic calling as special and individual witnesses of the Lord.[pp] That the world then did, and would yet more intensely hate them was a fact they had to face; but they were to remember that the world had hated their Master before them, and that they had been chosen and by ordination had been set apart from the world; therefore they must not hope to escape the world's hatred. The servant was not greater than his master, nor the apostle than his Lord, as on general principles they knew, and as they had been specifically told. They that hated them hated the Christ; and they that hated the Son hated the Father; great shall be the condemnation of such. Had the wicked Jews not closed their eyes and stopped their ears to the mighty works and gracious words of the Messiah, they would have been convinced of the truth, and the truth would have saved them; but they were left without cloak or excuse for their sin; and Christ affirmed that in their evil course had the scriptures been fulfilled in that they had hated Him without a cause.[qq] Then, reverting to the great and cheering promise of support through the coming of the Holy Ghost, the Lord said: "But when the Comforter is come, whom I will send unto you from the Father, even the Spirit of truth, which proceedeth from the Father, he shall testify of me: and ye also shall bear witness, because ye have been with me from the beginning."

These things had Jesus declared unto them that they might not "be offended," or in other words, taken by surprise, misled, and caused to doubt and stumble by the unprecedented events then impending. The apostles were forewarned of persecution, of their expulsion from

---

[pp] John 15:18–27.

[qq] Verse 25; compare Ps. 35:19; 69:4; 109:3.

the synagogs, and of a time in which hatred against them should be so bitter and the Satanic darkness of mind and spirit so dense that whosoever succeeded in killing one of them would profess that his foul deed had been done in God's service. In view of their overwhelming sorrow at the Lord's departure, He sought again to cheer them, saying: "Nevertheless I tell you the truth; It is expedient for you that I go away: for if I go not away, the Comforter will not come unto you; but if I depart, I will send him unto you."

The assured descent of the Holy Ghost, through whom they should be made strong to meet every need and emergency, was the inspiring theme of this part of the Lord's discourse. Many things which Christ yet had to say to His apostles, but which they were at that time unable to understand, the Holy Ghost would teach them. "Howbeit," said Jesus, "when he, the Spirit of truth, is come, he will guide you into all truth: for he shall not speak of himself; but whatsoever he shall hear, that shall he speak: and he will shew you things to come. He shall glorify me: for he shall receive of mine, and shall shew it unto you. All things that the Father hath are mine: therefore said I, that he shall take of mine, and shall shew it unto you."[rr]

Turning again to the matter of His departure, then so near as to be reckoned by hours, the Lord said, in amplified form of what He had before affirmed: "A little while, and ye shall not see me: and again, a little while, and ye shall see me, because I go to the Father."[ss] The apostles pondered and some questioned among themselves as to the Lord's meaning, yet so deep was the solemnity of the occasion that they ventured no open inquiry. Jesus knew of their perplexity and graciously explained that they would soon weep and lament while the world rejoiced; this had reference to His death; but He promised that their sorrow should be turned into joy; and this was based on His Resurrection to which they should be witnesses. He compared their then present and prospective state to that of a woman in travail, who in the after joy of blessed motherhood forgets her anguish. The happiness that awaited them would be beyond the power of man to take away; and thenceforth they should ask not of Christ alone, but of the Father

[rr] John 16:13–15; read verses 1–15.
[ss] John 16:16; compare 7:33; 13:33; 14:19.

in Christ's name; "And," said the Lord, "in that day ye shall ask me nothing. Verily, verily, I say unto you, Whatsoever ye shall ask the Father in my name, he will give it you. Hitherto have ye asked nothing in my name: ask, and ye shall receive, that your joy may be full."[tt] They were to be advanced to such honor and exalted recognition that they should approach the Father in prayer direct, but in the name of the Son; for they were beloved of the Father because they had loved Jesus, the Son, and had accepted Him as One sent by the Father.

The Lord again solemnly averred: "I came forth from the Father, and am come into the world: again, I leave the world, and go to the Father." The disciples were gratified at this plain avouchment, and exclaimed: "Lo, now speakest thou plainly, and speakest no proverb. Now are we sure that thou knowest all things, and needest not that any man should ask thee: by this we believe that thou camest forth from God." Their satisfaction threatened danger through over-confidence; and the Lord cautioned them, saying, that in an hour then close they should all be scattered, every man to his own, leaving Jesus alone, except for the Father's presence. In the same connection He told them that before the night had passed every one of them would be offended because of Him, even as it had been written: "I will smite the shepherd, and the sheep of the flock shall be scattered abroad."[uu] Peter, the most vehement of all in his protestations, had been told, as we have seen, that by cock-crow that night he would have thrice denied his Lord; but all of them had declared they would be faithful whatever the trial.[vv] In further affirmation of the material actuality of His Resurrection, Jesus promised the apostles that after He had risen from the grave He would go before them into Galilee.[ww]

In conclusion of this last and most solemn of the discourses delivered by Christ in the flesh, the Lord said: "These things I have spoken unto you, that in me ye might have peace. In the world ye shall have tribulation: but be of good cheer; I have overcome the world."[xx]

[tt] John 16:17, 23, 24; read verses 17–28.

[uu] Matt. 26:31; Mark 14:27; compare Zech. 13:7; see also Matt. 11:6.

[vv] Matt. 26:31–35; Mark 14:29–31.

[ww] Matt. 26:32; Mark 14:28; compare 16:7.

[xx] John 16:33.

THE CONCLUDING PRAYER

The impressive discourse to the apostles was followed by a prayer such as could be addressed to none but the Eternal Father, and such as none but the Son of that Father could offer.[yy] It has been called, and not inappropriately, the Lord's High-Priestly Prayer. In it Jesus acknowledged the Father as the source of His power and authority, which authority extends even to the giving of eternal life to all who are worthy: "And this is life eternal, that they might know thee the only true God, and Jesus Christ, whom thou hast sent." By way of reverent report as to the work assigned Him, the Son said: "I have glorified thee on the earth: I have finished the work which thou gavest me to do. And now, O Father, glorify thou me with thine own self with the glory which I had with thee before the world was." With unfathomable love the Lord pleaded for those whom the Father had given Him, the apostles then present, who had been called out from the world, and who had been true to their testimony of Himself as the Son of God. Of them but one, the son of perdition, had been lost. In the fervor of devoted supplication, the Lord pleaded:

"I pray not that thou shouldest take them out of the world, but that thou shouldest keep them from the evil. They are not of the world, even as I am not of the world. Sanctify them through thy truth: thy word is truth. As thou hast sent me into the world, even so have I also sent them into the world. And for their sakes I sanctify myself, that they also might be sanctified through the truth. Neither pray I for these alone, but for them also which shall believe on me through their word; that they all may be one; as thou, Father, art in me, and I in thee, that they also may be one in us: that the world may believe that thou hast sent me. And the glory which thou gavest me I have given them; that they may be one, even as we are one: I in them, and thou in me, that they may be made perfect in one; and that the world may know that thou hast sent me, and hast loved them, as thou hast loved me. Father, I will that they also, whom thou hast given me, be with me where I am; that they may behold my glory, which thou hast given me: for thou lovedst me before the foundation of the

[yy] John 17.

world. O righteous Father, the world hath not known thee: but I have known thee, and these have known that thou hast sent me. And I have declared unto them thy name, and will declare it: that the love wherewith thou hast loved me may be in them, and I in them."

When they had sung a hymn, Jesus and the Eleven went out to the Mount of Olives.ᶻᶻ

THE LORD'S AGONY IN GETHSEMANEᵃᵃᵃ

Jesus and the eleven apostles went forth from the house in which they had eaten, passed through the city gate, which was usually left open at night during a public festival, crossed the ravine of the Cedron, or more accurately Kidron, brook, and entered an olive orchard known as Gethsemane,ᵇᵇᵇ on the slope of Mount Olivet. Eight of the apostles He left at or near the entrance, with the instruction: "Sit ye here, while I go and pray yonder"; and with the earnest injunction: "Pray that ye enter not into temptation." Accompanied by Peter, James and John, He went farther; and was soon enveloped by deep sorrow, which appears to have been, in a measure, surprising to Himself, for we read that He "began to be sore amazed, and to be very heavy." He was impelled to deny Himself the companionship of even the chosen three; and, "Saith he unto them, My soul is exceeding sorrowful, even unto death: tarry ye here, and watch with me. And he went a little farther, and fell on his face, and prayed, saying, O my Father, if it be possible, let this cup pass from me: nevertheless not as I will, but as thou wilt." Mark's version of the prayer is: "Abba, Father, all things are possible unto thee; take away this cup from me; nevertheless not what I will, but what thou wilt."ᶜᶜᶜ

This part of His impassioned supplication was heard by at least one of the waiting three; but all of them soon yielded to weariness and ceased to watch. As on the Mount of Transfiguration, when the Lord appeared in glory, so now in the hour of His deepest humiliation,

---

ᶻᶻ Note 4, end of chapter.

ᵃᵃᵃ Matt. 26:36–46; Mark 14:32–42; Luke 22:39–46.

ᵇᵇᵇ Note 5, end of chapter.

ᶜᶜᶜ "Abba" is expressive of combined affection and honor, and signifies "Father." It is applied to the Eternal Father by Jesus in the passage above, and by Paul (Rom. 8:15; Gal. 4:6).

these three slumbered. Returning to them in an agony of soul Jesus found them sleeping; and addressing Peter, who so short a time before had loudly proclaimed his readiness to follow the Lord even to prison and death, Jesus exclaimed: "What, could ye not watch with me one hour? Watch and pray, that ye enter not into temptation"; but in tenderness added, "the spirit indeed is willing, but the flesh is weak." The admonition to the apostles to pray at that time lest they be led into temptation may have been prompted by the exigencies of the hour, under which, if left to themselves, they would be tempted to prematurely desert their Lord.

Aroused from slumber the three apostles saw the Lord again retire, and heard Him pleading in agony: "O my Father, if this cup may not pass away from me, except I drink it, thy will be done." Returning a second time He found those whom He had so sorrowfully requested to watch with Him sleeping again, "for their eyes were heavy"; and when awakened they were embarrassed or ashamed so that they wist not what to say. A third time He went to His lonely vigil and individual struggle, and was heard to implore the Father with the same words of yearning entreaty. Luke tells us that "there appeared an angel unto him from heaven, strengthening him"; but not even the presence of this super-earthly visitant could dispel the awful anguish of His soul. "And being in an agony he prayed more earnestly: and his sweat was as it were great drops of blood falling down to the ground."[ddd]

Peter had had a glimpse of the darksome road which he had professed himself so ready to tread; and the brothers James and John knew now better than before how unprepared they were to drink of the cup which the Lord would drain to its dregs.[eee]

When for the last time Jesus came back to the disciples left on guard, He said: "Sleep on now, and take your rest: behold, the hour is at hand, and the Son of man is betrayed into the hands of sinners." There was no use of further watching; already the torches of the approaching band conducted by Judas were observable in the distance. Jesus exclaimed: "Rise, let us be going: behold, he is at hand that doth betray me." Standing with the Eleven, the Lord calmly awaited the traitor's coming.

[ddd] Note 6, end of chapter.

[eee] John 13:37; Matt. 20:22; Mark 10:38, 39.

Christ's agony in the garden is unfathomable by the finite mind, both as to intensity and cause. The thought that He suffered through fear of death is untenable. Death to Him was preliminary to resurrection and triumphal return to the Father from whom He had come, and to a state of glory even beyond what He had before possessed; and, moreover, it was within His power to lay down His life voluntarily.^{fff} He struggled and groaned under a burden such as no other being who has lived on earth might even conceive as possible. It was not physical pain, nor mental anguish alone, that caused Him to suffer such torture as to produce an extrusion of blood from every pore; but a spiritual agony of soul such as only God was capable of experiencing. No other man, however great his powers of physical or mental endurance, could have suffered so; for his human organism would have succumbed, and syncope would have produced unconsciousness and welcome oblivion. In that hour of anguish Christ met and overcame all the horrors that Satan, "the prince of this world"^{ggg} could inflict. The frightful struggle incident to the temptations immediately following the Lord's baptism^{hhh} was surpassed and overshadowed by this supreme contest with the powers of evil.

In some manner, actual and terribly real though to man incomprehensible, the Savior took upon Himself the burden of the sins of mankind from Adam to the end of the world. Modern revelation assists us to a partial understanding of the awful experience. In March 1830, the glorified Lord, Jesus Christ, thus spake: "For behold, I, God, have suffered these things for all, that they might not suffer if they would repent, but if they would not repent, they must suffer even as I, which suffering caused myself, even God, the greatest of all, to tremble because of pain, and to bleed at every pore, and to suffer both body and spirit: and would that I might not drink the bitter cup and shrink—nevertheless, glory be to the Father, and I partook and finished my preparations unto the children of men."ⁱⁱⁱ

---

fff John 5:26, 27; and 10:17, 18.

ggg John 14:30.

hhh Page 120.

iii D&C 19:16–19; compare 18:11. See also 2 Ne. 9:5, 7, 21; Mosiah 3:7–14; 15:12; Alma 7:11–13; 11:40; 22:14; 34:8–15; 3 Ne. 11:11; 27:14, 15; and chapter 4 herein.

From the terrible conflict in Gethsemane, Christ emerged a victor. Though in the dark tribulation of that fearful hour He had pleaded that the bitter cup be removed from His lips, the request, however oft repeated, was always conditional; the accomplishment of the Father's will was never lost sight of as the object of the Son's supreme desire. The further tragedy of the night, and the cruel inflictions that awaited Him on the morrow, to culminate in the frightful tortures of the cross, could not exceed the bitter anguish through which He had successfully passed.

THE BETRAYAL AND THE ARREST[jjj]

During the period of the Lord's last and most loving communion with the Eleven, Judas had been busy in his treacherous conspiracy with the priestly authorities. It is probable that the determination to make the arrest that night was reached when Judas reported that Jesus was within the city walls and might easily be apprehended. The Jewish rulers assembled a body of temple guardsmen or police, and obtained a band of Roman soldiers under command of a tribune; this band or cohort was probably a detachment from the garrison of Antonia commissioned for the work of the night on requisition of the chief priests.[kkk] This company of men and officers representing a combination of ecclesiastical and military authority, set forth in the night with Judas at their head, intent on the arrest of Jesus. They were equipped with lanterns, torches, and weapons. It is probable that they were first conducted to the house in which Judas had left his fellow apostles and the Lord, when the traitor had been dismissed; and that finding the little company had gone out, Judas led the multitude to Gethsemane, for he knew the place, and knew also that "Jesus ofttimes resorted thither with his disciples."

While Jesus was yet speaking to the Eleven whom He had roused from slumber with the announcement that the betrayer was at hand, Judas and the multitude approached. As a preconcerted sign of

---

[jjj] Matt. 26:47–56; Mark 14:43–52; Luke 22:47–53; John 18:1–12.

[kkk] "Cohort," a term descriptive of a Roman body, and "military tribune" are more literal renderings of the Greek original than "band" and "captain" in John 18:3, 12. See revised version, margin.

identification the recreant Iscariot, with treacherous duplicity, came up with a hypocritical show of affection, saying, "Hail, master," and profaned his Lord's sacred face with a kiss.[lll] That Jesus understood the treacherous significance of the act appears in His pathetic, yet piercing and condemning reproach: "Judas, betrayest thou the Son of man with a kiss?" Then, applying the title with which the other apostles had been honored, the Lord said: Friend, do that for which thou art come.[mmm] It was a reiteration of the behest given at the supper table, "That thou doest, do quickly."

The armed band hesitated, though their guide had given the signal agreed upon. Jesus walked toward the officers, with whom stood Judas, and asked, "Whom seek ye?" To their reply, "Jesus of Nazareth," the Lord rejoined: "I am he." Instead of advancing to take Him, the crowd pressed backward, and many of them fell to the ground in fright. The simple dignity and gentle yet compelling force of Christ's presence proved more potent than strong arms and weapons of violence. Again He put the question, "Whom seek ye?" and again they answered, "Jesus of Nazareth." Then said Jesus: "I have told you that I am he; if therefore ye seek me, let these go their way." The last remark had reference to the apostles, who were in danger of arrest; and in this evidence of Christ's solicitude for their personal safety, John saw a fulfilment of the Lord's then recent utterance in prayer, "Of them which thou gavest me have I lost none."[nnn] It is possible that had any of the Eleven been apprehended with Jesus and made to share the cruel abuse and torturing humiliation of the next few hours, their faith might have failed them, relatively immature and untried as it then was; even as in succeeding years many who took upon themselves the name of Christ yielded to persecution and went into apostasy.[ooo]

When the officers approached and seized Jesus, some of the apostles, ready to fight and die for their beloved Master, asked, "Lord, shall we

[lll] The Greek text of Matt. 26:49, and Mark 14:45 clearly implies that Judas "kissed him much," that is many times, or effusively. See margin of revised version.

[mmm] This is a more nearly correct translation than "wherefore art thou come?" in the common version. See revised version. Matt. 26:50.

[nnn] John 18:9; compare 17:12.

[ooo] See *The Great Apostasy*, chaps. 4 and 5.

smite with the sword?" Peter, waiting not for a reply, drew his sword and delivered a poorly aimed stroke at the head of one of the nearest of the crowd, whose ear was severed by the blade. The man thus wounded was Malchus, a servant of the high priest. Jesus, asking liberty of His captors by the simple request, "Suffer ye thus far,"[ppp] stepped forward and healed the injured man by a touch. Turning to Peter the Lord rebuked his rashness, and commanded him to return the sword to its scabbard, with the reminder that "all they that take the sword shall perish with the sword." Then, to show the needlessness of armed resistance, and to emphasize the fact that He was submitting voluntarily and in accordance with foreseen and predicted developments, the Lord continued: "Thinkest thou that I cannot now pray to my Father, and he shall presently give me more than twelve legions of angels? But how then shall the scriptures be fulfilled, that thus it must be?"[qqq] And further, "the cup which my Father hath given me, shall I not drink it?"[rrr]

But, though surrendering Himself unresistingly, Jesus was not unmindful of His rights; and to the priestly officials, chief priests, captain of the temple guard, and elders of the people who were present, He voiced this interrogative protest against the illegal night seizure; "Are ye come out as against a thief with swords and staves for to take me? I sat daily with you teaching in the temple, and ye laid no hold on me. But all this was done, that the scriptures of the prophets might be fulfilled." Luke records the Lord's concluding words thus: "but this is your hour, and the power of darkness." Unheeding His question, and without deference to His submissive demeanor, the captain and the officers of the Jews bound Jesus with cords and led Him away, a Prisoner at the mercy of His deadliest enemies.

The eleven apostles, seeing that resistance was useless, not only on account of disparity of numbers and supply of weapons but chiefly because of Christ's determination to submit, turned and fled. Every one of them forsook Him, even as He had foretold. That they were really in jeopardy is shown by an incident preserved by Mark alone.

[ppp] Note 7, end of chapter.

[qqq] Compare Isa. 53:8.

[rrr] Note 8, end of chapter.

An unnamed young man, aroused from sleep by the tumult of the marching band, had sallied forth with no outer covering but a linen sheet. His interest in the arrest of Jesus and his close approach caused some of the guardsmen or soldiers to seize him; but he broke loose and escaped leaving the sheet in their hands.

NOTES TO CHAPTER 33

1. **The Day of the Passover Feast.**—Controversy has been rife for many centuries as to the day of the passover feast in the week of our Lord's death. That He was crucified on Friday, the day before the Jewish Sabbath, and that He rose a resurrected Being on Sunday, the day following the Sabbath of the Jews, are facts attested by the four Gospel-writers. From the three synoptists we infer that the last supper occurred on the evening of the first day of unleavened bread, and therefore at the beginning of the Jewish Friday. That the Lord's last supper was regarded by Himself and the apostles as a passover meal appears from Matt. 26:2, 17, 18, 19 and parallel passages, Mark 14:14–16; Luke 22:11–13; as also from Luke 22:7, 15. John, however, who wrote after the synoptists and who probably had their writings before him, as is indicated by the supplementary character of his testimony or "Gospel," intimates that the last supper of which Jesus and the Twelve partook together occurred before the Feast of the Passover (John 13:1, 2); and the same writer informs us that on the following day, Friday, the Jews refrained from entering the Roman hall of judgment, lest they be defiled and so become unfit to eat the passover (18:28). It should be remembered that by common usage the term "Passover" was applied not only to the day or season of the observance, but to the meal itself, and particularly to the slain lamb (Matt. 26:17; Mark 14:12, 14, 16; Luke 22:8, 11, 13, 15; John 18:28; compare 1 Cor. 5:7). John also specifies that the day of the Crucifixion was "the preparation of the passover" (19:14), and that the next day, which was Saturday, the Sabbath, "was an high day" (verse 31), that is a Sabbath rendered doubly sacred because of its being also a feast day.

Much has been written by way of attempt to explain this seeming discrepancy. No analysis of the divergent views of Biblical scholars on this subject will be attempted here; the matter is of incidental importance in connection with the fundamental facts of our Lord's betrayal and Crucifixion; for brief summaries of opinions and concise arguments the student may be referred to Smith's *Comprehensive Bible Dictionary*, article "Passover"; Edersheim's *Life and Times of Jesus the Messiah*, pp. 480–2, and 566–8; Farrar's *Life of Christ*, Appendix, Excursus 10; Andrews' *Life of Our Lord*, and Gresswell's *Dissertations*. Suffice it here to say that the apparent inconsistency may be explained by any of several assumptions. Thus, first, and very probably, the Passover referred to by John, for the eating of which the priests were desirous of keeping themselves free from Levitical defilement, may not have been the supper at which the paschal lamb was eaten, but the supplementary meal, the Chagigah. This later meal, the flesh part of which was designated as a sacrifice, had come to be regarded with veneration equal to that attaching to the paschal supper. Secondly; it is held by many authorities on Jewish antiquities that before, at, and after the time of Christ, two nights were devoted yearly to the paschal observance, during either of which the lamb might be eaten, and that this extension of time had been made in consideration of the increased population, which necessitated the ceremonial slaughtering of more lambs than could be slain on a single day; and in this connection it is interesting to note that Josephus (*Wars*, vi, ch. 9:3) records the number of lambs slain at a single Passover as 256,500. In the same paragraph, Josephus states that the lambs had to be slain between the ninth and the eleventh hour (3 to 5 p.m.). According to this explanation, Jesus and the Twelve may have partaken of the passover meal on the first of the two evenings, and the Jews who next day feared defilement may have deferred their observance until the second. Thirdly, the Lord's last paschal supper may have been eaten earlier than the time of general observance, He knowing that night to be His last in mortality. Supporters of this view explain the message to the man who provided the chamber for the last supper, "My time is at hand" (Matt. 26:18) as indicating a special urgency for the passover observance by Christ and the apostles, before the regularly appointed day. Some authorities assert that an error of one day had crept into the Jewish reckoning of time, and that Jesus ate the passover on the true date, while the Jews were a day behind. If "the preparation of the passover" (John 19:14) on Friday, the day of Christ's Crucifixion, means the slaughtering of the paschal lambs, our Lord, the real sacrifice of which all earlier altar victims had been but prototypes, died on the cross while the passover lambs were being slain at the temple.

2. Did Judas Iscariot Partake of the Sacrament of the Lord's Supper?—This question cannot be definitely answered from the brief accounts we have of the proceedings at the last supper. At best, only inference, not conclusion, is possible. According to the records made by Matthew and Mark, the Lord's announcement that there was a traitor among the Twelve was made early in the course of the meal; and the institution of the Sacrament occurred later. Luke records the prediction of treachery as following the administering of the sacramental bread and wine. All the synoptists agree that the Sacrament of Lord's Supper was administered before the sitting at the ordinary meal had broken up; though the Sacrament was plainly made a separate and distinct feature. John (13:2–5) states that the washing of feet occurred when supper was ended, and gives us good reason for inferring that Judas was washed with the rest (verses 10, 11), and that he later (verses 26–30) went out into the night for the purpose of betraying Jesus. The giving of a "sop" to Judas (verses 26, 27) even though supper was practically over, is not inconsistent with John's statement that the supper proper was ended before the washing of feet was performed; the act does not appear to have been so unusual as to cause surprise. To many it has appeared plausible, that because of his utter baseness Judas would not be permitted to participate with the other apostles in the holy ordinance of the Sacrament; others infer that he was allowed to partake, as a possible means of moving him to abandon his evil purpose even at that late hour, or of filling his cup of iniquity to overflowing. The writer's personal opinion is based on the last conception.

3. Washing of Feet.—The ordinance of the washing of feet was reestablished through revelation December 27, 1832. It was made a feature of admission to the school of the prophets, and detailed instructions relating to its administration were given (see D&C 88:140, 141). Further direction as to the ordinances involving washing were revealed January 19, 1841 (see D&C 124:37–39).

4. Discontinuity of the Lord's Last Discourse to the Apostles.—It is certain that part of the discourse following the last supper was delivered in the upper room where Christ and the Twelve had eaten; it is possible that the latter portion was spoken and the prayer offered (John 15, 16, 17) outdoors as Jesus and the Eleven wended their way toward the Mount of Olives. The 14th chapter of John ends with "Arise, let us go hence"; the next chapter opens with another section of the discourse. From Matthew 26:30–35, and Mark 14:26–31 we may infer that the prediction of Peter's denial of his Lord was made as the little company walked from the city to the mount. On the other hand, John (18:1) states that "when Jesus had spoken these words," namely, the whole discourse, and the concluding prayer, "he went forth with his disciples over the brook Cedron." Not one of our Lord's sublime utterances on that night of solemn converse with His own, and of communion between Himself and the Father, is affected by the circumstance of place.

5. Gethsemane.—The name means "oil press" and probably has reference to a mill maintained at the place for the extraction of oil from the olives there cultivated. John refers to the spot as a garden, from which designation we may regard it as an enclosed space of private ownership. That it was a place frequented by Jesus when He sought retirement for prayer, or opportunity for confidential converse with the disciples, is indicated by the same writer (John 18:1,2).

6. The Bloody Sweat.—Luke, the only Gospel-writer who mentions sweat and blood in connection with our Lord's agony in Gethsemane, states that "his sweat was as it were great drops of blood falling down to the ground" (22:44). Many critical expositors deny that there was an actual extrusion of blood, on the grounds that the evangelist does not positively affirm it, and that the three apostles, who were the only human witnesses, could not have distinguished blood from sweat falling in drops, as they watched from a distance in the night, even if the moon, which at the passover season was full, had been unobscured. Modern scripture removes all doubt. See D&C 19:16–19, also 18:11. See further a specific prediction of the bloody sweat, Mosiah 3:7.

7. "Suffer Ye thus Far."—Many understand these words, uttered by Jesus as He raised His hand to heal the wounded Malchus, to have been addressed to the disciples, forbidding their further interference. Trench (*Miracles*, 355) considers the meaning to be as follows: "Hold now; thus far ye have gone in resistance, but let it be no further; no more of this." The disputed interpretation is of little importance as to the bearing of the incident on the events that followed.

8. The Cup as a Symbol.—Our Lord's frequent mention of His foreseen sufferings as the cup of which the Father would have Him drink (Matt. 26:39, 42; Mark 14:36; Luke 22:42; John 18:11; compare Matt. 20:22; Mark 10:38; 1 Cor. 10:21) is in line with Old Testament usage of the term "cup" as a symbolic expression for a bitter or poisonous potion typifying experiences of suffering. See Psa. 11:6; 75:8; Isa. 51:17, 22; Jer. 25:15, 17; 49:12. In contrast, the opposite meaning is attached to the use of the term in some passages, e.g. Ps. 16:5; 23:5; 116:13; Jer. 16:7.

CHAPTER 34

THE TRIAL AND CONDEMNATION

THE JEWISH TRIAL

From Gethsemane the bound and captive Christ was haled before the Jewish rulers. John alone informs us that the Lord was taken first to Annas, who sent Him, still bound, to Caiaphas, the high priest;[a] the synoptists record the arraignment before Caiaphas only.[b] No details of the interview with Annas are of record; and the bringing of Jesus before him at all was as truly irregular and illegal, according to Hebrew law, as were all the subsequent proceedings of that night. Annas, who was father-in-law to Caiaphas, had been deposed from the high-priestly office over twenty years before; but throughout this period he had exerted a potent influence in all the affairs of the hierarchy.[c] Caiaphas, as John is careful to remind us, "was he, which gave counsel to the Jews, that it was expedient that one man should die for the people."[d]

At the palace of Caiaphas, the chief priests, scribes, and elders of the people were assembled, in a meeting of the Sanhedrin, informal or otherwise, all eagerly awaiting the result of the expedition led by Judas. When Jesus, the object of their bitter hatred and their predetermined victim, was brought in, a bound Prisoner, He was immediately put upon trial in contravention of the law, both written and traditional, of which those congregated rulers of the Jews professed to be such zealous supporters. No legal hearing on a capital charge could lawfully be

---

[a] John 18:13, 24.

[b] Matt. 26:57; Mark 14:53; Luke 22:54.

[c] Note 1, end of chapter.

[d] John 18:14; compare 11:49, 50.

held except in the appointed and official courtroom of the Sanhedrin. From the account given in the fourth Gospel we infer that the Prisoner was first subjected to an interrogative examination by the high priest in person.[e] That functionary, whether Annas, or Caiaphas is a matter of inference, inquired of Jesus concerning His disciples and His doctrines. Such a preliminary inquiry was utterly unlawful; for the Hebrew code provided that the accusing witnesses in any cause before the court should define their charge against the accused, and that the latter should be protected from any effort to make him testify against himself. The Lord's reply should have been a sufficient protest to the high priest against further illegal procedure. "Jesus answered him, I spake openly to the world; I ever taught in the synagogue, and in the temple, whither the Jews always resort; and in secret have I said nothing. Why askest thou me?—ask them which heard me, what I have said unto them: behold, they know what I said." This was a lawful objection against denying to a prisoner on trial his right to be confronted by his accusers. It was received with open disdain; and one of the officers who stood by, hoping perhaps to curry favor with his superiors, actually struck Jesus a vicious blow[f] accompanied by the question, "Answerest thou the high priest so?" To this cowardly assault the Lord replied with almost superhuman gentleness.[g] "If I have spoken evil, bear witness of the evil: but if well, why smitest thou me?" Combined with submissiveness, however, this constituted another appeal to the principles of justice; if what Jesus had said was evil, why did not the assailant accuse Him; and if He had spoken well, what right had a police officer to judge, condemn, and punish, and that too in the presence of the high priest? Law and justice had been dethroned that night.

"Now the chief priests, and elders, and all the council, sought false witness against Jesus, to put him to death."[h] Whether "all the council"

[e] John 18:19–23.

[f] The common text of John 18:22, says that the man "struck Jesus with the palm of his hand," that is to say slapped Him; such an act added humiliating insult to violence; the marginal reading of the revised version is "with a rod." There is lack of agreement on this point in the early Mss.

[g] Note 2, end of chapter.

[h] Matt. 26:59–61; Mark 14:55–59.

means a legal quorum, which would be twenty-three or more, or a full attendance of the seventy-two Sanhedrists, is of small importance. Any sitting of the Sanhedrin at night, and more particularly for the consideration of a capital charge, was directly in violation of Jewish law. Likewise was it unlawful for the council to consider such a charge on a Sabbath, a feast day, or on the eve on any such day. In the Sanhedrin, every member was a judge; the judicial body was to hear the testimony, and, according to that testimony and nought else, render a decision on every case duly presented. The accusers were required to appear in person; and they were to receive a preliminary warning against bearing false witness. Every defendant was to be regarded and treated as innocent until convicted in due course. But in the so-called trial of Jesus, the judges not only sought witnesses, but specifically tried to find false witnesses. Though many false witnesses came, yet there was no "witness" or testimony against the Prisoner, for the suborned perjurers failed to agree among themselves; and even the lawless Sanhedrists hesitated to openly violate the fundamental requirement that at least two concordant witnesses must testify against an accused person, for, otherwise, the case had to be dismissed.

That Jesus was to be convicted on some charge or other, and be put to death, had been already determined by the priestly judges; their failure to find witnesses against Him threatened to delay the carrying out of their nefarious scheme. Haste and precipitancy characterised their procedure throughout; they had unlawfully caused Jesus to be arrested at night; they were illegally going through the semblance of a trial at night; their purpose was to convict the Prisoner in time to have Him brought before the Roman authorities as early as possible in the morning—as a criminal duly tried and adjudged worthy of death. The lack of two hostile witnesses who would tell the same falsehoods was a serious hindrance. But, "at the last came two false witnesses, and said, This fellow said, I am able to destroy the temple of God, and to build it in three days." Others, however, testified: "We heard him say, I will destroy this temple that is made with hands, and within three days I will build another made without hands."[i] And so,

---

i Matt. 26:61 and Mark 14:58.

as Mark observes, even in this particular their "witness" or testimony did not agree. Surely in a case at bar, such discrepancy as appears between "I am able to" and "I will," as alleged utterances of the accused, is of vital importance. Yet this semblance of formal accusation was the sole basis of a charge against Christ up to this stage of the trial. It will be remembered that in connection with the first clearing of the temple, near the commencement of Christ's ministry, He had answered the clamorous demand of the Jews for a sign of His authority by saying, "Destroy this temple, and in three days I will raise it up." He spoke not at all of Himself as the one who would destroy; the Jews were to be the destroyers, He the restorer. But the inspired writer is particular to explain that Jesus "spake of the temple of his body," and not at all of those buildings reared by man.[j]

One may reasonably inquire as to what serious import could be attached to even such a declaration as the perjured witnesses claimed to have heard from the lips of Christ. The veneration with which the Jews professed to regard the Holy House, however wantonly they profaned its precincts, offers a partial but insufficient answer. The plan of the conspiring rulers appears to have been that of convicting Christ on a charge of sedition, making Him out to be a dangerous disturber of the nation's peace, an assailant of established institutions, and consequently an inciter of opposition against the vassal autonomy of the Jewish nation, and the supreme dominion of Rome.[k]

The vaguely defined shadow of legal accusation produced by the dark and inconsistent testimony of the false witnesses, was enough to embolden the iniquitous court. Caiaphas, rising from his seat to give dramatic emphasis to his question, demanded of Jesus: "Answerest thou nothing? what is it which these witness against thee?" There was nothing to answer. No consistent or valid testimony had been presented against Him; therefore He stood in dignified silence. Then Caiaphas, in violation of the legal proscription against requiring any person to testify in his own case except voluntarily and on his own initiative, not only demanded an answer from the Prisoner, but exercised the

---

[j] John 2:18–22.

[k] Note the accusation reported to Pilate that Jesus was guilty of "perverting the nation," Luke 23:2.

potent prerogative of the high-priestly office, to put the accused under oath, as a witness before the sacerdotal court. "And the high priest answered and said unto him, I adjure thee by the living God, that thou tell us whether thou be the Christ, the Son of God."[l] The fact of a distinct specification of "the Christ" and "the Son of God" is significant, in that it implies the Jewish expectation of a Messiah, but does not acknowledge that He was to be distinctively of divine origin. Nothing that had gone before can be construed as a proper foundation for this inquiry. The charge of sedition was about to be superseded by one of greater enormity—that of blasphemy.[m]

To the utterly unjust yet official adjuration of the high priest, Jesus answered: "Thou hast said: nevertheless I say unto you: Hereafter shall ye see the Son of man sitting on the right hand of power, and coming in the clouds of heaven." This expression "Thou hast said" was equivalent to—I am what thou hast said.[n] It was an unqualified avowal of divine parentage, and inherent Godship. "Then the high priest rent his clothes, saying, He hath spoken blasphemy; what further need have we of witnesses? behold, now ye have heard his blasphemy. What think ye? They answered and said, He is guilty of death."[o]

Thus the judges in Israel, comprising the high priest, the chief priests, the scribes and elders of the people, the Great Sanhedrin, unlawfully assembled, decreed that the Son of God was deserving of death, on no evidence save that of His own acknowledgment. By express provision the Jewish code forbade the conviction, specifically on a capital charge, of any person on his own confession, unless that was amply supported by the testimony of trustworthy witnesses. As in the Garden of Gethsemane Jesus had voluntarily surrendered Himself, so before the judges did He personally and voluntarily furnish the evidence upon which they unrighteously declared Him deserving of death. There could be no crime in the claim of Messiahship or divine Sonship, except that claim was false. We vainly search the record for

---

[l] Matt. 26:63–66; compare Mark 14:61–64.

[m] Pages 184 and 192.

[n] Compare Mark 14:62.

[o] Matt. 26:65, 66. Revised version reads: "He is worthy of death," and gives in margin a yet more literal rendering: "liable to" death.

even an intimation that inquiry was made or suggested as to the grounds upon which Jesus based His exalted claims. The action of the high priest in rending his garments was a dramatic affectation of pious horror at the blasphemy with which his ears had been assailed. It was expressly forbidden in the law that the high priest rend his clothes;[p] but from extra-scriptural writings we learn that the rending of garments as an attestation of most grievous guilt, such as that of blasphemy, was allowable under traditional rule.[q] There is no indication that the vote of the judges was taken and recorded in the precise and orderly manner required by the law.

Jesus stood convicted of the most heinous offense known in Jewry. However unjustly, He had been pronounced guilty of blasphemy by the supreme tribunal of the nation. In strict accuracy we cannot say that the Sanhedrists sentenced Christ to death, inasmuch as the power to authoritatively pronounce capital sentences had been taken from the Jewish council by Roman decree. The high-priestly court, however, decided that Jesus was worthy of death, and so certified when they handed Him over to Pilate. In their excess of malignant hate, Israel's judges abandoned their Lord to the wanton will of the attendant varlets, who heaped upon Him every indignity their brutish instincts could suggest. They spurted their foul spittle into His face;[r] and then, having blindfolded Him, amused themselves by smiting Him again and again, saying the while: "Prophesy unto us, thou Christ, Who is he that smote thee?" The miscreant crowd mocked Him, and railed upon Him with jeers and taunts, and branded themselves as blasphemers in fact.[s]

The law and the practice of the time required that any person found guilty of a capital offense, after due trial before a Jewish tribunal, should be given a second trial on the following day; and at this later hearing any or all of the judges who had before voted for conviction could reverse themselves; but no one who had once voted for acquittal could change his ballot. A bare majority was sufficient for

[p] Lev. 21:10.

[q] Josephus, *Wars*, ii, 15:2, 4; also 1 Maccabees 11:71.

[r] Matt. 26:67; Mark 14:65; compare Luke 18:32; see also Isa. 50:6.

[s] Matt. 26:68; Luke 22:62–65.

acquittal, but more than a majority was required for conviction. By a provision that must appear to us most unusual, if all the judges voted for conviction on a capital charge the verdict was not to stand and the accused had to be set at liberty; for, it was argued, a unanimous vote against a prisoner indicated that he had had no friend or defender in court, and that the judges might have been in conspiracy against Him. Under this rule in Hebrew jurisprudence the verdict against Jesus, rendered at the illegal night session of the Sanhedrists, was void, for we are specifically told that "they all condemned him to be guilty of death."[t]

Apparently for the purpose of establishing a shadowy pretext of legality in their procedure, the Sanhedrists adjourned to meet again in early daylight. Thus they technically complied with the requirement— that on every case in which the death sentence had been decreed the court should hear and judge a second time in a later session—but they completely ignored the equally mandatory provision that the second trial must be conducted on the day following that of the first hearing. Between the two sittings on consecutive days the judges were required to fast and pray, and to give the case on trial calm and earnest consideration.

Luke, who records no details of the night trial of Jesus, is the only Gospel-writer to give place to a circumstantial report of the morning session. He says: "And as soon as it was day, the elders of the people and the chief priests and the scribes came together, and led him into their council."[u] Some Biblical scholars have construed the expression, "led him into their council," as signifying that Jesus was condemned by the Sanhedrin in the appointed meeting-place of the court, viz. Gazith or the Hall of Hewn Stones, as the law of the time required; but against this we have the statement of John that they led Jesus directly from Caiaphas to the Roman hall of judgment.[v]

It is probable, that at this early daylight session, the irregular proceedings of the dark hours were approved, and the details of further procedure decided upon. They "took counsel against Jesus to put him to death"; nevertheless they went through the form of a second trial,

[t] Mark 14:64.
[u] Luke 22:66.
[v] John 18:28.

the issue of which was greatly facilitated by the Prisoner's voluntary affirmations. The judges stand without semblance of justification for calling upon the Accused to testify; they should have examined anew the witnesses against Him. The first question put to Him was, "Art thou the Christ? tell us." The Lord made dignified reply: "If I tell you, ye will not believe: and if I also ask you, ye will not answer me, nor let me go. Hereafter shall the Son of man sit on the right hand of the power of God." Neither did the question imply nor the answer furnish cause for condemnation. The whole nation was looking for the Messiah; and if Jesus claimed to be He, the only proper judicial action would be that of inquiring into the merit of the claim. The crucial question followed immediately: "Art thou then the Son of God? And he said unto them, Ye say that I am. And they said, What need we any further witness? for we ourselves have heard of his own mouth."[w]

Jehovah was convicted of blasphemy against Jehovah. The only mortal Being to whom the awful crime of blasphemy, in claiming divine attributes and powers, was impossible, stood before the judges of Israel condemned as a blasphemer. The "whole council," by which expression we may possibly understand a legal quorum, was concerned in the final action. Thus ended the miscalled "trial" of Jesus before the high priest and elders[x] of His people. "And straightway in the morning the chief priests held a consultation with the elders and scribes and the whole council, and bound Jesus, and carried him away, and delivered him to Pilate."[y] During the few hours that remained to Him in mortality, He would be in the hands of the Gentiles, betrayed and delivered up by His own.[z]

PETER'S DENIAL OF HIS LORD [aa]

When Jesus was taken into custody in the Garden of Gethsemane, all the Eleven forsook Him and fled. This is not to be accounted as

[w] Luke 22:66–71.

[x] Note 3, end of chapter.

[y] Mark 15:1; compare Matt. 27:1, 2; John 18:28.

[z] Note 4, end of chapter, gives further details of the unlawful irregularities of the Jewish trial of Jesus.

[aa] Matt. 26:58, 69–75; Mark 14:54, 66–72; Luke 22:54–62; John 18:15–18, 25–27.

certain evidence of cowardice, for the Lord had indicated that they should go.[bb] Peter and at least one other disciple followed afar off; and, after the armed guard had entered the palace of the high priest with their Prisoner, Peter "went in, and sat with the servants to see the end." He was assisted in securing admittance by the unnamed disciple, who was on terms of acquaintanceship with the high priest. That other disciple was in all probability John, as may be inferred from the fact that he is mentioned only in the fourth Gospel, the author of which characteristically refers to himself anonymously.[cc]

While Jesus was before the Sanhedrists, Peter remained below with the servants. The attendant at the door was a young woman; her feminine suspicions had been aroused when she admitted Peter, and as he sat with a crowd in the palace court she came up, and having intently observed him, said: "Thou also wast with Jesus of Galilee." But Peter denied, averring he did not know Jesus. Peter was restless; his conscience and the fear of identification as one of the Lord's disciples troubled him. He left the crowd and sought partial seclusion in the porch; but there another maid spied him out, and said to those nearby: "This fellow was also with Jesus of Nazareth"; to which accusation Peter replied with an oath: "I do not know the man."

The April night was chilly, and an open fire had been made in the hall or court of the palace. Peter sat with others at the fire, thinking, perhaps, that brazen openness was better than skulking caution as a possible safeguard against detection. About an hour after his former denials, some of the men around the fire charged him with being a disciple of Jesus, and referred to his Galilean dialect as evidence that he was at least a fellow countryman with the high priest's Prisoner; but, most threatening of all, a kinsman of Malthus, whose ear Peter had slashed with the sword, asked peremptorily: "Did not I see thee in the garden with him?" Then Peter went so far in the course of falsehood upon which he had entered as to curse and swear, and to vehemently declare for the third time, "I know not the man." As the last profane falsehood left his lips, the clear notes of a crowing cock broke upon

[bb] John 18:8, 9.
[cc] John 1:35, 40; 13:23; 19:26; 20:2; 21:7, 20, 24.

his ears,[dd] and the remembrance of his Lord's prediction welled up in his mind. Trembling in wretched realization of his perfidious cowardice, he turned from the crowd and met the gaze of the suffering Christ, who from the midst of the insolent mob looked into the face of His boastful, yet loving but weak apostle. Hastening from the palace, Peter went out into the night, weeping bitterly. As his later life attests, his tears were those of real contrition and true repentance.

CHRIST'S FIRST APPEARANCE BEFORE PILATE

As we have already learned, no Jewish tribunal had authority to inflict the death penalty; imperial Rome had reserved this prerogative as her own. The united acclaim of the Sanhedrists, that Jesus was deserving of death, would be ineffective until sanctioned by the emperor's deputy, who at that time was Pontius Pilate, the governor, or more properly, procurator, of Judea, Samaria, and Idumea. Pilate maintained his official residence at Caesarea,[ee] on the Mediterranean shore; but it was his custom to be present in Jerusalem at the times of the great Hebrew feasts, probably in the interest of preserving order, or of promptly quelling any disturbance amongst the vast and hetero-geneous multitudes by which the city was thronged on these festive occasions. The governor with his attendants was in Jerusalem at this momentous Passover season. Early on Friday morning, the "whole council," that is to say, the Sanhedrin, led Jesus, bound, to the judgment hall of Pontius Pilate; but with strict scrupulosity they refrained from entering the hall lest they become defiled; for the judgment chamber was part of the house of a Gentile, and somewhere therein might be leavened bread, even to be near which would render them ceremonially unclean. Let every one designate for himself the character of men afraid of the mere proximity of leaven, while thirsting for innocent blood!

In deference to their scruples Pilate came out from the palace; and, as they delivered up to him their Prisoner, asked: "What accusation bring ye against this man?" The question, though strictly proper and

---

[dd] Observe that Mark, who alone states that the Lord said to Peter "before the cock crow twice, thou shalt deny me thrice," (14:30) records a first crowing of the cock after Peter's first denial (v. 68) and a second crowing after the third denial (v. 72).

[ee] Caesarea Palestina, not Caesarea Philippi.

judicially necessary, surprised and disappointed the priestly rulers, who evidently had expected that the governor would simply approve their verdict as a matter of form and give sentence accordingly; but instead of doing so, Pilate was apparently about to exercise his authority of original jurisdiction. With poorly concealed chagrin, their spokesman, probably Caiaphas, answered: "If he were not a malefactor, we would not have delivered him up unto thee." It was now Pilate's turn to feel or at least to feign umbrage, and he replied in effect: Oh, very well; if you don't care to present the charge in proper order, take ye him, and judge him according to your law; don't trouble me with the matter. But the Jews rejoined: "It is not lawful for us to put any man to death."

John the apostle intimates in this last remark a determination on the part of the Jews to have Jesus put to death not only by Roman sanction but by Roman executioners ff for, as we readily may see, had Pilate approved the death sentence and handed the Prisoner over to the Jews for its infliction, Jesus would have been stoned, in accordance with the Hebrew penalty for blasphemy; whereas the Lord had plainly foretold that His death would be by crucifixion, which was a Roman method of execution, but one never practiced by the Jews. Furthermore, if Jesus had been put to death by the Jewish rulers, even with governmental sanction, an insurrection among the people might have resulted, for there were many who believed on Him. The crafty hierarchs were determined to bring about His death under Roman condemnation.

"And they began to accuse him, saying, We found this fellow perverting the nation, and forbidding to give tribute to Caesar, saying that he himself is Christ a King."gg It is important to note that no accusation of blasphemy was made to Pilate; had such been presented, the governor, thoroughly pagan in heart and mind, would probably have dismissed the charge as utterly unworthy of a hearing; for Rome with her many gods, whose number was being steadily increased by current heathen deification of mortals, knew no such offense as blasphemy in the Jewish sense. The accusing Sanhedrists hesitated not to substitute for blasphemy, which was the greatest crime known to the Hebrew code, the charge of high treason, which was the gravest offense

ff John 18:28–32.
gg Luke 23:2.

listed in the Roman category of crimes. To the vociferous accusations of the chief priests and elders, the calm and dignified Christ deigned no reply. To them He had spoken for the last time—until the appointed season of another trial, in which He shall be the Judge, and they the prisoners at the bar.

Pilate was surprised at the submissive yet majestic demeanor of Jesus; there was certainly much that was kingly about the Man; never before had such a One stood before him. The charge, however, was a serious one; men who claimed title to kingship might prove dangerous to Rome; yet to the charge the Accused answered nothing. Entering the judgment hall, Pilate had Jesus called.[hh] That some of the disciples, and among them almost certainly John, also went in, is apparent from the detailed accounts of the proceedings preserved in the fourth Gospel. Anyone was at liberty to enter, for publicity was an actual and a widely proclaimed feature of Roman trials.

Pilate, plainly without animosity or prejudice against Jesus, asked: "Art thou the King of the Jews? Jesus answered him, Sayest thou this thing of thyself, or did others tell it thee of me?" The Lord's counter-question, as Pilate's rejoinder shows, meant, and was understood to mean, as we might state it: Do you ask this in the Roman and literal sense—as to whether I am a king of an earthly kingdom—or with the Jewish and more spiritual meaning? A direct answer "Yes" would have been true in the Messianic sense, but untrue in the worldly signification; and "No" could have been inversely construed as true or untrue. "Pilate answered, Am I a Jew? Thine own nation and the chief priests have delivered thee unto me: what hast thou done? Jesus answered, My kingdom is not of this world: if my kingdom were of this world, then would my servants fight, that I should not be delivered to the Jews: but now is my kingdom not from hence. Pilate therefore said unto him, Art thou a king then? Jesus answered, Thou sayest that I am a king. To this end was I born, and for this cause came I into the world, that I should bear witness unto the truth. Every one that is of the truth heareth my voice."

It was clear to the Roman governor that this wonderful Man, with His exalted views of a kingdom not of this world, and an empire

---

hh John 18:33–38; compare Matt. 27:11; Mark 15:2; Luke 23:3, 4.

of truth in which He was to reign, was no political insurrectionist; and that to consider Him a menace to Roman institutions would be absurd. Those last words—about truth—were of all the most puzzling; Pilate was restive, and perhaps a little frightened under their import. "What is truth?" he rather exclaimed in apprehension than inquired in expectation of an answer, as he started to leave the hall. To the Jews without he announced officially the acquittal of the Prisoner. "I find in him no fault at all" was the verdict.

But the chief priests and scribes and elders of the people were undeterred. Their thirst for the blood of the Holy One had developed into mania. Wildly and fiercely they shrieked: "He stirreth up the people, teaching throughout all Jewry, beginning from Galilee to this place." The mention of Galilee suggested to Pilate a new course of procedure. Having confirmed by inquiry that Jesus was a Galilean, he determined to send the Prisoner to Herod, the vassal ruler of that province, who was in Jerusalem at the time.[ii] By this action Pilate hoped to rid himself of further responsibility in the case, and moreover, Herod, with whom he had been at enmity, might be placated thereby.

CHRIST BEFORE HEROD[jj]

Herod Antipas, the degenerate son of his infamous sire, Herod the Great,[kk] was at this time tetrarch of Galilee and Perea, and by popular usage, though without imperial sanction, was flatteringly called king. He it was who, in fulfilment of an unholy vow inspired by a woman's voluptuous blandishments, had ordered the murder of John the Baptist. He ruled as a Roman vassal, and professed to be orthodox in the observances of Judaism. He had come up to Jerusalem, in state, to keep the feast of the Passover. Herod was pleased to have Jesus sent to him by Pilate; for, not only was the action a gracious one on the part of the procurator, constituting as after events proved a preliminary to reconciliation between the two rulers,[ll] but it was a means of gratifying Herod's curiosity to see Jesus, of whom he had heard so much, whose

---

[ii] Luke 23:5–7.
[jj] Luke 23:8–12.
[kk] Pages 103–104, 107, 114-15.
[ll] Luke 23:12.

fame had terrified him, and by whom he now hoped to see some interesting miracle wrought.[mm]

Whatever fear Herod had once felt regarding Jesus, whom he had superstitiously thought to be the reincarnation of his murdered victim, John the Baptist, was replaced by amused interest when he saw the far-famed Prophet of Galilee in bonds before him, attended by a Roman guard, and accompanied by ecclesiastical officials. Herod began to question the Prisoner; but Jesus remained silent. The chief priests and scribes vehemently voiced their accusations; but not a word was uttered by the Lord. Herod is the only character in history to whom Jesus is known to have applied a personal epithet of contempt. "Go ye and tell that fox," He once said to certain Pharisees who had come to Him with the story that Herod intended to kill Him.[nn] As far as we know, Herod is further distinguished as the only being who saw Christ face to face and spoke to Him, yet never heard His voice. For penitent sinners, weeping women, prattling children, for the scribes, the Pharisees, the Sadducees, the rabbis, for the perjured high priest and his obsequious and insolent underling, and for Pilate the pagan, Christ had words—of comfort or instruction, of warning or rebuke, of protest or denunciation—yet for Herod the fox He had but disdainful and kingly silence. Thoroughly piqued, Herod turned from insulting questions to acts of malignant derision. He and his men-at-arms made sport of the suffering Christ, "set him at nought and mocked him"; then in travesty they "arrayed him in a gorgeous robe and sent him again to Pilate."[oo] Herod had found nothing in Jesus to warrant condemnation.

CHRIST AGAIN BEFORE PILATE[pp]

The Roman procurator, finding that he could not evade further consideration of the case, "called together the chief priests and the rulers

---

[mm] Matt. 14:1; Mark 6:14; Luke 9:7, 9.

[nn] Luke 13:31, 32.

[oo] Luke 23:11. Revised version reads, "arraying him in gorgeous apparel." Clarke *(Commentaries)* and many other writers assume that the robe was white, that being the usual color of dress amongst the Jewish nobility.

[pp] Luke 23:13–25; Matt. 27:15–31; Mark 15:6–20; John 18:39, 40; 19:1–16.

and the people," and "said unto them, Ye have brought this man unto me, as one that perverteth the people: and, behold, I, having examined him before you, have found no fault in this man touching those things whereof ye accuse him: No, nor yet Herod: for I sent you to him; and, lo, nothing worthy of death is done unto him. I will therefore chastise him, and release him." Pilate's desire to save Jesus from death was just and genuine; his intention of scourging the Prisoner, whose innocence he had affirmed and reaffirmed, was an infamous concession to Jewish prejudice. He knew that the charge of sedition and treason was without foundation; and that even the framing of such an accusation by the Jewish hierarchy, whose simulated loyalty to Caesar was but a cloak for inherent and undying hatred, was ridiculous in the extreme; and he fully realized that the priestly rulers had delivered Jesus into his hands because of envy and malice.[99]

It was the custom for the governor at the Passover season to pardon and release any one condemned prisoner whom the people might name. On that day there lay in durance, awaiting execution, "a notable prisoner, called Barabbas," who had been found guilty of sedition, in that he had incited the people to insurrection, and had committed murder. This man stood convicted of the very charge on which Pilate specifically and Herod by implication had pronounced Jesus innocent, and Barabbas was a murderer in addition. Pilate thought to pacify the priests and people by releasing Jesus as the subject of Passover leniency; this would be a tacit recognition of Christ's conviction before the ecclesiastical court, and practically an endorsement of the death sentence, superseded by official pardon. Therefore he asked of them: "Whom will ye that I release unto you? Barabbas, or Jesus which is called Christ?" There appears to have been a brief interval between Pilate's question and the people's answer, during which the chief priests and elders busied themselves amongst the multitude, urging them to demand the release of the insurrectionist and murderer. So, when Pilate reiterated the question: "Whether of the twain will ye that I release unto you?" assembled Israel cried "Barabbas." Pilate, surprised, disappointed, and angered, then asked: "What shall I

[99] Matt. 27:18; Mark 15:10.

do then with Jesus which is called Christ? They all say unto him, Let him be crucified. And the governor said, Why, what evil hath he done? But they cried out the more, saying, Let him be crucified."

The Roman governor was sorely troubled and inwardly afraid. To add to his perplexity he received a warning message from his wife, even as he sat on the judgment seat: "Have thou nothing to do with that just man: for I have suffered many things this day in a dream because of him." Those who know not God are characteristically superstitious. Pilate feared to think what dread portent his wife's dream might presage. But, finding that he could not prevail, and foreseeing a tumult among the people if he persisted in the defense of Christ, he called for water and washed his hands before the multitude—a symbolic act of disclaiming responsibility, which they all understood—proclaiming the while: "I am innocent of the blood of this just person: see ye to it." Then rose that awful self-condemnatory cry of the covenant people: "His blood be on us and on our children." History bears an appalling testimony to the literal fulfilment of that dread invocation.[rr] Pilate released Barabbas, and gave Jesus into the custody of the soldiers to be scourged.

Scourging was a frightful preliminary to death on the cross. The instrument of punishment was a whip of many thongs, loaded with metal and edged with jagged pieces of bone. Instances are of record in which the condemned died under the lash and so escaped the horrors of living crucifixion. In accordance with the brutal customs of the time, Jesus, weak and bleeding from the fearful scourging He had undergone, was given over to the half-savage soldiers for their amusement. He was no ordinary victim, so the whole band came together in the Pretorium, or great hall of the palace, to take part in the diabolical sport. They stripped Jesus of His outer raiment, and placed upon Him a purple robe.[ss] Then with a sense of fiendish realism they platted a crown of thorns, and placed it about the Sufferer's brows; a reed was put into His right hand as a royal scepter; and, as they bowed in a mockery of homage, they saluted Him with: "Hail, King of the Jews!" Snatching away the reed or rod, they brutally smote

[rr] Note 5, end of chapter.

[ss] Matthew says "scarlet," Mark and John say "purple."

Him with it upon the head, driving the cruel thorns into His quivering flesh; they slapped Him with their hands, and spat upon Him in vile and vicious abandonment.[tt]

Pilate had probably been a silent observer of this barbarous scene. He stopped it, and determined to make another attempt to touch the springs of Jewish pity, if such existed. He went outside, and to the multitude said: "Behold, I bring him forth to you, that ye may know that I find no fault in him." This was the governor's third definite proclamation of the Prisoner's innocence. "Then came Jesus forth, wearing the crown of thorns, and the purple robe. And Pilate saith unto them, Behold the man!"[uu] Pilate seems to have counted on the pitiful sight of the scourged and bleeding Christ to soften the hearts of the maddened Jews. But the effect failed. Think of the awful fact—a heathen, a pagan, who knew not God, pleading with the priests and people of Israel for the life of their Lord and King! When, unmoved by the sight, the chief priests and officers cried with increasing vindictiveness, "crucify him, crucify him," Pilate pronounced the fatal sentence, "Take ye him and crucify him," but added with bitter emphasis: "I find no fault in him."

It will be remembered that the only charge preferred against Christ before the Roman governor was that of sedition; the Jewish persecutors had carefully avoided even the mention of blasphemy, which was the offense for which they had adjudged Jesus worthy of death. Now that sentence of crucifixion had been extorted from Pilate, they brazenly attempted to make it appear that the governor's mandate was but a ratification of their own decree of death; therefore they said: "We have a law, and by our law he ought to die, because he made himself the Son of God." What did it mean? That awe-inspiring title, Son of God, struck yet deeper into Pilate's troubled conscience. Once more he took Jesus into the judgment hall, and in trepidation asked, "Whence art thou?" The inquiry was as to whether Jesus was human or superhuman. A direct avowal of the Lord's divinity would have frightened but could not have enlightened the heathen ruler; therefore Jesus gave no answer. Pilate was further surprised, and perhaps

[tt] Compare Luke 18:32.
[uu] Ecce Homo.

somewhat offended at this seeming disregard of his authority. He demanded an explanation, saying: "Speakest thou not unto me? knowest thou not that I have power to crucify thee, and have power to release thee?" Then Jesus replied: "Thou couldest have no power at all against me, except it were given thee from above: therefore he that delivered me unto thee hath the greater sin." The positions were reversed; Christ was the Judge, and Pilate the subject of His decision. Though not found guiltless, the Roman was pronounced less culpable than he or those who had forced Jesus into his power, and who had demanded of him an unrighteous committal.

The governor, though having pronounced sentence, yet sought means of releasing the submissive Sufferer. His first evidence of wavering was greeted by the Jews with the cry, "If thou let this man go, thou art not Caesar's friend: whosoever maketh himself a king speaketh against Caesar." Pilate took his place in the judgment seat, which was set up in the place of the Pavement, or Gabbatha, outside the hall. He was resentful against those Jews who had dared to intimate that he was no friend of Caesar, and whose intimation might lead to an embassy of complaint being sent to Rome to misrepresent him in exaggerated accusation. Pointing to Jesus, he exclaimed with unveiled sarcasm: "Behold your King!" But the Jews answered in threatening and ominous shouts: "Away with him, away with him, crucify him." In stinging reminder of their national subjugation, Pilate asked with yet more cutting irony, "Shall I crucify your King?" And the chief priests cried aloud: "We have no king but Caesar."

Even so was it and was to be. The people who had by covenant accepted Jehovah as their King, now rejected Him in Person, and acknowledged no sovereign but Caesar. Caesar's subjects and serfs have they been through all the centuries since. Pitiable is the state of man or nation who in heart and spirit will have no king but Caesar![vv]

Wherein lay the cause of Pilate's weakness? He was the emperor's representative, the imperial procurator with power to crucify or to save; officially he was an autocrat. His conviction of Christ's blamelessness and his desire to save Him from the cross are beyond question. Why

---

[vv] Note 6, end of chapter.

did Pilate waver, hesitate, vacillate, and at length yield contrary to his conscience and his will? Because, after all, he was more slave than freeman. He was in servitude to his past. He knew that should complaint be made of him at Rome, his corruption and cruelties, his extortions and the unjustifiable slaughter he had caused would all be brought against him. He was the Roman ruler, but the people over whom he exercised official dominion delighted in seeing him cringe, when they cracked, with vicious snap above his head, the whip of a threatened report about him to his imperial master, Tiberius.[ww]

JUDAS ISCARIOT [xx]

When Judas Iscariot saw how terribly effective had been the outcome of his treachery, he became wildly remorseful. During Christ's trial before the Jewish authorities, with its associated humiliation and cruelty, the traitor had seen the seriousness of his action; and when the unresisting Sufferer had been delivered up to the Romans, and the fatal consummation had become a certainty, the enormity of his crime filled Judas with nameless horror. Rushing into the presence of the chief priests and elders, while the final preparations for the Crucifixion of the Lord were in progress, he implored the priestly rulers to take back the accursed wage they had paid him, crying in an agony of despair: "I have sinned, in that I have betrayed the innocent blood." He may have vaguely expected a word of sympathy from the conspirators in whose wickedly skillful hands he had been so ready and serviceable a tool; possibly he hoped that his avowal might stem the current of their malignancy, and that they would ask for a reversal of the sentence. But the rulers in Israel repulsed him with disgust. "What is that to us?" they sneered, "see thou to that." He had served their purpose; they had paid him his price; they wished never to look upon his face again; and pitilessly they flung him back into the haunted blackness of his maddened conscience. Still clutching the bag of silver, the all too real remembrancer of his frightful sin, he rushed into the temple, penetrating even to the precincts of priestly reservation, and dashed the silver

---

ww Note 7, end of chapter.

xx Matt. 27:3–10; compare Acts 1:16–20.

pieces upon the floor of the sanctuary.[yy] Then, under the goading impulse of his master, the devil, to whom he had become a bond-slave, body and soul, he went out and hanged himself.

The chief priests gathered up the pieces of silver, and in sacrilegious scrupulosity, held a solemn council to determine what they should do with the "price of blood." As they deemed it unlawful to add the attainted coin to the sacred treasury, they bought with it a certain clay-yard, once the property of a potter, and the very place in which Judas had made of himself a suicide; this tract of ground they set apart as a burial place for aliens, strangers, and pagans. The body of Judas, the betrayer of the Christ, was probably the first to be there interred. And that field was called "Aceldama, that is to say, The field of blood".[zz]

NOTES TO CHAPTER 34

1. Annas, and His Interview with Jesus.—"No figure is better known in contemporary Jewish history than that of Annas; no person deemed more fortunate or successful, but also none more generally execrated than the late high priest. He had held the pontificate for only six or seven years; but it was filled by not fewer than five of his sons, by his son-in-law Caiaphas, and by a grandson. And in those days it was, at least for one of Annas' disposition, much better to have been than to be high priest. He enjoyed all the dignity of the office, and all its influence also, since he was able to promote to it those most closely connected with him. And while they acted publicly, he really directed affairs, without either the responsibility or the restraints which the office imposed. His influence with the Romans he owed to the religious views which he professed, to his open partisanship of the foreigner, and to his enormous wealth. . . .We have seen what immense revenues the family of Annas must have derived from the Temple booths, and how nefarious and unpopular was the traffic. The names of those bold, licentious, unscrupulous, degenerate sons of Aaron were spoken with whispered curses. Without referring to Christ's interference with that Temple-traffic, which, if His authority had prevailed, would of course have been fatal to it, we can understand how antithetic in every respect a Messiah, and such a Messiah as Jesus, must have been to Annas. . . . No account is given of what passed before Annas. Even the fact of Christ's being first brought to him is

---

[yy] Revised version of Matt. 27:5 reads, "And he cast down the pieces of silver into the sanctuary" instead of "in the temple," signifying that he flung the money into the Porch of the Holy House, as distinguished from the outer and public courts.

[zz] Acts 1:19; Matt. 27:8. Note 8, end of chapter.

only mentioned in the fourth Gospel. As the disciples had all forsaken Him and fled, we can understand that they were in ignorance of what actually passed, till they had again rallied, at least so far, that Peter and 'another disciple,' evidently John, 'followed Him into the palace of the high priest'—that is, into the palace of Caiaphas, not of Annas. For as, according to the three synoptic Gospels, the palace of the high priest Caiaphas was the scene of Peter's denial, the account of it in the fourth Gospel must refer to the same locality, and not to the palace of Annas."— Edersheim, *Life and Times of Jesus the Messiah*, vol. 2, pp. 547–8.

2. Christ's Forbearance when Smitten.—That Jesus maintained His equanimity and submissiveness even under the provocation of a blow dealt by a brutish underling in the presence of the high priest, is confirmatory of our Lord's affirmation that He had "overcome the world" (John 16:33). One cannot read the passage without comparing, perhaps involuntarily, the divine submissiveness of Jesus on this occasion, with the wholly natural and human indignation of Paul under somewhat similar conditions at a later time (Acts 23:1–5). The high priest Ananias, displeased at Paul's remarks, ordered someone who stood by to smite him on the mouth. Paul broke forth in angry protest: "God shall smite thee, thou whited wall: for sittest thou to judge me after the law, and commandest me to be smitten contrary to the law?" Afterward he apologized, saying that he knew not that it was the high priest who had given the command that he be smitten. See *Articles of Faith*, pp. 417–18, and Note 1 following the same lecture; and Farrar's *Life and Works of St. Paul*, pp. 539–40.

3. High Priests and Elders.—These titles as held by officials of the Jewish hierarchy in the time of Christ must not be confused with the same designations as applied to holders of the Higher or Melchizedek Priesthood. The high priest of the Jews was the presiding priest; he had to be of Aaronic descent to be a priest at all; he became high priest by Roman appointment. The elders, as the name indicates, were men of mature years and experience, who were appointed to act as magistrates in the towns, and as judges in the ecclesiastical tribunals, either in the Lesser Sanhedrins of the provinces, or in the Great Sanhedrin at Jerusalem. The term "elder" as commonly used among the Jews in the days of Jesus had no closer relation to eldership in the Melchizedek Priesthood than had the title "scribe." The duties of Jewish high priests and elders combined both ecclesiastical and secular functions; indeed both offices had come to be in large measure political perquisites. See "Elder" in Smith's *Bible Dictionary*. From the departure of Moses to the coming of Christ, the organized theocracy of Israel was that of the Lesser or Aaronic Priesthood, comprising the office of priest, which was confined to the lineage of Aaron, and the lesser offices of teacher and deacon, which were combined in the Levitical order. See "Orders and Offices in the Priesthood" by the author in *Articles of Faith*, pp. 204–9.

4. Illegalities of the Jewish Trial of Jesus.—Many volumes have been written on the so-called trial of Jesus. Only a brief summary of the principal items of fact and law can be incorporated here. For further consideration reference may be made to the following treatments: Edersheim, *Life and Times of Jesus the Messiah*; Andrews, *Life of Our Lord*; Dupin, *Jesus before Caiaphas and Pilate*; Mendelsohn, *Criminal Jurisprudence of the Ancient Hebrews*; Salvador, *Institutions of Moses*; Innes, *The Trial of Jesus Christ*; Maimonides, *Sanhedrin*; MM. Lemann, *Jesus before the Sanhedrin,*— Benny, *Criminal Code of the Jews*; and Walter M. Chandler, of the New York Bar, *The Trial of Jesus from a Lawyer's Standpoint*. The last named is a two volume work treating respectively, "The Hebrew Trial" and "The Roman Trial," and contains citations from the foregoing and other works.

Edersheim (vol. 2, pp. 556–58) contends that the night arraignment of Jesus in the house of Caiaphas was not a trial before the Sanhedrin, and notes the irregularities and illegalities of the procedure as proof that the Sanhedrin could not have done what was done that night. With ample citations in corroboration of the legal requirements specified, the author says: "But besides, the trial and sentence of Jesus in the palace of Caiaphas would have outraged every principle of Jewish criminal law and procedure. Such causes could only be tried, and capital sentence pronounced, in the regular meeting-place of the Sanhedrin, not, as here, in the high priest's palace; no process, least of all such an one, might be begun in the night, nor even in the afternoon, although if the discussion had gone on all day, sentence might be pronounced at night. Again, no process could take place on Sabbaths or feast-days, or even on the eves of them, although this would not have nullified proceedings; and it might be argued on the other side, that a process against one who had seduced the people should preferably be carried on, and sentence executed, on public feast-days, for the warning of all. Lastly, in capital cases there was a very elaborate system of warning, and cautioning witnesses; while it may safely be affirmed that at a regular trial Jewish judges, however prejudiced, would not have acted as the Sanhedrists and Caiaphas did on this occasion. . . . But although Christ was not tried and sentenced in a formal meeting of the Sanhedrin, there can, alas! be no question that His condemnation and death were the work, if not of the Sanhedrin, yet of the Sanhedrists—of the whole body of them ('all the council') in the sense of expressing what was the judgment and purpose of all the supreme council and leaders of Israel, with only very few exceptions. We bear in mind that the resolution to sacrifice Christ had for some time been taken."

The purpose in quoting the foregoing is to show on acknowledged and eminent authority, some of the illegalities of the night trial of Jesus, which, as shown by the above, and by the scriptural record, was conducted by the high priest and "the council" or Sanhedrin, in admittedly irregular and unlawful manner. If the Sanhedrists tried and condemned, yet were not in session as the Sanhedrin, the enormity of the proceeding is, if possible, deeper and blacker than ever.

In Chandler's excellent work (vol. 1, "The Hebrew Trial"), the record of fact in the case, and the Hebrew criminal law bearing thereon are exhaustively considered. Then follows an elaborate "Brief," in which the following points are set forth in order.

"Point 1: The arrest of Jesus was illegal," since it was effected by night, and through the treachery of Judas, an accomplice, both of which features were expressly forbidden in the Jewish law of that day.

"Point 2: The private examination of Jesus before Annas or Caiaphas was illegal"; for (1) it was made by night; (2) the hearing of any cause by a 'sole judge' was expressly forbidden; (3) as quoted from Salvador, 'A principle perpetually reproduced in the Hebrew scriptures relates to the two conditions of publicity and liberty.'

"Point 3: The indictment against Jesus was, in form, illegal. 'The entire criminal procedure of the Mosaic code rests upon four rules: certainty in the indictment; publicity in the discussion; full freedom granted to the accused; and assurance against all dangers or errors of testimony'—Salvador, p. 365. 'The Sanhedrin did not and could not originate charges; it only investigated those brought before it.'—Edersheim, vol. 1, p. 309. 'The evidence of the leading witnesses constituted the charge. There was no other charge; no more formal indictment. Until they spoke and spoke in the public assembly, the prisoner was scarcely an accused man.'—Innes, p. 41. 'The only prosecutors known to Talmudic criminal jurisprudence are the witnesses to the crime. Their duty is to bring the matter to the cognizance of the court, and to bear witness against the criminal. In capital cases they are the legal executioners also. Of an official accuser or prosecutor there is nowhere any trace in the laws of the ancient Hebrews.'—Mendelsohn, p. 110.

"Point 4: The proceedings of the Sanhedrin against Jesus were illegal because they were conducted at night. 'Let a capital offense be tried during the day, but suspend it at night.'—Mishna, Sanhedrin 4:1. 'Criminal cases can be acted upon by the various courts during daytime only, by the Lesser Sanhedrions from the close of the morning service till noon, and by the Great Sanhedrion till evening.'—Mendelsohn, p. 112.

"Point 5: The proceedings of the Sanhedrin against Jesus were illegal because the court convened before the offering of the morning sacrifice. 'The Sanhedrin sat from the close of the morning sacrifice to the time of the evening sacrifice.'—Talmud, Jer. San. 1:19. 'No session of the court could take place before the offering of the morning sacrifice.'—MM. Lemann, p. 109. 'Since the morning sacrifice was offered at the dawn of day, it was hardly possible for the Sanhedrin to assemble until the hour after that time.'—Mishna, Tamid, ch. 3.

"Point 6: The proceedings against Jesus were illegal because they were conducted on the day preceding a Jewish Sabbath; also on the first day of unleavened bread and the eve of the Passover.—'They shall not judge on the eve of the Sabbath nor on that of any festival.'—Mishna, San. 4:1. 'No court of justice in Israel was permitted to hold sessions on the Sabbath or any of the seven Biblical holidays. In cases of capital crime, no trial could be commenced on Friday or the day previous to any holiday, because it was not lawful either to adjourn such cases longer than over night, or to continue them on the Sabbath or holiday.'—Rabbi Wise, 'Martyrdom of Jesus,' p. 67.

"Point 7: The trial of Jesus was illegal because it was concluded within one day. 'A criminal case resulting in the acquittal of the accused may terminate the same day

on which the trial began. But if a sentence of death is to be pronounced, it cannot be concluded before the following day.'—Mishna, San. 4:1.

"*Point 8: The sentence of condemnation pronounced against Jesus by the Sanhedrin was illegal because it was founded upon His uncorroborated confession.* 'We have it as a fundamental principle of our jurisprudence that no one can bring an accusation against himself. Should a man make confession of guilt before a legally constituted tribunal, such confession is not to be used against him unless properly attested by two other witnesses.'—Maimonides, 4:2. 'Not only is self-condemnation never extorted from the defendant by means of torture, but no attempt is ever made to lead him on to self-incrimination. Moreover, a voluntary confession on his part is not admitted in evidence, and therefore not competent to convict him, unless a legal number of witnesses minutely corroborate his self-accusation.'—Mendelsohn, p. 133.

"*Point 9: The condemnation of Jesus was illegal because the verdict of the Sanhedrin was unanimous.* 'A simultaneous and unanimous verdict of guilt rendered on the day of the trial has the effect of an acquittal.'—Mendelsohn, p. 141. 'If none of the judges defend the culprit, i.e., all pronounce him guilty, having no defender in the court, the verdict of guilty was invalid and the sentence of death could not be executed.'—Rabbi Wise, *Martyrdom of Jesus*, p. 74.

"*Point 10: The proceedings against Jesus were illegal in that: (1) The sentence of condemnation was pronounced in a place forbidden by law; (2) The high priest rent his clothes; (3) The balloting was irregular.* 'After leaving the hall Gazith no sentence of death can be passed upon any one soever.'—Talmud, Bab. 'Of Idolatry' 1:8. 'A sentence of death can be pronounced only so long as the Sanhedrin holds its sessions in the appointed place.'—Maimonides, 14. See further Levit. 21:10; compare 10:6. 'Let the judges each in his turn absolve or condemn.'—Mishna, San. 15:5. 'The members of the Sanhedrin were seated in the form of a semicircle, at the extremity of which a secretary was placed, whose business it was to record the votes. One of these secretaries recorded the votes in favor of the accused, the other those against him.'—Mishna, San. 4:3. 'In ordinary cases the judges voted according to seniority, the oldest commencing; in a capital case the reverse order was followed.'—Benny, p. 73.

"*Point 11: The members of the Great Sanhedrin were legally disqualified to try Jesus.* 'Nor must there be on the judicial bench either a relation or a particular friend, or an enemy of either the accused or of the accuser.'—Mendelsohn, p. 108. 'Nor under any circumstances was a man known to be at enmity with the accused person permitted to occupy a position among the judges.'—Benny, p. 37.

"*Point 12: The condemnation of Jesus was illegal because the merits of the defense were not considered.* 'Then shalt thou enquire, and make search, and ask diligently.'—Deut. 13:14. 'The judges shall weigh the matter in the sincerity of their conscience.'—Mishna, San. 4:5. 'The primary object of the Hebrew judicial system was to render the conviction of an innocent person impossible. All the ingenuity of the Jewish legists was directed to the attainment of this end.'—Benny, p. 56.

Chandler's masterly statements of fact and his arguments on each of the foregoing points are commended to the investigator. The author tersely avers: "The pages of human history present no stronger case of judicial murder than the trial and Crucifixion of Jesus of Nazareth, for the simple reason that all forms of law were outraged and trampled under foot in the proceedings instituted against Him." (p. 216.)

5. "His Blood Be on Us, and on Our Children."—Edersheim (vol. 2, p. 578) thus forcefully comments on the acknowledgment of responsibility for the death of Christ: "The Mishna tells us that, after the solemn washing of hands of the elders and their disclaimer of guilt, priests responded with this prayer: 'Forgive it to thy people Israel, whom thou hast redeemed, O Lord, and lay not innocent blood upon thy people Israel.' But here, in answer to Pilate's words, came back that deep, hoarse cry: 'His blood be upon us,' and—God help us!—'on our children.' Some thirty years later, and on that very spot, was judgment pronounced against some of the best in Jerusalem; and among the 3,600 victims of the governor's fury, of whom not a few were scourged and crucified right over against the Pretorium, were many of the noblest of the citizens of Jerusalem. (Josephus, *Wars*, xiv, chap. 8:9). A few years more, and hundreds of crosses bore Jewish mangled bodies within sight of Jerusalem. And still have these wanderers seemed to bear, from century to century, and from land to land, that burden of blood; and still does it seem to weigh 'on us and on our children.'"

6. "We Have No King but Caesar."—"With this cry Judaism was, in the person of its representatives, guilty of denial of God, of blasphemy, of apostasy. It committed suicide, and ever since has its dead body been carried in show from land to land, and from century to century,—to be dead and to remain dead, till He come a second time, who is the resurrection and the life."—Edersheim, vol. 2, p. 581.

7. The Underlying Cause of Pilate's Surrender to the Jewish Demands.—Pilate knew what was right but lacked the moral courage to do it. He was afraid of the Jews, and more afraid of hostile influence at Rome. He was afraid of his conscience, but more afraid of losing his official position. It was the policy of Rome to be gracious and conciliatory in dealing with the religions and social customs of conquered nations. Pontius Pilate had violated this liberal policy from the early days of his procuratorship. In utter disregard of the Hebrew antipathy against images and heathen insignia, he had the legionnaires enter Jerusalem at night, carrying their eagles and standards decorated with the effigy of the emperor. To the Jews this act was a defilement of the Holy City. In vast multitudes they gathered at Caesarea, and petitioned the procurator that the standards and other images be removed from Jerusalem. For five days the people demanded and Pilate refused. He threatened a general slaughter, and was amazed to see the people offer themselves as victims of the sword rather than relinquish their demands. Pilate had to yield (Josephus, Ant. xviii, chap. 3:1; also *Wars*, ii, chap. 9:2, 3). Again he gave offense in forcibly appropriating the Corban, or sacred funds of the temple, to the construction of an aqueduct for supplying Jerusalem with water from the pools of Solomon. Anticipating the public protest of the people, he had caused Roman soldiers to disguise themselves as Jews; and with weapons concealed to mingle with the crowds. At a given signal these assassins plied their weapons and great numbers of defenceless Jews were killed or wounded (Josephus, Ant. xviii, chap. 3:2; and *Wars*, ii. chap. 9:3, 4). On another occasion, Pilate had grossly offended the people by setting up in his official residence at Jerusalem, shields that had been dedicated to Tiberius, and this "less for the honor of Tiberius than for the annoyance of the Jewish people." A petition signed by the ecclesiastical officials of the nation, and by others of influence, including four Herodian princes, was sent to the emperor, who reprimanded Pilate and directed that the shields be removed from Jerusalem to Caesarea (Philo. De Legatione ad Caium; sec. 38).

These outrages on national feeling, and many minor acts of violence, extortion and cruelty, the Jews held against the procurator. He realized that his tenure was insecure, and he dreaded exposure. Such wrongs had he wrought that when he would have done good, he was deterred through cowardly fear of the accusing past.

8. Judas Iscariot.—Today we speak of a traitor as a "Judas" or an "Iscariot." The man who made the combined name infamous has been for ages a subject of discussion among theologians and philosophers, and in later times the light of psychological analysis has been turned upon him. German philosophers were among the earliest to assert that the man had been judged in unrighteousness, and that his real character was of brighter tint than that in which it had been painted. Indeed some critics hold that of all the Twelve, Judas was the one most thoroughly convinced of our Lord's divinity in the flesh; and these apologists attempt to explain the betrayal as a deliberate and well-intended move to force Jesus into a position of difficulty from which He could escape only by the exercise of His powers of Godship, which, up to that time, He had never used in His own behalf.

We are not the invested judges of Judas nor of any other; but we are competent to frame and hold opinions as to the actions of any. In the light of the revealed word it appears that Judas Iscariot had given himself up to the cause of Satan while ostensibly serving the Christ in an exalted capacity. Such a surrender to evil powers could be accomplished only through sin. The nature and extent of the man's transgressions through the years are not told us. He had received the testimony that Jesus was the Son of God; and in the full light of that conviction he turned against his Lord, and betrayed Him to death. Modern revelation is no less explicit than ancient in declaring that the path of sin is that of spiritual darkness leading to certain destruction. If the man who is guilty of adultery, even in his heart only, shall, unless he repents, surely forfeit the companionship of the Spirit of God, and "shall deny the faith," and so the voice of God hath affirmed (see D&C 63:16), we cannot doubt that any and all forms of deadly sin shall poison the soul and, if not forsaken through true repentance, shall bring that soul to condemnation. For his trained and skillful servants, Satan will provide opportunities of service commensurate with their evil ability. Whatever the opinion of modern critics as to the good character of Judas, we have the testimony of John, who for nearly three years had been in close companionship with him, that the man was a thief (12:6); and Jesus referred to him as a devil (6:70), and as "the son of perdition" (17:12). See in this connection D&C 76:4–48.

That the evil proclivities of Judas Iscariot were known to Christ is evidenced by the Lord's direct statement that among the Twelve was one who was a devil; (John 6:70; compare 13:27; Luke 22:3); and furthermore that this knowledge was His when the Twelve were selected is suggested by the words of Jesus: "I know whom I have chosen," coupled with the explanation that in the choice He had made would the scriptures be fulfilled. As the sacrificial death of the Lamb of God was foreknown and foretold so the circumstances of the betrayal were foreseen. It would be contrary to both the letter and spirit of the revealed word to say that the wretched Iscariot was in the least degree deprived of freedom or agency in the course he followed to so execrable an end. His was the opportunity and privilege common to the Twelve, to live in the light of the Lord's immediate presence, and to receive from the source divine the revelation of God's purposes. Judas Iscariot was no victim of circumstances, no insensate tool guided by a superhuman power, except as he by personal volition gave himself up to Satan, and accepted a wage in the devil's employ. Had Judas been true to the right, other means than his perfidy would have operated to bring the Lamb to the slaughter. His ordination to the apostleship placed him in possession of opportunity and privilege above that of the uncalled and unordained; and with such blessed possibility of achievement in the service of God came corresponding capability to fall. A trusted and exalted officer of the government can commit acts of treachery and treason such as are impossible to the citizen who has never learned the secrets of State. Advancement implies increased accountability, even more literally so in the affairs of God's kingdom than in the institutions of men.

There is an apparent discrepancy between the account of Judas Iscariot's death given by Matthew (27:3–10) and that in Acts (1:16–20). According to the first, Judas hanged himself; the second states that he fell headlong, "and all his bowels gushed out." If both records be accurate, the wretched man probably hanged himself, and afterward fell, possibly through the breaking of the cord or the branch to which it was attached. Matthew says the Jewish rulers purchased the "field of blood"; the writer of the Acts quotes Peter as saying that Judas bought the field with the money he had received from the priests. As the ground was bought with the money that had belonged to Iscariot, and as this money had never been formally taken back by the temple officials, the field bought therewith belonged technically to the estate of Judas. The variations are of importance mainly as showing independence of authorship. The accounts agree in the essential feature, that Judas died a miserable suicide.

Concerning the fate of the "sons of perdition," the Lord has given a partial but awful account through a revelation dated February 16, 1832: "Thus saith the Lord, concerning all those who know my power, and have been made partakers thereof, and suffered themselves, through the power of the devil, to be overcome, and to deny the truth and defy my power—They are they who are the sons of perdition, of whom I say that it had been better for them never to have been born, For they are vessels of wrath, doomed to suffer the wrath of God, with the devil and his angels in eternity; Concerning whom I have said there is no forgiveness in this world nor in the world to come, Having denied the Holy Spirit after having received it, and having denied the Only Begotten Son of the Father—having crucified him unto themselves and put him to an open shame. These are they who shall go away into the lake of fire and brimstone, with the devil and his angels, And the only ones on whom the second death shall have any power. . . . Wherefore, he saves all except them: they shall go away into everlasting punishment, which is endless punishment, which is eternal punishment, to reign with the devil and his angels in eternity, where their worm dieth not, and the fire is not quenched, which is their torment; And the end thereof, neither the place thereof, nor their torment, no man knows. Neither was it revealed, neither is, neither will be revealed unto man, except to them who are made partakers thereof: Nevertheless I, the Lord, show it by vision unto many, but straightway shut it up again; Wherefore the end, the width, the height, the depth, and the misery thereof, they understand not, neither any man except them who are ordained unto this condemnation."—D&C 76:31–37, 44–48.

CHAPTER 35

DEATH AND BURIAL

ON THE WAY TO CALVARY[a]

Pontius Pilate, having reluctantly surrendered to the clamorous demands of the Jews, issued the fatal order; and Jesus, divested of the purple robe and arrayed in His own apparel, was led away to be crucified. A body of Roman soldiers had the condemned Christ in charge; and as the procession moved out from the governor's palace, a motley crowd comprising priestly officials, rulers of the Jews, and people of many nationalities, followed. Two convicted criminals, who had been sentenced to the cross for robbery, were led forth to death at the same time; there was to be a triple execution; and the prospective scene of horror attracted the morbidly minded, such as delight to gloat over the sufferings of their fellows. In the crowd, however, were some genuine mourners, as shall be shown. It was the Roman custom to make the execution of convicts as public as possible, under the mistaken and anti-psychological assumption that the spectacle of dreadful punishment would be of deterrent effect. This misconception of human nature has not yet become entirely obsolete.

The sentence of death by crucifixion required that the condemned person carry the cross upon which he was to suffer. Jesus started on the way bearing His cross. The terrible strain of the preceding hours, the agony in Gethsemane, the barbarous treatment He had suffered in the palace of the high priest, the humiliation and cruel usage to which He had been subjected before Herod, the frightful scourging under

---

[a] Matt. 27:31–33; Mark 15:20–22; Luke 23:26–33; John 19:16, 17.

Pilate's order, the brutal treatment by the inhuman soldiery, together with the extreme humiliation and the mental agony of it all, had so weakened His physical organism that He moved but slowly under the burden of the cross. The soldiers, impatient at the delay, peremptorily impressed into service a man whom they met coming into Jerusalem from the country, and him they compelled to carry the cross of Jesus. No Roman or Jew would have voluntarily incurred the ignominy of bearing such a gruesome burden; for every detail connected with the carrying out of a sentence of crucifixion was regarded as degrading. The man so forced to walk in the footsteps of Jesus, bearing the cross upon which the Savior of the world was to consummate His glorious mission, was Simon, a native of Cyrene. From Mark's statement that Simon was the father of Alexander and Rufus we infer that the two sons were known to the evangelist's readers as members of the early Church, and there is some indication that the household of Simon the Cyrenian came to be numbered with the believers.[b]

Among those who followed or stood and watched the death-procession pass, were some, women particularly, who bewailed and lamented the fate to which Jesus was going. We read of no man who ventured to raise his voice in protest or pity; but on this dreadful occasion as at other times, women were not afraid to cry out in commiseration or praise. Jesus, who had been silent under the inquisition of the priests, silent under the humiliating mockery of the sensual Herod and his coarse underlings, silent when buffeted and beaten by the brutal legionnaires of Pilate, turned to the women whose sympathizing lamentations had reached His ears, and uttered these pathetic and portentous words of admonition and warning: "Daughters of Jerusalem, weep not for me, but weep for yourselves, and for your children. For, behold, the days are coming, in the which they shall say, Blessed are the barren, and the wombs that never bare, and the paps which never gave suck. Then shall they begin to say to the mountains, Fall on us; and to the hills, Cover us. For if they do these things in a green tree, what shall be done in the dry?" It was the Lord's last testimony of the impending holocaust of destruction that was to follow the nation's

---

[b] Note 1, end of chapter.

rejection of her King. Although motherhood was the glory of every Jewish woman's life, yet in the terrible scenes which many of those there weeping would live to witness, barrenness would be accounted a blessing; for the childless would have fewer to weep over, and at least would be spared the horror of seeing their offspring die of starvation or by violence; for so dreadful would be that day that people would fain welcome the falling of the mountains upon them to end their sufferings.[c] If Israel's oppressors could do what was then in process of doing to the "Green Tree," who bore the leafage of freedom and truth and offered the priceless fruit of life eternal, what would the powers of evil not do to the withered branches and dried trunk of apostate Judaism?

Along the city streets, out through the portal of the massive wall, and thence to a place beyond but yet nigh unto Jerusalem, the cortege advanced. The destination was a spot called Golgotha, or Calvary, meaning "the place of a skull."[d]

THE CRUCIFIXION[e]

At Calvary the official crucifiers proceeded without delay to carry into effect the dread sentence pronounced upon Jesus and upon the two criminals. Preparatory to affixing the condemned to the cross, it was the custom to offer each a narcotic draught of sour wine or vinegar mingled with myrrh and possibly containing other anodyne ingredients, for the merciful purpose of deadening the sensibility of the victim. This was no Roman practice, but was allowed as a concession to Jewish sentiment. When the drugged cup was presented to Jesus He put it to His lips, but having ascertained the nature of its contents refused to drink, and so demonstrated His determination to meet death with faculties alert and mind unclouded.

Then they crucified Him, on the central cross of three, and placed one of the condemned malefactors on His right hand, the other on His left. Thus was realized Isaiah's vision of the Messiah numbered among the transgressors.[f] But few details of the actual Crucifixion are

[c] Note 2, end of chapter.
[d] Note 3, end of chapter.
[e] Matt. 27:34–50; Mark 15:23–37; Luke 23:33–46; John 19:18–30.
[f] Isa. 53:12; compare Mark 15:28; Luke 22:37.

given us. We know however that our Lord was nailed to the cross by spikes driven through the hands and feet, as was the Roman method, and not bound only by cords as was the custom in inflicting this form of punishment among some other nations. Death by crucifixion was at once the most lingering and most painful of all forms of execution. The victim lived in ever increasing torture, generally for many hours, sometimes for days. The spikes so cruelly driven through hands and feet penetrated and crushed sensitive nerves and quivering tendons, yet inflicted no mortal wound. The welcome relief of death came through the exhaustion caused by intense and unremitting pain, through localized inflammation and congestion of organs incident to the strained and unnatural posture of the body.[g]

As the crucifiers proceeded with their awful task, not unlikely with roughness and taunts, for killing was their trade and to scenes of anguish they had grown callous through long familiarity, the agonized Sufferer, void of resentment but full of pity for their heartlessness and capacity for cruelty, voiced the first of the seven utterances delivered from the cross. In the spirit of God-like mercy He prayed: *"Father, forgive them; for they know not what they do."* Let us not attempt to fix the limits of the Lord's mercy; that it would be extended to all who in any degree could justly come under the blessed boon thereof ought to be a sufficing fact. There is significance in the form in which this merciful benediction was expressed. Had the Lord said, "I forgive you," His gracious pardon may have been understood to be but a remission of the cruel offense against Himself as One tortured under unrighteous condemnation; but the invocation of the Father's forgiveness was a plea for those who had brought anguish and death to the Father's Well Beloved Son, the Savior and Redeemer of the world. Moses forgave Miriam for her offense against himself as her brother; but God alone could remit the penalty and remove the leprosy that had come upon her for having spoken against Jehovah's high priest.[h]

It appears that under Roman rule, the clothes worn by a condemned person at the time of execution became the perquisites of the executioners. The four soldiers in charge of the cross upon which

[g] Note 4, end of chapter.
[h] Num. 12.

the Lord suffered distributed parts of His raiment among themselves; and there remained His coat,[i] which was a goodly garment, woven throughout in one piece, without seam. To rend it would be to spoil; so the soldiers cast lots to determine who should have it; and in this circumstance the Gospel-writers saw a fulfilment of the psalmist's prevision: "They parted my garments among them, and upon my vesture did they cast lots."[j]

To the cross above the head of Jesus was affixed a title or inscription, prepared by order of Pilate in accordance with the custom of setting forth the name of the crucified and the nature of the offense for which he had been condemned to death. In this instance the title was inscribed in three languages, Greek, Latin, and Hebrew, one or more of which would be understood by every observer who could read. The title so exhibited read: *"This is Jesus the King of the Jews";* or in the more extended version given by John *"Jesus of Nazareth The King of the Jews."*[k] The inscription was read by many, for Calvary was close to the public thoroughfare and on this holiday occasion the passers-by were doubtless numerous. Comment was aroused; for, if literally construed, the inscription was an official declaration that the crucified Jesus was in fact King of the Jews. When this circumstance was brought to the attention of the chief priests, they excitedly appealed to the governor, saying: "Write not, The King of the Jews; but that he said, I am King of the Jews. Pilate answered, What I have written I have written." Pilate's action in so wording the title, and his blunt refusal to permit an alteration, may have been an intended rebuff to the Jewish officials who had forced him against his judgment and will to condemn Jesus; possibly, however, the demeanor of the submissive Prisoner, and His avowal of Kingship above all royalty of earth had impressed the mind if not the heart of the pagan governor with a conviction of Christ's unique superiority and of His inherent right of dominion; but, whatever the purpose behind the writing, the inscription stands in history as testimony of a heathen's consideration in contrast with Israel's ruthless rejection of Israel's King.[l]

[i] Revised version, marginal reading, "tunic."
[j] Matt. 27:35; Mark 15:24; Luke 23:34; John 19:23, 24; compare Ps. 22:18.
[k] Note 5, end of chapter.
[l] Pages 82–83 and 85–86.

The soldiers whose duty it was to guard the crosses, until loitering death would relieve the crucified of their increasing anguish, jested among themselves, and derided the Christ, pledging Him in their cups of sour wine in tragic mockery. Looking at the title affixed above the Sufferer's head, they bellowed forth the devil-inspired challenge: "If thou be the king of the Jews, save thyself." The morbid multitude, and the passers-by "railed on him, wagging their heads, and saying, Ah, thou that destroyest the temple, and buildest it in three days, save thyself, and come down from the cross." But worst of all, the chief priests and the scribes, the elders of the people, the unvenerable Sanhedrists, became ringleaders of the inhuman mob as they gloatingly exulted and cried aloud: "He saved others; himself he cannot save. If he be the King of Israel, let him now come down from the cross, and we will believe him. He trusted in God; let him deliver him now, if he will have him: for he said, I am the Son of God."[m] Though uttered in ribald mockery, the declaration of the rulers in Israel stands as an attestation that Christ had saved others, and as an intended ironical but a literally true proclamation that He was the King of Israel. The two malefactors, each hanging from his cross, joined in the general derision, and "cast the same in his teeth." One of them, in the desperation incident to approaching death, echoed the taunts of the priests and people: "If thou be Christ, save thyself and us."

The dominant note in all the railings and revilings, the ribaldry and mockery, with which the patient and submissive Christ was assailed while He hung, "lifted up" as He had said He would be,[n] was that awful "If" hurled at Him by the devil's emissaries in the time of mortal agony; as in the season of the temptations immediately after His baptism it had been most insidiously pressed upon Him by the devil himself.[o] That "If" was Satan's last shaft, keenly barbed and doubly envenomed, and it sped as with the fierce hiss of a viper. Was it possible in this the final and most dreadful stage of Christ's mission,

---

[m] Matt. 27:42, 43. The clause "if he be the King of Israel" in verse 42 of the common text is admittedly a mistranslation; it should read "He is the King of Israel." See revised version; also Edersheim, vol. 2, p. 596; compare Mark 15:32.

[n] John 3:14; 8:28; 12:32.

[o] Matt. 4:3, 6.

to make Him doubt His divine Sonship, or, failing such, to taunt or anger the dying Savior into the use of His superhuman powers for personal relief or as an act of vengeance upon His tormentors? To achieve such a victory was Satan's desperate purpose. The shaft failed. Through taunts and derision, through blasphemous challenge and diabolical goading, the agonized Christ was silent.

Then one of the crucified thieves, softened into penitence by the Savior's uncomplaining fortitude, and perceiving in the divine Sufferer's demeanor something more than human, rebuked his railing fellow, saying: "Dost not thou fear God, seeing thou art in the same condemnation? And we indeed justly; for we receive the due reward of our deeds: but this man hath done nothing amiss." His confession of guilt and his acknowledgment of the justice of his own condemnation led to incipient repentance, and to faith in the Lord Jesus, his companion in agony. "And he said unto Jesus, Lord, remember me when thou comest into thy kingdom."[p] To the appeal of penitence the Lord replied with such a promise as He alone could make: "Verily I say unto thee, To day shalt thou be with me in paradise."[q]

Among the spectators of this, the greatest tragedy in history, were some who had come in sympathy and sorrow. No mention is found of the presence of any of the Twelve, save one, and he, the disciple "whom Jesus loved," John the apostle, evangelist, and revelator; but specific record is made of certain women who, first at a distance, and then close by the cross, wept in the anguish of love and sorrow. "Now there stood by the cross of Jesus his mother, and his mother's sister, Mary the wife of Cleophas, and Mary Magdalene."[r]

In addition to the women named were many others, some of whom had ministered unto Jesus in the course of His labors in Galilee, and who were among those that had come up with Him to Jerusalem.[s] First in point of consideration among them all was Mary, the mother of Jesus, into whose soul the sword had pierced even as

[p] Luke 23:42; the revised version reads "when thou comest in thy kingdom."

[q] See chapter 36, following.

[r] John 19:25; compare Matt. 27:55, 56; Mark 15:40, 41; Luke 23:48, 49. See Note 6, end of chapter.

[s] See references last cited; and Luke 8:2, 3.

righteous Simeon had prophesied.ᵗ Jesus looking with tender compassion upon His weeping mother, as she stood with John at the foot of the cross, commended her to the care and protection of the beloved disciple, with the words, *"Woman, behold thy son!"* and to John, *"Behold thy mother!"* The disciple tenderly led the heart-stricken Mary away from her dying Son, and "took her unto his own home," thus immediately assuming the new relationship established by his dying Master.

Jesus was nailed to the cross during the forenoon of that fateful Friday, probably between nine and ten o'clock.ᵘ At noontide the light of the sun was obscured, and black darkness spread over the whole land. The terrifying gloom continued for a period of three hours. This remarkable phenomenon has received no satisfactory explanation from science. It could not have been due to a solar eclipse, as has been suggested in ignorance, for the time was that of full moon; indeed the Passover season was determined by the first occurrence of full moon after the spring equinox. The darkness was brought about by miraculous operation of natural laws directed by divine power. It was a fitting sign of the earth's deep mourning over the impending death of her Creator.ᵛ Of the mortal agony through which the Lord passed while upon the cross the Gospel-scribes are reverently reticent.

At the ninth hour, or about three in the afternoon, a loud voice, surpassing the most anguished cry of physical suffering issued from the central cross, rending the dreadful darkness. It was the voice of the Christ: *"Eloi, Eloi, lama sabachthani? which is, being interpreted, My God, my God, why hast thou forsaken me?"* What mind of man can fathom the significance of that awful cry? It seems, that in addition to the fearful suffering incident to crucifixion, the agony of Gethsemane had recurred, intensified beyond human power to endure. In that bitterest hour the dying Christ was alone, alone in most terrible reality. That the supreme sacrifice of the Son might be consummated in all its fulness, the Father seems to have withdrawn the support of His immediate Presence, leaving to the Savior of men the glory of complete victory over the forces of sin and death. The cry from the

---

ᵗ Luke 2:34, 35.

ᵘ Mark 15:25; see note 7, end of chapter.

ᵛ Compare Moses 7:37, 40, 48, 49, 56.

cross, though heard by all who were near, was understood by few. The first exclamation, *Eloi*, meaning *My God*, was misunderstood as a call for Elias.

The period of faintness, the conception of utter forsakenness soon passed, and the natural cravings of the body reasserted themselves. The maddening thirst, which constituted one of the worst of the crucifixion agonies, wrung from the Savior's lips His one recorded utterance expressive of physical suffering. *"I thirst"* He said. One of those who stood by, whether Roman or Jew, disciple or skeptic, we are not told, hastily saturated a sponge with vinegar, a vessel of which was at hand, and having fastened the sponge to the end of a reed, or stalk of hyssop, pressed it to the Lord's fevered lips. Some others would have prevented this one act of human response, for they said: "Let be, let us see whether Elias will come to save him." John affirms that Christ uttered the exclamation, "I thirst," only when He knew "that all things were now accomplished"; and the apostle saw in the incident a fulfilment of prophecy.[w]

Fully realizing that He was no longer forsaken, but that His atoning sacrifice had been accepted by the Father, and that His mission in the flesh had been carried to glorious consummation, He exclaimed in a loud voice of holy triumph: *"It is finished."* In reverence, resignation, and relief, He addressed the Father saying: *"Father, into thy hands I commend my spirit."*[x] He bowed His head, and voluntarily gave up His life.

Jesus the Christ was dead. His life had not been taken from Him except as He had willed to permit. Sweet and welcome as would have been the relief of death in any of the earlier stages of His suffering from Gethsemane to the cross, He lived until all things were accomplished as had been appointed. In the latter days the voice of the Lord Jesus has been heard affirming the actuality of His suffering and death, and the eternal purpose thereby accomplished. Hear and heed His words: "For, behold, the Lord your Redeemer suffered death in

---

[w] John 19:28; compare Ps. 69:21.

[x] The Gospel–writers leave us in some uncertainty as to which of the last two utterances from the cross,—"It is finished," and "Father, into thy hands I commend my spirit,"—was spoken first.

the flesh; wherefore he suffered the pain of all men, that all men might repent and come unto him."[y]

IMPORTANT OCCURRENCES
BETWEEN THE LORD'S DEATH AND BURIAL

The death of Christ was accompanied by terrifying phenomena. There was a violent earthquake; the rocks of the mighty hills were disrupted, and many graves were torn open. But, most portentous of all in Judaistic minds, the veil of the temple which hung between the Holy Place and the Holy of Holies[z] was rent from top to bottom, and the interior, which none but the high priest had been permitted to see, was thrown open to common gaze. It was the rending of Judaism, the consummation of the Mosaic dispensation, and the inauguration of Christianity under apostolic administration.

The Roman centurion and the soldiers under his command at the place of execution were amazed and greatly affrighted. They had probably witnessed many deaths on the cross, but never before had they seen a man apparently die of his own volition, and able to cry in a loud voice at the moment of dissolution. That barbarous and inhuman mode of execution induced slow and progressive exhaustion. The actual death of Jesus appeared to all who were present to be a miracle, as in fact it was. This marvel, coupled with the earthquake and its attendant horrors, so impressed the centurion that he prayed to God, and solemnly declared: "Certainly this was a righteous man." Others joined in fearsome averment: "Truly this was the Son of God." The terrified ones who spoke and those who heard left the place in a state of fear, beating their breasts, and bewailing what seemed to be a state of impending destruction.[aa] A few loving women, however, watched from a distant point, and saw all that took place until the Lord's body was laid away.

It was now late in the afternoon; at sunset the Sabbath would begin. That approaching Sabbath was held to be more than ordinarily sacred for it was a high day, in that it was the weekly Sabbath and a

---

[y] D&C 18:11; revelation given in June 1829; see also 19:16–19.

[z] See *The House of the Lord,* pages 59, 60.

[aa] Matt. 27:51–54; Mark 15:38, 39; Luke 23:47–49.

paschal holy day.[bb] The Jewish officials, who had not hesitated to slay their Lord, were horrified at the thought of men left hanging on crosses on such a day, for thereby the land would be defiled;[cc] so these scrupulous rulers went to Pilate and begged that Jesus and the two malefactors be summarily dispatched by the brutal Roman method of breaking their legs, the shock of which violent treatment had been found to be promptly fatal to the crucified. The governor gave his consent, and the soldiers broke the limbs of the two thieves with cudgels. Jesus, however, was found to be already dead, so they broke not His bones. Christ, the great Passover sacrifice, of whom all altar victims had been but suggestive prototypes, died through violence yet without a bone of His body being broken, as was a prescribed condition of the slain paschal lambs.[dd] One of the soldiers, to make sure that Jesus was actually dead, or to surely kill Him if He was yet alive, drove a spear into His side, making a wound large enough to permit a man's hand to be thrust thereinto.[ee] The withdrawal of the spear was followed by an outflow of blood and water,[ff] an occurrence so surprising that John, who was an eye-witness, bears specific personal testimony to the fact, and cites the scriptures thereby fulfilled.[gg]

THE BURIAL [hh]

A man known as Joseph of Arimathea, who was at heart a disciple of Christ, but who had hesitated to openly confess his conversion through fear of the Jews, desired to give the Lord's body a decent and honorable interment. But for some such divinely directed intervention, the body of Jesus might have been cast into the common grave of executed criminals. This man, Joseph, was "a counsellor; and he was a good man, and a just." It is expressly said of him that he "had not consented to the counsel and deed of them"; from which statement

[bb] John 19:31–37.

[cc] Deut. 21:23.

[dd] Ex. 12:46; Num. 9:12; Ps. 34:20; John 19:36; 1 Cor. 5:7.

[ee] John 20:27; 3 Ne. 11:14, 15.

[ff] Note 8, end of chapter.

[gg] John 19:34–37; compare Ps. 22:16, 17; Zech. 12:10; Rev. 1:7.

[hh] Matt. 27:57–61; Mark 15:42–47; Luke 23:50–56; John 19:38–42.

we infer that he was a Sanhedrist and had been opposed to the action of his colleagues in condemning Jesus to death, or at least had refrained from voting with the rest. Joseph was a man of wealth, station, and influence. He went in boldly unto Pilate and begged the body of Christ. The governor was surprised to learn that Jesus was already dead; he summoned the centurion and inquired as to how long Jesus had lived on the cross. The unusual circumstance seems to have added to Pilate's troubled concern. He gave command and the body of Christ was delivered to Joseph.

The body was removed from the cross; and in preparing it for the tomb Joseph was assisted by Nicodemus, another member of the Sanhedrin, the same who had come to Jesus by night three years before, and who at one of the conspiracy meetings of the council had protested against the unlawful condemnation of Jesus without a hearing.[ii] Nicodemus brought a large quantity of myrrh and aloes, about a hundredweight. The odorous mixture was highly esteemed for anointing and embalming, but its cost restricted its use to the wealthy. These two revering disciples wrapped the Lord's body in clean linen, "with the spices, as the manner of the Jews is to bury"; and then laid it in a new sepulchre, hewn in the rock. The tomb was in a garden, not far from Calvary, and was the property of Joseph. Because of the nearness of the Sabbath the interment had to be made with haste; the door of the sepulchre was closed, a large stone was rolled against it;[jj] and thus laid away the body was left to rest. Some of the devoted women, particularly Mary Magdalene, and "the other Mary," who was the mother of James and Joses, had watched the entombment from a distance; and when it was completed "they returned, and prepared spices and ointments; and rested the Sabbath day according to the commandment."

THE SEPULCHRE GUARDED [kk]

On the day following the "preparation," that is to say on Saturday, the Sabbath and "high day,"[ll] the chief priests and Pharisees came in a

[ii] John 3:1, 2; 7:50.

[jj] See revised version, Mark 15:46.

[kk] Matt. 27:62–66.

[ll] Note 9, end of chapter.

body to Pilate, saying: "Sir, we remember that that deceiver said, while he was yet alive, After three days I will rise again. Command therefore that the sepulchre be made sure until the third day, lest his disciples come by night, and steal him away, and say unto the people, He is risen from the dead: so the last error shall be worse than the first." It is evident that the most inveterate of the human enemies of Christ remembered His predictions of an assured resurrection on the third day after His death. Pilate answered with terse assent: "Ye have a watch: go your way, make it as sure as ye can." So the chief priests and Pharisees satisfied themselves that the sepulchre was secure by seeing that the official seal was affixed at the junction of the great stone and the portal, and that an armed guard was placed in charge.

NOTES TO CHAPTER 35

1. Simon the Cyrenian.—Simon, upon whom the cross of Jesus was laid, was a member of the Jewish colony in northern Africa, which had been established nearly three centuries before "the birth of Christ by Ptolemeus Lagi, who transported thither great numbers of Jews from Palestine (Josephus, *Antiquities*, xii, chap. 1). Cyrene, the home of Simon, was in the province of Libya; its site is within the present boundaries of Tunis. That the African Jews were numerous and influential is evidenced by the fact that they maintained a synagog in Jerusalem (Acts 6.9) for the accommodation of such of their number as visited the city. Rufus and his mother are mentioned in friendly reference by Paul over a quarter of a century after the death of Christ (Rom. 16:13). If this Rufus be one of the sons of Simon named by Mark (15:21), as tradition indicates, it is probable that Simon's family was prominently identified with the primitive Church. As to whether Simon had become a disciple before the Crucifixion, or was converted through his compulsory service in bearing the Lord's cross, or became a member of the Church at a later date, we are not definitely told.

2. Christ's Words to the Daughters of Jerusalem.—"The time would come, when the Old Testament curse of barrenness (Hosea 9:14) would be coveted as a blessing. To show the fulfilment of this prophetic lament of Jesus it is not necessary to recall the harrowing details recorded by Josephus (*Wars*, vi, 3:4), when a frenzied mother roasted her own child, and in the mockery of desperateness reserved the half of the horrible meal for those murderers who daily broke in upon her to rob her of what scanty food had been left her; nor yet other of those incidents, too revolting for needless repetition, which the historian of the last siege of Jerusalem chronicles. But how often, these many centuries, must Israel's women have felt that terrible longing for childlessness, and how often must the prayer of despair for the quick death of falling mountains and burying hills rather than prolonged torture (Hosea 10:8), have risen to the lips of Israel's sufferers! And yet, even so, these words were also prophetic of a still more terrible future (Rev. 6:10). For, if Israel had put such flame to its 'green tree' how terribly would the divine judgment burn among the dry wood of an apostate and rebellious people, that had so delivered up its Divine King and pronounced sentence upon itself by pronouncing it upon Him!"—Edersheim, *Life and Times of Jesus the Messiah*, vol. 2, p. 588.

Concerning the prayer that mountains fall to crush and hide, Farrar (*Life of Christ*, p. 645, note), says: "These words of Christ met with a painfully literal illustration when hundreds of the unhappy Jews at the siege of Jerusalem hid themselves in the darkest and vilest subterranean recesses, and when, besides those who were hunted out, no less than two thousand were killed by being buried under the ruins of their hiding places." A further fulfilment may be yet future. Consult Josephus, *Wars*, vi. 9:4. See also Hosea 9:12–16; 10:8; Isa. 2:10; compare Rev. 6:16.

3. "The Place of a Skull."—The Aramaic Hebrew name "Golgotha," the Greek "Kranion," and the Latin "Calvaria" or, as Anglicized, "Calvary," have the same meaning, and connote "a skull." The name may have been applied with reference to topographical features, as we speak of the brow of a hill; or, if the spot was the usual place of execution, it may have been so called as expressive of death, just as we call a skull a death's head. It is probable that the bodies of executed convicts were buried near the place of death; and if Golgotha or Calvary was the appointed site for execution, the exposure of skulls and other human bones through the ravages of beasts and by other means, would not be surprising; though the leaving of bodies or any of their parts unburied was contrary to Jewish law and sentiment. The origin of the name is of as little importance as are the many divergent suppositions concerning the exact location of the spot.

4. Crucifixion.—"It was unanimously considered the most horrible form of death. Among the Romans also the degradation was a part of the infliction, and the punishment if applied to freeman was only used in the case of the vilest criminals. . . . The criminal carried his own cross, or at any rate a part of it. Hence, figuratively, *to take, take up* or *bear one's cross is to endure suffering, affliction, or shame*, like a criminal on his way to the place of crucifixion (Matt. 10:38; 16:24; Luke 14:27, etc.). The place of execution was outside the city (1 Kgs. 21:13; Acts 7:58; Heb. 13:12), often in some public road or other conspicuous place. Arrived at the place of execution, the sufferer was stripped naked, the dress being the perquisite of the soldiers (Matt. 27:35). The cross was then driven into the ground, so that the feet of the condemned were a foot or two above the earth, and he was lifted upon it; or else stretched upon it on the ground and then lifted with it." It was the custom to station soldiers to watch the cross, so as to prevent the removal of the sufferer while yet alive. "This was necessary from the lingering character of the death, which sometimes did not supervene even for three days, and was at last the result of gradual benumbing and starvation. But for this guard, the persons might have been taken down and recovered, as was actually done in the case of a friend of Josephus. . . . In most cases the body was suffered to rot on the cross by the action of sun and rain, or to be devoured by birds and beasts. Sepulture was generally therefore forbidden; but in consequence of Deut. 21:22, 23 an express national exception was made in favor of the Jews (Matt. 27:58). This accursed and awful mode of punishment was happily abolished by Constantine." Smith's *Bible Dictionary*.

5. Pilate's Inscription.—"The King of the Jews."—No two of the Gospel-writers give the same wording of the title or inscription placed by Pilate's order above the head of Jesus on the cross; the meaning, however, is the same in all, and the unessential variation is evidence of individual liberty among the recorders. It is probable that there was actual diversity in the trilingual versions. John's version is followed in the common abbreviations used in connection with Roman Catholic figures of Christ: J. N. R. J.; or, inasmuch as "I" used to be an ordinary equivalent of "J,"—I. N. R. I.— "Jesus of Nazareth, King [Rex] of the Jews."

6. The Women at the Cross.—"According to the authorized version and revised version, only three women are named, but most modern critics hold that four are intended. Translate, therefore, 'His mother, and His mother's sister, (i.e. Salome, the mother of the evangelist [John]); and Mary the wife of Cleophas; and Mary Magdalene.'"—Taken from Dummelow's *Commentary* on John 19:25.

7. The Hour of the Crucifixion.—Mark (15:25) says: "And it was the third hour and they crucified him"; the time so specified corresponds to the hour from 9 to 10 a.m. This writer and his fellow synoptists, Matthew and Luke, give place to many incidents that occurred between the nailing of Christ to the cross and the sixth hour or the hour from 12 noon to 1 p.m. From these several accounts it is clear that Jesus was crucified during the forenoon. A discrepancy plainly appears between these records and John's statement (19:14) that it was "about the sixth hour" (noon) when Pilate gave the sentence of execution. All attempts to harmonize the accounts in this particular have proved futile because the discrepancy is real. Most critics and commentators assume that "about the sixth hour" in John's account is a misstatement, due to the errors of early copyists of the manuscript Gospels, who mistook the sign meaning 3rd for the signifying 6th.

8. The Physical Cause of Christ's Death.—While, as stated in the text, the yielding up of life was voluntary on the part of Jesus Christ, for He had life in Himself and no man could take His life except as He willed to allow it to be taken, (John 1:4; 5:26; 10:15–18) there was of necessity a direct physical cause of dissolution. As stated also the crucified sometimes lived for days upon the cross, and death resulted, not from the infliction of mortal wounds, but from internal congestion, inflammations, organic disturbances, and consequent exhaustion of vital energy. Jesus, though weakened by long torture during the preceding night and early morning, by the shock of the crucifixion itself, as also by intense mental agony, and particularly through spiritual suffering such as no other man has ever endured, manifested surprising vigor, both of mind and body, to the last. The strong, loud utterance, immediately following which He bowed His head and "gave up the ghost," when considered in connection with other recorded details, points to a physical rupture of the heart as the direct cause of death. If the soldier's spear was thrust into the left side of the Lord's body and actually penetrated the heart, the outrush of "blood and water" observed by John is further evidence of a cardiac rupture; for it is known that in the rare instances of death resulting from a breaking of any part of the wall of the heart, blood accumulates within the pericardium, and there undergoes a change by which the corpuscles separate as a partially clotted mass from the almost colorless, watery serum. Similar accumulations of clotted corpuscles and serum occur within the pleura. Dr. Abercrombie of Edinburgh, as cited by Deems (*Light of the Nations,* p. 682), "gives a case of the sudden death of a man aged seventy-seven years, owing to a rupture of the heart. In his case 'the cavities of the pleura contained *about three pounds of fluid,* but the lungs were sound.'" Deems also cites the following instance: "Dr. Elliotson relates the case of a woman who died suddenly. 'On opening the body the pericardium was found distended with *clear serum,* and a very large coagulum of blood, which had escaped through a spontaneous rupture of the aorta near its origin, without any other morbid appearance.' Many cases might be cited, but these suffice." For detailed treatment of the subject the student may be referred to Dr. Wm. Stroud's work *On the Physical Cause of the Death of Christ.* Great mental stress, poignant emotion either of grief or joy, and intense spiritual struggle are among the recognized causes of heart rupture.

The present writer believes that the Lord Jesus died of a broken heart. The Psalmist sang in dolorous measure according to his inspired prevision of the Lord's passion: "Reproach hath broken my heart; and I am full of heaviness: and I looked for some to take pity, but there was none; and for comforters, but I found none. They gave me also gall for my meat; and in my thirst they gave me vinegar to drink." (Ps. 69:20, 21; see also 22:14.)

9. The Request that Christ's Tomb be Sealed.—Many critics hold that the deputation called upon Pilate on Saturday evening, after the Sabbath had ended. This assumption is made on the ground that to do what these priestly officials did, in personally supervising the sealing of the tomb, would have been to incur defilement, and that they would not have so done on the Sabbath. Matthew's statement is definite—that the application was made on "the next day, that followed the day of the preparation." The preparation day extended from sunset on Thursday to the beginning of the Sabbath at sunset on Friday.

CHAPTER 36

IN THE REALM OF DISEMBODIED SPIRITS

Jesus the Christ died in the literal sense in which all men die. He underwent a physical dissolution by which His immortal spirit was separated from His body of flesh and bones, and that body was actually dead. While the corpse lay in Joseph's rock-hewn tomb, the living Christ existed as a disembodied Spirit. We are justified in inquiring where He was and what were His activities during the interval between His death on the cross and His emergence from the sepulchre with spirit and body reunited, a resurrected Soul. The assumption that most naturally suggests itself is that He went where the spirits of the dead ordinarily go; and that, in the sense in which while in the flesh He had been a Man among men, He was, in the disembodied state a Spirit among spirits. This conception is confirmed as a fact by scriptural attestation.

As heretofore shown[a] Jesus Christ was the chosen and ordained Redeemer and Savior of mankind; to this exalted mission He had been set apart in the beginning, even before the earth was prepared as the abode of mankind. Unnumbered hosts who had never heard the gospel, lived and died upon the earth before the birth of Jesus. Of those departed myriads many had passed their mortal probation with varying degrees of righteous observance of the law of God so far as it had been made known unto them, but had died in unblamable ignorance of the gospel; while other multitudes had lived and died as transgressors even against such moiety of God's law to man as they had learned and

---

[a] Chapters 2 and 3 herein.

such as they had professed to obey. Death had claimed as its own all of these, both just and unjust. To them went the Christ, bearing the transcendently glorious tidings of redemption from the bondage of death, and of possible salvation from the effects of individual sin. This labor was part of the Savior's foreappointed and unique service to the human family. The shout of divine exultation from the cross, "It is finished," signified the consummation of the Lord's mission in mortality; yet there remained to Him other ministry to be rendered prior to His return to the Father.

To the penitent transgressor crucified by His side, who reverently craved remembrance when the Lord should come into His kingdom,[b] Christ had given the comforting assurance: "Verily I say unto thee, Today shalt thou be with me in paradise." The spirit of Jesus and the spirit of the repentant thief left their crucified bodies and went to the same place in the realm of the departed.[c] On the third day following, Jesus, then a resurrected Being, positively stated to the weeping Magdalene: "I am not yet ascended to my Father." He had gone to paradise but not to the place where God dwells. Paradise, therefore, is not Heaven, if by the latter term we understand the abode of the Eternal Father and His celestialized children.[d] Paradise is a place where dwell righteous and repentant spirits between bodily death and resurrection. Another division of the spirit world is reserved for those disembodied beings who have lived lives of wickedness and who remain impenitent even after death. Alma, a Nephite prophet, thus spake of the conditions prevailing among the departed:

"Now concerning the state of the soul between death and the resurrection. Behold, it has been made known unto me, by an angel, that the spirits of all men, as soon as they are departed from this mortal body; yea, the spirits of all men, whether they be good or evil, are taken home to that God who gave them life. And then shall it come to pass that the spirits of those who are righteous, are received into a state of happiness, which is called paradise; a state of rest; a state of peace, where they shall rest from all their troubles and from

[b] Page 611.

[c] Note 1, end of chapter.

[d] Note the distinction by Paul in 2 Cor. 12:2–4.

all care, and sorrow, &c. And then shall it come to pass, that the spirits of the wicked, yea, who are evil; for behold, they have no part nor portion of the Spirit of the Lord; for behold, they chose evil works rather than good; therefore the spirit of the devil did enter into them, and take possession of their house; and these shall be cast out into outer darkness; there shall be weeping, and wailing, and gnashing of teeth; and this because of their own iniquity; being led captive by the will of the devil. Now this is the state of the souls of the wicked: yea, in darkness, and a state of awful, fearful, looking for the fiery indignation of the wrath of God upon them; thus they remain in this state, as well as the righteous in paradise, until the time of their resurrection."[e]

While divested of His body Christ ministered among the departed, both in paradise and in the prison realm where dwelt in a state of durance the spirits of the disobedient. To this effect testified Peter nearly three decades after the great event: "For Christ also hath once suffered for sins, the just for the unjust, that he might bring us to God, being put to death in the flesh, but quickened by the Spirit: By which also he went and preached unto the spirits in prison; Which sometime were disobedient, when once the longsuffering of God waited in the days of Noah, while the ark was a preparing, wherein few, that is, eight souls were saved by water."[f]

The disobedient who had lived on earth in the Noachian period are especially mentioned as beneficiaries of the Lord's ministry in the spirit world. They had been guilty of gross offenses, and had wantonly rejected the teachings and admonitions of Noah, the earthly minister of Jehovah. For their flagrant sin they had been destroyed in the flesh, and their spirits had endured in a condition of imprisonment, without hope, from the time of their death to the advent of Christ, who came as a Spirit amongst them. We are not to assume from Peter's illustrative mention of the disobedient antediluvians that they alone were included in the blessed opportunities offered through Christ's ministry in the spirit realm; on the contrary, we conclude in reason and consistency that all whose wickedness in the flesh had

[e] Alma 40:11–14.

[f] 1 Pet. 3:18–20; see Note 2, end of chapter.

brought their spirits into the prison house were sharers in the possibilities of expiation, repentance, and release. Justice demanded that the gospel be preached among the dead as it had been and was to be yet more widely preached among the living. Let us consider the further affirmation of Peter, as part of his pastoral admonition to the members of the primitive Church: "Who shall give account to him that is ready to judge the quick and the dead. For for this cause was the gospel preached also to them that are dead, that they might be judged according to men in the flesh, but live according to God in the spirit."[g]

That Jesus knew, while yet in the body, that His mission as the universal Redeemer and Savior of the race would not be complete when He came to die is sufficiently demonstrated by His words to the casuistical Jews, following the Sabbath day healing at Bethesda: "Verily, verily, I say unto you, The hour is coming, and now is, when the dead shall hear the voice of the Son of God: and they that hear shall live. For as the Father hath life in himself; so hath he given to the Son to have life in himself; and hath given him authority to execute judgment also, because he is the Son of man. Marvel not at this: for the hour is coming, in the which all that are in the graves shall hear his voice, and shall come forth; they that have done good, unto the resurrection of life; and they that have done evil, unto the resurrection of damnation."[h] The solemn truth, that through the Atonement of Christ salvation would be made possible to the dead as well as to the living, was revealed to the prophets centuries before the meridian of time. Isaiah was permitted to foresee the fate of the ungodly, and the state prepared for haughty and rebellious offenders against righteousness; but the dread vision was in part brightened by the deliverance that had been provided. "And it shall come to pass in that day, that the Lord shall punish the host of the high ones that are on high, and the kings of the earth upon the earth. And they shall be gathered together, as prisoners are gathered in the pit, and shall be shut up in the prison, and after many days shall they be visited."[i] To the same mighty prophet was shown the universality of the Savior's atoning victory, as comprising the

---

[g] 1 Pet. 4:5, 6. Note 2, end of chapter.

[h] John 5:25–29.

[i] Isa. 24:21, 22.

redemption of Jew and Gentile, living and dead; and convincingly he voiced the word of revelation: "Thus saith God the Lord, he that created the heavens, and stretched them out; he that spread forth the earth, and that which cometh out of it; he that giveth breath unto the people upon it, and spirit to them that walk therein: I the Lord have called thee in righteousness, and will hold thine hand, and will keep thee, and give thee for a covenant of the people, for a light of the Gentiles; to open the blind eyes, to bring out the prisoners from the prison, and them that sit in darkness out of the prison house."[j]

David, singing the praises of the Redeemer whose dominion should extend even to the souls in hell, shouted in joy at the prospect of deliverance: "Therefore my heart is glad, and my glory rejoiceth: my flesh also shall rest in hope. For thou wilt not leave my soul in hell; neither wilt thou suffer thine Holy One to see corruption. Thou wilt shew me the path of life: in thy presence is fullness of joy; at thy right hand there are pleasures for evermore."[k]

From these and other scriptures it is evident that the ministry of Christ among the disembodied was foreseen, predicted, and accomplished. The fact that the gospel was preached to the dead necessarily implies the possibility of the dead accepting the same and availing themselves of the saving opportunities thereof. In the merciful providence of the Almighty, provision has been made for vicarious service by the living for the dead, in the ordinances essential to salvation; so that all who in the spirit-world accept the word of God as preached to them, develop true faith in Jesus Christ as the one and only Savior, and contritely repent of their transgressions, shall be brought under the saving effect of baptism by water for the remission of sins, and be recipients of the baptism of the Spirit or the bestowal of the Holy Ghost.[l] Paul cites the principle and practice of baptism by the living for the dead as proof of the actuality of the resurrection: "Else what shall they do which are baptized for the dead, if the dead rise not at all? why are they then baptized for the dead?"[m] Free agency, the divine

[j] Isa. 42:5–7.

[k] Ps. 16:9–11.

[l] See *The Articles of Faith*, pp. 145–53, and *The House of the Lord*, pp. 63–93.

[m] 1 Cor. 15:29; see also *The House of the Lord*, p. 92.

birthright of every human soul, will not be annulled by death. Only as the spirits of the dead become penitent and faithful will they be benefited by the vicarious service rendered in their behalf on earth.

Missionary labor among the dead was inaugurated by the Christ; who of us can doubt that it has been continued by His authorized servants, the disembodied, who while in the flesh had been commissioned to preach the gospel and administer in the ordinances thereof through ordination in the Holy Priesthood? That the faithful apostles who were left to build up the Church on earth following the departure of its divine Founder, that other ministers of the word of God ordained to the Priesthood by authority in the Primitive as well as in the Latter-day Church, have passed from ministerial service among mortals to a continuation of such labor among the disembodied, is so abundantly implied in scripture as to be made a certainty. They are called to follow in the footsteps of the Master, ministering here among the living, and beyond among the dead.

The victory of Christ over death and sin would be incomplete were its effects confined to the small minority who have heard, accepted, and lived the gospel of salvation in the flesh. Compliance with the laws and ordinances of the gospel is essential to salvation. Nowhere in scripture is a distinction made in this regard between the living and the dead. The dead are those who have lived in mortality upon earth; the living are mortals who yet shall pass through the ordained change which we call death. All are children of the same Father, all to be judged and rewarded or punished by the same unerring justice, with the same interposition of benign mercy. Christ's atoning sacrifice was offered, not alone for the few who lived upon the earth while He was in the flesh, nor for those who were born in mortality after His death, but for all inhabitants of earth then past, present, and future. He was ordained of the Father to be a judge of both quick and dead;[n] He is Lord alike of living and dead,[o] as men speak of dead and living, though all are to be placed in the same position before Him; there will be but a single class, for all live unto Him.[p] While His body reposed in the tomb, Christ was

[n] Acts 10:42; 2 Tim. 4:1; 1 Pet. 4:5.

[o] Rom. 14:9.

[p] Luke 20:36, 38; *The Articles of Faith*, p. 145.

actively engaged in the further accomplishment of the Father's purposes, by offering the boon of salvation to the dead, both in paradise and in hell.

NOTES TO CHAPTER 36

1. Paradise.—The scriptures prove that at the time of the final judgment every man will stand before the bar of God, clothed in his resurrected body, and this, irrespective of his condition of righteousness or guilt. While awaiting resurrection, disembodied spirits exist in an intermediate state, of happiness and rest or of suffering and suspense, according to the course they have elected to follow in mortality. Reference to paradise as the abode of righteous spirits between the time of death and that of the resurrection is made by the prophet Nephi (2 Ne. 9:13), by a later prophet of the same name (4 Ne. 14), by Moroni; (Moroni 10:34); as also by Alma whose words are quoted in the text (Alma 40:12, 14). New Testament scripture is of analogous import (Luke 23:43; 2 Cor. 12:4; Rev. 2:7). The word "paradise" by its derivation through the Greek from the Persian, signifies a pleasant place, or a place of restful enjoyment. (See *Articles of Faith*, chap. 21, note 5). By many the terms "hades" and "sheol" are understood to designate the place of departed spirits, comprising both paradise and the prison realm; by others the terms are applied only to the latter, the place of the wicked, which is apart from paradise, the abode of the just.

The assumption that the gracious assurance given by Christ to the penitent sinner on the cross was a remission of the man's sins, and a passport into heaven, is wholly contrary to both the letter and spirit of scripture, reason, and justice. Confidence in the efficacy of death-bed professions and confessions on the basis of this incident is of the most insecure foundation. The crucified malefactor manifested both faith and repentance; his promised blessing was that he should that day hear the gospel preached in paradise; in the acceptance or rejection of the word of life he would be an agent unto himself. The requirement of obedience to the laws and ordinances of the gospel as an essential to salvation was not waived, suspended, or superseded in his case.

2. The Scripture Relating to Christ Among the Spirits in Prison.—The revised version of 1 Pet. 3:18–20 reads: "Because Christ also suffered for sins once, the righteous for the unrighteous, that he might bring us to God; being put to death in the flesh, but quickened in the spirit; in which also he went and preached unto the spirits in prison, which aforetime were disobedient, when the longsuffering of God waited in the days of Noah, while the ark was a preparing, wherein few, that is eight souls were saved through water." This is regarded by scholars as a closer approach to accuracy in translation than the common version. Certain important differences between the two versions will appear to the studious reader. The common version of the latter part of verse 18 and the whole of verse 19 reads: "being put to death in the flesh, but quickened, by the spirit: By which also he went and preached unto the spirits in prison." The revised text expresses the true thought that Christ was quickened, that is to say, was active, in His own spirit state, although His body was inert and in reality dead at the time; and that in that disembodied state He went and preached to the disobedient spirits. The later reading fixes the time of our Lord's ministry among the departed as the interval between His death and Resurrection.

CHAPTER 37

THE RESURRECTION AND THE ASCENSION

CHRIST IS RISEN

Saturday, the Jewish Sabbath, had passed, and the night preceding the dawn of the most memorable Sunday in history was well nigh spent, while the Roman guard kept watch over the sealed sepulchre wherein lay the body of the Lord Jesus. While it was yet dark, the earth began to quake; an angel of the Lord descended in glory, rolled back the massive stone from the portal of the tomb, and sat upon it. His countenance was brilliant as the lightning, and his raiment was as the driven snow for whiteness. The soldiers, paralyzed with fear, fell to the earth as dead men. When they had partially recovered from their fright, they fled from the place in terror. Even the rigor of Roman discipline, which decreed summary death to every soldier who deserted his post, could not deter them. Moreover, there was nothing left for them to guard; the seal of authority had been broken, the sepulchre was open, and empty.[a]

At the earliest indication of dawn, the devoted Mary Magdalene and other faithful women set out for the tomb, bearing spices and ointments which they had prepared for the further anointing of the body of Jesus. Some of them had been witnesses of the burial, and were conscious of the necessary haste with which the corpse had been wrapped with spicery and laid away by Joseph and Nicodemus, just before the beginning of the Sabbath; and now these adoring women came early to render loving service in a more thorough anointing and

---

[a] Matt. 28:1–4, see also verse 11.

external embalmment of the body. On the way as they sorrowfully conversed, they seemingly for the first time thought of the difficulty of entering the tomb. "Who shall roll us away the stone from the door of the sepulchre?" they asked one of another. Evidently they knew nothing of the seal and the guard of soldiery. At the tomb they saw the angel, and were afraid; but he said unto them: "Fear not ye: for I know that ye seek Jesus, which was crucified. He is not here: for he is risen, as he said. Come, see the place where the Lord lay. And go quickly, and tell his disciples that he is risen from the dead; and, behold, he goeth before you into Galilee; there shall ye see him: lo, I have told you."[b]

The women, though favored by angelic visitation and assurance, left the place amazed and frightened. Mary Magdalene appears to have been the first to carry word to the disciples concerning the empty tomb. She had failed to comprehend the gladsome meaning of the angel's proclamation "He is risen, as he said"; in her agony of love and grief she remembered only the words "He is not here," the truth of which had been so forcefully impressed by her own hasty glance at the open and tenantless tomb. "Then she runneth, and cometh to Simon Peter, and to the other disciple, whom Jesus loved, and saith unto them, They have taken away the Lord out of the sepulchre, and we know not where they have laid him."

Peter, and "that other disciple" who, doubtless, was John, set forth in haste, running together toward the sepulchre. John outran his companion, and on reaching the tomb stooped to look in, and so caught a glimpse of the linen cerements lying on the floor; but the bold and impetuous Peter rushed into the sepulchre, and was followed by the younger apostle. The two observed the linen grave-clothes, and lying by itself, the napkin that had been placed about the head of the corpse. John frankly affirms that having seen these things, he believed, and explains in behalf of himself and his fellow apostles, "For as yet they knew not the scripture, that he must rise again from the dead."[c]

The sorrowful Magdalene had followed the two apostles back to the garden of the burial. No thought of the Lord's restoration to life

[b] Matt. 28:5–7; compare Mark 16:1–7; Luke 24:1–8; John 20:1–2.
[c] John 20:1–10.

appears to have found place in her grief-stricken heart; she knew only that the body of her beloved Master had disappeared. While Peter and John were within the sepulchre, she had stood without, weeping. After the men had left she stooped and looked into the rock-hewn cavern. There she saw two personages, angels in white; one sat "at the head, and the other at the feet, where the body of Jesus had lain." In accents of tenderness they asked of her: "Woman, why weepest thou?" In reply she could but voice anew her overwhelming sorrow: "Because they have taken away my Lord, and I know not where they have laid him." The absence of the body, which she thought to be all that was left on earth of Him whom she loved so deeply, was a personal bereavement. There is a volume of pathos and affection in her words, "They have taken away my Lord."

Turning from the vault, which, though at that moment illumined by angelic presence, was to her void and desolate, she became aware of another Personage, standing near. She heard His sympathizing inquiry: "Woman, why weepest thou? whom seekest thou?" Scarcely lifting her tearful countenance to look at the Questioner, but vaguely supposing that He was the caretaker of the garden, and that He might have knowledge of what had been done with the body of her Lord, she exclaimed: "Sir, if thou have borne him hence, tell me where thou hast laid him, and I will take him away." She knew that Jesus had been interred in a borrowed tomb; and if the body had been dispossessed of that resting place, she was prepared to provide another. "Tell me where thou hast laid him," she pleaded.

It was Jesus to whom she spake, her beloved Lord, though she knew it not. One word from His living lips changed her agonized grief into ecstatic joy. "Jesus saith unto her, Mary." The voice, the tone, the tender accent she had heard and loved in the earlier days lifted her from the despairing depths into which she had sunk. She turned, and saw the Lord. In a transport of joy she reached out her arms to embrace Him, uttering only the endearing and worshipful word, "Rabboni," meaning My beloved Master. Jesus restrained her impulsive manifestation of reverent love, saying, "Touch me not;[d] for I

---

[d] Revised version, "Take not hold on me" (margin).

am not yet ascended to my Father," and adding, "but go to my brethren, and say unto them, I ascend unto my Father, and your Father; and to my God, and your God."[e]

To a woman, to Mary of Magdala, was given the honor of being the first among mortals to behold a resurrected Soul, and that Soul, the Lord Jesus.[f] To other favored women did the risen Lord next manifest Himself, including Mary the mother of Joses, Joanna, and Salome the mother of the apostles James and John. These and the other women with them had been affrighted by the presence of the angel at the tomb, and had departed with mingled fear and joy. They were not present when Peter and John entered the vault, nor afterward when the Lord made Himself known to Mary Magdalene. They may have returned later, for some of them appear to have entered the sepulchre, and to have seen that the Lord's body was not there. As they stood wondering in perplexity and astonishment, they became aware of the presence of two men in shining garments, and as the women "bowed down their faces to the earth" the angels said unto them: "Why seek ye the living among the dead? He is not here, but is risen: remember how he spake unto you when he was yet in Galilee, saying, The Son of man must be delivered into the hands of sinful men, and be crucified, and the third day rise again. And they remembered his words."[g] As they were returning to the city to deliver the message to the disciples, "Jesus met them, saying, All hail. And they came and held him by the feet, and worshipped him. Then said Jesus unto them, Be not afraid: go tell my brethren that they go into Galilee, and there shall they see me."[h]

One may wonder why Jesus had forbidden Mary Magdalene to touch Him, and then, so soon after, had permitted other women to hold Him by the feet as they bowed in reverence. We may assume that Mary's emotional approach had been prompted more by a feeling of personal yet holy affection than by an impulse of devotional worship such as the other women evinced. Though the resurrected Christ

[e] John 20:11–17.
[f] Mark 16:9.
[g] Luke 24:3–8.
[h] Matt. 28:9, 10.

manifested the same friendly and intimate regard as He had shown in the mortal state toward those with whom He had been closely associated, He was no longer one of them in the literal sense. There was about Him a divine dignity that forbade close personal familiarity. To Mary Magdalene Christ had said: "Touch me not; for I am not yet ascended to my Father." If the second clause was spoken in explanation of the first, we have to infer that no human hand was to be permitted to touch the Lord's resurrected and immortalized body until after He had presented Himself to the Father. It appears reasonable and probable that between Mary's impulsive attempt to touch the Lord, and the action of the other women who held Him by the feet as they bowed in worshipful reverence, Christ did ascend to the Father, and that later He returned to earth to continue His ministry in the resurrected state.

Mary Magdalene and the other women told the wonderful story of their several experiences to the disciples, but the brethren could not credit their words, which "seemed to them as idle tales, and they believed them not."[i] After all that Christ had taught concerning His rising from the dead on that third day,[j] the apostles were unable to accept the actuality of the occurrence; to their minds the resurrection was some mysterious and remote event, not a present possibility. There was neither precedent nor analogy for the stories these women told—of a dead person returning to life, with a body of flesh and bones, such as could be seen and felt—except the instances of the young man of Nain, the daughter of Jairus, and the beloved Lazarus of Bethany, between whose cases of restoration to a renewal of mortal life and the reported Resurrection of Jesus they recognized essential differences. The grief and the sense of irreparable loss which had characterized the yesterday Sabbath, were replaced by profound perplexity and contending doubts on this first day of the week. But while the apostles hesitated to believe that Christ had actually risen, the women, less skeptical, more trustful, knew, for they had both seen Him and heard His voice, and some of them had touched His feet.

[i] Luke 24:9–11; compare Mark 16:9–13.

[j] Note 1, end of chapter.

A PRIESTLY CONSPIRACY OF FALSEHOOD[k]

When the Roman guardsmen had sufficiently recovered from fright to make their precipitate departure from the sepulchre, they went to the chief priests, under whose orders they had been placed by Pilate,[l] and reported the supernatural occurrences they had witnessed. The chief priests were Sadducees, of which sect or party a distinguishing feature was the denial of the possibility of resurrection from the dead. A session of the Sanhedrin was called, and the disturbing report of the guard was considered. In the spirit in which these deceiving hierarchs had tried to kill Lazarus for the purpose of quelling popular interest in the miracle of his restoration to life, they now conspired to discredit the truth of Christ's Resurrection by bribing the soldiers to lie. These were told to say "His disciples came by night, and stole him away while we slept"; and for the falsehood they were offered large sums of money. The soldiers accepted the tempting bribe, and did as they were instructed; for this course appeared to them the best way out of a critical situation. If they were found guilty of sleeping at their posts, immediate death would be their doom;[m] but the Jews encouraged them by the promise: "If this come to the governor's ears, we will persuade him and secure you." It must be remembered that the soldiers had been put at the disposal of the chief priests, and presumably therefore were not required to report the details of their doings to the Roman authorities.

The recorder adds that until the day of his writing, the falsehood of Christ's body having been stolen from the tomb by the disciples was current among the Jews. The utter untenability of the false report is apparent. If all the soldiers were asleep—a most unlikely occurrence inasmuch as such neglect was a capital offense—how could they possibly know that any one had approached the tomb? And, more particularly, how could they substantiate their statement even if it were true, that the body was stolen and that the disciples were the grave-robbers?[n] The mendacious fiction was framed by the chief priests

[k] Matt.28:11–15.

[l] Matt. 27:65, 66.

[m] Compare Acts 12:19.

[n] Note 2, end of chapter.

and elders of the people. Not all the priestly circle were parties to it however. Some, who perhaps had been among the secret disciples of Jesus before His death, were not afraid to openly ally themselves with the Church, when, through the evidence of the Lord's Resurrection, they had become thoroughly converted. We read that but a few months later "a great company of the priests were obedient to the faith."°

CHRIST WALKS AND TALKS
WITH TWO OF THE DISCIPLES ᴾ

During the afternoon of that same Sunday, two disciples, not of the apostles, left the little band of believers in Jerusalem and set out for Emmaus, a village between seven and eight miles from the city. There could be but one topic of conversation between them, and on this they communed as they walked, citing incidents in the Lord's life, dwelling particularly upon the fact of His death through which their hopes of a Messianic reign had been so sadly blighted, and marveling deeply over the incomprehensible testimony of the women concerning His reappearance as a living Soul. As they went, engrossed in sorrowful and profound discourse, another Wayfarer joined them; it was the Lord Jesus, "but their eyes were holden that they should not know him." In courteous interest, He asked: "What manner of communications are these that ye have one to another, as ye walk, and are sad?" One of the disciples, Cleopas by name, replied with surprise tinged with commiseration for the Stranger's seeming ignorance: "Art thou only a stranger in Jerusalem, and hast not known the things which are come to pass there in these days?" Intent on drawing from the men a full statement of the matter by which they were so plainly agitated, the unrecognized Christ asked, "What things?" They could not be reticent. "Concerning Jesus of Nazareth" they explained, "which was a prophet mighty in deed and word before God and all the people: and how the chief priests and our rulers delivered him to be condemned to death, and have crucified him." In sorrowful mood they went on to tell how they had trusted that the now crucified Jesus would have proved to be the Messiah sent to redeem Israel; but alas! this was the third day since He

---

° Acts 6:7; compare John 12:42.

ᴾ Luke 24:13–32; compare Mark 16:12.

had been slain. Then, with brightening countenances, yet still perplexed, they told of certain women of their company who had astonished them that morning by saying that they had visited the sepulchre early and had discovered that the Lord's body was not there, but, "that they had also seen a vision of angels, which said that he was alive." Moreover, others besides the women had gone to the tomb, and had verified the absence of the body but had not seen the Lord.

Then Jesus, gently chiding His fellow travelers as foolish men and slow of heart in their hesitating acceptance of what the prophets had spoken, asked impressively, "Ought not Christ to have suffered these things, and to enter into his glory?" Beginning with the inspired predictions of Moses, He expounded to them the scriptures, touching upon all the prophetic utterances concerning the Savior's mission. Having continued with the two men to their destination Jesus "made as though he would have gone further," but they urged Him to tarry with them, for the day was already far spent. He so far acceded to their hospitable entreaty as to enter the house, and, as soon as their simple meal was prepared, to seat Himself with them at the table. As the Guest of Honor, He took the loaf, "blessed it and brake, and gave to them." There may have been something in the fervency of the blessing, or in the manner of the breaking and distributing the bread, that revived memories of former days; or, possibly, they caught sight of the pierced hands; but, whatever the immediate cause, they looked intently upon their Guest, "and their eyes were opened, and they knew him; and he vanished out of their sight." In a fulness of joyful wonderment they rose from the table, surprised at themselves for not having recognized Him sooner. One said to the other, "Did not our heart burn within us, while he talked with us by the way, and while he opened to us the scriptures?" Straightway they started to retrace their steps and hastened back to Jerusalem to confirm by their witness what, before, the brethren had been slow to believe.

THE RISEN LORD APPEARS TO THE DISCIPLES IN JERUSALEM AND EATS IN THEIR PRESENCE[q]

When Cleopas and his companion reached Jerusalem that night,

---

[q] Luke 24:33–48; John 20:19–23.

they found the apostles and other devoted believers assembled in solemn and worshipful discourse within closed doors. Precautions of secrecy had been taken "for fear of the Jews." Even the apostles had been scattered by the arrest, arraignment, and judicial murder of their Master; but they and the disciples in general rallied anew at the word of His Resurrection, as the nucleus of an army soon to sweep the world. The two returning disciples were received with the joyous announcement, "The Lord is risen indeed, and hath appeared to Simon." This is the sole mention made by the Gospel-writers of Christ's personal appearance to Simon Peter on that day. The interview between the Lord and His once recreant but now repentant apostle must have been affecting in the extreme. Peter's remorseful penitence over his denial of Christ in the palace of the high priest was deep and pitiful; he may have doubted that ever again would the Master call him His servant; but hope must have been engendered through the message from the tomb brought by the women, in which the Lord sent greetings to the apostles, whom for the first time He designated as His brethren,[r] and from this honorable and affectionate characterization Peter had not been excluded; moreover, the angel's commission to the women had given prominence to Peter by particular mention.[s] To the repentant Peter came the Lord, doubtless with forgiveness and loving assurance. The apostle himself maintains a reverent silence respecting the visitation, but the fact thereof is attested by Paul as one of the definite proofs of the Lord's Resurrection.[t]

Following the jubilant testimony of the assembled believers, Cleopas and his fellow traveler told of the Lord's companionship with them on the Emmaus road, of the things He had taught them, and of the manner in which He had become known unto them in the breaking of bread. As the little company communed together, "Jesus himself stood in the midst of them, and saith unto them, Peace be unto you." They were affrighted, supposing with superstitious dread that a ghost had intruded amongst them. But the Lord comforted them, saying "Why are ye troubled? and why do thoughts rise in your

[r] Matt. 28:10; John 20:17.
[s] Mark 16:7.
[t] 1 Cor. 15:5.

hearts? Behold my hands and my feet, that it is I myself: handle me, and see; for a spirit hath not flesh and bones, as ye see me have." Then He showed them the wounds in His hands and feet and side. "They yet believed not for joy," which is to say, they thought the reality, to which they all were witnesses, too good, too glorious, to be true. To further assure them that He was no shadowy form, no immaterial being of tenuous substance, but a living Personage with bodily organs internal as well as outward, He asked, "Have ye here any meat?" They gave Him a piece of broiled fish and other food[u] which He took "and did eat before them."

These unquestionable evidences of their Visitant's corporeity calmed and made rational the minds of the disciples; and now that they were composed and receptive the Lord reminded them that all things that had happened to Him were in accordance with what He had told them while He had lived amongst them. In His divine presence their understanding was quickened and enlarged so that they comprehended as never before the scriptures—the Law of Moses, the books of the prophets and the psalms—concerning Him. That His now accomplished death was a necessity, He attested as fully as He had predicted and affirmed the same aforetime. Then He said unto them: "Thus it is written, and thus it behoved Christ to suffer, and to rise from the dead the third day: and that repentance and remission of sins should be preached in his name among all nations, beginning at Jerusalem. And ye are witnesses of these things."

Then were the disciples glad. As He was about to depart the Lord gave them His blessing, saying, "Peace be unto you: as my Father hath sent me, even so send I you." This specification of men sent by authority points directly to the apostles; "And when he had said this, he breathed on them, and saith unto them, Receive ye the Holy Ghost: whose soever sins ye remit, they are remitted unto them; and whose soever sins ye retain, they are retained."[v]

---

[u] The words "and of an honeycomb" (Luke 24:42) are omitted from the revised version, and by many authorities are declared to be a spurious addition to the original text.

[v] John 20:21–23.

DOUBTING THOMAS[w]

When the Lord Jesus appeared in the midst of the disciples on the evening of the Resurrection Sunday, one of the apostles, Thomas, was absent. He was informed of what the others had witnessed, but was unconvinced; even their solemn testimony, "We have seen the Lord," failed to awaken an echo of faith in his heart. In his state of mental skepticism he exclaimed: "Except I shall see in his hands the print of the nails, and put my finger into the print of the nails, and thrust my hand into his side, I will not believe." Caution and charity must attend our judgment in any conclusion as to the incredulous attitude of this man. He could scarcely have doubted the well attested circumstance of the empty sepulchre, nor the veracity of Mary Magdalene and the other women as to the presence of angels and the Lord's appearing, nor Peter's testimony nor that of the assembled company; but he may have regarded the reported manifestations as a series of subjective visions; and the absence of the Lord's body may have been vaguely considered as a result of Christ's supernatural restoration to life followed by a bodily and final departure from earth. It was the corporeal manifestation of the risen Lord, the exhibition of the wounds incident to crucifixion, the invitation to touch and feel the resurrected body of flesh and bones, to which Thomas demurred. He had no such definite conception of the resurrection as would accord with a literal acceptance of the testimony of his brethren and sisters who had seen, heard, and felt.

A week later, for so the Jewish designation, "after eight days," is to be understood, therefore on the next Sunday, which day of the week afterward came to be known to the Church as the "Lord's Day" and to be observed as the Sabbath in place of Saturday, the Mosaic Sabbath,[x] the disciples were again assembled, and Thomas was with them. The meeting was held within closed and, presumably, guarded doors, for there was danger of interference by the Jewish officers. "Then came Jesus, the doors being shut, and stood in the midst, and said, Peace be unto you. Then saith he to Thomas, Reach hither thy finger, and behold my hands; and reach hither thy hand, and thrust it into my side: and be not faithless, but believing."

---

[w] John 20:24–29; compare Mark 16:14.

[x] Rev. 1:10; compare Acts 20:7; 1 Cor. 16:2.

The skeptical mind of Thomas was instantly cleansed, his doubting heart was purified; and a conviction of the glorious truth flooded his soul. In contrite reverence he bowed before his Savior, the while exclaiming in worshipful acknowledgment of Christ's Deity: "My Lord and my God." His adoration was accepted, and the Savior said: "Thomas, because thou hast seen me, thou hast believed: blessed are they that have not seen, and yet have believed."

AT THE SEA OF GALILEE[y]

The angel at the sepulchre and the risen Christ Himself had severally sent word to the apostles to go into Galilee, where the Lord would meet them as He had said before His death.[z] They deferred their departure until after the week following the Resurrection, and then once again in their native province, they awaited further developments. In the afternoon of one of those days of waiting, Peter said to six of his fellow apostles, "I go a fishing"; and the others replied, "We also go with thee." Without delay they embarked on a fishing boat; and though they toiled through the night, the net had been drawn in empty after every cast. As morning approached they drew near the land, disappointed and disheartened. In the early dawn they were hailed from the shore by One who asked: "Children, have ye any meat?"[aa] They answered "No." It was Jesus who made the inquiry, though none in the boat recognized Him. He called to them again, saying: "Cast the net on the right side of the ship, and ye shall find. They cast therefore, and now they were not able to draw it for the multitude of fishes." They did as directed and the result was so surprising as to appear to them miraculous; it must have aroused memories of that other remarkable draught of fishes, in the taking of which their fishermen's skill had been superseded; and at least three witnesses of the earlier miracle were now in the boat.[bb]

John, quick to discern, said to Peter, "It is the Lord"; and Peter, impulsive as ever, hastily girt his fisher's coat about him and sprang

[y] John 21:1–23.

[z] Matt. 28:10; Mark 16:7; compare Matt. 26:32, Mark 14:28.

[aa] The noun of address, "Children" is equivalent to our modern use of "Sirs," "Men" or "Lads." It was quite in harmony with the vernacular.

[bb] Luke 5:4–10.

into the sea, the sooner to reach land and prostrate himself at his Master's feet. The others left the vessel and entered a small boat in which they rowed to shore, towing the heavily laden net. On the land they saw a fire of coals, with fish broiling thereon, and alongside a supply of bread. Jesus told them to bring of the fish they had just caught, to which instruction the stalwart Peter responded by dashing into the shallows and dragging the net to shore. When counted, the haul was found to consist of a hundred and fifty-three great fishes; and the narrator is careful to note that "for all there were so many, yet was not the net broken."

Then Jesus said, "Come and dine"; and as the Host at the meal, He divided and distributed the bread and fish. We are not told that He ate with His guests. Everyone knew that it was the Lord who so hospitably served; yet on this, as on all other occasions of His appearing in the resurrected state, there was about Him an awe-inspiring and restraining demeanor. They would have liked to question Him, but durst not. John tells us that this was the "third time that Jesus shewed himself to his disciples, after that he was risen from the dead"; by which we understand the occasion to have been the third on which Christ had manifested Himself to the apostles, in complete or partial assembly; for, including also the appearing to Mary Magdalene, to the other women, to Peter, and to the two disciples on the country road, this was the seventh recorded appearance of the risen Lord.

When the meal was finished, "Jesus saith to Simon Peter, Simon, son of Jonas, lovest thou me more than these?" The question, however tenderly put, must have wrung Peter's heart, coupled as it was with the reminder of his bold but undependable protestation, "Though all men shall be offended because of thee, yet will I never be offended";[cc] followed by his denial that he had ever known the Man.[dd] To the Lord's inquiry Peter answered humbly, "Yea, Lord; thou knowest that I love thee." Then said Jesus, "Feed my lambs." The question was repeated; and Peter replied in identical words, to which the Lord responded, "Feed my sheep." And yet the third time Jesus asked, "Simon, son of

[cc] Matt. 26:33; Mark 14:29; compare Luke 22:33; John 13:37.

[dd] Matt. 26:70, 72, 74.

Jonas, lovest thou me?" Peter was pained and grieved at this reiteration, thinking perhaps that the Lord mistrusted him; but as the man had three times denied, so now was he given opportunity for a triple confession. To the thrice repeated question, Peter answered: "Lord, thou knowest all things; thou knowest that I love thee. Jesus saith unto him, Feed my sheep."

The commission "Feed my sheep" was an assurance of the Lord's confidence, and of the reality of Peter's presidency among the apostles. He had emphatically announced his readiness to follow his Master even to prison and death. Now, the Lord who had died said unto him: "Verily, verily, I say unto thee, When thou wast young, thou girdest thyself, and walkedst whither thou wouldst: but when thou shalt be old, thou shalt stretch forth thy hands, and another shall gird thee, and carry thee whither thou wouldst not." John informs us that the Lord so spake signifying the death by which Peter should find a place among the martyrs; the analogy points to crucifixion, and traditional history is without contradiction as to this being the death by which Peter sealed his testimony of the Christ.

Then said the Lord to Peter, "Follow me." The command had both immediate and future significance. The man followed as Jesus drew apart from the others on the shore; yet a few years and Peter would follow his Lord to the cross. Without doubt Peter comprehended the reference to his martyrdom, as his writings, years later, indicate.[ee] As Christ and Peter walked together, the latter, looking backward, saw that John was following, and inquired: "Lord, and what shall this man do?" Peter wished to peer into the future as to his companion's fate—was John also to die for the faith? The Lord replied: "If I will that he tarry till I come, what is that to thee? follow thou me." It was an admonition to Peter to look to his own course of duty, and to follow the Master, wherever the road should lead.

Concerning himself, John adds: "Then went this saying abroad among the brethren, that that disciple should not die: yet Jesus said not unto him, He shall not die; but, If I will that he tarry till I come, what is that to thee?" That John still lives in the embodied state, and

[ee] 2 Pet. 1:14.

shall remain in the flesh until the Lord's yet future advent, is attested by later revelation.[ff] In company with his martyred and resurrected companions, Peter and James, the "disciple whom Jesus loved" has officiated in the restoration of the Holy Apostleship in this the dispensation of the fulness of times.

OTHER MANIFESTATIONS
OF THE RISEN LORD IN GALILEE[gg]

Jesus had designated a mountain in Galilee whereon He would meet the apostles; and thither the Eleven went. When they saw Him at the appointed place, they worshiped Him. The record adds "but some doubted," by which may be implied that others beside the apostles were present, among whom were some who were unconvinced of the actual corporeity of the resurrected Christ. This occasion may have been that of which Paul wrote a quarter of a century later, concerning which he affirms that Christ "was seen of above five hundred brethren at once," of whom, though some had died, the majority remained at the time of Paul's writing, living witnesses to his testimony.[hh]

To those assembled on the mount Jesus declared: "All power is given unto me in heaven and in earth." This could be understood as nothing less than an affirmation of His absolute Godship. His authority was supreme, and those who were commissioned of Him were to minister in His name, and by a power such as no man could give or take away.

THE FINAL COMMISSION AND THE ASCENSION

Throughout the forty days following His Resurrection, the Lord manifested Himself at intervals to the apostles, to some individually and to all as a body,[ii] and instructed them in "the things pertaining to the kingdom of God."[jj] The record is not always specific and definite as to time and place of particular events; but as to the purport of the

[ff] D&C 7; compare 3 Ne. 28:1–12.

[gg] Matt. 28:16–18.

[hh] 1 Cor. 15:6.

[ii] Note 3, end of chapter.

[jj] Acts 1:3.

Lord's instruction during this period there exists no cause for doubt. Much that He said and did is not written [kk] but such things as are of record, John assures his readers, "are written, that ye might believe that Jesus is the Christ, the Son of God; and that believing ye might have life through his name."[ll]

As the time of His ascension drew nigh, the Lord said unto the eleven apostles: "Go ye into all the world, and preach the gospel to every creature. He that believeth and is baptized shall be saved; but he that believeth not shall be damned. And these signs shall follow them that believe; In my name shall they cast out devils; they shall speak with new tongues; they shall take up serpents; and if they drink any deadly thing, it shall not hurt them; they shall lay hands on the sick, and they shall recover."[mm] In contrast with their earlier commission, under which they were sent only "to the lost sheep of the house of Israel,"[nn] they were now to go to Jew and Gentile, bond and free, to mankind at large, of whatever nation, country, or tongue. Salvation, through faith in Jesus the Christ, followed by repentance and baptism, was to be freely offered to all; the rejection of the offer thenceforth would bring condemnation. Signs and miracles were promised to "follow them that believe," thus confirming their faith in the power divine; but no intimation was given that such manifestations were to precede belief, as baits to catch the credulous wonder-seeker.

Assuring the apostles anew that the promise of the Father would be realized in the coming of the Holy Ghost, the Lord instructed them to remain in Jerusalem, whither they had now returned from Galilee, until they would be "endued with power from on high";[oo] and He added: "For John truly baptized with water; but ye shall be baptized with the Holy Ghost not many days hence."[pp]

---

kk John 20:30; compare 21:25, remembering that the latter passage may have reference to occurrences both before and after the Lord's death.

ll John 20:31.

mm Mark 16:15–18.

nn Matt. 10:5, 6.

oo "Clothed with power from on high" according to revised version, Luke 24:29.

pp Acts 1:5; see also Luke 24:49; and compare John 14:16, 17, 26; 15:26; 16:7,13.

In that last solemn interview, probably as the risen Savior led the mortal Eleven away from the city toward the old familiar resort on the Mount of Olives, the brethren, still imbued with their conception of the kingdom of God as an earthly establishment of power and dominion, asked of Him, "Lord, wilt thou at this time restore again the kingdom to Israel?" Jesus answered, "It is not for you to know the times or the seasons, which the Father hath put in his own power. But ye shall receive power, after that the Holy Ghost is come upon you: and ye shall be witnesses unto me both in Jerusalem, and in all Judea, and in Samaria, and unto the uttermost part of the earth."[qq] Their duty was thus defined and emphasized: "Go ye therefore, and teach all nations, baptizing them in the name of the Father, and of the Son, and of the Holy Ghost: teaching them to observe all things whatsoever I have commanded you: and, lo, I am with you alway, even unto the end of the world. Amen."[rr]

When Christ and the disciples had gone "as far as to Bethany," the Lord lifted up His hands, and blessed them; and while yet He spake, He rose from their midst, and they looked upon Him as He ascended until a cloud received Him out of their sight. While the apostles stood gazing steadfastly upward, two personages, clothed in white apparel, appeared by them; these spake unto the Eleven, saying: "Ye men of Galilee, why stand ye gazing up into heaven? this same Jesus, which is taken up from you into heaven, shall so come in like manner as ye have seen him go into heaven."[ss]

Worshipfully and with great joy the apostles returned to Jerusalem, there to await the coming of the Comforter. The Lord's ascension was accomplished; it was as truly a literal departure of a material Being as His Resurrection had been an actual return of His spirit to His own corporeal body, theretofore dead. With the world abode and yet abides the glorious promise, that Jesus the Christ, the same Being who ascended from Olivet in His immortalized body of flesh and bones, shall return, descending from the heavens, in similarly material form and substance.

[qq] Acts 1:7, 8; compare Matt. 24:36; Mark 13:32.
[rr] Matt. 28:19, 20.
[ss] Acts 1:9–11; see also Luke 24:50, 51.

NOTES TO CHAPTER 37

1. Precise Time and Manner of Christ's Emergence from the Tomb Not Known.—
Our Lord definitely predicted His Resurrection from the dead on the third day,
(Matt. 16:21; 17:23; 20:19; Mark 9:31; 10:34; Luke 9:22; 13:32; 18:33), and the
angels at the tomb (Luke 24:7), and the risen Lord in Person (Luke 24:46) verified
the fulfilment of the prophecies; and apostles so testified in later years (Acts 10:40;
1 Cor. 15:4). This specification of the third day must not be understood as meaning
after three full days. The Jews began their counting of the daily hours with sunset;
therefore the hour before sunset and the hour following belonged to different days.
Jesus died and was interred during Friday afternoon. His body lay in the tomb, dead,
during part of Friday (first day), throughout Saturday, or as we divide the days, from
sunset Friday to sunset Saturday, (second day), and part of Sunday (third day). We
know not at what hour between Saturday sunset and Sunday dawn he rose.

The fact that an earthquake occurred, and that the angel of the Lord descended
and rolled the stone from the portal of the tomb in the early dawn of Sunday—for
so we infer from Matt. 28:1, 2—does not prove that Christ had not already risen.
The great stone was rolled back and the inside of the sepulchre exposed to view, so
that those who came could see for themselves that the Lord's body was no longer
there; it was not necessary to open the portal in order to afford an exit to the
resurrected Christ. In His immortalized state He appeared in and disappeared from
closed rooms. A resurrected body, though of tangible substance, and possessing all
the organs of the mortal tabernacle, is not bound to earth by gravitation, nor can it
be hindered in its movements by material barriers. To us who conceive of motion
only in the directions incident to the three dimensions of space, the passing of a
solid, such as a living body of flesh and bones, through stone walls, is necessarily
incomprehensible. But that resurrected beings move in accordance with laws
making such passage possible and to them natural, is evidenced not only by the
instance of the risen Christ, but by the movements of other resurrected personages.
Thus, in September, 1823, Moroni, the Nephite prophet who had died about A.D.
400, appeared to Joseph Smith in his chamber, three times during one night, coming
and going without hindrance incident to walls of roof (see JS-H 2:43; also *Articles of
Faith*, pp. 9–11). That Moroni was a resurrected man is shown by his corporeity
manifested in his handling of the metallic plates on which was inscribed the record
known to us as the Book of Mormon. So also resurrected beings possess the power of
rendering themselves visible or invisible to the physical vision of mortals.

2. Attempts to Discredit the Resurrection Through Falsehood.—The inconsistent
assertion that Christ had not risen but that His body had been stolen from the
tomb by the disciples, has been sufficiently treated in the text. The falsehood is its
own refutation. Unbelievers of later date, recognizing the palpable absurdity of this
gross attempt at misrepresentation, have not hesitated to suggest other hypotheses,
each of which is conclusively untenable. Thus, the theory based upon the impossible

assumption that Christ was not dead when taken from the cross, but was in a state of coma or swoon, and that He was afterward resuscitated, disproves itself when considered in connection with recorded facts. The spear-thrust of the Roman soldier would have been fatal, even if death had not already occurred. The body was taken down, handled, wrapped and buried by members of the Jewish council, who cannot be thought of as actors in the burial of a living man; and so far as subsequent resuscitation is concerned, Edersheim (vol. 2, p. 626) trenchantly remarks: "Not to speak of the many absurdities which this theory involves, it really shifts—if we acquit the disciples of complicity—the fraud upon Christ Himself." A crucified person, removed from the cross before death and subsequently revived, could not have walked with pierced and mangled feet on the very day of his resuscitation, as Jesus did on the road to Emmaus. Another theory that has had its day is that of unconscious deception on the part of those who claimed to have seen the resurrected Christ, such persons having been victims of subjective but unreal visions conjured up by their own excited and imaginative condition. The independence and marked individuality of the several recorded appearings of the Lord disprove the vision theory. Such subjective visual illusions as are predicated by this hypothesis, presuppose a state of expectancy on the part of those who think they see; but all the incidents connected with the manifestations of Jesus after His Resurrection were directly opposed to the expectations of those who were made witnesses of His resurrected state.

The foregoing instances of false and untenable theories regarding the Resurrection of our Lord are cited as examples of the numerous abortive attempts to explain away the greatest miracle and the most glorious fact of history. The Resurrection of Jesus Christ is attested by evidence more conclusive than that upon which rests our acceptance of historical events in general. Yet the testimony of our Lord's rising from the dead is not founded on written pages. To him who seeks in faith and sincerity shall be given an individual conviction which shall enable him to reverently confess as exclaimed the enlightened apostle of old: "Thou art the Christ, the Son of the living God." Jesus, who is God the Son, is not dead. "I know that my Redeemer liveth." (Job 19:25.)

3. Recorded Appearances of Christ Between Resurrection and Ascension.—
1. To Mary Magdalene, near the sepulchre (Mark 16:9, 10; John 20:14).
2. To other women, somewhere between the sepulchre and Jerusalem (Matt. 28:9).
3. To two disciples on the road to Emmaus (Mark 16:12; Luke 24:13).
4. To Peter, in or near Jerusalem (Luke 24:34; 1 Cor. 15:5).
5. To ten of the apostles and others at Jerusalem (Luke 24:36; John 20:19).
6. To the eleven apostles at Jerusalem (Mark 16:14; John 20:26).
7. To the apostles at the Sea of Tiberias, Galilee, (John 21).
8. To the eleven apostles on a mountain in Galilee (Matt. 28:16).
9. To five hundred brethren at once (1 Cor. 15:6); locality not specified, but probably in Galilee.

10. To James (1 Cor. 15–7). Note that no record of this manifestation is made by the Gospel-writers.

11. To the eleven apostles at the time of the ascension, Mount of Olives, near Bethany (Mark 16:19; Luke 24:50, 51).

The Lord's manifestations of Himself to men subsequent to the ascension will be considered later.

CHAPTER 38

THE APOSTOLIC MINISTRY

MATTHIAS ORDAINED TO THE APOSTLESHIP[a]

After witnessing the Lord's ascension from Olivet, the eleven apostles returned to Jerusalem filled with joy and thoroughly suffused with the spirit of adoring worship. Both in the temple and in a certain upper room, which was their usual place of meeting, they continued in prayer and supplication, often in association with other disciples, including Mary the mother of the Lord, some of her sons, and the little sisterhood of faithful women who had ministered to Jesus in Galilee and had followed Him thence to Jerusalem and to Calvary.[b] The disciples, most of whom had been dispersed by the tragic events of that last and fateful Passover, had gathered again, with renewed and fortified faith, about the great fact of the Lord's Resurrection. Christ had become "the first-fruits of them that slept," "the first begotten of the dead," and "the first-born" of the race to rise from death to immortality.[c] They knew that not only had the grave been compelled to give up the body of their Lord, but that a way had been provided for the striking of the fetters of death from every soul. Immediately following the Resurrection of the Lord Jesus, many righteous ones who had slept in the tomb had been resurrected, and had appeared in Jerusalem, revealing themselves unto many.[d] The universality of the resurrection of the dead was soon to become a prominent feature of apostolic teaching.

[a] Acts 1:15–26.

[b] Luke 24:52, 53; Acts 1:12–14.

[c] 1 Cor. 15:20; Rev. 1:5; Col. 1:18.

[d] Matt. 27:52, 53.

The first official act undertaken by the apostles was the filling of the vacancy in the council of the Twelve, occasioned by the apostasy and suicide of Judas Iscariot. Sometime between the ascension of Christ and the feast of Pentecost, when the Eleven and other disciples, in all about a hundred and twenty, were together "with one accord in prayer and supplication," Peter laid the matter before the assembled Church, pointing out that the fall of Judas had been foreseen,ᵉ and citing the psalmist's invocation: "Let his habitation be desolate, and let no man dwell therein: and his bishoprick let another take."ᶠ Peter affirmed the necessity of completing the apostolic quorum; and he thus set forth the qualifications essential in the one who should be ordained to the Holy Apostleship; "Wherefore of these men which have companied with us all the time that the Lord Jesus went in and out among us, beginning from the baptism of John, unto that same day that he was taken up from us, must one be ordained to be a witness with us of his resurrection." Two faithful disciples were nominated by the Eleven, Joseph Barsabas and Matthias. In earnest supplication the assembly besought the Lord to indicate whether either of these men, and if so which, was to be chosen for the exalted office; then, "they gave forth their lots; and the lot fell upon Matthias; and he was numbered with the eleven apostles."

The proceeding throughout is deeply significant and instructive. The Eleven fully realized that on them lay the responsibility, and in them was vested the authority, to organize and develop the Church of Christ; that the council or quorum of the apostles was limited to a membership of twelve; and that the new apostle, like themselves, must be competent to testify in special and personal witness concerning the earthly ministry, death, and Resurrection of the Lord Jesus. The selection of Matthias was accomplished in a general assembly of the primitive Church; and while the nominations were made by the apostles, all present appear by implication to have had a voice in the matter of installation. The principle of authoritative administration through

---

ᵉ Acts 1:16; compare Ps. 41:9; see also John 13:18.

ᶠ Acts 1:20. The revised version substitutes on a preponderance of authority "office" or, (marginal reading), "overseership," for the erroneous rendering "bishoprick" in the common version. Compare Ps. 109:8.

common consent of the membership, so impressively exemplified in the choosing of Matthias, was followed, a few weeks later, by the selection of "seven men of honest report, full of the Holy Ghost and wisdom," who having been sustained by the vote of the Church, were set apart to a special ministry by the laying-on of the apostles' hands.[g]

THE BESTOWAL OF THE HOLY GHOST[h]

At the time of Pentecost, which fell on the fiftieth day after the Passover,[i] and therefore, at this particular recurrence, about nine days after Christ's ascension, the apostles "were all with one accord in one place," engaged in their customary devotions, and waiting, as instructed, until they would be endowed with a particular bestowal of power from on high.[j] The promised baptism by fire and the Holy Ghost befell them on that day. "Suddenly there came a sound from heaven as of a rushing mighty wind, and it filled all the house where they were sitting. And there appeared unto them cloven tongues like as of fire, and it sat upon each of them. And they were all filled with the Holy Ghost, and began to speak with other tongues, as the Spirit gave them utterance."

The "sound from heaven as of a rushing mighty wind" was heard abroad;[k] and a multitude gathered about the place. The visible manifestation of "cloven tongues like as of fire," by which each of the Twelve was invested, was seen by those within the house, but apparently not by the gathering crowds. The apostles spoke to the multitude, and a great miracle was wrought, by which "every man heard them speak in his own language"; for the apostles, now richly gifted, spake in many tongues, as the Holy Ghost, by whom they had been endowed, gave them utterance. There were present men from many lands and of many nations, and their languages were diverse. In amazement some of them said: "Behold, are not all these which speak

[g] Acts 6:1–6; Note 1, end of chapter.

[h] Acts 2:1–41. Note 7, end of chapter.

[i] Note 2, end of chapter.

[j] Luke 24:49; Acts 1:4, 5, 8.

[k] Acts 2:6, in a better rendering than that of the common text (see revised version) reads: "And when this sound was heard, the multitude came together."

Galileans? And how hear we every man in our own tongue, wherein we were born?" While many were impressed by the preternatural ability of the brethren, others in mocking tones said the men were drunken. This instance of Satanic prompting to inconsiderate speech is especially illustrative of inconsistency and rash ineptitude. Strong drink gives to no man wisdom; it steals away his senses and makes of him a fool.

Then Peter, as the president of the Twelve, stood up and proclaimed in behalf of himself and his brethren: "Ye men of Judea, and all ye that dwell at Jerusalem, be this known unto you, and hearken to my words: for these are not drunken, as ye suppose, seeing it is but the third hour of the day." It was the Jewish custom, particularly on festival days, to abstain from food and drink until after the morning service in synagog, which was held about the third hour, or nine o'clock in the forenoon. The apostle cited ancient prophecy embodying the promise of Jehovah that He would pour out His Spirit upon all flesh, so that wonders would be wrought, even as those there present witnessed.[1] Then boldly did Peter testify of Jesus of Nazareth, whom he characterized as "a man approved of God among you by miracles and wonders and signs, which God did by him in the midst of you, as ye yourselves also know"; and, reminding them, in accusing earnestness, of the awful crime to which they had been in some degree parties, he continued: "Him, being delivered by the determinate counsel and foreknowledge of God, ye have taken, and by wicked hands have crucified and slain: whom God hath raised up, having loosed the pains of death: because it was not possible that he should be holden of it." Citing the inspired outburst of the psalmist, who had sung in jubilant measure of the soul that should not be left in hell, and of the flesh that should not see corruption, he showed the application of these scriptures to the Christ; and fearlessly affirmed: "This Jesus hath God raised up, whereof we all are witnesses. Therefore being by the right hand of God exalted, and having received of the Father the promise of the Holy Ghost, he hath shed forth this, which ye now see and hear." With increasing fervency, fearing neither derision nor

---

[1] Joel 2:28,29; compare Zech. 12:10.

violence, and driving home to the hearts of his enthralled listeners the fearful fact of their guilt, Peter proclaimed as in voice of thunder: "Therefore let all the house of Israel know assuredly, that God hath made that same Jesus, whom ye have crucified, both Lord and Christ."

The power of the Holy Ghost could not be resisted; to every earnest soul it carried conviction. They that heard were pricked in their hearts, and in contrition cried out to the apostles: "Men and brethren, what shall we do?" Now that they were prepared for the message of salvation, It was given without reserve. "Repent," answered Peter, "and be baptized every one of you in the name of Jesus Christ for the remission of sins, and ye shall receive the gift of the Holy Ghost. For the promise is unto you, and to your children, and to all that are afar off, even as many as the Lord our God shall call."

To the apostles' testimony, to the exhortation and warning, the people responded with profession of faith and repentance. Their joy was comparable to that of the spirits in prison, to whom the disembodied Christ had borne the authoritative word of redemption and salvation. Those who repented and confessed their belief in Christ at that memorable Pentecost were received into the Church by baptism, to the number of about three thousand. That their conversion was genuine and not the effect of a passing enthusiasm, that they were literally born again through baptism into a newness of life, is evidenced by the fact that they endured in the faith—"and they continued stedfastly in the apostles' doctrine and fellowship, and in breaking of bread, and in prayers." So devoted were these early converts, so richly blessed with the outpouring of the Holy Ghost was the Church in those days, that the members voluntarily disposed of their individual possessions and had all things in common. To them faith in the Lord Jesus Christ was of greater worth than the wealth of earth.[m] Among them, there was nothing called "mine" or "thine," but all things were theirs in the Lord.[n] Signs and wonders followed the apostles, "and the Lord added to the church daily such as should be saved."

Through the bestowal of the Holy Ghost the apostles had become changed men. As made clear to them by the Spirit of Truth, the

[m] Note 3, end of chapter.

[n] Acts 2:44–46; 4:32–37; 6:1–4.

scriptures constituted a record of preparation for the events to which they were special and ordained witnesses. Peter, who but a few weeks earlier had quailed before a serving-maid, now spoke openly, fearing none. Seeing once a lame beggar at the Gate Beautiful which led into the temple court, he took the afflicted one by the hand, saying: "Silver and gold have I none; but such as I have give I thee: In the name of Jesus Christ of Nazareth rise up and walk."° The man was healed and leaped in the exuberance of his newly found strength; then he went with Peter and John into the temple, praising God aloud. An amazed crowd, which grew to include about five thousand men, gathered around the apostles in Solomon's Porch; and Peter, observing their wonderment, seized on the occasion to preach to them Jesus the Crucified. He ascribed all praise for the miracle to the Christ whom the Jews had delivered up to be slain, and in unambiguous accusation declared: "The God of Abraham, and of Isaac, and of Jacob, the God of our fathers, hath glorified his Son Jesus; whom ye delivered up, and denied him in the presence of Pilate, when he was determined to let him go. But ye denied the Holy One and the Just, and desired a murderer to be granted unto you; and killed the Prince of life, whom God hath raised from the dead; whereof we are witnesses." In merciful recognition of the ignorance in which they had sinned, he exhorted them to expiatory penitence, crying: "Repent ye therefore, and be converted, that your sins may be blotted out, when the times of refreshing shall come from the presence of the Lord; and he shall send Jesus Christ, which before was preached unto you: whom the heaven must receive until the times of restitution of all things, which God hath spoken by the mouth of all his holy prophets since the world began." There was no encouragement to a belief that their sins could be annulled by wordy profession; a due season of repentance was their privilege, if so be they would believe.

As Peter and John thus testified, the priests and the captain of the temple, together with the ruling Sadducees, came upon them toward evening, and put them in prison to await the action of the judges next day.ᵖ On the morrow they were arraigned before Annas, Caiaphas,

---

° Acts 3:6; read the entire chapter.

ᵖ Acts 4:1–22.

and other officials, who demanded of them by what power or in whose name they had healed the lame man. Peter, impelled by the power of the Holy Ghost, answered: "Be it known unto you all, and to all the people of Israel, that by the name of Jesus Christ of Nazareth, whom ye crucified, whom God raised from the dead, even by him doth this man stand here before you whole. This is the stone which was set at nought of you builders, which is become the head of the corner. Neither is there salvation in any other: for there is none other name under heaven given among men, whereby we must be saved."[q]

The hierarchy learned to their consternation that the work they had sought to destroy through the Crucifixion of Jesus Christ was spreading now as it had never spread before. In desperation they commanded the apostles, "Not to speak at all nor teach in the name of Jesus." But Peter and John answered boldly: "Whether it be right in the sight of God to hearken unto you more than unto God, judge ye. For we cannot but speak the things which we have seen and heard." This rejoinder of righteous defiance the priestly rulers dared not openly resent; they had to content themselves with threats.

The Church grew with surprising rapidity; "believers were the more added to the Lord, multitudes both of men and women." So abundantly was the gift of healing manifest through the ministrations of the apostles that as formerly to Christ, now to them, the people flocked, bringing their sick folk and those possessed of evil spirits; and all were healed. So great was the faith of the believers that they laid their afflicted ones on couches in the streets, "that at the least shadow of Peter passing by might overshadow some of them."[r]

The high priest and his haughty Sadducean associates caused the apostles to be again arrested and thrown into the common prison. But that night the angel of the Lord opened the dungeon doors and brought the prisoners forth, telling them to go into the temple and further proclaim their testimony of the Christ. This the apostles did, and were so engaged when the Sanhedrin assembled to put them on trial. The officers who were sent to bring the prisoners to the judgment hall returned, saying: "The prison truly found we shut with all safety,

[q] Acts 4:8–12; compare Ps. 118:22; Isa. 28:16; Matt. 21:42.
[r] Acts 5:12–17.

and the keepers standing without before the doors; but when we had opened, we found no man within." As the judges sat in impotent consternation, an informer appeared with the word that the men they wanted were at that moment preaching in the courts. The captain and his guard arrested the apostles a third time, and brought them in, but without violence, for they feared the people. The high priest accused the prisoners by question and affirmation: "Did not we straitly command you that ye should not teach in this name? and, behold, ye have filled Jerusalem with your doctrine, and intend to bring this man's blood upon us." Yet, how recently had those same rulers led the rabble in the awful imprecation, "His blood be on us, and on our children."[s]

Peter and the other apostles, undaunted by the august presence, and undeterred by threatening words or actions, answered with the direct counter-charge that they who sat there to judge were the slayers of the Son of God. Ponder well the solemn affirmation: "We ought to obey God rather than men. The God of our fathers raised up Jesus, whom ye slew and hanged on a tree. Him hath God exalted with his right hand to be a Prince and a Saviour, for to give repentance to Israel, and forgiveness of sins. And we are his witnesses of these things; and so is also the Holy Ghost, whom God hath given to them that obey him."

Closing, locking, bolting their hearts against the testimony of the Lord's own, the chief priests, scribes, and elders of the people counseled together as to how they could put these men to death. There was at least one honorable exception among the murderously inclined councilors. Gamaliel, who was a Pharisee and a noted doctor of the law, the teacher of Saul of Tarsus afterward known through conversion, works, and divine commission, as Paul the apostle,[t] rose in the council, and having directed that the apostles be removed from the hall, warned his colleagues against the injustice they had in mind. He cited the cases of men falsely claiming to have been sent of God, everyone of whom had come to grief with utter and most ignominious failure of his seditious plans; so would these men come to nought if the work they

[s] Matt. 27:25; compare 23:35.
[t] Acts 22:3.

professed proved to be of men; "But," added the dispassionate and learned doctor, "if it be of God, ye cannot overthrow it; lest haply ye be found even to fight against God."[u] Gamaliel's advice prevailed for the time being, to the extent of causing the apostles' lives to be spared; but the council, in contravention of justice and propriety, had the prisoners beaten. Then the brethren were discharged with the renewed injunction that they speak not in the name of Jesus. They went out rejoicing that they were counted worthy to suffer stripes and humiliation in defense of the Lord's name; and daily, both in the temple, and by house to house visitation, they valiantly taught and preached Jesus the Christ. Converts to the Church were not confined to the laity; a great company of the priests swelled the number of the disciples, who multiplied greatly in Jerusalem.[v]

STEPHEN THE MARTYR; HIS VISION OF THE LORD[w]

First among the "seven men of honest report" who were set apart under the hands of the apostles to administer the common store of the Church community, was Stephen, a man eminent in faith and good works, through whom the Lord wrought many miracles. He was zealous in service, aggressive in doctrine, and fearless as a minister of Christ. Some of the foreign Jews, who maintained a synagog in Jerusalem, engaged Stephen in disputation, and being unable "to resist the wisdom and the spirit by which he spake," conspired to have him charged with heresy and blasphemy. He was brought before the council on the word of men suborned to witness against him; and these averred that they had "heard him speak blasphemous words against Moses, and against God." The perjured accusers further testified that he had repeatedly spoken blasphemously against the temple, and the law, and had even declared that Jesus of Nazareth would some day destroy the temple, and change the Mosaic ceremonies. The charge was utterly false in spirit and fact, though possibly in a sense partly true in form; for, judging by what we have of record concerning Stephen's character and works, he was a zealous preacher of the word

---

[u] Acts 5:33–40.

[v] Acts 6:7.

[w] Acts 6:8–15; and 7.

as a world religion, through which the exclusiveness and alleged sanctity of Jerusalem as the holy city and of the now desecrated temple as the earthly abiding-place of Jehovah, would be abrogated; furthermore he seems to have realized that the law of Moses had been fulfilled in the mission of the Messiah.

When the Sanhedrists looked upon him, his face was illumined, and they saw it "as it had been the face of an angel." In answer to the charge, he delivered an address, which on critical analysis appears to have been extemporaneous, nevertheless it is strikingly logical and impressive in argument. The delivery was abruptly terminated, however, by a murderous assault.[x] In effective epitome Stephen traced the history of the covenant people from the time of Abraham down, showing that the patriarchs, and in turn Moses and the prophets, had lived and ministered in progressive preparation for the development of which those present were witnesses. He pointed out that Moses had foretold the coming of a Prophet, who was none other than Jehovah, whom their fathers had worshipped in the wilderness, before the tabernacle, and later in the temple; but, he affirmed, "the most High dwelleth not in temples made with hands," the most gorgeous of which could be but small to Him who said: "Heaven is my throne, and earth is my footstool."[y]

It is plain to be seen that Stephen's speech was not one of vindication, and far from a plea in his own defense; it was a proclamation of the word and purposes of God by a devoted servant who had no thought for personal consequences. In forceful arraignment he thus addressed His judges: "Ye stiffnecked and uncircumcised in heart and ears, ye do always resist the Holy Ghost: as your fathers did, so do ye. Which of the prophets have not your fathers persecuted? and they have slain them which shewed before of the coming of the Just One; of whom ye have been now the betrayers and murderers." Maddened at this direct accusation, the Sanhedrists "gnashed on him with their teeth." He knew that they thirsted for his blood; but, energized by the Holy Ghost, he looked steadfastly upward, and exclaimed in rapture: "Behold I see the heavens opened, and the Son of man standing on

[x] Acts 7:1–53.

[y] Isa. 66:1, 2; see also Matt. 5:34, 35; 23:22.

the right hand of God."[z] This is the first New Testament record of a manifestation of Christ to mortal eyes by vision or otherwise, subsequent to His ascension. The priestly rulers cried aloud, and stopped their ears to what they chose to regard as blasphemous utterances; and, rushing upon the prisoner with one accord, they hurried him outside the city walls and stoned him to death. True to his Master, he prayed: "Lord Jesus, receive my spirit"; and then, crushed to earth, he cried with a loud voice: "Lord, lay not this sin to their charge. And when he had said this, he fell asleep."

So died the first martyr for the testimony of the risen Christ. He was slain by a mob comprising chief priests, scribes, and elders of the people. What cared they that no sentence had been pronounced against him, or that they were acting in reckless defiance of Roman law? Devout men bore the mangled body to its burial; and all the disciples lamented greatly. Persecution increased, and members of the Church were scattered through many lands, wherein they preached the gospel and won many to the Lord. The blood of Stephen the martyr proved to be rich and virile seed, from which sprang a great harvest of souls.[aa]

CHRIST MANIFESTS HIMSELF TO SAUL OF TARSUS, LATER KNOWN AS PAUL THE APOSTLE

Among the disputants who, when defeated in discussion, conspired against Stephen and brought about his death, were Jews from Cilicia.[bb] Associated with them was a young man named Saul, a native of the Cilician city of Tarsus. This man was an able scholar, a forceful controversialist, an ardent defender of what he regarded as the right, and a vigorous assailant of what to him was wrong. Though born in Tarsus he had been brought to Jerusalem in early youth and had there grown up a strict Pharisee and an aggressive supporter of Judaism. He was a student of the law under the tutelage of Gamaliel, one of the most eminent masters of the time;[cc] and had the confidence

[z] Acts 7:56. Note this exceptional application of the title, Son of Man, to Christ by anyone other than Himself.

[aa] Acts 8:4; 11:19.

[bb] Acts 6:9.

[cc] Acts 22:3; compare 5:34.

of the high priest.[dd] His father, or perhaps an earlier progenitor, had acquired the rank of Roman citizenship, and Saul was a born heir to that distinction. Saul was a violent opponent of the apostles and the Church, and had made himself a party to the death of Stephen by openly consenting thereunto and by holding in personal custody the garments of the false witnesses while they stoned the martyr.

He wrought havoc in the Church by entering private houses and haling thence men and women suspected of belief in the Christ, and these he caused to be cast into prison.[ee] The persecution in which he took so prominent a part caused a scattering of the disciples throughout Judea, Samaria, and other lands; though the apostles remained and continued their ministry in Jerusalem.[ff] Not content with local activity against the Church, "Saul, yet breathing out threatenings and slaughter against the disciples of the Lord, went unto the high priest, and desired of him letters to Damascus to the synagogues, that if he found any of this way, whether they were men or women, he might bring them bound unto Jerusalem."[gg]

As Saul and his attendants neared Damascus they were halted by an occurrence of awe-inspiring grandeur.[hh] At noontide there suddenly appeared a light far exceeding the brightness of the sun, and in this dazzling splendor the whole party was enveloped, so that they fell to the ground in terror. In the midst of the unearthly glory, a sound was heard, which to Saul alone was intelligible as an articulate voice; he heard and understood the reproving question spoken in the Hebrew tongue: "Saul, Saul, why persecutest thou me?" In trepidation he inquired: "Who art thou, Lord?" The reply sounded the heart of Saul to its depths: "I am Jesus of Nazareth, whom thou persecutest"; and continued, as in sympathetic consideration of the persecutor's situation

---

dd In view of Saul's social status and recognized ability, many believe him to have been a member of the Sanhedrin; but for this assumption we find no definite warrant in scripture.

ee Acts 7:58; 8:1–3.

ff Acts 8:1.

gg Acts 9:1, 2. Observe that "way" here used for the first time to connote the gospel or religion of Christ, occurs frequently in Acts (16:17; 18:25, 26; 19:9, 23; 22:4; 24:14, 22).

hh Three versions of this manifestation and its immediate results appear in Acts (9:3–29; 22:6–16; and 26: 12–18): the first is the historian's narrative, while the others are given as reports of Saul's own words.

and the renunciation that would be required of him: "It is hard for thee to kick against the pricks."[ii] The enormity of his hostility and enmity against the Lord and His people filled the man's soul with horror, and in trembling contrition he asked: "Lord, what wilt thou have me to do?" The reply was: "Arise, and go into the city, and it shall be told thee what thou must do." The brilliancy of the heavenly light had blinded Saul. His companions led him into Damascus, where, at the house of Judas, in the street called Straight, he sat in darkness for three days, during which period he neither ate nor drank.

There lived in that city a faithful disciple named Ananias, to whom the Lord spake, instructing him to visit Saul and minister unto him that he might be healed of his blindness. Ananias was astonished at the commission, and ventured to remind the Lord that Saul was a notorious persecutor of the saints, and had come at that time to Damascus to arrest and put in bonds all believers. But the Lord answered: "Go thy way: for he is a chosen vessel unto me, to bear my name before the Gentiles, and kings, and the children of Israel: for I will shew him how great things he must suffer for my name's sake." Ananias went to Saul, laid his hands upon the penitent sufferer, saying: "Brother Saul, the Lord, even Jesus, that appeared unto thee in the way as thou camest, hath sent me, that thou mightest receive thy sight, and be filled with the Holy Ghost." The physical obstruction to vision was removed; scaly particles fell from the eyes of Saul, and his sight was restored. Without delay or hesitation, he was baptized. When strengthened by food he communed with the disciples at Damascus and straightway began to preach in the synagogs, declaring Jesus to be the Son of God.[jj]

When Saul returned to Jerusalem, the disciples were doubtful of his sincerity, they having known of him as a violent persecutor; but Barnabas, a trusted disciple, brought him to the apostles, told of his miraculous conversion and testified of his valiant service in preaching the word of God. He was received into fellowship, and afterward was ordained under the hands of the apostles.[kk] His Hebrew name, Saul,

---

[ii] Note 4, end of chapter.
[jj] Note 4, end of chapter.
[kk] Acts 9:26–28; 13:2, 3.

was in time substituted by the Latin Paulus, or as to us, Paul.[ll] In view of his commission to carry the Gospel to the Gentiles, the use of his Roman name may have been of advantage, and particularly so as he was a Roman citizen and therefore could claim the rights and exemptions attaching to the status of citizenship.[mm]

It is no part of our present purpose to follow even in outline the labors of the man thus peremptorily and miraculously called into the ministry; the fact of Christ's personal manifestations to him is the sole subject of present consideration. While in Jerusalem Paul was blessed with a visual manifestation of the Lord Jesus, accompanied by the giving of specific instructions. His own testimony is to this effect: "While I prayed in the temple, I was in a trance; and saw him saying unto me, Make haste, and get thee quickly out of Jerusalem: for they will not receive thy testimony concerning me." In explanation of his rejection by the people, Paul confessed his evil past, saying, "Lord, they know that I imprisoned and beat in every synagogue them that believed on thee: and when the blood of thy martyr Stephen was shed, I also was standing by, and consenting unto his death, and kept the raiment of them that slew him." To this the Lord replied: "Depart; for I will send thee far hence unto the Gentiles."[nn] Once again, as he lay a prisoner in the Roman castle, the Lord stood by him in the night, and said: "Be of good cheer, Paul: for as thou hast testified of me in Jerusalem, so must thou bear witness also at Rome."[oo]

Paul's personal witness that he had seen the resurrected Christ is explicit and emphatic. With his enumeration of some of the risen Lord's appearances he associates his own testimony, as addressed to the Corinthian saints, in this wise: "For I delivered unto you first of all that which I also received, how that Christ died for our sins according to the scriptures; and that he was buried, and that he rose again the third day according to the scriptures: and that he was seen of Cephas, then of the Twelve: after that, he was seen of above five hundred brethren at once; of whom the greater part remain unto this present,

[ll] Acts 13:9

[mm] Acts 16:37–40; 22:25–28; 23:27; 25:11; 26:32; 28:19.

[nn] Acts 22:17–21.

[oo] Acts 23:11.

but some are fallen asleep. After that, he was seen of James; then of all the apostles. And last of all he was seen of me also, as of one born out of due time. For I am the least of the apostles, that am not meet to be called an apostle, because I persecuted the church of God."[pp]

CLOSE OF THE APOSTOLIC MINISTRY— THE REVELATION THROUGH JOHN

The period of apostolic ministry continued until near the close of the first century of our era, approximately sixty to seventy years from the time of the Lord's ascension. In the course of that epoch the Church experienced both prosperity and vicissitude. At first the organized body increased in membership and influence in a manner regarded as phenomenal, if not miraculous.[qq] The apostles and the many other ministers who labored under their direction in graded positions of authority strove so effectively to spread the word of God, that Paul writing approximately thirty years after the ascension affirmed that the gospel had already been carried to every nation, or, to use his words, "preached to every creature under heaven."[rr] Through the agency of the Holy Ghost Christ continued to direct the affairs of His Church on the earth; and His mortal representatives, the apostles, traveled and taught, healed the afflicted, rebuked evil spirits, and raised the dead to a renewal of life.[ss]

We are without record of any direct or personal appearance of Christ to mortals between the manifestations to Paul and the revelation to John on the isle of Patmos. Tradition confirms John's implication that he had been banished thither "for the word of God, and for the testimony of Jesus Christ."[tt] He avers that what he wrote, now known as the book of Revelation, is "The Revelation of Jesus Christ, which God gave unto him, to shew unto his servants things which must shortly come to pass; and he sent and signified it by his angel unto his servant John."[uu] The

---

[pp] 1 Cor. 15:3–9.

[qq] Note 5, end of chapter.

[rr] Col. 1:23; see verse 6; also *The Great Apostasy,* 1:20, 21.

[ss] Acts 9:36–43.

[tt] Rev. 1:9. See note 6, end of chapter.

[uu] Rev. 1:1; read the whole chapter.

apostle gives a vivid description of the glorified Christ as seen by him; and of the Lord's words he made record as follows: "Fear not; I am the first and the last: I am he that liveth, and was dead; and, behold, I am alive for evermore, Amen; and have the keys of hell and of death."ᵛᵛ John was commanded to write to each of the seven churches, or branches of the Church of Christ, then existing in Asia, administering reproof, admonition and encouragement, as the condition of each required.

The final ministry of John marked the close of the apostolic administration in the primitive Church. His fellow apostles had gone to their rest, most of them having entered through the gates of martyrdom, and although it was his special privilege to tarry in the flesh until the Lord's advent in glory,ʷʷ he was not to continue his service as an acknowledged minister, known to and accepted by the Church. Even while many of the apostles lived and labored, the seed of apostasy had taken root in the Church and had grown with the rankness of pernicious weeds. This condition had been predicted, both by Old Testament prophets ˣˣ and by the Lord Jesus.ʸʸ The apostles also spake in plain prediction of the growth of the Apostasy all too grievously apparent to them as then in progress.ᶻᶻ Personal manifestations of the Lord Jesus to mortals appear to have ceased with the passing of the apostles of old, and were not again witnessed until the dawn of the Dispensation of the Fulness of Times.

NOTES TO CHAPTER 38

1. Presiding Authority and Common Consent.—"Another instance of official action in choosing and setting apart men to special office in the Church arose soon after the ordination of Matthias. It appears that one feature of the Church organization in early apostolic days was a common ownership of material things, distribution being made according to need. As the members increased, it was found impracticable

---

ᵛᵛ Rev. 1:10–20.

ʷʷ Page 642 herein.

ˣˣ Isa. 24:1–6; Amos 8:11, 12.

ʸʸ Matt. 24:4, 5, 10–13, 23–26.

ᶻᶻ Acts 20:17–31, particularly 29, 30; 1 Tim. 4:1–3; 2 Tim. 4:1–4; 2 Thes. 2:3, 4, 7, 8; 2 Pet. 2:1–3, read the entire chapter and observe its application to conditions in the world today; Jude 3, 4, 17–19; Rev. 13:4, 6–9; 14:6, 7. See *The Great Apostasy,* chapter 2.

for the apostles to devote the necessary attention and time to these temporal matters, so they called upon the members to select seven men of honest report, whom the apostles would appoint to take special charge of these affairs. These men were set apart by prayer and by the laying on of hands. The instance is instructive as showing that the apostles realized their possession of authority to direct in the affairs of the Church, and that they observed with strictness the principle of common consent in the administration of their high office. They exercised their priestly powers in the spirit of love, and with due regard to the rights of the people over whom they were placed to preside."—The author, *The Great Apostasy,* 1:19.

2. Pentecost.—The name means "fiftieth" and was applied to the Jewish feast that was celebrated fifty days after the second day of unleavened bread, or the Passover day. It is also known as "the feast of weeks" (Ex. 34:22; Deut. 16:10), because according to the Hebrew style, it fell seven weeks, or a week of weeks, after the Passover; as "the feast of harvest" (Ex. 23:16); and as "the day of the first-fruits" (Num. 28:26). Pentecost was one of the great feasts in Israel, and was of mandatory observance. Special sacrifices were appointed for the day, as was also an offering suitable to the harvest season, comprizing two leavened loaves made of the new wheat; these were to be waved before the altar and then given to the priests (Lev. 23:15–20). Because of the unprecedented events that characterized the first Pentecost after our Lord's ascension, the name has become current in Christian literature as expressive of any great spiritual awakening or unusual manifestation of divine grace.

3. Having All Things in Common.—No condition recorded of the early apostolic ministry expresses more forcefully the unity and devotion of the Church in those days than does the fact of the members establishing a system of common ownership of property (Acts 2:44, 46; 4:32–37; 6:1–4). One result of this community of interest in temporal things was a marked unity in spiritual matters; they "were of one heart and of one soul." Lacking nothing, they lived in contentment and godliness. Over thirty centuries earlier the people of Enoch had rejoiced in a similar condition of oneness, and their attainments in spiritual excellence were so effective that "the Lord came and dwelt with his people; . . . And the Lord called his people Zion, because they were of one heart and one mind, and dwelt in righteousness; and there was no poor among them." (Moses 7:16–18.) The Nephite disciples grew in holiness, as "they had all things common among them, every man dealing justly, one with another." (3 Ne. 26:19; see also 4 Ne. 1:2–3.) A system of unity in material affairs has been revealed to the Church in this current dispensation, (D&C 82:17, 18; 51:10–13, 18; 104:70–77), to the blessings of which the people may attain as they learn to replace selfish concern by altruism, and individual advantage by devotion to the general welfare.—See *Articles of Faith,* 24:439–40.

4. Saul's Conversion.—The sudden change of heart by which an ardent persecutor of the saints was so transformed as to become a true disciple, is to the average mind a miracle. Saul of Tarsus was a devoted student and observer of the law, a strict Pharisee. We find no intimation that he ever met or saw Jesus during the Lord's life in the flesh; and his contact with the Christian movement appears to have been brought about through disputation with Stephen. In determining what he would call right and what wrong the young enthusiast was guided too much by mind and too little by heart. His learning, which should have been his servant, was instead his master. He was a leading spirit in the cruel persecution of the first converts to Christianity; yet none can doubt his belief that even in such he was rendering service to Jehovah (compare John 16:2). His unusual energy and superb ability were misdirected. As soon as he realized the error of his course, he turned about, without counting risk, cost, or the certainty of persecution and probable martyrdom. His repentance was as genuine as had been his persecuting zeal. All through his ministry he was tortured by the past (Acts 22:4, 19, 20; 1 Cor. 15:9; 2 Cor. 12:7; Gal. 1:13); yet he found a measure of relief in the knowledge that he had acted in good conscience (Acts 26:9–11). It was "hard for him to kick against the pricks" (revised version "goad," Acts 9:5; 26:14) of tradition, training, and education; yet he hesitated not. He was a chosen instrument for the work of the Lord (Acts 9:15); and promptly he responded to the Master's will. Whatever of error Saul of Tarsus had committed through youthful zeal, Paul the apostle gave his all—his time, talent, and life—to expiate. He was preeminently the Lord's apostle to the Gentiles; and this opening of the doors to others than Jews was the main contention between himself and Stephen. In accordance with the divine and fateful purpose, Paul was called to do the work, in opposition to which he had been a participant in the martyrdom of Stephen. At the Lord's word of direction Paul was ready to preach Christ to the Gentiles; only by a miracle could the Jewish exclusiveness of Peter and the Church generally be overcome (Acts 10; and 11:1–18).

5. Rapid Growth of the Primitive Church.—Eusebius, who wrote in the early part of the fourth century, speaking of the first decade after the Savior's ascension, says: "Thus, then, under a celestial influence and cooperation, the doctrine of the Savior, like the rays of the sun, quickly irradiated the whole world. Presently, in accordance with divine prophecy, the sound of His inspired evangelists and apostles had gone throughout all the earth, and their words to the ends of the world. Throughout every city and village, like a replenished barn floor, churches were rapidly abounding and filled with members from every people. Those who, in consequence of the delusions that had descended to them from their ancestors, had been fettered by the ancient disease of idolatrous superstition, were now liberated by the power of Christ, through the teachings and miracles of His messengers."—(Eusebius, *Eccles. Hist.*, Book 1, ch. 3.)

6. Patmos.—A small island in the Icarian section of the Aegean Sea. Dr. John R. Sterret writes of it in the *Standard Bible Dictionary* as follows: "A volcanic island of the Sporades group, now nearly treeless. It is characterized by an indented coast and has a safe harbor. By the Romans it was made a place of exile for the lower class of criminals. John, the author of 'Revelation' was banished thither by Domitian, A.D. 94. According to tradition he lived there at hard labor for eighteen months."

7. The Holy Ghost Given.—In answer to a question as to whether the Holy Ghost was received by the apostles at or before Pentecost, a statement was published by the First Presidency of the Church on February 5, 1916 (see *Deseret News* of that date), from which statement the following excerpts are taken: "The answer to this question depends upon what is meant by 'receiving' the Holy Ghost. If reference is made to the promise of Jesus to His apostles about the endowment or gift of the Holy Ghost by the presence and ministration of the 'personage of Spirit,' called the Holy Ghost by revelation (D&C 130:22), then the answer is, it was not until the day of Pentecost that the promise was fulfilled. But the divine essence called the Spirit of God, or Holy Spirit, or Holy Ghost, by which God created or organized all things, and by which the prophets wrote and spoke, was bestowed in former ages, and inspired the apostles in their ministry long before the day of Pentecost. . . . We read that Jesus, after His Resurrection, breathed upon His disciples and said, 'Receive ye the Holy Ghost.' But we also read that He said, 'Behold, I send the promise of my Father upon you: but tarry ye in the city of Jerusalem, until ye be endued with power from on high' (John 20:22; Luke 24:49). We read further: 'For the Holy Ghost was not yet given; because that Jesus was not yet glorified.' (John 7:39.) Thus the promise was made, but the fulfilment came after, so that the Holy Ghost sent by Jesus from the Father did not come in person until the day of Pentecost, and the cloven tongues of fire were the sign of His coming."

CHAPTER 39

MINISTRY OF THE RESURRECTED CHRIST
ON THE WESTERN HEMISPHERE

By considering the apostolic ministry in immediate sequence to our study of the Lord's ascension from the Mount of Olives, we have departed from the chronological order of the several personal manifestations of the risen Savior to mortals; for very soon after His final farewell to the apostles in Judea He visited His "other sheep," not of the eastern fold, whose existence He had affirmed in that impressive sermon concerning the Good Shepherd and His sheep.[a] Those other sheep who were to hear the Shepherd's voice and eventually be made part of the united fold, were the descendants of Lehi who, with his family and a few others, had left Jerusalem 600 B.C. and had crossed the great deep to what we now know as the American continent, whereon they had grown to be a mighty though a divided people.[b]

THE LORD'S DEATH SIGNALIZED BY
GREAT CALAMITIES ON THE AMERICAN CONTINENT
As already set forth in these pages, the birth of Jesus at Bethlehem had been made known to the Nephite nation on the western hemisphere by divine revelation; and the glad event had been marked by the appearance of a new star, by a night devoid of darkness so that two days and the night between had been as one day, and by other wonderful occurrences, all of which had been predicted through the prophets of the western world.[c] Samuel the Lamanite, who through

[a] John 10:16; compare 3 Ne. 15:17–21.

[b] See pages 47 and 53 herein.

[c] Pages 47–50.

faithfulness and good works had become a prophet, mighty in word and deed, duly chosen and commissioned of God, had coupled with his predictions of the glorious occurrences that were to mark the birth of Christ, prophecies of other signs—of darkness, terror, and destruction—by which the Savior's death on the cross would be signalized.[d] Every prophetic word concerning the phenomena that were to attend the Lord's birth had been fulfilled; and many people had been brought thereby to believe in Christ as the promised Redeemer; but, as is usual with those whose belief rests on miracles, many among the Nephites "began to forget those signs and wonders which they had heard, and began to be less and less astonished at a sign or a wonder from heaven, insomuch that they began to be hard in their hearts, and blind in their minds, and began to disbelieve all which they had heard and seen."[e]

Thirty and three years had sped their course since the illumined night and the other signs of Messiah's advent; then, on the fourth day of the first month, or, according to our calendar, during the first week of April, in the thirty-fourth year, there arose a great and terrible tempest, with thunderings, lightnings, and both elevations and depressions of the earth's surface, so that the highways were broken up, mountains were sundered, and many cities were utterly destroyed by earthquake, fire, and the inrush of the sea. For three hours the unprecedented holocaust continued; and then thick darkness fell, in the which it was found impossible to kindle a fire; the awful gloom was like unto the darkness of Egypt[f] in that its clammy vapors could be felt. This condition lasted until the third day, so that a night a day and a night were as one unbroken night, and the impenetrable blackness was rendered the more terrible by the wailing of the people, whose heart-rending refrain was everywhere the same, "O that we had repented before this great and terrible day."[g]

Then, piercing the darkness, came a Voice,[h] before which the frightful chorus of human lamentation was silenced; "Wo, wo, wo unto

[d] Hel. 14:14–27.

[e] 3 Ne. 2:1.

[f] Ex. 10:21–23.

[g] 3 Ne. 8:5–25; compare Hel. 14:20–27.

[h] 3 Ne. 9.

this people" resounded throughout the land. The Voice proclaimed increasing woes except the people should repent. Destruction had befallen because of wickedness, and the devil was then laughing over the number of the dead and the retributive cause of their destruction. The extent of the dread calamity was detailed; cities that had been burned with their inhabitants, others that had sunk into the sea, yet others buried in the earth, were enumerated; and the divine reason for this widespread destruction was plainly set forth—that the wickedness and abominations of the people might be hidden from the face of the earth. Those who had lived to hear were declared to be the more righteous of the inhabitants; and to them hope was offered on conditions of more thorough repentance and reformation.

The identity of the Voice was thus made known: "Behold, I am Jesus Christ the Son of God. I created the heavens and the earth, and all things that in them are. I was with the Father from the beginning. I am in the Father, and the Father in me; and in me hath the Father glorified his name." The Lord commanded that the people should no longer serve Him with bloody sacrifices and burnt offerings; for the law of Moses was fulfilled; and thenceforth the only acceptable sacrifice would be the broken heart and the contrite spirit; and such should never be rejected. The humble and repentant the Lord would receive as His own. "Behold," He said, "for such I have laid down my life, and have taken it up again; therefore repent, and come unto me ye ends of the earth, and be saved."

The Voice ceased; and through the space of many hours of continuing darkness vociferous lamentations were hushed, for the people were convicted of their guilt and silently wept in astonishment over what they had heard, and in hopeful anticipation of the salvation that had been offered. A second time the Voice was heard, as in sorrow over those who had refused to accept the Savior's succor; for often had He protected them, more often would He have so done had they been willing, and yet in the future would He cherish them, "as a hen gathereth her chickens under her wings" if they would repent and live in righteousness. On the morning of the third day the darkness dispersed, seismic disturbances ceased, and the storms abated. As the pall was lifted from the land the people saw how profound had been the convulsions of earth, and how great had been their loss of kindred and friends. In their contrition and humiliation they remembered the predictions of the prophets, and knew that the mandate of the Lord had been executed upon them.[i]

Christ had risen; and following Him many of the righteous dead on the western continent rose from their graves, and appeared as resurrected, immortalized beings among the survivors of the land-wide destruction; even as in Judea many of the saints had been raised immediately after the Resurrection of Christ.[j]

FIRST VISITATION OF JESUS CHRIST TO THE NEPHITES [k]

About six weeks or more after the events last considered,[l] a great multitude of the Nephites had assembled at the temple in the land called Bountiful,[m] and were earnestly discoursing with one another over the great changes that had been wrought in the land, and particularly concerning Jesus Christ, of whose atoning death the predicted signs had been witnessed in all their tragic details. The prevailing spirit of the assembly was that of contrition and reverence. While thus congregated they heard a sound as of a Voice from above; but both a first and a second utterance were to them unintelligible. As they listened with rapt intentness, the Voice was heard a third time, and it said unto them: *"Behold my beloved Son, in whom I am well pleased, in whom I have glorified my name: hear ye him."*[n]

While gazing upward in reverent expectation, the people beheld a Man, clothed in a white robe, who descended and stood among them. He spake, saying: "Behold, I am Jesus Christ, whom the prophets testified shall come into the world; and behold, I am the light and the life of the world; and I have drunk out of that bitter cup which the Father hath given me, and have glorified the Father in taking upon me the sins of the world, in the which I have suffered the will of the Father in all things from the beginning." The multitude prostrated

---

[i] 3 Ne. 10.

[j] Hel. 14:25; 3 Ne. 23:7–13; compare Matt. 27:52, 53.

[k] 3 Ne. 11–18 inclusive.

[l] 3 Ne. 10:18. Bear in mind that Christ's ascension took place forty days after His Resurrection.

[m] Note 1, end of chapter.

[n] 3 Ne. 11:7; compare Matt. 3:17; Mark 1:11; Luke 9:35; JS–H 1:17.

themselves in adoration for they remembered that their prophets had foretold that the Lord would appear among them after His Resurrection and ascension.°

As He directed, the people arose, and one by one came to Him, and did see and feel the prints of the nails in His hands and feet, and the spear-wound in His side. Moved to adoring utterance, with one accord they cried: "Hosanna! blessed be the name of the Most High God!" then, falling at the feet of Jesus, they worshiped Him.

Summoning Nephi and eleven others to approach, the Lord gave them authority to baptize the people after His departure, and prescribed the mode of baptism with particular injunction against disputation in the matter or alteration of the given form, as witness the Lord's words:

"Verily I say unto you, that whoso repenteth of his sins through your words, and desireth to be baptized in my name, on this wise shall ye baptize them: behold, ye shall go down and stand in the water, and in my name shall ye baptize them. And now behold, these are the words which ye shall say, calling them by name, saying, Having authority given me of Jesus Christ, I baptize you in the name of the Father, and of the Son, and of the Holy Ghost. Amen. And then shall ye immerse them in the water, and come forth again out of the water. And after this manner shall ye baptize in my name, for behold, verily I say unto you, that the Father, and the Son, and the Holy Ghost are one; and I am in the Father, and the Father in me, and the Father and I are one. And according as I have commanded you thus shall ye baptize. And there shall be no disputations among you, as there hath hitherto been; neither shall there be disputations among you concerning the points of my doctrine, as there hath hitherto been."ᴾ

The people in general, and particularly the Twelve, chosen as stated, were impressively warned against contention over matters of doctrine, the spirit of which was declared to be of the devil, "who is the father of contention." The doctrine of Jesus Christ was set forth in simple yet comprehensive summary in these words:

"Behold, verily, verily, I say unto you, I will declare unto you my doctrine. And this is my doctrine, and it is the doctrine which the

---

° 3 Ne. 11:12; compare 1 Ne. 12:6; 2 Ne. 26:1, 9; Alma 16:20.
ᴾ 3 Ne. 11:23–28; compare D&C 20:72–74.

Father hath given unto me; and I bear record of the Father and the Father beareth record of me, and the Holy Ghost beareth record of the Father and me, and I bear record that the Father commandeth all men, everywhere, to repent and believe in me; And whoso believeth in me, and is baptized, the same shall be saved; and they are they who shall inherit the kingdom of God. And whoso believeth not in me, and is not baptized, shall be damned."[q]

Repentance, and humility akin to that of the innocent trusting child were the prerequisites for baptism, without which none could inherit the kingdom of God. With the incisiveness and simplicity that had characterized His teachings in Palestine, the Lord thus instructed His newly chosen Twelve:

"Verily, verily, I say unto you, that this is my doctrine, and whoso buildeth upon this, buildeth upon my rock, and the gates of hell shall not prevail against them. And whoso shall declare more or less than this, and establish it for my doctrine, the same cometh of evil, and is not built upon my rock, but he buildeth upon a sandy foundation, and the gates of hell standeth open to receive such, when the floods come and the winds beat upon them. Therefore go forth unto this people, and declare the words which I have spoken unto the ends of the earth."[r]

Then, turning to the multitude, Jesus admonished them to give heed to the teachings of the Twelve, and continued with a discourse embodying the sublime principles He had taught among the Jews in the Sermon on the Mount.[s] The Beatitudes, the Lord's Prayer, and the same splendid array of ennobling precepts are set forth, and the same wealth of effective comparison and apt illustration appear, in both Matthew's and Nephi's versions of this unparalleled address; but a significant difference is observed in every reference to the fulfilment of the Mosaic law; for where the Jewish scriptures record the Lord's words as pointing to a fulfilment then incomplete, the corresponding expressions in the Nephite account are in the past tense, the law having been already fulfilled in its entirety through the death and

q 3 Ne. 11:31–34; compare Mark 16:15, 16; see also John 12:48.

r 3 Ne. 11:39–41.

s 3 Ne. chaps. 12, 13, 14; compare Matt. chaps. 5, 6, 7.

Resurrection of Christ. Thus, to the Jews Jesus had said: "Till heaven and earth pass, one jot or one tittle shall in no wise pass from the law, till all be fulfilled"; but to the Nephites: "For verily I say unto you, one jot nor one tittle hath not passed away from the law, but in me it hath all been fulfilled."[t]

Many marveled over this matter, wondering what the Lord would have them do concerning the law of Moses; "for they understood not the saying that old things had passed away, and that all things had become new." Jesus, conscious of their perplexity, proclaimed in plainness that He was the Giver of the law, and that by Him had it been fulfilled and therefore abrogated. His affirmation is particularly explicit:

"Behold I say unto you, that the law is fulfilled that was given unto Moses. Behold, I am he that gave the law, and I am he who covenanted with my people Israel: therefore, the law in me is fulfilled, for I have come to fulfil the law; therefore it hath an end. Behold, I do not destroy the prophets, for as many as have not been fulfilled in me, verily I say unto you, shall all be fulfilled. And because I said unto you, that old things hath passed away, I do not destroy that which hath been spoken concerning things which are to come. For behold, the covenant which I have made with my people is not all fulfilled; but the law which was given unto Moses, hath an end in me."[u]

Addressing Himself to the Twelve He affirmed that never had the Father commanded Him to inform the Jews concerning the existence of the Nephites, except indirectly by mention of other sheep not of the Jewish fold; and as, "because of stiffneckedness and unbelief," they had failed to comprehend His words, the Father had commanded Him to say no more with reference either to the Nephites or to the third fold—comprising "the other tribes of the house of Israel, whom the Father hath led away out of the land." To the Nephite disciples Jesus taught many other matters that had been withheld from the Jews, who through unfitness to receive had been left in ignorance. Even the Jewish apostles had wrongly supposed that those "other sheep" were the Gentile nations, not realizing that the carrying of the

---

[t] Matt. 5:18, and 3 Ne. 12:18; compare 46, 47; 15:2–10; and 9:17–20. See Note 2, end of chapter.

[u] 3 Ne. 15:4–8.

gospel to the Gentiles was part of their particular mission, and oblivious to the fact that never would Christ manifest Himself in person to those who were not of the house of Israel. Through the promptings of the Holy Ghost and under the ministrations of men commissioned and sent would the Gentiles hear the word of God; but to the personal manifestation of the Messiah they were ineligible.[v] Great, however, will be the Lord's mercies and blessings to the Gentiles who accept the truth, for unto them the Holy Ghost shall bear witness of the Father and of the Son; and all of them who comply with the laws and ordinances of the gospel shall be numbered in the house of Israel. Their conversion and enfoldment with the Lord's own will be as individuals, and not as nations, tribes, or peoples.[w]

The adoring multitude, numbering about two thousand five hundred souls, thought that Jesus was about to depart; and they tearfully yearned to have Him remain. He comforted them with the assurance that He would return on the morrow, and admonished them to ponder upon the things He had taught, and to pray in His name to the Father for understanding. He had already informed the Twelve, and now stated to the people, that He would show Himself and minister "unto the lost tribes of Israel, for they are not lost unto the Father, for he knoweth whither he hath taken them." Voicing the compassion He felt, the Lord directed the people to fetch their afflicted ones, the lame, halt, maimed, blind and deaf, the leprous, and the withered; and when these were brought He healed them, every one. Then, as He commanded, parents brought their little children, and placed them in a circle around Him. The multitude bowed in prayer; and Jesus prayed for them; "And," wrote Nephi, "no tongue can speak, neither can there be written by any man, neither can the hearts of men conceive so great and marvellous things as we both saw and heard Jesus speak; and no one can conceive of the joy which filled our souls at the time we heard him pray for us unto the Father." The prayer being ended, Jesus bade the multitude arise; and joyfully He exclaimed: "Blessed are ye because of your faith. And now behold, my joy is full." Jesus wept. Then He took the children, one by one, and blessed them, praying unto the Father for each.

[v] 3 Ne. 15:11–24.
[w] 3 Ne. 16:4–20.

"And when he had done this he wept again, and he spake unto the multitude, and saith unto them, behold your little ones. And as they looked to behold, they cast their eyes towards heaven, and they saw the heavens open, and they saw angels descending out of heaven as it were, in the midst of fire; and they came down and encircled those little ones about, and they were encircled about with fire; and the angels did minister unto them."[x]

The Lord Jesus sent for bread and wine, and caused the people to sit down. The bread He brake and blessed, and gave thereof to the Twelve; these, having eaten, distributed bread to the multitude. The wine was blessed, and all partook, the Twelve first, and afterward the people. With impressiveness similar to that attending the institution of the Sacrament of the Lord's Supper among the apostles in Jerusalem, Jesus made plain the sanctity and significance of the ordinance, saying that authority for its future administration would be given; and that it was to be participated in by all who had been baptized into fellowship with Christ, and was always to be observed in remembrance of Him, the bread being the sacred emblem of His body, the wine the token of His blood that had been shed. By express commandment, the Lord forbade the sacrament of bread and wine to all but the worthy; "For," He explained, "whoso eateth and drinketh my flesh and blood unworthily, eateth and drinketh damnation to his soul; therefore if ye know that a man is unworthy to eat and drink of my flesh and blood, ye shall forbid him." But the people were forbidden to cast out from their assemblies those from whom the Sacrament was to be withheld, if so be they would but repent and seek fellowship through baptism.[y]

The necessity of prayer was explicitly emphasized by the Lord, the commandment to pray being given to the Twelve and to the multitude separately. Individual supplication, family devotions, and congregational worship were thus enjoined:

"Therefore ye must always pray unto the Father in my name; and whatsoever ye shall ask the Father in my name, which is right, believing

---

[x] 3 Ne. 17:22–24; read entire chapter.

[y] 3 Ne. 18:1–14, 27–34; compare 1 Cor. 11:23–30. For the prescribed manner of administering the Sacrament, see Moro. 4 and 5; compare D&C 20:75–79.

that ye shall receive, behold it shall be given unto you. Pray in your families unto the Father, always in my name, that your wives and your children may be blessed. And behold, ye shall meet together oft, and ye shall not forbid any man from coming unto you when ye shall meet together, but suffer them that they may come unto you, and forbid them not; but ye shall pray for them, and shall not cast them out; and if it so be that they come unto you oft, ye shall pray for them unto the Father, in my name."[z]

The Lord then touched with His hand each of the Twelve, investing them, in words unheard by others, with power to confer the Holy Ghost by the imposition of hands upon all repentant and baptized believers.[aa] As he finished the ordination of the Twelve, a cloud overshadowed the people, so that the Lord was hidden from their sight; but the twelve disciples "saw and did bear record that he ascended again into heaven."

CHRIST'S SECOND VISITATION TO THE NEPHITES[bb]

On the morrow a yet greater multitude assembled in expectation of the Savior's return. Throughout the night messengers had spread the glorious tidings of the Lord's appearing, and of His promise to again visit His people. So great was the assembly that Nephi and his associates caused the people to separate into twelve bodies, to each of which one of the disciples was assigned to impart instruction and to lead in prayer. The burden of supplication was that the Holy Ghost should be given unto them. Led by the chosen disciples the whole vast concourse approached the water's edge, and Nephi, going first, was baptized by immersion; he then baptized the eleven others whom Jesus had chosen. When the Twelve had come forth out of the water, "they were filled with the Holy Ghost, and with fire. And behold, they were encircled about as if it were fire; and it came down from heaven, and the multitude did witness it, and do bear record; and angels did come down out of heaven, and did minister unto them. And it came to pass that while the angels were ministering unto the

[z] 3 Ne. 18:19–23.
[aa] 3 Ne. 18:36, 37; Moro. 2:1–3.
[bb] 3 Ne 19–25 and 26:1–5.

disciples, behold, Jesus came and stood in the midst, and ministered unto them."[cc]

Thus Jesus appeared in the midst of the disciples and ministering angels. At His command the Twelve and the multitude knelt in prayer; and they prayed unto Jesus, calling Him their Lord and their God. Jesus separated Himself by a little space, and in humble attitude prayed, saying in part: "Father, I thank thee that thou hast given the Holy Ghost unto these whom I have chosen; and it is because of their belief in me, that I have chosen them out of the world. Father, I pray thee that thou wilt give the Holy Ghost unto all them that shall believe in their words." The disciples were yet fervently praying to Jesus when He returned to them; and as He looked upon them with merciful and approving smile, they were glorified in His presence, so that their countenances and their apparel shone with a brilliancy like unto that of the face and garments of the Lord, even so that "there could be nothing on earth so white as the whiteness thereof." A second and a third time Jesus retired and prayed unto the Father; and while the people comprehended the meaning of His prayer, they confessed and bare record that "so great and marvellous were the words which he prayed, that they cannot be written, neither can they be uttered by man." The Lord rejoiced in the faith of the people, and to the disciples He said: "So great faith have I never seen among all the Jews; wherefore I could not shew unto them so great miracles, because of their unbelief. Verily I say unto you, there are none of them that have seen so great things as ye have seen; neither have they heard so great things as ye have heard."[dd] Then the Lord administered the Sacrament in manner as on the yesterday; but both the bread and the wine were provided without human aid. The sanctity of the ordinance was thus expressed: "He that eateth this bread, eateth of my body to his soul, and he that drinketh of this wine, drinketh of my blood to his soul, and his soul shall never hunger nor thirst, but shall be filled."

This was followed by instructions concerning the covenant people, Israel, of whom the Nephites were a part, and of the relation they would bear to the Gentile nations in the future development of

[cc] Note 3, end of chapter.

[dd] 3 Ne. 19:35 36; read the entire chapter.

the divine purpose. Jesus declared Himself to be that Prophet whose coming Moses had foretold, and the Christ of whom all the prophets had testified. The temporary supremacy of the Gentiles, whereby the further scattering of Israel would be accomplished, and the eventual gathering of the covenant people, were predicted, with frequent reference to the inspired utterances of Isaiah bearing thereon.[ee] The future of Lehi's descendants was pictured as a dwindling in unbelief through iniquity; in consequence of which the Gentiles would grow to be a mighty people on the western continent, even though that land had been given as an ultimate inheritance to the house of Israel. The establishment of the then future but now existent American nation, characterized as "a free people," was thus foretold and God's purpose therein explained: "For it is wisdom in the Father that they should be established in this land, and be set up as a free people by the power of the Father, that these things might come forth from them unto a remnant of your seed, that the covenant of the Father may be fulfilled which he hath covenanted with his people, O house of Israel."[ff]

As a sign of the time in which the gathering of the several branches of Israel from their long dispersion should take place, the Lord specified the prosperity of the Gentiles in America, and their agency in bringing the scriptures to the degraded remnant of Lehi's posterity or the American Indians.[gg] It was made plain that all Gentiles who would repent, and accept the gospel of Christ through baptism, should be numbered among the covenant people and be made partakers of the blessings incident to the last days, in which the New Jerusalem would be established on the American continent. The joyful account of gathered Israel as Jehovah had given it aforetime through the mouth of His prophet Isaiah, was repeated by the resurrected Jehovah to His Nephite flock.[hh] Admonishing them to ponder the words of the prophets, which were of record amongst them, and to give heed to the new scriptures He had made known, and especially commanding the Twelve to teach the people further concerning the

[ee] 3 Ne. 20; see references to Isaiah given therein.

[ff] 3 Ne. 21:4.

[gg] 3 Ne. 21:1–7; for prophecies concerning subsequent events see remainder of chapter.

[hh] 3 Ne. 22; compare Isa. 54.

things He had expounded, the Lord informed them of the revelations given through Malachi, and directed that the same be written.[ii]

The prophecies so reiterated by Him who had inspired Malachi to utterance, were at that time obviously of the future, and are even yet unfulfilled in their entirety. The advent of the Lord, to which these scriptures testify, is yet future; but that the time is now near—that "great and dreadful day of the Lord"—is attested by the fact that Elijah who was to come before that day, has appeared in the discharge of his particular commission—that of turning the hearts of the living children to their dead progenitors, and the hearts of the departed fathers to their still mortal posterity.[jj]

The personal ministry of Christ on the occasion of this second visitation lasted three days, during which He gave the people many scriptures, such as had been before given unto the Jews, for so the Father had commanded; and He expounded unto them the purposes of God, from the beginning until the time at which Christ shall return in His glory; "And even unto the great and last day, when all people, and all kindreds, and all nations and tongues shall stand before God, to be judged of their works, whether they be good or whether they be evil; if they be good, to the resurrection of everlasting life; and if they be evil, to the resurrection of damnation, being on a parallel, the one on the one hand, and the other on the other hand, according to the mercy, and the justice, and the holiness which is in Christ, who was before the world began." In merciful ministration He healed their afflicted folk, and raised a man from the dead. At later but unspecified times, He showed Himself among the Nephites, and "did break bread oft, and bless it, and give it unto them."[kk]

After His second ascension from among them, the spirit of prophecy was manifest among the people, and this extended even to children and babes, many of whom spake of marvelous things, as the Spirit gave them utterance. The Twelve entered upon their ministry with

---

[ii] 3 Ne. 24 and 25; compare Mal. 3 and 4.

[jj] D&C 110:13–16. Elijah appeared in the Kirtland Temple April 3, A.D. 1836, and committed to the Church the keys of authority for vicarious work in behalf of the dead. See chapter 41 herein.

[kk] 3 Ne. 26:4, 5, 13–15.

vigor, teaching all who would hear, and baptizing those who, through repentance, sought communion with the Church. Upon all who thus complied with the requirements of the gospel, the Holy Ghost was bestowed; and those so blessed lived together in love, and were called the Church of Christ.[ll]

CHRIST'S VISITATION TO HIS CHOSEN TWELVE AMONG THE NEPHITES [mm]

Under the administration of the twelve ordained disciples the Church grew and prospered in the land of Nephi.[nn] The disciples, as special witnesses of the Christ, traveled, preached, taught, and baptized all who professed faith and showed forth repentance. On a certain occasion the Twelve were assembled in "mighty prayer and fasting," seeking instruction on a particular matter which, notwithstanding the Lord's injunction against contention, had given rise to disputation among the people. As they supplicated the Father in the Son's name, Jesus appeared amongst them, and asked: "What will ye that I shall give unto you?" Their answer was: "Lord, we will that thou wouldst tell us the name whereby we shall call this church; for there are disputations among the people concerning this matter." They had provisionally called the community of baptized believers the Church of Christ; but, apparently this true and distinguishing name had not been generally accepted without question.

"And the Lord said unto them, Verily, verily, I say unto you, why is it that the people should murmur and dispute because of this thing? Have they not read the scriptures, which say ye must take upon you the name of Christ, which is my name? for by this name shall ye be called at the last day; and whoso taketh upon him my name, and endureth to the end, the same shall be saved at the last day; therefore whatsoever ye shall do, ye shall do it in my name; therefore ye shall call the church in my name; and ye shall call upon the Father in my name, that he will bless the church for my sake; And how be it my church, save it be called in my name? for if a church be

<hr>

[ll] 3 Ne. 26:14–21.

[mm] 3 Ne. 26, 27, and 28:1–12.

[nn] Note 1, end of chapter.

called in Moses' name, then it be Moses' church; or if it be called in the name of a man, then it be the church of a man; but if it be called in my name, then it is my church, if it so be that they are built upon my gospel. Verily I say unto you, that ye are built upon my gospel; therefore ye shall call whatsoever things ye do call, in my name; therefore if ye call upon the Father, for the church, if it be in my name, the Father will hear you; and if it so be that the church is built upon my gospel, then will the Father shew forth his own works in it; but if it be not built upon my gospel, and is built upon the works of men, or upon the works of the devil, verily I say unto you, they have joy in their works for a season, and by and by the end cometh, and they are hewn down and cast into the fire, from whence there is no return; for their works do follow them, for it is because of their works that they are hewn down; therefore remember the things that I have told you."[oo]

In such wise did the Lord confirm as an authoritative bestowal, the name which, through inspiration, had been assumed by His obedient children, *The Church of Jesus Christ.* The Lord's explanation as to the one and only Name by which the Church could be appropriately known is cogent and convincing. It was not the church of Lehi or Nephi, of Mosiah or Alma, of Samuel or Helaman; else it should have been called by the name of the man whose church it was, even as today there are churches named after men;[pp] but being the Church established by Jesus Christ, it could properly bear none other name than His.

Jesus then reiterated to the Nephite Twelve many of the cardinal principles He had before enunciated to them and to the people at large; and commanded that His words be written, excepting certain exalted communications which He forbade them to write. The importance of preserving as a priceless treasure the new scriptures He had given was shown, with assurance that in heaven records were kept of all things done by divine direction. The Twelve were told that they were to be the judges of their people; and in view of such investiture they were admonished to diligence and godliness.[qq] The Lord was

---

[oo] 3 Ne. 27:4–12.

[pp] E.g. of Calvin, Luther, Wesley; see also *The Great Apostasy,* 10:21, 22.

[qq] Note the assurance of a similar commission promised the Jewish apostles: Matt. 19:28; Luke 22:30. See also 1 Ne. 12:9.

made glad by the faith and ready obedience of the Nephites amongst whom He had ministered; and to the twelve special witnesses He said: "And now behold, my joy is great, even unto fulness, because of you, and also this generation; yea, and even the Father rejoiceth, and also all the holy angels, because of you and this generation; for none of them are lost. Behold, I would that ye should understand; for I mean them who are now alive of this generation; and none of them are lost; and in them I have fulness of joy." His joy, however, was mingled with sorrow because of the apostasy into which the later generations would fall; this He foresaw as a dire condition that would attain its climax in the fourth generation from that time.[rr]

THE THREE NEPHITES

In loving compassion the Lord spoke unto the twelve disciples, one by one, asking: "What is it that ye desire of me, after that I am gone to the Father?"[ss] All but three expressed the desire that they might continue in the ministry until they had reached a goodly age, and then in due time be received by the Lord into His kingdom. To them Jesus gave blessed assurance, saying: "After that ye are seventy and two years old, ye shall come unto me in my kingdom, and with me ye shall find rest." He turned to the three who had reserved the request they ventured not to express;

"And he said unto them, Behold, I know your thoughts, and ye have desired the thing which John, my beloved, who was with me in my ministry, before that I was lifted up by the Jews, desired of me; therefore more blessed are ye, for ye shall never taste of death, but ye shall live to behold all the doings of the Father, unto the children of men, even until all things shall be fulfilled, according to the will of the Father, when I shall come in my glory, with the powers of heaven; and ye shall never endure the pains of death; but when I shall come in my glory, ye shall be changed in the twinkling of an eye from mortality to immortality: and then shall ye be blessed in the kingdom of my Father."[tt]

[rr] 3 Ne. 27:32 and references given therewith.

[ss] 3 Ne. 28:1; read verses 1–12.

[tt] 3 Ne. 28:6–8.

The blessed three were assured that in the course of their prolonged life they should be immune to pain, and should know sorrow only as they grieved for the sins of the world. For their desire to labor in bringing souls unto Christ as long as the world should stand, they were promised an eventual fulness of joy, even like unto that to which the Lord Himself had attained. Jesus touched each of the nine who were to live and die in the Lord, but the three who were to tarry till He would come in His glory He did not touch. "And then he departed."

A change was wrought in the bodies of the Three Nephites, so that, while they remained in the flesh, they were exempt from the usual effects of physical vicissitude. The heavens were opened to their gaze; they were caught up, and saw and heard unspeakable things. "And it was forbidden them that they should utter; neither was it given unto them power that they could utter the things which they saw and heard." Though they lived and labored as men among their fellows, preaching, baptizing, and conferring the Holy Ghost upon all who gave heed to their words, the enemies to the truth were powerless to do them injury. Somewhat later than a hundred and seventy years after the Lord's last visitation, malignant persecution was waged against the Three. For their zeal in the ministry they were cast into prison; but "the prisons could not hold them, for they were rent in twain." They were incarcerated in underground dungeons; "But they did smite the earth with the word of God, insomuch that by his power they were delivered out of the depths of the earth; and therefore they could not dig pits sufficient to hold them." Thrice they were cast into a furnace of fire, but received no harm; and three times were they thrown into dens of ravenous beasts, but, "behold they did play with the beasts, as a child with a suckling lamb, and received no harm."[uu] Mormon avers that in answer to his prayers the Lord had made known unto him that the change wrought upon the bodies of the Three was such as to deprive Satan of all power over them, and that "they were holy, and that the powers of the earth could not hold them; and in this state they were to remain until the judgment day of

---

[uu] 3 Ne. 28:13–23; compare 4 Ne. 1:14, 29–33.

Christ; and at that day they were to receive a greater change, and to be received into the kingdom of the Father to go no more out, but to dwell with God eternally in the heavens."ᵛᵛ For nearly three hundred years, and possibly longer, the Three Nephites ministered visibly among their fellows; but as the wickedness of the people increased these special ministers were withdrawn, and thereafter manifested themselves only to the righteous few. Moroni, the last prophet of the Nephites, when engaged in completing the record of his father, Mormon, and adding thereto matters of his own knowledge, wrote concerning these three disciples of the Lord, that they "did tarry in the land until the wickedness of the people was so great, that the Lord would not suffer them to remain with the people; and whether they be upon the face of the land no man knoweth. But behold, my father and I have seen them, and they have ministered unto us."ʷʷ Their ministry was to be extended to Jews and Gentiles, amongst whom they labor unrecognized as of ancient birth; and they are sent unto the scattered tribes of Israel, and to all nations, kindreds, tongues and peoples, from whom they have brought and are bringing many souls unto Christ, "that their desire may be fulfilled, and also because of the convincing power of God which is in them."ˣˣ

GROWTH OF THE CHURCH FOLLOWED BY THE APOSTASY OF THE NEPHITE NATION

The Church of Jesus Christ developed rapidly in the land of Nephi, and brought to its faithful adherents unprecedented blessings. Even the hereditary animosity between Nephites and Lamanites was forgotten; and all lived in peace and prosperity. So great was the unity of the Church that its members owned all things in common, and "therefore they were not rich and poor, bond and free, but they were all made free, and partakers of the heavenly gift."ʸʸ Populous cities replaced the desolation of ruin that had befallen at the time of the Lord's Crucifixion. The land was blessed, and the people rejoiced in

---

ᵛᵛ 3 Ne. 28:39, 40.

ʷʷ Morm. 8:10, 11; see also 3 Ne. 28:26–32, 36–40; 4 Ne. 1:14, 37; Ether 12:17.

ˣˣ 3 Ne. 28:27–32.

ʸʸ 4 Ne. 1:3; read 1:23.

righteousness. "And it came to pass that there was no contention in the land, because of the love of God which did dwell in the hearts of the people. And there were no envyings, nor strifes, nor tumults, nor whoredoms, nor lyings, nor murders, nor any manner of lasciviousness; and surely there could not be a happier people among all the people who had been created by the hand of God."[zz] Nine of the twelve special witnesses chosen by the Lord passed at appointed times to their rest, and others were ordained in their stead. The state of blessed prosperity and of common ownership continued for a period of a hundred and sixty-seven years; but soon thereafter came a most distressing change. Pride displaced humility, display of costly apparel superseded the simplicity of happier days; rivalry led to contention, and thence the people "did have their goods and their substance no more common among them, and they began to be divided into classes, and they began to build up churches unto themselves, to get gain, and began to deny the true church of Christ."[aaa] Man-made churches multiplied, and persecution, true sister to intolerance, became rampant. The red-skinned Lamanites reverted to their degraded ways, and developed a murderous hostility against their white brothers; and all manner of corrupt practices became common among both nations. For many decades the Nephites retreated before their aggressive foes, making their way northeastward through what is now the United States. About A.D. 400 the last great battle was fought near the hill Cumorah;[bbb] and the Nephite nation became extinct.[ccc] The degenerate remnant of Lehi's posterity, the Lamanites or American Indians, have continued until this day. Moroni, the last of the Nephite prophets, hid away the record of his people in the hill Cumorah, whence it has been brought forth by divine direction in the current dispensation. That record is now before the world translated through the gift and power of God, and published to the edification of all nations, as the BOOK OF MORMON.

[zz] 4 Ne. 1:15, 16.

[aaa] 4 Ne. 1:25, 26.

[bbb] Near Manchester, Ontario County, New York.

[ccc] See Morm. 1–9; and Moro. 10.

NOTES TO CHAPTER 39

1. The Land Bountiful.—This comprised the northerly part of South America, extending to the Isthmus of Panama. On the north it was bounded by the Land of Desolation, which embraced Central America, and, in later Nephite history, an indefinite extent north of the Isthmus. The South American continent in general is called, in the Book of Mormon, the Land of Nephi.

2. The Jewish and Nephite Versions of the "Sermon on the Mount."—As indicated in the text, one of the most impressive contrasts between the Sermon on the Mount and the virtual repetition of the discourse by our Lord on the occasion of His visit to the Nephites, is that of prediction concerning the fulfilment of the law of Moses in the first delivery, and unqualified affirmation in the second that the law had been fulfilled. Among the Beatitudes certain differences appear, in each of which the Nephite sermon is more explicit. Thus, instead of, "Blessed are the poor in spirit" (Matt. 5:3), we read, "Blessed are the poor in spirit who come unto me" (3 Ne. 12:3). Instead of, "Blessed are they which do hunger and thirst after righteousness; for they shall be filled" (Matthew), we read, "And blessed are all they who do hunger and thirst after righteousness, for they shall be filled with the Holy Ghost" (Nephi). Instead of, "for righteousness' sake," (Matthew) we have "for my name's sake," (Nephi). For the difficult passage, "Ye are the salt of the earth: but if the salt have lost his savour, wherewith shall it be salted?" (Matthew), we have the clearer expression, "I give unto you to be the salt of the earth; but if the salt shall lose its savor, wherewith shall the earth be salted?" (Nephi). And, as already noted, in place of "one jot or one tittle shall in no wise pass from the law, till all be fulfilled" (Matthew), we have "one jot nor one tittle hath not passed away from the law, but in me it hath all been fulfilled" (Nephi). Variations in succeeding verses are incident to this prospective fulfilment (Matthew), and affirmed accomplishment (Nephi). Instead of the strong analogy concerning the plucking out of an offending eye, or the severing of an evil hand (Matthew), we find: "Behold, I give unto you a commandment, that ye suffer none of these things to enter into your heart; for it is better that ye should deny yourselves of these things, wherein ye will take up your cross, than that ye should be cast into hell" (Nephi). Following the illustrative instances of the gospel requirements superseding those of the law, the Nephite record presents this splendid summation: "Therefore those things which were of old time, which were under the law in me, are all fulfilled. Old things are done away, and all things have become new; therefore I would that ye should be perfect even as I, or your Father who is in heaven is perfect."

In Matthew's report of the sermon, little distinction is made between the precepts addressed to the multitude in general, and the instructions given particularly to the Twelve. Thus, Matthew 6:25–34 was spoken inferentially to the apostles; for they and not the people were to lay aside all worldly pursuits; in the sermon delivered to the Nephites the distinction is thus made clear: "And now it came to pass that when Jesus had spoken these words, he looked upon the twelve whom he had chosen, and said unto them, Remember the words which I have spoken. For behold, ye are they whom I have chosen to minister unto this people. Therefore I say unto you, take no thought for your life, what ye shall eat, or what ye shall drink; nor yet for your body, what ye shall put on. Is not the life more than meat, and the body than raiment?" etc. (See 3 Ne. 13:25–34). Matthew 7 opens with "Judge not that ye be not judged," without intimation as to its general or special application; 3 Nephi 14 begins "And now it came to pass that when Jesus had spoken these words, he turned again to the multitude, and did open his mouth unto them again, saying, Verily, verily, I say unto you, judge not, that ye be not judged." A careful, verse-by-verse comparison between the Sermon on the Mount as recorded by Matthew, and the risen Lord's discourse to His people on the western continent is earnestly recommended to every student.

3. Baptisms Among the Nephites After the Lord's Visitation.—We read that before the second appearing of Christ to the Nephites, the chosen Twelve were baptized (3 Ne. 19:10–13). These men had doubtless been baptized before, for Nephi had been empowered not only to baptize but to ordain others to the requisite authority for administering baptism (3 Ne. 7:23–26). The baptism of the disciples on the morn of the Savior's second visit, was in the nature of a rebaptism, involving a renewal of covenants, and confession of faith in the Lord Jesus.

It is possible that in the earlier Nephite baptisms some irregularity in mode or impropriety in the spirit of administering the ordinance may have arisen; for, as we have seen the Lord enjoined upon the people in connection with the instructions concerning baptism that disputations must cease. (3 Ne. 11:28–33.)

As to second or later baptisms, the author has written elsewhere (see *Articles of Faith*, 7:142–45) practically as follows. Rebaptisms recorded in scripture are few, and in each instance the special circumstances justifying the action are apparent. Thus, we read of Paul baptizing certain disciples at Ephesus, though they had already been immersed after the manner of John's baptism. But in this case the apostle was evidently unconvinced that the baptism had been solemnized by due authority, or that the believers had been properly instructed as to the import of the ordinance. When he tested the efficacy of their baptism by asking "Have ye received the Holy Ghost since ye believed?" they answered him, "We have not so much as heard whether there be any Holy Ghost." Then asked he in seeming surprise, "Unto what then were ye baptized? and they said, Unto John's baptism. Then said Paul, John verily baptized with the baptism of repentance, saying unto the people, that they should believe on him which should come after him, that is, on Christ Jesus. When they heard this, they were baptized in the name of the Lord Jesus." (See Acts 19:1–6.)

In the Church today a repetition of the baptismal rite on an individual is allowable under certain specific conditions. Thus, if one, having entered the Church by baptism, withdraws from it, or is excommunicated therefrom, and afterward repents and desires to regain his standing in the Church, he can do so only through baptism. However, such is a repetition of the initiatory ordinance as previously administered. There is no ordinance of "rebaptism" in the Church distinct in nature, form, or purpose, from other baptism; and, therefore, in administering baptism to a subject who has been formerly baptized, the form of the ceremony is exactly the same as in first baptisms.

CHAPTER 40

THE LONG NIGHT OF APOSTASY

For over seventeen hundred years on the eastern hemisphere, and for more than fourteen centuries on the western, there appears to have been silence between the heavens and the earth.[a] Of direct revelation from God to man during this long interval, we have no authentic record. As already shown, the period of apostolic ministry on the eastern continent probably terminated before the dawn of the second century of the Christian era. The passing of the apostles was followed by the rapid development of a universal apostasy as had been foreseen and predicted.[b]

In the accomplishment of this great falling away, external and internal causes cooperated. Among the disintegrating forces acting from without, the most effective was the persistent persecution to which the saints were subjected, incident to both Judaistic and pagan opposition. Vast numbers who had professed membership and many who had been officers in the ministry deserted the Church; while a few were stimulated to greater zeal under the scourge of persecution. The general effect of opposition from the outside—of external causes of decline in faith and works considered as a whole—was the defection of individuals, resulting in a widespread *apostasy from the Church.* But immeasurably more serious was the result of internal dissension, schism and disruption, whereby an absolute *apostasy of the Church* from the way and word of God was brought about.

---

a Note 1, end of chapter.

b No extended account of the Apostasy of the primitive Church can be attempted here; the reader is referred to special works treating this important subject. See the author's *The Great Apostasy.*

Judaism was the earliest oppressor of Christianity, and became the instigator and abettor of the succeeding atrocities incident to pagan persecution. Open and vigorous hostility of the Roman powers against the Christian Church became general during the reign of Nero, (beginning about A.D. 64), and continued with occasional respites of a few months or even years at a time to the close of Diocletian's reign (about A.D. 305). The inhuman cruelty and savage barbarity to which were subjected those who dared profess the name of Christ during these centuries of heathen domination are matters of accepted history.[c] When Constantine the Great came to the throne in the first quarter of the fourth century, a radical change was inaugurated in the attitude of the state toward the church. The emperor straightway made the so-called Christianity of the time the religion of his realm; and zealous devotion to the church became the surest recommendation to imperial favor. But the church was already in great measure an apostate institution and even in crude outline of organization and service bore but remote resemblance to the Church of Jesus Christ, founded by the Savior and builded through the instrumentality of the apostles. Whatever vestiges of genuine Christianity may have possibly survived in the church before, were buried beyond the sight of man by the abuses that followed the elevation of the churchly organization to secular favor through the decree of Constantine. The emperor, even though unbaptized, made himself the head of the church, and priestly office was more sought after than military rank or state preferment. The spirit of apostasy, by which the church had become permeated before Constantine threw about it the mantle of imperial protection and emblazoned it with the insignia of state, now was roused to increased activity as the leaven of Satan's own culture flourished under the conditions most favorable for such fungoid growth.

The bishop of Rome had already asserted supremacy over his fellows in the episcopate; but when the emperor made Byzantium his capital, and renamed it in his own honor, Constantinople, the bishop of that city claimed equality with the Roman pontiff. The claim was contested; the

[c] See *The Great Apostasy,* chaps. 4 and 5.

ensuing dissension divided the church; and the disruption has persisted until the present day, as is evidenced by the existing distinction between the Roman Catholic and the Greek Catholic churches.

The Roman pontiff exercised secular as well as spiritual authority; and in the eleventh century arrogated to himself the title of *Pope*, signifying *Father*, in the sense of paternal ruler in all things. During the twelfth and thirteenth centuries the temporal authority of the pope was superior to that of kings and emperors; and the Roman church became the despotic potentate of nations, and an autocrat above all secular states. Yet this church, reeking with the stench of worldly ambition and lust of dominance, audaciously claimed to be the Church established by Him who affirmed: "My kingdom is not of this world." The arrogant assumptions of the Church of Rome were not less extravagant in spiritual than in secular administration. In her loudly asserted control over the spiritual destinies of the souls of men, she blasphemously pretended to forgive or retain individual sins, and to inflict or remit penalties both on earth and beyond the grave. She sold permission to commit sin and bartered for gold charters of indulgent forgiveness for sins already done. Her pope, proclaiming himself the vicar of God, sat in state to judge as God Himself; and by such blasphemy fulfilled the prophecy of Paul following his warning in relation to the awful conditions antecedent to the Second Coming of the Christ: "Let no man deceive you by any means: for that day shall not come, except there come a falling away first, and that man of sin be revealed, the son of perdition; Who opposeth and exalteth himself above all that is called God, or that is worshipped; so that he as God sitteth in the temple of God, shewing himself that he is God."[d]

In her unrestrained abandon to the license of arrogated authority, the Church of Rome hesitated not to transgress the law of God, change the ordinances essential to salvation, and ruthlessly break the everlasting covenant, thereby defiling the earth even as Isaiah had foretold.[e] She altered the ordinance of baptism, destroying its symbolism and associating with it imitations of pagan rites; she corrupted the Sacrament of the Lord's Supper and befouled the doctrine

[d] 2 Thes. 2:3, 4.
[e] Isa. 24:5.

thereof by the vagary of *transubstantiation*;[f] she assumed to apply the merits of the righteous to the forgiveness of the sinner in the unscriptural and wholly repellent dogma of *supererogation*; she promoted idolatry in most seductive and pernicious forms; she penalized the study of the holy scriptures by the people at large; she enjoined an unnatural state of celibacy upon her clergy; she revelled in unholy union with the theories and sophistries of men, and so adulterated the simple doctrines of the gospel of Christ as to produce a creed rank with superstition and heresy; she promulgated such perverted doctrines regarding the human body as to make the divinely formed tabernacle of flesh appear as a thing fit only to be tortured and contemned; she proclaimed it an act of virtue insuring rich reward to lie and deceive if thereby her own interests might be subserved; and she so thoroughly departed from the original plan of Church organization as to make of herself a spectacle of ornate display, fabricated by the caprice of man.[g]

The most important of the internal causes by which the Apostasy of the primitive Church was brought about may be thus summarized: (1) The corrupting of the simple doctrines of the gospel of Christ by admixture with so-called philosophic systems. (2) Unauthorized additions to the prescribed rites of the Church and the introduction of vital alterations in essential ordinances. (3) Unauthorized changes in Church organization and government.[h]

Under the tyrannous repression incident to usurped and unrighteous domination by the Roman church, civilization was retarded and for centuries was practically halted in its course. The period of retrogression is known in history as the Dark Ages. The fifteenth century witnessed the movement known as the Renaissance or Revival of Learning; there was a general significantly rapid awakening among men, and a determined effort to shake off the stupor of indolence and ignorance was manifest throughout the civilized world. By historians and

[f] The false doctrine of "transubstantiation" is to the effect that the bread and wine administered as emblems of Christ's flesh and blood in the Sacrament of the Lord's Supper are transmuted by priestly consecration into the actual flesh and blood of Jesus Christ. See *The Great Apostasy*, 8:16–19.

[g] *The Great Apostasy*, chaps. 6, 7, 8.

[h] *The Great Apostasy*, 6:14, 15; for comprehensive treatment of the subject see chaps. 6 to 9 inclusive.

philosophers the revival has been regarded as an unconscious and spontaneous prompting of the "spirit of the times"; it was a development predetermined in the Mind of God to illumine the benighted minds of men in preparation for the restoration of the gospel of Jesus Christ, which was appointed to be accomplished some centuries later.[i]

With the renewal of intellectual activity and effort in material betterment, there came, as a natural and inevitable accompaniment, protest and revolt against the ecclesiastical tyranny of the age. The Albigenses in France had risen in insurrection against churchly despotism during the thirteenth century; and in the fourteenth, John Wickliffe of Oxford University had boldly denounced the corruption of the Roman church and clergy, and particularly the restrictions imposed by the papal hierarchy on the popular study of the scriptures. Wickliffe gave to the world a version of the Holy Bible in English. These manifestations of independent belief and action the papal church sought to repress and punish by force. The Albigenses had been subjected to inhuman cruelties and unrestrained slaughter. Wickliffe was the subject of severe and persistent persecution; and though he died in his bed the vindictiveness of the Roman church was unsated until she had caused his body to be exhumed and burned and the ashes scattered abroad. John Huss and Jerome of Prague were prominent on the continent of Europe in agitation against papal despotism, and both fell martyrs to the cause. Though the church had become apostate to the core, there were not lacking men brave of heart and righteous of soul, ready to give their lives to the furtherance of spiritual emancipation.

A notable revolt against the papacy occurred in the sixteenth century, and is known as the Reformation. This movement was begun in 1517 by Martin Luther, a German monk; and it spread so rapidly as soon to involve the whole domain of popedom. Formal *protests* against the despotism of the papal church were formulated by the representatives of certain German principalities and other delegates at a diet or general council held at Spires A.D. 1529; and the reformers were thenceforth known as *Protestants*. An independent church was

---

[i] Note 2, end of chapter.

proposed by John, Elector of Saxony, a constitution for which was prepared at his instance by Luther and his colleague, Melanchthon. The *Protestants* were discordant. Being devoid of divine authority to guide them in matters of church organization and doctrine, they followed the diverse ways of men, and were rent within while assailed from without. The Roman church, confronted by determined opponents, hesitated at no extreme of cruelty. The court of the Inquisition, which had been established in the latter part of the fifteenth century under the infamously sacrilegious name of the "Holy Office," became intoxicated with the lust of barbarous cruelty in the century of the Reformation, and inflicted indescribable tortures on persons secretly accused of heresy.

In the early stages of the Reformation instigated by Luther, the king of England, Henry VIII, declared himself a supporter of the pope, and was rewarded by a papal bestowal of the distinguishing title "Defender of the Faith." Within a few years, this same British sovereign was excommunicated from the Roman church, because of impatient disregard of the pope's authority in the matter of Henry's desire to divorce Queen Catherine so that he could marry one of her maids. The British parliament, in 1534, passed the Act of Supremacy, by which the nation was declared free from all allegiance to papal authority. By Act of Parliament the king was made the head of the church within his own dominions. Thus was born the Church of England, a direct result of the licentious amours of a debauched and infamous king. With blasphemous indifference to the absence of divine commission, with no semblance of priestly succession, an adulterous sovereign created a church, provided therein a "priesthood" of his own, and proclaimed himself supreme administrator in all matters spiritual.

With the conflict between Catholicism and Protestantism in Great Britain the student of history is familiar. Suffice it here to say that the mutual hatred of the two contending sects, the zeal of their respective adherents, their professed love of God and devotion to Christ's service, were chiefly signalized by the sword, the ax, and the stake. Revelling in the realization of at least a partial emancipation from the tyranny of priestcraft, men and nations debauched their newly acquired liberty of thought, speech, and action, in a riot of abhorrent excess. The mis-called Age of Reason, and the atheistical abominations culminating in the French Revolution stand as ineffaceable testimony of what man may become when glorying in his denial of God.

Is it to be wondered at, that from the sixteenth century onward, churches of man's contriving have multiplied with phenomenal rapidity? Churches and churchly organizations professing Christianity as their creed have come to be numbered by hundreds. On every side is heard in this day, "Lo, here is Christ" or "Lo, there." There are sects named from the circumstances of their origin—as the Church of England; others after their famous founders or promoters—as Lutheran, Calvinist, Wesleyan; some are known by peculiarities of doctrine or plan of administration—as Methodist, Presbyterian, Baptist, Congregationalist; but down to the third decade of the nineteenth century there was no church on earth affirming name or title as the Church of Jesus Christ. The only organization called a church existing at that time and venturing to assert claim to authority by succession was the Catholic church, which for centuries had been apostate and wholly bereft of divine authority or recognition. If the "mother church" be without a valid priesthood, and devoid of spiritual power, how can her offspring derive from her the right to officiate in the things of God? Who would dare to affirm that man can originate a priesthood which God is bound to honor and acknowledge? Granted that men may and do create among themselves societies, associations, sects, and even "churches" if they choose so to designate their organizations; granted that they may prescribe rules, formulate laws, and devise plans of operation, discipline, and government, and that all such laws, rules, and schemes of administration are binding upon those who assume membership—granted all these rights and powers— whence can such human institutions derive the authority of the Holy Priesthood, without which there can be no Church of Christ?[j]

The apostate condition of Christendom has been frankly admitted by many eminent and conscientious representatives of the several churches, and by churches as institutions. Even the Church of England acknowledges the awful fact in her official declaration of degeneracy, as set forth in the *"Homily Against Peril of Idolatry,"* in these words:

---

[j] This paragraph is in part a paraphrase of *The Great Apostasy,* 10:21, 22.

"So that laity and clergy, learned and unlearned, all ages, sects, and degrees of men, women, and children of whole Christendom—an horrible and most dreadful thing to think—have been at once drowned in abominable idolatry; of all other vices most detested of God, and most damnable to man; and that by the space of eight hundred years and more."[k]

Let it not be concluded that through the night of the universal apostasy, long and dark as it was, God had forgotten the world. Mankind had not been left wholly to itself. The Spirit of God was operative so far as the unbelief of men permitted. John the apostle, and the Three Nephite disciples,[l] were ministering among men, though unknown. But through the centuries of spiritual darkness men lived and died without the administration of a contemporary apostle, prophet, elder, bishop, priest, teacher, or deacon. Whatever of the form of Godliness existed in the churches of human establishment was destitute of divine power. The time foreseen by the inspired apostle had fully come—mankind in general refused to endure sound doctrine, but, having itching ears, did they heap to themselves teachers, after their own lusts, and verily had they turned away their ears from the truth to follow after fables.[m] The first quarter of the nineteenth century witnessed the cumulative fulfilment of the conditions predicted through the prophet Amos: "Behold, the days come, saith the Lord God, that I will send a famine in the land, not a famine of bread, nor a thirst for water, but of hearing the words of the Lord: And they shall wander from sea to sea, and from the north even to the east, they shall run to and fro to seek the word of the Lord, and shall not find it."[n]

Throughout the period of apostasy the windows of heaven had been shut toward the world, so as to preclude all direct revelation from God, and particularly any personal ministration or theophany of the Christ. Mankind had ceased to know God; and had invested the utterances of prophets and apostles of old, who had known Him,

[k] Note 3, end of chapter.

[l] Page 642 and 684–86.

[m] See 2 Tim. 4:1–4; also *The Great Apostasy,* 2:30.

[n] Amos 8:11, 12.

with a pall of mystery and fancy, so that the True and the Living God was no longer believed to exist; but in His place the sectaries had tried to conceive of an incomprehensible being, devoid of "body, parts, or passions," an immaterial nothing.[o]

But it had been determined in the councils of heaven, that after many centuries of benighted ignorance the world should be illumined anew by the light of truth. Through the operation of the genius of intelligence, which is the Spirit of Truth, the soul of the race had been undergoing a preparation, like unto the deep plowing of a field, for the planting of the gospel afresh. The principle of the mariner's compass was revealed by the Spirit; the material embodiment thereof was invented by man; and by its aid the unknown oceans were explored. Toward the end of the fifteenth century Columbus was led by the inspiration of God to the discovery of the New World, whereon dwelt the degenerate posterity of Lehi, a dark-skinned remnant of the house of Israel—the American Indians. In due time the good ships *Mayflower* and *Speedwell* brought to the western world the Pilgrim Fathers, as the vanguard of a host escaping from exile and seeking a new home wherein they could worship according to the dictates of their consciences. The coming of Columbus and the later immigration of the Puritan Pilgrims had been predicted nearly six hundred years before Christ; their respective missions had been as truly appointed unto them as has been the sending of any prophet with a message to deliver and a work to do.[p] The war between the American Colonies and the Mother Country, and the victorious issue thereof in the emancipation of the American nation once and forever from monarchial rule, had been foretold as further steps in the preparation for the restoration of the gospel. Time was allowed for the establishment of a stable government, for the raising up of men chosen and inspired to frame and promulgate the Constitution of the United States, which promises to every man a full measure of political and religious freedom. It was not meet that the precious seed of the restored gospel be thrown upon unplowed soil, hardened by intolerance, and fit to produce only thorns of bigotry and rank weeds of mental

[o] See Church of England *Book of Common Prayer,* Articles of Religion 1. Note 4, end of chapter.

[p] See 1 Ne. 13:10–13. Note 5, end of chapter.

and spiritual serfdom. The gospel of Jesus Christ is the embodiment of liberty; it is the truth that shall make free every man and every nation who will accept and obey its precepts.

At the appointed time, the Eternal Father and His Son Jesus the Christ appeared to man upon the earth, and inaugurated the Dispensation of the Fulness of Times.

NOTES TO CHAPTER 40

1. Cessation of Revelation on the Western Hemisphere.—"The eastern world had lost this knowledge of the Lord earlier than the western hemisphere. Upon the land of North America, four hundred years after the birth of our Savior and Master, there stood at least one man who knew the Lord God Almighty as a distinct personality, a Being capable of communicating Himself to man. That man was Moroni, the son of Mormon, whose testimony abides now and must abide through all the ages to come."—George Q. Cannon, *Life of Joseph Smith*, p. 21. See Moro. 10:27–34.

2. Results of the Great Apostasy Divinely Overruled for Eventual Good.—The thoughtful student cannot fail to see in the progress of the great apostasy and its results the existence of an overruling power operating toward eventual good, however mysterious its methods. The heartrending persecutions to which the saints were subjected in the early centuries of our era, the anguish, the torture, the bloodshed incurred in defense of the testimony of Christ, the rise of an apostate church, blighting the intellect and leading captive the souls of men—all these dread conditions were foreknown to the Lord. While we cannot say or believe that such exhibitions of human depravity and blasphemy of heart were in accordance with the divine will, certainly God willed to permit full scope to the free agency of man, in the exercise of which agency some won the martyr's crown, and others filled the flagon of their iniquity to overflowing. Not less marked is the divine permission in the revolts and rebellions, in the revolutions and reformations, that developed in opposition to the darkening influence of the apostate church. Wickliffe and Huss, Luther and Melanchthon, Zwingli and Calvin, Henry VIII in his arrogant assumption of priestly authority, John Knox in Scotland, Roger Williams in America—these and a host of others builded better than they knew, in that their efforts laid in part the foundation of the structure of religious freedom and liberty of conscience—and this in preparation for the restoration of the gospel as had been divinely predicted.— *The Great Apostasy*, 10:19, 20.

3. Declaration of a General Apostasy by the Church of England.—The *Book of Homilies,* from which the quotation given in the text is taken, was published about the middle of the sixteenth century. The official proclamation of a universal apostasy was made prominently current, for the Homilies were "appointed to be read in churches" in lieu of sermons under certain conditions. In the statement cited, the Church of England solemnly avers that a state of apostasy affecting all ages, sects, and degrees throughout whole Christendom, had prevailed for eight hundred years prior to the establishment of the church making the declaration. That this affirmation remains effective today, as both confession and profession of the Church of England, appears from the fact that the homily "Against Peril of Idolatry" and certain other homilies are specifically ratified and endorsed, and withal prescribed "to be read in Churches by the Ministers diligently and distinctly that they may be understanded of the people." See "Articles of Religion" xxxv, in current issues of Church of England, *Book of Common Prayer.*

4. The "Creed of Athanasius."—At the Council of Nice, convoked by the emperor, Constantine, A.D. 325, a formal statement of belief concerning the Godhead was adopted. Later a modification was issued, known as the "Creed of Athanasius," and though the authorship is questioned, the creed has a place in the ritual of some of the Protestant churches. No more conclusive evidence that men had ceased to know God need be adduced than the Athanasian Creed. As confessed by the Church of England in this day, and as published in the official ritual (see *Prayer Book*) "The Creed of Saint Athanasius" is this: "We worship one God in Trinity, and Trinity in Unity; neither confounding the Persons: nor dividing the Substance. For there is one Person of the Father, another of the Son: and another of the Holy Ghost. But the Godhead of the Father, of the Son, and of the Holy Ghost, is all one: the Glory equal, the Majesty co-eternal. Such as the Father is, such is the Son: and such is the Holy Ghost. The Father uncreate, the Son uncreate: and the Holy Ghost uncreate. The Father incomprehensible, the Son incomprehensible: and the Holy Ghost incomprehensible. The Father eternal, the Son eternal: and the Holy Ghost eternal. And yet they are not three eternals: but one eternal. As also there are not three incomprehensibles, nor three uncreated: but one uncreated, and one incomprehensible. So likewise the Father is Almighty, the Son Almighty: and the Holy Ghost Almighty. And yet they are not three Almighties: but one Almighty. So the Father is God, the Son is God: and the Holy Ghost is God. And yet they are not three Gods: but one God. So likewise the Father is Lord, the Son Lord, and the Holy Ghost Lord. And yet not three Lords: but one Lord."

Then follows this strange confession of what is at once required by "Christian verity," and forbidden by the "Catholick Religion": "For like as we are compelled by the Christian verity: to acknowledge every Person by himself to be God and Lord; so are we forbidden by the Catholick Religion: to say, There be three Gods, or three Lords."

5. The Mission of Columbus and Its Results.—Unto Nephi, son of Lehi, was shown the future of his people, including the degeneracy of a branch thereof, afterward known as Lamanites and in modern times as American Indians. The coming of a man from among the Gentiles, across the deep waters, was revealed in such plainness as to positively identify that man with Columbus; and the coming of other Gentiles to this land, out of captivity, is equally explicit. The revelation is thus recorded by Nephi to whom it was given: "And it came to pass that I looked and beheld many waters; and they divided the Gentiles from the seed of my brethren. And it came to pass that the angel said unto me, Behold the wrath of God is upon the seed of thy brethren. And I looked and beheld a man among the Gentiles who was separated from the seed of my brethren by the many waters; and I beheld the Spirit of God, that it came down and wrought upon the man; and he went forth upon the many waters, even unto the seed of my brethren, who were in the promised land. And it came to pass that I beheld the Spirit of God, that it wrought upon other Gentiles; and they went forth out of captivity, upon the many waters." (1 Ne. 13:10–13). The establishment of a great Gentile nation on the American continent, the subjugation of the Lamanites or Indians, the war between the newly established nation and Great Britain, or "their mother Gentiles," and the victorious outcome of that struggle for independence, are set forth with equal clearness in the same chapter.

CHAPTER 41

Personal Manifestations of God the Eternal Father and of His Son Jesus Christ in Modern Times

A NEW DISPENSATION

In the year of our Lord 1820 there lived at Manchester, Ontario County, state of New York, a worthy citizen named Joseph Smith. His household comprised his wife and their nine children. The third son and fourth child of the family was Joseph Smith Jr., who at the time of which we speak was in his fifteenth year. In the year specified, New York and adjacent states were swept by a wave of intense agitation in religious matters; and unusual zeal was put forth by ministers of the numerous rival sects to win converts to their respective folds. The boy Joseph was profoundly affected by this intense excitement, and was particularly puzzled and troubled over the spirit of confusion and contention manifest through it all. As our present subject has to do with him specifically, and in view of the transcendent importance of his testimony to the world, his own account of what ensued is given herewith.

"Some time in the second year after our removal to Manchester, there was in the place where we lived an unusual excitement on the subject of religion. It commenced with the Methodists, but soon became general among all the sects in that region of country. Indeed, the whole district of country seemed affected by it, and great multitudes united themselves to the different religious parties, which created no small stir and division amongst the people, some crying, 'Lo, here!' and others, 'Lo, there!' Some were contending for the Methodist faith, some for the Presbyterian, and some for the Baptist.

"For notwithstanding the great love which the converts to these different faiths expressed at the time of their conversion, and the great zeal manifested by the respective clergy, who were active in getting up and promoting this extraordinary scene of religious feeling, in order to have everybody converted, as they were pleased to call it, let them join what sect they pleased—yet when the converts began to file off, some to one party and some to another, it was seen that the seemingly good feelings of both the priests and the converts were more pretended than real; for a scene of great confusion and bad feeling ensued; priest contending against priest, and convert against convert; so that all their good feelings one for another, if they ever had any, were entirely lost in a strife of words and a contest about opinions.

"I was at this time in my fifteenth year. My father's family was proselyted to the Presbyterian faith, and four of them joined that church, namely—my mother Lucy; my brothers Hyrum and Samuel Harrison; and my sister Sophronia.

"During this time of great excitement, my mind was called up to serious reflection and great uneasiness; but though my feelings were deep and often poignant, still I kept myself aloof from all these parties, though I attended their several meetings as often as occasion would permit. In process of time my mind became somewhat partial to the Methodist sect, and I felt some desire to be united with them; but so great were the confusion and strife among the different denominations, that it was impossible for a person young as I was, and so unacquainted with men and things, to come to any certain conclusion who was right and who was wrong.

"My mind at times was greatly excited, the cry and tumult were so great and incessant. The Presbyterians were most decided against the Baptists and Methodists, and used all the powers of either reason or sophistry to prove their errors, or, at least, to make the people think they were in error. On the other hand, the Baptists and Methodists in their turn were equally zealous in endeavoring to establish their own tenets and disprove all others.

"In the midst of this war of words and tumult of opinions, I often said to myself, What is to be done? Who of all these parties are right; or, are they all wrong together? If any one of them be right, which is it, and how shall I know it?

"While I was laboring under the extreme difficulties caused by the contests of these parties of religionists, I was one day reading the Epistle of James, first chapter and fifth verse, which reads: *If any of you lack wisdom, let him ask of God, that giveth to all men liberally, and upbraideth not; and it shall be given him.*

"Never did any passage of scripture come with more power to the heart of man than this did at this time to mine. It seemed to enter with great force into every feeling of my heart. I reflected on it again and again, knowing that if any person needed wisdom from God, I did; for how to act I did not know, and unless I could get more wisdom than I then had, I would never know; for the teachers of religion of the different sects understood the same passages of scripture so differently as to destroy all confidence in settling the question by an appeal to the Bible.

"At length I came to the conclusion that I must either remain in darkness and confusion, or else I must do as James directs, that is, ask of God. I at length came to the determination to 'ask of God,' concluding that if He gave wisdom to them that lacked wisdom, and would give liberally, and not upbraid, I might venture.

"So, in accordance with this, my determination to ask of God, I retired to the woods to make the attempt. It was on the morning of a beautiful, clear day, early in the spring of eighteen hundred and twenty. It was the first time in my life that I had made such an attempt, for amidst all my anxieties I had never as yet made the attempt to pray vocally.

"After I had retired to the place where I had previously designed to go, having looked around me, and finding myself alone, I kneeled down and began to offer up the desires of my heart to God. I had scarcely done so, when immediately I was seized upon by some power which entirely overcame me, and had such an astonishing influence over me as to bind my tongue so that I could not speak. Thick darkness gathered around me, and it seemed to me for a time as if I were doomed to sudden destruction.

"But, exerting all my powers to call upon God to deliver me out of the power of this enemy which had seized upon me, and at the very moment when I was ready to sink into despair and abandon myself to destruction—not to an imaginary ruin, but to the power of some actual being from the unseen world, who had such marvelous power as I had never before felt in any being—just at this moment of great alarm, I saw a pillar of light exactly over my head, above the brightness of the sun, which descended gradually until it fell upon me.

"It no sooner appeared than I found myself delivered from the enemy which held me bound. When the light rested upon me I saw two personages, whose brightness and glory defy all description, standing above me in the air. One of them spake unto me, calling me by name, and said, pointing to the other—*This is my beloved Son, hear him!*

"My object in going to inquire of the Lord was to know which of all the sects was right, that I might know which to join. No sooner, therefore, did I get possession of myself, so as to be able to speak, than I asked the personages who stood above me in the light, which of all the sects was right—and which I should join.

"I was answered that I must join none of them, for they were all wrong; and the personage who addressed me said that all their creeds were an abomination in his sight; that those professors were all corrupt; that 'they draw near to me with their lips, but their hearts are far from me; they teach for doctrines the commandments of men, having a form of godliness, but they deny the power thereof.'

"He again forbade me to join with any of them; and many other things did he say unto me, which I cannot write at this time. When I came to myself again, I found myself lying on my back, looking up into heaven.

"Some few days after I had this vision, I happened to be in company with one of the Methodist preachers, who was very active in the before mentioned religious excitement; and, conversing with him on the subject of religion, I took occasion to give him an account of the vision which I had had. I was greatly surprised at his behavior; he treated my communication not only lightly, but with great contempt, saying, it was all of the devil, that there were no such things as visions or revelations in these days; that all such things had ceased with the apostles, and that there would never be any more of them.

"I soon found, however, that my telling the story had excited a great deal of prejudice against me among professors of religion, and was the cause of great persecution, which continued to increase; and though I was an obscure boy, only between fourteen and fifteen years of age, and my circumstances in life such as to make a boy of no consequence in the world, yet men of high standing would take notice sufficient to excite the public mind against me, and create a bitter persecution; and this was common among all the sects—all united to persecute me.

"It caused me serious reflection then, and often has since, how very strange it was that an obscure boy, of a little over fourteen years of age, and one, too, who was doomed to the necessity of obtaining a scanty maintenance by his daily labor, should be thought a character of sufficient importance to attract the attention of the great ones of the most popular sects of the day, and in a manner to create in them a spirit of the most bitter persecution and reviling. But strange or not, so it was, and it was often the cause of great sorrow to myself.

"However, it was nevertheless a fact that I had beheld a vision. I have thought since, that I felt much like Paul, when he made his defense before King Agrippa, and related the account of the vision he had when he saw a light, and heard a voice; but still there were but few who believed him; some said he was dishonest, others said he was mad; and he was ridiculed and reviled. But all this did not destroy the reality of his vision. He had seen a vision, he knew he had, and all the persecution under heaven could not make it otherwise; and though they should persecute him unto death, yet he knew, and would know to his latest breath, that he had both seen a light, and heard a voice speaking unto him, and all the world could not make him think or believe otherwise.

"So it was with me. I had actually seen a light, and in the midst of that light I saw two personages, and they did in reality speak to me; and though I was hated and persecuted for saying that I had seen a vision, yet it was true; and while they were persecuting me, reviling me, and speaking all manner of evil against me falsely for so saying, I was led to say in my heart: Why persecute me for telling the truth? I have actually seen a vision, and who am I that I can withstand God, or why does the world think to make me deny what I have actually seen? For I had seen a vision; I knew it, and I knew that God knew it, and I could not deny it, neither dared I do it, at least I knew that by so doing I would offend God, and come under condemnation.

"I had now got my mind satisfied so far as the sectarian world was concerned; that it was not my duty to join with any of them, but to continue as I was until further directed. I had found the testimony of

James to be true, that a man who lacked wisdom might ask of God, and obtain, and not be upbraided."[a]

In this wise was ushered in the Dispensation of the Fulness of Times.[b] The darkness of the long night of apostasy was dispelled; the glory of the heavens once more illumined the world; the silence of centuries was broken; the voice of God was heard again upon the earth. In the spring of A.D. 1820 there was one mortal, a boy not quite fifteen years old, who knew as well as that he lived, that the current human conception of Deity as an incorporeal essence of something possessing neither definite shape nor tangible substance was as devoid of truth in respect to both the Father and the Son as its statement in formulated creeds was incomprehensible. The boy Joseph knew that both the Eternal Father and His glorified Son, Jesus Christ, were in form and stature, perfect Men; and that in Their physical likeness mankind had been created in the flesh.[c] He knew further that the Father and the Son were individual Personages, each distinct from the other—a truth fully attested by the Lord Jesus during His mortal existence, but which had been obscured if not buried by the sophistries of human unbelief. He realized that the unity of the Godhead was a oneness of perfection in purpose, plan, and action, as the scriptures declare it to be, and not an impossible union of personalities, as generations of false teachers had tried to impress. This resplendent theophany confirmed the fact of a universal apostasy, with the inevitable corollary—that the Church of Christ was nowhere existent upon the earth. It effectively dissipated the delusion that direct revelation from the heavens had forever ceased; and affirmatively proved the actuality of personal communication between God and mortals.

For the fourth time since the Savior's birth in the flesh, the voice of the Father had attested the Son's authority in matters pertaining to earth and man.[d] In this latter-day revelation of Himself, as on the earlier occasions, the Father did no more than affirm the fact of the Son's identity, and command that He be obeyed.

[a] JS–H 1:25–26; also *History of The Church of Jesus Christ of Latter–day Saints*, vol. 1, pp. 2–8.

[b] Eph. 1:9, 10. Note 1, end of chapter.

[c] Note 5, end of chapter.

[d] For earlier instances, see pages 122, 350, and 672.

"A MESSENGER SENT FROM THE PRESENCE OF GOD"[e]

For about three and a half years following the glorious appearing of the Father and the Son to Joseph Smith, the youthful revelator was left to himself, so far as further manifestations from heaven were concerned. The period was one of probation. He was subjected to the sneers of youths of his age, and to aggressive persecution on the part of older men, "who," as he very justly and somewhat accusingly remarks, "ought to have been my friends and to have treated me kindly, and if they supposed me to be deluded to have endeavored in a proper and affectionate manner to have reclaimed me."[f] He pursued his usual vocation, that of farm work in association with his father and brothers, from whom he received kindness, consideration, and sympathy; and in spite of raillery, abuse, and denunciation from the community at large he remained firm and faithful in his solemn avouchment that he had seen and heard both the Eternal Father and Jesus the Christ, and that he had been instructed to join none of the contending sects or churches because they were all fundamentally wrong.

On the night of the 21st of September 1823, while engaged in fervent prayer to God in the solitude of his chamber, Joseph observed the room become illuminated until the light exceeded that of a cloudless noon. A glorious personage appeared within the room, standing a little space above the floor. Both the body of the visitant and the loose robe he wore were of exquisite whiteness. Calling Joseph by name he announced himself as Moroni, "a messenger sent from the presence of God"; and informed the young man that the Lord had a work for him to do, and that his name should come to be spoken of both for good and for evil among all nations, kindreds, and tongues. The angel told of a record engraven on plates of gold, which contained an account of the former inhabitants of the American continent, and the fulness of the everlasting gospel as delivered by the Savior to those ancient people; and furthermore, that with the record were a breastplate, and the Urim and Thummim, which had been prepared by divine instrumentality for use in translating the book. The place at which the plate and the other sacred things were deposited was shown to Joseph in vision, and

[e] JS–H 1:29–54, 59; also *History of the Church*, vol. 1, pp. 10–16, 18.
[f] JS–H 1:28.

so clear was the demonstration that he readily recognized the spot when he visited it next day.

The angel quoted several passages from the Old and one from the New Testament, some verbatim, and some with small variations from the Biblical version. Joseph's statement concerning the scriptures cited by Moroni is as follows:

"He first quoted part of the third chapter of Malachi, and he quoted also the fourth or last chapter of the same prophecy, though with a little variation from the way it reads in our Bibles. Instead of quoting the first verse as it reads in our books, he quoted it thus:

"For behold, the day cometh that shall burn as an oven, and all the proud, yea, and all that do wickedly, shall burn as stubble; for they that come shall burn them, saith the Lord of Hosts, that it shall leave them neither root nor branch.

"And again, he quoted the fifth verse thus: *Behold, I will reveal unto you the Priesthood, by the hand of Elijah the prophet, before the coming of the great and dreadful day of the Lord.*

"He also quoted the next verse differently: *And he shall plant in the hearts of the children the promises made to the fathers, and the hearts of the children shall turn to their fathers; if it were not so, the whole earth would be utterly wasted at his coming.*

"In addition to these, he quoted the eleventh chapter of Isaiah, saying that it was about to be fulfilled. He quoted also the third chapter of Acts, twenty-second and twenty-third verses, precisely as they stand in our New Testament. He said that that prophet was Christ; but the day had not yet come when they who would not hear his voice should be cut off from among the people, but soon would come.

"He also quoted the second chapter of Joel, from the twenty-eighth verse to the last. He also said that this was not yet fulfilled but was soon to be. And he further stated that the fulness of the Gentiles was soon to come in."[g]

The messenger departed, and the light disappeared with him. Twice during the same night, however, the angel returned, each time repeating what had been said at his first appearing and adding words

---

g JS–H 1:36–41; and *History of the Church,* vol. 1, pp. 12, 13.

of instruction and caution. On the next day Moroni appeared to the young man again, and directed him to inform his father of the visitations and commandments he had received. Joseph's father instructed him to obey the messenger's instructions and testified that they were given of God. Joseph then went to the locality specified by the angel, on the side of a hill called in the record Cumorah, and immediately identified the spot that had been shown him in vision. By the aid of a lever he removed a large stone, which proved to be the cover of a stone box wherein lay the plates and other articles described by Moroni. The angel appeared at the place, and forbade Joseph to remove the contents of the box at that time. The young man replaced the massive stone lid and left the spot.

Four years later, the plates, the Urim and Thummim, and the breastplate were delivered into Joseph's keeping by the angel Moroni. This Moroni, who now came as a resurrected being, was the last survivor of the Nephite nation; he had completed the record, and then shortly before his death had hidden away the same in the hill Cumorah, whence it was brought forth through his instrumentality and delivered to the modern prophet and seer, Joseph Smith, September 22, 1827. That record, or, strictly speaking a part thereof, is now accessible to all; it has been translated through divine instrumentality and is now published in many languages as the Book of Mormon.[h]

THE AARONIC PRIESTHOOD
CONFERRED BY JOHN THE BAPTIST

On the 15th of May, 1829, Joseph Smith and his scribe in the work of translating the Nephite record, Oliver Cowdery, retired to a secluded glade to pray. Their special purpose was to inquire of the Lord concerning the ordinance of baptism for the remission of sins, some account of which they had found on the plates. Joseph writes:

"While we were thus employed, praying and calling upon the Lord, a messenger from heaven descended in a cloud of light, and having laid his hands upon us, he ordained us, saying:

[h] Morm. 6:6; Moro. 10:2.

"Upon you my fellow servants, in the name of Messiah, I confer the Priesthood of Aaron, which holds the keys of the ministering of angels, and of the Gospel of repentance, and of baptism by immersion for the remission of sins; and this shall never be taken again from the earth, until the sons of Levi do offer again an offering unto the Lord in righteousness." [i]

The angelic visitor stated that his name was John, the same who is designated in the New Testament, John the Baptist; and that he had acted in ordaining the two under the direction of Peter, James, and John, who held the keys of the Higher or Melchizedek Priesthood. He explained that the Aaronic Priesthood did not comprise "the power of laying on hands for the gift of the Holy Ghost";[j] but he predicted that the Higher Priesthood, having this power, would be conferred later. By his express direction, Joseph baptized Oliver, and the latter in turn baptized Joseph, by immersion in water.

THE MELCHIZEDEK PRIESTHOOD
CONFERRED BY PETER, JAMES, AND JOHN

Shortly after their ordination to the Lesser or Aaronic Priesthood, Joseph Smith and Oliver Cowdery were visited by the presiding apostles of old, Peter, James, and John, who conferred upon them the Melchizedek Priesthood and ordained them to the Holy Apostleship. In a later revelation the Lord Jesus thus specifically acknowledges the respective ordinations as having been done by His will and commandment:

"Which John I have sent unto you, my servants, Joseph Smith, Jun., and Oliver Cowdery, to ordain you unto this first priesthood which you have received, that you might be called and ordained even as Aaron. . . . And also with Peter, and James, and John, whom I have sent unto you, by whom I have ordained you and confirmed you to be apostles, and special witnesses of my name, and bear the keys of your ministry, and of the same things which I revealed unto them: Unto whom I have committed the keys of my kingdom, and a dispensation of the gospel for the last times; and for the fulness of times, in the which I will gather together in one all things, both which are in heaven, and which are on the earth."[k]

---

[i] JS–H 1:68, 69; D&C 13; *History of the Church*, vol. 1, p. 39.

[j] Note 2 and 6, end of chapter.

[k] D&C 27:8, 12, 13.

ESTABLISHMENT OF THE CHURCH
OF JESUS CHRIST OF LATTER-DAY SAINTS

On the sixth day of April A.D. 1830, the Church of Jesus Christ of Latter-day Saints was formally organized, at Fayette, Seneca County, New York, in accordance with the secular law governing the establishment of religious associations. The persons actually participating in the organization numbered but six, such being the minimum required by law in such an undertaking; many others were present however, some of whom had already received the ordinance of baptism for the remission of sins. By revelation to Joseph Smith, the Lord had previously specified the day on which the organization was to be effected, and had made known His plan of Church government— with detailed instructions as to the requisite conditions for membership; the indispensability of baptism by immersion, and the precise manner in which the initiatory ordinance was to be administered; the manner of confirming baptized believers as members of the Church; the duties of elders, priests, teachers, and deacons in the Church; the exact procedure to be followed in the administration of the Sacrament of the Lord's Supper; the order of Church discipline, and the method of transferring members from one branch to another.[l] The baptized converts present at the organization were called upon to express their acceptance or rejection of Joseph Smith and Oliver Cowdery as elders in the Church; and in accordance with the unanimous vote in the affirmative the ordination or setting apart of these two men as respectively first and second elder in the new organization was performed.[m]

While the Book of Mormon had been in course of translation, particularly during the two years immediately preceding the organization of the Church, several revelations had been given through Joseph the prophet and seer, relating to the work of translation and to the preparatory labor necessary to the establishment of the Church as an institution among men. The Author of these several revelations declared Himself definitely to be Jesus Christ, God, the Son of God, the Redeemer, the Light and Life of the World, Alpha and Omega, Christ

[l] D&C 20.

[m] D&C 20:2, 3; compare 21:11; see also *History of the Church*, vol. 1, pp. 40, 41.

the Lord, the Lord and Savior.[n] As early as A.D. 1829, the calling of
the Twelve Apostles was indicated, and appointment was made for the
searching out of the Twelve who should stand before the world as
special witnesses of the Christ; these were subsequently ordained to
the Holy Apostleship, and the council or quorum of the Twelve has
been recognized, and instructions concerning their exalted duties
have been given, in numerous revelations of later dates.[o]

In such manner has the Church of Jesus Christ been reestablished
upon the earth, with all the powers and authority pertaining to the
Holy Priesthood as committed by the Lord Jesus to His apostles in
the period of His personal ministry. The inauguration of a new
dispensation of the gospel, with a restoration of the Priesthood, was
absolutely necessary; since through the Apostasy of the primitive
Church there lived not a man empowered to speak or administer in
the name of God or His Christ. John the Revelator saw in his vision
of the last days an angel bringing anew "the everlasting gospel to preach
unto them that dwell on the earth, and to every nation, and kindred,
and tongue, and people, saying with a loud voice, Fear God, and give
glory to him; for the hour of his judgment is come: and worship him
that made heaven, and earth, and the sea, and the fountains of waters."[p]

Such an angelic embassage would have been but a needless and
empty display, and therefore an impossibility, had the everlasting
gospel remained upon the earth with its powers of priesthood perpetuated by succession. The scriptural assurances of a restoration in the
last days through direct bestowal from the heavens is conclusive proof
of the actuality of the universal apostasy. Moroni came to Joseph
Smith as "a messenger sent from the presence of God," and delivered
a record containing "the fulness of the everlasting gospel," as it had been
imparted to the Lord's people in ancient times; and the worldwide
distribution of the Mormon, and of other publications embodying
the revealed word in modern times, and the ministry of thousands
who labor in the authority of the Holy Priesthood combine as the

[n] D&C 5, 6, 8, 10–12, 14–20.

[o] D&C 18:27, 31–36; 20:38–44; 84:63, 64; 95:4; 107:23–25; 112:1, 14, 21; 118;
124:127–130.

[p] Rev. 14:6, 7.

loud voice addressed to every nation, crying: "Fear God, and give glory to him; for the hour of his judgment is come."

FURTHER COMMUNICATIONS
FROM THE HEAVENS TO MAN

Following the organization of the Church as heretofore described, direct communication between the Lord Jesus Christ and His prophet Joseph was frequent, as the needs of the Church required. Numerous revelations were given, and these are accessible to all who will read.[q] A marvelous manifestation was granted to the prophet and his associate in the presidency of the Church, Sidney Rigdon, the record of which appears as follows:

"We, Joseph Smith, Jun., and Sidney Rigdon, being in the Spirit on the sixteenth of February, in the year of our Lord, one thousand eight hundred and thirty-two, by the power of the Spirit our eyes were opened and our understandings were enlightened, so as to see and understand the things of God—even those things which were from the beginning before the world was, which were ordained of the Father, through his Only Begotten Son, who was in the bosom of the Father, even from the beginning, of whom we bear record, and the record which we bear is the fulness of the gospel of Jesus Christ, who is the Son, whom we saw and with whom we conversed in the heavenly vision; For while we were doing the work of translation, which the Lord had appointed unto us, we came to the twenty-ninth verse of the fifth chapter of John, which was given unto us as follows. Speaking of the resurrection of the dead, concerning those who shall hear the voice of the Son of Man, and shall come forth; they who have done good in the resurrection of the just, and they who have done evil in the resurrection of the unjust. Now this caused us to marvel, for it was given unto us of the Spirit; and while we meditated upon these things, the Lord touched the eyes of our understandings and they were opened, and the glory of the Lord shone round about; and we beheld the glory of the Son, on the right hand of the Father, and received of his fulness; and saw the holy angels, and they who are

---

[q] See D&C and *History of the Church.*

sanctified before his throne, worshiping God, and the Lamb, who worship him for ever and ever. And now, after the many testimonies which have been given of him, this is the testimony last of all, which we give of him, that he lives; for we saw him, even on the right hand of God, and we heard the voice bearing record that he is the Only Begotten of the Father—that by him and through him, and of him the worlds are and were created, and the inhabitants thereof are begotten sons and daughters unto God."[r]

The vision was followed by further revelation both through sight and hearing; and the Lord showed unto His servants and proclaimed aloud the fate of the wicked and the characteristic features of the varied degrees of glory provided for the souls of mankind in the hereafter. The several states of graded honor and exaltation pertaining to the telestial, the terrestrial, and the celestial kingdoms were revealed, and the ancient scriptures relating thereto were illumined with the new light of simplicity and literalness.[s]

PERSONAL APPEARING OF THE LORD JESUS CHRIST IN THE KIRTLAND TEMPLE

In less than three and a half years after its organization the Church began the erection of the first temple of modern times at Kirtland, Ohio. The work was undertaken in compliance with a revelation from the Lord requiring this labor at the hands of His people. The Church membership was small; the people were in poverty; the period was one of determined opposition and relentless persecution.[t] Be it understood that to the Latter-day Saints a temple is more than chapel, church, tabernacle, or cathedral; it is no place of common assembly even for purposes of congregational worship, but an edifice sacred to the ordinances of the Holy Priesthood—distinctively and essentially a House of the Lord. The temple at Kirtland stands today, a substantial and stately building; but it is no longer in possession of the people who reared it by unmeasured sacrifice of time, substance, and effort extending through years of self-denial and suffering. Its cornerstones

[r] D&C 76:11–24; also *History of the Church* under date specified.

[s] See D&C 76:25–119; also *The Articles of Faith*, pp. 91–93; 405–11.

[t] See *The House of the Lord*, pp. 114–23.

were laid July 23, 1833, and the completed structure was dedicated March 27, 1836. The dedicatory service was made ever memorable by a Pentecostal outpouring of the Spirit of the Lord accompanied by the visible presence of angels. In the evening of the same day the several quorums of priesthood assembled in the house, and a yet greater manifestation of divine power and glory was witnessed. On the succeeding Sunday—April 3, 1836—after a service of solemn worship, including the administration of the Lord's Supper, the prophet Joseph and his counselor, Oliver Cowdery, retired for prayer within the veils enclosing the platform and pulpit reserved for the presiding authorities of the Melchizedek Priesthood. They bear this solemn testimony to the personal appearing of the Lord Jesus Christ at that time and place:

"The veil was taken from our minds, and the eyes of our understanding were opened. We saw the Lord standing upon the breast work of the pulpit, before us, and under his feet was a paved work of pure gold in color like amber. His eyes were as a flame of fire, the hair of his head was white like the pure snow, his countenance shone above the brightness of the sun, and his voice was as the sound of the rushing of great waters, even the voice of Jehovah, saying—I am the first and the last, I am he who liveth, I am he who was slain, I am your advocate with the Father. Behold, your sins are forgiven you, you are clean before me, therefore lift up your heads and rejoice, let the hearts of your brethren rejoice, and let the hearts of all my people rejoice, who have, with their might, built this house to my name. For behold, I have accepted this house, and my name shall be here, and I will manifest myself to my people in mercy in this house, Yea I will appear unto my servants, and speak unto them with mine own voice, if my people will keep my commandments, and do not pollute this holy house, Yea the hearts of thousands and tens of thousands shall greatly rejoice in consequence of the blessings which shall be poured out, and the endowment with which my servants have been endowed in this house; and the fame of this house shall spread to foreign lands, and this is the beginning of the blessing which shall be poured out upon the heads of my people. Even so. Amen."[u]

---

[u] D&C 110:1–10; also *History of the Church* under date specified.

After the Savior's withdrawal, the two mortal prophets were visited by glorified beings, each of whom had officiated on earth as a specially commissioned servant of Jehovah, and now came to confer the authority of his particular office upon Joseph and Oliver, thus uniting all the powers and authorities of olden dispensations in the restored Church of Christ, which characterizes the last and greatest dispensation of history. This is the record:

"After this vision closed, the heavens were again opened unto us, and Moses appeared before us, and committed unto us the keys of the gathering of Israel from the four parts of the earth, and the leading of the ten tribes from the land of the north. After this, Elias appeared, and committed the dispensation of the gospel of Abraham, saying, that in us, and our seed, all generations after us should be blessed. After this vision had closed, another great and glorious vision burst upon us, for Elijah the prophet, who was taken to heaven without tasting death, stood before us, and said—Behold, the time has fully come, which was spoken of by the mouth of Malachi, testifying that he (Elijah) should be sent before the great and dreadful day of the Lord come, to turn the hearts of the fathers to the children, and the children to the fathers, lest the whole earth be smitten with a curse. Therefore the keys of this dispensation are committed into your hands, and by this ye may know that the great and dreadful day of the Lord is near, even at the doors."[v]

JESUS THE CHRIST IS WITH HIS CHURCH TODAY

Right gloriously has the Lord brought about a fulfilment of the promises uttered through the mouths of His holy prophets in by-gone ages—to restore the gospel with all its former blessings and privileges; to bestow anew the Holy Priesthood with authority to administer in the name of God; to reestablish the Church bearing His name and founded upon the rock of divine revelation; and to proclaim the message of salvation to all nations, kindreds, tongues, and peoples. In spite of persecution both mobocratic and judicially sanctioned, in spite of assaults, drivings, and slaughter, the Church has developed with

[v] D&C 110:11–16. Note 5, end of chapter.

marvelous rapidity and strength since the day of its organization. Joseph, the prophet, and his brother Hyrum, the patriarch of the Church, were brutally slain as martyrs to the truth at Carthage, Illinois, June 27, 1844. But the Lord raised up others to succeed them; and the world learned in part and yet shall know beyond all question that the Church so miraculously established in the last days is not the church of Joseph Smith nor of any other man, but in literal verity, the Church of Jesus Christ. The Lord has continued to make known His mind and will through prophets, seers, and revelators whom He has successively chosen and appointed to lead His people; and the voice of divine revelation is heard in the Church today. As provided for in its revealed plan and constitution, the Church is blessed by the ministry of prophets, apostles, high priests, patriarchs, seventies, elders, bishops, priests, teachers, and deacons.[w] The spiritual gifts and blessings of old are again enjoyed in rich abundance.[x] New scriptures, primarily directed to present duties and current developments in the purposes of God, yet which illuminate and make plain in simplicity the scriptures of old, have been given to the world through the channel of the restored priesthood; and other scriptures shall yet be written. The united membership of the Church proclaims:

"We believe all that God has revealed, all that He does now reveal, and we believe that He will yet reveal many great and important things pertaining to the Kingdom of God."[y]

The predicted gathering of Israel from their long dispersion is in progress under the commission given by the Lord through Moses. The "mountain of the Lord's house" is already established in the top of the mountains, and all peoples flow unto it; while the elders of the Church go forth among the nations, saying: "Come ye, and let us go up to the mountain of the Lord, to the house of the God of Jacob; and he will teach us of his ways, and we will walk in his paths: for out of Zion shall go forth the law, and the word of the Lord from Jerusalem."[z]

---

[w] See "Plan of Government in the Restored Church," in *The Articles of Faith*, pp. 204–12.

[x] See "Spiritual Gifts" in *The Articles of Faith*, chapter 12.

[y] No. 9 of *The Articles of Faith of The Church of Jesus Christ of Latter-day Saints.*

[z] Isa. 2:2, 3; compare Micah 4:1, 2; see also D&C 29:8.

Within sacred temples, the living are officiating vicariously in behalf of the dead; and the hearts of mortal children are turned with affectionate concern toward their departed ancestors, while disembodied hosts are praying for the success of their posterity, yet in the flesh, in the service of salvation.^{aa} The saving gospel is offered freely to all, for so hath its Author commanded. Through the medium of the press, and by the personal ministrations of men invested with the Holy Priesthood whom the Church sends out by thousands, this Gospel of the Kingdom is today preached throughout the world. When such witness among the nations is made complete, "then shall the end come"; and the nations "shall see the Son of Man coming in the clouds of heaven, with power and great glory."^{bb}

NOTES TO CHAPTER 41

1. The Dispensation of the Fulness of Times.—"Now the thing to be known is, what the fulness of times means, or the extent and authority thereof. It means this, that the dispensation of the fulness of times is made up of all the dispensations that ever have been given since the world began, until this time. Unto Adam first was given a dispensation. It is well known that God spake to him with His own voice in the garden, and gave him the promise of the Messiah. And unto Noah also was a dispensation given; for Jesus said, 'As it was in the days of Noe, so shall it be also in the days of the coming of the Son of Man'; and as the righteous were saved then, and the wicked destroyed, so it will be now. And from Noah to Abraham, and from Abraham to Moses, and from Moses to Elias, and from Elias to John the Baptist, and from then to Jesus Christ, and from Jesus Christ to Peter, James, and John, the Apostles all having received in their dispensation by revelation from God, to accomplish the great scheme of restitution, spoken by all the holy Prophets since the world began; the end of which is, the dispensation of the fulness of times, in which all things shall be fulfilled have been spoken of since the earth was made."—See *Millennial Star*, vol. 16, p. 220.

2. Limitations of the Aaronic Priesthood.—After conferring the Lesser or Aaronic Priesthood upon Joseph Smith and Oliver Cowdery, the officiating angel, who had been known while a mortal being as John the Baptist, explained that the authority he had imparted did not extend to the laying-on of hands for the bestowal of the Holy Ghost, the latter ordinance being a function of the Higher or Melchizedek

---

^{aa} See *The House of the Lord,* pp. 63–109.

^{bb} JS–M 1:31, 36; compare Matt. 24:14, 30.

Priesthood. Consider the instance of Philip, (not the apostle Philip), whose ordination empowered him to baptize, though a higher authority than his was requisite for the conferring of the Holy Ghost; and consequently the apostles Peter and John went down to Samaria to officiate in the case of Philip's baptized converts (Acts 8:5, 12–17). See D&C 20:41, 46.

3. Priesthood and Office Therein.—It is important to know that although Joseph Smith and Oliver Cowdery had been ordained to the Holy Apostleship, and therefore to a fulness of the Melchizedek Priesthood, by Peter, James, and John, it was necessary that they be ordained as elders in the Church. When they received the Melchizedek Priesthood from the three ancient apostles, there was no organized Church of Jesus Christ, and consequently no need of Church officers, such as elders, priests, teachers, or deacons. As soon as the Church was established, officers were chosen therein and these were ordained to the requisite office or grade in the Priesthood. Moreover, the principle of common consent in the conduct of Church affairs was observed in this early action of the members in voting to sustain the men nominated for official positions, and has continued to be the rule of the Church to this day. It is pertinent to point out further that in conferring upon Joseph and Oliver the Aaronic Priesthood, John the Baptist did not ordain them to the office of priest, teacher, or deacon. These three offices are included in the Aaronic, as are the offices of elder, seventy, high priest, etc., in the Melchizedek Priesthood. Read D&C 20:38–67; *Articles of Faith*, 11.

4. Modern Temples.—The Lord's gracious promise given in the Kirtland Temple—to appear unto His servants at times then future, and to speak unto them with His own voice, provided the people would keep His commandments and not pollute that holy house—has been in no wise abrogated nor forfeited through the enforced relinquishment of the Kirtland Temple by the Latter-day Saints. The people were compelled to flee before the fury of mobocratic persecution; but they hastened to erect another and yet more splendid sanctuary at Nauvoo, Illinois, and were again dispossessed by lawless mobs. In the valleys of Utah the Church has erected four great temples, each more stately than the last; and in these holy houses the sacred ordinances pertaining to salvation and exaltation of both the living and the dead are in uninterrupted progress. The temples of the present dispensation, in the order of their completion, and designated according to location, are those of Kirtland, Ohio; Nauvoo, Illinois; St. George, Logan, Manti, and Salt Lake City, Utah; Cardston, Canada; and Laie, Hawaii. See *House of the Lord*.

5. Consistency of the Church's Claim to Authority.—The proofs of order and system in the restoration of authority to officiate in particular functions pertaining to the priesthood are striking, and go to prove the continued validity, beyond the grave, of authoritative ordination on earth. The keys of the Aaronic order, comprizing authority to baptize for the remission of sins, were brought by John the

Baptist, who had been especially commissioned in that order of priesthood in the time of Christ. The apostleship, comprizing all powers inherent in the Melchizedek Priesthood, was restored by the presiding apostles of old, Peter, James, and John. Then, as has been seen, Moses conferred the authority to prosecute the work of gathering; and Elijah, who, not having tasted death, held a peculiar relation to both the living and the dead, delivered the authority of vicarious ministry for the departed. To these appointments by heavenly authority should be added that given by Elias, who appeared to Joseph Smith and Oliver Cowdery, and "committed the dispensation of the gospel of Abraham." It is evident, then, that the claims made by the Church with respect to its authority are complete and consistent as to the source of the powers professed and the channels through which such have been delivered again to earth. Scripture and revelation, both ancient and modern, support as unalterable law the principle that no one can delegate to another an authority which the giver does not possess.

6. Cessation of the Melchizedek Administration in Ancient Times.—The Higher or Melchizedek Priesthood was held by the patriarchs from Adam to Moses. Aaron was ordained to the priest's office, as were his sons; but that Moses held superior authority is abundantly shown (Num. 12:1–8). After Aaron's death his son Eleazar officiated in the authority of the Lesser Priesthood; and even Joshua had to take counsel and authority from him (Num. 27:18–23). From the ministry of Moses to that of Jesus Christ, the Lesser Priesthood alone was operative upon the earth, excepting only the instances of specially delegated authority of the higher order such as is manifest in the ministrations of certain chosen prophets, Isaiah, Jeremiah, Ezekiel, and others. It is evident that these prophets, seers, and revelators were individually and specially commissioned; but it appears that they had not authority to call and ordain successors, for in their time the Higher Priesthood was not existent on earth in an organized state with duly officered quorums. Not so with the Aaronic and Levitical Priesthood, however. The matter is made particularly plain through latter-day revelation. See D&C 84:23–28; read the entire section; also *House of the Lord*, pp. 198–200.

CHAPTER 42

JESUS THE CHRIST TO RETURN

THE LORD'S SECOND ADVENT
PREDICTED IN ANCIENT SCRIPTURE

"Ye men of Galilee, why stand ye gazing up into heaven? this same Jesus, which is taken up from you into heaven, shall so come in like manner as ye have seen him go into heaven."[a] So spake the white-robed angels to the eleven apostles as the resurrected Christ ascended from their midst on Olivet. The scriptures abound in predictions of the Lord's return.

By the "Second Advent" we understand not the personal appearing of the Son of God to a few, such as His visitation to Saul of Tarsus, to Joseph Smith in 1820, and again in the Kirtland Temple in 1836; nor later manifestations to His worthy servants as specifically promised;[b] but His yet future coming in power and great glory, accompanied by hosts of resurrected and glorified beings, to execute judgment upon the earth and to inaugurate a reign of righteousness.

The prophets of both hemispheres, who lived prior to the meridian of time, said comparatively little concerning the Lord's Second Coming; their souls were too full of the merciful plan of redemption associated with the Savior's birth into mortality to permit them to dwell upon the yet more distant consummation appointed for the last days. Certain of them, however, were permitted to behold in vision the working out of the divine purposes even to the end of time; and these

---

[a] Acts 1:11.

[b] See also D&C 110:8; compare 36:8; 42:36; 97:15, 16; 109:5; 124:27; 133:2.

testified with unsurpassed fervency concerning the glorious coming of Christ in the final dispensation. Enoch, the seventh from Adam, prophesied saying, "Behold the Lord cometh with ten thousands of his saints, to execute judgment upon all."[c] In a more extended account of the Lord's revelations to Enoch than is included in the Bible, we read that after this righteous prophet had been shown the scenes of Israel's history, down to and beyond the death, Resurrection and ascension of Jesus Christ, he pleaded with God, saying: "I ask thee if thou wilt not come again on the earth. And the Lord said unto Enoch: As I live, even so will I come in the last days, in the days of wickedness and vengeance, to fulfil the oath which I have made unto you concerning the children of Noah. . . . And it came to pass that Enoch saw the day of the coming of the Son of Man, in the last days, to dwell on the earth in righteousness for the space of a thousand years."[d] Isaiah, in rapturous contemplation of the eventual triumph of righteousness, exclaimed: "Say to them that are of a fearful heart, Be strong, fear not: behold, your God will come with vengeance, even God with a recompence; he will come and save you"; and again: "Behold, the Lord God will come with strong hand, and his arm shall rule for him: behold, his reward is with him, and his work before him."[e] The conditions specified were not realized in the earthly life of the Redeemer; moreover the context clearly shows that the prophet's words are applicable to the last days only—the time of the ransomed of the Lord, the time of restitution, and of the triumph of Zion.

Of all Biblical scriptures relating to our subject, the utterances of the Christ Himself in the course of His earthly ministry are most direct and certain. Many of these we have already considered in the narrative of the Savior's life; the few following are sufficient for present demonstration. "For the Son of man shall come in the glory of his Father with his angels; and then he shall reward every man according to his works."[f] To the apostles and the people generally He proclaimed: "Whosoever therefore shall be ashamed of me and of my

[c] Jude 14, 15; compare Gen. 5:18; see next reference following.
[d] Moses 7:59, 60, 65. Note 1, end of chapter.
[e] Isa. 35:4; and 40:10; see also Ps. 50:3; Mal. 3:1; 4:5, 6; compare Note 1, chapter 11 herein.
[f] Matt. 16:27.

words in this adulterous and sinful generation; of him also shall the Son of man be ashamed, when he cometh in the glory of his Father with the holy angels."ᵍ When a bound prisoner before proud Caiaphas, Jesus answered the unlawful adjuration of the corrupt high priest, by affirming: "I say unto you, Hereafter shall ye see the Son of man sitting on the right hand of power, and coming in the clouds of heaven."ʰ

The apostles had been so impressed with the Master's assurance that He would return to earth in power and glory, that they eagerly questioned as to the time and signs of His coming.ⁱ He stated explicitly, though at the time they failed to comprehend Him, that many great events would intervene between His departure and return, including the long era of darkness associated with the Apostasy.ʲ But as to the certainty of His advent in glory, as Judge, and Lord, and King, Jesus left no excuse for dubiety in the minds of His apostles. After the ascension, throughout the course of apostolic administration, the future coming of the Lord was preached with earnest emphasis.ᵏ

Book of Mormon prophecies concerning the advent of the Lord in the last days are specific and definite. On the occasion of His appearing to the Nephites on the American continent shortly after His ascension from the Mount of Olives, Christ preached the gospel to assembled multitudes; "And he did expound all things, even from the beginning until the time that he should come in his glory"; and the events to follow, "even unto the great and last day."ˡ In granting the wish of the three Nephite disciples who desired to continue their ministry in the flesh throughout the generations to come, the Lord said unto them:

"Ye shall live to behold all the doings of the Father, unto the children of men, even until all things shall be fulfilled, according to the will of

---

ᵍ Mark 8:38; compare Luke 9:26.

ʰ Matt. 26:64.

ⁱ Matt. 24:3; Mark 13:26; Luke 21:7; Acts 1:6.

ʲ Matt. 24; see chaps. 32 and 40 herein.

ᵏ See Acts 3:20, 21; 1 Cor. 4:5; 11:26; Philip. 3:20; 1 Thes. 1:10; 2:19; 3:13; 4:15–18; 2 Thes. 2:1, 8; 1 Tim. 6:14, 15; Titus 2:13; James 5:7, 8; 1 Pet. 1:5–7; 4:13; 1 Jn. 2:28; 3:2; Jude 14, etc.

ˡ 3 Ne. 26:3, 4.

the Father, when I shall come in my glory, with the powers of heaven; And ye shall never endure the pains of death; but when I shall come in my glory, ye shall be changed in the twinkling of an eye from mortality to immortality: and then shall ye be blessed in the kingdom of my Father."ᵐ

THE COMING OF THE LORD PROCLAIMED THROUGH MODERN REVELATION

To the Church of Jesus Christ, restored and reestablished in these the last days, the word of the Lord has come repeatedly, declaring the actuality of His second advent and the nearness of that glorious yet dreadful event. But a few months after the Church was organized, the voice of Jesus Christ was heard, admonishing the elders to vigilance and proclaiming as follows:

"For the hour is nigh, and the day soon at hand when the earth is ripe: and all the proud, and they that do wickedly, shall be as stubble, and I will burn them up, saith the Lord of Hosts, that wickedness shall not be upon the earth; for the hour is nigh, and that which was spoken by mine apostles must be fulfilled; for as they spoke so shall it come to pass; for I will reveal myself from heaven with power and great glory, with all the hosts thereof, and dwell in righteousness with men on earth a thousand years, and the wicked shall not stand."ⁿ

In the month following, the Lord gave instructions to certain elders, concluding with these portentous words:

"Wherefore, be faithful, praying always, having your lamps trimmed and burning, and oil with you, that you may be ready at the coming of the Bridegroom: for behold, verily, verily, I say unto you, that I come quickly. Even so. Amen."ᵒ

Again we read in a later revelation:

"And blessed are you because you have believed; and more blessed are you because you are called of me to preach my gospel, to lift up your voice as with the sound of a trump, both long and loud, and cry repentance unto a crooked and perverse generation, preparing the

ᵐ 3 Ne. 28:7, 8; see also 29:2.

ⁿ D&C 29:9–11.

ᵒ D&C 33:17, 18.

way of the Lord for his second coming; for behold, verily, verily, I say unto you, the time is soon at hand, that I shall come in a cloud with power and great glory, and it shall be a great day at the time of my coming, for all nations shall tremble."[P]

The Lord Jesus addressed a general revelation to His Church in March 1831, through which His earlier predictions uttered to the Twelve shortly before His betrayal were made plain, and the assurances of His glorious coming were thus reiterated:

"Ye look and behold the fig-trees, and ye see them with your eyes, and ye say when they begin to shoot forth, and their leaves are yet tender, that summer is now nigh at hand; even so it shall be in that day when they shall see all these things, then shall they know that the hour is nigh. And it shall come to pass that he that feareth me shall be looking forth for the great day of the Lord to come, even for the signs of the coming of the Son of man: And they shall see signs and wonders, for they shall be shown forth in the heavens above, and in the earth beneath; and they shall behold blood, and fire, and vapors of smoke; and before the day of the Lord shall come, the sun shall be darkened, and the moon be turned into blood, and stars fall from heaven; and the remnant shall be gathered unto this place, and then they shall look for me, and, behold, I will come; and they shall see me in the clouds of heaven, clothed with power and great glory, with all the holy angels; and he that watches not for me shall be cut off."[q]

So near is the consummation that the intervening period is called "today"; and, in applying this time designation in the year 1831, the Lord said:

"Behold, now it is called today (until the coming of the Son of man), and verily it is a day of sacrifice, and a day for the tithing of my people; for he that is tithed shall not be burned (at his coming); For after today cometh the burning: this is speaking after the manner of the Lord; for verily I say, tomorrow all the proud and they that do wickedly shall be as stubble; and I will burn them up, for I am the Lord of hosts: and I will not spare any that remain in Babylon.

[P] D&C 34:4–8.

[q] D&C 45:37–44; compare this section with Matt. 24, and Luke 21:5–36. See also D&C 49:23–28.

Wherefore, if ye believe me, ye will labor while it is called today."[r]

THE TIME AND ACCOMPANIMENTS
OF THE LORD'S COMING

The date of the future advent of Christ has never been revealed to man. To the inquiring apostles who labored with the Master, He said: "But of that day and hour knoweth no man, no, not the angels of heaven, but my Father only."[s] In the present age, a similar declaration has been made by the Father: "I, the Lord God, have spoken it, but the hour and the day no man knoweth, neither the angels in heaven, nor shall they know until he comes."[t] Only through watchfulness and prayer may the signs of the times be correctly interpreted and the imminence of the Lord's appearing be apprehended. To the unwatchful and the wicked the event will be as sudden and unexpected as the coming of a thief in the night.[u] But we are not left without definite information as to precedent signs. Biblical prophecies bearing upon this subject we have heretofore considered.[v] As later scriptures affirm: "Before the great day of the Lord shall come, Jacob shall flourish in the wilderness, and the Lamanites shall blossom as the rose. Zion shall flourish upon the hills and rejoice upon the mountains, and shall be assembled together unto the place which I have appointed."[w] War shall become so general that every man who will not take arms against his neighbor must of necessity flee to the land of Zion for safety.[x] Ephraim shall assemble in Zion on the western continent, and Judah shall be again established in the east; and the cities of Zion and Jerusalem shall be the capitals of the world empire, over which Messiah shall reign in undisputed authority. The Lost Tribes shall be brought forth from the place where God has hidden them through the centuries and receive their long deferred

---

[r] D&C 64:23–25.

[s] Matt. 24:36; compare Mark 13:32–37.

[t] D&C 49:7; the context shows that the words are those of the Father.

[u] 1 Thes. 5:2; 2 Pet. 3:10; compare Matt. 24:43, 44; 25:13; Luke 12:39, 40.

[v] Page 532.

[w] D&C 49:24, 25.

[x] D&C 45:68–71.

blessings at the hands of Ephraim. The people of Israel shall be restored from their scattered condition.[y]

In addressing the elders of His Church in 1832, the Lord urged upon them the imperative need of devoted diligence, and said:

"Abide ye in the liberty wherewith ye are made free; entangle not yourselves in sin but let your hands be clean, until the Lord come; For not many days hence and the earth shall tremble and reel to and fro as a drunken man, and the sun shall hide his face, and shall refuse to give light, and the moon shall be bathed in blood, and the stars shall become exceeding angry, and shall cast themselves down as a fig that falleth from off a fig tree. And after your testimony cometh wrath and indignation upon the people; For after your testimony cometh the testimony of earthquakes, that shall cause groanings in the midst of her, and men shall fall upon the ground, and shall not be able to stand. And also cometh the testimony of the voice of thunderings, and the voice of lightnings, and the voice of tempests, and the voice of the waves of the sea, heaving themselves beyond their bounds. And all things shall be in commotion; and surely, men's hearts shall fail them; for fear shall come upon all people; And angels shall fly through the midst of heaven, crying with a loud voice, sounding the trump of God, saying, Prepare ye, prepare ye, O inhabitants of the earth; for the judgment of our God is come: behold, and lo! the Bridegroom cometh, go ye out to meet him."[z]

A characteristic of present-day revelation is the reiteration of the fact that the event is nigh at hand, "even at the doors." The fateful time is repeatedly designated in scripture, "the great and dreadful day of the Lord."[aa] Fearful indeed will it be to individuals, families, and nations, who have so far sunk into sin as to have forfeited their claim to mercy. The time is not that of the final judgment—when the whole race of mankind shall stand in the resurrected state before the bar of God— nevertheless it shall be a time of unprecedented blessing unto the righteous and of condemnation and vengeance upon the wicked.[bb] With

---

[y] D&C 133:7–14, 21–35; *The Articles of Faith,* chaps. 18, 19.

[z] D&C 88:86–92.

[aa] D&C 110:14, 16; compare Joel 2:31; Mal. 4:5; 3 Ne. 25:5.

[bb] D&C 29:11–17.

Christ shall come those who have already been resurrected; and His approach shall be the means of inaugurating a general resurrection of the righteous dead, while the pure and just who are still in the flesh shall be instantaneously changed from the mortal to the immortal state and shall be caught up with the newly resurrected to meet the Lord and His celestial company, and shall descend with Him. To this effect did Paul prophesy: "Even so them also which sleep in Jesus will God bring with him. . . . For the Lord himself shall descend from heaven with a shout, with the voice of the archangel, and with the trump of God: and the dead in Christ shall rise first: Then we which are alive and remain shall be caught up together with them in the clouds, to meet the Lord in the air."^{cc} Compare the promise made to the Three Nephites: "And ye shall never endure the pains of death; but when I shall come in my glory, ye shall be changed in the twinkling of an eye from mortality to immortality."^{dd} Of the superlative glories awaiting the righteous when the Lord shall come, we have received in this day a partial description as follows: "And the face of the Lord shall be unveiled; and the saints that are upon the earth, who are alive, shall be quickened, and be caught up to meet him."^{ee} The heathen nations shall be redeemed and have part in the First Resurrection.^{ff}

THE KINGDOM OF HEAVEN TO COME

The coming of Christ in the last days, accompanied by the apostles of old^{gg} and by the resurrected saints, is to mark the establishment of the Kingdom of Heaven upon earth. The faithful apostles who were with Jesus in His earthly ministry are to be enthroned as judges of the whole house of Israel;^{hh} they will judge the Nephite Twelve, who in turn will be empowered to judge the descendants of Lehi, or that branch of the Israelitish nation which was established upon the western continent.ⁱⁱ

cc 1 Thes. 4:14–17.
dd 3 Ne.28:8.
ee D&C 88:95–98.
ff Note 2, end of chapter.
gg D&C 29:12.
hh D&C 29:12; compare Matt. 19:28; Luke 22:30.
ii 3 Ne. 27:27; compare 1 Ne. 12:9, 10; Morm. 3:18, 19.

While the expressions "Kingdom of God" and "Kingdom of Heaven" are used in the Bible synonymously or interchangeably, later revelation gives to each a distinctive meaning. The Kingdom of God is the Church established by divine authority upon the earth; this institution asserts no claim to temporal rule over nations; its sceptre of power is that of the Holy Priesthood, to be used in the preaching of the gospel and in administering its ordinances for the salvation of mankind living and dead. The Kingdom of Heaven is the divinely ordained system of government and dominion in all matters, temporal and spiritual; this will be established on earth only when its rightful Head, the King of kings, Jesus the Christ, comes to reign. His administration will be one of order, operated through the agency of His commissioned representatives invested with the Holy Priesthood. When Christ appears in His glory, and not before, will be realized a complete fulfilment of the supplication: "Thy kingdom come. Thy will be done in earth, as it is in heaven."

The Kingdom of God has been established among men to prepare them for the Kingdom of Heaven which shall come; and in the blessed reign of Christ the King shall the two be made one. The relationship between them has been revealed to the Church in this wise:

"Hearken, and lo, a voice as of one from on high, who is mighty and powerful, whose going forth is unto the ends of the earth, yea, whose voice is unto men—Prepare ye the way of the Lord, make his paths straight. The keys of the kingdom of God are committed unto man on the earth, and from thence shall the gospel roll forth unto the ends of the earth, as the stone which is cut out of the mountain without hands, shall roll forth, until it has filled the whole earth; Yea, a voice crying—Prepare ye the way of the Lord, prepare ye the supper of the Lamb, make ready for the Bridegroom; Pray unto the Lord, call upon his holy name, make known his wonderful works among the people; Call upon the Lord, that his kingdom may go forth upon the earth, that the inhabitants thereof may receive it, and be prepared for the days to come, in the which the Son of man shall come down in heaven, clothed in the brightness of his glory, to meet the kingdom of God which is set up on the earth; Wherefore may the kingdom of God go forth, that the kingdom of heaven may come, that thou, O God, mayest be glorified in heaven so on earth, that thy enemies may be subdued: for thine is the honour, power and glory, for ever and ever. Amen."[jj]

THE MILLENNIUM

The inauguration of Christ's reign on earth is to be the beginning of a period that shall be distinct in many important particulars from all precedent and subsequent time; and the Lord shall reign with His people a thousand years. The government of individuals, communities and nations throughout this Millennium is to be that of a perfect theocracy, with Jesus the Christ as Lord and King. The more wicked part of the race shall have been destroyed; and during the period Satan shall be bound "that he should deceive the nations no more, till the thousand years should be fulfilled"; while the just shall share with Christ in rightful rule and dominion. The righteous dead shall have come forth from their graves, while the wicked shall remain unresurrected until the thousand years be past.[kk] Men yet in the flesh shall mingle with immortalized beings; children shall grow to maturity and then die in peace or be changed to immortality "in the twinkling of an eye."[ll] There shall be surcease of enmity between man and beast; the venom of serpents and the ferocity of the brute creation shall be done away, and love shall be the dominant power of control. Among the earliest revelations on the subject is that given to Enoch; and in this the return of that prophet and his righteous people with Christ in the last days was thus assured:

"And the Lord said unto Enoch: Then shalt thou and all thy city meet them there, and we will receive them into our bosom, and they shall see us; and we will fall upon their necks, and they shall fall upon our necks, and we will kiss each other; And there shall be mine abode, and it shall be Zion, which shall come forth out of all the creations which I have made; and for the space of a thousand years the earth shall rest. And it came to pass that Enoch saw the day of the coming of the Son of Man, in the last days, to dwell on the earth

---

[jj] D&C 65. For a fuller treatment of this subject as also the distinction between Church and Kingdom, see *The Articles of Faith,* pp. 365–68.

[kk] Rev. 20:1–6; compare D&C 43:18.

[ll] D&C 63:50–51; 101:30; compare 1 Cor. 15:51–57.

in righteousness for the space of a thousand years."[mm]

In these latter days the Lord has thus spoken, requiring preparation for the Millennial era, and describing in part the glories thereof:

"And prepare for the revelation which is to come, when the veil of the covering of my temple, in my tabernacle, which hideth the earth, shall be taken off, and all flesh shall see me together. And every corruptible thing, both of man, or of the beasts of the field, or of the fowls of the heavens, or of the fish of the sea, that dwell upon all the face of the earth, shall be consumed; And also that of element shall melt with fervent heat; and all things shall become new, that my knowledge and glory may dwell upon all the earth. And in that day the enmity of man, and the enmity of beasts, yea, the enmity of all flesh, shall cease from before my face. And in that day whatsoever any man shall ask, it shall be given unto him. And in that day Satan shall not have power to tempt any man. And there shall be no sorrow because there is no death. In that day an infant shall not die until he is old, and his life shall be as the age of a tree, and when he dies he shall not sleep, (that is to say in the earth,) but shall be changed in the twinkling of an eye, and shall be caught up, and his rest shall be glorious. Yea, verily I say unto you, in that day when the Lord shall come, he shall reveal all things."[nn]

The Millennium is to precede the time designated in scriptural phrase "the end of the world." When the thousand years are passed, Satan shall be loosed for a little season, and the final test of man's integrity to God shall ensue. Such as are prone to impurity of heart shall yield to temptation while the righteous shall endure to the end.[oo] A revelation to this effect was given the Church in 1831, in part as follows:

"For the great Millennium, of which I have spoken by the mouth of my servants, shall come; For Satan shall be bound, and when he is loosed again, he shall only reign for a little season, and then cometh the end of the earth; And he that liveth in righteousness shall be changed in the twinkling of an eye, and the earth shall pass away so as

---

[mm] Moses 7:63–65.

[nn] D&C 101:23–32; compare Isa. 65:17–25 and 11:6–9; see also D&C 29:11, 22; 43:30; 63:51.

[oo] Rev. 20:7–15.

by fire; And the wicked shall go away into unquenchable fire, and their end no man knoweth on earth, nor ever shall know, until they come before me in judgment. Hearken ye to these words: Behold, I am Jesus Christ, the Saviour of the world. Treasure these things up in your hearts, and let the solemnities of eternity rest upon your minds."[pp]

THE CELESTIAL CONSUMMATION

The vanquishment of Satan and his hosts shall be complete. The dead, small and great, all who have breathed the breath of life on earth, shall be resurrected—every soul that has tabernacled in flesh, whether good or evil—and shall stand before God, to be judged according to the record as written in the books.[qq] So shall be brought to glorious consummation the mission of the Christ. "Then cometh the end, when he shall have delivered up the kingdom to God, even the Father; when he shall have put down all rule and all authority and power. For he must reign, till he hath put all enemies under his feet. The last enemy that shall be destroyed is death. For he hath put all things under his feet."[rr] Then shall the Lord Jesus "deliver up the kingdom, and present it unto the Father spotless, saying—I have overcome and have trodden the wine-press alone, even the wine-press of the fierceness of the wrath of Almighty God. Then shall he be crowned with the crown of his glory, to sit on the throne of his power to reign for ever and ever."[ss] The earth shall pass to its glorified and celestialized condition, an eternal abode for the exalted sons and daughters of God.[tt] Forever shall they reign, kings and priests to the Most High, redeemed, sanctified, and exalted through their Lord and God JESUS THE CHRIST.

NOTES TO CHAPTER 42

1. **Enoch,** spoken of by Jude as "the seventh from Adam," was the father of Methuselah. In Genesis 5:24 we read: "And Enoch walked with God; and he was not; for God took him." From the Lord's revelation to Moses we learn that Enoch

[pp] D&C 43:30–34. See also *The Articles of Faith*, pp. 358–71.
[qq] Rev. 20:11–15.
[rr] 1 Cor. 15:24–27.
[ss] D&C 76:107, 108.
[tt] Note 3, end of chapter.

was a mighty man, favored of God because of his righteousness, and a leader of and revelator to his people. Through his agency a city was built, the inhabitants of which excelled in righteous living to such an extent that they were of one heart and one mind and had no poor among them. It was called the City of Holiness or Zion. The residue of the race were all corrupt in the sight of the Lord. Enoch and his people were taken from the earth and are to return with Christ at His coming. (Moses 7:12–21, 68, 69; compare D&C 45:11, 12.)

2. Heathen in the First Resurrection.—"And then shall the heathen nations be redeemed, and they that knew no law shall have part in the first resurrection; and it shall be tolerable for them." (D&C 45:54.) Such is the word of the Lord with respect to those benighted peoples who live and die in ignorance of the laws of the gospel. This affirmation is sustained by other scriptures, and by a consideration of the principles of true justice according to which humanity is to be judged. Man shall be accounted blameless or guilty according to his deeds as interpreted in the light of the law under which he is required to live. It is inconsistent with our conception of a just God to believe Him capable of inflicting condemnation upon any one for non-compliance with a requirement of which the person had no knowledge. Nevertheless, the laws of the gospel cannot be suspended even in the case of those who have sinned in darkness and ignorance; but it is reasonable to believe that the plan of redemption shall afford such benighted ones an opportunity of learning the laws of God; and, as fast as they so learn, will obedience be required on pain of the penalty.

3. Regeneration of the Earth.—In speaking of the graded and progressive glories provided for His creations, and of the laws of regeneration and sanctification, the Lord has thus spoken through revelation in the present dispensation: "And again, verily I say unto you, the earth abideth the law of a celestial kingdom, for it filleth the measure of its creation, and transgresseth not the law. Wherefore it shall be sanctified; yea, notwithstanding it shall die, it shall be quickened again, and shall abide the power by which it is quickened, and the righteous shall inherit it." (D&C 88:25, 26.) This appointed change, by which the earth shall pass to the condition of a celestialized world, is referred to in numerous scriptures as the institution of "a new heaven and a new earth" (Rev. 21:1, 3,4; Ether 13:9; D&C 29:23).

INDEX